CompTIA® Network+ (N10-004) Cert Guide

Mike Harwood

Pearson
800 East 96th Street
Indianapolis, Indiana 46240 USA

CompTIA® Network+ (N10-004) Cert Guide

ISBN-13: 978-0-7897-4559-0

ISBN-10: 0-7897-4559-3

Library of Congress Cataloging-in-Publication Data

Harwood, Mike.

   CompTIA Network+ (N10-004) cert guide / Mike Harwood. — 1st ed.
      p. cm.
   Includes index.
   ISBN 978-0-7897-4559-0 (hardcover w/cd) 1. Computer networks—Examinations—Study guides. 2. Telecommunications engineers—Certification. 3. Electronic data processing personnel—Certification. I. Title.
   TK5105.5.H37168 2011
   004.6—dc22   2010024692

Printed in the United States of America

First Printing: August 2010

Trademarks

Warning and Disclaimer

Bulk Sales

Que Publishing offers excellent discounts on this book when ordered in quantity for bulk purchases or special sales. For more information, please contact

   U.S. Corporate and Government Sales
   1-800-382-3419
   corpsales@pearsontechgroup.com
For sales outside of the U.S., please contact
   International Sales
   international@pearson.com

Associate Publisher
Dave Dusthimer

Acquisitions Editor
Betsy Brown

Development Editor
Dayna Isley

Managing Editor
Sandra Schroeder

Project Editor
Mandie Frank

Copy Editor
Apostrophe Editing Services

Indexer
Tim Wright

Proofreader
Williams Woods Publishing Services

Technical Editors
Chris Crayton
Timothy L. Warner

Publishing Coordinator
Vanessa Evans

Multimedia Developer
Dan Scherf

Designer
Gary Adair

Composition
Mark Shirar

Contents at a Glance

Elements on the CD-ROM:

Table of Contents

Chapter 2   **Media and Connectors   61**

About the Author

Mike Harwood (MCSE, A+, Network+, Server+, Linux+) has more than 14 years experience in information technology and related fields. He has held a number of roles in the IT field including network administrator, instructor, technical writer, website designer, consultant, and online marketing strategist. Mike has been a regular on-air technology contributor for CBC radio and has coauthored numerous computer books, including the *Network+ Exam Cram* published by Pearson.

Dedication

This book is dedicated to the grandparents: to Frank and Marlane King whose enthusiasm, support, and sense of adventure make them grandparents a father wants for his daughters, Breanna, Paige, and Delaney; and to Ellen and Stu Jones who are always supportive, wise, and eager to provide the grandchildren with adventures and lifelong memories. And of course to my loving, supportive wife, Linda, who keeps me on track.

Acknowledgments

The creation of a book is not a simple process and requires the talents and dedication from many people to make it happen. With this in mind, I would like to thank the folks at Pearson for their commitment to this project.

Specifically, I would like to say thanks to Betsy Brown for overseeing the project and keeping things moving. A special thanks to Dayna Isley for outstanding editing and focus. Let's not forget the technical editors Chris Crayton and Tim Warner who checked and rechecked to ensure that the project stayed on target technically—a truly difficult task considering the number of facts presented and the conflicting information that seems to be part of the networking world.

Finally, I am very thankful to my family and friends who once again had to put up with me while I worked my way through another project. Hopefully, a trip to the Magic Kingdom will make it up to you.

About the Reviewers

Chris Crayton is an author, technical editor, technical consultant, security consultant, and trainer. Formerly, he worked as a networking instructor at Keiser College (2001 Teacher of the Year); as a network administrator for Protocol, an electronic customer relationship management (eCRM) company; and at Eastman Kodak Headquarters as a computer and network specialist. Chris has authored several print and online books, including *The A+ Exams Guide*, Second Edition (CRM/Cengage Learning, 2008), *Microsoft Windows Vista 70-620 Exam Guide Short Cut* (O'Reilly,2007), *CompTIA A+ Essentials 220-601 Exam Guide Short Cut* (O'Reilly, 2007), *A+ Adaptive Exams* (Charles River Media, 2002), *The A+ Exams Guide*, *The A+ Certification and PC Repair Handbook* (Charles River Media, 2005), and *The Security+ Exam Guide* (Charles River Media, 2003). He is also co-author of the *CompTIA Security+ Study Guide & DVD Training System*, Second Edition (Syngress, 2007). Chris is also a technical editor/reviewer for several major publishing companies, including Pearson, McGraw-Hill, Charles River Media, Thomson/Cengage Learning, Wiley, O'Reilly, Syngress, and Apress. He holds MCSE, MCP+I, A+, and Network+ certifications.

We Want to Hear from You!

As the reader of this book, *you* are our most important critic and commentator. We value your opinion and want to know what we're doing right, what we could do better, what areas you'd like to see us publish in, and any other words of wisdom you're willing to pass our way.

As an associate publisher for Que Publishing, I welcome your comments. You can email or write me directly to let me know what you did or didn't like about this book—as well as what we can do to make our books better.

Please note that I cannot help you with technical problems related to the topic of this book. We do have a User Services group, however, where I will forward specific technical questions related to the book.

When you write, please be sure to include this book's title and author as well as your name, email address, and phone number. I will carefully review your comments and share them with the author and editors who worked on the book.

Email: feedback@quepublishing.com
Mail: Dave Dusthimer
Associate Publisher
Pearson Education
800 East 96th Street
Indianapolis, IN 46240 USA

Reader Services

Visit our website and register this book at www.pearsonitcertification.com/title/
9780789745590 for convenient access to any updates, downloads, or errata that
might be available for this book.

Introduction

The CompTIA Network+ exam has become the leading introductory-level network certification available today. Network+ is recognized by both employers and industry giants such as Microsoft and Novell as providing candidates with a solid foundation of networking concepts, terminology, and skills. The Network+ exam covers a broad range of networking concepts to prepare candidates for the technologies they are likely to be working with in today's network environments.

This book is your one-stop shop. Everything you need to know to pass the exam is in here. You do not need to take a class in addition to buying this book to pass the exam. However, depending on your personal study habits or learning style, you might benefit from buying this book *and* taking a class.

Exam Preps are meticulously crafted to give you the best possible learning experience for the particular characteristics of the technology covered and the actual certification exam. The instructional design implemented in the *Exam Preps* reflects the task- and experience-based nature of CompTIA certification exams. The *Exam Preps* provide the factual knowledge base you need for the exams but then take it to the next level, with exercises and exam questions that require you to engage in the analytic thinking needed to pass the Network+ exam.

CompTIA recommends that the typical candidate for this exam have a minimum of 9 months experience in network support and administration. In addition, CompTIA recommends that candidates have preexisting hardware knowledge such as CompTIA A+ certification.

How This Book Helps You

This book takes you on a self-guided tour of all the areas covered by the Network+ exam and teaches you the specific skills you need to achieve your certification. The book also contains helpful hints, tips, real-world examples, and exercises.

Exam Objectives and Chapter Organization

Every objective you need to know for the Network+ exam is covered in this book. Table I-1 shows the full list of exam objectives and the chapter in which they are covered. In addition to this table, each chapter begins by specifiying the objectives to be covered.

Table I.1   CompTIA Network+ Exam Objectives

Exam Topic	Chapter
1.0 Network Technologies	
1.1 Explain the function of common networking protocols	4
TCP	
FTP	
UDP	
TCP/IP suite	
DHCP	
TFTP	
DNS	
HTTP(S)	
ARP	
SIP (VoIP)	
RTP (VoIP)	
SSH	
POP3	
NTP	
IMAP4	
Telnet	
SMTP	
SNMP2/3	
ICMP	
IGMP	
TLS	

1.2 Identify commonly used TCP and UDP default ports   4

TCP ports:
    FTP — 20, 21
    SSH — 22
    TELNET — 23
    SMTP — 25
    DNS — 53
    HTTP — 80
    POP3 — 110
    NTP — 123
    IMAP4 — 143
    HTTPS — 443
UDP ports:
    TFTP — 69
    DNS — 53
    BOOTPS/DHCP — 67
    SNMP — 161

1.3 Identify the following address formats   5

IPv6
IPv4
MAC addressing

1.4 Given a scenario, evaluate the proper use of the following addressing technologies and   5
addressing schemes

Addressing technologies:
    Subnetting
    Classful vs. classless (e.g. CIDR, Supernetting)
    NAT
    PAT
    SNAT
    Public vs. private
    DHCP (static, dynamic APIPA)
Addressing schemes:
    Unicast
    Multicast
    Broadcast

| *2.1 Categorize standard cable types and their properties* | 2 |

Type:

    CAT3, CAT5, CAT5e, CAT6

    STP, UTP

    Multimode fiber, single-mode fiber

    Coaxial

        RG-59

        RG-6

    Serial

    Plenum vs. Non-plenum

Properties:

    Transmission speeds

    Distance

    Duplex

    Noise immunity (security, EMI)

    Frequency

| *2.2 Identify common connector types* | 2 |

RJ-11

RJ-45

BNC

SC

ST

LC

RS-232

| *2.3 Identify common physical network topologies* | 1 |

Star

Mesh

Bus

Ring

Point to point

Point to multipoint

Hybrid

| *2.4 Given a scenario, differentiate and implement appropriate wiring standards* | 2 |

568A

568B

Straight vs. cross-over

Rollover

Loopback

2.5 Categorize WAN technology types and properties   8

Type:

  Frame relay

  E1/T1

  ADSL

  SDSL

  VDSL

  Cable modem

  Satellite

  E3/T3

  OC-x

  Wireless

  ATM

  SONET

  MPLS

  ISDN BRI

  ISDN PRI

  POTS

  PSTN

Properties

  Circuit switch

  Packet switch

  Speed

  Transmission media

  Distance

2.6 Categorize LAN technology types and properties   6

Types:

    Ethernet

    10BaseT

    100BaseTX

    100BaseFX

    1000BaseT

    1000BaseX

    10GBaseSR

    10GBaseLR

    10GBaseER

    10GBaseSW

    10GBaseLW

    10GBaseEW

    10GBaseT

Properties

    CSMA/CD

    Broadcast

    Collision

    Bonding

    Speed

    Distance

2.7 Explain common logical network topologies and their characteristics   1

Peer to peer

Client/server

VPN

VLAN

2.8 Install components of wiring distribution   2

Vertical and horizontal cross connects

Patch panels

66 block

MDFs

IDFs

25 pair

100 pair

110 block

Demarc

Demarc extension

Smart jack

Verify wiring installation

Verify wiring termination

3.0 Network Devices

3.1 Install, configure and differentiate between common network devices   3

Hub

Repeater

Modem

NIC

Media converters

Basic switch

Bridge

Wireless access point

Basic router

Basic firewall

Basic DHCP server

3.2 Identify the functions of specialized network devices   3

Multilayer switch

Content switch

IDS/IPS

Load balancer

Multifunction network devices

DNS server

Bandwidth shaper

Proxy server

CSU/DSU

4.7 Given a scenario, troubleshoot common connectivity issues and select an appropriate   11
solution

Physical issues:

> Cross talk
> Nearing crosstalk
> Near End crosstalk
> Attenuation
> Collisions
> Shorts
> Open impedance mismatch (echo)
> Interference

Logical issues:

> Port speed
> Port duplex mismatch
> Incorrect VLAN
> Incorrect IP address
> Wrong gateway
> Wrong DNS
> Wrong subnet mask

Issues that should be identified but escalated:

> Switching loop
> Routing loop
> Route problems
> Proxy arp
> Broadcast storms

Wireless issues:

> Interference (bleed, environmental factors)
> Incorrect encryption
> Incorrect channel
> Incorrect frequency
> ESSID mismatch
> Standard mismatch (802.11 a/b/g/n)
> Distance
> Bounce
> Incorrect antenna placement

6.0 Network Security

6.1 Explain the function of hardware and software security devices 14

Network based firewall

Host based firewall

IDS

IPS

VPN concentrator

6.2 Explain common features of a firewall 14

Application layer vs. network layer

Stateful vs. stateless

Scanning services

Content filtering

Signature identification

Zones

6.3 Explain the methods of network access security 14

Filtering:

  ACL

    MAC filtering

    IP filtering

  Tunneling and encryption

    SSL VPN

    VPN

    L2TP

    PPTP

    IPSEC

  Remote access

    RAS

    RDP

    PPPoE

    PPP

    VNC

    ICA

6.4 Explain methods of user authentication   15

PKI

Kerberos

AAA

   RADIUS

   TACACS+

Network access control

   802.1x

CHAP

MS-CHAP

EAP

6.5 Explain issues that affect device security   15

Physical security

Restricting local and remote access

Secure methods vs. unsecure methods

   SSH, HTTPS, SNMPv3, SFTP, SCP

   TELNET, HTTP, FTP, RSH, RCP, SNMPv1/2

6.6 Identify common security threats and mitigation techniques   15

Security threats

   DoS

   Viruses

   Worms

   Attackers

   Man in the middle

   Smurf

   Rogue access points

   Social engineering (phishing)

Mitigation techniques

   Policies and procedures

   User training

   Patches and updates

This book contains 15 chapters, plus appendixes, as follows:

- **Chapter 1, "Introduction to Computer Networking"**—Introduces some fundamental networking concepts including physical and logical network topologies and their characteristics.

- **Chapter 2, "Media and Connectors"**—Explores network media, a key network infrastructure component. The chapter includes media types and characteristics, media connectors, wiring standards, specialized wiring, and wiring distribution.

- **Chapter 3, "Networking Components and Devices"**—Covers common networking infrastructure hardware including switches, routers, and more specialized network devices, such as load balancers, multilevel switches, and more.

- **Chapter 4, "Understanding the TCP/IP Protocol Suite"**—Reviews the key individual protocols found within the TCP/IP protocol.

- **Chapter 5, "TCP/IP Addressing and Routing"**—Covers everything TCP/IP including subnetting, addressing, and more for both IPv6 and IPv4. The chapter also includes network routing and routing protocols.

- **Chapter 6, "Ethernet Networking Standards"**—Covers all the aspects of Ethernet networking standards including speeds, access methods, and other characteristics.

- **Chapter 7, "Wireless Networking"**—Reviews wireless networking including the protocols used, access points, characteristics of wireless standards, wireless troubleshooting, and securing wireless communications.

- **Chapter 8, "Wide Area Networking"**—Reviews the technologies used to create wide area networks including standards, WAN implementations, and switching methods.

- **Chapter 9, "OSI Model"**—Reviews the OSI model and maps protocols and network hardware to each level.

- **Chapter 10, "Network Performance and Optimization"**—Looks at disaster recovery, fault tolerant measures, high availability, and quality of service (QoS). It also examines uptime, latency, and high bandwidth applications.

- **Chapter 11, "Troubleshooting Procedures and Best Practices"**—Looks at the art of troubleshooting from isolating the symptoms all the way to finding the solution and documenting the procedures.

- **Chapter 12, "Command-Line Networking Tools"**—Reviews the command-line tools used in networking troubleshooting and procedures and identifies the output from each of the command-line tools.

- **Chapter 13, "Network Management Tools and Documentation Procedures"**—Covers aspects of documentation procedures including wiring schematics and network diagrams; the chapter also reviews some network management tools including packet sniffers, cable testers, toner probes, and more.

- **Chapter 14, "Network Access Security"**—Reviews network security hardware and procedures including firewalls, IDS and IPS, security protocols, and remote access protocols.

- **Chapter 15, "Security Technologies and Malicious Software"**—Covers malicious software including viruses, Trojan horses, and worms. The chapter also explores authentication protocols and secure and unsecure protocols.

The following appendix is printed in the book:

- **Appendix A, "Answers to the Review Questions"**—Includes the answers to all the review questions from Chapters 1 through 15.

The appendixes included on the CD-ROM are

- **Appendix B, "Memory Tables"**—Holds the key tables and lists from each chapter with some of the content removed. You can print this appendix, and as a memory exercise, complete the tables and lists. The goal is to help you memorize facts that can be useful on the exams.

- **Appendix C, "Memory Tables Answer Key"**—Contains the answer key for the exercises in Appendix B.

- **Glossary**—Contains definitions for all the terms listed in the "Define Key Terms" section at the conclusion of Chapter 1–15.

Instructional Features

This book provides multiple ways to learn and reinforce the exam material. Following are some of the helpful methods:

- **Focus questions**—Each chapter ends with a list of questions related to specific exam objectives to keep in mind when preparing for the exam.

- **Foundation topics**—This main section of each chapter covers all the important information related to the exam objectives.

- **Key topics**—An icon marks the tables, figures, and lists you need to memorize.

- **Key terms**—A list of key terms appears at the end of each chapter. Write the definition of each key term, and check your work in the Glossary at the end of the book.

- **Exercises**—Found at the end of the chapters in the "Apply Your Knowledge" section, exercises are performance-based opportunities for you to learn and assess your knowledge.

- **Review questions**—The review questions at the end of each chapter offer an opportunity to test your comprehension of the topics discussed within the chapter.

- **Practice exam**—The CD-ROM accompanying this book includes a practice exam that tests you on all the Network+ exam topics.

Network Hardware and Software Requirements

As a self-paced study guide, *Network+ Cert Guide* is meant to help you understand concepts that must be refined through hands-on experience. To make the most of your studying, you need to have as much background on and experience with both common operating systems and network environments as possible. The best way to do this is to combine studying with work on actual networks. These networks need not be complex; the concepts involved in configuring a network with only a few computers follow the same principles as those involved in configuring a network that has hundreds of connected systems. This section describes the recommended requirements you need to form a solid practice environment.

To fully practice some of the exam objectives, you need to create a network with two (or more) computers networked together. To do this, you need an operating system. CompTIA maintains that the exam is vendor-neutral, and for the most part, it appears to be. However, if there were a slight tilt in the exam questions, it would be toward Microsoft Windows. Therefore, you would do well to set up a small network using a Microsoft server platform such as Windows servers. In addition, you need clients with operating systems such as Windows Vista, Linux, and Mac. When you actually get into it, you might want to install a Linux server as well because you are most certainly going to work with Linux servers in the real world. The following is a detailed list of the hardware and software requirements needed to set up your network:

- A network operating system such as Windows Server or Linux

- Client operating system software such as Windows XP, Mac OS X, or Linux

- Modern PC offering up-to-date functionality including wireless support

- A minimum 1.5GB of free disk space

- A CD-ROM or DVD drive

- A network interface card (NIC) for each computer system

- Network cabling such as Category 5 or higher unshielded twisted-pair

- A two-port (or more) miniport hub to create a test network

- Wireless devices

It's easy to obtain access to the necessary computer hardware and software in a corporate business environment. It can be difficult, however, to allocate enough time within the busy workday to complete a self-study program. Most of your study time will occur after normal working hours, away from the everyday interruptions and pressures of your regular job.

Advice on Taking the Exam

Keep this advice in mind as you study:

- **Read all the material**—CompTIA has been known to include material that is not expressly specified in the objectives. This book includes additional information that is not reflected in the objectives to give you the best possible preparation for the examination—and for your real-world experiences to come.

- **Complete the exercises in each chapter**—They can help you gain experience in using the specified methodology or approach. CompTIA exams might require task- and experienced-based knowledge and require you to have an understanding of how certain network procedures are accomplished.

- **Use the review questions to assess your knowledge**—Don't just read the chapter content; use the review questions to find out what you know and what you don't know. If you struggle, study some more, review, and then assess your knowledge again.

- **Complete the practice exam included on the CD-ROM**—Utilize the practice exam included with this book to assess whether you have retained the information you learned in this book and are prepared to take the exam.

Remember that the primary objective is not to pass the exam but to understand the material. When you understand the material, passing the exam should be simple. Knowledge is a pyramid; to build upward, you need a solid foundation. This book and the Network+ certification are designed to ensure that you have that solid foundation.

Good luck!

This chapter covers CompTIA Network+ objectives 2.3 and 2.7. Upon completion of this chapter, you will be able to answer the following questions:

- What is a network?

- What are the characteristics of a peer-to-peer network?

- How do systems in a client/server network communicate?

- What is the function of a VLAN?

- What is a virtual private network?

- What are the common wired LAN topologies?

- What are wireless topologies?

CHAPTER 1

Introduction to Computer Networking

By itself, the computer sitting on your desk is a powerful personal and business tool. Link that system with 1, 2, or even 1,000 other computers, and the possibilities and potential of your system become almost endless. That is the nature of networking.

Companies of all sizes depend on a collection of interconnected computers to conduct business. These computer networks make possible most of the applications and services used in corporate and home environments. Email, print sharing, real-time communication, file sharing, and videoconferencing would all be unavailable (or pointless) without networks.

The CompTIA Network+ exam is designed to prepare people to work with and around computer networks. The CompTIA objectives introduce basic networking concepts and design, laying the foundation for a solid, comprehensive understanding of networking fundamentals. This book closely follows the CompTIA objectives, clearly explaining each objective and highlighting the important concepts most likely to appear on the exam.

This chapter examines some of the fundamental principles that affect modern networking. These include a discussion about peer-to-peer and client/server computing and the differences between local area networks (LAN), wide area networks (WAN), and metropolitan area networks (MAN). This chapter also looks at network topologies, VLANs, VPNs, wireless topologies, and the physical and logical arrangements of devices on a network.

Foundation Topics

What Is a Network?

By definition, a *network* is a group of connected computers. The group can be as small and simple as two computers and a printer set up in a house or as large and complex as a multisite network that supports thousands of computers and hundreds of printers and other devices. Regardless of the size and complexity of a network, its fundamental function is to enable you to communicate and share data and resources.

Although the basic purpose of a network has not changed since the first network was created, the way in which we build and use networks has evolved in an amazing way. In a not-too-distant past, networks were a luxury that only the largest companies and governments could afford, but they now have become a vital business tool that hundreds of millions of people rely on every day.

NOTE: The Internet   It might seem as though a small network in your house is different from a network such as the Internet, but you would be surprised how much the two have in common. For example, the PCs on a home network most likely communicate in the same way as systems on the Internet. Also, the Internet has clients and servers just like a small network might have. The Internet uses certain devices, such as network routers, that are not as common in a home network, but the basic building blocks of both networks are the same. The term *Internet* is derived from the term *internetwork*, which describes a group of connected networks.

The operation of a network needs to be transparent to the people who use it. Users, for example, need to print to a printer connected to the network just as easily as if it were attached to their own PCs. They also need to access files this easily. The degree of transparency of a network depends on how good the network's structure is and, to a certain extent, how well the network is managed. (But no matter how well a network is managed, problems will occasionally crop up.)

If the purpose of a network is to share resources among computer systems, what types of information and services are shared on a network—and why? All networks, regardless of their design or size, perform one or all of a number of network functions. The following are some common reasons for implementing a network:

■ **Communication**—Increased communication is one of the primary purposes of a network. Networks enable a variety of communications, including videoconferencing, real-time chats, and email. Many organizations have grown so dependent on network communications that without it, they cannot function.

■ **Sharing hardware**—Printing is the best example of hardware sharing. Without a network, each computer that requires printing capabilities would need a printer connected directly to it—and that would be impractical and costly. Although printers are almost certainly the most popular devices shared on networks, other devices are often shared as well, including scanners, optical drives, tape drives, and other removable media.

- **Sharing data**—Linking users on the same system makes it easy for them to share files with others on the network. However, because people can access the data across the network, access to both the data and the network must be carefully controlled. Fortunately, network operating systems provide mechanisms that enable you to secure data so that access can be controlled.

- **Sharing applications**—Networking makes it possible for numerous users to share a single application. This makes it unnecessary to install the same application on several computer systems; instead, the application can be run from a central location. Such a strategy is often used on medium to large networks, where it is difficult and time consuming to install and maintain applications on numerous individual systems. Application sharing is also important for centralized systems such as databases; users rely on networks to access and use such systems.

- **Data backup and retrieval**—A network makes it possible to store data in a central location. When the data is in a central location, it is easier to back up and retrieve. The importance of this benefit cannot be overstated. No matter how much money is invested in a computer network, the data that travels on it has the most value.

Because of these network functions, the majority of businesses and increasing numbers of home users have networks. Given such advantages, the decision often is not whether to set up a network but what type of network to create. The next section explores some of the options.

LANs and WANs

Networks are categorized according to how many locations they span. A network confined to a single location is known as a local area network (LAN). Networks that span multiple geographic locations are known as wide area networks (WAN). The following sections examine the characteristics of these types of networks.

A LAN is confined to a single geographic location, such as a single building, office, or school. LANs are created with networking media that are fast but that can cover a limited distance. Figure 1.1 shows an example of a LAN.

A WAN is a network that spans multiple geographic locations. WANs are generally slower than LANs and are considerably more expensive to run. WANs are all about data throughput, and the more you need, the more you spend. WANs connect LANs to create an *internetwork*. Figure 1.2 shows an example of a WAN.

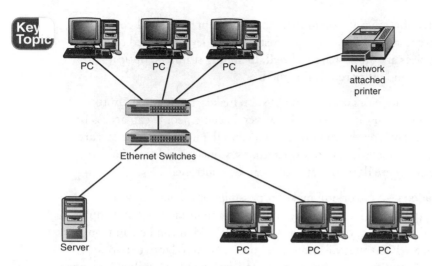

Figure 1.1   An example of a LAN.

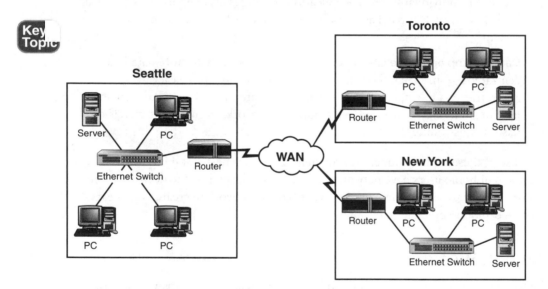

Figure 1.2   An example of a WAN.

WANs often use different technologies from LANs. WAN technologies are discussed in Chapter 8, "Wide Area Networking."

TIP: LAN/WAN Technologies   An understanding of the technologies used in both LANs and WANs is required for the Network+ test. These technologies are covered in detail throughout the rest of this book.

NOTE: When Does a LAN Become a WAN?   Technically, a LAN never becomes a WAN. If the definitions of LAN and WAN were taken literally and applied to a working model that had three connected sites, the portions of the network confined within each site would be LANs, and the network elements connecting the sites would be called the WAN. Another distinction between a LAN and a WAN is that, to function, a WAN relies on an Internet service provider (ISP) or telecommunications company (Telco) to provide a link. The ISP link can be a variety of technologies including digital (T1 lines), ISDN lines, and even analog lines. Avoid the temptation to refer to the entire internetwork as a WAN, because WANs and LANs employ different technologies.

MANs, CANs, and PANs

In addition to LANs and WANs, you might also encounter metropolitan area networks (MANs), campus area networks (CANs), personal area networks (PANs) in discussions of network layouts.

A MAN is confined to a certain geographic area, such as a university campus or a city. No formal guidelines dictate the differences between a MAN and a WAN; technically, a MAN is a WAN. Perhaps for this reason, the term *MAN* is used less frequently than *WAN*. If any distinction exists, it's that a MAN is smaller than a WAN. A MAN is almost always bigger than a LAN and usually smaller than or equal to a WAN. MANs utilize an ISP or Telco provider.

A CAN is a network that spans a defined single location (such as an office complex with multiple buildings or a college campus) but is not large enough to be considered a WAN.

A PAN is a small network design typically associated with a single person. A common implementation of a PAN is using wireless technologies. A wireless personal area network (WPAN) refers to the technologies involved in connecting devices in close proximity to exchange data or resources. An example might be connecting a laptop with a PDA to synchronize an address book. Because of their small size and the nature of the data exchange, WPAN devices lend themselves well to ad hoc wireless networking. *Ad hoc wireless networks* have devices, such as wireless network interface cards, that connect to each other directly and not through a wireless access point. Ad hoc wireless networks are discussed later in this chapter.

Now that you understand the purpose and function of networks and how networks are classified based on size, in the following section you look at the specific types of computer networks, including peer-to-peer, client/server, virtual private, and virtual local area networks.

Peer-to-Peer Versus Client/Server Networks

Wired networks use two basic models: peer-to-peer and client/server. The model used by an organization depends on the role of the network and what the users require from it. You will probably encounter both network models; therefore, you need to understand how these models work and their strengths and weaknesses.

The Peer-to-Peer Networking Model

Peer-to-peer networking, sometimes referred to as a workgroup, is a low-cost, easily implemented network solution generally used in small network environments that need to share a few files and maybe some hardware, such as printers. As its name suggests, on a peer-to-peer network all systems are equal, or *peers*. Each system can share hardware or files and access the same resources on other systems.

> **NOTE:** **Peer-to-Peer Home Networks** Peer-to-peer networks are often seen in residential settings, where home computers are linked together to share an Internet connection, printers, or files. All popular workstation PC operating systems offer peer-to-peer network functionality.

A peer-to-peer network offers no centralized data storage or centralized control over the sharing of files or resources. In a sense, everyone on a peer-to-peer network is a network administrator and can share resources as they see fit. They have the option to grant all users on the network complete access to their computers, including printers and files, or they can choose not to share anything. Figure 1.3 shows an example of a peer-to-peer network.

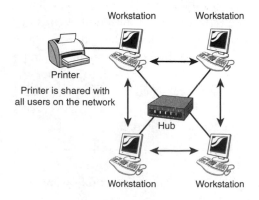

Resources of each system are made available to other
systems on the network

Figure 1.3 An example of a peer-to-peer network.

The peer-to-peer model works well on networks that have 10 or fewer computers, but as a network grows, it becomes more complicated. Peer-to-peer networking is often referred to as *decentralized networking* because the network files, data, and administration are not handled from a central location. This arrangement can lead to huge problems, especially in large networks. For example, locating specific files can become difficult because the files might be on multiple computers. Data backup cannot be performed from a central location; each computer must be backed up individually. Decentralized networking can also be difficult in terms of network security because security is controlled by individual computer users instead of administered from a central location. This decentralized security model requires that each user have a user account and password defined on every system that user will access. With no way of synchronizing passwords between the systems, this can quickly become a problem. Many users have problems remembering just one or two passwords, let alone a dozen.

Given the complexity and drawbacks of using peer-to-peer networking, you might wonder why anyone would use it. Many small companies begin with a peer-to-peer network because it's the easiest and least expensive type to install. After the networks grow too big, they switch to the client/server model, which is discussed in the next section.

> **NOTE: Peer-to-Peer Network Size**   A peer-to-peer network can link an unlimited number of PCs; no standards define a maximum. The only limits are the practicality of managing multiple systems in a peer-to-peer model and the restrictions of the operating system used on the workstations.

Advantages of Peer-to-Peer Networks

The following are three of the advantages of using the peer-to-peer networking model:

- **Cost**—Because peer-to-peer networking does not require a dedicated server, such networks are cost-effective. This makes them an attractive option in environments where money is tight.

- **Ease of installation**—The built-in support for peer-to-peer networking in modern operating systems makes installing and configuring a peer-to-peer network a straightforward process.

- **Maintenance**—A small peer-to-peer network is easy to maintain and does not require specialized staff or training. This makes the peer-to-peer network design cost-effective.

Disadvantages of Peer-to-Peer Networks

The following are some of the disadvantages of using the peer-to-peer networking model:

- **Security**—In a decentralized model, a networkwide security policy cannot be enforced from a server; rather, security needs to be applied to each computer and resource individually.

- **Data backup**—Because files and data are located on individual computers, each system must have its data backed up individually.

- **Resource access**—In a decentralized approach, it can be difficult to locate resources on the network. Printers and files can be distributed among numerous computer systems.

- **Limited numbers of computers**—Peer-to-peer networking is effective only on small networks (fewer than 10 computers).

As you can see, the disadvantages of peer-to-peer networking outweigh the advantages. Therefore, client/server networks are far more popular in corporate or business environments than peer-to-peer networks.

The Client/Server Networking Model

Client/server networking—or *server-based networking*, as it is commonly called—is the network model you are most likely to see in the corporate world. The server-based network model is scalable, enabling additional computers or other networked devices to be added with little difficulty. Perhaps the greatest benefit of this model is that it enables for centralized management of all network services, security, and streamlined backup procedures. Figure 1.4 shows an example of a client/server network.

As you might have gathered, two types of computers are required for the server-based model: the client and the server. Figure 1.5 shows the relationship between client and server computers. These two computer systems are often different from each other, and each plays a unique role on a network.

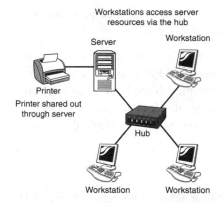

Figure 1.4 An example of a client/server network.

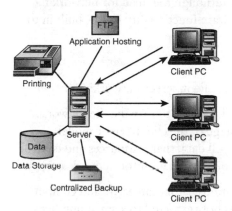

Figure 1.5 The relationship between client and server computers.

Servers

Servers are the workhorses of the network. They respond to the numerous requests that come from client computers, such as requests for files, network authentication, and access to shared hardware resources. Network administration—including network security, backups, and network monitoring—is done from the server.

To perform their functions, server computers require additional resources and computing power. Server systems often use specialized hardware and software in fault-tolerant configurations to ensure that they remain operational. When a server fails and goes offline, it cannot respond to requests from client systems, and its functions are unavailable. This situation can be frustrating for users and costly for an organization.

In addition to requiring specific hardware, servers also require a network operating system. A network operating system stands above ordinary desktop operating systems; it has unique features and functions that enable an administrator to manage, monitor, and administer the data and resources of the server and the users who connect to it. In addition, network operating systems are designed to be resilient in case of the kind of downtime previously discussed.

A network can have a single server that offers more than one network service or hundreds of servers, each performing a dedicated task. For example, one server might be used only to authenticate users, and another might be used to store an applications database. Some of the most common roles for dedicated servers include acting as file and print servers, application servers, web servers, database servers, firewall servers, and proxy servers.

Client Computers

Client computers are the other half of the client/server model. Client computers connect to the network and access the resources of the server. Software is needed to enable the client to connect to the network, although the need for networking has become so fundamental that the client software functionality is now built in to desktop operating systems.

Advantages of Client/Server Networking

The following are some of the advantages of the client/server networking model:

- **Centralized management and security**—The ability to manage the network from a single location is the biggest advantage of the client/server model. From a server, you can perform backups of all data, share resources and control access to those resources, manage user accounts, and monitor network activity.

- **Scalability**—In a server-based network, administrators can easily add computers and devices. In addition, the network is not restricted to a small number of computers. In a client/server network, the number of clients is limited by factors such as licensing and network capacity rather than by the operating system's capability to support them.

- **Simplified backups**—On server-based networks, files and folders typically reside in a single location or a small number of locations and are therefore easier to back up than the files on a peer-to-peer network. Scheduling backups to occur at regular intervals is easier with a centralized network design.

Disadvantages of Client/Server Networking

The following are some of the disadvantages of the client/server networking model:

- **High cost**—A server-based network requires additional hardware and software, so it can be a costly venture. The costs of the client/server model include the costs of the network operating system and at least one server system, replete with specialized server hardware. Also, because the client/server model can support far more systems than the peer-to-peer model, networking devices such as hubs, routers, and switches are often needed.

- **Administration requirements**—Client/server networks require additional administrative skills over those required on a peer-to-peer network. In particular, the technical abilities of the administrator need to be greater. Organizations that use the server-based model often need technically skilled people to manage and maintain the network and the servers.

- **Single points of failure**—In a client/server model, the client systems depend on servers to provide network services. If the server fails, the clients can't access the services that reside on the server. Great effort and expense are needed to ensure the high availability of network servers.

Given the limitations of the peer-to-peer network design, such networks are used in only a few situations. On the other hand, the client/server networking model is versatile, and its shortcomings are overshadowed by its capabilities and advantages. You will spend most of your time working with server-based networks of all shapes and sizes.

> **NOTE: Hybrid Networks**   The distinction between networks that use a peer-to-peer design and those that use a client/server design is not always clear. Today's operating systems let client computers share resources with other systems in a peer-to-peer configuration and also be connected to a server. Such an arrangement is sometimes referred to as a *hybrid network*. Although this model takes advantage of the benefits of both network models, it is also susceptible to their combined shortcomings.

Distributed and Centralized Computing

Although they're less of an issue than in the past, you need to be familiar with two important networking concepts: distributed and centralized computing. These concepts are not directly related to the server-based/peer-to-peer discussion, although by definition a peer-to-peer and server-based network model are examples of a distributed computing model.

The terms *distributed* and *centralized computing* describe the location on a network where the processing takes place. In an environment such as a mainframe, the processing is performed on a centralized system that also stores all the data. In such a model, no data processing or data storage occurs on the client terminal. In contrast, in a distributed processing environment, processing is performed in more than one place. If a network has servers and workstations, processing can take place on the server or on the client.

It is relatively unusual for a company to have just a centralized computing environment. A company is far more likely to have a server-based network, which would fall under the banner of distributed computing, and perhaps a mainframe accessed from the same PCs as the server-based network, which would fall under the banner of centralized computing. A good example of such an environment might be a company that books hotel reservations for customers, in which the booking system is held on a mainframe, but the email system used to correspond with clients is held on a PC-based server and accessed through client software on the PCs.

Virtual Private Networks (VPN)

In the mid-1990s, Microsoft, IBM, and Cisco began working on a technology called *tunneling* By 1996, more companies had become interested and involved in the work, and from their efforts virtual private networks (VPN) became one of the most popular methods of remote access. But before you can understand why VPNs became so popular, you must first know a bit more about them.

Essentially, a VPN extends a LAN by establishing a remote connection using a public network such as the Internet. A VPN provides a secure point-to-point dedicated link between two points over a public IP network. Figure 1.6 shows how a VPN enables remote access for a remote client to a private network.

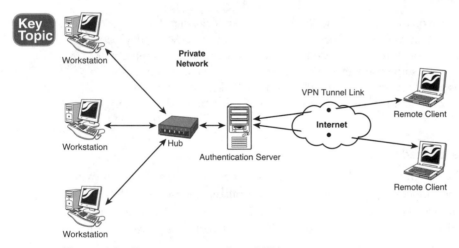

Figure 1.6   Remote access using a VPN.

For many companies, the VPN link provides the perfect method to expand their networking capabilities and reduce their costs. By using the public network (Internet), a company does not need to rely on expensive private leased lines to establish and maintain the remote connection. Using the Internet to facilitate the remote connection, the VPN enables network connectivity over a possibly long physical distance. In this respect, a VPN is a form of WAN.

> **NOTE: Using the VPN**   Many companies use a VPN to provide a cost-effective method of establishing a connection between remote clients and a private network. VPN can also be used for connecting one private LAN with another, known as *LAN-to-LAN internetworking*. For security reasons, it is possible to use a VPN to provide controlled access within an intranet.

Components of the VPN Connection

A VPN enables anyone with an Internet connection to use the infrastructure of the public network to connect to the main network and access resources as if the user were logged on to the network locally. It also enables two networks to connect to each other securely.

Many elements are involved in establishing a VPN connection, including the following:

- **VPN client**—The computer that initiates the connection to the VPN server. Referring back to Figure 1.6, you can notice that the VPN clients are the laptop computer systems labeled *remote clients*.

- **VPN server**—Authenticates connections from VPN clients.

- **Access method**—As mentioned, a VPN is most often established over a public network such as the Internet; however, some VPN implementations use a private intranet. The network used must be IP-based.

- **VPN protocols**—Protocols are required to establish, manage, and secure the data over the VPN connection. The Point-to-Point Tunneling Protocol (PPTP) and the Layer 2 Tunneling Protocol (L2TP) are commonly associated with VPN connections. These protocols, and their supporting authentication and encryption protocols, enable authentication and encryption in VPNs. Authentication enables VPN clients and servers to correctly establish the identity of people on the network. Encryption enables potentially sensitive data to be guarded from the general public.

VPNs have become popular because they enable the public Internet to be safely utilized as a WAN connectivity solution.

TIP: VPN Connections   VPNs support analog modems, Integrated Services Digital Network (ISDN) wireless connections, and dedicated broadband connections such as cable and Digital Subscriber Line (DSL). You should remember this for the exam.

VPN Pros and Cons

As with any technology, pros and cons exist. Fortunately with VPN technology, these are clear cut, and even the cons typically do not prevent an organization from using VPNs in their networks. There are several benefits to using a VPN in your network, but like any other technology there are some drawbacks. The following list highlights the good and the bad of VPNs:

- **Reduced cost**—By using the public network, no need exists to rent dedicated lines between remote clients and a private network. Additionally, a VPN also can replace remote access servers and long-distance dial-up network connections commonly used in the past by business travelers needing to access their company intranet. This eliminates long-distance phone charges.

- **Network scalability**—The cost to an organization of building a dedicated private network might be reasonable at first but increases exponentially as the organization grows. The Internet enables an organization to grow its remote client base without having to increase or modify an internal network infrastructure.

- **Simplified administration**—With a VPN network, adding and removing clients is a straightforward process. Authentication work is managed from the VPN authentication server, and client systems can be easily configured for automatic VPN access.

Disadvantages of using a VPN include the following:

- **Security and setup complexity**—Using a VPN, data is sent over a public network and therefore may be at risk of data being captured and compromised. This risk is minimized as much as possible with the use of various security protocols and proper configuration. VPN administrators need an understanding of security protocols and an ability to properly setup, configure, and manage a VPN connection.

- **Reliability**—The reliability of the VPN communication is dependant upon the public network and is not under an organization's direct control. Instead, the solution relies on an ISP and its quality of service (QoS).

Chapter 8 and Chapter 14, "Network Access Security" describe additional details related to VPNs.

Virtual Local Area Network (VLAN)

The word *virtual* is used often—perhaps too often—in the computing world. In the case of virtual LANs (VLAN), the word *virtual* does little to help explain the technology. Perhaps a more descriptive name for the VLAN concept might have been *segmented*. For now at least, we use virtual.

> **NOTE: 802.1Q**   802.1Q is the Institute of Electrical and Electronics Engineers (IEEE) specification developed to ensure interoperability of VLAN technologies from the various vendors.

VLANs are used for network segmentation, a strategy that significantly increases the performance capability of the network, removes potential performance bottlenecks, and can even increase network security. A VLAN is a group of connected computers that acts as if it is on its own network segments, even though it might not be. A VLAN is a group of logically connected systems and configured through an interface on a switch or router. For instance, suppose that you work in a three-story building in which the advertising employees are spread over all three floors. A VLAN can let all the advertising personnel be combined and access network resources as if they were connected on the same segment. This virtual segment can be isolated from other network segments. In effect, it would appear to the advertising group that it was on a network by itself.

TIP: VLANs   VLANs enable you to create multiple broadcast domains on a single switch. In essence, this is the same as creating separate networks for each

VLANs offer some clear advantages, such as creating logical segmentation of a network that gives administrators flexibility beyond the restrictions of the physical network design and cable infrastructure. VLANs enable for easier administration because the network can be divided into well-organized sections. Further, you can increase security by isolating certain network segments from others. For example, you can segment the marketing personnel from finance or the administrators from the students. VLANs can ease the burden on overworked routers and reduce broadcast storms. The following list summarizes the benefits of VLANs:

- **Increased security**—By creating logical (virtual) boundaries, network segments can be isolated.

- **Increased performance**—By reducing broadcast traffic throughout the network, VLANs free up bandwidth.

- **Organization**—Network users and resources that are linked and communicate frequently can be grouped together in a VLAN.

- **Simplified administration**—With a VLAN the network administrator's job is easier when moving users between LAN segments, recabling, addressing new stations, and reconfiguring switches and routers.

VLAN Membership

You can use several methods to determine VLAN membership or determine how devices are assigned to a specific VLAN. The methods include protocol-based VLANs, port-based VLANs, and MAC address-based VLANs, as described in the following sections.

Protocol-Based VLANs

With protocol-based VLAN membership, computers are assigned to VLANs by using the protocol that is in use and the Layer 3 address. For example, it enables the IP subnet to have its own VLAN.

When we say Layer 3 address, we refer to one of the most important networking concepts, the Open Systems Interconnect (OSI) reference model. This conceptual model, created by the International Organization for Standardization (ISO) in 1978 and revised in 1984, describes a network architecture that enables data to be passed between computer systems. There are seven layers in total, which are discussed in detail in Chapter 9, "OSI Model." In brief, Layer 3, known as the network layer, identifies the mechanisms by which data can be moved between two networks or systems. One mechanism is transport protocols, which in the case of TCP/IP is the IP protocol.

It is important to note that although VLAN membership can be based on Layer 3 information, this has nothing to do with routing or routing functions. The IP addresses are used only to determine the membership in a particular VLAN—not to determine routing.

Port-Based VLANs

Port-based VLANs require that specific ports on a network switch be assigned to a VLAN. For example, ports 1 through 4 can be assigned to marketing, ports 5 through 7 can be assigned to sales, and so on. Using this method, a switch determines VLAN membership by taking note of the port used by a particular packet. Figure 1.7 shows how the ports on a server could be used for port-based VLAN membership.

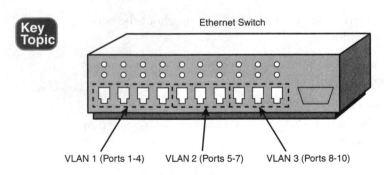

Figure 1.7   Port-based VLAN membership.

MAC Address-Based VLANs

The Media Access Control (MAC) address is a unique 12-digit hexadecimal number stamped into every network interface card. Every device that will be used on a network has a unique address built in to it. It is hardwired and cannot be physically modified. As you might have guessed, the MAC address-based VLAN assigns membership according to the MAC address of the workstation. To do this, the switch must keep track of the MAC addresses that belong to each VLAN. The advantage of this method is that a workstation computer can be moved anywhere in an office without needing to be reconfigured; because the MAC address does not change, the workstation remains a member of a particular VLAN. Table 1.1 provides an example of the membership of a MAC address-based VLAN.

Table 1.1   MAC Address-Based VLANs

MAC Address	VLAN	Description
44-45-53-54-00-00	1	Sales
44-45-53-54-13-12	2	Marketing
44-45-53-54-D3-01	3	Administration
44-45-53-54-F5-17	1	Sales

VLAN Segmentation

The capability to logically segment a LAN provides a new level of administrative flexibility, organization, and security. Whether the LAN is segmented using the protocol, MAC address, or port, the result is the same; the network is segmented. The segmentation is used for several reasons, including security, organization, and performance. To get a better idea of how this works, let's look at a network without using a VLAN. Figure 1.8 shows this network design.

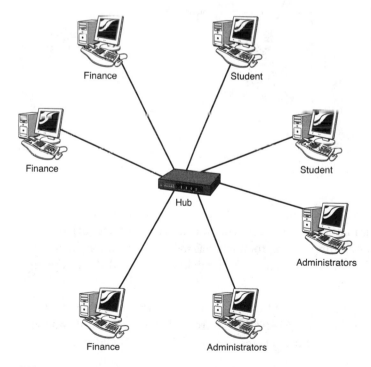

Figure 1.8   Network configuration without using a VLAN.

In Figure 1.8, all systems on the network can see each other. That is, the student computers can see both the administrator and finance computers. In terms of security, this is not a good arrangement. Figure 1.9, on the other hand, shows how this same network might look using a VLAN. Notice that the three network users are separated using the VLAN. To these users, the other networks are invisible.

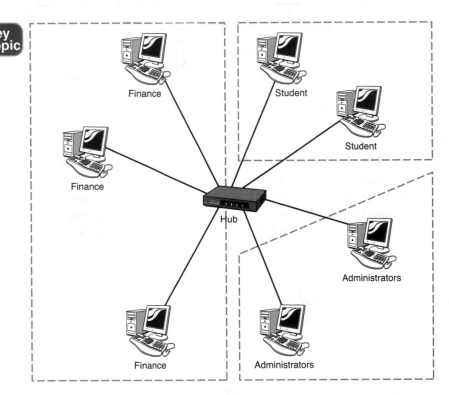

Figure 1.9   Network configuration using VLAN.

LAN Topologies

The term *network topology* refers to the layout of a network. The type of topology affects what networking method is used, and what media types and network devices are required. Topologies are important;, they serve as the foundation for the information you'll learn in the following sections. You will likely be asked about topologies on the Network+ exam.

Before we look at the different types of topologies, we must first examine one of the most confusing networking principles: the difference between physical and logical topologies. Then we examine the specific physical LAN topologies in use today: bus, star, ring, mesh, and wireless.

Physical and Logical Topologies

Network topologies can be defined on a physical level or on a logical level. The *physical topology* refers to how a network is physically constructed—that is, how it actually looks. The *logical topology* refers to how a network looks to the devices that use it—in other words, how it actually functions. In a number of commonly implemented network models, the physical topology differs from the logical topology. It can be difficult to appreciate what that means, so let's use an example.

The most commonly implemented network model is a physical star/logical bus topology. In this configuration, computers connect to a central devices, called a *hub* or more likely in today's networks, a *switch*, which gives the network the appearance of a star (or a reasonable facsimile thereof). However, the devices attached to the star see the network as a linear bus topology and use the topology based on its logical characteristics.

NOTE: Network Topologies   Understanding network topologies and their characteristics is an objective for the Network+ exam. Therefore, you should make sure that you understand the concept of topologies. This includes both wired and wireless topologies.

NOTE: How Did We Get Here?   The physical/logical topology discussion can be confusing, so let's examine its background. When networks were first created, they followed a simple path. For example, the first Ethernet network was a physical and logical bus (single length of cable). As you will see in upcoming sections, however, this physical bus approach has a number of disadvantages; therefore, alternatives were sought. In this case, the solution was to move away from the single cable segment approach and instead use different types of cable on a physical star. The media access method and the networking system remained the same, however, resulting in a physical star/logical bus topology.

Bus Topology

The bus network is called a *trunk*, or *backbone*. Computers connect to this backbone, as shown in Figure 1.10.

Figure 1.10   An example of the bus topology.

The computers can connect to the backbone by a cable, known as a *drop cable*, or more commonly, directly to the backbone via T connectors. At each end of the cable, terminators prevent the signal from bouncing back down the cable. In addition, one end of the cable should be grounded. More information on the specific connectors and cables used in different network implementations is provided in Chapter 2, "Media and Connectors."

NOTE: Ethernet Standards   The most common implementation of a linear bus is the Institute of Electrical and Electronics Engineers (IEEE) 802.3a standard, 10Base2, which is an Ethernet standard. Ethernet standards are covered in Chapter 6, "Ethernet Networking Standards."

Bus topologies are easy and inexpensive to implement because a single-segment bus topology doesn't require any special networking equipment. However, they are notoriously difficult to troubleshoot, and a single break in the network cable renders the entire segment useless. For this and a number of other reasons, such as limited speed capacity, bus topologies have been largely replaced with the physical star topology. Table 1.2 lists the main features, advantages, and disadvantages of bus topologies.

Table 1.2   Features, Advantages, and Disadvantages of the Linear Bus Topology

Features	Advantages	Disadvantages
Uses a single length of cable.	It is inexpensive and easy to implement.	It cannot be expanded easily. Doing so may render the network inaccessible while the expansion is performed.
Devices connect directly to the cable.	It doesn't require special equipment.	A break in the cable renders the entire segment unusable.
The cable must be terminated at both ends.	It requires less cable than other topologies.	It is difficult to troubleshoot.

Star Topology

In a star topology, each device on the network connects to a centralized device via a separate cable. This arrangement creates a point-to-point network connection between the two devices and gives the overall appearance of a star. Figure 1.11 shows an example of the star topology.

Figure 1.11   An example of the star topology.

Multiple stars can be rearranged into a treelike structure known as a *hierarchical star*. The hierarchical star enables for high levels of flexibility and expandability. Depending on the networking equipment used, it also makes it possible to manage traffic and isolate high-traffic areas of the network. Figure 1.12 shows an example of a hierarchical star topology.

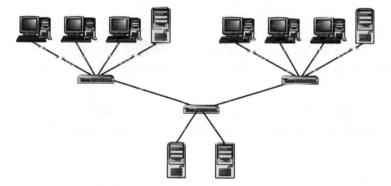

Figure 1.12   An example of the hierarchical star topology.

One of the biggest advantages of the star topology is that computers can be connected to and disconnected from the network without affecting any other systems. Thus it's easy to add systems to or remove systems from the network. In addition, the failure of a system or the cable it uses to attach likewise generally has no effect on other stations on the network. However, in the star topology, all devices on the network connect to a central device, and this central device creates a single point of failure on the network.

The star topology is the most widely implemented network design in use today; you will definitely encounter it in the real world. Working with and troubleshooting a star topology can be tricky, however, and you need to know what to look for and where to look.

Table 1.3 provides the features, advantages, and disadvantages of the physical star topology.

Table 1.3   Features, Advantages, and Disadvantages of the Physical Star Topology

Features	Advantages	Disadvantages
Devices connect to a central point.	It can be easily expanded without disruption to existing systems.	It requires additional networking equipment to create the network layout.
Each system uses an individual cable to attach.	A cable failure affects only a single system.	It requires considerably more cable than other topologies, such as the linear bus.
Multiple stars can be combined to create a hierarchical star.	It is easy to troubleshoot.	Centralized devices create a single point of failure.

Ring Topology

In the ring topology, the network layout forms a complete ring. Computers connect to the network cable directly or, far more commonly, through a specialized network device.

On a ring network, data travels in one direction, passing from one computer to the next until it reaches the intended destination. Figure 1.13 shows an example of the ring topology.

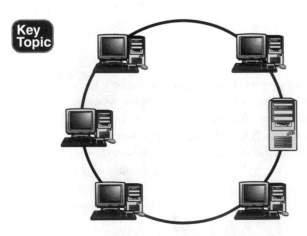

Figure 1.13   An example of the ring topology.

Ring topologies are more difficult to install and configure than other topologies because breaking the loop disrupts the entire network. Even if network devices are used to create the ring, the ring must still be broken if a fault occurs or the network needs to be expanded. To negate the problem of a broken ring making the network unavailable, you can configure dual rings so that one ring can be used if the other fails.

The ring network can be a physical ring topology with each node connecting directly to the ring, or it can be a logical ring topology. In a logical ring, each node connects to a central device known as an Multi-Station Access Unit (MSAU). The function of the ring is performed within the MSAU. The logical ring topology network would have the appearance of a physical star because each node connects to a central device.

Ring topologies are relatively uncommon; the physical star layout is by far the most popular topology. For this reason, you are unlikely to actually install a ring topology. Table 1.4 shows the features, advantages, and disadvantages of the ring topology.

Table 1.4   Features, Advantages, and Disadvantages of the Ring Topology

Feature	Advantage	Disadvantage
Devices are connected in a closed loop or ring.	It is easy to troubleshoot. Also, it can be implemented in a fault-tolerant configuration using dual rings.	A cable network break can disrupt the entire network. Also adding or removing computers to the network creates network disruption for all users.

Wired Mesh Topology

The mesh network topology is all about link redundancy. A mesh network uses multiple connections between network devices to ensure that if one link should fail, an alternative path exists for data to travel and reach its destination. The goal of the mesh network is to provide maximum reliability and redundancy for the network but this capability comes at a price. Establishing these redundant links can be costly in terms of wiring, support, and maintenance.

The two types of mesh topologies are full and partial. A full wired mesh topology interconnects every node with every other node on the network. As you might imagine, the complexity and cost of this topology can be significant. Full mesh is usually reserved for backbone networks.

A partial wired mesh interconnects some or most nodes, but others nodes do not have redundant links. Typically, mission critical servers and systems are fully meshed, whereas some other less-critical systems are left to traditional single nonredundant links. Partial mesh topology is commonly found in peripheral networks connected to a full meshed backbone.

Figure 1.14 shows an example of the mesh topology.

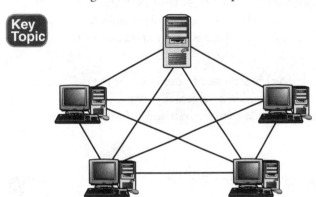

Figure 1.14   An example of the full mesh topology.

NOTE: Fault Tolerance   The mesh layout is the most fault tolerant of all the network topologies. Redundant links exist between all nodes, and the failure of a single link does not affect the overall functionality of the network.

Given the relative ease with which the other topologies can be created and the complexity of the mesh layout, you should not be surprised to learn that wired networks using the mesh layout are few and far between. You are unlikely to see a mesh layout in a LAN setting. The mesh topology is sometimes adopted in WAN configurations that require direct connections between every geographic site.

Table 1.5 lists the features, advantages, and disadvantages of the mesh topology.

Table 1.5   Features, Advantages, and Disadvantages of the Mesh Topology

Features	Advantages	Disadvantages
A full mesh uses point-to-point connectivity between all devices.	Multiple links provide fault tolerance and redundancy.	It is difficult to implement.

A partial mesh uses point-to-point connectivity between devices, but not all of them.	The network can be expanded with minimal or no disruption.	It can be expensive because it requires specialized hardware and cable.

Wireless Network Topologies

The widespread interest in networks without wires and the push toward obtaining "anywhere, anytime" Internet access has encouraged rapid growth in wireless standards and related technologies. The IEEE 802.11 wireless standards in particular have experienced considerable success. Several wireless standards fall under the 802.11 banner, each with its own speeds, radio frequencies, and transmission ranges. These standards create the possibility for wireless local area networking (WLAN) and put the possibility of complete mobile computing within reach.

When working with wireless technologies, you need to be aware of several types of topologies. These include the infrastructure, or managed, wireless topology; the ad-hoc, or unmanaged, wireless topology; point-to-point wireless design; point-to-multipoint; mesh wireless; and hybrid topologies.

Infrastructure Wireless Topology

The infrastructure wireless topology is commonly used to extend a wired LAN to include wireless devices. Wireless devices communicate with the wired LAN through a base station known as an access point (AP). The AP forms a bridge between a wireless and wired LAN, and all transmissions between wireless stations or between a system and a wired network client go through the AP. APs are not mobile and must stay connected to the wired network; therefore, they become part of the wired network infrastructure, thus the name. In infrastructure wireless networks, several APs can provide wireless coverage for a large area with signal regeneration hardware such as repeaters and wireless access point extenders used to increase signal range. The infrastructure topology can also use a single access point to provide coverage for a small area, such as a single home or small building. Figure 1.15 shows an example of an infrastructure wireless network using a single AP.

NOTE: **Wireless BSS and ESS**   In the wireless infrastructure mode, the wireless network consists of at least one AP connected to the wired network infrastructure and a set of wireless end stations, as shown in Figure 1.15. This configuration is referred to as a basic service set (BSS).

In an extended service set (ESS) two or more BSSs combine to form a single subnetwork. Traffic is forwarded from one BSS to another to smooth the progress of movement.

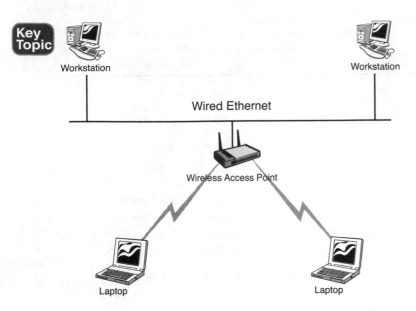

Figure 1.15 Wireless infrastructure topology.

Ad Hoc Wireless Networking

In a wireless ad hoc topology, devices communicate directly between themselves without using an access point. This peer-to-peer network design is commonly used to connect a small number of computers or wireless devices. For example, an ad hoc wireless network can be set up temporarily between laptops in a boardroom or to connect two systems in a home instead of a wired solution. The ad hoc wireless design provides a quick method to share files and resources between a small number of systems. Figure 1.16 shows an example of an ad hoc network design.

> **NOTE: Ad Hoc Wireless Topology**   The ad hoc, or unmanaged, network design does not use an AP. All wireless devices connect directly to each other.

Point-to-Point, Point-to–Multipoint, and Mesh-Wireless Topology

When setting up a wireless network, you can choose from several other topologies. These include the point-to-point, point-to–multipoint, and wireless-mesh configurations.

Point-to-Point Networks

As the name suggests, in a point-to-point (PtP) wireless configuration, the communication link travels from one node directly to one other node. Wireless point-to-point systems are often used in wireless backbone systems, such as microwave relay communications, or as a replacement for a single wired communication cable. Figure 1.17 shows a point-to-point wireless configuration.

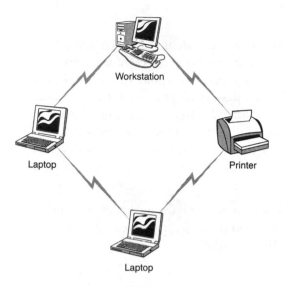

Figure 1.16   An ad hoc wireless topology.

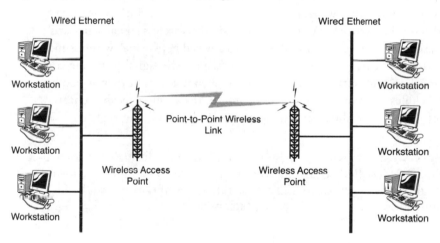

Figure 1.17   A point-to-point wireless topology.

As seen in Figure 1.17, the point-to-point wireless link connects two remote locations. Not having to run cable, such as fiber, makes it an economical way to provide a communication link. However, in a typical point-to-point wireless configuration, no redundancy exists. This means if the wireless link should fail, communication between the locations will not be available.

The point-to-point link is often used for organizations that need a direct link between two remote office buildings. These point-to-point wireless connections are typically easy to install and require no external outdoor casing, cables, and other accessories. Because there is no need for the cabling infrastructure, a point-to-point wireless solution is a cost-effective method for connecting two remote locations.

Point-to-Multipoint

A point-to-multipoint (PtMP) wireless connection is designed to link multiple wired networks. Signals in point-to-multipoint networks travel from a central node, such as a base station of a cellular system, an access point of a WLAN, or a satellite. The function of the multipoint wireless topology is to interconnect multiple locations enabling them to access and share resources. Multipoint networks use a base station as the "hub" and client networks as the connection points communicating with the base station. These point-to-multipoint networks are used in wireless Internet service providers (WISP), large corporate campuses, interconnected branch offices, and more.

The reliability of the PtMP network topology relies on the quality of the central node and each connecting node. The location of the central node is important to ensure the range and strength of the wireless signal.

Mesh Networks

Mesh networks are common in the wireless networking world. In the wireless mesh network, as with the wired mesh, each network node is interconnected to other nodes on the network. With a wired mesh, the wireless signal starts at a wireless base station (access point) attached to a wired network. A wireless mesh network extends the transmission distance by relaying the signal from one computer to another. Unlike the wired mesh where a complex and expensive collection of physical cables are required to create the mesh, the wireless mesh is cheap to implement. Figure 1.18 shows an example of a wireless mesh network.

> **TIP: Wireless Mesh**   A wireless mesh network is created through the connection of wireless APs installed at each network user's locale. Data signals in a wireless mesh rely on all nodes to propagate signals. Wireless mesh networks can be identified by the interconnecting signals between each node.

The wireless mesh network has several key advantages. Because a wireless mesh network is interconnected with one or more nodes on the network, multiple paths exist for data to travel to reach its destination. When a new node is added, it provides new paths for other nodes, which in turn improves network performance and decreases congestion. Advantages of the wireless mesh include the following:

- **Self-healing**—Wireless mesh networks are known as self–healing, which refers to the networks' capability to adapt to network failure and function even if a node is moved from one location to another. Self-healing in a wireless mesh environment is possible because of the interconnected links between devices and because of the actual wireless media.

- **Scalable**—Wireless mesh networks are highly scalable. Using wireless, it is possible to add new systems to the network without the need for expensive cables.

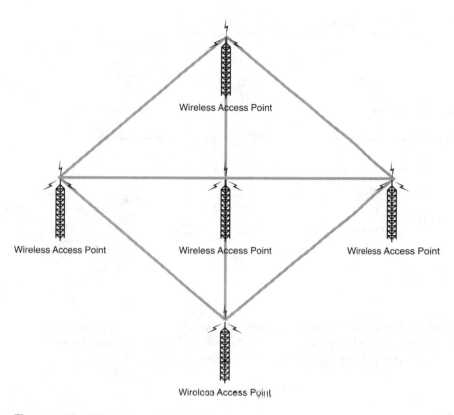

Figure 1.18 Wireless mesh topology.

- **Reliability**—Of all network topologies, the mesh network provides the greatest reliability. The redundant number of paths for the data to travel ensures that data can reach its destination.

- **Cost**—One of the disadvantages of the wired mesh is the cost associated with running the cabling and the support costs of such a complex network. Wireless mesh networks are essentially self-configuring and do not have the cabling requirements. Therefore, systems can be added, removed, and relocated with little cost or disruption to the network.

Hybrid Topologies

As you might expect, topology designs are not black and white. Many of the topologies we see in large networking environments are a hybrid of physical topologies. An example of a hybrid topology is the star-bus, which is a combination of the star topology and the bus topology. Figure 1.19 shows how this MIGHT look in a network implementation.

Another example of a hybrid topology is the star-wired ring topology, which is the combination of the physical star topology and the physical ring topology.

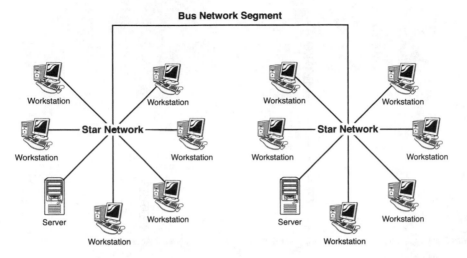

Figure 1.19   A star-bus topology.

> **NOTE: Another Meaning**   The term *hybrid topology* also can refer to the combination of wireless and wired networks. For the Network+ exam, however, the term *hybrid* most likely refers to the combination of physical networks.

Summary

This chapter provides an overview of the functions and purposes of computer networks. Key among the functions of the network are increased communication, both in real-time and via email; sharing of hardware between multiple users; reduction in overall cost and support of multiple devices; and the capability to share files.

Two network models are identified in this chapter: peer-to-peer networking and client/server networking. Peer-to-peer networking is restricted to networks with few users and does not use a centralized server. Peer-to-peer networks are most commonly seen in home network environments and in small offices.

The client/server model is more common and familiar than the peer-to-peer model, especially in larger networks. The client/server model uses a dedicated server and offers many advantages over the peer-to-peer network model. Perhaps most notable of these advantages is the capability to centrally manage the network, although the cost and administration requirements are higher than those of peer-to-peer networks.

Two other network models discussed are VPNs and VLANs. VPNs provide a means to securely connect remote users to a private network. VPNs use a variety of protocols to make and secure the connection. VLANs provide a way to segregate a network. Three ways that a VLAN does this are port-based VLANs, protocol-based VLANs, and MAC-based VLANs.

Networks have both physical and logical topologies. The physical topology refers to the way the network is physically laid out, including media, computers, and other networking devices such as hubs or switches. The logical topology refers to how data is transmitted around the network. Common network topologies include star, ring, bus, and mesh. Each of these topologies offers distinct advantages and disadvantages and various levels of fault tolerance.

Wireless networks are typically implemented using ad hoc or infrastructure network design. Wireless topologies include point-to-point, point-to–multipoint, and wireless-mesh design.

Exam Preparation Tasks

Review All the Key Topics

Review the most important topics in the chapter, noted with the key topics icon in the outer margin of the page. Table 1.6 lists a reference of these key topics and the page numbers on which each is found.

Table 1.6 Key Topics for Chapter 1

Key Topic Element	Description	Page Number
Figure 1.1	An example of a local area network	26
Figure 1.2	An example of a wide area network	26
Figure 1.6	Remote access using a VPN	34
Figure 1.7	Port based VLAN membership	38
Table 1.1	MAC address VLAN membership	39
Table 1.2	Features, advantages, and disadvantages of the linear bus topology	42
Figure 1.9	Network configuration using a VLAN	40
Figure 1.10	An example of a bus topology	41
Figure 1.11	An example of a star topology	43
Figure 1.12	An example of the hierarchical star topology	43
Table 1.3	Features, advantages, and disadvantages of the physical star topology	44

Table 1.6   Key Topics for Chapter 1

Key Topic Element	Description	Page Number
Figure 1.13	An example of a ring topology	44
Table 1.4	Features, advantages, and disadvantages of the ring topology	45
Figure 1.14	An example of a full mesh topology	46
Table 1.5	Features, advantages, and disadvantages of the mesh topology	46
Figure 1.15	Wireless infrastructure topology	48
Figure 1.16	An ad hoc wireless topology	49

Complete the Tables and Lists from Memory

Print a copy of Appendix B, "Memory Tables," (found on the CD), or at least the section for this chapter, and complete the tables and lists from memory. Appendix C, "Memory Tables Answer Key," also on the CD, includes completed tables and lists to check your work.

Define Key Terms

Define the following key terms from this chapter, and check your answers in the Glossary.

- Star
- Mesh
- Bus
- Ring
- Point-to-point
- Point-to-multipoint
- LAN
- WAN
- MAN
- MAC address
- Hybrid
- Peer to peer
- Client/server

- Topology
- VPN
- VLAN

Apply Your Knowledge

Exercise 1.1 Comparing LAN Topologies

You have been asked to recommend a topology for a new network. You have been asked to consider all options and prepare a document that shows how they compare. To complete your task, you decide to create a chart showing the advantages and disadvantages of the various network topologies. For this exercise, complete the following chart and check your answers with the tables presented earlier in this chapter:

Estimated time: 10 minutes

Topology Type	Key Features	Advantages	Disadvantages
Star			
Bus			
Wired Mesh			
Ring			
Wireless Infrastructure			
Wireless Mesh			

Review Questions

You can find the answers to these questions in Appendix A.

1. Which of the following is a disadvantage of the physical bus topology?
  a. Has complex cabling requirements
  b. Is prone to cable faults
  c. Requires a dedicated server
  d. Requires a dedicated hub

2. Which of the following are valid ways to assign computers to a VLAN? (Choose all the best answers.)
  a. Protocol assignment
  b. Port-based assignment
  c. NetBIOS computer name
  d. MAC address

3. Which of the following statements best describes a VPN?

   a. It is any protocol that enables remote clients to log in to a server over a network such as the Internet.

   b. It provides a system whereby only screen display and keyboard and mouse input travel across the link.

   c. It is a secure communication channel across a public network such as the Internet.

   d. It is a protocol used for encryption of user IDs and passwords.

4. Which of the following topologies offers the greatest level of redundancy?

   a. Mesh

   b. Star

   c. Bus

   d. Ring

5. You are the administrator for a local company. Recently a second branch of the company has opened across town. You need to connect the two networks in a cost-effective manner. Which of the following solutions could you use?

   a. VLAN

   b. Star

   c. VPN

   d. LAN

6. Which of the following is required to establish a VPN connection? (Choose all correct answers.)

   a. VPN server

   b. VPN client

   c. VPN protocols

   d. VPN MAC identification

7. You have just been hired as the administrator for a large corporation. The network connects two star network segments with a bus network. Which of the following network types is used?

   a. Bus

   b. Star bus

   c. Ad-hoc

   d. Mesh

8. Which network topology is represented in the following diagram?

    a. Bus

    b. Star

    c. Logical ring

    d. Mesh

9. You have recently added several wireless clients to your company's network. Each client will access the network through a wireless access point. Which of the following topologies are you using?

    a. Wireless token ring

    b. Wireless mesh topology

    c. Infrastructure

    d. Ad hoc

10. Which of the following topologies has a single connection between each node on the network and a centralized device?

    a. Ring

    b. Mesh

    c. Star

    d. Bus

11. You have been asked to connect two office locations together. A wireless link has been specified. Which of the following strategies would you use to connect the two offices?

    a. Point to point

    b. Wireless mesh

    c. PtMP

    d. Ad hoc

12. Which topology is represented in the following diagram?

    a. Star topology

    b. Star bus

    c. Ad hoc

    d. Infrastructure

13. What is the name for a network that connects two geographically separate locations?

   a. PAN

   b. LAN

   c. DAN

   d. WAN

14. Which network topology is represented in the following diagram?

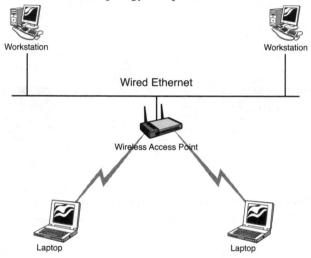

   a. Bus

   b. Star

   c. Mesh

   d. Ring

15. Which of the following is a feature of the physical star topology?

   a. It requires less cable than other physical topologies.

   b. The network is easy to expand.

   c. Apart from the cable and connectors, no other equipment is required to create the network.

   d. There is no single point of failure.

16. The 802.11 standard describes what kind of network?

   a. Wired mesh

   b. Contention

   c. Wireless

   d. Star bus

17. A mainframe is an example of what computing model?
   a. Segregated
   b. Distributed
   c. Centralized
   d. Decentralized

18. Which of the following network topologies offers the greatest level of redundancy but the highest implementation cost?
   a. Wireless mesh
   b. Wired mesh
   c. Hybrid star
   d. Bus network

19. Which network topology is represented in the following diagram?

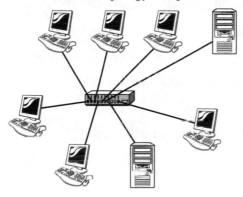

   a. Star
   b. Bus
   c. Mesh
   d. Ring

20. Which of the following technologies are used for network segmentation?
   a. VLAN
   b. VPN
   c. Hybrids
   d. PtMP

This chapter covers CompTIA Network+ objectives 2.1, 2.2, 2.4, and 2.8. Upon completion of this chapter, you will be able to answer the following questions:

- What are the characteristics of various network media?

- What connectors are used with network cabling?

- Where is coaxial cable used?

- What is the difference between plenum and nonplenum cabling?

- What are commonly used network topologies?

- What are the various wiring standards?

- How is cabling distributed in a network environment?

CHAPTER 2

Media and Connectors

To provide effective technical support, administrators must have a solid understanding of the logical standards and physical media used on today's networks. *Logical standards* define characteristics such as the configuration of the network, the speed at which the network operates, and how devices access the network *Physical media* refers to the cabling and connectors used to create the network.

Although you might think that knowledge of such things would be relevant only when designing or building a new network, you would be surprised at how frequently existing networks are expanded, upgraded, or reconfigured. When performing any of these tasks, your knowledge of standards and media will come into play. This is because the standards and media define and dictate such criteria as the maximum distance between devices, the capability of media to with stand outside interference, and even how much space is required in wiring closets and equipment cabinets.

Foundation Topics

Networking Media

As identified in Chapter 1, "Introduction to Computer Networking," a network is a group of connected computers. The computers on a traditional local area network (LAN) are connected by physical network media. Many types of media are used to connect network devices, and each type offers unique characteristics that you must understand to determine the media's suitability for a given network environment.

Before discussing the various network media, this section identifies some of the terms and general considerations relevant to network media.

NOTE: Media   Because not all networks use traditional cable, the term media is used. This term encompasses copper-based and fiber-optic cable and wireless media types.

Choosing the correct network media is an important consideration because the media forms the foundation for the entire network. When you work with any media, you must be aware of the factors that influence its suitability for a given network implementation. Some of the most common media considerations include interference, transmission speed, media length, and installation and repair. The following sections discuss each.

Media Interference

As a data signal travels through a specific media, it might be subjected to a type of interference known as *electromagnetic interference* (*EMI*). Common sources of EMI include computer monitors and fluorescent lighting fixtures—basically, anything that creates an electromagnetic field. If a network cable is too close to such devices, the signal within the cable can become corrupted. As you might expect, some network media are more susceptible than others to the effects of EMI. Copper-based media are prone to EMI and are managed using levels of shielding within the cable, whereas fiber-optic media using light transmissions do not suffer from EMI interference.

In most networks, standard cable provides sufficient resistance so that EMI isn't a problem. However, you might work in some environments where such interference is a major concern. This is often the case when running cabling through ceilings, air ducts, or elevator shafts where interference is often present. In such instances, it becomes important to understand which media offer the greatest resistance to EMI and when EMI resistant cabling should be used.

> **NOTE: EMI-Resistant Cable Cost**   Cables designed for greater resistance to EMI cost more than those that aren't.

EMI is just one of the threats to network transmissions. Data signals can also be subjected to something commonly referred to as *cross talk*, which occurs when signals from two cables or wires in close proximity to one another interfere with each other. As a result, the signals on both cables might become corrupted. When you troubleshoot intermittent network problems, it might be worth your time to confirm that cross talk or EMI is not at the root of your problems.

Data Transmission Rates

One of the more important media considerations is the supported data transmission rate or speed. Different media types are rated to certain maximum speeds, but whether they are used to this maximum depends on the networking standard used and the network devices connected to the network.

> **NOTE: Bandwidth**   The transmission rate of media is sometimes referred to incorrectly as the bandwidth. In truth, the term bandwidth refers to the width of the range of electrical frequencies, or amount of channels that the media can support. Bandwidth correlates to the amount of data that can traverse the media at one time, but other factors determine what the maximum speed supported by a cable

Transmission rates are normally measured by the number of data bits that can traverse the media in a single second. In the early days of data communications, this measurement was expressed as bits per second (bps), but today's networks are measured in Mbps (megabits per second) and Gbps (gigabits per second).

> **NOTE: Also Known As**   In your studies, you might see megabits per second and gigabits per second referred to as Mbit/s and Gbit/s. These are used interchangeably with Mbps and Gbps. More details on speeds and their abbreviations are covered in Chapter 13, "Network Management Tools and Documentation Procedures."

The different types of network media vary in the transmission rates they can accommodate. If you work on a network that accommodates huge amounts of data, transmission rates are a crucial consideration. In contrast, many older networks in small offices might occasionally share only files and maybe a printer. In such an environment, transmission rate is not a big issue.

Media Length

Not all networks have the same design. Some are isolated to a single office building, and others span large distances. For large network implementations, *media length* (that is, the maximum distance over which a certain type of media can be used) might be a factor in the network administrator's choice of network media. Each media has a recommended maximum length, and surpassing these recommendations can cause intermittent network problems that are often difficult to troubleshoot.

All types of media have maximum lengths because a signal weakens as it travels farther from its point of origin. If the signal travels far enough, it can weaken so much that it becomes unusable. The weakening of data signals as they traverse the media is referred to as *attenuation*.

Copper-based media is particularly susceptible to attenuation, although different types of copper cable offer varying degrees of resistance to weakening signals. Some copper media, such as shielded twisted-pair (STP), use a special shielding inside the cable, which helps protect the signal from outside interference. As a result, the distance a signal can travel increases.

Another strategy commonly employed to compensate for attenuation is *signal regeneration*. The cable does not perform the regeneration process; rather, network devices such as switches or repeaters handle signal regeneration. These devices strengthen the signal as it passes, and in doing so, they increase the distance the signal can travel. Network devices, such as hubs, routers, and switches, are covered in Chapter 3, "Networking Components and Devices."

TIP: Attenuation   For the Network+ exam, you will be expected to know what attenuation is and how it affects a network.

Fiber-optic cable does not suffer from attenuation. Instead, it suffers from a condition called *chromatic dispersion*, which refers to the weakening of the light strength as it travels over distance. Although the scientific processes behind chromatic dispersion and attenuation are different, the end result is the same. Signals get weaker and at some point become unusable unless they are regenerated.

Some cable types, such as fiber optic, offer support for long distances; other types, such as twisted-pair, offer support for much shorter distances (a fraction of the distance of fiber). Some unbound media (wireless media) don't have an exact figure for the allowable distance because so many variables can limit the effective range.

Secure Transmission and Physical Media

Physical media provides a relatively secure transmission medium, because to gain access to the signal on the cable, a person must physically access it—that is, the person must tap into the cable. Fiber-optic cable is more secure than copper-based media because the light transmissions and glass or plastic construction make it particularly hard to tap into. When it comes to security, wireless media is another topic entirely and is discussed in Chapter 7, "Wireless Networking."

Installation and Repair

Some network media are easier to manage and install than others. This might seem like a minor consideration, but in real-world applications, it can be important. For example, fiber-optic cable is far more complex to install and troubleshoot than twisted-pair. It's so complicated that special tools and training are often needed to install a fiber-optic-based network. It is important to be aware of what you are in for when it's time to implement or repair the network media.

NOTE: Plenum Cables Plenum is the mysterious space that resides between the false, or drop, ceiling and the true ceiling. This space is typically used for the air conditioning or heating ducts. It might also hold a myriad of cables, including telephone, electrical, and network cables. The cables that occupy this space must be plenum-rated. Plenum cables are coated with a nonflammable material, often Teflon or Kynar, and do not give off toxic fumes if they catch fire. As you might imagine, plenum-rated cables cost more than regular cables, but they are mandatory when cables are not run through a conduit. As an added bonus, plenum-rated cables suffer from less attenuation than nonplenum cables.

Simplex, Half-Duplex, and Full-Duplex

Those who do not know about duplexing might assume that network transmissions travel in any direction through the media. Specific dialog control modes determine the direction in which data can flow through the network media. The three dialog modes are simplex, half-duplex, and full-duplex.

The *simplex* mode enables only one-way communication through the media. A good example of simplex is a car radio: There is only one transmitting device, and all other devices are receiving devices. A simplex dialog mode uses the full bandwidth of the media for transmitting the signal. The advantages of the simplex dialog mode can be seen in many applications, but networks are not among them.

NOTE: Simplex Transmission A broadcast message—that is, one that is sent to all nodes on the network—is a good example of a simplex transmission. Remember this for the exam.

Half-duplex enables each device to both transmit and receive, but only one of these processes can occur at one time. Many networks are configured for and support only half-duplex communication. A good example of half-duplex transmission is a modem that can either transmit or receive but not both simultaneously. The transmitting device can use the entire bandwidth of the media.

If at all possible, the preferred method of communication on networks is *Full-duplex*, which enables devices to receive and transmit simultaneously. On a network, devices that can use full-duplexing can double their transfer rates provided the devices they connect to also support the higher speed. For instance, a 100Mbps network card connected to a switch in full-duplex mode can operate at 200Mbps and therefore significantly increase the transmission speed. An example of full-duplex is a telephone conversation, where both parties talk (send) and listen (receive) simultaneously.

NOTE: Know the Difference   Half-duplex enables two-way communication over a single channel. Full-duplex provides two-way communication by using different channels for sending and receiving signals. For the exam, know the differ-

---

Networking Terminology

The term *segment* is used extensively in discussions of network media. However, what *segment* means appears to be open to some interpretation. Technically speaking, a segment is simply a section of a larger entity. In networking, a segment is a part of the network or a single length of cable. You can just as easily say that one computer is on the same segment as another because you can say that each computer is on its own segment. In this case, the cable type affects the definition of *segment*. The first statement is correct if you use coaxial cable; the second is correct if you use twisted-pair.

Cable Media

Having now examined some of the general considerations that surround network media, the next step is to look at the different types of media commonly used on modern networks. Discussions of network media might not be the most glamorous part of computer networking but are important both for the Network+ exam and the real world.

Network media can be divided into two distinct categories: cable and wireless, sometimes referred to as *bound* and *unbound* media. Cable media come in three common types: twisted-pair, coaxial, and fiber optic.

Even with the rapid growth of wireless networking, you will still spend much of your administrative time managing cable media. Cable media provide a physical connection between networked devices—for example, a copper cable running from a desktop computer to a hub or switch in the server room. Data transmissions pass through the cable to their destination.

The materials used to construct cable media include

- **Metal (normally copper)**—Copper-based cable is widely used to connect LANs and wide area networks (WANs).

■ **Glass or plastic**—Optical cable, which uses glass or plastic, is mainly used for large-scale network implementations or over long distances.

The following sections review the various types of cable media and the networks on which they are used.

Twisted-Pair Cable

Now and for the foreseeable future, twisted-pair cable is the network media of choice. It is relatively inexpensive, easy to work with, and well suited to the needs of the modern network. There are two distinct types of twisted-pair cable: unshielded twisted-pair (UTP) and shielded twisted-pair (STP). UTP is by far the most common implementation of twisted-pair cable and is used for both telephone systems and computer networks.

STP, as its name implies, adds extra shielding within the casing, so it copes with interference and attenuation better than regular UTP. Because of this shielding, cable distances for STP can be greater than for UTP; but, unfortunately, the additional shielding also makes STP more costly than regular UTP.

NOTE: What's with the Twist?   Ever wonder why twisted-pair wiring is twisted? In the ongoing battle with interference and attenuation, it was discovered that twisting the wires within a cable resulted in greater signal integrity than running the wires parallel to one another. UTP cable is particularly susceptible to cross talk, and increasing the number of twists per foot in the wire achieves greater resistance against interference. The technique of twisting wires together is not limited to network cable; some internal and external SCSI cables employ a similar strategy.

Several categories of twisted-pair cabling exist, and the early categories are most commonly associated with voice transmissions. The categories are specified by the Electronics Industries Association/Telecommunications Industries Association (EIA/TIA). EIA/TIA is an organization that focuses on the development of standards for electronic components, electronic information, telecommunications, and Internet security. These standards are important to ensure uniformity of components and devices.

NOTE: MHz   When talking about cabling, it is important to understand the distinction between Hertz and bits per second in relation to bandwidth. When we talk about bandwidth and a bits per second rating, we refer to a rate of data transfer. For example, Category 5 cable has a 100Mbps rate of data transfer. When we refer to MHz and bandwidth, we talk about the width range of frequency of the media. MHz refers to megahertz

Key Topic

■ **Category 1**—Voice-grade UTP telephone cable. Because of its susceptibility to interference and attenuation and its low bandwidth capability, Category 1 UTP is not practical for network applications.

- **Category 2**—Data-grade cable capable of transmitting data up to 4Mbps. Category 2 cable is too slow for networks. It is unlikely that you will encounter Category 2 used on any network today.

- **Category 3**—Data-grade cable capable of transmitting data up to 10Mbps with a possible bandwidth of 16MHz. Years ago, Category 3 was the cable of choice for twisted-pair networks. As network speeds pushed the 100Mbps speed limit, Category 3 became ineffective.

- **Category 4**—Data-grade cable that has potential data throughput of 16Mbps. Category 4 cable was often implemented in the IBM Token Ring networks. Category 4 cable is no longer used.

- **Category 5**—Data-grade was typically used with Fast Ethernet operating at 100Mbps with a transmission range of 100 meters. Although Category 5 was a popular media type, the cable is an outdated standard with newer implementations using the 5e standard. Category 5, despite being used primarily for 10/100 Ethernet networking, can go faster. The IEEE 802.11ae standard specifies 1000Mbps over Category 5 cable. More on IEEE standards can be found in Chapter 6, "Ethernet Networking Standards."

- **Category 5e**—Data-grade cable used on networks that run at 10/100 Mbps and even theoretically specifies 1000Mbps depending on the implementation. However, actual speeds would likely be a lot less. Category 5e cabling can be used up to 100 meters, depending on the network and standard used. Category 5e cable provides a minimum of 100MHz of bandwidth.

- **Category 6**—High-performance UTP cable capable of transmitting data up to 10Gbps. Category 6 has a minimum of 250MHz of bandwidth and specifies cable distances up to 100 meter cable length with 10/100/1000Mbps transfer, along with 10Gbps over shorter distances. Category 6 cable is typically made up of four twisted-pairs of copper wire, but its capabilities far exceed those of other cable types. Category 6 twisted-pair use a *longitudinal separator*, which separates each of the four pairs of wires from each other. This extra construction significantly reduces the amount of cross talk in the cable and enables for the faster transfer rates.

- **Category 6a**—Category 6a (augmented 6) offers improvements over Category 6 by offering a minimum of 500MHz of bandwidth. It specifies transmission distances up to 100 meters and is used with 10Gbps networking standards such as 10Gbase-T.

TIP: Determining Cable Categories   If you work on an existing network that is a few years old, you might need to determine which category of cable is used on the network. The easiest way to do this is simply to read the cable. The category number should be clearly printed on it.

TIP: Cables Don't Have Speeds   For the Network+ exam, be aware of the transfer rates at which commonly implemented network standards operate, rather than what the maximum speed supported by a cable might be. It is the networking equipment, manufactured to meet certain IEEE standards, that defines transfer rates of the network, not the network cabling. All the network cabling needs to do is support that speed as a minimum.

Coaxial Cable

At one time, almost all networks used coaxial cable. Times have changed, and coax has fallen out of favor, giving way to faster and more durable cable options. That is not to say that you won't work with coax at some point. Many environments have been using coax and continue to do so because their network needs do not require an upgrade to another media—at least not yet. Many small offices continue to use coax on their networks, so we include it in our discussion.

Coaxial cable resembles standard TV cable and is constructed using an outside insulation cover, braided metal shielding, and a copper wire at the center, as shown in Figure 2.1. The shielding and insulation help combat attenuation, cross talk, and EMI. Some coax is available with dual and even quad shielding.

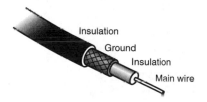

Insulation
Ground
Insulation
Main wire

Figure 2.1   Coaxial cable construction.

Two types of coax are used in networking: thin coax and thick coax. Neither is particularly popular anymore, but you are most likely to encounter thin coax.

Even though thin coax is by far the most widely used type of coax, you are unlikely to encounter it unless you support an older network. As the name suggests, it is thin—at least compared to other forms of available coax. Thin coax, also called Thinnet, is only .25 inches in diameter, making it fairly easy to install. In networking uses, it has a maximum cable length of 185 meters (that is, just more than 600 feet). If longer lengths of thin coax are used, data signals sent along the cable will suffer from attenuation, compromising data integrity. Table 2.1 summarizes the types of thin coax cable.

Table 2.1   Thin Coax Types

Cable Type	Description
RG 59 /U	A type of coaxial cable used to generate low-power video connections. The RG-59 cable cannot be used over long distances owing to its high-frequency power losses. In such cases, RG-6 cables are used instead.
RG 6	Often used for cable TV and cable modems.

In network implementations, thin coax typically runs from computer to computer and uses Bayonet Neill Concelman (BNCs) to connect to network devices. Figure 2.2 shows BNC T connectors and terminators, which are often used with thin coax.

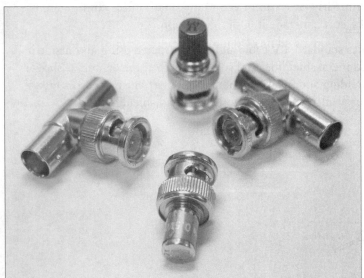

Figure 2.2   BNC T connectors and terminators.

NOTE: BNC Connectors   BNC connectors are also sometimes referred to as British Naval Connectors. Fortunately, CompTIA uses just the acronym, so you don't need to worry about this for the Network+ exam.

Fiber-Optic Cable

Fiber-optic cable takes a step away from traditional copper-based media, and unlike standard networking cables, which use electrical signals to send data transmissions, fiber uses light. As a result, fiber-optic transmissions are not susceptible to EMI or cross talk, giving fiber cable an obvious advantage over copper-based media. In addition, fiber-optic cable is highly resistant to the signal weakening, referred to as chromatic dispersion, which was mentioned earlier in the section "Media Length." All this enables data signals on a fiber-optic cable to travel distances measured in kilometers rather than meters, as with copper-based media. Further advantages of fiber-optic cable include that it's small in diameter, lightweight, and offers significantly faster transmission speeds than other cable media. Because of the construction of fiber cable and that it uses light transmission rather than electronic signals, it is resistant to signal tampering and eavesdropping making it more secure. Quite simply, fiber beats twisted-pair from almost every angle. Then why aren't all networks using fiber cable? The same reason we don't all drive Porsches: cost.

Several factors help ensure that we will continue to use twisted-pair and copper-based media in network environments. First, a fiber solution is costly in comparison to UTP-based cable implementations, eliminating it from many small- to mid-sized companies that simply do not have the budget to support a fiber-optic solution. The second drawback of fiber is that it can be more complex to install than UTP. Creating custom lengths of fiber-optic cable requires trained professionals and specialized tools. In contrast, custom lengths of UTP cabling can be created easily with commonly available tools. Third, fiber technology is incompatible with much of the existing electronic network infrastructure, meaning that to use fiber-optic cable, much of the current network hardware needs to be retrofitted or upgraded, and that can be a costly commitment.

A fiber-optic cable consists of several components, including the optic core at the center, optic cladding, insulation, and outer jacket. The optic core is responsible for carrying the light signal and is commonly constructed of plastic or glass. Figure 2.3 shows an example of the components of a fiber-optic cable.

Two types of optical fiber are commonly available: single-mode and multimode. Multimode fiber (MMF) has a larger core than single-mode. This larger core enables hundreds of light rays to flow through the fiber simultaneously. Single-mode fiber (SMF), on the other hand, has a small core that enables only a single light beam to pass. The light transmissions in single-mode fiber pass through the core in a direct line, like a flashlight beam. The numerous light beams in multimode fiber bounce around inside the core, inching toward their destination. Because light beams bounce within the core, the light beams slow down, reduce in strength, and take some time to travel along the cable. For this reason, single-mode fiber's speed and distance are superior to those of multimode.

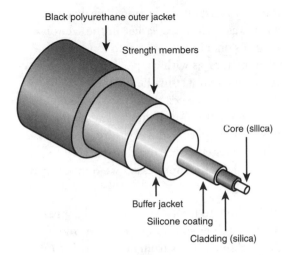

Figure 2.3   Fiber-optic cable.

Fiber cable can also have a variety of internal compositions (glass or plastic core), and the size of the core inside the cable, measured in microns, can vary. Some of the common types of fiber-optic cable include the following:

- 62.5 micron core/125 micron cladding multimode
- 50 micron core/125 micron cladding multimode
- 8.3 micron core/125 micron cladding single mode

NOTE: Fiber-Optic Cable Transmission Rates   The rate at which fiber-optic cable can transmit data is determined by the mode used and whether the fiber core is glass or plastic.

Media Connectors

All forms of network media need to be physically attached to the networked devices in some way. Media connectors provide the interface between the cables and the devices to which they attach (similar to the way an electrical cord connects a television and an electrical outlet). This section explores the common connectors you are likely to encounter in your work and, perhaps more important, on the Network+ exam.

NOTE: Know the Connectors   You will be expected to identify the various media connectors and know which connectors are used with which cable.

RJ Connectors

The connector you are most likely to encounter on modern networks is the RJ-45 (registered jack) connector. RJ-45 connectors bear a passing resemblance to the familiar RJ-11 connectors used with common telephone connections. The difference between the two connectors is that the RJ-11 connector supports six wires, whereas the RJ-45 network connector supports eight. Both RJ-11 and RJ-45 connectors are associated with twisted-pair cable. Figure 2.4 shows RJ-45 connectors, whereas Figure 2.5 shows RJ-11 connectors.

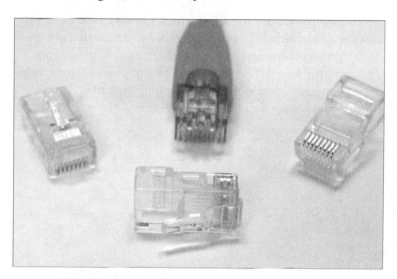

Figure 2.4   RJ-45 connectors.

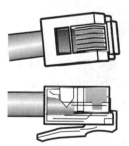

Figure 2.5   RJ-11 connectors.

F-Type Connectors and RG-59/RG-6 Cables

F-Type connectors are used for attaching coaxial cable to devices. This includes RG-59 and RG-6 cables. In the world of modern networking, F-Type connectors are most commonly associated with connecting Internet modems to cable or satellite Internet providers' equipment. However, they are also used for connecting to some proprietary peripherals.

> **NOTE: F is Not for Fiber**   Because of its name, people often mistakenly assume that an F-Type connector is used with fiber-optic cabling. It is not. The F-Type connector is used only with coaxial or copper-based cables, including RG-59 and RG-6 cables.

F-Type connectors screw into place, ensuring a firm contact between the cable and device. Hand tightening is all that should be required to make the contact; the use of tools such as pliers to tighten connections is not recommended. Should a connector prove difficult to remove, however, you can use a pair of pliers or grips with a light pressure. F-Type connectors have a "nut" on the connection to assist this process. Figure 2.6 shows an example of an F-Type connector.

Figure 2.6   An F-Type connector.

RS-232 Standard

RS-232 (Recommended Standard-232) is a TIA/EIA standard for serial transmission between computers and peripheral devices such as modems, mice, and keyboards. The RS-232 standard was introduced in the 1960s and is still used today. However, today we have the third revision of the RS-232 standard appropriately named RS-232C. In most cases today, peripheral devices are more commonly connected using USB or wireless connections. In normal operation, RS-232 has a limit of about 50 feet with a data transfer rate of about 20kbps. RS-232 commonly uses a 25-pin DB-25 connector or a 9-pin DB-9 (aka DE-9) connector. Figure 2.7 shows an example of RS-232 standard connectors.

Serial connectors need to attach to serial cables. Serial cables often use 4–6 wires to attach to the connectors and, similar to other cable types, can come in both an unshielded and shielded type. Shielding reduces interference and EMI for the cable. The distance a length of serial cable can run varies somewhat. This depends on the characteristics of the serial port and the quality of the serial cable. The RS-232 standard specifies serial cable distances up to 50 feet and a transfer speed up to 20kbps. Other serial standards increase this range and speed.

Fiber Connectors

Several types of connectors are associated with fiber-optic cable. Which one is used is determined by the fiber implementation. Figure 2.8 shows some of the different fiber connectors you might encounter when working with fiber networks.

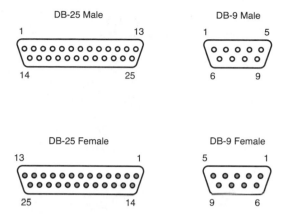

Figure 2.7   RS-232 DB connectors.

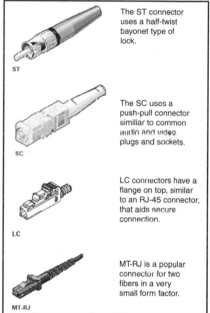

Figure 2.8   Fiber connectors. (Reproduced with permission from Computer Desktop Encyclopedia. 1981–2001. The Computer Language Co. Inc., www.computerlanguage.com.)

TIP: Fiber-Optic Connectors   For the Network+ exam, you will be expected to identify the various fiber-optic connectors. Specifically, the CompTIA Network+ exam objectives refer to the SC, ST, MT-RJ, and LC connectors.

IEEE 1394 (FireWire)

The IEEE 1394 interface, also known as FireWire, is more commonly associated with the attachment of peripheral devices such as digital cameras or printers than network connections. However, it is possible to create small networks with IEEE 1394 cables, which is why discussion of the connectors is included here.

The IEEE 1394 interface comes in a 4- or 6-pin version, both of which are shown in Figure 2.9.

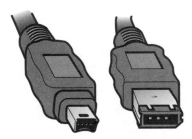

Figure 2.9   4-pin (left) and 6-pin (right) IEEE 1394 (FireWire) connectors.

Universal Serial Bus Connectors (USB)

Universal Serial Bus (USB) ports are now a common sight on both desktop and laptop computer systems. Like IEEE 1394, USB is associated more with connecting consumer peripherals such as MP3 players and digital cameras than with networking. However, many manufacturers now make wireless network cards that plug directly into a USB port. Most desktop and laptop computers have between two and four USB ports, but USB hubs are available that provide additional ports if required.

A number of connectors are associated with USB ports, but the two most popular are Type A and Type B. Type A connectors are the more common of the two and are the type used on PCs. Although many peripheral devices also use a Type A connector, an increasing number now use a Type B. Figure 2.10 shows a Type A connector and a Type B connector.

Cable Summary

Be prepared: The CompTIA Network+ exam requires you to identify the basic characteristics of each cable type discussed in this section. In particular, you will be expected to know which cables offer the greatest resistance to interference and attenuation, and you must identify which type of cable is best suited for a particular network environment. Table 2.2 summarizes the characteristics of the various cable media.

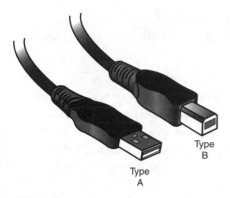

Type
B

Type
A

Figure 2.10   Type A and Type B USB connectors.

Table 2.2   Cable Media Characteristics

Media	Resistance to Attenuation	Resistance to EMI/Cross Talk	Cost of Implementation	Difficulty of Implementation
UTP	Low	Low	Low	Low
STP	Moderate	Moderate	Moderate	Low
Thin coax	Moderate	Moderate	Low	Low
Fiber-optic	Very high*	Perfect	Very high	Moderate

*Technically, the weakening of signals as they travel along a fiber-optic cable is considered chromatic dispersion, not attenuation.

Wiring Standards and Specialized Cable

When it comes to working with networks, we need to understand how different cabling standards and ways of wiring network cable come into play. Some situations call for a specialized cable, such as networking two computers directly together. In this section we review some wiring standards and types of specialized cable.

568A and 568B Wiring Standards

568A and 568B are telecommunications standards from the Telecommunications Industry Association (TIA) and the Electronics Industry Association (EIA). These 568 standards specify the pin arrangements for the RJ-45 connectors on UTP or STP cables. The number 568 references the order in which the wires within the Cat 5, Cat3, and Cat6 cable are terminated and attached to the connector.

The 568A and 568B standards are quite similar; the difference is the order in which the pins are terminated. The signal is the same for both, and both are used for patch cords in an Ethernet network.

Network media may not always come with connectors attached, or you might need to make custom length cables. As a network administrator, this is when you need to know something about how these standards actually work. Before you can crimp on the connectors, you need to know which order the individual wires will be attached to the connector. Figure 2.11 shows the pin number assignments for the 568A and 568B standards. Pin numbers are read left to right with the connector tab facing down.

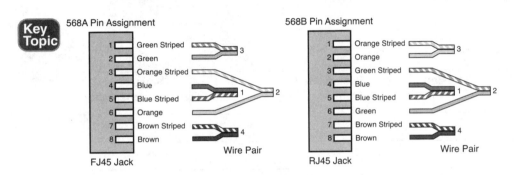

Figure 2.11   Pin assignments for the 568A and 568B standard.

Straight Versus Crossover Cable

Two types of cables can connect devices to hubs and switches: crossover cables and straight-through cables. The difference between the two types is that in a crossover cable, two sets of wires are crossed; in a straight-through cable, all the wires run straight through.

Specifically, in a crossover cable, wires 1 and 3 and wires 2 and 6 are crossed: Wire 1 at one end becomes wire 3 at the other end, wire 2 at one end becomes wire 6 at the other end, and vice versa in both cases. You can see the differences between the two cables in Figure 2.12 and Figure 2.13. Figure 2.12 shows the pinouts for a straight-through cable, and Figure 2.13 shows the pinouts for a crossover cable.

NOTE: Crossover Function   The crossover cable can be used to directly network two PCs together without using a hub or switch. This is done because the cable performs the function of switching. Crossover cable is also used to uplink connectivity devices; that is, switch to switch or switch to router. The next chapter covers using a straight-through cable and crossover cable to interconnect hubs and switches.

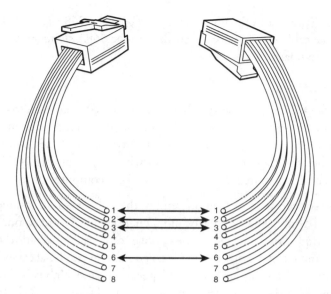

Figure 2.12   Pinouts for a straight-through twisted-pair cable.

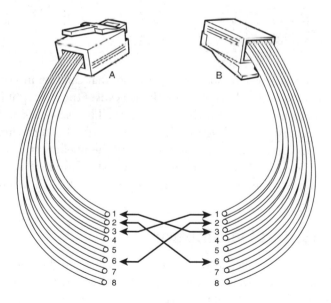

Figure 2.13   Pinouts for a crossover twisted-pair cable.

To make a crossover Ethernet cable, you need to use both the 568A and 568B standards. One end of the cable can be wired according to the 568A standard and the other with the 568B standard.

Rollover and Loopback Cables

The rollover cable is a Cisco proprietary cable used to connect a computer system to a router, switch, or firewall console port. The rollover cable resembles an Ethernet UTP cable; however, it is not possible to use on anything but Cisco equipment. Like UTP cable, the rollover cable has eight wires inside and an RJ-45 connector on each end that connects to the router and the computer port.

As far as pinouts are concerned, pin 1 on one end of the rollover cable connects to pin 8 at the other end of the cable; similarly, pin 2 connects pin 7, and so on. The ends are simply reversed. After one end of the rollover cable is connected to the PC and the other to the Cisco terminal, the Cisco equipment can be accessed from the computer system using a program such as HyperTerminal, which is included with Microsoft Windows products up to Windows XP and HyperACCESS for Windows Vista and Windows 7. Alternatively, any Telnet client can establish a console connection to a Cisco networking device.

NOTE: Rollover   For the Network+ exam, remember that the rollover cable is a proprietary cable used to connect a PC to a Cisco router.

A loopback cable, also known as a loopback plug, is a tool that can test and isolate network problems. If made correctly, the loopback plug causes the link light on a device such as a network interface card (NIC) to come on. This is a quick and cheap way to test simple network cabling problems. The loopback plug redirects outgoing data signals back to the system. The system will then believe it is both sending and receiving data. The loopback plug is a troubleshooting tool used to test the device to see if it is sending and receiving properly. The loopback cable uses UTP cable and RJ-45 connectors.

Components of Wiring Distribution

So far in this chapter we have looked at various types of media and the associated connectors. In this final section we look at wiring in the closet, the place in networks where we connect the cables and networking devices. These rooms are often called the wiring closet or the telecommunications room. These telecommunication rooms contain the key network devices such as the hubs, routers, switches, servers, and the like.

In this telecommunications room the network media, such as patch cables, connect network devices to horizontal cables and the rest of the network. In this final section of the chapter, we look at some of the components found in the wiring closet, including cross connects, horizontal and vertical cabling, patch panels, and punch-down blocks. You also learn about two types of wiring closets and the importance of the demarcation point.

Network Cross Connects

The cable that runs throughout a network can be divided into two distinct sections: the horizontal cable that connects client systems to the network and vertical (backbone) cabling that runs between floors to connect different locations on the network. Both of these cable types have to be consolidated and distributed from a location; this location is a wiring closet.

In terms of cable distribution, there are three types: the horizontal cross connect, the intermediate cross connect, and the vertical or main cross connect. The term *cross connect* refers to the point at which the cables running throughout the network meet and connect. For example, the term *horizontal cross connect* refers to the distribution point for the horizontal cable.

The main or vertical cross connect is the location where outside cables enter the building for distribution. This can include Internet and phone cabling. The intermediate cross connect is typically used in larger networks and provides an intermediate cross connect between the main and horizontal cross connects. The horizontal cross connect is the location where the vertical and horizontal connections meet.

Horizontal Cabling

Within the telecommunications room, horizontal cabling connects the telecommunication room to the end user. Specifically, the horizontal cabling extends from the telecommunications outlet, or network outlet with RJ-45 connectors, at the client end, and includes all cable from that outlet to the telecommunication room to the horizontal cross connect. As mentioned, the term *horizontal cross connect* refers to the distribution point for the horizontal cable. The horizontal cross connect includes all connecting hardware, such as patch panels and patch cords. The horizontal cross connect is the termination point for all network horizontal cable. Figure 2.14 shows horizontal cabling.

Horizontal cabling runs within walls and ceilings and is therefore referred to as permanent cable or structure cable. The length of cable running from the horizontal connects and the telecommunication outlet on the client side should not exceed 90 meters. Patch cables typically should not exceed 5 meters. The reason for this suggestion lies in the 100-meter segment restriction of twisted-pair cable.

NOTE: Horizontal Wiring   Horizontal wiring includes all cabling run from the wallplate or network connection to the telecommunications closet. The outlets, cable, and cross connects in the closet are all part of the horizontal wiring, which gets its name because the cable typically runs horizontally above ceilings or along the floor.

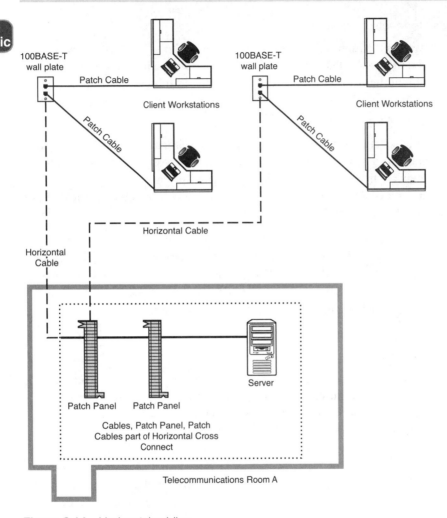

Figure 2.14 Horizontal cabling.

Vertical Cable

A vertical cable, or backbone cable, refers to the media used to connect telecommunication rooms, server rooms, and remote locations and offices. Vertical cable can connect locations outside of the local LAN and requiring high-speed connections. Therefore, vertical cable is often fiber-optic cable or high-speed UTP cable. Figure 2.15 shows the relationship between horizontal cable and vertical cable.

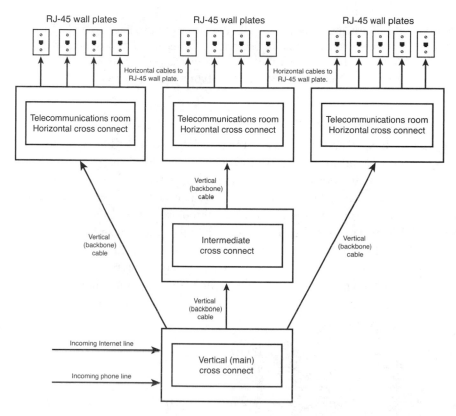

Figure 2.15 Vertical and horizontal cabling.

Patch Panels

If you ever looked in a telecommunications room, you have probably seen a distribution block, more commonly called a patch panel. A *patch panel* is a freestanding or wall-mounted unit with a number of RJ-45 port connections on the front. In a way, it looks like a wall-mounted hub without the light-emitting diodes (LEDs). The patch panel provides a connection point between network equipment such as hubs and switches and the ports to which PCs connect, which are normally distributed throughout a building. Figure 2.16 shows three patch panels.

Figure 2.16 A selection of patch panels. (Photo courtesy of TRENDware International, www.trendware.com.)

> **NOTE: Direct Cable Connections**   Not all environments use patch panels. In some environments, cables are run directly between systems and a hub or switch. This is an acceptable method of connectivity, but it is not as easy to make tidy as a structured cabling system that uses a patch panel system and wall or floor sockets.

Type 66 and Type 110 Punchdown Blocks

Predating the patch panel and still in use is the punchdown block. The wires from a telephony or UTP cable are attached to the punchdown block using a tool called a *punchdown tool*. Each punchdown block has a series of *insulation displacement connectors (IDCs)*, which are metal tabs in which wires are placed. Because the connector strips the insulation on the wire, it is a rather grandiose name. To use the punchdown tool, you place one wire at a time in the tip of the tool and push it into the connectors attached to the punchdown block. The wire insulation is stripped, and the wires are firmly embedded into the metal connector. Figure 2.17 shows an example of a typical punchdown tool and IDC connectors in a punchdown block.

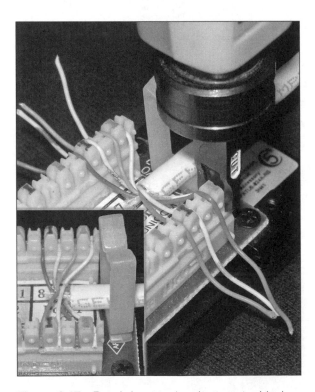

Figure 2.17   Punchdown tool and connector block.

Using a punchdown tool is much faster than using wire strippers to prepare each individual wire and then twisting the wire around a connection pole or tightening a screw to hold the wire in place. In many environments, cable tasks are left to a specialized cable contractor. In others, the administrator is the one with the task of connecting wires to a patch panel.

The two main types of punchdown blocks used are type 66 and type 110. Type 66 is of older design and not as widely used as type 110. The 66 is a block used to connect wiring for telephone systems and other low-speed network systems. Like all punchdown blocks, a punchdown tool is used to force solid wire into metal slots on the 66 block.

The 66 block has 50 rows of IDC contacts to accommodate 25 pair. The 66 block was primarily used for voice communication and, although approved for Category 5, may not be suitable owing to cross-talk problems. Also, although approved for Category 5 cable, it is limited to 16MHz.

For many years, the 66 block was standard in wiring closets and telecommunication rooms. Although the 66 block was used for low-speed data networks, it found its greatest use in voice applications. The 110 block replaced the 66 block for data communications because it supports higher frequencies and less cross talk. With its 50 rows of IDC connectors, the 66 block enabled for 25 pairs of wires to be connected. The 110 block uses different types of connections enabling for 25, 50, 100, 200, and 300 wire pairs.

A 110 block has two separate components: the 110-IDC connectors, which are used to terminate the wires, and the 110 wiring block, on which the connectors are attached. A 110 block consists of multiple 110 terminating connectors; there is a connector for each cable that must be terminated. The 110 block is typically mounted to the wall with each 110 connector visible from the front.

A 110 wiring block usually has several rows of 110 terminating connectors attached. Individual wires are placed into a connector block using a punchdown tool. Similar to that of the 66 block, when the wires are punched into the IDC with the punchdown tool, the cable sheathing is pierced, and metal to metal contact occurs. Figure 2.17 shows a 110 punchdown tool placing wires in a 110 block.

> **NOTE: 110 Block**   The 110 block improves on the 66 block by supporting higher frequencies and less cross talk and therefore supports higher-speed networks.

MDF and IDF

Main Distribution Frame (MDF and Intermediate Distribution Frame (IDF) define types of wiring closets. The main wiring closet for a network typically holds the majority of the network gear, including routers, switches, wiring, servers, and so on. This is also typically the wiring closet where outside lines run into the network. This main wiring closet is known as the MDF. One of the key components in the MDF is a primary patch panel. The network connector jacks attached to this patch panel lead out to the building for network connections.

In some networks, multiple wiring closets are used. When this is the case, the MDF connects to these secondary wiring closets, or IDFs, using a backbone cable. This backbone cable can be UTP, fiber, or even coaxial. In today's high-speed networks, UTP Gigabit Ethernet or high-speed fiber are the media of choice. Figure 2.18 shows the relationship between the MDF and the IDF.

Relationship between MDF and IDF

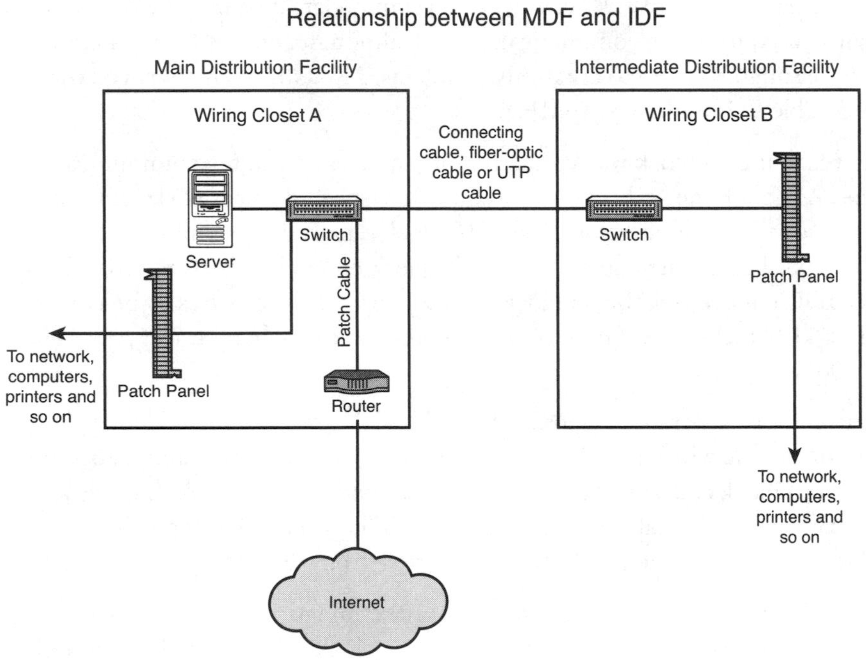

Figure 2.18   Relationship between MDFs and IDFs.

Demarcation Point

The demarcation point of a network refers to the connection point between the ISP's part of the network and the customer's portion of the network. This point is important for network administrators because it distinguishes the portion of the network the administrator is responsible for from the section the ISP is responsible for. As an example, for those who have high-speed Internet, the ISP can support everything from the cable modem back to their main distribution center. This is why, if a modem fails, it is replaced by the ISP and not by the customer. This is true for all connecting wiring to that point as well.

As mentioned previously, knowing the location of the demarcation point is essential because it marks the point where the customer (or administrator) is responsible should a problem occur, and who should pay for that problem. The ISP is responsible to ensure that the network is functional up to the demarcation point, and the customer/administrator is responsible to ensure everything from that point is operational.

The demarcation point is the point at which the ISP places its services in your network. There is not always a choice where this demarcation is placed. This means that a company might have six floors of offices and the demarcation point is in the basement and not practical for the network. This is when you need a demarcation extension, which extends the demarcation point to a more functional location. This might sound simple but involves knowledge of cabling distances and other infrastructure-related requirements. The demarcation extension can be the responsibility of the administrator or for a fee, ISPs can provide them.

As you might imagine, we need some form of hardware at the demarcation point. This is the smart jack also known as the Network Interface Device (NID). The smart jack performs several primary functions, including

- **Loopback feature**—Built in to the smart jack and, like the Ethernet loopback cable, is used for testing purposes. In this case, the loopback feature enables for remote testing so technicians do not always need to be called to visit the local network to isolate problems.

- **Signal amplification**—The smart jack has the capability to amplify signals. This feature is similar to that of the function of repeaters in an Ethernet network.

- **Surge protection**—Lighting and other environmental conditions can cause electrical surges that can quickly damage equipment. Many smart jacks include protection from environmental situations.

- **Remote alarms**—Enables the owner to identify if something goes wrong with the smart jack and therefore the connections at the demarcation point.

NOTE: Demarc Point   DEMARC is the telephone company or ISP term for where their facilities or wires end and where yours begin.

Verify Wiring Installation and Termination

After a segment of network cable has been placed where it needs to go, whether run through the plenum or connecting a patch cable, the final task is wiring termination. *Termination* refers to the process of connecting the network cable to the wall jack, plug, or patch panel. Termination is generally a straightforward process with little difficulty. You can quickly test if the wiring and termination work if the LED on the connected network card is lit. Also, if connecting a client system, you can ping other devices on the network if all is working.

If you have run the wiring and completed termination and a system cannot access the network and the link light is not lit, there are few things to look for when troubleshooting the wiring installation and termination.

Verify termination and wiring installation link light on the device (switch/NIC) not lit

- If connecting a patch cable to a PC or switch and no link light is lit, verify that the patch cable is good by switching it with a known working one.

- If it is a homemade patch cable, ensure that the RJ-45 connector is properly attached.

- Ensure that the RJ-45 connector is properly seated in the wall jack and NIC or switch port.

- If no link light is lit when connecting to a switch, change to another port on the switch. Sometimes a single port can be faulty.

- Verify that the correct patch cable is used. It is possible that a rollover cable or crossover cable might be used accidentally.

- Verify that the cables used are the correct standard. For example, the patch cable is a 568A or 568B.

If the link light on a device is lit and intermittent problems occur

- Try replacing the cable with a known working one.

- Verify where the network cable is run. Ensure that a plenum-rated cable is used if it runs through ceilings or duct work.

- Look for heavy bends or partial breaks in the network cable.

- Verify that shielded cabling is used in areas of potentially high interference.

- Check for the length of the cable run. Remember, the total run of cable should be about 100 meters. If the cable length exceeds this limit, you could experience intermittent signals errors that are hard to track down and troubleshoot.

Make or Buy?

During your networking career, you will most certainly encounter the debate about whether to crimp your own twisted-pair network cables or buy them. The arguments for making cables always seem to hinge on cost-savings. The arguments against crimping cables are often much more solid. Purchasing cables from a reputable maker ensures that the cables you install will work every time. The same cannot be said of homemade cables. In addition, when you factor in the time it takes to make a cable or troubleshoot a poorly made one, the cost-savings are lessened. However, in some instances you'll have no choice but to make cables—for example, when special-distance cables are required.

Summary

Networks are often complex in design, maintenance, and implementation, and the basics—such as network standards, media, and connectors—are often forgotten. But these elements are the foundation blocks of a network.

Several types of cable are used on modern networks, including coaxial, twisted-pair, and fiber-optic cable. Each cable has different strengths and weaknesses, making some types of cable more suitable than others in a given network environment. Part of the role of the network administrator is to identify the characteristics of the various cable types and to know how to troubleshoot them when required.

Each of these cable types requires the appropriate connector. By far the most commonly used connector type today is the RJ-45 connector, which is used with twisted-pair cable. Other connector types include SC and ST and LC connectors for fiber-optic cable and BNCs for thin coax cable.

To add clients to an existing network, you need to identify the connectors and cables already in use on the network. By using observation techniques—examining the cables and connectors already in use—you can find out what you need to know to correctly add computers to the network.

Several key characteristics and considerations determine a media's suitability for a specific network environment. These considerations include cross talk, attenuation, EMI, bandwidth, installation, and repair. You need to understand each of these to determine the appropriate media for a network.

Networks use dialog modes to determine the direction that transmissions flow over the network media. Three dialog modes are used: simplex, half-duplex, and full-duplex. Simplex enables only one-way communication; half-duplex enables two-way communication, but devices cannot send and receive simultaneously; and full-duplex enables devices to simultaneously receive and transmit.

Important specialized cables used on networks have different pin configurations, including rollover and crossover cables. The determination of pin configurations of straight-through cable are governed by the 568A and 568B standards.

Exam Preparation Tasks

Review all the Key Topics

Review the most important topics in the chapter, noted with the key topics icon in the outer margin of the page. Table 2.3 lists a reference of these key topics and the page numbers on which each is found.

Table 2.3   Key Topics for Chapter 2

Key Topic Element	Description	Page Number
UTP Bullets	Twisted-pair categories	67
Figure 2.1	Coaxial cable construction	69
Table 2.1	Coaxial cable types	70
Figure 2.2	BNC T connectors and terminators	70
Figure 2.4	RJ-45 connectors	73
Figure 2.7	RS-232 DB connectors	75
Figure 2.8	Fiber connectors	75
Table 2.2	Cable media characteristics	77
Figure 2.11	Pin assignments for the 568A and 568B standard	78
Figure 2.12	Pinouts for a straight-through twisted-pair cable	79
Figure 2.14	Horizontal cabling	82
Figure 2.18	Relationship between MDFs and IDFs	86

Complete the Tables and Lists from Memory

Print a copy of Appendix B, "Memory Tables" (found on the CD), or at least the section for this chapter, and complete the tables and lists from memory. Appendix C, "Memory Tables Answer Key," also on the CD, includes completed tables and lists to check your work.

Define Key Terms

Define the following key terms from this chapter, and check your answers in the Glossary.

■   568A

■   568B

■   Coaxial

■   Demarc

■   EMI

■   F-Type

■   IEEE 1394

■   IDF

- LC

- Loopback

- MDF

- Media

- MMF

- MTRJ

- Patch Panel

- Plenum

- Rollover

- RJ-11

- RJ-45

- SC

- SMF

- ST

- STP

- Straight

- Crossover

- UTP

Apply Your Knowledge

Exercise 2.1 Identifying Cable Costs

In this project, you use the Internet to identify cable characteristics and associated costs.

In this chapter we looked at the network media, connectors, and standards—all of which are essential to networks. As a network administrator, you need to have a detailed knowledge of network media and their associated connectors. When you are called on to troubleshoot or implement a network, this knowledge can prove invaluable.

A common task for network administrators is to source out the costs of cable and connectors. Consider the following scenario: You have been contracted by BootCo, a maker of snowshoes and outdoor gear, to begin the process of implementing a network. BootCo requires a network of 25 systems and needs to know the costs associated with the media for the network. The network cable lengths are as follows:

6 cables at 22 meters each

10 cables at 18 meters each

4 cables at 9 meters each

5 cables at 72 meters each

In this exercise, you determine the difference in cost of using Category 5e cable or Category 6 cable. You also determine the cost difference in buying premade cables or making your own.

Estimated time: 20 minutes

1. Get on the Internet and from a search engine, look for a company that sells network cable. The search is likely to return many results, and you might need to restrict your search to local vendors.
2. Browse a vendor's website and locate UTP Category 5e and Category 6 cable.
3. You need to price out the cables based on the previously stated lengths. Also remember that you need 50 connectors and a special tool called an RJ-45 crimper if you are going to make the cables yourself. The crimper is a special tool used to attach the RJ-45 connectors to the twisted-pair cable.
4. Continue to search the site for the costs for the Category 5e and Category 6 cable. To get a better idea of costs, you might need to find information from several vendors.
5. Compare the cost of buying bulk cable and connectors to the cost of buying premade cables and connectors.

Exercise 2.2 Media Troubleshooting

Knowing what cable to use for a specific purpose is an important skill for network administrators. Suppose you were brought in to troubleshoot a network suffering from slow network speeds and intermittent data loss. You isolate the problem to a length of cable run through the ceiling. The specs for the cable are as follows:

- Nonplenum
- Meets or exceeds all CAT 3 standards
- Compliance to TIA/EIA-568-B.2 and IEC /ISO 11801 standards
- Unshielded twisted-pair
- PVC polyvinyl chloride jacket

What recommendation would you make given these specifications?

Exercise Solution

Sometimes when working with older networks, administrators encounter problems with out-of-date cabling. This sometimes occurs when a network is upgraded but some cable segments are not updated. In this scenario, you need to select a plenum-rated cable to address the intermittent signal errors likely related because the cable runs through the ceiling. Also, it is Category 3 cable, which needs to be upgraded to accommodate today's network speeds. The specs should look like the following:

CMR riser plenum-rated cable

Meets or exceeds all CAT5e standards

Compliance to TIA/EIA-568-B.2 and IEC /ISO 11801 standards

24 AWG solid, bare copper cable

50 conductor

PVC polyvinyl chloride jacket

UL Listed E198134

Review Questions

You can find answers to the review questions in Appendix A, "Answers to the Review Questions."

1. Which of the following connectors are associated with the RS-232 standard? (Choose two.)
   a. DB-25
   b. F-Type
   c. DE-9
   d. DB-45

2. Which of the following statements are true of 568A and 568B wiring standards?
   a. The 568 standards specify the pin arrangements for the RJ-45 connectors on coaxial cable and UTP cable.
   b. The 568 standards specify the pin arrangements for the F-Type connectors on UTP or STP cables.
   c. The 568 standards specify the pin arrangements for the RJ-45 connectors on UTP cable.
   d. The 568 standards specify the pin arrangements for fiber connectors.

3. You are connecting some equipment at a client's home. You notice that one of the cables provided with the equipment has an F-Type connector on it. Which of the following tasks are you most likely performing?
   a. Connecting a printer to a FireWire port
   b. Creating a peer-to-peer network using IEEE1394 cables

    c. Connecting a cable Internet modem

    d. Creating a peer-to-peer network with STP cabling

4. Which of the following copper-based media offers speeds up to 10Gbps and has a minimum of 250 MHz of bandwidth?

    a. Category 6b

    b. Single-mode fiber

    c. Multimode fiber

    d. Category 6

5. You are working on an older network and are required to add a client. The network is using Category 5 UTP cable. Which connector should you use?

    a. SC

    b. ST

    c. RJ-45

    d. RJ-11

6. Which of the following cable types are coated with a nonflammable material, often Teflon or Kynar, and do not give off toxic fumes if they catch fire?

    a. 1000BaseFX

    b. Plenum grade

    c. Nonplenum grade

    d. Coaxial

7. While reviewing the specifications for a new network installation, you notice that the design calls for RJ-45 and SC connectors. The network is a high-speed design capable of supporting speeds up to 1000Mbps. What two types of network cable will the specifications call for?

    a. Thin coax and UTP

    b. RJ-11 and fiber optic

    c. Cat 6 UTP and fiber optic

    d. Cat 5 UTP and fiber optic

8. Which of the following terms describes interference created by individual wires within a network cable such as UTP?

    a. Attenuation

    b. Cross talk

    c. FDM

    d. Disruption

9. Which of the following cable types connect a computer system to a Cisco router or switch?

    a. Loopback

    b. Loopunder

    c. Rollover

    d. Rollback

10. What is the maximum distance a signal can travel over multimode fiber?

    a. 10,000 meters

    b. 412 meters

    c. 500 meters

    d. 100 meters

11. Which of the following is used to redirect the outgoing signal back to the system to test a port or network card?

    a. Loopback cable

    b. Rollover cable

    c. UTP diagnostic cable

    d. Interfeed cable

12. Which of the following media types offers the greatest resistance to interference?

    a. STP

    b. Unshielded fiber

    c. Fiber optic

    d. UTP

13. You are adding a new switch to the existing network. Which of the following technologies enable you to uplink connectivity devices; that is, switch to switch or switch to router?

    a. Crossover cable

    b. Straight through cable

    c. Standard UTP cable

    d. Standard STP cable

14. You are working in a wiring closet of a large corporation. The patch panel used has 50 rows of IDC contacts. Which type of patch panel is your company using?

    a. 100 punchblock

    b. 110 punchblock

    c. 66 punchblock

    d. 60 punchblock

15. Which of the following connectors is not associated with fiber-optic cabling?

    a. F-Type

    b. SC

    c. ST

    d. LC

16. Which of the following terms identifies the loss in signal strength as a signal travels through a media?

    a. Cross talk

    b. EMI

    c. Plenum

    d. Attenuation

17. You are a running cable in a new network. You are running a series of cable from the wiring closet to the telecommunications port for the client systems. What type of cable are you running?

    a. Horizontal cable

    b. MDF cable

    c. Vertical cable

    d. IDF cable

18. Which fiber-optic mode enables the fastest transfer rates?

    a. SC

    b. ST

    c. Single-mode

    d. Multimode

19. A company that transfers sensitive data has asked you to install a media highly resistant to eavesdropping and signal tampering. Which of the following media would you recommend?

    a. STP

    b. UTP

    c. FTP

    d. Fiber

20. You need to network two client systems together, but you do not have a switch or hub. Which of the following cable types could you use?

    a. Rollback

    b. Loopback

    c. Loop connector

    d. Crossover

This chapter covers CompTIA Network+ objectives 3.1, 3.2, and 3.3. Upon completion of this chapter, you will be able to answer the following questions:

- What is the function of a network hub and switch?
- What are the functions of specialized network devices?

CHAPTER 3

Networking Components and Devices

So far this book has examined topologies, and cable types and connectors. These are all integral parts of the network. This chapter focuses on another— networking hardware. These are the physical components that make the network function. This chapter explores the networking devices you are most likely to see in today's network environments and the function they perform. Each of these devices fulfills a specific role within a network; however, only the largest and most complex environments use all of them.

Foundation Topics

Common Network Devices

A network uses any number of network devices, which include switches, routers, bridges, firewalls, modems, access points (APs), and more. Network administrators must not only have familiarity with these devices but also must know how to configure and monitor them. In this section we explore some of the devices you will see on most networks and some specialized devices.

Hubs

Hubs are simple network devices, and their simplicity is reflected in their low cost. Small hubs with four or five ports (often referred to as *workgroup hubs*) cost less than $50; with the requisite cables, they provide everything needed to create a small network. Hubs with more ports are available for networks that require greater capacity. Figure 3.1 shows an example of a workgroup hub, and Figure 3.2 shows an example of the type of hub you might see on a corporate network.

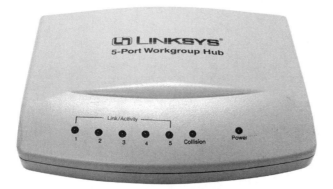

Figure 3.1   A workgroup hub.

Figure 3.2   A high-capacity, or high-density, hub.

Computers connect to a hub via a length of twisted-pair cabling. In addition to ports for connecting computers, even an inexpensive hub generally has a port designated as an uplink port that enables the hub to connect to another hub to create larger networks. The "Working with Hubs and Switches" section later in this chapter presents a detailed discussion of this feature. Figure 3.3 shows how a hub connects to a client workstation.

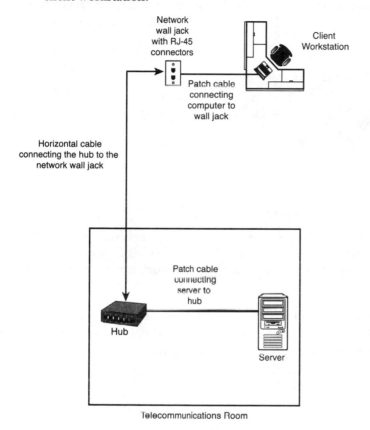

Figure 3.3 Hub and workstation connection.

NOTE: Token Ring and MSAUs Both hubs and switches are used in Ethernet networks. Token-ring networks, which are few and far between, use special devices called *multistation access units (MSAU)* to create the network. In some cases, MSAUs are referred to as *token-ring switches;* but because of the way token ring operates, these devices perform a different function from the hubs and switches discussed in this section.

Most hubs are referred to as either active or passive. *Active* hubs regenerate a data signal before forwarding it to all the ports on the device and require a power supply. Small workgroup hubs normally use an external power adapter, but on larger units the power supply is built in. *Passive* hubs, which today are seen only on older networks, do not need power and don't regenerate the data signal.

Regeneration of the signal aside, the basic function of a hub is to take data from one of the connected devices and forward it to all the other ports on the hub. This method of operation is inefficient because, in most cases, the data is intended for only one of the connected devices. Thus, the hub system of forwarding data to all devices connected to it is unnecessary. You can see a representation of how a hub works in Figure 3.4.

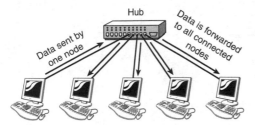

Figure 3.4   How a hub works.

> **NOTE: Broadcasting**   The method of sending data to all systems regardless of the intended recipient is referred to as *broadcasting*. On busy networks, broadcast communications can have a significant impact on overall network performance.

Because of the inefficiencies of the hub system and the constantly increasing demand for more bandwidth, hubs are all but replaced with switches. As you see in the next section, switches offer distinct advantages over hubs.

Network Switches

On the surface, a *switch* looks much like a hub. Despite their similar appearance, switches are far more efficient than hubs and are more desirable for today's network environments. Figure 3.5 shows an example of a 32-port Ethernet switch. If you refer back to Figure 3.2, you notice similarities in the appearance of the high-density hub and this switch.

Figure 3.5   A 32-port Ethernet switch. (Photo courtesy TRENDware International, www.trendware.com.)

As with a hub, computers connect to a switch via a length of twisted-pair cable. Multiple switches are often interconnected to create larger networks. Despite their similarity in appearance and their identical physical connections to computers, switches offer significant operational advantages over hubs.

As discussed in the preceding section, a hub forwards data to all ports, regardless of whether the data is intended for the system connected to the port. This arrangement is inefficient; however, it requires little intelligence on the part of the hub, which is why hubs are inexpensive.

Rather than forwarding data to all the connected ports, a switch forwards data only to the port to which the destination system is connected. It looks at the Media Access Control (MAC) addresses of the devices connected to it to determine the correct port. A *MAC address* is a unique number stamped into every NIC. By forwarding data only to the system to which the data is addressed, the switch decreases the amount of traffic on each network link dramatically. In effect, the switch literally channels (or *switches*, if you prefer) data between the ports. Figure 3.6 illustrates how a switch works.

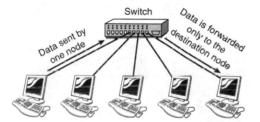

Figure 3.6 How a switch works.

When two devices attempt to transmit at the same time on a network, collisions occur. Such collisions cause the performance of the network to degrade. By channeling data only to the connections that should receive it, switches reduce the number of collisions that happen on the network. As a result, switches provide significant performance improvements over hubs.

Switches can also further improve performance over the performance of hubs by using a mechanism called *full-duplex*. On a standard network connection, the communication between the system and the switch or hub is called *half-duplex*. In a half-duplex connection, data can be either sent or received on the wire but not at the same time. Because switches manage the data flow on the connection, a switch can operate in full-duplex mode—it can send and receive data on the connection at the same time. In a full-duplex connection, the maximum data throughput is double that for a half-duplex connection; for example, 10Mbps becomes 20Mbps, and 100Mbps becomes 200Mbps. As you can imagine, the difference in performance between a 100Mbps network connection and a 200Mbps connection is considerable.

TIP: Half-duplex   It's important to remember that a full-duplex connection has a maximum data rate of double the standard speed, and a half-duplex connection is the standard speed. The term *half-duplex* can sometimes lead people to believe that the connection speed is half of the standard, which is not the case. To remember this, think of the half-duplex figure as half the full-duplex figure, not half the standard figure.

The secret of full-duplex lies in the switch. As discussed previously in this section, switches can isolate each port and effectively create a single segment for each port on the switch. Because only two devices are on each segment (the system and the switch), and because the switch is calling the shots, no collisions occur. No collisions mean no need to detect collisions; thus, a collision-detection system is not needed with switches. The switch drops the conventional carrier-sense multiple-access with collision detection (CSMA/CD) media access method and adopts a far more efficient communication method. On a network that uses CSMA/CD, when a system wants to send data to another system, it first checks to see whether the network media is free. If it doesn't check, the network would be flooded with data, and collisions between data will occur. CSMA/CD is covered in Chapter 6, "Ethernet Networking Standards."

NOTE: Microsegmentation   The process of direct communication between sender and receiver that switches perform to decrease collisions is called *microsegmentation.*

To use a full-duplex connection, you basically need three components: a switch, the appropriate cable, and a NIC (and driver) that supports full-duplex communication. Given these requirements, and that most modern NICs are full-duplex-ready, you might think everyone would be using full-duplex connections. However, the reality is a little different. In some cases, the NIC is not configured to operate in full-duplex mode.

TIP: Troubleshooting Network Connection Speed   Most NICs can automatically detect the speed of the network connection they are connected to. However, although the detection process is normally reliable, on some occasions it might not work correctly. If you troubleshoot a network connection and the autodetect feature is turned on, try setting the speed manually (preferably to a low speed) and then give it another go. If you use a managed switch, you might have to do the same configuration at the switch end of the connection.

All Switches Are Not Created Equal

Having learned the advantages of using a switch and having looked at the speeds associated with the network connections on the switch, you could assume that one switch is just as good as another. This is not the case. Switches are rated by the number of packets per second (pps) they can handle. When you're buying network switches, it might be necessary to look at the pps figures before making a decision.

Switching Methods

Switches use three methods to deal with data as it arrives:

- **Cut-through**—In a cut-through configuration, the switch begins to forward the packet as soon as it is received. No error checking is performed on the packet, so the packet is moved through quickly. The downside of cut-through is that because the integrity of the packet is not checked, the switch can propagate errors.

- **Store-and-forward**—In a store-and-forward configuration, the switch waits to receive the entire packet before beginning to forward it. It also performs basic error checking.

- **Fragment-free**—Building on the speed advantages of cut-through switching, fragment-free switching works by reading only the part of the packet that enables it to identify fragments of a transmission.

As you might expect, the store-and-forward process takes longer than the cut-through method, but it is more reliable. In addition, the delay caused by store-and-forward switching increases with the packet size. The delay caused by cut-through switching is always the same—only the address portion of the packet is read, and this is always the same size, regardless of the size of the data packet. The difference in delay between the two protocols is high. On average, cut-through switching is 30 times faster than store-and-forward switching.

It might seem that cut-through switching is the obvious choice, but today's switches are fast enough to use store-and-forward switching and still deliver high performance. On some managed switches, you can select the switching method you want to use.

NOTE: Latency   Latency refers to the delay in communication between a sending and receiving device. Some communications have a short latency, whereas communication of others, such as a base station dish and a satellite, can have a long latency. The higher the latency, the bigger the delay in sending the data.

Advanced Switch Features

As mentioned previously, switches are more complex than hubs. Today's switches do far more than the switches of just a few years ago. In this section we look at a few of the more advanced features that switches perform.

Power over Ethernet (PoE)

The purpose of Power over Ethernet (PoE) is described in the name. Essentially, PoE is a technology that enables electrical power to be transmitted over twisted-pair Ethernet cable. The power is transferred, along with data, to provide power to remote devices. These devices can include remote switches, wireless access points, Voice over IP (VoIP) equipment, and more.

One of the key advantages of PoE is the centralized management of power. For instance, without PoE, all remote devices need to be powered independently. In the case of a power outage, each of these devices requires an uninterruptible power supply (UPS) to continue operation. A UPS is a battery pack that enables devices to operate for a period of time. With PoE supplying power, a UPS is required only in the main facility. In addition, centralized power management enables administrators to power up or power down remote equipment.

NOTE: VLAN and Spanning Tree   VLAN and spanning tree were outlined in the CompTIA objectives for this chapter. VLANs, however, are discussed in Chapter 1, "Introduction to Computer Networking," and Chapter 11, "Troubleshooting Procedures and Best Practices," and the Spanning Tree Protocol is discussed later in this chapter along with the discussion of routers.

Trunking

In computer networking, the term *trunking* refers to the use of multiple network cables or ports in parallel to increase the link speed beyond the limits of any one single cable or port. Sound confusing? Those who have network experience might have heard the term *link aggregation*, which is essentially the same concept and refers to using multiple cables to increase the throughput. The higher capacity trunking link is used to connect switches to form larger networks.

Port Mirroring

As you might imagine, administrators need a way to monitor network traffic and monitor how well a switch is working. This is the function of *port mirroring*. To use port mirroring, administrators configure a copy of all inbound and outbound traffic to go to a certain port. A protocol analyzer is used to examine the data sent to the port and therefore is not interrupting the flow of regular traffic.

TIP: Port Mirroring   Remember for the exam that port mirroring enables administrators to monitor the traffic outbound and inbound to the switch.

Port Authentication

As the name implies, port authentication is authenticating users on a port-by-port basis. One standard that specifies port authentication is the 802.1X standard often associated with wireless security. Systems that attempt to connect to a LAN port must be authenticated. Those systems authenticated can access the LAN, and those that are not authenticated get no further. More information on the 802.1X standard and port authentication is in Chapter 7, "Wireless Networking."

Working with Hubs and Switches

Despite the advantages of switches over hubs, hubs are still widely used in older networks. Whether working with hubs or switches, you need to be aware of some of their characteristics when troubleshooting a network. For instance, if performance-monitoring tools show network bottlenecks or a congested network, the hubs might need to be replaced with switches for increased performance. This is especially important when you work with both hubs and switches in a production environment.

NOTE: Production Environments   The term *production* describes a working, or live, computing environment.

Hub and Switch Ports

Hubs and switches have two types of ports: medium dependent interface (MDI) and medium dependent interface crossover (MDI-X). The two types of ports differ in their wiring. As the X implies, an MDI-X port's wiring is crossed; this occurs because the transmit wire from the connected device must be wired to the receive line on the other. Rather than use a crossover cable, you can use the simpler straight-through cable to connect systems to the switch or hub.

NOTE: MDI-X or MDI   The majority of the ports on a hub/switch are normally MDI-X ports, and hosts (PCs, routers) usually come equipped with MDI ports.

On most modern hubs and switches, a special port called the *uplink port* enables you to connect two hubs and switches to create larger networks. Because the aim of this type of network connection is to make each hub or switch think that it is part of a larger network, the connection for the port is not crossed; a straight-through network cable connects the two hubs or switches. When you connect ports, remember that MDI-X is crossed MDI. If there is one device with MDI port and one device with MDI-X port, a straight-through cable is required. If both are MDI ports, a crossover cable is needed. Today, however, newer switches/routers have autosense ports, which means that you can use any type of cable (crossover or straight), and it will detect and cross lines if necessary. Figure 3.7 shows the uplink port on an Ethernet switch.

Figure 3.7   The uplink port on an Ethernet switch.

TIP: Crossing Over   In the absence of an uplink port, you can connect two hubs or switches by using MDI-X ports, but you must use a crossover cable to do

NOTE: Hub Ports   Instead of having a dedicated uplink port, some switches and hubs have a port that you can change between MDI and MDI-X by pushing a button. If you use the port to connect a computer, make sure that it is set to MDI-X. If you connect to another hub or switch, make sure that it's set to MDI.

How Many Is Too Many?

Although Ethernet standards state that you can have as many as 1,024 nodes on a network, the practical maximum can be much lower. The number of nodes you can accommodate depends on a number of factors. Using switches instead of hubs makes a *huge* difference, particularly if you use the full-duplex features of these devices. The amount of traffic generated by clients also has a significant effect, as does the type of traffic. On a more subtle level, you must consider the quality of the networking components and devices you use.

Hubs and switches are sometimes equipped with a network connection for another cable type, such as coaxial. Switches that accommodate different media types, such as fiber-optic cable and UTP, are called *hybrid switches*. Other higher-end devices have empty sockets into which you can plug connectivity modules of choice. This approach enables you to create fast networks. For example, three 24-port 10/100 Ethernet switches could be connected to each other by a Gigabit Ethernet fiber-optic connection. This would create a fast network structure in which switch-to-system communication can occur at 200Mbps (in full-duplex mode) and switch-to-switch communication can occur at Gigabit Ethernet speeds. The result is a fast local area network (LAN).

TIP: Switches—Read the Label   Switches are often labeled as 10/100/1000Mbps switches. This label normally means that the ports on the switch can operate at 10Mbps, 100Mbps, or 1000Mbps. Don't take it for granted, though. Some older switches have 10Mbps ports for connecting systems and 100Mbps ports for uplinking. Because no guidelines exist for labeling devices, some of those older switches are referred to as 10/100/1000 switches. Always check the specifications before buying a switch.

Hub and Switch Indicator Lights

Both hubs and switches use light-emitting diodes (LEDs) to indicate certain connection conditions. A link light on the hub indicates the existence of a live connection. On higher-end devices, additional lights might indicate activity, the speed of the connection, whether the connection is at half- or full-duplex, and sometimes errors or collisions. The LEDs provide an immediate visual indicator about the status of the device, so familiarizing yourself with their function is a worthwhile exercise.

Rack-Mount, Stackable, and Freestanding Devices

Some hubs and switches, and many other networking devices, are designed to be placed in a rack, whereas others are labeled as stackable or freestanding. Rack-mount devices are designed for placement into equipment racks, which are a common sight in computer rooms. The racks are approximately 19 inches wide; devices designed to be rack mounted are slightly smaller than freestanding devices so they can fit in the racks. Small metal brackets are screwed to the sides of the devices to enable them to be fitted into the racks.

If you don't have racks, you need to use stackable or freestanding devices. These devices can literally be placed on top of one another. Many network equipment manufacturers realize that not everyone has racks, and make their equipment usable in either a rack or a freestanding configuration.

Managed Hubs and Switches

Both hubs and switches come in managed and unmanaged versions. A managed device has an interface through which it can be configured to perform certain special functions. For example, it might enable for port mirroring, which can be useful for network monitoring, or enable ports to be specified to operate at a certain speed. Because of the extra functionality of a managed device, and because of the additional components required to achieve it, managed devices are considerably more expensive than unmanaged devices. When you specify switches or hubs, consider the need for manageability carefully. If a switch will be used to connect servers to the network, a managed device might make the most sense—the extra functionality might come in handy. On parts of the network that accommodate client computers, unmanaged devices generally suffice.

> **NOTE: Port Density**   Excluding the small workgroup hubs, hubs and switches normally have 8, 16, 24, or 32 ports each, although variations are available. To help you compare prices between devices, manufacturers often quote a price per port. In some cases, a higher-density device with more ports can cost significantly less per port than a device with fewer ports.

At this time, switches are still more expensive than hubs with equivalent capacity, but the gap is narrowing quickly. Some manufacturers have stopped producing hubs and instead are putting all their efforts into developing switches. This would seem to be a sound strategy. In all but the smallest networks or companies with the most restrictive budgets, hubs are obsolete. In new implementations, hubs are unlikely to be specified and installed.

Repeaters

As mentioned in Chapter 2, "Media and Connectors," data signals weaken as they travel down a particular media. This is known as *attenuation*. To increase the distance a signal can travel, we can use repeaters. Repeaters increase the usable length of the cable and are commonly used with coaxial network configurations. Because coaxial networks have now fallen out of favor, and because the functionality of repeaters has been built in to other devices, such as hubs and switches, repeaters are rarely used independently.

Bridges

Bridges are networking devices that connect networks. Sometimes it is necessary to divide networks into segments to reduce the amount of traffic on each larger subnet or for security reasons. When divided, the bridge connects the two subnets and manages the traffic flow between them. Today, network switches have largely replaced bridges.

A bridge functions by blocking or forwarding data, based on the destination MAC address written into each frame of data. If the bridge believes the destination address is on a network other than that from which the data was received, it can forward the data to the other networks to which it is connected. If the address is not on the other side of the bridge, the data is blocked from passing. Bridges "learn" the MAC addresses of devices on connected networks by "listening" to network traffic and recording the network from which the traffic originates. Figure 3.8 shows a representation of a bridge.

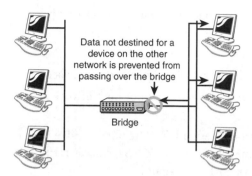

Figure 3.8   How a bridge works.

> **NOTE: Manual Bridge Configuration**   Some early bridge implementations required you to manually enter the information for each device on the network. Fortunately, bridges are now of the learning variety, and manual configuration is no longer necessary.

The advantages of bridges are simple and significant. By preventing unnecessary traffic from crossing onto other network segments, a bridge can dramatically reduce the amount of network traffic on a segment. Bridges also make it possible to isolate a busy network from a not-so-busy one, thereby preventing pollution from busy nodes.

Bridge Implementation Considerations

Although implementing bridges can offer huge improvements in performance, you must factor in a number of considerations. The first is bridge placement. Generally, you should follow the 80/20 rule for bridge placement: 80% of the traffic should not cross the bridge; that is, it should be local traffic. Only 20% of the traffic should cross a bridge to another segment. The rule is easy to understand, but accurately determining the correct location for the bridge to accommodate the rule is another matter.

Another, potentially more serious, consideration is bridging loops, which can be created when more than one bridge is used on a network. Multiple bridges can provide fault tolerance or improve performance. Bridging loops occur when multiple bridges become confused about where devices are on the network.

As an example of bridging loops, imagine that you have a network with two bridges, as depicted in Figure 3.9. During the learning process, the following steps occur, as shown in Figure 3.10:

1. The north bridge receives a packet from Interface A and determines that it is for a system that is not on Network Z.

2. The bridge forwards the packet to Network X.

3. Now the south bridge sees a packet originating on Network X on Interface C.

4. Because the south bridge thinks the destination system is not on Network X, it forwards the packet to Network Z.

5. The north bridge picks up the packet from Network Z. The north bridge determines that the destination system is not on Network Z, so it forwards the packet to Network X, and the whole process begins again.

Spanning Tree Protocol (STP) is used with network bridges and switches and with the help of the spanning-tree algorithm (STA) avoids or eliminate loops on a Layer 2 network.

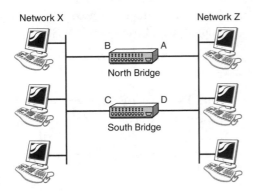

Figure 3.9   A network with two bridges.

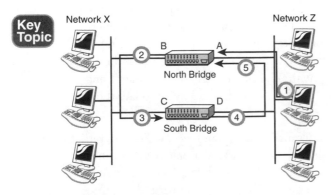

Figure 3.10   A bridging loop.

NOTE: Layer 2?   As a heads up, when we talk about STP, we talk about Layer 2 of the OSI model, and both bridges and switches work at Layer 2. Routers work at Layer 3. The OSI model and how it relates to network hardware is reviewed in Chapter 9, "OSI Model."

The STA enables a bridge or switch to dynamically work around loops in a network's topology. Both STA and STP were developed to prevent loops in the network and provide a way to route around any failed network bridge or ports. If the network topology changes, or if a switch port or bridge fails, STA creates a new spanning tree, notifies the other bridges of the problem, and routes around it. STP is the protocol, and STA is the algorithm STP uses to correct loops.

If a problem occurs with a particular port, the STP protocol can perform a number of actions, including blocking the port, disabling the port, or forwarding data destined for that port to another port. It does this to ensure that no redundant links or paths are found in the spanning tree and that only a single active path exists between any two network nodes.

STP uses bridge protocol data units (BPDUs) to identify the status of ports and bridges across the network. BPDUs are simple data messages exchanged between switches and contain information on ports and provide status of those ports to other switches. If BPDU messages finds a loop in the network, they are managed by shutting down a particular port or bridge interface.

Redundant paths and potential loops can be avoided within ports in several ways:

- **Blocking**—A blocked port will accept BDPU messages but will not forward those messages on.

- **Disabled**—The port is offline and does not accept BPDU messages.

- **Forwarding**—The port is part of the active spanning-tree topology and will forward BPDU messages to other switches.

- **Learning**—In a learning state, the port is not part of the active spanning-tree topology but can take over if another port fails. Learning ports receive BPDUs and identify changes to the topology when made.

- **Listening**—A listening port receives BPDU messages and monitors for changes to the network topology.

Most of the time, ports will be either in forwarding or blocked states. When a disruption occurs to the topology or a bridge or switch fails for some reason, listening and learning states will be used.

NOTE: STP   STP is defined in the IEEE 802.1d standard. IEEE and related standards are discussed in Chapter 6.

Types of Bridges

Three types of bridges are used in networks. You don't need detailed knowledge of how each bridge works, but you should have an overview:

■ **Transparent bridge**—Invisible to the other devices on the network. Transparent bridges perform only the function of blocking or forwarding data based on the MAC address; the devices on the network are oblivious to these bridges' existence. Transparent bridges are by far the most popular types of bridges.

■ **Translational bridge**—Converts from one networking system to another. As you might have guessed, it translates the data it receives. Translational bridges are useful for connecting two different networks, such as Ethernet and token-ring networks. Depending on the direction of travel, a translational bridge can add or remove information and fields from the frame as needed.

■ **Source-route bridge**—Designed by IBM for use on token-ring networks. The source-route bridge derives its name from the fact that the entire route of the frame is embedded within the frame. This enables the bridge to make specific decisions about how the frame should be forwarded through the network. The diminishing popularity of token ring makes the chances that you'll work with a source-route bridge slim.

NOTE: Identify the Bridge   On the Network+ exam, you might be asked to identify the purpose of a certain type of bridge.

As switches become ever cheaper, bridges have been overtaken by switches in terms of functionality and performance. Expect to be working with switches more often than with bridges.

Routers

Routers are an increasingly common sight in any network environment, including a small home office that uses one to connect to an ISP and a corporate IT environment where racks of routers manage data communication with disparate remote sites. Routers make internetworking possible, and in view of this, they warrant detailed attention.

Routers are network devices that direct data around the network. By examining data as it arrives, the router can determine the destination address for the data; then, by using tables of defined routes, the router determines the best way for the data to continue its journey. Unlike bridges and switches, which use the hardware-configured MAC address to determine the destination of the data, routers use the software-configured network address to make decisions. This approach makes routers more functional than bridges or switches, and it also makes them more complex because they have to work harder to determine the information.

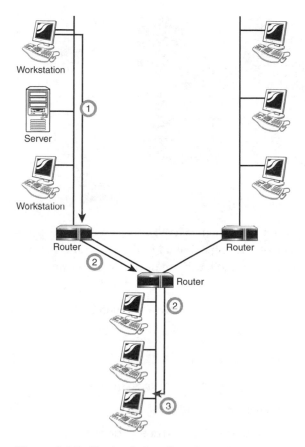

Figure 3.11 The basic function of a router.

The following steps explain the basic function of a router, as illustrated in Figure 3.11.

1. Data is sent to the router.

2. The router determines the destination address and forwards it to the next step in the journey.

3. The data reaches its destination.

The basic requirement for a router is that it must have at least two network interfaces. If they are LAN interfaces, the router can manage and route the information between two LAN segments. More commonly, a router provides connectivity across wide area network (WAN) links. Figure 3.12 shows a router with two LAN ports (marked AUI 0 and AUI 1) and two WAN ports (marked Serial 0 and Serial 1). This router can route data between two LAN segments and two WAN segments.

A router can be either a dedicated hardware device or a server system that has at least two network interfaces installed in it. As part of their functionality, all common network operating systems offer the capability to act as routers.

Figure 3.12 A router with two LAN ports and two WAN ports.

Dedicated hardware routers offer greater performance levels than server-based solutions, but they have the disadvantage of offering a limited range of features for their cost. However, the attraction of a dedicated hardware device often outweighs this factor.

The following are some of the advantages of dedicated hardware routers:

■ Typically faster than server-based routers

■ Generally more reliable than server-based routers

■ Easier to harden against attacks than server-based routing solutions

The following are some of the disadvantages of dedicated hardware routers:

■ More expensive than server-based router solutions; extra functionality might need to be purchased.

■ Often require specialized skills and knowledge to manage them.

■ Limited to a small range of possible uses.

The capabilities of a router depend on the features it has. A basic router might route only one protocol between two network interfaces of the same type. A more advanced router can act as a gateway between two networks and two protocols. In addition, it can offer firewall services, security and authentication, or remote access functionality such as virtual private networking.

NOTE: Brouters A *brouter* is a device that routes traffic that can be routed and bridges anything that cannot be routed. Because bridges have been replaced by the more flexible routers, brouters have also fallen out of favor.

The topic of routing is complex, and the routing information provided in this chapter is the most basic of tutorials. Chapter 5, "TCP/IP Routing and Addressing," expands the discussion of routers by describing the protocols that routers use. Although this book describes the aspects of routing that you need to know for the exam, you should seek out further sources of information if you work with routers on a daily basis.

Gateways

The term *gateway* is applied to any device, system, or software application that can perform the function of translating data from one format to another. The key feature of a gateway is that it converts the format of the data, not the data itself.

> **NOTE: Gateways Versus Default Gateways**   Don't confuse gateways, which are discussed in this section, with default gateways, which are discussed in Chapter 5. The two perform different roles on a network.

Software gateways can be found everywhere. Many companies use an email system such as Microsoft Exchange or Novell GroupWise. These systems transmit mail internally in a certain format. When email needs to be sent across the Internet to users using a different email system, the email must be converted to another format, usually to Simple Mail Transfer Protocol (SMTP). This conversion process is performed by a software gateway.

Another good (and often used) example of a gateway involves the Systems Network Architecture (SNA) gateway, which converts the data format used on a PC to that used on an IBM mainframe or minicomputer. A system that acts as an SNA gateway sits between the client PC, and the mainframe and translates requests and replies from both directions. Figure 3.13 shows how this would work in a practical implementation.

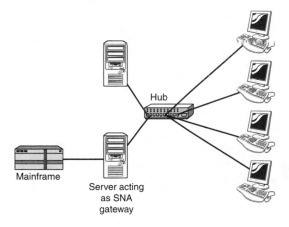

Figure 3.13 An SNA gateway.

If it seems from the text in this section that we are vague about what a gateway is, it's because there is no definite answer. The function of a gateway is specific, but how the gateway functionality is implemented is not.

No matter what their use, gateways slow the flow of data and can therefore potentially become bottlenecks. The conversion from one data format to another takes time, and so the flow of data through a gateway is always slower than the flow of data without one.

Modems

Modem is a contraction of the terms *modulator* and *demodulator*. Modems perform a simple function: They translate digital signals from a computer into analog signals that can travel across conventional phone lines. The modem modulates the signal at the sending end and demodulates at the receiving end.

Modems provide a relatively slow method of communication. The fastest modem available on the market today has a maximum speed of 56Kbps. Compare that to the speed of a 100/1000Mbps network connection, and you'll find that the modem is simply to slow. Today's modems are limited to browsing simple web pages or occasionally downloading small files but are wholly unsuitable for downloading large files and browsing heavy graphic websites. As a result, many people prefer to use other remote access methods, including ISDN, discussed in Chapter 8, "Wide Area Networking," and cable/DSL access.

Modems are available as internal devices that plug into expansion slots in a system; external devices that plug into serial or USB ports; PCMCIA cards designed for use in laptops; and specialized devices designed for use in systems, such as hand-held computers. In addition, many laptops now come with integrated modems. For large-scale modem implementations, such as at an ISP, rack-mounted modems are also available. Figure 3.14 shows an internal modem and a PCMCIA modem.

Figure 3.14   An internal modem (left) and a PCMCIA modem (right).

Modems are controlled through a series of commands known as the Hayes AT command set. Hayes was a company that, for many years, led the field in the development of modems and modem technology. The AT commands enable you to control a modem and configure and diagnose it. Table 3.1 lists some of the most commonly used AT commands.

Table 3.1   Commonly Used AT Modem Commands

Command	Result
ATA	Answers an incoming call
ATH	Hangs up the current connection
ATZ	Resets the modem
ATI3	Displays modem identification information

NOTE: Know the AT Command   On the Network+ exam, you might be asked to identify the correct AT command to be used in a given situation.

Modem Connection Speeds

The actual speed you obtain on a modem connection depends on a variety of factors, including the quality of the line you use and the speed of the modem. For example, you might find that even with a 56Kbps modem, the most you can get on a certain connection is 53Kbps. If you try the same connection again on a different phone line, you might get a higher or lower rate. Quality of the connection aside, two factors govern the maximum speed attainable by your modem: the speed of the Universal Asynchronous Receiver/Transmitter (UART) chip in your system (which controls the serial ports) and the speed of the modem.

In older systems, the UART chips were capable of only slow speeds, making them unable to keep up with fast modems. Today, most systems have UART chips capable of speeds well in excess of those offered by modems. Now the modem, not the UART chip, is the bottleneck. Table 3.2 lists the types of commonly used UART chips and their associated speeds.

Table 3.2   UART Chips and Their Associated Speeds

UART Chip	Speed (bps)
8250	9,600
16450	115,200
16550	115,200

Table 3.2   UART Chips and Their Associated Speeds

UART Chip	Speed (bps)
16650	430,800
16750	921,600
16950	921,600

Modem speeds can be expressed in either baud rate or bits per second (bps). The *baud rate* refers to the number of times a signal changes in each second, and the *bps rate* is the number of bits of data that can be sent or received in a second. Although the figures are identical in some modems, in others the bps rate is higher than the baud rate. The baud rate is actually not as important, and the higher the bps figure, the better. Most modern modems offer bps rates far greater than the baud rate.

To make it easier to compare modems, standards have been created that define the data throughput of the modem and what features it provides. These are sometimes referred to as the *V standards*, and you can use them when buying a modem to determine the modem's capabilities.

Network Interface Cards (NIC)

NICs—sometimes called network cards—are the mechanisms by which computers connect to a network. NICs come in all shapes and sizes, and they come in prices to suit all budgets. Consider the following when buying a NIC:

■ **Network compatibility**—Sometimes people order the wrong type of NIC for the network. Given the prevalence of Ethernet networks, you are likely to need to specify network compatibility only when buying a NIC for another networking system.

■ **Bus compatibility**—Newly purchased NICs will almost certainly use the Peripheral Component Interconnect Express (PCIe) bus.

■ **Port compatibility**—Generally a NIC has only one port, for twisted-pair cabling. If you want some other connectivity, you need to be sure to specify your card accordingly; for example, you might need a fiber-optic or coaxial cable port.

> **NOTE: Combo Cards**   Sometimes a NIC has a twisted-pair socket, a coaxial connector, and an attachment unit interface (AUI) port. These cards are referred to as *combo* cards. Today, the dominance of twisted-pair cabling means that most NICs have only a twisted-pair connection.

■ **Hardware compatibility**—Before installing a network card into a system, you must verify compatibility between the network card and the operating system on the PC in which you install the NIC. If you use good-quality network cards from a recognized manufacturer, such verification should be little more than a formality.

NOTE: NIC terminology Many terms are used to refer to NICs, such as *network card, network adapter,* and *LAN adapter.* All refer to the same thing.

Types of Network Interfaces

Network interfaces come as add-in expansion cards or as PCMCIA cards used in laptop systems. In some cases, rather than have an add-in NIC, the network interface is embedded into the motherboard. Figure 3.15 shows an example of an add-in NIC. Figure 3.16 shows a PCMCIA network card, and Figure 3.17 shows a built-in network interface in a laptop system.

Figure 3.15 An expansion NIC.

NOTE: Combo Cards Did you notice that the cards used in Figure 3.14 and 3.16 are the same card? This is not a mistake; the PCMCIA card is both a modem and a NIC.

The False Economy of NICs

The difference between an inexpensive network card and an expensive one is less than you might think; but even so, people are tempted to go for the low-cost option. In many cases, this turns out to be a false economy. Not only do higher-end cards tend to be easier to install, they also are generally easier to troubleshoot as well. An hour spent trying to troubleshoot a misbehaving inexpensive network card can negate any cost-savings from the purchase. This is particularly relevant on server systems, where a problem network card will not only cause you frustration but also will most likely cause the users of the server problems. If you work on server systems, it's worth investigating fault-tolerant network card configurations, such as adapter teaming.

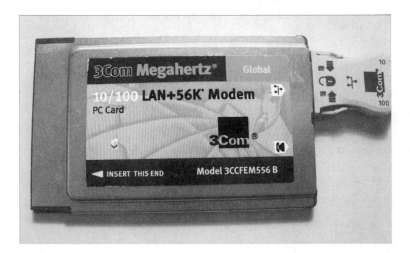

Figure 3.16   A PCMCIA NIC.

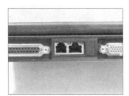

Figure 3.17   A built-in network interface on a laptop system.

A network interface typically has at least two LEDs that indicate certain conditions:

- **Link light**—Indicates whether a network connection exists between the card and the network. An unlit link light is an indicator that something is awry with the network cable or connection.

- **Activity light**—Indicates network activity. Under normal conditions, the light should flicker sporadically and often. Constant flickering might indicate a busy network or a problem somewhere on the network worth investigating.

- **Speed light**—Indicates that the interface is connected at a certain speed. This feature is normally found on Ethernet NICs that operate at 100Mbps/1000Mbps—and then only on certain cards.

Some network cards combine the functions of certain lights by using dual-color LEDs. PCMCIA cards sometimes have no lights, or the lights are incorporated into the media adapter that comes with the card. You can see an example in Figure 3.18.

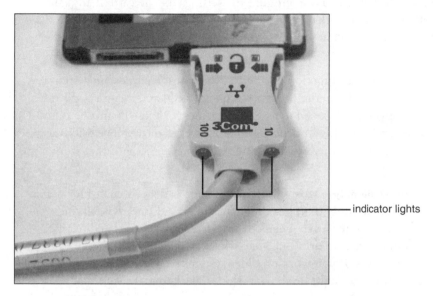

indicator lights

Figure 3.18 Indicator lights on a media adapter for a PCMCIA NIC.

Installing Network Cards

At some point in your networking career, it is likely that you will have to install a NIC into a system. For that reason, an understanding of the procedures and considerations related to NIC installations is useful.

> **TIP: Avoid ESD**   When installing any component in a system, you need to observe proper and correct procedures to guard against electrostatic discharge (ESD). ESD can cause components to fail immediately or degrade so that it fails at some point in the future. Proper ESD precautions include wearing an antistatic wrist strap and properly grounding yourself.

Here are some of the main points to consider:

- **Drivers**—Almost every NIC is supplied with a driver disk, but the likelihood of the drivers on the disk being the latest drivers is slim. Always make sure that you have the latest drivers by visiting the website of the NIC manufacturer. The drivers play an important role in the correct functioning of the NIC, so spend a few extra minutes to make sure that the drivers are installed and configured correctly.

- **NIC configuration utilities**—In days gone by, NICs were configured with small groups of pins known as *jumpers*, or with small plastic blocks of switches known as *dip switches*. Unless you work with old equipment, you are unlikely to encounter dip switches. Although these methods were efficient and easy to use, they have now largely been abandoned in favor of software configuration utilities, which enable you to configure the settings for the card (if any) and to test whether the card works properly. Other utilities can be used through the operating system to obtain statistical information, help, and a range of other features.

■ **System resources**—To function correctly, NICs must have certain system resources allocated to them: the interrupt request (IRQ) and memory addresses. In some cases, you might need to assign the values for these manually. In most cases, you can rely on plug-and-play, which assigns resources for devices automatically and even the software driver needed to make the hardware work with the operating system.

■ **Physical slot availability**—Most modern PCs have at least three or four usable expansion slots. Not only that, but the increasing trend toward component integration on the motherboard means that devices such as serial and parallel ports and sound cards are now built in to the system board and therefore don't use up valuable slots. If you work on older systems or systems that have a lot of add-in hardware, you might be short of slots. Check to make sure that a slot is available before you begin.

■ **Built-in network interfaces**—A built-in network interface is a double-edged sword. The upsides are that it doesn't occupy an expansion slot, and hardware compatibility with the rest of the system is almost guaranteed. The downside is that a built-in component is not upgradeable. For this reason, you might find install an add-in NIC and at the same time disable the onboard network interface. Disabling the onboard interface is normally a straightforward process, achieved by going into the BIOS setup screen or, on some systems, a system configuration utility. In either case, consult the documentation that came with the system or look for information on the manufacturer's website.

As time goes on, NIC and operating system manufacturers are making it increasingly easy to install NICs in systems of all sorts and sizes. By understanding the requirements of the card and the correct installation procedure, you should install cards simply and efficiently.

Media Converters

Network technologies change at a rapid pace, and administrators are always on the lookout to find cost-effective ways to increase network performance. The demand for higher speeds and greater distances keeps us, as administrators, on our toes. The process of incorporating new technology with older infrastructure is made easier with media converters.

Network media converters interconnect different types of cables within an existing network. For example, the media converter connects newer Gigabit Ethernet technologies with older 100BaseT networks.

This ability to combine networks, increases networking flexibility, while decreasing the cost of having to retrofit the network to accommodate new technology. Converters come in many shapes and sizes to connect to a variety of networks. This includes coax, twisted-pair, single-mode, or multimode fiber. Converters can be designed to work with any network type, including Ethernet, Fast Ethernet, Gigabit Ethernet, Asynchronous Transfer Mode (ATM), fiber distributed data interface (FDDI), and token ring.

TIP: Converters   By using media converters, companies do not need to dismantle the current wiring infrastructures. Media converters enable us to use existing infrastructure while keeping pace with changing technologies.

Firewalls

Today, firewalls are an essential part of a network's design. A *firewall* is a networking device, either hardware- or software-based, that controls access to your organization's network. This controlled access is designed to protect data and resources from outside threats. To do this, firewalls are typically placed at entry/exit points of a network. For example, a firewall might be placed between an internal network and the Internet. After the firewall is in place, it can control access in and out of that point.

Although firewalls typically protect internal networks from public networks, they also control access between specific network segments within a network. For example, you might place a firewall between the accounts department and the sales department segments of the network.

As mentioned, firewalls can be implemented through software or through a dedicated hardware device. Organizations implement software firewalls through network operating systems (NOS) such as Linux/UNIX, Windows servers, and Mac OS servers. The firewall is configured on the server to enable or permit certain types of network traffic. In small offices and for regular home use, a firewall is commonly installed on the local system and configured to control traffic. Many third-party firewalls are available.

Hardware firewalls are used in networks of all sizes today. Hardware firewalls are often dedicated network devices that you can implement with little configuration and use to protect all systems behind it from outside sources. Hardware firewalls are readily available and often combined with other devices. For example, many broadband routers and wireless APs have firewall functionality built in. In such a case, the router or AP might have a number of ports available to plug systems into.

You can find a complete discussion of firewalls in Chapter 14, "Network Access Security."

DHCP Server

Without question, the easiest way to assign TCP/IP information to client systems is to use a Dynamic Host Configuration Protocol (DHCP) server. On a network running TCP/IP, each computer must have a unique IP address to be recognized and be part of the network. Briefly, a *protocol* is a method of communicating between computers.

Computers on a network using TCP/IP require specific network settings to connect to the network. First among these settings is the IP address. An IPv4 address consists of *four octets*, or four sets of 8 bits—represented in decimal form—for example, 192.168.2.1. Each computer on the network must have one of these numbers to perform network functions through TCP/IP. The number must be unique to the PC and must be within a certain range to enable the PC to connect to other systems. A complete discussion of TCP/IP and addressing is covered in Chapter 5.

There was a time when all IP addresses were entered manually into the network settings of each client workstation. Manually set, or static, IP addresses are difficult to maintain in large networks. Adding to the time it takes to individually set the IP addresses is that each address must be unique. Duplicate IP addresses prevent a successful connection to the network for the second system to log on with the duplicate IP address. All network services will be unavailable to the workstations that logs on second. When you set static IP addresses, it is essential to track assigned IP addresses carefully to prevent duplicating addresses and to make future expansion and troubleshooting easier.

In larger networks, the assignment of manual addresses can be a nightmare, especially when IP addressing schemes can be changed and computers can be moved, retired, or replaced. That's where DHCP comes in. DHCP does the job of assigning IP addresses, eliminating the need to assign IP addresses individually and making the job of network administrators considerably easier. When a DHCP server runs on a network, the workstation boots up and requests an IP address from the server. The server responds to the request and automatically assigns an IP address to the computer for a given period of time, known as a *lease*. The workstation acknowledges the reception of the IP address, and the workstation has all the information it needs to become part of the network. This communication between the server and the workstation happens completely automatically and is invisible to the computer user.

Because of their capability to efficiently distribute IP addresses to network workstations, DHCP servers are widely used in client/server environments. People working with networks will most certainly encounter DHCP servers. The critical nature of DHCP services means that companies often choose to run more than one DHCP server.

> **NOTE: Where's AP**   The objectives specify a discussion of wireless access points (APs), which are covered with the rest of wireless information in Chapter 7.

Specialized Network Devices

A network is composed of many pieces of hardware. Some, such as firewalls and DHCP servers, are in most networks. Devices that are more specialized, such as load balancers and proxy servers, are not found in every network environment. CompTIA lists the devices described in the following sections as specialized networking devices. We take a quick look at what they are designed to do.

Multilayer and Content Switches

It used to be that networking devices and the function they perform were separate. We had bridges, routers, hubs, and more, but they were separate devices. Over time, the functions of some individual network devices became integrated into a single device. This is true of multilayer switches.

A multilayer switch is one that can operate at both the Layer 2 and Layer 3 of the OSI model. The OSI model is covered in Chapter 9, but for now, this means that the multilayer device can operate both as a switch and as a router. Also known as a Layer 3 switch, the multilayer switch is a high-performance device that actually supports the same routing protocols that routers do. It is a regular switch directing traffic within the LAN, but it can forward packets between subnets as well.

> **NOTE: 2 for 1**   A multilayer switch operates as both a router and a switch.

A content switch is another specialized device. A content switch is not as common on today's networks, mostly because of cost. A content switch examines the network data it receives, decides where the content is intended to go, and forwards it there. The content switch has the capability to identify the application that data is targeted for by associating it with a port. For example, if data is using the SMTP port, the data could be forwarded to an SMTP server.

Content servers can help with load balancing because they can distribute requests across servers and target data only to the servers needing the data, or distribute data between application servers. For example, if multiple mail servers are used, the content switch can distribute requests between the servers, thereby sharing the load evenly. This is why the content switch is sometimes referred to as a load-balancing switch.

> **NOTE: Content Switching**   A content switch can distribute incoming data to specific application servers and help distribute the load.

Intrusion Detection and Prevention Systems

Administrators can use several methods to help secure the network. In addition to a firewall, an intrusion detection system (IDS) and intrusion prevention system (IPS) can be used. Both are designed to help identify unwanted network access and traffic, but they work in slightly different ways.

An IDS is either a hardware or software device that constantly monitors inbound and outbound network traffic. The IDS uses built-in parameters to flag and document any traffic it determines to be suspicious or potentially dangerous. But that is where the IDS stops. It does not actively try to manage the threat; rather, it identifies the threat and then the administrator must monitor the IDS system to see what the problem might be. Although it doesn't try to fix the potential threat, the IDS can be configured to send an alert, notifying the administrator of a potential threat and security breach.

In operation, an IDS system compares the inbound and outbound traffic to a large database of attack signatures. Attack signatures are known elements of a particular attack. Just as we have fingerprints, certain attacks can be identified by their features. In this way, the IDS system can identify attacks that have already been identified elsewhere and can pinpoint them entering or leaving the network. An IDS system is only as good as the database it uses to identify attacks, which makes it important to keep the database up to date.

An IDS system can be deployed as host-based (resident to a single system) or network-based (watches all network traffic). In either case, an IDS system cannot replace a firewall because it has different functions. The firewall monitors secures access between two networks, such as a business and the Internet, and prevents unwanted traffic from entering the network. The IDS system inspects an intrusion after it has taken place—that is, after it has passed the firewall. An IDS also watches for threats from within the network, whereas the firewall operates on the network perimeter.

An IDS system looks to flag potential threats. In contrast, the IPS is more proactive and tries to manage them on its own. Similar to an IDS, the IPS monitors both inbound and outbound traffic and looks for potential threats. But where an IDS flags and documents the threat, the IPS takes immediate action, trying to remove the threat. Where an IDS might flag a network intruder, the IPS will try to immediately shut the intruder out. The actions an IPS takes are established by the network administrator. You can find more information about IDS and IPS in Chapter 14.

Load Balancer

Network servers are the workhorses of the network. We rely on them to hold and distribute data, maintain backups, secure network communications, and more. A single server often cannot maintain the workload. This is where load balancing comes into play. *Load balancing* is a technique in which the workload is distributed between several servers. This feature can increase network performance, reliability, and availability.

> **NOTE: Share the Load**   Remember for the exam that load balancing increases redundancy and, therefore, availability to data.

A load balancer can be either a hardware device or software specially configured to balance the load. You can learn more about load balancing and its importance in the network in Chapter 10, "Network Performance and Optimization."

Multifunction Network Devices

It used to be that each device on a network had its own purpose. We had a firewall, routers, repeaters, and hubs, to name a few. Multifunction network devices combine the function of these individual devices into a single unit. Let's look at a wireless access point used by home users or small companies for wireless access to the Internet. Those of you who have experience with these devices know they are multifunction network devices. They have combined functionality, including firewall, DHCP server, wireless access point, switch, gateway, and router. One device under $100 can perform all these functions. These multifunction devices make it easier for administrators to tend to the network. Fewer devices need to be managed, and all configurations can be handled remotely.

Multifunction devices can offer some advantages over multiple independent devices or software packages. Suppose an organization maintains antivirus, firewall, content-filtering, and IDS/IPS software on a single or even on several servers. This organization must pay for the cost of the software on each of the servers the operating system, and the personnel to maintain the systems. All this can be replaced with a single multifunction network device.

DNS Server

A domain name system (DNS) server performs a basic but vital role for many organizations. The function of a DNS server is relatively simple in that it provides name resolution from hostnames to IP addresses. The measures to which the server will go to provide a successful resolution, however, are not so simple. In addition to consulting its own databases for the requested information, a DNS server also contacts other DNS servers as needed to get the necessary information. This process can involve a large number of queries.

As you might know, each device on a network requires a unique IP address so that it can provide services to clients. Rather than rely on the flawed human memory to remember these addresses, DNS enables us to use easy-to-remember hostnames, such as comptia.org, to access these hosts. When we type `www.comptia.org` into a web browser, our configured DNS server takes the request and searches through a system of DNS servers to find out the correct TCP/IP address that relates to www.comptia.org. After the DNS server has ascertained the correct TCP/IP address, that address is returned to the client, which then contacts the IP address directly. To speed up subsequent requests for the same address, the DNS server adds the address to its cache. For a workstation to send requests to the DNS server, the TCP/IP address of the DNS server must be provided to the workstations. This can be done manually, or the address can be included in the information supplied by a DHCP server.

Before DNS was used, resolution of hostnames to IP addresses was (and still is, in some cases) performed through static text files called Hosts files. These text files quickly became too large to manage easily and were replaced by DNS.

The function of DNS remains largely hidden from most users, but our reliance on the system is amazingly high. In January 2001, a Microsoft employee made a configuration change to one of Microsoft's DNS servers. The change caused an error that rendered some Microsoft-hosted websites, including the popular Hotmail system, inaccessible for a number of hours. The servers were up and running, but they could not be reached.

Most common operating systems provide the capability to act as a DNS server. Some implementations are more sophisticated than others, but the basic principle of hostname-to-TCP/IP-address resolution remains the same.

The amount of computing power required by a DNS server is proportional to the number of DNS requests that it handles. Within an organization, records might be configured for only a relatively small number of hosts, and only a small number of client requests might occur. In such an environment, it would be unlikely to have a server dedicated to DNS functions. In contrast, a DNS server for an ISP would need to be powerful enough to accommodate perhaps millions of requests per hour.

> **TIP: DNS Server**   A DNS server answers client requests to translate hostnames to IP addresses.

Bandwidth Shaper

The demand for bandwidth on networks has never been higher. Internet and intranet applications demand a high amount of bandwidth. Administrators have to ensure that despite these demands, adequate bandwidth is available for mission critical applications whereas few resources are dedicated to spam or peer-to-peer downloads. To do this, we need to monitor network traffic to ensure that data flows as required.

The term *bandwidth shaping* describes the mechanisms used to control bandwidth usage on the network. Bandwidth shaping is typically done using software installed on a network server. From this server, administrators can control who uses bandwidth, for what, and when. Bandwidth shaping establishes priorities to data traveling to and from the Internet and within the network.

A bandwidth shaper essentially performs two key functions: monitoring and shaping. Monitoring includes identifying where bandwidth usage is high and at what time of day. After that information is obtained, administrators can customize or shape bandwidth usage for the best needs of the network. Figure 3.19 shows an example of a bandwidth shaper.

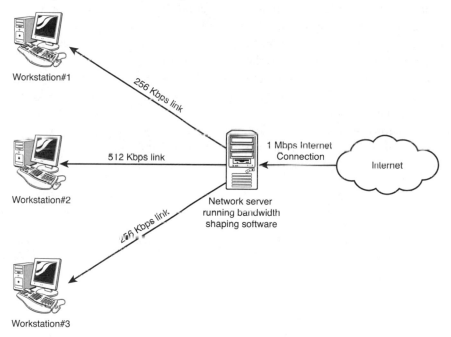

Figure 3.19   Bandwidth shaper.

Proxy Server

Proxy servers are typically part of a firewall system; they have become so integrated with firewalls that the distinction between the two can sometimes be lost. However, proxy servers perform a unique role in the network environment—a role that is separate from that of a firewall. For the purposes of this book, a proxy server is defined as a server that sits between a client computer and the Internet, looking at the web page requests sent by the client. For example, if a client computer wants to access a web page, the request is sent to the proxy server rather than directly to the Internet. The proxy server first determines whether the request is intended for the Internet or for a web server locally. If the request is intended for the Internet, the proxy server sends the request out as if it had originated the request. When the information is returned by the Internet web server, the proxy server returns the information to the client.

Although a delay might be induced by the extra step of going through the proxy server, the process is largely transparent to the client that originated the request. Because each request a client sends to the Internet is channeled through the proxy server, the proxy server can provide certain functionality over and above forwarding requests.

One feature is that proxy servers can greatly improve network performance through a process called *caching*. When a caching proxy server has answered a request for a web page, the server makes a copy of all or part of that page in its cache. Then, when the page is requested again, the proxy server answers the request from the cache rather than going back out to the Internet. For example, if a client on a network requests the web page www.comptia.org, the proxy server can cache the contents of that web page. When a second client computer on the network attempts to access the same site, that client can retrieve it from the proxy server cache, and accessing the Internet is not necessary. This greatly increases the response time to the client and can significantly reduce the bandwidth needed to fulfill client requests. An example of this is shown in Figure 3.20.

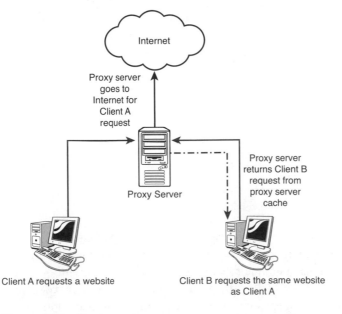

Figure 3.20   Proxy server.

Nowadays, speed is everything, and the capability to quickly access information from the Internet is a crucial concern for some organizations. Proxy servers and their capability to cache web content accommodate this need for speed.

An example of this speed might be found in a classroom. If a teacher asks 30 students to access a specific URL (Uniform Resource Locator), without a proxy server, all 30 requests are sent into cyberspace and subjected to the delays or other issues that can arise. The classroom scene with a proxy server is quite different. Only 1 request of the 30 finds its way to the Internet; the other 29 are filled by the proxy server's cache. Web page retrieval can be almost instantaneous.

However, caching has one potential drawback. When you log on to the Internet, you get the latest information, but this is not always so when information is retrieved from a cache. For some web pages, it is necessary to go directly to the Internet to ensure that the information is up to date.

Another key feature of proxy servers is that network administrators have the ability to filter client requests. If a server administrator wants to block access to certain websites, a proxy server enables this control, making it easy to completely disallow access to some websites. If you find it necessary to block out numerous websites, however, the job of maintaining proxy servers gets a little more complicated.

Determining which websites users can or cannot access is typically done through something called an access control list (ACL). The ACL is a list of allowable or nonallowed websites. As you might imagine, compiling such a list can be a monumental task. Given that millions of websites exist and new ones are created daily, how would it be possible to target and disallow access to the "questionable" ones? One approach is to reverse the situation and deny access to all pages except those that appear in an "allowed" list. This approach has a high administrative overhead and can greatly limit the productive benefits available from Internet access.

Understandably, it is impossible to maintain a list that contains the locations of all sites that contain questionable content. In fairness, that is not what proxy servers were designed to do. However, by maintaining a list, proxy servers are better able to provide a greater level of control than that of an open system, and along the way, they can make the retrieval of web pages far more efficient.

CSUs/DSUs

A Channel Service Unit/Data Service Unit (CSU/DSU) acts as a translator between the LAN data format and the WAN data format. Such a conversion is necessary because the technologies used on WAN links are different from those used on LANs. Some consider a CSU/DSU as a type of digital modem; but unlike a normal modem, which changes the signal from digital to analog, a CSU/DSU changes the signal from one digital format to another. Figure 3.21 shows how a CSU/DSU might fit into a network.

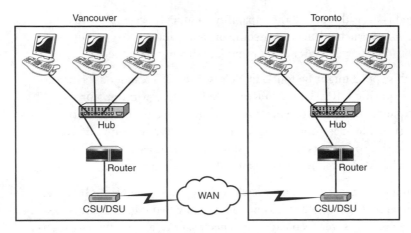

Figure 3.21   How a CSU/DSU is used in a network.

A CSU/DSU has physical connections for the LAN equipment, normally via a serial interface, and another connection for a WAN. Traditionally, the CSU/DSU has been in a separate box from other networking equipment; however, the increasing use of WAN links means that some router manufacturers are now including the CSU/DSU functionality in routers or are providing the expansion capability to do so.

Network Devices Summary

The information in this chapter is important for the Network+ exam. To summarize the coverage of network devices, we have placed some of the key points about each device in Table 3.3. You should learn this information well.

Table 3.3   Network Devices Summary

Device	Function/Purpose	Key Points
Hub	Connects devices on an Ethernet twisted-pair network.	A hub does not perform any tasks besides signal regeneration.
Switch	Connects devices on a twisted-pair network	A switch forwards data to its destination by using the MAC address embedded in each packet.
Repeater	Regenerates data signals	The function a repeater provides is typically built in to other devices, such as switches.
Bridge	Connects LANs to reduce overall network traffic	A bridge enables or prevents data from passing through it by reading the MAC address.
Router	Connects networks together	A router uses the software-configured network address to make forwarding decisions.

Table 3.3 Network Devices Summary

Device	Function/Purpose	Key Points
Gateway	Translates from one data format to another	Gateways can be hardware- or software-based. Any device that translates data formats is called a gateway.
CSU/DSU	Translates digital signals used on a LAN to those used on a WAN	CSU/DSU functionality is sometimes incorporated into other devices, such as a router with a WAN connection.
Modem	Provides serial communication capabilities across phone lines.	Modems modulate the digital signal into analog at the sending end and perform the reverse function at the receiving end.
Network interface card	Enables systems to connect to the network	Network interfaces can be add-in expansion cards, PCMCIA cards, or built-in interfaces.
Media converter	Interconnects older technology with new	Hardware device that connects newer Gigabit Ethernet technologies with older 100BaseT networks or older copper standards with fiber.
Firewall	Provides controlled data access between networks	Firewalls can be hardware- or software-based and are an essential part of a network's security strategy.
DHCP server	Automatically distributes IP information	DHCP assigns all IP information, including IP address, subnet mask, DNS, gateway, and more.
Multilayer switch	Works as a switch and as a router	Operates on Layer 2 and Layer 3 of OSI model as a switch and can perform router function.
Content switch	Forwards data by application	Content switches can identify and forward data by its port and application.
Load balancer	Distributes network load	Load balancing increases redundancy by distributing load to multiple servers.
Multifunction devices	Combine network services	Hardware devices that combine multiple network services into a single device, reducing cost and easing administrative difficulty.
DNS server	Provides name resolution from hostnames to IP addresses.	A DNS server answers clients' requests to translate hostnames to IP addresses.
Bandwidth shaper	Manages network bandwidth	The bandwidth shaper monitors and controls bandwidth usage.

Table 3.3 Network Devices Summary

Device	Function/Purpose	Key Points
Proxy server	Manages client Internet requests	Serves two key network functions: increasing network performance by caching, and filtering outgoing client requests.

Summary

Many devices create networks. Every network except the simplest, single-segment coaxial networks uses one or more of these devices. Knowledge of the purpose of the devices discussed in this chapter is vital for the Network+ exam and for the real world.

Hubs and switches provide a mechanism to connect devices to a network created with twisted-pair cabling. Switches offer a speed advantage over hubs because they can use full-duplex communications. They also create dedicated paths between devices, reducing the number of collisions that occur. Both hubs and switches are available in managed and unmanaged varieties.

Bridges enable network traffic to be confined to certain network segments, thereby reducing the amount of network traffic. On Ethernet networks, bridges provide the additional benefit of reduced collisions.

Routers are devices that connect networks and thereby create internetworks. Because routers use software-configured network addresses instead of hardware-defined MAC addresses, they can provide more functionality than bridges. Routers either can be dedicated hardware devices or can be implemented through software on server systems.

Multilayer and content switches are listed as specialized network devices in the CompTIA objectives. Multilayer switches operate as both a switch and a router. Content switches forward data to its associated application server.

Bandwidth shapers are used on a network to manipulate how bandwidth is used. Load balancers are used to distribute the processing and data traffic between devices. It prevents network resources from being overloaded.

DNS servers are used on a network designed to resolve hostname to IP addresses. DHCP servers automatically assign IP addressing information to client systems. A gateway is a device that translates from one data format to another; it can be a hardware device or a software application. A CSU/DSU is an example of a gateway: CSUs/DSUs translate from the data format used on LANs to that used on

WANs. A modem, which translates a signal from digital to analog so that it can be transmitted across a conventional phone line, is another example of a gateway.

NICs are the point of connectivity between devices and the network. NICs can be add-in expansion cards, PCMCIA devices for laptops, or devices built in to the system board.

On a network, each NIC is identified by a unique MAC address. MAC addresses are assigned by the manufacturers that produce the devices, although the high-level assignment of addresses is managed and carried out by the IEEE.

Other network devices include firewalls, converters, proxy servers, and repeaters. Firewalls protect one network from another, converters connect new and old technology, proxy servers provide caching and filtering services, and repeaters regenerate data signals to enable them to travel farther.

If you get a chance to use all the hardware devices discussed in this chapter, count yourself lucky. Almost every environment uses some of them, but few use them all.

Exam Preparation Tasks

Review All the Key Topics

Review the most important topics in the chapter, noted with the key topics icon in the outer margin of the page. Table 3.4 lists a reference of these key topics and the page numbers on which each is found.

Table 3.4   Key Topics for Chapter 3

Key Topic Element	Description	Page Number
Figure 3.3	Hub and workstation connection	101
Figure 3.6	How a switch works	103
List	How a switch forwards data	105
Figure 3.8	How a bridge works	111
Figure 3.10	A bridging loop	112
Table 3.1	AT modem commands	119
Figure 3.19	Bandwidth shaping	131
Table 3.3	Network devices summary	134

Complete the Tables and Lists from Memory

Print a copy of Appendix B, "Memory Tables" (found on the CD), or at least the section for this chapter, and complete the tables and lists from memory. Appendix C, "Memory Tables Answer Key," also on the CD, includes completed tables and lists to check your work.

Define Key Terms

- Hub
- Repeater
- Modem
- NIC
- Media converters
- Basic switch
- Bridge
- Access points
- Router
- Firewall
- DHCP server
- PoE
- Spanning tree
- Trunking
- Port mirroring
- Port authentication
- Multilayer switch
- Content switching
- Load balancer
- Multifunction network devices
- DNS server
- Bandwidth shaper
- Proxy server
- CSU/DSU

Apply Your Knowledge

Exercise 3.1 Determining MAC Addresses for Network Cards

This chapter identifies the characteristics and functions of network devices. In an ideal world, this project would require hands-on experience with these devices, but this is not an ideal world, and access to this equipment is not always easy. Therefore, we include two exercises that you might be required to perform if such devices are used on your network.

This project assumes that you use a Windows-based system. You need an installed NIC with a working driver.

Estimated time: 10 minutes

1. Open a command window by selecting Start, Run. In the command box, type cmd and then click OK.

2. At the command prompt, type `ipconfig /all`. The MAC address of your NIC is displayed in the Physical Address line.

3. Open a web browser and go to the following website: http://standards.ieee.org/regauth/oui/oui.txt.

4. Using the Find functionality in your web browser, type in the first three octets of your physical address. The find function locates the entry that corresponds with the address of your NIC. Is the manufacturer of your NIC the company you expected it to be? Some NIC manufacturers rebrand cards manufactured by another company. For that reason, the MAC address might correspond to a manufacturer that is different from the brand name of the card.

Exercise 3.2 Viewing the IP Information on Your System

In this chapter we discussed gateways, DHCP servers, and DNS servers. In this exercise we identify all of these on a client system and whether DHCP is enabled.

Estimated time: 5 minutes

1. Open a command window by selecting Start, Run. In the command box, type cmd.exe and then click OK.

2. At the command prompt, type `ipconfig /all`.

3. A long window of information displays. Scroll down the list; can you find the address of the default gateway? Through this device, you are routed forward to the Internet.

4. Do you see the IP address of the DNS server? The device with this IP address is responsible for converting your hostname to the IP address.

5. Finally, find the IP address of the DHCP server. If DHCP is enabled, you see the IP address of the DHCP server.

6. If you work from home using a home router for this exercise, you can put the IP address of the DHCP or DNS server into your browser. This takes you to a logon window and enables you to configure the device.

Review Questions

You can find answers to the review questions in Appendix A, "Answers to Review Questions."

1. Several users on your network are downloading from peer-to-peer networks, tying up bandwidth during peak hours. Which of the following manages network bandwidth?

   a. Load balancer

   b. Load toner

   c. Bandwidth toner

   d. Bandwidth shaper

2. You have recently been hired as a network administrator for a large company. The company uses a multilayer switch. What is the function of the switch on the network? (Select two.)

   a. Route traffic between subnets

   b. Route traffic between DNS servers on the local LAN

   c. Operate as a Layer 2 network switch

   d. Switch data based on content

3. Which of the following technologies are responsible for answering client requests to translate hostnames to IP addresses?

   a. Balancing server

   b. DNS server

   c. Proxy server

   d. DHCP server

4. A bridge makes forwarding decisions based on what information?

   a. IP address

   b. MAC address

   c. Binary address

   d. IRQ address

5. What information does a switch use to determine the port to which data should be sent?

   a. The IP address of the connected device

   b. The priority of the connected device

   c. The MAC address of the connected device

   d. The Ethernet address of the connected device

6. Which of the following network devices performs filtering and caching web pages for client Internet requests?

   a. Proxy server

   b. DNS server

   c. DHCP server

   d. RAS server

7. Which of the following best describes the function of PoE?

   a. Routes data to PPP ports

   b. Provides power over twisted-pair cable

   c. Increases speeds of twisted-pair cable

   d. Trunks switch ports

8. What is the purpose of the uplink port on a hub or switch? (Select three)

   a. It enables for satellite connections.

   b. It enables hubs or switches to be connected together.

   c. It enables computers to connect to the device.

   d. It provides a spare port, which can be used if another port fails.

9. By what method does a router determine the destination address for a packet?

   a. It looks at the MAC address of the sender.

   b. It looks for the MAC address of the destination.

   c. It looks for the software-configured network address for the destination.

   d. It looks at the FCS field of the packet.

10. Which of the following devices was specifically designed to deal with attenuation?

   a. Switch

   b. Passive hub

   c. DHCP server

   d. Repeater

11. Which of the following are valid port states when routing with STP? (Select two.)

   a. Disabled

   b. Listening

   c. Paused

   d. Suspended

12. What is the difference between an active hub and a passive hub?

    a. An active hub has management capabilities.

    b. An active hub forwards the data only to the ports that need it.

    c. An active hub channels bandwidth to a given connection if the connection becomes too slow.

    d. An active hub regenerates the signal before forwarding it.

13. Which of the following devices is typically used to protect private internal networks from public ones?

    a. DHCP server

    b. Firewall

    c. Active hub

    d. Protective switch

14. Which of the following technologies enables power to be sent over regular UTP cable?

    a. PoE

    b. PoDNS

    c. PoC

    d. PoUTP

15. What is the maximum speed of a 16550 UART chip?

    a. 64,000bps

    b. 115,200bps

    c. 430,800bps

    d. 921,600bps

16. What is the name of the bridging method used to segregate Ethernet networks?

    a. Source-route

    b. Invisible

    c. Cut-through

    d. Transparent

17. You have been called to support a network. When you arrive, you notice that multiple lines run between the switch and the server. This is an example of which of the following technologies?

    a. Routing

    b. Basing

    c. Trunking

    d. Port mirroring

18. A CSU/DSU is used in which of the following network configurations?
    a. When converting from a token-ring network to an Ethernet network
    b. When converting a digital signal to an analog signal
    c. When converting from the digital signals used on a LAN to the digital signals used on a WAN
    d. When converting from the digital signal format used on a LAN to the analog signal format used on a WAN

19. A router makes its forwarding decisions based on which of the following information?
    a. IP address
    b. ARP address
    c. Binary address
    d. Frame address

20. You are given the task of upgrading a new NIC in the company file and print server. Which of the following should you determine before buying a replacement card? (Choose all correct answers.)
    a. Bus compatibility
    b. Network compatibility
    c. Hardware compatibility
    d. Cooling requirements

This chapter covers CompTIA Network+ objectives 1.1 and 1.2. Upon completion of this chapter, you will be able to answer the following questions:

- What are the function of TCP/IP protocols?

- Which protocols are used with TCP ports?

- Which protocols are used with UDP ports?

CHAPTER 4

Understanding the TCP/IP Protocol Suite

In networks, as in everyday life, rules and procedures govern communication. The rules and procedures that enable devices on a network to communicate with each other are referred to as *protocols*. Some protocols deal specifically with the process of transferring data from one system to another, and others are responsible for route discovery and providing client functionality.

This chapter focuses on the TCP/IP protocol suite. TCP/IP is not a single protocol but rather an entire collection of protocols, each designed to perform a different function on the network. Understanding how TCP/IP works requires an understanding of those protocols within the TCP/IP protocol suite. This chapter examines some of the characteristics of the protocols found within TCP/IP and their function. Understanding these characteristics is important for the Network+ exam.

Foundation Topics

A Brief Introduction to Protocols

When computers were restricted to stand-alone systems, little need existed for mechanisms to communicate between them. However, it wasn't long before the need to connect computers for the purpose of sharing files and printers became a necessity. Establishing communication between network devices required more than a length of cabling; a method or a set of rules was needed to establish how systems would communicate. Protocols provide that method.

It would be nice if a single protocol facilitated communication among all devices, but this is not the case. You can use a number of protocols on a network, each of which has its own features, advantages, and disadvantages. What protocol you choose can have a significant impact on the functioning and performance of the network.

Protocols are grouped into *protocol suites*. Each protocol suite defines a complete set of protocols that allow the devices to communicate. Within each protocol suite are a variety of protocols, which can be broken down into three distinct categories:

- **Application protocols**—Provide client functionality

- **Transport protocols**—Provide mechanisms for moving data around the network

- **Network protocols**—Perform the underlying tasks that enable the movement of data

The main protocol used today to facilitate network communication is Transmission Control Protocol/Internet Protocol (TCP/IP), which is a comprehensive protocol suite. TCP/IP is available for all common platforms, including Windows, Linux, UNIX, Mac OS, and Novell systems. Although TCP/IP reigns supreme today, it used to have some significant competition, including

- **Internetwork Packet Exchange/Sequenced Packet Exchange (IPX/SPX)**— Developed by Novell, IPX/SPX is a set of protocols originally designed for use on Novell networks. It is now less popular than it once was because of the impact of TCP/IP.

- **AppleTalk**—Designed for use on networks that use Macintosh systems, AppleTalk is an advanced suite of protocols that provides high levels of functionality. Like IPX/SPX, it is also now less popular than it once was because of the impact of TCP/IP.

In addition to these protocol suites, certain other protocols, such as NetBIOS Extended User Interface (NetBEUI), were previously commonly used on smaller networks. Because these protocols are no longer widely deployed, they have been left out of this version of the Network+ objectives and out of this book.

To get an idea of exactly how protocols facilitate communication between devices, let's look at the role protocols play at the sending and receiving computers. In the data communication process, the information that passes between computers on a network goes through certain steps at both the sending and receiving devices. The following sections discuss what takes place at each end of the communication process.

Protocols from the Sending Device

For a computer to send data, the following steps must be performed; keep in mind that these are general steps—the actual processes taken at the sending device are far more complex:

1. The protocol is responsible for breaking the data into smaller parts and sent through the network.
2. Within each individual packet, network addressing information is attached. Network addressing identifies the destination for the packet and the route it travels to a destination.
3. The data is prepared for transmission and sent through the network interface card (NIC) and on to the network.

You can match steps 1 through 3 to the OSI model, starting with the application layer and ending with the physical layer, where the data is passed from the NIC to the network media. The OSI model is discussed in detail in Chapter 9, "OSI Model."

Protocols on the Receiving Device

The steps for the receiving device are similar to those for the sending device, but they occur in the opposite order:

1. When data reaches the destination computer, the data is taken off the network media and in through the system's NIC.
2. The addressing information added by the sending computer is stripped from the packets.
3. The data packets are reassembled.
4. The reassembled packets are passed to the specific application for use.

To accomplish these steps, the same protocol must be used on the sending and receiving devices. It is possible for two devices that use different protocols to communicate with each other, but a *gateway*—an intermediary device that has the capability to translate between two formats—is needed. For more information on gateways, refer to Chapter 3, "Networking Components and Devices."

Transmission Control Protocol/Internet Protocol (TCP/IP) Protocol Suite

In the dynamic IT industry, technologies come and go; new and improved methods, procedures, and equipment replace the old at a staggering pace. TCP/IP is one of the few exceptions to the rule. Not only has it survived in a state similar to its original, but as other networking protocols have fallen away, networks' dependency on TCP/IP has increased. There might have been pretenders to the protocol crown, but TCP/IP is truly the champion.

In the late 1970s and early 1980s, the U.S. Department of Defense Advanced Research Projects Agency (ARPA) needed a system that would enable it to share the resources of its expensive mainframe computer systems. From this, the ARPANET—the forerunner of today's Internet—was developed.

The original ARPANET network used a communication protocol known as NCP, but limitations were soon discovered, and a new protocol was needed to meet the new networking demands. That new protocol was TCP/IP, which soon became the unquestioned leader in the protocol arena; increasingly, networks of all shapes and sizes were using it.

The history of the Internet and the development of TCP/IP have been closely linked and continue to be so today. ARPANET was retired in 1989, but its functions were steadily improved, and today we have the Internet. TCP/IP has always been at the root of the Internet; if you work in network environments that require Internet access, you can expect to use the TCP/IP protocol. All the major network operating systems include support for TCP/IP.

Although TCP/IP is often referred to as a single protocol, the TCP/IP suite is composed many protocols. Each of the protocols in the TCP/IP suite provides a different function, and together they provide the functionality we know as TCP/IP.

The TCP/IP protocol suite got its name from the two main protocols in the suite: TCP and the IP. TCP is responsible for providing reliable transmissions from one system to another, and IP is responsible for addressing and route selection. The following sections describe TCP, IP, and the other protocols that make up the TCP/IP protocol suite.

> **NOTE: Request For Comments**   As we work through this chapter and through the book, the term *Request For Comments (RFC)* is used. RFCs are standards published by the Internet Engineering Task Force (IETF) that describe methods, behaviors, research, or innovations applicable to the operation of the Internet and Internet-connected systems. Each new RFC has an associated reference number. Looking up this number gives you information on the specific technology. For more information on RFCs go to the Internet Engineering Task Force online (www.ietf.org).

Internet Protocol (IP)

IP, which is defined in RFC 791, is the protocol used to transport data from one node on a network to another. IP is connectionless, which means that it doesn't guarantee the delivery of data; it simply makes a best effort to do so. To ensure that transmissions sent via IP are completed, a higher-level protocol such as TCP is required.

NOTE: IP and the OSI Model   IP operates at the network layer of the OSI model. Refer to Chapter 9 for more on protocols and the OSI model.

In addition to providing best-effort delivery, IP also performs fragmentation and reassembly tasks for network transmissions. Fragmentation is necessary because the maximum transmission unit (MTU) size is limited in IP. In other words, network transmissions that are too big to traverse the network in a single packet have to be broken into smaller chunks and reassembled at the other end. Another function of IP is addressing. IP addressing is a complex subject; refer to Chapter 5, "TCP/IP Addressing and Routing," for a complete discussion.

Transmission Control Protocol (TCP)

TCP, which is defined in RFC 793, is a connection-oriented protocol that uses IP as its transport protocol. Being connection-oriented means that TCP establishes a mutually acknowledged session between two hosts before communication takes place. TCP provides reliability to IP communications. Specifically, TCP adds features such as flow control, sequencing, and error detection and correction. For this reason, higher-level applications that need guaranteed delivery use TCP rather than its lightweight and connectionless brother, UDP.

When TCP wants to open a connection with another host, it follows this procedure:

1. It sends a message called a SYN to the target host.
2. The target host opens a connection for the request and sends back an acknowledgment message called an ACK (or SYN ACK).
3. The host that originated the request sends back another acknowledgment, saying that it has received the ACK message and that the session is ready to be used to transfer data.

When the data session is completed, a similar process is used to close the session. This three-step session establishment and acknowledgment process is referred to as the *TCP three-way handshake*.

NOTE: TCP and the OSI Model   TCP operates at the transport layer of the OSI model.

TCP is a reliable protocol because it has mechanisms that can accommodate and handle errors. These mechanisms include *timeouts*, which cause the sending host to automatically retransmit data if its receipt is not acknowledged within a given time period.

NOTE: SYN Flooding   A problem with the TCP SYN/ACK system is that the TCP/IP protocol stack assumes that each of the SYN requests it receives is genuine. Although this is normally the case, hackers can also exploit this trust as a weakness by using an attack known as a SYN flood. In a SYN flood, large numbers of SYN requests are directed at a host, but the source address to which the system attempts to send an ACK is false; therefore, no acknowledgment of the ACK occurs. The host, assuming that the lack of response is attributable to a network problem, keeps the SYN connections open for a period of time as a "just in case" precaution. During this time, the connection cannot be used by another host. If enough false SYN requests are directed at a server, the result is that no connections are left to service legitimate requests. To guard against this occurrence, some applications and operating systems have strategies that determine when a false connection is made, which helps prevent SYN flooding.

NOTE: Half-Open Connections   A SYN flood produces a high number of half-open connections on the target host. Most routers nowadays can be configured to guard against this problem.

User Datagram Protocol (UDP)

UDP, which is defined in RFC 768, is the brother of TCP. Like TCP, UDP uses IP as its transport protocol, but the big difference is that UDP does not guarantee delivery like TCP does. In a sense, UDP is a "fire and forget" protocol; it assumes that the data sent will reach its destination intact. Actually, the process of checking whether data is delivered is left to upper-layer protocols.

NOTE: UDP and the OSI Model   UDP operates at the transport layer of the OSI model.

Unlike TCP, with UDP there is no establishment of a session between the sending and receiving hosts, which is why UDP is referred to as a connectionless protocol. The upshot of this is that UDP has a much lower overhead than TCP. A TCP packet header has 14 fields, whereas a UDP packet header has 4. Therefore, UDP is much more efficient than TCP. In applications that don't need the added features of TCP, UDP is much more economical in terms of bandwidth and processing effort.

> **NOTE: Connection-Oriented**   TCP is a connection-oriented protocol that uses IP as its transport protocol. This is in contrast to UDP, which is a connectionless protocol.

File Transfer Protocol (FTP)

As its name suggests, File Transfer Protocol (FTP provides for the uploading and downloading of files from a remote host running FTP server software. In addition to uploading and downloading files, FTP enables you to view the contents of folders on an FTP server and rename and delete files and directories if you have the necessary permissions. FTP, which is defined in RFC 959, uses TCP as a transport protocol to guarantee delivery of packets.

FTP has security mechanisms used to authenticate users. However, rather than create a user account for every user, you can configure FTP server software to accept anonymous logons. When you do this, the username is anonymous, and the password is normally blank. Most FTP servers that offer files to the general public operate in this way.

In addition to being popular as a mechanism for distributing files to the general public over networks such as the Internet, FTP is also popular with individuals and organizations that need to frequently exchange large files across a LAN.

> **NOTE: FTP and the OSI Model**   FTP is an application layer protocol.

All the common network operating systems offer FTP server capabilities, although whether you use them depends on whether you need FTP services. All popular workstation operating systems offer FTP client functionality, although it is common to use third-party utilities such as CuteFTP and FileZilla instead.

FTP assumes that files being uploaded or downloaded are straight text (that is, ASCII) files. If the files are not text, which is likely, the transfer mode must be changed to binary. With sophisticated FTP clients, such as CuteFTP, the transition between transfer modes is automatic. With more basic utilities, you have to perform the mode switch manually.

Unlike some of the other protocols discussed in this chapter that perform tasks transparently to the user, FTP is an application layer service called upon frequently. Therefore, it can be useful to know some of the commands supported by FTP. If you use a client such as CuteFTP, you might never need to use these commands, but they are useful to know in case you use a command-line FTP client. Table 4.1 lists some of the most commonly used FTP commands.

Table 4.1   Commonly Used FTP Commands

Command	Purpose
ls	Lists the files in the current directory on the remote system
cd	Changes working directory on the remote host
lcd	Changes working directory on the local host
put	Uploads a single file to the remote host
get	Downloads a single file from the remote host
mput	Stands for *multiple put* and uploads multiple files to the remote host
mget	Downloads multiple files from the remote host
binary	Switches transfers into binary mode
ascii	Switches transfers into ASCII mode (the default)

TIP: FTP Commands   rk+ exam, you might be asked to identify the appropriate FTP command to use in a given situation.

Secure Shell (SSH)

Created by students at the Helsinki University of Technology, Secure Shell (SSH) is a secure alternative to Telnet. SSH provides security by encrypting data as it travels between systems. This makes it difficult for hackers using packet sniffers and other traffic detection systems. It also provides more robust authentication systems than Telnet.

Two versions of SSH are available: SSH1 and SSH2. Of the two, SSH2 is considered more secure. The two SSH versions are not compatible. So, if you use an SSH client program, the server implementation of SSH that you connect to must be the same version.

Although SSH, like Telnet, is primarily associated with UNIX and Linux systems, implementations of SSH are available for all commonly used computing platforms, including Windows and Macintosh. As previously discussed, SSH is the foundational technology for the Secure File Transfer Protocol (SFTP).

TIP: SSH and Secure Communications   For the exam, you should remember that SSH is a more secure alternative to Telnet.

Secure File Transfer Protocol (SFTP)

One of the big problems associated with FTP is that it is considered insecure. Even though simple authentication methods are associated with FTP, it is still susceptible to relatively simple hacking approaches. In addition, FTP transmits data between sender and receiver in an unencrypted format. By using a packet sniffer, a hacker could easily copy packets from the network and read the contents. In today's high-security computing environments, a more robust solution is needed.

That solution is the Secure File Transfer Protocol, which, based on the Secure Shell (SSH) technology, provides robust authentication between sender and receiver. It also provides encryption capabilities, which means that even if packets are copied from the network, their contents will remain hidden from prying eyes.

SFTP is implemented through client and server software available for all commonly used computing platforms.

> **NOTE: Which SFTP Is It?**   In an industry dominated by acronyms, it should come as no surprise that two protocols have the same acronym. In this case, the SFTP acronym describes both the Secure File Transfer Protocol and the Simple File Transfer Protocol. If you research additional information for the Network+ exam, make sure that you read about the Secure File Transfer Protocol.

Trivial File Transfer Protocol (TFTP)

A variation on FTP is Trivial File Transfer Protocol (TFTP), which is also a file transfer mechanism; however, TFTP does not have either the security capability or the level of functionality that FTP has. TFTP, which is defined in RFC 1350, is most often associated with simple downloads, such as those associated with transferring firmware to a device such as a router and booting diskless workstations.

Another feature that TFTP does not offer is directory navigation. Whereas in FTP, commands can be executed to navigate around and manage the file system, TFTP offers no such capability. TFTP requires that you request not only exactly what you want but also the particular location. Unlike FTP, which uses TCP as its transport protocol to guarantee delivery, TFTP uses UDP.

> **NOTE: TFTP and the OSI Model**   TFTP is an application layer protocol that uses UDP, which is a connectionless transport layer protocol. For this reason, TFTP is referred to as a connectionless file transfer method.

Simple Mail Transfer Protocol (SMTP)

The SMTP protocol defines how mail messages are sent between hosts. SMTP uses TCP connections to guarantee error-free delivery of messages. SMTP is not overly sophisticated and requires the destination host to always be available. For this reason, mail systems spool incoming mail so that users can read it later. How the user then reads the mail depends on how the client accesses the SMTP server.

NOTE: **Sending and Receiving Mail** SMTP can be used for both sending and receiving mail. The Post Office Protocol (POP) and Internet Message Access Protocol (IMAP) can be used only for receiving mail.

Hypertext Transfer Protocol (HTTP)

HTTP is the protocol that enables text, graphics, multimedia, and other material to be downloaded from an HTTP server. HTTP defines what actions can be requested by clients and how servers should answer those requests.

In a practical implementation, HTTP clients (that is, web browsers) make requests in an HTTP format to servers running HTTP server applications (that is, web servers). Files created in a special language such as Hypertext Markup Language (HTML) are returned to the client, and the connection is closed.

TIP: **HTTP and TCP** HTTP is connection-oriented protocol that uses TCP as a transport protocol. You should know this for the exam.

HTTP uses a uniform resource locator (URL) to determine what page should be downloaded from the remote server. The URL contains the type of request (for example, http://), the name of the server contacted (for example, www.microsoft.com), and optionally the page requested (for example, /support). The result is the syntax that Internet-savvy people are familiar with: http://www.microsoft.com/support.

Hypertext Transfer Protocol Secure (HTTPS)

One of the downsides of using HTTP is that HTTP requests are sent in clear text. For some applications, such as e-commerce, this method of exchanging information is not suitable—a more secure method is needed. The solution is HTTPS, which uses a system known as Secure Sockets Layer (SSL), which encrypts the information sent between the client and the host.

For HTTPS to be used, both the client and server must support it. All popular browsers now support HTTPS, as do web server products, such as Microsoft Internet Information Services (IIS), Apache, and almost all other web server applications that provide sensitive applications. When you access an application that uses HTTPS, the URL starts with https rather than http—for example, https://www.amazon.com.

NOTE: **HTTPS** E-commerce sites such as online banking or purchasing should use HTTPS on their site. Look for the HTTPS connections for payment transactions on the e-commerce sites and for sensitive data transfers between corporate information systems.

Post Office Protocol Version 3/Internet Message Access Protocol Version 4 (POP3/IMAP4)

Both POP3, which is defined in RFC 1939, and IMAP4, the latest version of which is defined in RFC 1731, are mechanisms for downloading, or pulling, email from a server. They are necessary because, although the mail is transported around the network via SMTP, users cannot always read it immediately, so it must be stored in a central location. From this location, it needs to be downloaded, which is what POP and IMAP enable you to do.

POP and IMAP are popular, and many people now access email through applications such as Microsoft Outlook and Mozilla, which are POP and IMAP clients.

One of the problems with POP is that the password used to access a mailbox is transmitted across the network in clear text. This means that someone could determine your POP password with relative ease. This is an area in which IMAP offers an advantage over POP. It uses a more sophisticated authentication system, which makes it more difficult for someone to determine a password.

NOTE: POP and IMAP   POP and IMAP can be used to download, or pull, email from a server, but they cannot be used to send mail. That function is left to SMTP, which can both send and receive.

NOTE: Web-Based Mail—The Other, Other Email   Although accessing email by using POP and IMAP has many good points, such systems rely on servers to hold the mail until it is downloaded to the client system. In today's world, a more sophisticated solution to anytime/anywhere email access is needed. For many people, that solution is web-based mail. Having an Internet-based email account enables you to access your mail from anywhere and from any device that supports a web browser. Recognizing the obvious advantages of such a system, all the major email systems have, for some time, included web access gateway products.

Telnet

Telnet, which is defined in RFC 854, is a virtual terminal protocol. It enables sessions to be opened on a remote host and then for commands to be executed on that remote host. For many years, Telnet was the method by which multiuser systems such as mainframes and minicomputers were accessed by clients. It was also the connection method of choice for UNIX systems. Today, Telnet is still commonly used for accessing routers and other managed network devices.

One of the problems with Telnet is that it is not secure. As a result, remote session functionality is now almost always achieved by using alternatives such as SSH.

NOTE: Telnet and UNIX/Linux   Telnet is used to access UNIX and Linux systems.

Internet Control Message Protocol (ICMP)

Internet Control Message Protocol (ICMP), defined in RFC 792, is a protocol that works with the Network layer to provide error checking and reporting functionality. In effect, ICMP is a tool that IP uses in its quest to provide best-effort delivery.

ICMP can be used for a number of functions. Its most common function is probably the widely used and incredibly useful `ping` utility. `ping` sends a stream of ICMP echo requests to a remote host. If the host can respond, it does so by sending echo reply messages back to the sending host. In that one simple process, ICMP enables the verification of the protocol suite configuration of both the sending and receiving nodes and any intermediate networking devices.

However, ICMP's functionality is not limited to the use of the `ping` utility. ICMP also can return error messages such as Destination Unreachable and Time Exceeded messages. (The former message is reported when a destination cannot be contacted and the latter when the Time-To-Live [TTL] of a datagram has been exceeded.)

In addition to these and other functions, ICMP performs *source quench*. In a source quench scenario, the receiving host cannot handle the influx of data at the same rate as the data is sent. To slow down the sending host, the receiving host sends ICMP source quench messages, telling the sender to slow down. This action prevents packets from dropping and having to be re-sent.

ICMP is a useful protocol. Although ICMP operates largely in the background, the `ping` utility alone makes it one of the most valuable of the protocols discussed in this chapter.

Address Resolution Protocol (ARP) and Reverse Address Resolution Protocol (RARP)

Address Resolution Protocol (ARP), defined in RFC 826, is responsible for resolving IP addresses to Media Access Control (MAC) addresses. When a system attempts to contact another host, IP first determines whether the other host is on the same network it is on by looking at the IP address. If IP determines that the destination is on the local network, it consults the ARP cache to see whether it has a corresponding entry.

If no entry exists for the host in the ARP cache, a broadcast on the local network asks the host with the target IP address to send back its MAC address. The communication is sent as a broadcast because without the target system's MAC address, the source system cannot communicate directly with the target system.

Because the communication is a broadcast, every system on the network picks it up. However, only the target system replies because it is the only device whose IP address matches the request. The target system, recognizing that it is the target of the ARP request, replies directly to the source system. It can do this because the ARP request contains the MAC address of the system that sent it. If the destination host is determined to be on a different subnet than the sending host, the ARP process is performed against the default gateway and then repeated for each step of the journey between the sending and receiving hosts.

The Reverse Address Resolution Protocol (RARP) performs the same function as ARP, but in reverse. In other words, it resolves MAC addresses to IP addresses. RARP makes it possible for applications or systems to learn their own IP address from a router or DNS server. Such a resolution is useful for tasks such as performing reverse lookups in DNS. RARP is defined in RFC 903.

NOTE: ARP Functions   The function of ARP is to resolve the IP address of a system to the MAC address of the interface on that system.

Network Time Protocol (NTP)

Network Time Protocol (NTP), defined in RFC 1305, is the part of the TCP/IP protocol suite that facilitates the communication of time between systems. The idea is that one system configured as a time provider transmits time information to other systems that can be both the time receivers and the time providers to other systems.

Time synchronization is important in today's IT environment because of the distributed nature of applications. Two good examples of situations in which time synchronization is important are email and directory services systems. In each of these cases, having time synchronized between devices is important because without it there would be no way of keeping track of changes to data and applications.

In many environments, external time sources such as radio clocks, global positioning system (GPS) devices, and Internet-based time servers are used as sources for NTP time. In others, the real time clock of the system is used. Regardless of what source is used, the time information is communicated between devices by using NTP.

NOTE: NTP Rules   Specific guidelines dictate how NTP should be used. You can find these "rules of engagement" at http://support.ntp.org/bin/view/Servers/RulesOfEngagement.

NTP server and client software is available for a variety of platforms and devices. If you are looking for a way to ensure time synchronization between devices, look to NTP as a solution.

Network News Transfer Protocol (NNTP)

The Transfer Protocol (NNTP) is a protocol associated with the posting and retrieval of messages from newsgroups. A *newsgroup* is the name given to a discussion forum hosted on a remote system. By using NNTP client software, like that included with many common email clients, users can post, reply, and retrieve messages.

Although web-based discussion forums are replacing newsgroups, demand for newsgroup access remains high. The distinction between web-based discussion forums and NNTP newsgroups is that in newsgroups, messages are retrieved from the server to be read. In contrast, on a web-based discussion forum the messages are not downloaded. They are simply viewed from a remote location.

NNTP, defined in RFC 3977, is an application layer protocol that uses TCP as its transport mechanism.

Secure Copy Protocol (SCP)

The Secure Copy Protocol (SCP) is another protocol based on SSH technology. SCP provides a secure means to copy files between systems on a network. SSH technology encrypts data as it travels across the network, thereby securing it from eavesdropping. It is intended as a more secure substitute for the Remote Copy Protocol (RCP). SCP is available as a command-line utility or as part of application software for most commonly used computing platforms.

Lightweight Directory Access Protocol (LDAP)

The Lightweight Directory Access Protocol is a protocol that provides a mechanism to access and query directory services systems. In the context of the Network+ exam, these directory services systems are most likely to be Novell Directory Services (NDS), Microsoft Active Directory, and Apple Open Directory. Although LDAP supports command-line queries executed directly against the directory database, most LDAP interactions will be via utilities such as an authentication program (network logon) or locating a resource in the directory through a search utility.

Internet Group Management Protocol (IGMP)

Internet Group Management Protocol (IGMP) is the protocol within the TCP/IP protocol suite that manages multicast groups. It enables, for example, one computer on the Internet to target content to a specific group of computers that will receive content from the sending system. This is in contrast to unicast messaging in which data is sent to a single computer or network device and not a group or a broadcast message that goes to all systems.

Multicasting is a mechanism by which groups of network devices can send and receive data between the members of the group at one time, instead of sending messages to each device in the group separately. The multicast grouping is established by each device being configured with the same multicast IP address. These multicast IP addresses are from the IPv4 Class D range including 224.0.0.0 to 239.255.255.255 address ranges. IGMP registers devices into a multicast group and discovers what other devices on the network are members of the same multi-cast group. Common applications for multicasting include groups of routers on an internetwork and videoconferencing clients. For more information on unicast and multicast addressing for both IPv4 and IPv6, refer to Chapter 5.

Domain Name System (DNS)

DNS performs an important function on TCP/IP-based networks. It resolves hostnames, such as www.examcram.com, to IP addresses, such as 209.202.161.67. Such a resolution system makes it possible for people to remember the names of, and refer to frequently used hosts, using the easy-to-remember hostnames rather than the hard-to-remember IP addresses.

> **NOTE: Platform-Independent**   Like other TCP/IP-based services, DNS is a platform-independent protocol. Therefore, it can be used on Linux, UNIX, Windows, NetWare, and almost every other platform.

In the days before the Internet, the network that was to become the Internet used a text file called HOSTS to perform name resolutions. The file was regularly updated with changes and distributed to other servers. The following is a sample of some entries from a HOSTS file:

```
192.168.3.45     server1  s1              #The main
                                           file and
                                           print server
192.168.3.223    mail     mailserver #The email server
```

As you can see, the IP address of the host is listed, along with the corresponding hostname. It is possible to add to a HOSTS file aliases of the server names, which in this example are s1 and mailserver. All the entries have to be added manually, and each system to perform resolutions must have a copy of the file.

> **TIP: The HOSTS File**   On the Network+ exam, you might be asked to identify the purpose and function of a HOSTS file.

> **NOTE: Comments in a HOSTS File**   A comment in a HOSTS file is preceded by a number (pound) sign (#).

Even when the Internet was growing at a relatively slow pace, using the HOSTS file was both cumbersome and prone to error. It was obvious that as the network grew, a more automated and dynamic method of performing name resolution was needed. DNS became that method.

NOTE: Resolution via the HOSTS File   HOSTS file resolution is still supported by practically every platform. If you need to resolve only a few hosts that will not change often or at all, you can still use the HOSTS file for this.

DNS solves the problem of name resolution by offering resolution through servers configured to act as name servers. The name servers run DNS server software, which enables them to receive, process, and reply to requests from systems that want to resolve hostnames to IP addresses. Systems that query DNS servers for a hostname-to-IP address mapping are referred to as *resolvers*. Figure 4.1 shows an example of the DNS resolution process.

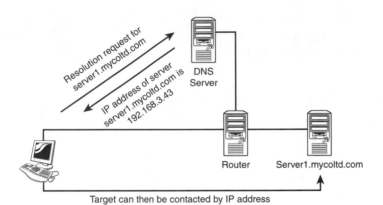

Figure 4.1   The DNS resolution process.

Because the DNS namespace, discussed in the following section, is large, a single server cannot hold all the records for the entire namespace. As a result, there is a good chance that a given DNS server might not resolve the request for a certain entry. In this case, the DNS server asks another DNS server whether it has an entry for the host.

NOTE: DDNS   One of the problems with DNS is that despite all its automatic resolution capabilities, entries and changes to those entries must still be performed manually. A strategy to solve this problem is to use Dynamic DNS (DDNS), a newer system that enables hosts to be automatically registered with the DNS server.

The DNS Namespace

DNS operates in what is referred to as the *DNS namespace*. This space has logical divisions organized in a hierarchical structure. At the top level are domains such as

.com (commercial) and .edu (educational), and domains for countries, such as .uk (United Kingdom) and .de (Germany). Below the top level are subdomains associated with organizations or commercial companies, such as Red Hat and Microsoft. Within these domains, hosts or other subdomains can be assigned. For example, the server ftp.redhat.com would be in the redhat.com domain. Or another domain called, for instance, development, could be created, and hosts could be placed in that (that is, ftp.development.redhat.com). Figure 4.2 shows a graphical representation of a DNS hierarchical namespace.

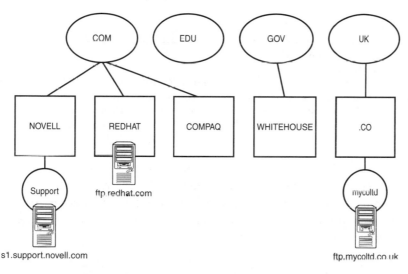

Figure 4.2   An example of a DNS hierarchical namespace.

NOTE: FQDNs   The domain name, along with any subdomains, is referred to as the fully qualified domain name (FQDN) because it includes all the components from the top of the DNS namespace to the host. For this reason, many people refer to DNS as resolving FQDNs to IP addresses.

The lower domains are largely open to use in whatever way the domain name holder sees fit. However, the top-level domains are not as flexible. Table 4.2 lists a selection of the most widely used top-level DNS domain names. Recently, a number of top-level domains were added, mainly to accommodate the increasing need for hostnames.

Table 4.2   Selected Top-Level Domains in the DNS Namespace

Top-Level Domain Name	Intended Purpose
com	Commercial organizations

Table 4.2   Selected Top-Level Domains in the DNS Namespace

Top-Level Domain Name	Intended Purpose
edu	Educational organizations/establishments
gov	U.S. government organizations/establishments
net	Network providers/centers
org	Not-for-profit/other organizations
mil	Military
arpa	Reverse lookup
de	A country-specific domain, in this case Germany*

*In addition to country-specific domains, many countries have created subdomains that follow roughly the same principles as the original top-level domains (for example, .co.uk, .gov.nz).

It should be noted that although the assignment of domain names is supposed to conform to the structure in Table 4.2, the assignment of names is not as closely controlled as you might think. It's not uncommon for some domain names to be used for other purposes. In particular, the .net and .org namespaces have been used for purposes other than what was intended.

NOTE: Reverse Lookup   Although the primary function of DNS is to resolve hostnames to IP addresses, it is also possible to have DNS perform an IP address-to-hostname resolution. This process is called *reverse lookup*.

Types of DNS Entries

Although the most common entry in a DNS database is an A (address) record, which maps a hostname to an IP address, DNS can hold numerous other types of entries, as well. Some of particular note are the MX (mail exchanger) record, which is used to map entries that correspond to mail exchanger systems; and CNAME, or canonical record name, which can be used to create alias records for a system. A system can have an A record and then multiple CNAME entries for its aliases. A DNS table with all these types of entries might look like this:

```
fileserve.mycoltd.com   IN   A    192.168.33.2
email.mycoltd.com       IN   A    192.168.33.7
fileprint.mycoltd.com   IN CNAME fileserver.mycoltd.com
mailer.mycoltd.com      IN  MX  10    email.mycoltd.com
```

As you can see, rather than map to an actual IP address, the CNAME and MX record entries map to another host, which DNS in turn can resolve to an IP address.

DNS in a Practical Implementation

In a real-world scenario, whether you use DNS is almost a nonissue. If you have Internet access, you will most certainly use DNS, but you are likely to use the DNS facilities of your ISP rather than have your own internal DNS server. However, if you operate a large, complex, multiplatform network, you might find that internal DNS servers are necessary. The major network operating system vendors are aware that you might need DNS facilities in your organization, so they include DNS server applications with their offerings.

It is common practice for workstations to be configured with the IP addresses of two DNS servers for fault tolerance. Figure 4.3 shows an example.

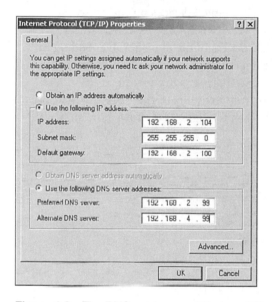

Figure 4.3   The DNS entries on a Windows XP system.

The importance of DNS, particularly in environments in which the Internet is heavily used, cannot be overstated. If DNS facilities are not accessible, the Internet effectively becomes unusable, unless you can remember the IP addresses of all your favorite sites.

Simple Network Management Protocol (SNMP)

Simple Network Management Protocol (SNMP) enables network devices to communicate information about their state to a central system. It also enables the central system to pass configuration parameters to the devices. There are three versions of SNMP:

- **SNMPv1**—Operates over UDP SNMPv1 and is widely used; the main network-management protocol used.

■ **SNMPv2**—Operates much the same as SNMPv1 but adds improvements in the areas of security, performance, and confidentiality.

■ **SNMPv3**—The latest version of SNMP adds additional security features and remote configuration abilities.

NOTE: SNMP is Not an NMS   SNMP is a protocol that facilitates network management functionality. It is not, in itself, a network management system (NMS).

Components of SNMP

In an SNMP configuration, a central system known as a *manager* acts as the central communication point for all the SNMP-enabled devices on the network. On each device to be managed and monitored via SNMP, software called an *SNMP agent* is set up and configured with the IP address of the manager. Depending on the configuration, the SNMP manager then communicates with and retrieves information from the devices running the SNMP agent software. In addition, the agent can communicate the occurrence of certain events to the SNMP manager as they happen. These messages are known as *traps*. Figure 4.4 shows how an SNMP system works.

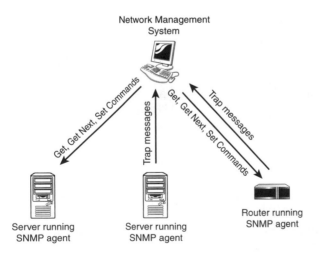

Figure 4.4   How SNMP works.

SNMP Management Systems

An SNMP management system is a computer running a special piece of software called a network management system (NMS). These software applications can be free, or they can cost thousands of dollars. The difference between the free applications and those that cost a great deal of money normally boils down to functionality and support. All NMS systems, regardless of cost, offer the same basic functionality. Today, most NMS applications use graphical maps of the network to locate a device and then query it. The queries are built in to the application and are triggered by a point and click. You can issue SNMP requests from a command-line utility, but with so many tools available, it is simply not necessary.

NOTE: Trap Managers   Some people refer to SNMP managers or NMSs as trap managers. This reference is misleading because NMS can do more than just accept trap messages from agents.

Using SNMP and an NMS, it is possible to monitor all the devices on a network, including switches, hubs, routers, servers, and printers, and any device that supports SNMP, from a single location. Using SNMP, you can see the amount of free disk space on a server in Jakarta or reset the interface on a router in Helsinki—all from the comfort of your desk in San Jose. Such power, though, does bring with it some considerations. For example, because an NMS gives you the ability to reconfigure network devices, or at least get information from them, it is common practice to implement an NMS on a secure workstation platform, such as a Linux or Windows server, and to place the NMS PC in a secure location.

SNMP Agents

Although the SNMP manager resides on a PC, each device that is part of the SNMP structure also needs to have SNMP functionality enabled. This is performed through a software component called an *agent*.

An SNMP agent can be any device capable of running a small software component that facilitates communication with an SNMP manager. SNMP agent functionality is supported by almost any device designed to be connected to a network.

In addition to providing a mechanism for managers to communicate with them, agents can tell SNMP managers when something happens. When a certain condition is met on a device running an SNMP agent, a trap is sent to the NMS, and the NMS then performs an action, depending on the configuration. Basic NMS systems might sound an alarm or flash a message onscreen. Other, more advanced, products can send a pager message, dial a cell phone, or send an email message.

Management Information Bases (MIB)

Although the SNMP trap system might be the most commonly used aspect of SNMP, the manager-to-agent communication is not just a one-way street. In addition to reading information from a device using the SNMP commands Get and Get Next, SNMP managers can also issue the Set command. Having just three commands might make SNMP seem like a limited mechanism, but this is not the case. The secret of SNMP's power is in how it uses those three commands.

To demonstrate how SNMP commands work, imagine that you and a friend each have a list on which the following four words are written: four, book, sky, and table. If you, as the manager, ask your friend for the first value, she, acting as the agent, will reply "four." This is analogous to an SNMP Get command. Now, if you ask for the next value, she would reply "book." This is analogous to an SNMP Get Next command. If you then say "set green," and your friend changes the word *book* to *green*, you will have performed the equivalent of an SNMP Set command. Sound simplistic? Well, if you can imagine expanding the list to include 100 values, you can see how you could navigate and set any parameter in the list, using just those three commands. The key, though, is to make sure that you and your friend have exactly the same list, which is where Management Information Bases (MIBs) come in.

SNMP uses databases of information called MIBs to define what parameters are accessible, which of the parameters are read-only, and which are capable of being set. MIBs are available for thousands of devices and services, covering every imaginable need.

TIP: Finding a MIB   If you want to find a MIB for a device on your network, MIB Central (www.mibdepot.com) provides a searchable database of nearly 2,400 MIBs for a wide range of equipment.

To ensure that SNMP systems offer cross-platform compatibility, MIB creation is controlled by the International Organization for Standardization (ISO). An organization that wants to create a MIB can apply to the ISO. The ISO then assigns the organization an ID under which it can create MIBs as it sees fit. The assignment of numbers is structured within a conceptual model called the *hierarchical name tree*.

SNMP Communities

Another feature of SNMP that enables for manageability is communities. *SNMP communities* are logical groupings of systems. When a system is configured as part of a community, it communicates only with other devices that have the same community name. In addition, it accepts Get, Get Next, or Set commands only from an SNMP manager with a community name it recognizes. Typically, two communities are defined by default: a public community intended for read-only use and a private community intended for read-and-write operations.

Whether you use SNMP depends on how many devices you have and how distributed your network infrastructure is. Even in environments that have only a few devices, SNMP can be useful because it can act as your eyes and ears, notifying you if a problem on the network occurs.

Dynamic Host Configuration Protocol (DHCP)

Dynamic Host Configuration Protocol (DHCP), defined in RFC 2131, enables ranges of IP addresses, known as *scopes*, to be defined on a system running a DHCP server application. When another system configured as a DHCP client is initialized, it asks the server for an address. The server then assigns an address from the DHCP scope to the client for a predetermined amount of time, known as the *lease*. Figure 4.5 shows a representation of DHCP.

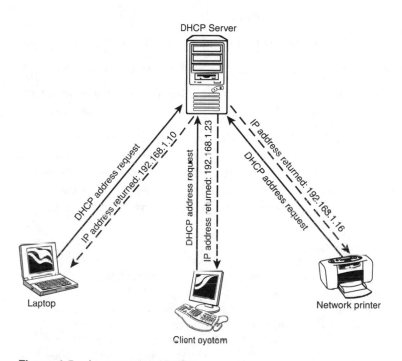

Figure 4.5 An example of DHCP.

At various points during the lease, the client attempts to renew the lease from the server. If the server cannot perform a renewal, the lease expires at 100%, and the client stops using the address.

In addition to an IP address and the subnet mask, the DHCP server can supply many other pieces of information, although exactly what can be provided depends on the DHCP server implementation. In addition to the address information, the default gateway is often supplied, along with DNS information.

In addition to having DHCP supply a random address from the scope, it's also possible to configure it to supply a specific address to a client. Such an arrangement is known as a *reservation*. Reservations are a means by which you can still use DHCP for a system but at the same time guarantee that it will always have the same IP address. Some devices on a network require the same IP address, and other network systems rely on that IP address for communication. For example, if a system maps to a network printer using the printers IP address, it must be the same or the client cannot connect.

The advantages of using DHCP are numerous:

■   Administrators do not have to manually configure each system.

■   Human error such as the assignment of duplicate IP addresses is eliminated.

■   Reconfiguring systems is unnecessary if they move from one subnet to another or if you decide to make a wholesale change of the IP addressing structure.

The downsides are that DHCP traffic is broadcast-based and thus generates network traffic, albeit a small amount. Also, the DHCP server software must be installed and configured on a server, which can place additional processor load (again, minimal) on that system. From an administrative perspective, after the initial configuration, DHCP is about as maintenance free as a service can get, with only occasional monitoring normally required.

NOTE: Platform Independence   DHCP is a protocol-dependent service, but it is not platform-dependent. This means that you can use, for instance, a Linux DHCP server for a network with Windows clients or a Novell DHCP server with Linux clients. Although the DHCP server offerings in the various network operating systems might differ slightly, the basic functionality is the same across the board. Likewise, the client configuration for DHCP servers running on a different operating system platform is the same as for DHCP servers running on the same base operating system platform.

To better understand how DHCP works, it is worth spending a few minutes looking at the processes that occur when a DHCP-enabled client connects to the network. When a system configured to use DHCP comes onto the network, it broadcasts a special packet that looks for a DHCP server. This packet is known as the DHCPDISCOVER packet. The DHCP server, which is always on the lookout for DHCPDISCOVER broadcasts, picks up the packet and compares the request with the scopes that it has defined. If it finds that it has a scope for the network from which the packet originated, it chooses an address from the scope, reserves it, and sends the address, along with any other information, such as the lease duration, to the client. This is known as the DHCPOFFER packet. Because the client still does not have an IP address, this communication is also achieved via broadcast.

When the client receives the offer, it looks at the offer to determine whether it is suitable. If more than one offer is received, which can happen if more than one DHCP server is configured, the offers are compared to see which is best. *Best* in this context can involve a variety of criteria but is normally the length of the lease. When the selection process is complete, the client notifies the server that the offer has been accepted, through a packet called a DHCPREQUEST packet, at which point the server finalizes the offer and sends the client an acknowledgment. This last message, which is sent as a broadcast, is known as a DHCPACK packet. When the client system has received the DHCPACK, it initializes the TCP/IP suite and can communicate on the network. Figure 4.6 shows a representation of the DHCP process between a server and a client.

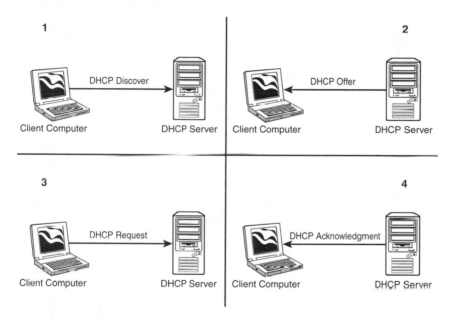

Figure 4.6   The DHCP process.

NOTE: What if the DHCP Server Is on a Different Subnet from the Client?
A common question about DHCP is, "What happens if the DHCP server is on a different subnet from the client?" Normally, a router is configured not to forward a broadcast, but if the router is configured appropriately, it recognizes that the broadcast packet is a DHCP discovery packet, and it therefore forwards the packet. When it does, however, it embeds in the packet information about which network the packet originated from. This enables the DHCP server to match the source network address with one of its ranges. This strategy enables a single DHCP server to serve the entire internetwork. If the router doesn't accommodate DHCP forwarding, a special service called a DHCP relay agent can be configured on a server. The DHCP relay agent forwards DHCP packets directly to the DHCP server instead of using broadcasts, enabling packets to traverse the routers.

NOTE: Another lesser used automatic addressing protocol is BOOTP. Originally created so that diskless workstations could obtain information—such as the TCP/IP address, subnet mask, and default gateway—needed to connect to the network. Such a system was necessary because diskless workstations had no way of storing the information. More information on bootp is covered in Chapter 5.

Transport Layer Security

The Transport Layer Security (TLS) protocol is a security protocol designed to ensure privacy between communicating client/server applications. When a server and client communicate, TLS ensures that no one can eavesdrop and intercept or otherwise tamper with the data message. TLS is the successor to SSL.

TLS is composed of two layers: The first is the TLS Record Protocol, which uses a reliable transport protocol such as TCP and ensures that the connection made between systems is private using data encryption. The TLS Handshake Protocol is used for authentication between the client and the server. Chapter 13, "Network Management Tools and Documentation Procedures" covers authentication, encryption, and more on security protocols.

Session Initiation Protocol

We all know that long distance calls are expensive, in part because it is costly to maintain phone lines and employ technicians to keep those phones ringing. Voice over IP (VoIP) is a cheaper alternative for our phone service. VoIP technology enables voice conversations to occur by traveling through IP packets and via the Internet. VoIP avoids the high cost of regular phone calls by using the existing infrastructure of the Internet; no monthly bills or expensive long distance charges are required. But how does it work?

Like every other type of network communication, VoIP requires protocols to make the magic happen. In the case of VoIP, one such protocol is the Session Initiation Protocol (SIP), which is an application layer protocol designed to establish and maintain multimedia sessions such as Internet telephony calls. This means that SIP can create communication sessions for such features as audio/videoconferencing, online gaming, and person-to-person conversations over the Internet. SIP does not operate alone; it uses TCP or UDP as transport protocols. Remember, TCP enables guaranteed delivery of data packets, whereas UDP is a fire-and-forget transfer protocol.

NOTE: SIP Security Services   SIP also includes a suite of security services, which includes denial-of-service prevention, authentication (both user to user and proxy to user), integrity protection, and encryption and privacy services.

Real-time Transport Protocol (RTP)

Through the Internet or over our networks, we can use a variety of multimedia services such as video conferencing, VoIP, and streaming audio. The demand for these types of real-time applications is increasing, creating the need for protocols to support them. Currently, TCP and UDP are widely used Internet transport protocols; however, both were not designed with real-time applications in mind. The Real-Time Transport Protocol (RTP) was designed specifically for the transport of real-time applications. Although RTP might be known as a transport protocol, it still requires other protocols for transport, often UDP. Using UDP, RTP does not guarantee delivery of multimedia data. UDP is most often used because applications using RTP are less sensitive to packet loss, but typically sensitive to delays.

> **TIP: RTP**   For the Network+ exam, remember that RTP is the Internet-standard protocol for the transport of real-time data, including audio and video. RTP does not guarantee delivery of data.

RTP is responsible to carry the data that has real-time properties. It combines this transport responsibility with the Real-time Transport Protocol Control Protocol (RTCP). The function of the RTCP is to monitor the data delivery, looking for dropped data packets, and to help ensure quality of service (QoS).

TCP/IP Protocol Suite Summary

Table 4.3 summarizes the details of each of the protocols discussed in the preceding sections. You can use this table for review before you take the Network+ exam.

Table 4.3 TCP/IP Protocol Suite Summary

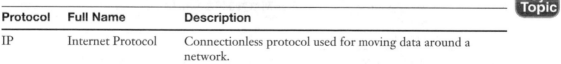

Protocol	Full Name	Description
IP	Internet Protocol	Connectionless protocol used for moving data around a network.
TCP	Transmission Control Protocol	Connection-oriented protocol that offers flow control, sequencing, and retransmission of dropped packets.
UDP	User Datagram Protocol	Connectionless alternative to TCP used for applications that do not require the functions offered by TCP.
FTP	File Transfer	Protocol Protocol for uploading and downloading files to and from a remote host; also accommodates basic file management tasks.
SFTP	Secure File Transfer Protocol	Protocol for securely uploading and downloading files to and from a remote host. Based on SSH security.

Table 4.3   TCP/IP Protocol Suite Summary

Protocol	Full Name	Description
TFTP	Trivial File Transfer Protocol	File transfer protocol that does not have the security or error checking of FTP. TFTP uses UDP as a transport protocol and is therefore connectionless.
SMTP	Simple Mail Transfer Protocol	Mechanism for transporting email across networks.
HTTP	Hypertext Transfer Protocol	Protocol for retrieving files from a web server.
HTTPS	Hypertext Transfer Protocol Secure	Secure protocol for retrieving files from a web server.
POP3/IMAP	Post Office Protocol Internet Message Access Protocol version 3/version 4	Used for retrieving email from a server on which the email is stored. Can be used only to retrieve mail. IMAP and POP cannot be used to send mail.
Telnet	Telnet	Enables sessions to be opened on a remote host.
SSH	Secure Shell	Enables secure sessions to be opened on a remote host.
ICMP	Internet Control Message Protocol	Used on IP-based networks for error reporting, flow control, and route testing.
ARP	Address Resolution Protocol	Resolves IP addresses to MAC addresses to enable communication between devices.
RARP	Reverse Address Resolution Protocol	Resolves MAC addresses to IP addresses.
NTP	Network Time Protocol	Used to communicate time synchronization information between devices.
NNTP	Network News Transport Protocol	Facilitates the access and downloading of messages from newsgroup servers.
SCP	Secure Copy Protocol	Enables files to be copied securely between two systems. Uses SSH technology to provide encryption services.
LDAP	Lightweight Directory Access Protocol	Protocol used to access and query directory services systems such as Novell Directory Services and Microsoft Active Directory.

Table 4.3 TCP/IP Protocol Suite Summary

Protocol	Full Name	Description
IGMP	Internet Group Management Protocol	Provides a mechanism for systems within the same multicast group to register and communicate with each other.
DNS	Domain Name System	Resolves hostnames to IP addresses.
DHCP	Dynamic Host Configuration Protocol	Automatically assigns TCP/IP information.
SNMP	Simple Network Management Protocol	SNMP monitors and controls network devices; manages configurations, statistics collection, performance, and security; and reports network management information to a management console.
TLS	Transport Layer Security	A security protocol designed to ensure privacy between communicating client/server applications.
SIP	Session Initiation Protocol	SIP is an application layer protocol designed to establish and maintain multimedia sessions such as Internet telephony calls.
RTP	Real-time	Transport Protocol The Internet-standard protocol used for the transportation of real-time data.

Identifying Common TCP/IP Port Numbers

The TCP/IP protocol suite offers so many services and applications that a mechanism is needed to identify to which protocol the incoming communications should be sent. That mechanism is a TCP/IP port.

Each TCP/IP protocol or application has a port associated with it. When a communication is received, the target port number is checked to see what protocol or service it is destined for. The request is then forwarded to that protocol or service. Take, for example, HTTP, whose assigned port number is 80. When a web browser forms a request for a web page, the request is sent to port 80 on the target system. When the target system receives the request, it examines the port number, and when it sees that the port is 80, it forwards the request to the web server application.

You can understand ports by thinking about the phone system of a large company. You can dial a central number (analogous to the IP address) to reach the switchboard, or you can append an extension number to get to a specific department directly (analogous to the port number). Another analogy is an apartment block. An apartment block has a single street address, but each apartment in the building has its own apartment number.

TCP/IP has 65,535 ports available, but they are broken down into three designations:

- **Well-known ports**—The port numbers range from 0 to 1023.

- **Registered ports**—The port numbers range from 1024 to 49151. Registered ports are used by applications or services that need to have consistent port assignments.

- **Dynamic or private ports**—The port numbers range from 49152 to 65535. These ports are not assigned to any protocol or service in particular and can be used for any service or application.

It is common for protocols to establish communication on one of the well-known ports and then move to a port in the dynamic range for the rest of the conversation. It's a bit like using a CB radio, in that you try to get a "breaker" on Channel 19, but then you go to another channel to have a conversation, leaving 19 open for others.

NOTE: IANA   You can obtain a list of port numbers from Internet Assigned Numbers Authority (IANA) at www.iana.org/assignments/port-numbers.

Understanding some of the most common TCP/IP port assignments is important because administrators are often required to specify port assignments when working with applications and configuring security for a network. Table 4.4 shows some of the most well-known port assignments. For the Network+ exam, concentrate on the information provided in Table 4.4, and you should be able to answer any port-related questions you might receive.

Table 4.4   Some of the Most Common TCP/IP Suite Protocols and Their Port Assignments

Protocol	Port Assignment	TCP/UDP Service
FTP	20	TCP
FTP	21	TCP
SSH	22	TCP
Telnet	23	TCP
SMTP	25	TCP
DNS	53	UDP/TCP
TFTP	69	UDP
HTTP	80	TCP/UDP

POP3	110	TCP
NNTP	119	TCP
NTP	123	TCP
IMAP4	143	TCP
SNMP	161	UDP
HTTPS	443	TCP
BOOTPS/DHCP	67	UDP

TIP: Port Numbers   Expect to know what port numbers are used for each protocol for the Network+ exam.

You might have noticed in Table 4.4 that FTP has two ports associated with it. Port 20 is considered the Data port, whereas Port 21 is considered the Control port. In practical use, FTP connections use Port 21. Port 20 is rarely used in modern implementations.

Although these are the standard ports for each of these protocols, in some cases it's possible to assign other port numbers to services. For example, you might choose to have one web server application listen to the default port 80 while another listens to a different port. The result would be that if a user accesses the server but specifies a different port number, the user would be directed to the other web server application running on the server.

Summary

This chapter introduces the TCP/IP protocol used in all modern network environments. A protocol is a set of rules that governs how communication and the exchange of data takes place between devices on a network.

The TCP/IP protocol suite is composed of several individual protocols. Each individual protocol provides a different function for the protocol suite. Some protocols, such as RTP, UDP, and TCP, are transport protocols; others, such as POP3, IMAP, and SMTP, are used for email. Knowing each protocol and its function is an important part of network administration.

Each protocol within the TCP/IP protocol suite requires a port through which to access and leave a system. These ports can be blocked to prevent a certain protocol from functioning on that system.

Exam Preparation Tasks

Review All the Key Topics

Review the most important topics in the chapter, noted with the key topics icon in the outer margin of the page. Table 4.5 lists a reference of these key topics and the page numbers on which each is found.

Table 4.5 Key Topics for Chapter 4

Key Topic Element	Description	Page Number
Table 4.1	Commonly used FTP commands	152
Table 4.2	Selected top level DNS domains	161
Table 4.3	Protocol Suite summary	171
List	TCP/IP ports	174
Table 4.4	TCP/IP Protocol port assignments	174

Complete the Tables and Lists from Memory

Print a copy of Appendix B, "Memory Tables" (found on the CD), or at least the section for this chapter, and complete the tables and lists from memory. Appendix C, "Memory Tables Answer Key," also on the CD, includes completed tables and lists to check your work.

Define Key Terms

Define the following key terms from this chapter, and check your answers in the Glossary.

- TCP
- FTP
- UDP
- TCP/IP suite
- DHCP
- TFTP
- DNS
- HTTP(S)

- ARP
- SIP (VoIP)
- RTP (VoIP)
- SSH
- POP3
- NTP
- IMAP4
- Telnet
- SMTP
- SNMP2/3
- ICMP
- IGMP
- TLS

Apply Your Knowledge

Exercise 4.1 Testing Ports on Your Computer

As mentioned previously, protocols enter and leave a computer system using ports. If these ports are not properly configured, intruders can enter through them. In this exercise you test the security of your computer's ports.

Estimated time: 10 minutes

1. Open your web browser and go to http://www.grc.com. Click the ShieldsUP! logo on the screen.
2. Scroll down the page until you find the link ShieldsUP! It is red and on the left side of the screen.
3. Select the Proceed button to continue.
4. On this screen you can choose what you would like to have scanned. Choose the All Service Ports option, as shown in Figure 4.7.
5. Your system will be scanned, and any potential security breaches will be noted.

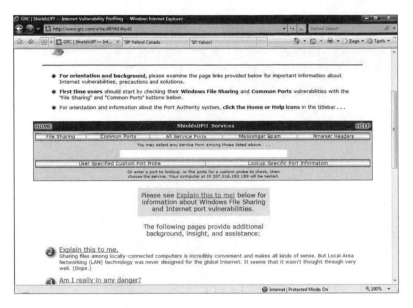

Figure 4.7   Scanning options.

Exercise 4.2 Troubleshooting Scenario

You are an engineer for a systems implementation company. A new client calls to ask whether you can provide some guidance on how to configure a new firewall it wants to implement. The client has a relatively small network with only 16 client systems and two file servers. The client provides the following summary of the services that it wants to allow through the firewall:

■   Users should send and receive email from Microsoft Outlook. An ISP hosts the users' mailboxes.

■   Users should browse both nonsecure and secure web pages. The company uses the ISP's DNS servers.

■   Users should access remote servers to download files via FTP.

■   A timing device in one of the servers maintains time for the entire network, but that server needs access to a time source hosted on the Internet.

■   Users should access Internet-based newsgroups.

Based on the information provided, what protocols would you inform the client to allow through the firewall, and what port numbers are associated with those protocols?

Exercise 4.2 Solution

Based on the information provided, you would likely recommend configuring the firewall to allow SMTP (port 25) traffic for sending email and POP3 (110) for receiving email. Nonsecure browsing would require HTTP (80), and secure browsing would require HTTPS (443). Name resolutions would be performed via DNS (53). FTP access would require ports 20 and 21 to be opened. Time information is transmitted using the NTP protocol (123). Newsgroup access is facilitated through the NNTP protocol on port 119.

Review Questions

1. What is the function of HTTP?
   a. It enables files to be retrieved from web servers.
   b. It provides a mechanism for time synchronization information to be communicated between hosts.
   c. It enables virtual terminal sessions to be opened on a remote host.
   d. It resolves NetBIOS names to IP addresses.

2. On a DHCP server, what term is given to the period of time for which a system is assigned an address?
   a. Own time
   b. Reservation
   c. Lease
   d. Assignment time

3. Which of the following are considered transport protocols? (Choose the two best answers.)
   a. TCP
   h. IP
   c. UDP
   d. NCP

4. When using FTP, which command would you use to upload multiple files at once?
   a. mget
   b. put
   c. mput
   d. get

5. During a discussion, your ISP's technical support representative mentions that you might have been using the wrong FQDN. Which TCP/IP-based network service is the representative referring to?

   a. DHCP

   b. RTP

   c. SNMP

   d. DNS

6. What is the function of ARP?

   a. It resolves MAC addresses to IP addresses.

   b. It secures RARP transfers.

   c. It resolves IP addresses to MAC addresses.

   d. It resolves hostnames to IP addresses.

7. What is the function of NTP?

   a. It provides a mechanism for the sharing of authentication information.

   b. It accesses shared folders on a Linux system.

   c. It communicates utilization information to a central manager.

   d. It communicates time synchronization information between systems.

8. Which port is assigned to the POP3 protocol?

   a. 21

   b. 123

   c. 443

   d. 110

9. When you configure a new server application, the manual tells you to allow access through port 443. What kind of application are you configuring?

   a. Virtual terminal application

   b. Web-based email application

   c. FTP server

   d. Secure website

10. What is the purpose of a reverse lookup in DNS?

    a. It resolves IP addresses to hostnames.

    b. It identifies potential DNS intrusions.

    c. It resolves hostnames to IP addresses.

    d. It enables you to see who owns a particular domain name.

11. In SNMP, what message is sent by a system if a threshold is triggered?

    a. Alert

    b. Trap

    c. Catch

    d. Signal

12. Which of the following port ranges is described as "well known"?

    a. 0 to 1023

    b. 1024 to 49151

    c. 49152 to 65535

    d. 65535 to 78446

13. Which of the following is considered an application protocol?

    a. TCP

    b. IP

    c. UDP

    d. FTP

14. Which of the following protocols is the Internet-standard protocol for the transport of real-time data?

    a. RCP

    b. RIP

    c. RTP

    d. SCP

15. Which of the following protocols is associated with network management?

    a. SNMP

    b. TCP

    c. IP

    d. UDP and TCP

16. You are troubleshooting a network and find that you can ping the IP address of a remote system but not its hostname. Which of the following protocols might not be functioning correctly?

    a. SNMP

    b. SCP

    c. DNS

    d. RTP

17. Which of the following top-level domain names is reserved for educational websites?

    a. .lib

    b. .educate

    c. .edu

    d. .univ

18. While tightening security on a computer system, you close port 23. Which of the following services would be affected?

   a. FTP

   b. SMTP

   c. Telnet

   d. SSH

19. TCP is an example of what kind of transport protocol?

   a. Connection-oriented

   b. Connection-reliant

   c. Connection-dependent

   d. Connectionless

20. Because of security concerns, you have been asked to block ports 143 and 25. Which of the following services are blocked?

   a. TFTP

   b. IMAP4

   c. SMTP

   d. DNS

This chapter covers CompTIA Network+ objectives 1.3, 1.4, 1.5, and 1.6. This chapter covers the following subjects:

- What are valid MAC addresses and how are they used?

- What is an IPv4 address?

- How are IPv4 addresses subnetted?

- What is the difference between public and private addressing schemes?

- How are IPv6 addresses used on a network?

- What are routing protocols and how are they used?

- What are NAT, PAT, and SNAT?

CHAPTER 5

TCP/IP Addressing and Routing

Transmission Control Protocol/Internet Protocol (TCP/IP) is so dominant that it warrants its own chapter. Numerous other chapters in this book also provide coverage of the many aspects of TCP/IP. This chapter deals with TCP/IP addressing for both IPv4 and IPv6, MAC addressing, routing, and routing protocols. These are some of the common technologies network administrators work with daily. Expect the content presented in this chapter to be well represented on the Network+ exam. We start by looking at MAC addressing.

Foundation Topics

Identifying MAC Addresses

You might already know that devices use MAC addresses, but you might not yet understand why MAC addresses exist, how they are assigned, and what they consist of. This section explains those details.

> **NOTE: A MAC Address Is the Physical Address**   A MAC address is sometimes referred to as a *physical address* because it is physically embedded in the interface. Sometimes it is also referred to as a *network address*, which is incorrect. A *network address* is the logical protocol address assigned to the network to which the interface is connected.

A MAC address is a 6-byte (48-bit) hexadecimal address that enables a NIC to be uniquely identified on the network. The MAC address forms the basis of network communication, regardless of the protocol used to achieve network connection. Because the MAC address is so fundamental to network communication, mechanisms are in place to ensure no possibility of duplicate addresses.

To combat the possibility of duplicate MAC addresses being assigned, the Institute of Electrical and Electronics Engineers (IEEE) took over the assignment of MAC addresses. But rather than be burdened with assigning individual addresses, the IEEE instead decided to assign each manufacturer an ID and then let the manufacturer further allocate IDs. The result is that in a MAC address, the first three bytes define the manufacturer, and the manufacturer assigns the last three bytes.

For example, consider the MAC address of the computer on which this book is being written: 00:D0:59:09:07:51. The first three bytes (00:D0:59) identify the manufacturer of the card; because only this manufacturer can use this address, the first three bytes are known as the Organizational Unique Identifier (OUI). The last three bytes (09:07:51) are then referred to as the Universal LAN MAC address. They make this interface unique. You can find a complete listing of organizational MAC address assignments at http://standards.ieee.org/regauth/oui/oui.txt.

> **TIP: MAC Address**   Because MAC addresses are expressed in hexadecimal, only the numbers 0 through 9 and the letters A through F can be used. If you get a Network+ exam question about identifying a MAC address and some of the answers contain letters and numbers other than 0 through 9 and the letters A through F, you can discount those answers immediately.

You can discover the MAC address of the NIC in various ways, depending on what system or platform you work on. Table 5.1 defines various platforms and the method you can use to view the MAC address of an interface.

Table 5.1   Methods of Viewing the MAC Addresses of NICs

Platform	Method
Windows 2003/XP/Vista/7	Run `ipconfig /all` from a command prompt.
Linux/some UNIX	Run the `ifconfig -a` command.
Novell NetWare	Run the `config` command.
Cisco router	Run the `sh int <interface name>` command.

Figure 5.1 shows the `ipconfig /all` command run on a Windows server system. The MAC address is defined on the physical address line of the output.

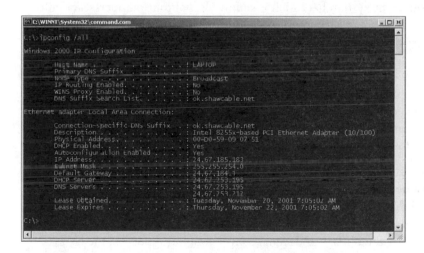

Figure 5.1   The output from the **`ipconfig /all`** command on a Windows server system.

Understanding IPv4 Addressing Fundamentals

Addressing is perhaps the most challenging aspect of TCP/IP. It's certainly a topic that often has many people scratching their heads for a while. This section looks at how IP addressing works for IPv4. In today's IT environment, and certainly in the immediate future, IPv4 will remain the protocol of choice for networking. However, IPv6 is poised and ready to take over in the next few years. For now, though, IPv4 knowledge is critical both for real-world application and the Network+ exam.

General IP Addressing Principles

To communicate on a network using the TCP/IP protocol, each system has to be assigned a unique address. The address defines both the number of the network to which the device is attached and the address of the node on that network. In other words, the IP address provides two pieces of information. It's a bit like a street name and a house number of a person's home address.

> **NOTE: IP Terminology**   Two important phrases in IP addressing are *network address* and *host address*. The IP address defines both, but you must understand that the network address and the node address are different from one another. You need to be aware, also, that some people call the network address the *network ID* and the host address the *host ID*.

Each device on a logical network segment must have the same network address as all the other devices on the segment. All the devices must have different node addresses.

So how does the system know which part of the address is the network part and which is the node part? That is the function of a *subnet mask*. On its own, an IP address is no good to the system because it is simply a set of four numbers. The subnet mask is used in concert with the IP address to determine which portion of the IP address refers to the network address and which refers to the node address.

IPv4 Addressing

An IPv4 address (which this book refers to as an *IP address* from now on) is composed of four sets of 8 bits, or octets. The result is that IP addresses are 32 bits in length. Each bit in each octet is assigned a decimal value. The leftmost bit has a value of 128, followed by 64, 32, 16, 8, 4, 2, and 1, left to right.

Each bit in the octet can be either a 1 or a 0. This numbering system is called *binary*. If the value is 1, it is counted as its equivalent decimal value, and if it is 0, it is ignored. If all the bits are 0, the value of the octet is 0. If all the bits in the octet are 1, the value is 255, which is 128 + 64 + 32 + 16 + 8 + 4 + 2 + 1. Figure 5.2 shows a chart representing the binary-to-decimal conversion. In Figure 5.2, the chart is used to derive the decimal of 195.

128	64	32	16	8	4	2	1
1	1	0	0	0	0	1	1

Figure 5.2   A binary-to-decimal conversion chart showing how 195 is derived.

By using the set of 8 bits and manipulating the 1s and 0s, any value between 0 and 255 can be obtained for each octet. Table 5.2 shows a few examples of this.

Table 5.2 Examples of Numbers Derived Through Binary

Decimal Value	Binary Value	Decimal Calculation
10	00001010	8 + 2 = 10
192	11000000	128 + 64 = 192
205	11001101	128 + 64 + 8 + 4 + 1 = 205
223	11011111	128 + 64 + 16 + 8 + 4 + 2 + 1 =223

The IP address is composed of four sets of these bits, each of which is separated by a period. For this reason, an IP address is expressed in dotted-decimal notation.

IP addresses are grouped into logical divisions called *classes*. In the IPv4 address space are five address classes (A through E), although only three are used for assigning addresses to clients. Class D is reserved for multicast addressing, and Class E is reserved for future development.

Of the three classes available for address assignments, each uses a fixed-length subnet mask to define the separation between the network and the node address. A Class A address uses only the first octet to represent the network portion; a Class B address uses two octets; and a Class C address uses three octets. The upshot of this system is that Class A has a small number of network addresses but a large number of possible host addresses. Class B has a larger number of networks but a smaller number of hosts, and Class C has an even larger number of networks and an even smaller number of hosts. The exact numbers are provided in Table 5.3.

Table 5.3 IPv4 Address Classes and the Number of Available Network/Host Addresses

Address Class	Range	Number of Networks	Number of Hosts per Network	Binary Value of First Octet
A	1–126	126	16,777,214	00000001–01111110
B	128–191	16384	65,534	10xxxxxx
C	192–223	2,097,152	254	110xxxxx
D	224–239	NA	NA	1110xxxx
E	240–255	NA	NA	1111xxxx

Notice in Table 5.3 that the network number 127 is not included in any of the ranges. The 127 network ID is reserved for the local loopback. The local loopback is a function built in to the TCP/IP protocol suite and can be used for troubleshooting purposes.

Each of the classes of an IP address used for address assignment has a standard subnet mask associated with it. Table 5.4 lists the default subnet masks.

Table 5.4 Default Subnet Masks Associated with IP Address Classes

Address Class	Default Subnet Mask
A	255.0.0.0
B	255.255.0.0
C	255.255.255.0

TIP: Address Classes   For the Network+ exam, be prepared to identify into which class a given address falls and the default subnet mask for a given class.

NOTE: Subnet Masks   Like an IP address, a subnet mask is a 32-bit address expressed in dotted-decimal format. Unlike an IP address, though, a subnet mask performs just one function: It defines which parts of the IP address refer to the network address and which refer to the node address. For systems to be on the same network, they must have the same subnet mask. Even a 1-bit difference in the subnet mask means that the systems are on different networks.

IPv4 Address Types

The IPv4 has three primary types of address types: unicast, broadcast, and multicast. It is important to distinguish the three types:

- **Unicast**—With unicast addresses, a single address is specified. Data sent with unicast addressing is delivered to a specific node identified by the address. It is a point-to-point address link.

- **Broadcast**—At the opposite end of the spectrum of unicast addressing is the broadcast address. A broadcast address is an IP address that you can use to target all systems on a subnet or network instead of single hosts. In other words, a broadcast message goes to everyone on the network.

- **Multicast**—Multicasting is a mechanism by which groups of network devices can send and receive data between the members of the group at one time, instead of sending messages to each device in the group separately. This helps optimize the network by making better use of bandwidth. The multicast grouping is established by each device being configured with the same multicast IP address.

TIP: Address Types   Before taking the Network+ exam, be sure you can differentiate between unicast, multicast, and broadcast IPv4 addressing.

Distributing IPv4 Addresses to the Network

Having established the need for each system on a TCP/IP-based network to have a unique address, we can now go on to look at how those systems receive their addresses. There are two basic ways in which a system can receive an address: *static* and *dynamic*. Microsoft Windows systems also provide an additional feature, called *automatic* or *self-addressing*, but in essence this is a variation of dynamic addressing, so we will examine it under that heading.

Static Addressing

Static addressing refers to the manual assignment of IP addresses to a system. In other words, a person has to physically configure the system with the correct IP address. There are problems with this approach, most notably that of human error. Configuring one system with the correct address is simple, but in the course of configuring, for instance, a few hundred systems, mistakes are likely. If the IP addresses are entered incorrectly, the system will most likely not connect to other systems on the network. If a client system were misconfigured with the IP address of a server, it could even prevent anyone from connecting to the server, because both systems might disable their network interfaces as a result of the conflict.

Another drawback of static addressing is reconfiguration. If the IP addressing scheme for the organization changes, each system must again be manually reconfigured. In a large organization with hundreds or thousands of systems, such a reconfiguration could take a considerable amount of time and manpower, even if it occurs only infrequently. These drawbacks to static addressing are so significant that nearly all networks use dynamic IP addressing.

NOTE: Sometimes You Need Static   Some systems such as web servers should always be configured with static IP addresses

Dynamic Addressing

Dynamic addressing refers to the assignment of IP addresses automatically. On modern networks the mechanism used to do this is the Dynamic Host Configuration Protocol (DHCP). DHCP is a protocol, part of the TCP/IP protocol suite, that enables a central system to provide client systems with IP addresses. Assigning addresses automatically with DHCP alleviates the burden of address configuration and reconfiguration that occurs with static IP addressing. More information on DHCP can be found in Chapter 4, "Understanding the TCP/IP Protocol Suite."

Bootstrap Protocol (BOOTP)

BOOTP was originally created so that diskless workstations could obtain information—such as the TCP/IP address, subnet mask, and default gateway— needed to connect to the network. Such a system was necessary because diskless workstations had no way of storing the information.

When a system configured to use BOOTP is powered up, it broadcasts for a BOOTP server (BOOTPS)on the network. If such a server exists, it compares the MAC address of the system issuing the BOOTP request with a database of entries. From this database, it supplies the system with the appropriate information. It can also notify the workstation of a file that it must run on BOOTP.

If you use BOOTP, you should be aware that, like DHCP, it is a broadcast-based system. Therefore, routers must be configured to forward BOOTP broadcasts.

APIPA and IPv4

Automatic Private IP Addressing (APIPA) is a feature introduced with Windows 98 and included in all subsequent Windows versions. The function of APIPA is that a system can provide itself with an IP address if it cannot receive an address dynamically from a DHCP server. In such an event, APIPA assigns the system an address from the 169.254.0.0 address range and configures the subnet mask (255.255.0.0). However, it doesn't configure the system with a default gateway address. As a result, communication is limited to the local network.

> **NOTE: Inability to Obtain an Address from a DHCP Server**   If a system that does not support APIPA cannot get an address from a DHCP server, the default action is to configure itself with an IP address of 0.0.0.0. Keep this in mind when troubleshooting IP addressing problems on non-APIPA platforms.

The idea behind APIPA is that systems on a segment can communicate with each other if a DHCP server failure occurs. In reality, the limited usability of APIPA makes it little more than a measure of last resort. For example, imagine that a system is powered on while the DHCP server is operational and receives an IP address of 192.168.100.2. Then the DHCP server fails. Now if the other systems on the segment are powered on and cannot get an address from the DHCP server because it is down, they would self-assign addresses in the 169.254.0.0 address range via APIPA. The systems with APIPA addresses can talk to each other, but they cannot talk to a system that received an address from the DHCP server. Likewise, any system that received an IP address via DHCP would be unable to talk to systems with APIPA assigned addresses. This, and the absence of a default gateway, is why. As an addressing tool, APIPA is of limited use in real-world environments; however, when an APIPA address does appear, it is an indicator to administrators that a addressing problem has occurred and that the client computer is not receiving an IP lease from a DHCP server.

> **NOTE: APIPA—Smarter Than It Looks**   How does APIPA know what address to assign to the system? Before assigning an address, it broadcasts that address on the network. The default action of TCP/IP is to generate an error if it hears from

another system with the same address. If APIPA hears this error, it broadcasts another address, and another, from the 169.254.0.0 range until it receives no errors. It then assigns that address to the system. All this occurs invisibly in the background on the computer.

Zeroconf

Zero Configuration (Zeroconf) answers the call for a means of networking computer systems without requiring configuration time or technical know-how. This approach is becoming increasingly necessary as we use a larger number and wider variety of computing devices in a networked scenario. Although zero configuration networking is obviously of use in creating small ad-hoc networks with computers, its real purpose is to provide a simple means of connecting other "noncomputer" type devices—for example, the garage door opener and the house lights.

Following are three basic requirements for a system to support Zeroconf. First, the system must assign itself an IP address (APIPA) without the need for a DHCP server. Second, the system must resolve the hostname of another system to an IP address without the use of a DNS server. Finally, a system must locate or advertise services on the network without a directory services system like Microsoft's Active Directory. Zeroconf is supported by Mac and Windows operating systems, and by Linux and UNIX.

Broadcast Addresses and "This Network"

Two important concepts> to keep in mind when working with TCP/IP are broadcast addresses and the addresses used to refer to "this network." When referring to "this network," the host ID portion of the address is expressed as 0s. So, for network number 192.168, the reference would be 192.168.0.0. For a Class A network number 12, it would be 12.0.0.0.

Broadcast addresses work much the same way as "this network" addresses, except that the host ID portion of the address is set to 255, to reflect that the message is going to be sent to all the hosts on this network. Using the preceding examples, the broadcast addresses would be 192.168.255.255 and 12.255.255.255.

Classless Interdomain Routing (CIDR)

Classless interdomain routing (CIDR) is a method of assigning addresses outside the standard Class A, B, and C structure. Specifying the number of bits in the subnet mask as a specific number provides more flexibility than with the three standard class definitions.

Using CIDR, addresses are assigned using a value known as the *slash*. The actual value of the slash depends on how many bits of the subnet mask are used to express the network portion of the address. For example, a subnet mask that uses all 8 bits from the first octet and 4 from the second would be described as /12, or "slash 12." A subnet mask that uses all the bits from the first three octets would be called /24. Why the slash? In actual addressing terms, the CIDR value is expressed after the address, using a slash. So the address 192.168.2.1/24 means that the IP address of the node is 192.168.2.1, and the subnet mask is 255.255.255.0.

Default Gateways

Default gateways are the means by which a device can access hosts on other networks for which it does not have a specifically configured route. Most workstation configurations default to just using default gateways rather than having any static routes configured. This enables workstations to communicate with other network segments or with other networks, such as the Internet.

> **TIP: Default Gateways**   For the Network+ exam, you will be expected to identify the purpose and function of a default gateway.

When a system wants to communicate with another device, it first determines whether the host is on the local network or a remote network. If the host is on a remote network, the system looks in the local routing table to determine whether it has an entry for the network on which the remote host resides. If it does, it uses that route. If it does not, the data is sent to the default gateway.

> **NOTE: Default Gateway Must Be Local**   Although it might seem obvious, it's worth mentioning that the default gateway must be on the same network as the nodes that use it.

In essence, the default gateway is simply the path out of the network for a given device. Figure 5.3 shows an example of how a default gateway fits into a network infrastructure.

If a system is not configured with any static routes or a default gateway, it is limited to operating on its own network segment.

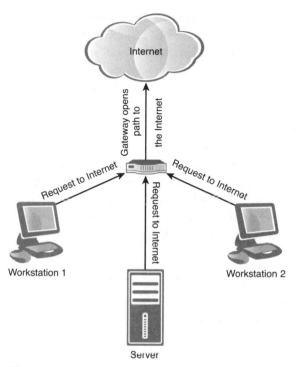

Figure 5.3   The role of a default gateway.

Understanding Subnetting

Now that we have looked at how IP addresses are used, we can discuss the process
of subnetting. *Subnetting* is a process by which bits from the node portion of an address are used to create more networks than you would have if you used the default
subnet mask.

> **NOTE: IP Subnetting**   IP subnetting is a complex task, and it is difficult to
> explain fully in the space available in this book. The information provided in this
> section
> is sufficient to answer any subnetting-related questions you might see on the
> Network+ exam. This material goes into more detail than is required. In the real

To illustrate subnetting, let's use an example. Suppose that you have been assigned
the Class B address 150.150.0.0. Using this address and the default subnet mask,
you could have a single network (150.150) and can use the rest of the address as
node addresses. This would give you many possible node addresses, which in reality is probably not useful. So you can "borrow" bits from the node portion of the
address to use as network addresses. This reduces the number of nodes per network, but chances are, you will still have more than enough.

The simplest use of subnetting in this example would be to use a subnet mask of 255.255.255.0 instead of the default Class B subnet mask of 255.255.0.0. This would give you 254 subnetworks (150.150.1 through 150.150.254.0) and 254 nodes on each of those networks. The only problem arises if you need more than 254 nodes on each network. You then have to use a process referred to as *partial-octet* or *fractional subnetting*.

In partial-octet/fractional subnetting, only part of the octet is used to create more networks, and the rest of the octet is still available for assigning as node addresses. Here's how it works. Using the example of 150.150.0.0, suppose that you want to create six networks. To do that, you need to take enough bits from the third octet to create six network addresses; at the same time, you need to preserve as many node addresses as possible. If you take the first 3 bits, you can use combinations of the bits to create values as the network addresses. Table 5.5 shows the values.

Table 5.5   Values of Subnets When Using 3 Bits from an Octet

Binary Value	Decimal Value
000	0
001	32
010	64
011	96
100	128
101	160
110	192
111	224

Because no portion of the address can be all 0s or all 1s, you can't use the 000 and 111 combinations. Therefore, you lose the network assignments of 0 and 224. You are conveniently left with six possible networks.

The bits you are taking are from the left side of the octet. To take this a step further, imagine that you use 5 bits of the octet instead of 3, as in the previous example. Using 5 bits, you would be taking the 128, 64, 32, 16, and 8 binary positions. The network numbers you could use would be 8, 16, 24, 32, 40, 48, 56, 64, and so on up to 248, in multiples of 8, which is the lowest number of the set that was used. In each instance, the available network IDs can be derived by taking the lowest number used, which in the first example is 32 and in this example is 8, and then multiplying up from there.

NOTE: A Little Subnet Math   You can use a calculation to work out how many networks you'll get from a number of bits. For example, 2 to the power of the number of masked bits minus 2 equals the number of networks, and 2 to the power of the number of unmasked bits minus 2 gives you the number of nodes on the network. You have to subtract 2 from the total in each case because you can't have a portion of the address as all 1s or all 0s. Here is the actual equation: $2^n - 2 = x$. Where n is the number of masked bits (or in the case of calculating hosts, the number of unmasked bits).

Let's look at another example. Imagine that you have been assigned the network ID 211.106.15.0. You need to have at least four networks. What would the subnet mask be, and what are the network IDs that you could use?

The subnet mask would be 255.255.255.224. To create four networks, you would need to use 3 bits (128, 64, and 32). This would give you six possible networks (32, 64, 96, 128, 160, and 192). It's simple! Remember, as discussed earlier, that you can't use the values corresponding to all 0s or all 1s when working with subnets, which is why the network numbers 0 and 224 are not included.

The network addresses that can be derived from an address of 211.106.15.0 and a subnet mask of 255.255.255.224 are shown in Table 5.6, along with the usable address ranges for each network.

Table 5.6 Subnetted Network > Addresses from the Address 211.106.15.0

Network Address	Usable Address Range
211.106.15.32	211.106.15.33–211.106.15.63
211.106.15.64	211.106.15.65–211.106.15.95
211.106.15.96	211.106.15.97–211.106.15.127
211.106.15.128	211.106.15.129–211.106.15.159
211.106.15.160	211.106.15.161–211.106.15.191
211.106.15.192	211.106.15.193–211.106.15.223

The question often on people's minds is, "Okay, but how does this work in the real world?" Using the 211.106.15.0 example as a base, let's look at how the addressing would occur on the client systems. A system with the address 211.106.15.122 would be on the network 211.106.15.96, and the host ID would be 26 (96 + 26 = 122). The value of the third octet is the combination of the network address and the host ID.

As you can see, the use of subnetting makes addressing seem more complex, but when you are used to the calculations involved, it's straightforward.

There are two main reasons for subnetting. First, it allows you to use IP address ranges more effectively. Second, it provides increased security and manageability to IP networking by providing a mechanism to create multiple networks rather than having just one. Using multiple networks confines traffic to only the network that it needs to be on, which reduces overall network traffic levels. Multiple subnets also create more broadcast domains, which in turn reduces network wide broadcast traffic.

NOTE: Subnetting Help   All this subnetting math can get a bit confusing. To get a better idea of subnetting, check out the subnetting calculator at www.subnet-calculator.com.

Public and Private IP Address Schemes

IP addressing involves many considerations, not the least important of which are public and private networks. A *public network* is a network to which anyone can connect. The best and perhaps only pure example of such a network is the Internet. A *private network* is any network to which access is restricted. A corporate, school, or home network would be considered a private network.

The main difference between public and private networks, apart from that access to a private network is tightly controlled and access to a public network is not, is that the addressing of devices on a public network must be considered carefully, whereas addressing on a private network has a little more latitude.

As you learned in the section "General IP Addressing Principles," earlier in this chapter, for hosts on a network to communicate by using TCP/IP, they must have unique addresses. The address defines the logical network each host belongs to and the host's address on that network. On a private internetwork with, for example, three logical networks and 100 nodes on each network, addressing is not a particularly complex task. On a network on the scale of the Internet, however, addressing is more involved.

Each device on the Internet must be assigned a unique address, often referred to as a> *registered address* because it is assigned to a specific party. If two devices have the same address, chances are that neither will communicate. Therefore, the assignment of addresses is carefully controlled by various organizations. Originally, the organization responsible for address assignments was the Internet Assigned Numbers Authority (IANA), but it has since delegated some of the addressing responsibility to other organizations. Around the world, three organizations shoulder the responsibility for assigning IP addresses. In the Americas and parts of the Caribbean, address assignments are the responsibility of the American Registry for Internet Numbers (ARIN); in the Asia Pacific region, it is the Asia Pacific Network Information Centre (APNIC); and in Europe, the Middle East, and parts of Africa, it is Réseaux IP Européens Network Coordination Centre (RIPE NCC). Between them, these organizations ensure that there are no IP address space conflicts and that the assignment of addresses is carefully managed.

NOTE: IPv4 Assignments   You can view the IP address range assignments for IPv4 at www.iana.org/assignments/ipv4-address-space.

If you connect a system directly to the Internet, you need to get a valid registered IP address from one of these organizations. Alternatively, you can obtain an address from an ISP. Because of the nature of their business, ISPs have large blocks of IP addresses that they can then use to assign to their clients. If you need a registered IP address, getting one from an ISP will almost certainly be a simpler process than going through a regional numbers authority. Getting a number from an ISP is the way most people get addresses. Some ISPs' plans include blocks of registered IP addresses, working on the principle that businesses are going to want some kind of permanent presence on the Internet. Of course, if you discontinue your service with the ISP, you can no longer use the IP address the ISP provided.

Private Address Ranges

To provide flexibility in addressing, and to prevent an incorrectly configured network from polluting the Internet, certain address ranges are set aside for private use. These address ranges are called *private ranges* because they are designated for use only on private networks. These addresses are special because Internet routers are configured to ignore any packets they see marked with these addresses. This means that if a network "leaks" onto the Internet, it won't make it any further than the first router it encounters.

Three private address ranges are defined in RFC 1918, one each from Classes A, B, and C. You can use whichever range you want, although the Class A and Class B address ranges offer more addressing options than does Class C. Table 5.7 defines the address ranges.

Table 5.7   Private Address Ranges

Class	Address Range	Default Subnet Mask
A	10.0.0.0–10.255.255.255	255.0.0.0
B	172.16.0.0–172.31.255.255	255.255.0.0
C	192.168.0.0–192.168.255.255	255.255.255.0

As you can see, the ranges offer a myriad of addressing possibilities. Even the Class C range offers 254 networks, with 254 nodes on each network, which is more than sufficient for the majority of network installations.

> **TIP: Private Address Ranges**   For the Network+ exam, be prepared to identify the benefit of using a private IP address range, which provides a degree of flexibility in addressing without requiring the use of registered IP addresses.

There is no requirement to use private addresses. Many organizations choose not to use them and instead use an addressing scheme of another range. Such a strategy is fine if there is no chance the data from the network will find its way on to a public network. Given that the private ranges are created for this reason and are flexible in terms of accommodating addresses, there is no reason not to use them.

Practical Uses of Public and Private IP Addressing

Having established the purpose of both public and private networks, and of public and private IP addressing, we can now look at how these fit into a practical scenario. It is common practice for a company to have only a handful of registered IP addresses and to configure the internal, private network by using one of the private addressing schemes. Figure 5.4 shows the most basic example.

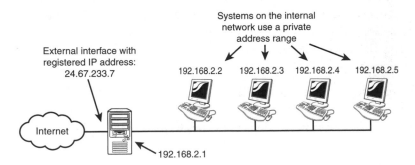

Figure 5.4   A basic example of public and private network address assignments.

The network in Figure 5.4 could provide Internet access to clients through the proxy server system. The external interface of the proxy server would have a registered IP address, and all the systems on the internal network would use one of the private ranges.

In this example, the external interface of the proxy server could use an ISP-assigned DHCP address. But what if the company wanted to have the same address all the time for a web server or a web access gateway for its email system? Then you would need to consider how you would assign IP addresses to the systems so that they could be accessed by an outside source.

IPv6 Addressing

The current Internet Protocol Version 4 (IPv4) has served as the protocol for the Internet for almost 30 years. When IPv4 was in development 30 years ago, it would have been impossible for its creators to imagine or predict the future demand for IP devices and therefore IP addresses.

> **NOTE: Ever Wonder About IPv5?**   IPv5 was an experimental protocol that never went anywhere. Although the protocol IPv5 has fallen into obscurity, the name has been reserved and we now have IPv6.

As mentioned earlier, IPv4 uses a 32-bit addressing scheme, giving IPv4 a total of 4,294,967,296 possible unique addresses that can be assigned to IP devices. More than 4 billion addresses might sound like a lot, and it is. However, the number of IP-enabled devices increases daily at a staggering rate. It is also important to remember that not all these addresses can be used by public networks. Many are reserved for private addresses and are not available for public use. This reduces the number of addresses that can be allocated as public Internet addresses.

The IPv6 project started in the mid 1990s, well before the threat of IPv4 limitations was upon us. Now network hardware and software is equipped and ready to deploy IPv6 addressing. There are a number of improvements with IPv6; most notable is its capability to handle growth for public networks. IPv6 uses a 128-bit addressing scheme, enabling a total number of possible addresses to 340,282,366,920,938,463,463,374,607,431,768,211,456.

This section shows how to identify IPv6 addresses and describes IPv6 address types.

Identifying IPv6 Addresses

As previously discussed, IPv4 uses a dotted-decimal notation, 8 bits converted to its decimal equivalent and separated by periods. An example of an IPv4 address is 192.168.2.1. .

Because of the 128-bit structure of the IPv6 addressing scheme, it looks quite a bit different from IPv4 addresses. An IPv6 address is divided along 16-bit boundaries, and each 16-bit block is converted to a 4-digit hexadecimal number and separated by colons. The resulting representation is called colon-hexadecimal. Let's look at how it works. Figure 5.5 shows an IPv6 address from a Windows Vista system.

Two IPv6 addresses are listed in Figure 5.5: the link local IPv6 address, which we discuss later, and the external IPv6 address. The external IPv6 address is

    2001:0:4137:9e50:3cde:37d1:3f57:fe93

You can simplify an IPv6 address by removing the leading zeros within each 16-bit block. All zeros cannot be removed, however, because each address block must

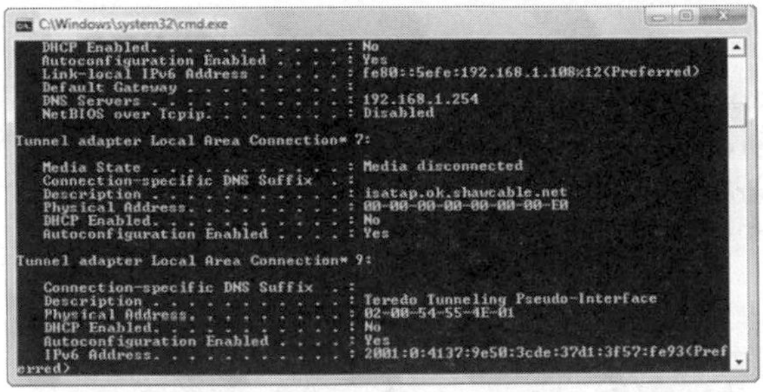

Figure 5.5 IPv6 addresses in a Windows Vista dialog screen.

have at least a single digit. The address shown in Figure 5.5 suppresses the zeros. Removing the zero suppression, the address representation becomes

2001:0000:4137:9e50:3cde:37d1:3f57:fe93

Some of the IPv6 addresses you will work with have sequences of zeros. When this occurs the number is often abbreviated to make it easier to read. In the preceding example we saw that a single zero represented a number set in the hexadecimal form. To further simplify the representation of IPv6 addresses, a contiguous sequence of 16-bit blocks set to 0 in the colon hexadecimal format can be compressed to "::", known as *double-colon*. For example, you can compress the IPv6 address of 2001:0000:0000:0000:3cde:37d1:3f57:fe93 to 2001::3cde:37d1:3f57:fe93.

However, there are limits to how we can reduce the IPv6 zeros. Zeros within the IPv6 address cannot be eliminated when they are not first in the number sequence. For instance, 2001:4000:0000:0000:0000:0000:0000:0003 cannot be compressed as 2001:4::3. This would actually appear as 2001:4000::3.

When you look at an IPv6 address using a double colon (::), how do you know exactly what numbers are represented? The formula is to subtract the number of blocks from 8 and then multiple the number by 16. So in the address 2001:4000::3, there are three blocks used (2001, 4000, and 3). The equation is

8 – 3X16 = 80

Therefore, the total number of bits represented by the double colon in this example is 80.

NOTE: Zeros   The process of removing zeros can be used only once in an IPv6 address. Using the double colons more than once would make it impossible to determine the number of 0 bits represented by each instance of double colons.

IPv6 Address Types

Another difference between IPv4 and IPv6 is in the address types. IPv4 addressing was discussed earlier in this chapter in the section "IPv4 Addressing." When it comes to IPv6 addresses, there are several types of addresses:

- **Unicast IPv6 addresses**—A unicast address specifies a single interface. Data packets sent to a unicast destination travel from the sending host to the destination host. It is a direct line of communication.

- **Multicast addresses**—As with IPv4 addresses, *multicasting* sends and receives data between groups of nodes, sending IP messages to that group rather than to every node on the LAN (broadcast) or just one other node (unicast). The prefix used for IPv6 multicast addresses is FF00::/8.

- **Anycast addresses**—Anycast addresses represent the middle ground between the unicast addresses and multicast addresses. Anycast delivers messages to any one node in the multicast group.

A few types of addresses fall under the unicast banner:

- **Global unicast addresses**—Global unicast addresses are the equivalent of IPv4 public addresses. These addresses are routable and travel throughout the network. The prefix used > for global unicast addresses is 2000::/3.

- **Link-local address**—Link-local addresses are those addresses designated for use on a single local network. Link-local addresses are automatically configured on all interfaces. This automatic configuration is equivalent to the 169.254.0.0/16 automatically assigned IPv4 addressing. The prefix used for a link-local address is fe80::/10. On a single link IPv6 network with no router, link-local addresses are used to communicate between devices on the link.

- **Unique local addresses**—Unique local addresses are equivalent to the IPv4 private address space (10.0.0.0/8, 172.16.0.0/12, and 192.168.0.0/16). Like IPv4, in which private address ranges are used in private networks, IPv6 uses unique local addresses that will not interfere with global unicast addresses. In addition, routers will not forward unique local traffic outside the site. Unlike link-local addresses, unique local addresses are not automatically configured and must be assigned either through stateless or stateful address configuration processes. The prefix used for the unique local address is (FC00::/7).

NOTE: Site-Local Addresses   In 2003, RFC 3513 defined the block fec0::/10 as site-local addresses. However, some confusion existed over what "site" meant. The result is that site local addresses were scrapped, and unique local addresses were introduced.

NOTE: Stateful Versus Stateless   You might come across the terms stateful and stateless configuration. Stateless refers to IP autoconfiguration, where administrators need not manually input configuration information. In a stateful configuration, network devices obtain address information from a server.

NOTE: **Reserved IPv6 Addresses** In IPv4, an address (127.0.0.1) is reserved as the loopback address. IPv6 has the same reservation. IPv6 address 0:0:0:0:0:0:0:1 is reserved as the loopback address.

Table 5.8 shows a comparison between IPv4 and IPv6 addressing.

Table 5.8 Comparing IPv4 and IPv6

Address Feature	IPv4 Address	IPv6 Address
Loopback address	127.0.0.1	0:0:0:0:0:0:0:1 (::1)
Networkwide addresses	IPv4 public address ranges	Global unicast IPv6 addresses
Private network addresses	10.0.0.0 172.16.0.0 192.168.0.0	Unique local addresses ranges (FC00::/7)
Autoconfigured addresses	IPv4 automatic private IP addressing (169.254.0.0)	Link-local addresses of FE80:: prefix.

TIP: **Private Address** For the Network+ exam remember that fe80:: is a private link-local address.

Differentiating Between Routable and Routing Protocols

Routers rely on two types of network protocols to make the routing magic happen: routable protocols and routing protocols. We examine them separately in the next sections.

Routable Protocols

Large internetworks need protocols that enable systems to be identified by the address of the network to which they are attached and by an address that uniquely identifies them on that network. Network protocols that provide both of these features are said to be *routable*. The most common routable protocol used on today's network is TCP/IP.

Recall that TCP/IP was developed in the 1970s by the Department of Defense, which needed a protocol to use on its WAN. TCP/IP's flexibility, durability, and functionality meant that it soon became the WAN protocol of choice and also became the standard for LANs. Today, most networks use TCP/IP in some fashion, even if the main LAN protocol is something other than TCP/IP. TCP/IP is a huge topic, and anyone in networking must understand it.

TCP/IP is a protocol suite composed of numerous individual protocols. Within TCP/IP, the routing protocols used are the Routing Information Protocol (RIP and RIPv2), Open Shortest Path First (OSPF), Intermediate System-to-Intermediate System (IS-IS), Border Gateway Protocol (BGP), and Enhanced Interior Gateway Routing Protocol (EIGRP). RIP, RIPv2, and BGP are distance-vector routing protocols, and OSPF and IS-IS are link-state routing protocols. You learn what this means in the next section.

Some routers are capable of routing more than one protocol at a time, a feature known as *multiprotocol routing*. Multiprotocol routing brings with it a number of considerations, not the least of which is that a multiprotocol router might need to work considerably harder than a router working with only a single protocol. This is the case not only because more than one protocol exists, but because there might also be multiple routing protocols.

Routing Protocols

Routing protocols are the means by which routers communicate with each other. This communication is necessary so that routers can learn the network topology and changes that occur in it. The two methods to assign routes for the network are static and dynamic routing.

With static routing, network route information must be manually entered by the administrator into a routing table. There are two main disadvantages of this approach: First, manually entering routes is time-consuming and susceptible to human error. Second, if the topology of the network changes, the routers must be manually reconfigured. Therefore, static routing is generally used only in the smallest of environments. In environments with more than a handful of routers, dynamic routing is the preferred option.

Dynamic routing uses routing protocols designed to dynamically discover paths to network destinations and how to get to them. Using these routing protocols, the network router must learn the routes available on the network first. The router can then sort through its list of routes and choose the best path for data to follow. The routing protocols can also communicate to other routers, informing them of all discovered routes.

NOTE: Metrics   In routing, the term *metric* describes the "cost" or number of 'hops' associated with a certain route. The metric can be a combination of factors, including the number of routers between a router's position and the destination, the time it takes to complete the journey, and even a value that can be assigned by an administrator to discourage use of a certain route. Under normal circumstances, routers choose the route with the lowest metric or shortest number of hops between routers.

The two types of routing protocols are *distance-vector* and *link-state protocols*. Each has a different strategy for dealing with router-to-router communication.

Distance-Vector Routing Protocols

With distance-vector routing protocols, each router communicates all the routes it knows about to all other routers to which it is directly attached (that is, its *neighbors*). Because each router in the network knows only about the routers to which it is attached, it doesn't know how to complete the entire journey; instead, it only knows how to make the next hop. *Hops* are the means by which distance-vector routing protocols determine the shortest way to reach a given destination. Each router constitutes one hop; so if a router is four hops away from another router, there are three routers, or hops, between itself and the destination. Distance-vector protocols can also use a time value known as a *tick*, which enables the router to make a decision about which path is quickest if given the choice of more than one (a common situation on networks with redundant links).

The frequency with which routers send route updates depends on the routing protocol used, but it is usually between 10 and 60 seconds. At each update, the entire routing table of the sender is sent to the other connected routers. When the other routers receive the information, they check it against the existing information; if there are any changes, they alter their routing tables accordingly.

This constant update cycle is one of the problems of distance-vector routing protocols because it can lead to large amounts of network traffic. Furthermore, after the initial learning period, the updates should (hopefully) be irrelevant; the chances of the network topology changing every 30 seconds or so are slim, and if you do have such a network, some troubleshooting might be in order.

When a change does occur on the network, it might take some time for all the routers to learn of the change. The process of each router learning about the change and updating its routing tables is known as *convergence*. In a small network, convergence might not take long; but in larger networks, those with, for instance, more than 20 routers, it might take some time to complete. Rather than cause the routers to wait for the updates, you can configure *triggered updates*, which are sent when a topology change is detected. Using triggered updates can significantly improve the convergence speed of distance-vector–based networks.

You can also use *hold-down timers* to improve convergence. A hold-down timer prevents a router from trying to make too many changes too quickly. When a router receives a change about a route, it makes the change and then applies a hold-down timer to the change. The hold-down timer prevents further changes from being made to that route within the defined time period. Hold-down timers are particularly useful when an unreliable router keeps going on and off the network. If hold-down timers are not applied, updates to the routing tables on routers would continually be changing, and the network might never converge.

In some configurations, distance-vector routing protocols can lead to routing loops. *Routing loops* occur when a router tells another router about a route that it heard about from the same router. For example, consider the router layout in Figure 5.6. If Router C becomes unable to access Router D through Network 1, it removes the route from its table and sends the update to Router B; Router B removes the route. But if Router B receives an update from Router A before it sends an update to Router A, the route is reinstated because according to Router A, it can still access Network 1. Now Router B begins to send anything destined for Network 1 back to Router A, which duly sends it back to Router B, and so on, thus creating a routing loop. Each time the route is added to the table, the hop count for the route increases—a problem known as the *count to infinity*.

Figure 5.6   How routing loops occur.

You can use two strategies to prevent routing loops when using distance-vector routing protocols:

- **Split horizon**—The split horizon algorithm addresses the problem of routing loops by not advertising routes back on the interface from which they are learned. In other words, to use Figure 5.6 as an example, Router C would not advertise back to Router B any route that it learned from Router B. Basically, Router C figures that, because it learned about the route from Router B, Router B must be nearer to the destination than it is.

- **Split horizon with poison reverse**—With this strategy, also known as *poison reverse*, routers do advertise routes back on the interfaces from which they were learned, but they do so with a hop count of infinity. The value used for infinity (which seems like an impossible situation) depends on the routing protocol used. Again using the example from Figure 5.6, Router C would advertise to Router B the routes it learned from Router B, but it would also add the infinite hop count. In other words, Router C would say, "I know about Router A, but I can't reach it myself." This way, Router B would never try to add the route to Router A through Router C, because according to Router C, it can't reach Router A.

Several distance-vector protocols are in use today, including the following:

■ **Routing Information Protocol (RIP)**—The RIP protocol route metric is limited to a maximum of 15 hops. One of the downsides of the protocol is that the original specification required router updates to be transmitted every 30 seconds. On smaller networks this can be okay; however, this causes huge traffic on larger networks. The original RIP also did not support router authentication, leaving it vulnerable to attacks.

■ **RIPv2**—This second version of RIP deals with the shortcomings of the original design. RIPv2 includes authentication to enable for secure transmissions and changes from networkwide broadcast discovery using multicast to reduce network traffic. However, to maintain compatibility with RIP, RIPv2 still supports a limit of 15 hops.

■ **Border Gateway Protocol (BGP)**—BGP is a routing protocol often associated with the Internet. BGP can be used between gateway hosts on the Internet. BGP examines the routing table, which contains a list of known routers, the addresses they can reach, and a cost metric associated with the path to each router so that the best available route is chosen. BGP communicates between the routers using the TCP protocol.

■ **Enhanced Interior Gateway Routing Protocol (EIGRP)**—EIGRP is a protocol that enables routers to exchange information more efficiently than with earlier network protocols. EIGRP uses its neighbors to help determine routing information. Routers configured to use EIGRP keep copies of its neighbors' routing information and query these tables to help find the best possible route for transmissions to follow. EIGRP uses the Diffusing-Update Algorithm (DUAL) to determine the best route to a destination.

Link-State Routing Protocols

A router that uses a link-state protocol differs from a router that uses a distance-vector protocol because it builds a map of the entire network and then holds that map in memory. On a network that uses a link-state protocol, routers send out link-state advertisements (LSAs) that contain information about what networks they are connected to. The LSAs are sent to every router on the network, thus enabling the routers to build their network maps.

When the network maps on each router are complete, the routers update each other at a given time, just like a distance-vector protocol does, but the updates occur much less frequently with link-state protocols than with distance-vector protocols. The only other circumstance under which updates are sent is if a change in the topology is detected, at which point the routers use LSAs to detect the change and update their routing tables. This mechanism, combined with the fact that routers hold maps of the entire network, makes convergence on a link-state-based network occur quickly.

Although it might seem like link-state protocols are an obvious choice over distance-vector protocols, routers on a link-state-based network require more powerful hardware and more RAM than those on a distance-vector-based network. Not only do the routing tables have to be calculated, but they must also be stored. A router that uses distance-vector protocols need to maintain only a small database of the routes accessible by the routers to which it is directly connected. A router that uses link-state protocols must maintain a database of the routers in the entire network.

Link-state protocols include the following:

■ **Open Shortest Path First (OSPF)**—Based on the shortest path first (SPF) algorithm to find the least cost path to any destination in the network. In operation, each router using OSPF sends out a list of its neighbors to other routers on the network. From this information, routers can determine the network design and can determine the shortest path for data to travel.

■ **Intermediate System to Intermediate System (IS-IS)**—Discovers the shortest path for data travel using the SPF algorithm. IS-IS routers distribute topology information to other routers, enabling them to make the best path decisions.

TIP: Identify the Protocols   Be prepared to identify both the link-state and distance-vector routing protocols used on TCP/IP networks.

IGP Versus EGP

Now that we have talked about routing protocols, we should clarify the difference between Interior Gateway Protocols (IGP) and Exterior Gateway Protocols (EGP). The IGP identifies the protocols used to exchange routing information between routers within a LAN or interconnected LANs. IGP is not a protocol but describes a category of link-state routing protocols that support a single, confined geographic area such as a local area network. IGP protocols fall into two categories: distance-vector protocols (including RIP and IGRP) and link-state protocols (including OSPF and IS-IS).

Whereas IGP protocols are geographically confined, EGP protocols are used for routing information outside of the network, such as the Internet. On the Internet, an EGP is required. EGP defines distance-vector protocols commonly used between hosts on the Internet to exchange routing table information. BGP is an example of an EGP.

NAT, PAT, and SNAT

We have had many acronyms in this chapter, and we are going to end with three more: Network Address Translation (NAT), Port Address Translation (PAT), and Static Network Address Translation (SNAT).

The basic principle of NAT is that many computers can "hide" behind a single IP address; or more specifically, NAT is a form of or IP masquerading in which entire addresses, usually consisting of private network addresses behind a single IP address in another, often public address space. So, it often involves hiding the IP addresses of an organization's private addresses from the public ones used on the Internet. This strategy adds a level of security by making it difficult to see internal addresses from an external source. Using NAT means that only one registered IP address is needed on the external interface of the system acting as the gateway between the internal and external networks.

NOTE: NAT and Proxy Servers   Don't confuse NAT with proxy servers. The proxy service is different from NAT, but many proxy server applications do include NAT functionality.

NAT enables you to use whatever addressing scheme you like on your internal networks, although it is common practice to use the private address ranges, which were discussed earlier in the chapter.

When a system is >performing NAT service, it funnels the requests given to it to the Internet. To the remote host, the request looks like it is originating from a single address. The system performing the NAT function keeps track of who asked for what and makes sure that when the data is returned, it is directed to the correct system. Servers that provide NAT functionality do so in different ways. For example, it is possible to statically map a specific internal IP address to a specific external one (known as the *one-to-one NAT method*) so that outgoing requests are always tagged with the same IP address. Alternatively, if you have a group of public IP addresses, you can have the NAT system assign addresses to devices on a first-come, first-served basis. Either way, the basic function of NAT is the same. Figure 5.7 shows a representation of NAT.

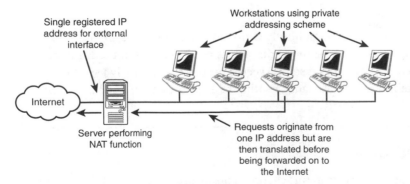

Figure 5.7   An example of NAT.

A few variations exist on NAT, each designed for a slightly different purpose. Some of these NAT variations include Port Address Translation (PAT), Static Network Address Translation (SNAT), and Dynamic Network Address Translation (DNAT).

- **PAT**—NAT enables administrators to conserve public IP addresses and at the same time secure the internal network. PAT is a variation on NAT. With PAT, all systems on the LAN are translated to the same IP address but with a different port number assignment. PAT is used when multiple clients want to access the Internet. However, with not enough public IP addresses available, you need to map the inside clients to a single public IP address. When packets come back into the private network, they are routed to their destination with a table within PAT that tracks the public and private port numbers.

- **SNAT and DNAT**—SNAT maps a private IP address directly to a static unchanging public IP address. This enables an internal system, such as a mail server, to have an unregistered (private) IP address and still be reachable over the Internet. In contrast, in a DNAT configuration, a private IP address is mapped to a public IP address using a pool of public IP addresses.

Summary

This chapter focuses on IP addressing, both for IPv4 and for IPv6. IP addressing is a major topic, and it is important for network administrators to understand it. Of particular importance are the structure of the addresses and the classes in which they fit. Understanding subnetting allows network administrators to use the allocated IP address space in the most efficient way possible.

An important component of configuring TCP/IP addressing on a system is the default gateway. Without a default gateway address, a system can communicate only with other systems on the same subnet.

This chapter also examined the purpose of private and public networks and their role in a TCP/IP network environment. As the IP address space continues to be depleted, such concepts will become increasingly important.

Routing is an important part of network administration. Two types of routing technologies are commonly used, link state and distance vector. Both of these have various protocols associated with them.

A network that uses TCP/IP has a number of services that offer needed functionality. Services such as DHCP and NAT offer a solution to the time-consuming and sometimes problematic task of IP addressing. DNS offers name resolution services that can enable users to access hosts by using easy-to-remember names rather than TCP/IP addressing.

Exam Preparation Tasks

 ## Review All the Key Topics

Review the most important topics in the chapter, noted with the Key Topics icon in the outer margin of the page. Table 5.9 lists a reference of these key topics and the page numbers on which each is found.

Table 5.9 Key Topics for Chapter 5

Key Topic Element	Description	Page Number
Table 5.1	Methods of viewing the MAC addresses of NICs	187
Figure 5.1	The output from the `ipconfig /all` command	187
Table 5.2	Examples of numbers derived through binary	189
Table 5.3	IPv4 address classes and the number of available network/host addresses	189
Table 5.4	Default subnet masks	190
List	IPv4 address types	190
Table 5.6	Subnetted network addresses from the address 211.106.15.0	197
Table 5.7	Private address ranges	199
Table 5.8	Comparing IPv4 and IPv6	204

Define Key Terms

Define the following key terms from this chapter, and check your answers in the Glossary.

- IPv6
- IPv4
- MAC addressing
- Subnetting
- NAT
- PAT

- SNAT

- DHCP

- Unicast

- Multicast

- Broadcast

- Link state

- OSPF

- IS-IS

- Distance vector

- RIP

- RIPv2

- BGP

- EIGRP

- IGP

- EGP

- Next hop

- Convergence

Apply Your Knowledge

Exercise 5.1 Identifying Your MAC Address

Each device on the network has a MAC address imprinted on the NIC. This address is used both to identify machines and as a filter for firewalls. In this exercise, you identify the MAC address of your computer. This exercise assumes you use a Windows operating system.

Estimated time: 5 minutes

1. Choose Start, Run and in the space provided, type **cmd**.

2. At the command prompt type **ipconfig /all.**

3. The command will issue all TCP/IP information on the system and the MAC address.

4. After you see the MAC address listed, identify which parts of the address identify the Organizational Unique Identifier (OUI) and the Universal LAN MAC

address. To discover the manufacturer of your network device, try to find them at http://standards.ieee.org/regauth/oui/oui.txt.

Exercise 5.2 Discovering Your DHCP Server Address

If you are behind a router at home or using a computer at the office, it is likely you are getting your TCP/IP information from a DHCP server. In this exercise we check the address of the DHCP server. Also, if you cannot connect to your network, this can also show if you are receiving an address via APIPA.

Estimated time: 5 minutes

1. Choose Start, Run and in the space provided, type **cmd**.

2. At the command prompt type **ipconfig /all.**

3. The command issues all TCP/IP information on the system, including the address of your DHCP server. The printout will look something like the following.

```
Physical Address. . . . . . . . . : 00-1E-4C-43-FA-55
DHCP Enabled. . . . . . . . . . . : Yes
Autoconfiguration Enabled . . . . : Yes
Link-local IPv6 Address . . . . . :
fe80::c1bf:c044:8e7c:e27f%8(Preferr
IPv4 Address. . . . . . . . . . . : 192.168.1.64(Preferred)
Subnet Mask . . . . . . . . . . . : 255.255.255.0
Lease Obtained. . . . . . . . . . : Sunday, April 19, 2009 2:17:31 PM
Lease Expires . . . . . . . . . . : Monday, April 20, 2009 2:17:31 PM
Default Gateway . . . . . . . . . : 192.168.1.254
DHCP Server . . . . . . . . . . . : 192.168.1.254
DHCPv6 IAID . . . . . . . . . . . : 167778686
DNS Servers . . . . . . . . . . . : 192.168.1.254
                                    192.168.1.254
```

Exercise 5.3 Releasing and Renewing IP Information

If you cannot see a valid DHCP server and you have an address in the 169.x.x.x range, you are not on the network and getting your IP information from APIPA. If you get no IP information or an IP address of 0.0.0.0, you have lost all network connectivity, and APIPA is likely not configured.

This exercise attempts to release IP information and renew it from a DHCP server. This is a troubleshooting step sometimes done when a DHCP server exists and a system does not recognize it.

Estimated time: 5 minutes

To release an IP address from the command line:

1. Choose Start, Run and in the space provided, type **cmd** to open a command prompt.

2. At the command prompt, type **ipconfig /all** to view current IP information.

3. After you see the IP information, you can release it by typing the following command: **ipconfig /release**.

4. At the command prompt, type **ipconfig /all** to see that the IP information has gone.

To renew the IP information from the command line:

1. Choose Start, Run and in the space provided, type **cmd** to open a command prompt.

2. At the command prompt, type **ipconfig /all** to view current IP information.

3. After you see the information, you can renew it by typing the following command: **ipconfig /renew**.

4. At the command prompt, type **ipconfig /all** to see that the IP information has returned.

Make sure you type a space after ipconfig and a forward slash before release.

After you have released your IP address, you need to renew it by using the command **ipconfig /renew**. (Again, remember the space after ipconfig and the forward slash before renew.)

Exercise 5.4 Configuring IP Information

In the following table you see six IP addresses. For each line, identify what class the IP address falls into and also provide the default subnet mask for that class. You can compare your answers with the solution table. The first entry is completed as an example.

IP Address	Class	Subnet Mask
151.76.24.77	B	255.255.0.0
129.43.202.105		
65.231.78.101		
207.19.113.72		
192.168.43.102		
7.15.104.24		

Solution Table

IP Address	Class	Subnet Mask
151.76.24.77	B	255.255.0.0
129.43.202.105	B	255.255.0.0
65.231.78.101	A	255.0.0.0
207.19.113.72	C	255.255.255.0
192.168.43.102	C	255.255.255.0
7.15.104.24	A	255.0.0.0

Review Questions

You can find answers to these questions in Appendix A, "Answers to Review Questions."

1. Which of the following is a link-state routing protocol used on TCP/IP networks?
   a. RIP
   b. ARP
   c. OSPF
   d. NLSP

2. You are configuring a firewall to use NAT. In the configuration, you map a private IP address directly to a persistent public IP address. What form of NAT is used?
   a. NAT
   b. DNAT
   c. SNAT
   d. All options provided are correct.

3. Which of the following statements best describes split horizon?
   a. Routes are advertised back on the interface from which they were learned, with a metric of 16.
   b. Routes are advertised back on the interface from which they were learned, with a metric of 0.
   c. Routes are not advertised back on the interface from which they were learned.
   d. Routes are advertised back on the interface from which they were learned, with a metric of 16, and on all other interfaces they are advertised back on the interface from which they were learned, with a metric of 0.

4. In a network that uses distance-vector routing protocols, what information is included in the update sent out by each router?

   a. Details of the routers that it is directly managed by

   b. A map of the entire network, with hop counts valued from its current position

   c. Details of all the routers it knows about

   d. Details of its own configuration

5. What condition can arise if routers advertise a route back to the router from which it was learned?

   a. Count to infinity

   b. Infinity loop

   c. Countless hop

   d. Count to 16

6. What term is used by routers to describe each step necessary to reach a destination?

   a. Hop

   b. Jump

   c. Skip

   d. Leap

7. Which of the following is a distance-vector routing protocol used on TCP/IP networks?

   a. ARP

   b. NLSP

   c. OSPF

   d. RIP

8. You decide to move your network from NetBEUI to TCP/IP. For the external interfaces, you decide to obtain registered IP addresses from your ISP, but for the internal network, you choose to configure systems by using one of the private address ranges. Of the following address ranges, which one would you *not* consider?

   a. 192.168.0.0 to 192.168.255.255

   b. 131.16.0.0 to 131.16.255.255

   c. 10.0.0.0 to 10.255.255.255

   d. 172.16.0.0 to 172.31.255.255

9. Which of the following addresses is a Class B address?

   a. 129.16.12.200

   b. 126.15.16.122

   c. 211.244.212.5

   d. 193.17.101.27

10. Consider the IP address 195.16.17.8. Assuming that the default subnet mask is being used, which part of the address would be considered the network address?
    a. 195.16
    b. 195.16.17
    c. 16.17.8
    d. 17.8

11. Which of the following protocols is associated with EGP?
    a. BGP
    b. OSPF
    c. RIPv2
    d. RIPv1

12. Which of the following is the correct broadcast address for the Class A network 14?
    a. 14.255.255.0
    b. 14.0.0.0
    c. 255.255.255.255
    d. 14.255.255.255

13. What is the IPv6 equivalent of 127.0.0.1? (Select two.)
    a. 0:0:0:0:0:0:0:1
    b. 0:0:0:0:0:0:0:24
    c. ::1
    d. ::24

14. You ask your ISP to assign a public IP address for the external interface of your Windows 2008 server, which is running a proxy server application. In the email message you receive that contains the information, the ISP tells you that you have been assigned the IP address 203.15.226.12/24. When you fill out the subnet mask field on the IP configuration dialog box on your system, what subnet mask should you use?
    a. 255.255.255.255
    b. 255.255.255.0
    c. 255.255.240.0
    d. 255.255.255.240

15. Which of the following technologies are designed to "hide" behind a single IP address?
    a. NAS
    b. DHCP
    c. Multicasting
    d. NAT

16. Which of the following address types are associated with IPv6? (Choose all that apply.)

   a. Broadcast

   b. Multicast

   c. Unicast

   d. Anycast

17. Which of the following addresses is a valid IPv6 address?

   a. 211.16.233.17.12.148.201.226

   b. 42DE:7E55:63F2:21AA:CBD4:D773:CC21:554F

   c. 42DE:7E55:63G2:21AT:CBD4:D773:CC21:554F

   d. 42DE:7E55:63F2:21AA

18. Which of the address types sends data to all systems on a subnet or network instead of single hosts?

   a. Multicast

   b. Unicast

   c. Broadcast

   d. Anycast

19. Which of the following IPv6 address types are associated with IPv4 private address ranges?

   a. Link-local addresses

   b. Unique local address

   c. Global address

   d. Unicast addresses

20. Which of the following IPv6 address types are associated with IPv4 automatic 169.254.0.0 addressing?

   a. Link-local addresses

   b. Unique local address

   c. Global address

   d. Unicast addresses

21. Which of the following represents a valid MAC address?

   a. 00:G0:59:09:07:5F

   b. 00-D0-59-09-07-51

   c. 00:D0:59:09:07:51

   d. 00-D0:5C:09:07:51

This chapter covers CompTIA Network+ objective 2.6. Upon completion of this chapter, you will be able to answer the following questions:

■ What are the features of CSMA/CD?

■ How do broadcasts and collisions impact network performance?

■ What are the transmission rates of Ethernet technologies?

■ What are the characteristics of 100Base Ethernet technologies?

■ What are the characteristics of 1000Base networking?

■ What are the characteristics of 10GBase Ethernet technologies

■ What are the various Ethernet standards?

CHAPTER 6

Ethernet Networking Standards

As discussed in Chapter 1, "Introduction to Computer Networking," a topology defines the structure of a network, and network standards define how it works. As early as the 1970s, it was apparent that networks were going to play a large role in future corporate environments. Many manufacturers saw the computing and network trend and became increasingly active in network component development. These companies realized that for their products to work together, standards would be necessary to ensure compatibility. The task of producing the standards fell to an international body called the Institute of Electrical and Electronics Engineers (IEEE).

The IEEE developed a set of standards called the 802 project. These standards are still used today, although there have been many changes and additions along the way. By using the standards defined by the IEEE, manufacturers can be sure that their products will work with products from other companies that adhere to the standards.

Some of the IEEE 802 standards define only certain technologies, whereas others, such as the 802.3 standard, define entire networking systems. The following are some of the most important IEEE 802 standards:

- **802.1, bridging and management**—Defines the systems for managing networks and specifies technologies for making sure that the network is available to users and responding to requests. It defines internetwork communications standards between devices and includes specifications for routing and bridging.

- **802.2, the LLC sublayer**—Defines specifications for the Logical Link Control (LLC) sublayer in the 802 standard series.

- **802.3, CSMA/CD**—Defines the carrier-sense multiple-access with collision detection (CSMA/CD) media access method used in Ethernet networks. This is the most popular networking standard used today.

- **802.4, a token passing bus (rarely used)**—Defines the use of a token-passing system on a linear bus topology.

- **802.5, token ring networks**—Defines token ring networking, also known as token ring access.

- **802.6, metropolitan area network (MAN)**—Defines a data transmission method called distributed queue dual bus (DQDB), which is designed to carry voice and data on a single link.

- **802.7, Broadband Technical Advisory**—Defines the standards and specifications of broadband communications methods.

- **802.8, Fiber-Optic Technical Advisory**—Provides assistance to other IEEE 802 committees on subjects related to the use of fiber optics.

- **802.9, integrated voice and data networks**—Defines the advancement of integrated voice and data networks.

- **802.10, network security**—Defines security standards that make it possible to safely and securely transmit and exchange data.

- **802.11, wireless networks**—Defines standards for wireless LAN communication.

- **802.12, 100BaseVG-AnyLAN**—Defines standards for high-speed LAN technologies.

For the Network+ exam and day-to-day real-life networking, some of these standards are more important than others. This chapter primarily focuses on the 802.3 Ethernet standards and their characteristics, such as access methods (CSMA/CD), signaling type (baseband/broadband), their speeds, and the distances they support. Chapter 7, "Wireless Networking," discusses 802.11 wireless standards.

Foundation Topics

Characteristics Specified in the IEEE 802 Standards

The IEEE standards specify the characteristics of the networking systems, including speed, access methods, topologies, and media. Although you don't need detailed knowledge of all these IEEE standards in real-world applications, a general understanding of these standards will be an asset.

Speed

Many factors contribute to the speed of a network. The standard defines the maximum speed of a networking system. The speed normally is measured in megabits per second (Mbps), although some faster network systems use gigabits per second (that is, Gbps, where 1Gbps is equivalent to 1000Mbps).

NOTE: Bandwidth   The term *bandwidth* has become a gray area in the network world. In everyday use it sometimes describes the amount of data that can travel over a network connection in a given time period. This is technically not accurate; that definition more closely defines data throughput. Bandwidth refers to the width of the range of electrical frequencies, or amount of channels that the media can support. Bandwidth correlates to the amount of data that can traverse the media at one time, but other factors determine what the maximum speed supported by a cable will be.

Some networks are faster than others. For example, a token ring (802.5) network has a maximum speed of 16Mbps. Many Ethernet networks (802.3 variants) operate at 100Mbps and far beyond. However, the maximum speed attainable on a network can be affected by many factors. Networks that achieve 100% of their potential bandwidth are few and far between.

Access Methods

Access methods govern the way in which systems access the network media and send data. Access methods are necessary to ensure that systems on the network can communicate with each other. Without an access method, it would be impossible for two systems to communicate at the exclusion of every other system. Access methods ensure that everyone gets an opportunity to use the network.

Several access methods are used in networks; the most popular are CSMA/CD and CSMA/CA, and a distant third would be token passing. Other methods, such as demand priority are sometimes found as well. We look at each of these access methods separately.

Carrier Sense Multiple Access/Collision Detection

Carrier Sense Multiple Access/Collision Detection (CSMA/CD) is defined in the IEEE 802.3 standard. CSMA/CD is the most common media access method because it is associated with 802.3 Ethernet networking, which is by far the most popular networking system.

On a network that uses CSMA/CD, when a system wants to send data to another system, it first checks to see whether the network media is free. It must do this because each piece of network media used in a LAN can carry only one signal at a time. If the sending node detects that the media is free, it transmits, and the data is sent to the destination. It seems simple.

Now, if it always worked like this, you wouldn't need the CD part of CSMA/CD. Unfortunately, in networking, as in life, things do not always go as planned. The problem arises when two systems attempt to transmit at exactly the same time. It might seem like a long shot that two systems will pick the same moment to send data, but we are dealing with communications that occur many times in a single second—and most networks have more than two machines. Imagine that 200 people are in a room. The room is silent, but then two people decide to say something at exactly the same time. Before they start to speak, they check (listen) to see whether someone else is speaking; because no one else is speaking, they begin to talk. The result is two people speaking at the same time, which is similar to a network collision.

Collision detection works by detecting fragments of the transmission on the network media that result when two systems try to talk at the same time. The two systems wait for a randomly calculated amount of time before attempting to transmit again. This amount of time—a matter of milliseconds—is known as the *backoff*.

When the backoff period has elapsed, the system attempts to transmit again. If the system doesn't succeed on the second attempt, it keeps retrying until it gives up and reports an error.

NOTE: Contention   CSMA/CD is known as a contention media access method because systems contend for access to the media.

The upside of CSMA/CD is that it has relatively low overhead, meaning that not much is involved in the workings of the system. The downside is that as more systems are added to the network, more collisions occur, and the network becomes slower. The performance of a network that uses CSMA/CD degrades exponentially as more systems are added. Its low overhead means that CSMA/CD systems theoretically can achieve greater speeds than high-overhead systems, such as token passing. However, because collisions take place, the chances of all that speed translating into usable bandwidth are relatively low.

NOTE: Equal Access   On a network that uses CSMA/CD, every node has equal access to the network media.

Despite its problems, CSMA/CD is an efficient system. As a result, rather than replace it with some other technology, workarounds have been created that reduce the likelihood of collisions. One such strategy is the use of network switches that create multiple collision domains and therefore reduce the impact of collisions on performance. See Chapter 3, "Networking Components and Devices," to learn about using switches.

Table 6.1 summarizes the advantages and disadvantages of the CSMA/CD access method.

Table 6.1   Advantages and Disadvantages of CSMA/CD

Advantages	Disadvantages
Has low overhead	Collisions degrade network performance.
Utilizes all available bandwidth when possible	Priorities cannot be assigned to certain nodes.
	Performance degrades exponentially as devices are added.

CSMA/CA

Instead of collision detection as with CSMA/CD, the Carrier-Sense Multiple Access with Collision Avoidance (CSMA/CA) access method uses signal avoidance rather than detection. In a networked environment, CSMA/CA is the access mechanism used with the 802.11 wireless standards.

On CSMA/CA networks, each computer signals its intent to transmit data signals before any data is actually sent. When a networked system detects a potential collision, it waits before sending out the transmission enabling systems to avoid transmission collisions. The CSMA/CA access method uses a random backoff time that determines how long to wait before trying to send data on the network. When the backoff time expires, the system will again "listen" to verify a clear channel on which to transmit. If the media is still busy, another backoff interval is initiated that is less than the first. The process continues until the wait time reaches zero, and the media is clear.

CSMA/CA uses a broadcast method to notify its intention to transmit data. Network broadcasts create a considerable amount of network traffic and can cause network congestion, which could slow down the entire network. Because CSMA/CD and CSMA/CA differ only in terms of detection and avoidance, they share similar advantages and disadvantages, as shown previously in Table 6.1.

NOTE: CSMA/CA in Action   The CSMA/CA access method uses a "listen before talking" strategy. Any system wanting to transmit data must first verify that the channel is clear before transmitting, thereby avoiding potential collisions.

Token Passing

Although token passing, defined in the IEEE 802.5 standard, was previously a popular media access method, the domination of Ethernet networking has pushed it far into the background. Although it might not be popular, it is clever.

On a token-passing network, a special data frame called a *token* is passed among the systems on the network. The network has only one token, and a system can send data only when it has possession of the token. When the data arrives, the receiving computer sends a verification message to the sending computer. The sender then creates a new token, and the process begins again. Standards dictate how long a system can have control over the token.

One of the big advantages of the token-passing access method is the lack of collisions. Because a system can transmit only when it has the token, no contention exists. Even under heavy load conditions, the speed of a token-passing system does not degrade in the same way as a contention-based method such as CSMA/CD. In a practical scenario, this makes token passing more suitable than other access methods for applications such as videoconferencing.

However, token passing does have drawbacks. The creation and passing of the token generate overhead on the network, which reduces the maximum speed. In addition, the software and hardware requirements of token-passing network technologies are more complex—and therefore more costly—than those of other media access methods.

Bonding

Ethernet bonding, also referred to as channel bonding, is a strategy used to increase the speed of a communication channel and to add redundancy to the link. Ethernet bonding requires one or two network interfaces installed on the host and combined together to increase throughput. If one of the network interfaces should fail, there is another to continue service.

Bonding is also used with wireless networking such as 802.11n that uses two adjacent Wi-Fi channels simultaneously to double the bandwidth of the wireless link compared to 802.11b/g. The theoretical speeds of 802.11n networks cannot be reached without using a bonding configuration.

Topology

As discussed in Chapter 1, topologies dictate both the physical and logical layouts of the network. Remember that topologies include bus, star, ring, mesh, and wireless. Each of the IEEE LAN standards can be implemented by using the topology specified within the standard. Some standards, such as 802.3 (Ethernet), have multiple physical topologies but always use the same logical topology.

Media

Each IEEE defines what media are available to transport the signal around the network. The term *media*, which is the plural of *medium*, generically describes the methods by which data is transported from one point to another. Common network media types include twisted-pair cable, coaxial cable, infrared, radio frequency, and fiber-optic cable. See Chapter 2, "Media and Connectors," for a detailed discussion of media types.

Differentiating Between Baseband and Broadband Signaling

Two types of signaling methods transmit information over network media: baseband and broadband. Before we get any further into 802.3 standards, we should clarify the difference between the two.

TIP: Baseband and Broadband   Be prepared to identify the characteristics of baseband and broadband for the Network+ exam.

Baseband

Baseband transmissions typically use digital signaling over a single wire; the transmissions themselves take the form of either electrical pulses or light. The digital signal used in baseband transmission occupies the entire bandwidth of the network media to transmit a single data signal. Baseband communication is bidirectional, enabling computers to both send and receive data using a single cable. However, the sending and receiving cannot occur on the same wire at the same time.

NOTE: Ethernet and Baseband   Ethernet networks use baseband transmissions; notice the word "base"—for example, 100BaseT or 100BaseFX.

Using baseband transmissions, it is possible to transmit multiple signals on a single cable by using a process known as Time-Division Multiplexing (TDM), which divides a single channel into time slots. The key thing about TDM is that it doesn't change how baseband transmission works, only the way data is placed on the cable.

Broadband

Whereas baseband uses digital signaling, broadband uses analog signals in the form of optical or electromagnetic waves over multiple transmission frequencies. For signals to be both sent and received, the transmission media must be split into two channels. Alternatively, two cables can be used: one to send and one to receive transmissions.

Multiple channels are created in a broadband system by using a multiplexing technique known as *Frequency-Division Multiplexing (FDM)*, which enables broadband media to accommodate traffic going in different directions on a single media at the same time.

Ethernet Standards

Now that you have learned about the characteristics defined by the IEEE standards, let's examine the standards. Make sure that you are completely familiar with the information provided in each of the following sections before you take the Network+ exam.

TIP: The 802.3Standards   Pay special attention to the 802.3 standards. You can expect a question regarding the characteristics of the various standards on the Network+ exam.

NOTE: 10Base2 Coverage   Even though it is not specifically stated in the CompTIA Network+ objectives, we have included a little coverage on 10Base2 because there is still a chance that you might encounter it in the real world. Also, you never know when CompTIA might choose to include 10Base2 as a wrong answer for a question related to one of the other networking standards discussed in this section. When taking an exam, knowing what something isn't can be as useful as knowing what it is!

10Base2

10Base2, which is defined as part of the IEEE 802.3a standard, specifies data transmission speeds of 10Mbps and a total segment length of 185 meters using RG-58 coaxial cable. The 10Base2 standard specifies a physical bus topology and uses Bayonet Neill Concelman (BNC) connectors with 50-ohm terminators at each end of the cable. One of the physical ends of each segment must be grounded.

NOTE: What Is Base?   When discussing network standards, the word *base*, as in 10Base2, defines that the media can carry only one data signal per wire, or channel, at one time.

10Base2 networks enable a maximum of five segments with only three of those segments populated. Each of the three populated segments can have a maximum of 30 nodes attached. 10Base2 requires a minimum of .5 meters between nodes. For the network to function properly, the segment must be complete. With this in mind, the addition or removal of systems on a 10Base2 network might make the entire network unusable.

NOTE: Cable Break   The coax cable used in 10Base2 networks is prone to cable breaks. A break anywhere in the cable makes the entire network inaccessible.

NOTE: Coaxial and the 5-4-3 Rule   When working with Ethernet networks that use coaxial media, the 5-4-3 rule applies. The rule specifies that the network is limited to a total of five cable segments. These five segments can be connected using no more than four repeaters, and only three segments on the network can be populated.

10BaseT

The 10BaseT LAN standard specifies an Ethernet network that commonly uses unshielded twisted-pair cable; however, in some implementations that require a greater resistance to interference and attenuation, shielded twisted-pair (STP) can be used. STP has extra shielding to combat interference. For more information on the STP and other forms of cabling, refer to Chapter 2.

10BaseT uses baseband transmission and has a maximum physical segment length of 100 meters. As with the coaxial cabling standards, repeaters are sometimes used to extend the maximum segment length, although the repeating capability is now often built in to networking devices used in twisted-pair networks. 10BaseT specifies transmission speeds of 10Mbps and can use several categories of UTP cable, including Categories 3, 4, and 5 (all of which use RJ-45 connectors). 10BaseT takes advantage of the multiple wires inside twisted-pair cable to create independent transmit and receive paths, which means that a full-duplex mode can be optionally supported. The maximum number of computers supported on a 10BaseT network is 1,024.

All 10BaseT networks use a point-to-point network design, with one end of the connection attaching to the network card and the other to a hub or switch. These point-to-point connections result in a physical star topology. See Chapter 3 for information on the devices used in twisted-pair networks.

NOTE: Crossover Cable   You can link two computer systems directly, without the use of a hub by using a specially constructed crossover cable. Crossover cables are also sometimes used to establish other same device connections, such as when connecting two hubs or two switches to create a larger network.

Table 6.2 summarizes the characteristics of the 10BaseT standard.

Table 6.2 Summary of 10BaseT Characteristics

Characteristic	Description
Transmission method	Baseband
Speed	10Mbps
Total distance/segment	100 meters (328 feet)
Cable type	Category 3, 4, or 5 UTP or STP
Connector	RJ-45

Make or Buy?

During your networking career, you will most certainly encounter the debate about whether to crimp your own twisted-pair network cables or buy them. The arguments for making cables always seem to hinge on cost-savings. The arguments against crimping cables are often much more solid. Purchasing cables from a reputable maker ensures that the cables you install will work every time. The same cannot be said of homemade cables. In addition, when you factor in the time it takes to make a cable or troubleshoot a poorly made one, the cost-savings are lessened. However, in some instances you have no choice but to make cables—for example, when specific cable length cables are desired

---

10BaseFL

10BaseFL is an implementation of 10Mbps Ethernet over fiber-optic cabling. 10BaseFL's primary advantage over 10BaseT is that it can be used over distances up to 2 kilometers. However, given the availability of other faster networking standards, such as 100BaseFX (discussed later), you are unlikely to encounter many 10BaseFL implementations.

Fast Ethernet

There was a time when 10Mbps networks were considered fast enough, but those days are long gone. Today, companies and home users alike demand more data throughput than is available with 10Mbps network solutions. For such networks, Fast Ethernet is the most commonly used network design. Fast Ethernet standards are specified in the IEEE 802.3u standard. Three standards are defined by 802.3u: 100BaseTX, 100BaseT4, and 100BaseFX.

NOTE: Fast Ethernet Lingo Fast Ethernet is often referred to as 100BaseX, which also refers collectively to the 100BaseTX, 100BaseT4, and 100BaseFX standards.

100BaseTX

100BaseTX is a Fast Ethernet networking design and is one of three 802.3u standards. As its name suggests, 100BaseTX transmits network data at speeds up to 100Mbps, the speeds at which most LANs operate today. 100BaseTX is most often implemented with UTP cable, but it can use STP; therefore, it suffers from the same 100-meter distance limitations as other UTP-based networks. 100BaseTX uses Category 5, 5e, or 6 UTP cable, and like 10BaseT, it uses independent transmit and receive paths and can therefore support full-duplex operation. 100BaseTX is without question the most common Fast Ethernet standard.

100BaseT4

100BaseT4 is the second Fast Ethernet standard specified under 802.3u. It can use Category 3, 4, 5, 5e, and 6 UTP cable, and it uses all four of the available pairs of wires within the cable, limiting full-duplex transfer. 100BaseT4 is similar in other respects to 100BaseTX: Its cable distance is limited to 100 meters, and its maximum transfer speed is 100Mbps. 100BaseT4 is not widely implemented, but it is sometimes used in environments where cable, such as Category 3 cable, exists.

> **NOTE: Limited Implementation**   100BaseT4 is not a common implementation of Fast Ethernet. As a result, it is not included in the CompTIA objectives for the Network+ exam.
>
> **Repeaters** Fast Ethernet repeaters are sometimes needed when you connect segments that use 100BaseTX, 100BaseT4, or 100BaseFX.

100BaseFX

100BaseFX is the IEEE standard for running Fast Ethernet over fiber-optic cable. Because of the expense of fiber implementations, 100BaseFX is largely limited to use as a network backbone. 100BaseFX can use two-strand multimode fiber or single-mode fiber media. The maximum segment length for half-duplex multimode fiber is 412 meters, but when used in full-duplex mode over multimode fiber, distances can reach 2 kilometers. Using full-duplex single-mode fiber, 100BaseFX can reach distances up to 10,000 meters. 100BaseFX often uses SC or ST fiber connectors.

Fast Ethernet Comparison

Table 6.3 summarizes the characteristics of the 802.3u Fast Ethernet specifications.

Table 6.3   Summary of 802.3u Fast Ethernet Characteristics

Characteristic	100BaseTX	100BaseT4	100BaseFX
Transmission method	Baseband	Baseband	Baseband

Table 6.3   Summary of 802.3u Fast Ethernet Characteristics

Characteristic	100BaseTX	100BaseT4	100BaseFX
Speed	100Mbps	100Mbps	100Mbps
Distance	100 meters	100 meters	412 meters (multimode, half duplex); 2 kilometers (multimode, full duplex); 10,000 meters (single mode, full duplex)
Cable type	UTP, STP	Category 3 or higher	Fiber optic
Connector type	RJ-45	RJ-45	SC, ST

Gigabit Ethernet

Fast Ethernet and the Fast Ethernet standards are still used today. However, in many modern network environments, real-time applications and heavier network use means something faster than Fast Ethernet and 100Mbps networking is required. This has led to the development of Gigabit Ethernet.

Gigabit Ethernet describes the Ethernet implementations that provide the potential for 1000Mbps (1Gbps) bandwidth. Gigabit Ethernet standards are available that define the use of both fiber- and copper-based media. The Gigabit standards include 1000BaseX and 1000BaseT.

1000BaseX

1000BaseX refers collectively to three distinct standards: 1000BaseLX, 1000BaseSX, and 1000BaseCX.

Both 1000BaseSX and 1000BaseLX are laser standards used over fiber. *LX* refers to *long wavelength laser*, and *SX* refers to *short wavelength laser*. Both the SX and LX wave lasers can be supported over two types of multimode fiber-optic cable: fibers of 62.5 micron and 50 micron diameters. Only LX wave lasers support the use of single-mode fiber. Chapter 2 provides information on the difference between the types of fiber-optic cable.

At the end of the day, the differences between 1000BaseLX and the 1000BaseSX have to do with cost and transmission distance. 1000BaseLX can transmit over 316 meters in half duplex for both multimode fiber and single-mode fiber, 550 meters for full-duplex multimode fiber, and 5,000 meters for full-duplex single-mode fiber. Although 1000BaseSX is less expensive than 1000BaseLX, it cannot match the distances achieved by 1000BaseLX.

1000BaseCX moves away from the fiber cable and uses shielded copper wire. Segment lengths in 1000BaseCX are severely restricted; the maximum cable distance is 25 meters. Because of the restricted cable lengths, 1000BaseCX networks are not widely implemented. Table 6.4 summarizes the characteristics of Gigabit Ethernet 802.3z standards.

Table 6.4   Summary of IEEE 802.3z Gigabit Ethernet Characteristics

Characteristic	1000BaseSX	1000BaseLX	1000BaseCX
Transmission method	Baseband	Baseband	Baseband
Transfer rate	1000Mbps	1000Mbps	1000Mbps
Distance	Half-duplex 275 meters (62.5 micron multimode fiber); half-duplex 316 meters (50 micron multimode and single-mode fiber); 275 meters (62.5 micron multimode fiber):full duplex 550 meters (50 micron multimode fiber)	Half-duplex 316 (50 micron multimode and single-mode fiber); full-duplex 550 meters (multimode fiber); 5000 (single-mode fiber)	25 meters for both full-duplex and half-duplex operations
Cable type	62.5/125 and 50/125 multimode fiber	62.5/125 and 50/125 multimode fiber; two 10-micron single-mode optical fibers	Shielded copper cable
Connector type	Fiber connectors	Fiber connectors	9-pin shielded connector

1000BaseT

1000BaseT, sometimes referred to as 1000BaseTX, is another Gigabit Ethernet standard, and it is given the IEEE 802.3ab designation. The 802.3ab standard specifies Gigabit Ethernet over Category 5 UTP cable. The standard enables for full-duplex transmission using the four pairs of twisted cable. To reach data transfer rates of 1000Mbps over copper, a data transmission speed of 250Mbps is achieved using Cat 5e or Cat6 cabling. Table 6.5 summarizes the characteristics of 1000BaseT.

Table 6.5 Summary of 1000BaseT Characteristics

Characteristic	Description
Transmission method	Baseband
Maximum transfer rate	1000Mbps
Total distance/segment	100 meters
Cable type	Category 5 or better
Connector type	RJ-45

10Gigabit Ethernet

In the never-ending quest for faster data transmission rates, network standards are always pushed to the next level. In today's networking environments, that level is 10 Gigabit Ethernet, also referred to as 10GbE. As the name suggests, 10GbE has the capability to provide data transmission rates of up to 10 gigabits per second. That's 10,000Mbps, or 100 times faster than most modern LAN implementations. There are a number of 10GbE implementations; this section explores the 10GBaseSR/SW, 10GBaseLR/LW, 10GBaseER/EW, and 10GBaseT standards highlighted in the Network+ objectives.

Designed primarily as a WAN and MAN connectivity medium, 10GbE was ratified as the IEEE 802.3ae standard in June 2002. Many networking hardware manufacturers now market 10GbE equipment. Although 10GbE network implementations are expensive, companies such as ISPs that require extremely high-speed networks have been relatively quick to implement 10GbE.

10GBaseSR/SW

The IEEE 802.3ae 10 Gigabit Ethernet specification includes a serial interface referred to as 10GBaseS that is designed for transmission on multimode fiber. Two Ethernet standards that fall under the S category include 10GBaseSR and 10GBaseSW. Both SR and SW are designed for deployment over short wavelength multimode fiber. The distance for both classifications ranges from as little as 2 meters to 300 meters. The difference between the two classifications is that SR is designed for use over dark fiber. In the networking world, dark fiber refers to "unlit" fiber, or fiber that is not in use and connected to any other equipment. The 10GBaseSW standard is designed for longer distance data communications and connects to SONET equipment. SONET stands for Synchronous Optical Network. It is a fiber-optic transmission system for high-speed digital traffic. SONET is discussed in Chapter 8, "Wide Area Networking."

TIP: Go the Distance   10GBaseSR/SW is designed for LAN or MAN implementations, with a maximum distance of 300 meters using 50 micron multimode fiber cabling. 10GBaseSR can also be implemented with 62.5 micron multimode fiber cabling but is limited to 33 meters.

10GBaseLR/LW

The 10GBaseLR/LW Ethernet standards offer greater distances by using single-mode fiber rather than multimode fiber. Refer to Chapter 2 for a discussion of the differences between single-mode and multimode fiber.

Both the LR and LW standards are designed to be used over long-wavelength single-mode fiber, giving it a potential transmission range of anywhere from 2 meters to 10 kilometers. This transmission range makes the standards available for LAN, MAN, and WAN deployments. As with the previous standards, the LR standard is used with dark fiber where the LW standard is designed to connect to SONET equipment.

10GBaseER/EW

For wide area networks that require greater transmission distances, the Ethernet 10GBaseER/EW standards come into play. Both the ER and EW Gigabit standards are deployed with extra long wavelength single-mode fiber. This medium provides transmission distances ranging from 2 meters to 40 kilometers. As with the previous two standards, ER is deployed over dark fiber (dark fiber refers to the optical fiber infrastructure currently in place but is not currently used), whereas the EW standard is used primarily with SONET equipment. Table 6.6 outlines the characteristics of the 10GbE standards.

Table 0.0   Summary of 802.3ae Characteristics

Fiber	62.5 Micron MMF	50 Micron MMF	SMF
SR/SW	Up to 33 meters	300 meters	Not used
LR/LW	Not used	Not used	10 kilometers
ER/EW	Not used	Not used	40 kilometers

TIP: IEEE Standards   10 Gigabit Ethernet is defined in the IEEE 802.3ae standard.

NOTE: 10GBASELX4   Providing a common ground between the 802.3ae standards is one known as 10GBaseLX4. It is a hybrid of the other standards and can be used over both single-mode and multimode fiber. In application, the lx4 standard can reach distances ranging from 2 to 300 meters using multimode fiber and anywhere from 2 to 10 kilometers using single-mode fiber.

10GBaseT

The final standard outlined in the Network+ objectives is the 802.3an Ethernet standard, which brings 10-gigabit speed to regular copper cabling. Although transmission distances might not be that of fiber, it enables a potential upgrade from 1000-gigabit networking to 10-gigabit networking using the current wiring infrastructure.

The 10GBaseT standard specifies 10-gigabit transmissions over UTP or STP twisted-pair cables. The standard calls for a cable specification of Category 6 or Category 6a to be used. With Category 6, the maximum transmission range is 55 meters; with the augmented Category 6a cable, transmission range increases to 100 meters. Category 6 and 6a cables are specifically designed to reduce attenuation and crosstalk, making 10-gigabit speeds possible. The 802.3an standard specifies RJ-45 networking connectors. Table 6.7 outlines the characteristics of the 802.3an standard.

Table 6.7   Summary of 802.3an Characteristics

Characteristic	Description
Transmission method	Baseband
Speed	10-gigabit
Total distance/segment	100 meters (328 feet) Category 6a cable
Total distance/segment	55 meters Category 6 cable
Cable type	Category 6, 6a UTP or STP
Connector	RJ-45

Summary

Access methods are the methods by which data is sent onto the network. The most common access methods are CSMA/CD, which uses a collision detection and contention method, CSMA/CA, and token passing.

The IEEE defines several LAN standards, including 802.2 (the LLC layer), 802.3 (Ethernet), 802.5 (token ring), and 802.11 (wireless). Each of these standards identifies specific characteristics, including the network's media, speed, access method, and topology.

This chapter focused on the 802.3 Ethernet networking standards. Several sub-standards fall under the 802.3 banner specifying different characteristics for network deployment. Each of the 802.3 standards use the CSMA/CD access method. Of the Ethernet standards, the 802.3ae and 802.3an offer the greatest speeds. The 802.3ae standard specifies 10-gigabit speeds over fiber cable, whereas 802.3an offers 10-gigabit speeds over copper cabling.

Exam Preparation Tasks

Review all the Key Topics

Review the most important topics in the chapter, noted with the key topics icon in the outer margin of the page. Table 6.8 lists a reference of these key topics and the page numbers on which each is found.

Table 6.8   Key Topics for Chapter 6

Key Topic Element	Description	Page Number
Table 6.1	Advantages and disadvantages of CSMA/CD	225
Table 6.2	Summary of 10BaseT characteristics	230
Table 6.3	Summary of 802.3u Fast Ethernet characteristics	231
Table 6.4	Characteristics of Gigabit Ethernet 802.3z standards	233
Table 6.5	Summary of 1000BaseT	234
List	IEEE 802 standards	221

Complete the Tables and Lists from Memory

Print a copy of Appendix B, "Memory Tables" (found on the CD), or at least the section for this chapter, and complete the tables and lists from memory. Appendix C, "Memory Tables Answer Key," also on the CD, includes completed tables and lists to check your work.

Define Key Terms

Define the following key terms from this chapter, and check your answers in the Glossary.

- Media
- Bandwidth

- Baseband/broadband
- Duplexing
- Ethernet
- 10BaseT
- 100BaseTX
- 100BaseFX
- 1000BaseT
- 1000BaseX
- 10GBaseSR
- 10GBaseLR
- 10GBaseER
- 10GBaseSW
- 10GBaseLW
- 10GBaseEW
- 10GBaseT
- CSMA/CD
- Broadcast
- Collision
- Bonding
- Speed
- Distance

Apply Your Knowledge

Exercise 6.1 Network Recommendations

Understanding the commonly used IEEE 802.3 networking standards is an important part of a network administrator's knowledge. It enables the administrator to understand the current network and plan for future needs. In this exercise you do just that.

You have been called in to make recommendations for an organization called MiPa Incorporated. Recently MiPi has seen huge growth in sales. MiPA currently has a single office but needs to expand to include two more offices around town.

Both branch offices will be about 5 to 10 kilometers away. MiPa currently uses Category 5e cable and wants to continue using its current infrastructure to save cost. MiPa has asked for a detailed table outlining its network options.

Complete the following steps:

Step 1.   Complete the following table to identify potential solutions for MiPA.

Step 2.   Write a simple report to MiPa outlining your recommendations for its future network needs. Explain why you are making the recommendation.

The following table lists some of the common standards, but various pieces of information are missing. Your task is to complete the table. You can check your answers against the information provided in the solution table.

Standard	Speed	Baseband or Broadband	Media	Maximum Distance
	1000Mbps		UTP	100 meters
10Base2			50 micron multimode fiber	300 meters
1000BaseSX			Single-mode fiber	
				40,000 meters
	100Mbps		UTP	100 meters
1000BaseCX				
10GBaseSW				
10GBaseLW				
10GBaseEW				

Exercise 6.1 Solution Table

Standard	Speed	Baseband or Broadband	Media	Maximum Distance
1000BaseT	1000Mbps	Base	UTP	100 meters
10GbaseSR	10Gbps	Base	50 micron multi-mode fiber	300 meters
1000BaseSX	1000Mbps	Base	Single-mode fiber	5,000 meters
1000BaseCX	1000Mbps	Base	STP	25 meters
10GBaseSW	10Gbps	Base	62.5 MMF/50MMF	33Meters (62.5 MMF)/300meters (50 MMF)
10GBaseLW	10Gbps	Base	Single-mode fiber	10+ Kilometers
10GBaseEW	10Gbps	Base	Single-mode fiber	40+ Kilometers
10GbaseER	10Gbps	Base	Single-mode fiber	40,000 meters
100BaseTX	100Mbps	Base	UTP	100 meters

Review Questions

You can find the answers to these questions in Appendix A.

1. Which of the following 10 Gigabit Ethernet standards has the greatest maximum transmission distance?
   a. 10GBaseSR
   b. 10GBaseER
   c. 10GBaseLR
   d. 10GBaseXR

2. What kind of access method is CSMA/CD?
   a. Contention
   b. Demand priority
   c. Collision avoidance
   d. Token passing

3. Which of the following IEEE specifications does CSMA/CD relate to?
   a. 802.2
   b. 802.3
   c. 802.4
   d. 802.5

4. You need to connect two servers located 600 meters apart. You require a direct connection without the use of signal regeneration. Which of the following Ethernet standards would you employ?

   a. 10BaseT with Category 5e cable

   b. 100BaseT with Category 6 cable

   c. 100BaseT with Category 5e cable

   d. 100BaseFX

5. You have been called as a consultant for MiPa. They currently have a network using Category 6 cable and need 10-gigabit network speeds. Which of the following statements are true?

   a. This is not possible with this cable.

   b. This is possible but with transmission distance limited to 100 meters.

   c. This is possible but with transmission distance limited to 55 meters.

   d. This is possible but with transmission distance limited to 155 meters.

6. You have been asked to develop the specifications for a new storage wide area network. The new link will provide a direct connection between two office blocks 3,200 meters apart. The specifications call for the fastest connection possible using currently ratified standards. Which of the following 802.3 standards are you most likely to recommend?

   a. 100BaseFX

   b. 10GBaseER

   c. 10GBaseSR

   d. 10GBaseWR

7. Which of the following standards can be implemented over multimode fiber with a transmission range of 300 meters?

   a. 10GBaseSW

   b. 10GBaseEW

   c. 10GBaseLW

   d. 10GBaseRW

8. Which of the following Ethernet standards is associated with 802.3an?

   a. 10BaseT

   b. 1000BaseTX

   c. 1000BaseT

   d. 10GBaseT

9. As a network administrator, you have been asked to recommend a networking standard that can support data transfers of up to 100Mbps using the existing Category 3 cable and the CSMA/CD access method. Which of the following best suits your needs?

   a. 100BaseTX

   b. 100BaseFX

   c. 100BaseVG-AnyLAN

   d. 100BaseT4

10. Which of the following standards are specified by 802.3u? (Select all that apply.)

   a. 10GBaseT

   b. 100BaseFX

   c. 100BaseTX

   d. 100BaseT4

11. Which of the following are associated with IEEE 802.3z? (Choose the three best answers.)

   a. 1000BaseLX

   b. 1000BaseCX

   c. 10GBaseSR

   d. 1000BaseSX

12. Which of the following media types offers the greatest distance?

   a. 10GBaseT

   b. 1000BaseCX

   c. 1000BaseT

   d. 10GBaseLW

13. What is the maximum transfer distance defined by the 1000BaseT standard?

   a. 250 meters

   b. 100 meters

   c. 1,000 meters

   d. 550 meters

14. Which of the following is an advantage of 100BaseFX over 100BaseTX?

   a. 100BaseFX is faster than 100BaseTX.

   b. 100BaseFX implementations are cheaper than 100BaseTX implementations.

   c. 100BaseFX can be implemented over existing Category 3 or 4 UTP cabling.

   d. 100BaseFX can be implemented over greater distances than 100BaseTX.

15. Which of the following standards can be implemented over copper cable? (Select two.)

   a. 1000BaseCX

   b. 1000BaseSW

   c. 10GBaseT

   d. 10GBaseLW

16. Which of the following is true of the 802.3ab standard?

   a. Specifies 1-gigabit transfer over Category 5 cable

   b. Specifies 100-megabit transfer over Category 5 cable

   c. Specifies 1-gigabit transfer over Category 4 cable

   d. Specifies 200-megabit transfer over Category 4 cable

17. You are a network administrator for a large company. Transfer speeds have been too slow, and you have been asked to recommend a 1000Mbps network solution. The network requires a transfer distance of 3,500 meters. Which of the following would you recommend?

    a. 1000BaseCX

    b. 1000BaseLX

    c. 10GBaseT

    d. 1000BaseSX

18. Which fiber-optic mode enables the fastest transfer rates?

    a. SC

    b. ST

    c. Single mode

    d. Multimode

19. You have been asked to recommend a network solution to a large organization. They are requesting a network solution that must enable for 10-gigabit speeds but uses the existing Category 6 infrastructure. Which of the following might you recommend?

    a. 802.3ae

    b. 10GBaseCX

    c. 802.3an

    d. 1000BaseLX

20. Baseband sends transmissions in which of the following forms?

    a. Digital

    b. Analog

    c. Digital and analog

    d. RF

This chapter covers CompTIA Network+ objectives 1.7 and 3.4. Upon completion of this chapter, you will be able to answer the following questions:

- What are the components that create wireless networks?
- What are the characteristics of 802.11 wireless standards?
- How is spread spectrum technology used in wireless networking?
- What is the function of the beacon management frame?
- What are the factors that cause wireless interference?
- How can wireless networks be secured?

CHAPTER 7

Wireless Networking

One of the bigger changes in the networking world since the release of the previous Network+ exam is in wireless networking. Networks of all shapes and sizes incorporate wireless segments. Home wireless networking has also grown significantly in the past few years.

As you know, wireless networking enables users to connect to a network using radio waves instead of wires. Network users within range of a wireless transceiver (transmitter/receiver), known as an access point (AP), can move around an office freely without needing to plug in to a wired infrastructure. The benefits of wireless networking clearly have led to its growth.

Today, wireless local area networks (WLAN) provide a flexible and secure data communications system used to augment an Ethernet LAN or in some cases to replace it altogether. This chapter explores the many facets of wireless networking starting with some of the devices and technologies that make wireless networking possible.

Foundation Topics

Understanding Wireless Devices

In a common wireless implementation, an AP connects to the wired network from a fixed location using standard cabling. The wireless AP receives and then transmits data between the wireless LAN and the wired network infrastructure.

Client systems communicate with a wireless AP using wireless LAN adapters. Such adapters are built in to, or added to, devices such as PC cards in laptops, PDAs, or desktop computers. Wireless LAN adapters provide the communication point between the client system and the airwaves via an antenna.

This section describes the role of APs and antennas in a wireless network.

Wireless Access Point

Wireless APs are both a transmitter and receiver (transceiver) device used for wireless LAN (WLAN) radio signals. An AP is typically a separate network device with a built-in antenna, transmitter, and adapter. APs use the wireless infrastructure network mode to provide a connection point between WLANs and a wired Ethernet LAN. Recall from Chapter 1, "Introduction to Computer Networking," that wireless networks use the ad-hoc network topology and the infrastructure topology. The ad hoc is a peer-to-peer network design, and the infrastructure topology uses an AP. APs also typically have several ports enabling a way to expand the network to support additional clients.

Depending on the size of the network, one or more APs might be required. Additional APs enable access to more wireless clients and expand the range of the wireless network. Each AP is limited by a *transmissions range*, which is the distance a client can be from an AP and still get a useable signal. The actual distance depends on the wireless standard used and the obstructions and environmental conditions between the client and the AP. Factors affecting wireless transmission ranges are covered later in this chapter. Figure 7.1 shows an example of an AP in a network configuration.

NOTE: Wireless Access Points   An AP can also operate as a bridge connecting a standard wired network to wireless devices or as a router passing data transmissions from one access point to another.

TIP: AP Range   If you use a wireless device that loses its connection, you might be too far away from the AP.

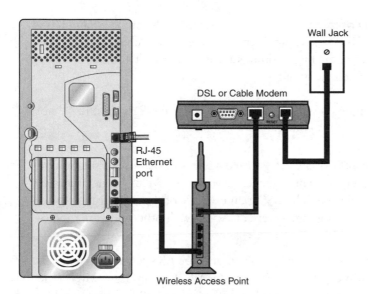

Figure 7.1   APs connect WLANs and a wired Ethernet LAN.

As mentioned, an AP is used in an infrastructure wireless network design. Used in the infrastructure mode, the AP receives transmissions from wireless devices within a specific range and transmits those signals to the network beyond. This network can be a private Ethernet network or the Internet. In infrastructure wireless networking, there can be multiple access points to cover a large area or only a single access point for a small area, such as a single home or small building.

NOTE: An AP for All Seasons   Because wireless networks are sometimes deployed in environments other than inside a warm, dry building, some manufacturers offer rugged versions of APs. These devices are sealed against the elements, making them suitable for placement in locations where nonrugged devices would not survive. If you implement a wireless network, consider whether using these rugged devices are warranted.

When working with wireless APs, you need to understand many terms and acronyms. In this section we define some of the more common wireless acronyms you will see both on the exam and in any wireless networking documentation.

■ **Service Set Identifier (SSID)**—A network name needed to connect to a wireless AP. It is like a workgroup name used with Windows networking. 802.11 wireless networks use the SSID to identify all systems belonging to the same network. Client stations must be configured with the SSID to be authenticated to the AP. The AP might broadcast the SSID, enabling all wireless clients in the area to see the SSID of the AP. For security reasons, APs can be configured to not broadcast the SSID or to cloak them. This means that client systems need to be given the SSID name by an administrator instead of it automatically being discovered by the client system.

NOTE: SSIDs One element of wireless security involves configuring the AP not to broadcast the SSID name. This configuration is done on the AP.

- **Basic Service Set (BSS)**—Refers to a wireless network that uses a single AP and one or more wireless clients connecting to the AP. Many home offices are an example of a BSS design. The BSS is an example of the infrastructure wireless topology. Wireless topologies were discussed with other network topologies in Chapter 1.

- **Extended Service Set (ESS)**—Refers to two or more BSS sets connected, therefore using multiple APs. The ESS creates WLANs or larger wireless networks and is a collection of APs and clients. Connecting BSS systems enable clients to roam between areas and maintain the wireless connection without having to reconfigure between BSSs.

- **Extended Service Set Identifier (ESSID)**—The ESSID and the SSID are used interchangeably, but there is a difference between the two. The SSID is the name used with BSS networks, and the ESSID is the network name used with an ESS wireless network design. With an ESS, not all APs necessarily use the same name.

- **Basic Service Set Identifier (BSSID)**—Refers to the MAC address of the BSS AP. The BSSID is not to be confused with the SSID, which is the name of the wireless network.

- **Basic Service Area (BSA)**—When troubleshooting or designing wireless networks, the BSA is an important consideration. The BSA refers to the coverage area of the AP. The BSA for an AP depends on many factors, including the strength of the AP antenna, interference in the area, and whether an omnidirectional or directional antenna is used.

TIP: Know the Acronyms Several of the acronyms provided in the preceding bulleted list are sure to be on the Network+ exam. Be sure you can identify the function of each before writing the exam.

Wireless Antennas

A *wireless* antenna is an integral part of overall wireless communication. Antennas come in many shapes and sizes, with each one designed for a specific purpose. Selecting the right antenna for a particular network implementation is a critical consideration and one that could ultimately decide how successful a wireless network will be. In addition, using the right antennas can save money on networking costs because you need fewer antennas and access points.

Many small home network adapters and access points come with a nonupgradeable antenna, but higher-grade wireless devices require that you decide which antenna to use. Selecting an antenna takes careful planning and requires an understanding of what range and speed you need for a network. The antenna is designed to help wireless networks do the following:

- Work around obstacles

- Minimize the effects of interference

- Increase signal strength

- Focus the transmission, which can increase signal speed

The following sections explore some of the characteristics of wireless antennas.

Antenna Ratings

When a wireless signal is low and influenced by heavy interference, it might be possible to upgrade the antennas to create a more solid wireless connection. To determine the strength of an antenna, we refer to its *gain value*. But how do we determine the gain value?

Consider a huge wireless tower emanating circular waves in all directions. If you could see these waves, you would see the data waves forming a sphere around the tower. The signals around the antenna flow equally in all directions (including up and down). An antenna that does this has a 0dbi gain value and is referred to as an *isotropic antenna*. The isotropic antenna rating provides a base point for measuring actual antenna strength.

An antenna's gain value represents the difference between the 0dBi isotropic and the power of the antenna. For example, a wireless antenna advertised as a 15dBi antenna is 15 times stronger than the hypothetical isotropic antenna. The higher the decibel figure, the higher the gain.

NOTE: dBi   The *dB* in the designation stands for *decibels*, and the *i* references the hypothetical isotropic antenna.

When looking at wireless antennas, remember that a higher gain value means stronger send and receive signals. In terms of performance, the general rule is that every 3dB of gain added doubles the effective power output of an antenna.

Types of Wireless Antennas

When selecting an antenna for a particular wireless implementation, you must determine the type of coverage used by an antenna. In a typical configuration, a wireless antenna can be either *omnidirectional* or *directional*. The choice between the two depends on the wireless environment.

An omnidirectional antenna is designed to provide a 360-degree dispersed wave pattern. This type of antenna is used when coverage in all directions from the antenna is required. Omnidirectional antennas are good to use when a broad-based signal is required. For example, by providing an even signal in all directions, clients can access the antenna and associated access point from various locations. Because of the dispersed nature of omnidirectional antennas, the signal is weaker overall and therefore accommodates shorter signal distances. Omnidirectional antennas are great in an environment in which there is a clear line of sight between the senders and receivers. The power is evenly spread to all points, making omnidirectional antennas well suited for home and small office applications.

Directional antennas are designed to focus the signal in a particular direction. This focused signal enables for greater distances and a stronger signal between two points. The greater distances enabled by directional antennas allow a viable alternative for connecting locations, such as two offices, in a point-to-point configuration.

Directional antennas are also used when you need to tunnel or thread a signal through a series of obstacles. This concentrates the signal power in a specific direction and enables you to use less power for a greater distance than an omnidirectional antenna. Figure 7.2 shows an example of a directional and an omnidirectional antenna beam.

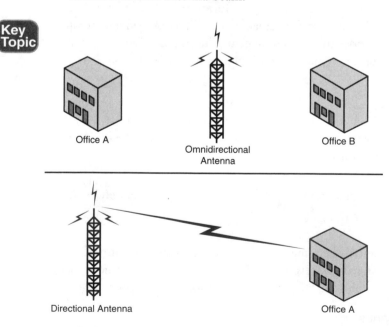

Figure 7.2   Directional antenna signal.

NOTE: Polarization   In the wireless world, *polarization* refers to the direction that the antenna radiates wavelengths. This direction can either be vertical, horizontal, or circular. Today, vertical antennas are perhaps the most common. As far as configuration is concerned, both the sending and receiving antennas should be set to the same polarization.

Data Rate Versus Throughput

When talking about wireless transmissions, it is important to distinguish between *throughput* and *data rate*. From time to time these terms are used interchangeably, but technically speaking, they are different. As shown later in this chapter, each wireless standard has an associated data rate. For instance, the 802.11g wireless standard lists a data rate of up to 54Mbps. This represents the potential maximum data rate at which devices using this standard can send and receive data. However, in network data transmissions, many factors prevent the data rate from reaching this end-to-end theoretical maximum. For instance, data packets include overhead such as routing information, checksums, and error recovery data. Although this might all be necessary, it can impact overall data rate.

The number of clients on the network can also impact the data rate; the more clients, the more collisions. Depending on the network layout, collisions can have a significant impact on end-to-end transmission. Wireless network signals degrade as they pass through obstructions such as walls or doors; the signal speed deteriorates with each obstruction.

All these factors leave us with the actual throughput of wireless data transmissions. Throughput represents the actual transfer rate to expect from wireless transmissions. In practical application, wireless transmissions will be approximately one-half or less of the listed data rate. This means that we could hope for about 20–25Mbps for 802.11g and not the listed rate of 54Mbps. Depending on the wireless setup, the transmission rate could be much less.

802.11 Wireless Standards

802.11 represents the IEEE designation for wireless networking. Several wireless networking specifications exist under the 802.11 banner. The Network+ objectives focus on 802.11, 802.11a, 802.11b, 802.11g, and 802.11n. All these standards use the Ethernet protocol and the CSMA/CA access method.

NOTE: CSMA/CA   CSMA/CA defines a media access method for wireless networking. CSMA/CA was discussed in Chapter 6, "Ethernet Networking Standards."

The 802.11 wireless standards can differ in terms of speed, transmission ranges, and frequency used but are similar in terms of actual implementation. All standards can use either an infrastructure or ad-hoc network design, and each can use the same security protocols. The ad-hoc and infrastructure wireless topologies were discussed in Chapter 1.

The IEEE 802.11 standards include

- **IEEE 802.11**—There were two variations on the initial 802.11 wireless standard. Both offered 1 or 2Mbps transmission speeds and the same radio frequency (RF) of 2.4GHz. The difference between the two was in the way in which data traveled through the RF media. One used frequency hopping spread spectrum (FHSS), and the other used direct sequence spread spectrum (DSSS). These technologies are discussed in the next section. The original 802.11 standards are far too slow for modern networking needs and are now no longer deployed.

- **IEEE 802.11a**—In terms of data rate, the 802.11a standard was far ahead of the original 802.11 standards. 802.11a specifies data rates of up to 54Mbps, but communications typically take place at 6Mbps, 12Mbps, or 24Mbps. 802.11a is not compatible with other wireless standards 802.11b and 802.11g.

- **IEEE 802.11b**—The 802.11b standard provides for a maximum transmission data rate of 11Mbps. However, devices were designed to be backward compatible with previous standards that provided for speeds of 1, 2, and 5.5Mbps. 802.11b offers a transmission range of up to 100ft with 11Mbps data rate and 300ft operating a 1Mbps data rate. 802.11b uses a 2.4GHz RF range and is compatible with 802.11g.

- **IEEE 802.11g**—802.11g is a popular wireless standard today. On average, 802.11g offers wireless transmission over distances of 150 feet and a data rate of 54Mbps compared with the 11Mbps of the 802.11b standard. Like 802.11b, 802.11g operates in the 2.4GHz range and is therefore compatible with it.

- **IEEE 802.11n**—The newest of the wireless standards listed in the Network+ objectives is 802.11n. The goal of the 802.11n standard is to significantly increase throughput in both the 2.4 GHz and the 5 GHz frequency range. The baseline goal of the standard is to reach speeds of 100 Mbps but given the right conditions, it is estimated that the 802.11n data rates might reach a staggering 600 Mbps. In practical operation, 802.11n speeds will be much less.

Table 7.1 highlights the characteristics of the various 802.11 wireless standards.

Table 7.1   802.11 Wireless Standards

IEEE Standard	Frequency/ Media	Speed	Topology	Transmission Range	Access Method
802.11	2.4GHz RF	1 to 2Mbps	Ad hoc/ infrastructure	20 feet indoors.	CSMA/CA
802.11a	5GHz	Up to 54Mbps	Ad hoc/ infrastructure	25 to 75 feet indoors; range can be affected by building materials.	CSMA/CA
802.11b	2.4GHz	Up to 11Mbps	Ad hoc/ infrastructure	Up to 150 feet indoors; range can be affected by building materials.	CSMA/CA
802.11g	2.4GHz	Up to 54Mbps	Ad hoc/ infrastructure	Up to 150 feet indoors; range can be affected by building materials.	CSMA/CA
802.11n	2.4GHz/5GHz	Up to 600Mbps	Ad hoc/ infrastructure	175+ feet indoors; range can be affected by building materials.	CSMA/CA

Want More Wireless?

Wireless developments continue at a rapid pace. Though not specifically outlined in the objectives, IEEE 802.15 and IEEE 802.16 are other wireless standards worth mentioning. 802.15 is a wireless standard specifying characteristics for wireless personal area networks (WPAN). The original 802.15 version specified technologies for WPANs such as those using the Bluetooth standard. Bluetooth is often used to provide wireless links between portable digital devices, including notebook computers, peripherals, cellular telephones, beepers, and consumer electronic devices. 802.16 specifies standards for broadband wireless communications using metropolitan area networks (MAN). The original 802.16 standard identified a fixed point-to-multipoint broadband wireless system operating in the 10–66GHz licensed spectrum. The 802.16a specified non-line-of-sight extensions in the 2–11GHz spectrum, delivering up to 70Mbps at distances up to 31 miles. Known as the *WirelessMAN specification*, 802.16 standards with faster speeds can accommodate bandwidth demanding applications. Further, the increased range of up to 30 miles provides a true end-to-end solution.

802.16 standards are in a position to take wireless to the next level. Imagine using high-speed wireless links to establish a connection backbone between geographically separate locations. This could replace cumbersome and expensive solutions used today such as T1 or T3 links. Another version of 802.16, 802.16e is expected to enable connections for mobile devices.

The Magic Behind 802.11n

Following on the heels of 802.11g is the 802.11n standard. It is significantly faster and travels greater distances than its predecessor. But how is this done? 802.11n takes the best from the 802.11 standards and mixes in some new features to take wireless to the next level. First among these new technologies is multiple input multiple output (MIMO).

MIMO is unquestionably the biggest development for 802.11n and the key to the new speeds. Essentially, MIMO uses multiplexing to increase range and speed of wireless networking. Multiplexing is a technique that combines multiple signals for transmission over a single line or media. MIMO enables the transmission of multiple data streams traveling on different antennas in the same channel at the same time. A receiver reconstructs the streams that have multiple antennas as well. By using multiple paths, MIMO provides a significant capacity gain over conventional single antenna systems, along with more reliable communication.

In addition to all these improvements, 802.11n enables channel bonding that will essentially double the data rate again. The 802.11b and 802.11g wireless standards use a single channel to send and receive information. With channel bonding, it is possible to use two channels at the same time. As you might guess, the capability to use two channels at once increases performance. It is expected that bonding can help increase wireless transmission rates from the 54Mbps offered with the 802.11g standards to a theoretical maximum of 600Mbps.

> **NOTE: Channel Surfing**   In wireless networking a single channel is 20MHz in width. When two channels are bonded they are a total of 40MHz. 802.11n systems can use either the 20MHz channels or the 40MHz channel.

Wireless Radio Channels

Radio frequency (RF) channels are important parts of wireless communications. A *channel* is the band of RF used for the wireless communication. Each IEEE wireless standard specifies the channels that can be used. The 802.11a standard specifies radio frequency ranges between 5.15 and 5.875GHz. In contrast, 802.11b and 802.11g standards operate between the 2.4 to 2.4835GHz range.

> **NOTE: That Hertz**   Hertz (Hz) is the standard of measurement for radio frequency. Hertz is used to measure the frequency of vibrations and waves, such as sound waves and electromagnetic waves. One hertz is equal to one cycle per second (1Hz). Radio frequency is measured in kilohertz (one thousand cycles per second), megahertz (one million cycles per second), or gigahertz (one billion cycles per second).

As far as channels are concerned, 802.11a has a wider frequency band, enabling more channels and therefore more data throughput. As a result of the wider band,

802.11a supports up to eight nonoverlapping channels. 802.11b/g standards use the smaller band and support only up to three nonoverlapping channels.

It is recommended that the nonoverlapping channels be used for communication. In the United States, 802.11b/g use 11 channels for data communication; three of these—channels 1, 6, and 11—are nonoverlapping channels. Most manufacturers set their default channel to one of the nonoverlapping channels to avoid transmission conflicts. With wireless devices, you have the option of selecting which channel your WLAN operates on to avoid interference from other wireless devices that operate in the 2.4GHz frequency range.

When troubleshooting a wireless network, be aware that overlapping channels can disrupt the wireless communications. For example, in many environments, APs are inadvertently placed close together—perhaps two access points in separate offices located next door to each other or between floors. Signal disruption can result if channel overlap exists between the access points. The solution is to try to move the access point to avoid the problem with the overlap, or change channels to one of the other nonoverlapping channels—for example, switch from channel 6 to channel 11.

You would typically change the channel of a wireless device only if a channel overlap occurs with another device. If a channel must be changed, it must be changed to another nonoverlapping channel.

NOTE: Troubleshooting Utilities   When troubleshooting a wireless problem in Windows, you can use the `ipconfig` command to see the status of IP configuration. Similarly, you can use the `ifconfig` command in Linux. In addition, Linux users can use the `iwconfig` command to view the state of your wireless network adapter. Using `iwconfig`, you can view such important information as the link quality, AP MAC address, data rate, and encryption keys, which can be helpful in ensuring that the parameters within the network are consistent.

TIP: Channel Separation   IEEE 802.11g/b wireless systems communicate with each other using radio frequency signals in the band between 2.4GHz and 2.5GHz. Neighboring channels are 5MHz apart. Applying two channels that enable the maximum channel separation can decrease the amount of channel cross talk and provide a noticeable performance increase over networks with minimal channel separation.

Table 7.2 outlines the available wireless channels. When deploying a wireless network, it is recommended that you use channel 1, grow to use channel 6, and add channel 11 when necessary, because these three channels do not overlap.

Table 7.2   RF Channels for 802.11b/g

Channel	Frequency Band
1	2412MHz
2	2417MHz
3	2422MHz
4	2427MHz
5	2432MHz
6	2437MHz
7	2442MHz
8	2447MHz
9	2452MHz
10	2457MHz
11	2462MHz

NOTE: Why Do They Overlap?   When looking at Table 7.2, remember that the RF channels listed (2412 for channel 1, 2417 for 2, and so on) are actually the center frequency that the transceiver within the radio and access point uses. There is only 5MHz separation between the center frequencies, and an 802.11b signal occupies approximately 30MHz of the frequency spectrum. As a result, data signals fall within about 15MHz of each side of the center frequency and overlap with several adjacent channel frequencies. This leaves you with only three channels (channels 1, 6, and 11 for the United States) that you can use without causing interference between access points.

Table 7.3 shows the channel ranges for 802.11a; 802.11n has the option of using both channels used by 802.11a and b/g.

Table 7.3   RF Channels for 802.11a

Channel	Frequency Band
36	5180MHz
40	5200MHz
44	5220MHz
48	5240MHz
52	5260MHz
56	5280MHz

60	5300MHz
64	5320MHz

NOTE: War Driving   The advent of wireless networking has led to a new phenomenon: *war driving*. Armed with a laptop with an 802.11 capable wireless NIC, it is possible to drive around metropolitan areas seeking out wireless networks. When one is found, users can attempt to gain access to the network over the wireless connection. Such practices are illegal, although little can be done to prevent them other than using the built-in security features of 802.11. The problem is, not many installations use these features. If you are responsible for a network that has a wireless element, be sure to implement all the security features available. Not doing so is tantamount to allowing anyone into your building and letting him use one of your PCs to access the server.

Spread Spectrum Technology

Spread spectrum refers to the manner in which data signals travel through a radio frequency. With spread spectrum, data does not travel straight through a single RF band; this type of transmission is known as *narrowband transmission*. Spread spectrum requires that data signals either alternate between carrier frequencies or constantly change their data pattern. Although the shortest distance between two points is a straight line (narrowband), spread spectrum is designed to trade off bandwidth efficiency for reliability, integrity, and security. Spread spectrum signal strategies use more bandwidth than in the case of narrowband transmission, but the trade-off is a data signal that is clearer and easier to detect. This chapter reviews three types of spread spectrum technologies: frequency hopping, direct sequence, and Orthogonal Frequency Division Multiplexing (OFDM).

Frequency-Hopping Spread Spectrum (FHSS) Technology

Frequency-Hopping Spread Spectrum (FHSS) requires the use of narrowband signals that change frequencies in a predictable pattern. The term *frequency hopping* refers to hopping of data signals between narrow channels. For example, consider the 2.4GHz frequency band used by 802.11b. This range is divided into 70 narrow channels of 1MHz each. Somewhere between 20 and several hundred milliseconds, the signal hops to a new channel following a predetermined cyclical pattern.

Because data signals using FHSS switch between RF bands, they have a strong resistance to interference and environmental factors. The FHSS signal strategy makes it well suited for installations designed to cover a large geographical area and where the use of directional antennas to minimize the influence of environmental factors is not possible.

FHSS is not the preferred spread spectrum technology for today's wireless standards. However, FHSS is used for some lesser-used standards and for cellular deployments for fixed Broadband Wireless Access (BWA), where the use of DSSS is virtually impossible because of its limitations.

Direct-Sequence Spread Spectrum (DSSS) Technology

With Direct-Sequence Spread Spectrum (DSSS) transmissions, the signal is spread over a full transmission frequency spectrum. For every bit of data sent, a redundant bit pattern is also sent. This 32-bit pattern is called a *chip*. These redundant bits of data provide for both security and delivery assurance. Transmissions are safe and reliable because the system sends so many redundant copies of the data, and only a single copy is required to have complete transmission of the data or information. DSSS can minimize the effects of interference and background noise.

As for a comparison between the two, DSSS has the advantage of providing higher security and signal delivery than FHSS, but it is a sensitive technology, affected by many environmental factors.

Orthogonal Frequency Division Multiplexing

Orthogonal Frequency Division Multiplexing (OFDM) is a transmission technique that transfers large amounts of data over 52 separate, evenly spaced frequencies. OFDM splits the radio signal into these separate frequencies and simultaneously transmits them to the receiver. By splitting the signal and transferring over different frequencies, the amount of cross talk interference is reduced. OFDM is associated with 802.11a, 802.11g amendments, and 802.11n wireless standards.

FHSS, DSSS, OFDM, and 802.11 Standards

The original 802.11 standard had two variations, both offering the same speeds but differing in the RF spread spectrum used. One of the original 802.11 standards used FHSS. This 802.11 variant used the 2.4GHz radio frequency band and operated with a 1 or 2Mbps data rate. Since this original standard, wireless implementations have favored DSSS.

The second 802.11 variation uses DSSS and specifies a 2Mbps peak data rate with optional fallback to 1Mbps in noisy environments. 802.11, 802.11b, and 802.11g use the DSSS spread spectrum. This means that the underlying modulation scheme is similar between each standard, enabling all DSSS systems to coexist with 2, 11, and 54Mbps 802.11 standards. As a comparison, it is like the migration from the older 10Mbps Ethernet networking to the more commonly implemented 100Mbps standard. The speed was different, but the underlying technologies were similar, enabling for an easier upgrade.

Table 7.4 provides a comparison of wireless standards and spread spectrum used.

Table 7.4 Comparison of IEEE 802.11 Standards

IEEE Standard	RF Used	Spread Spectrum	Data Rate (Mbps)
802.11	2.4GHz	FHSS	1/2
802.11	2.4GHz	DSSS	1/2
802.11a	5GHz	OFDM	54
802.11b	2.4GHz	DSSS	11
802.11g	2.4GHz	DSSS	54
802.11n	2.4/5GHz	OFDM	600 (theoretical)

Beacon Management Frame

Within wireless networking is a frame type known as the beacon management frame (beacon). Beacons are an important part of the wireless network because it is their job to advertise the presence of the access point so systems can locate it. Wireless clients automatically detect the beacons and attempt to establish a wireless connection to the AP.

The beacon frame is sent out by the AP in an infrastructure network design. Client stations will send out beacons only if connected in an ad-hoc network design. There are several parts of the beacon frame, all of which are used by the client system to learn about the AP before attempting to join the network. This information includes the following:

- **Channel information**—The channel used by the AP.

- **Supported data rates**—The data transfer rates identified by the AP configuration.

- **SSID**—The name of the wireless network name.

- **Time stamp**—Synchronization information. The time stamp is used by the client system to synchronize its clock with the AP.

These beacons are transmitted from the AP about every 10 seconds. The beacon frames add overhead to the network; therefore, some APs enable you to reduce the amount of beacons sent. With home networks, constant beacon information is not necessary.

Before a client system can attempt to connect to an AP, it must first locate it. There are two methods for AP discovery: passive and active. In passive detection, the client system listens for the beacon frames to discover the AP. After it is detected, the beacon frame provides the information necessary for the system to access the AP.

With active scanning, the client station transmits another type of management frame known as a *probe request*. The probe request goes out from the client system looking for a specific SSID or any SSID within its area. After the probe request is sent, all APs in the area with the same SSID reply with another frame, the *probe response*. The information contained in the probe response is the same information included with the beacon frame. This information enables the client to access the system.

> **TIP: Beacon**   Be prepared to identify the role of wireless beacons on the Network+ exam.

Configuring and Troubleshooting the Wireless Connection

Now that we have reviewed key wireless settings, let's take a look at an actual wireless connection configuration. Figure 7.3 shows the configuration screen of a wireless access point.

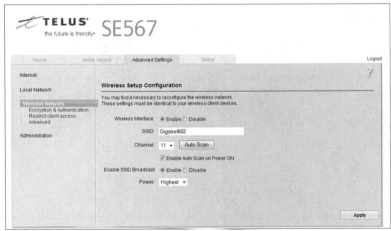

Figure 7.3   Wireless configuration information.

As you can see from the screen capture, the settings for this wireless router are clearly laid out. For instance, you can see that the wireless connection uses an SSID password of Gigaset602 and wireless channel 11. Each wireless access point might differ in the layout but all have similar configuration options.

The configuration screen on a wireless AP enables you to adjust many settings for troubleshooting or security reasons. This section identifies some of the common settings and terms used on an AP.

- **SSID**—This configuration uses an SSID of Gigaset602. The SSID can be changed in a large network to help identify its location or network segment. For troubleshooting, if a client cannot access a base station, make sure that they are both using the same SSID. Incompatible SSIDs are sometimes found when clients move computers, such as laptops, between different wireless networks. They obtain an SSID from one network, and, if the system is not rebooted, the old SSID won't enable communication to a different base station.

- **Channel**—This connection is set to use channel 11. To access this network, all systems must use this channel. If needed, the channel can be changed using the drop-down menu. The menu lists channels 1 through 11.

- **SSID broadcast**—In their default configuration, wireless access points typically broadcast the SSID name into the air at regular intervals. This feature of SSID broadcast is intended to enable clients to easily discover the network and roaming between WLANs. The problem with SSID broadcasting is that it makes it a little easier to get around security. SSIDs are not encrypted or protected in any way. Anyone can snoop and get a look at the SSID and attempt to join the network.

- **Authentication**—Typically, you can set three options for the authentication to be used:
  - **WEP-open**—The simplest of the three authentications methods because it does not perform any type of client verification. It is a weak form of authentication because there is no proof of identity.
  - **WEP-shared**—Requires that a WEP key be configured on both the client system and the access point. This makes authentication with WEP-shared mandatory and therefore more secure for wireless transmission.
  - **WPA-PSK**—Wi-Fi Protected Access with Pre-Shared Key (WPA-PSK) is a stronger form of encryption in which keys are automatically changed and authenticated between devices after a specified period of time or after a specified number of packets has been transmitted.

- **Wireless Mode**—To access the network, the client must use the same wireless mode as the AP. Today most users configure the network for 802.11g/n for the faster speeds or a combination of 802.11b/g/n because they are compatible.

- **DTIM Period**—Wireless transmissions can broadcast to all systems; that is, they can send messages to all clients on the wireless network. Multiple broadcast messages are known as multicast or broadcast traffic. Delivery traffic indication message (DTIM) is a feature used to ensure that when the multicast or broadcast traffic is sent, all systems are awake to hear the message. The DTIM setting specifies how often the DTIM message is sent within the beacon frame. The DTIM setting by default is 1. This means that the DTIM message will be sent with every beacon. If the DTIM is set to 3, every third beacon will include a wake up call.

- **Maximum Connection Rate**—The transfer rate is typically set to Auto by default. This enables the maximum connection speed. However, it is possible to drop the speed down to increase the distance that the signal travels and boost signal strength due to poor environmental conditions.

- **Network Type**—This is where the network can be set to use the ad-hoc or infrastructure network design.

> **TIP:** **AP Settings**   For the Network+ exam, ensure you can identify the various settings used to establish connection between a client and an AP.

Configuring Communications Between Wireless Devices

To work with wireless networks, it is important to have a basic understanding of the communication that occurs between wireless devices. If using an infrastructure wireless network design, there are two key parts to the network: the wireless client, also known as the station (STA), and the AP. The AP acts as a bridge between the STA and the wired network.

As with other forms of network communication, before transmissions between devices can occur, the wireless AP and the client must first begin to talk to each other. In the wireless world, this is a two-step process involving *association* and *authentication*.

The association process occurs when a wireless adapter is first turned on. The client adapter immediately begins to scan across the wireless frequencies for wireless APs, or if using ad-hoc mode, other wireless devices. When the wireless client is configured to operate in infrastructure mode, the user can choose a wireless AP to connect with. This process might also be automatic with the AP selection based on the SSID, signal strength, and frame error rate. Finally, the wireless adapter switches to the assigned channel of the selected wireless AP and negotiates the use of a port.

If at any point, the signal between the devices drops below an acceptable level, or if the signal becomes unavailable for any reason, the wireless adapter initiates another scan looking for an AP with stronger signals. When the new AP is located, the wireless adapter selects the new AP and associates with it. This is known as *reassociation*.

> **NOTE:** **Roaming Around**   The 802.11 standards enable a wireless client to roam between multiple APs. An AP transmits a beacon signal every so many milliseconds and includes a time stamp for client synchronization and an indication of supported data rates. A client system uses the beacon message to identify the

strength of the existing connection to an AP. If the connection is too weak, the roaming client attempts to associate itself with a new AP. This enables the client system to roam between distances and APs.

With the association process complete, the authentication process begins. After the devices associate, keyed security measures are applied before communication can take place. On many APs, authentication can be set to either *authentication*. The default setting is typically open authentication, which enables access with only the SSID and the correct WEP key for the AP. The problem with open authentication is that if you don't have other protection or authentication mechanisms in place, your wireless network is totally open to intruders. When set to shared-key mode, the client must meet security requirements before communication with the AP can occur.

After security requirements are met, you have established IP-level communication. This means that wireless standard requirements have been met, and Ethernet networking takes over. Basically, a switch occurs between 802.11 to 802.3 standards. The wireless standards create the physical link to the network, enabling regular networking standards and protocols to use the link. This is how the physical cable is replaced, but to the networking technologies there is no difference between regular cable media or wireless media.

Several components combine to enable wireless communications between devices. Each of these must be configured on both the client and the AP:

- **(Extended)Service Set Identifier (SSID/ESSID)**—Whether your wireless network uses infrastructure mode or ad-hoc mode, an SSID is required. The SSID is a configurable client identification that enables clients to communicate to a particular base station. Only client systems configured with the same SSID as the AP can communicate with it. SSIDs provide a simple password arrangement between base stations and clients.

- **Wireless channel**—RF channels are important parts of wireless communications. A *channel* refers to the band of frequency used for the wireless communication. Each standard specifies the channels that can be used. The 802.11a standard specifies radio frequency ranges between 5.15 and 5.875GHz. In contrast, 802.11b and 802.11g/n standards operate between the 2.4 to 2.4835GHz ranges. Fourteen channels are defined in the IEEE 802.11b/g/n channel set, 11 of which are available in North America.

- **Security features**—IEEE 802.11 provides for security using two methods: authentication and encryption. Authentication refers to the verification of the client system. In the infrastructure mode, authentication is established between an AP and each station. Wireless encryption services must be the same on the client and the AP for communication to occur.

> **NOTE: Default Settings**   Wireless devices ship with default SSIDs, security set-tings, channels, passwords, and usernames. To protect yourself, it is strongly recom-mended that you change these default settings. Today, many Internet sites list the default settings used by manufacturers with their wireless devices. This information is used by people who want to gain unauthorized access to your wireless devices.

Troubleshooting Wireless Signals

Because wireless signals travel through the atmosphere, they are susceptible to dif-ferent types of interference than standard wire networks. Interference weakens wireless signals and is therefore an important consideration when working with wireless networking.

Interference is unfortunately inevitable, but the trick is to minimize the levels of interference. Wireless LAN communications are typically based on radio fre-quency signals that require a clear and unobstructed transmission path.

The following are some factors that cause interference:

- **Physical objects**—Trees, masonry, buildings, and other physical structures are some of the most common sources of interference. The density of the materi-als used in a building's construction determines the number of walls the RF signal can pass through and still maintain adequate coverage. Concrete and steel walls are particularly difficult for a signal to pass through. These struc-tures will weaken or at times completely prevent wireless signals.

- **Radio frequency interference**—Wireless technologies such as 802.11b/g use an RF range of 2.4GHz, and so do many other devices, such as cordless phones, microwaves, and so on. Devices that share the channel can cause noise and weaken the signals.

- **Electrical interference**—Electrical interference comes from devices such as computers, refrigerators, fans, lighting fixtures, or any other motorized de-vices. The impact that electrical interference has on the signal depends on the proximity of the electrical device to the wireless access point. Advances in wireless technologies and in electrical devices have reduced the impact these types of devices have on wireless transmissions.

- **Environmental factors**—Weather conditions can have a huge impact on wire-less signal integrity. Lightning, for example, can cause electrical interference, and fog can weaken signals as they pass through.

Many wireless implementations are found in the office or at home. Even when outside interference such as weather is not a problem, plenty of wireless obstacles exist around the office. Table 7.5 highlights a few examples to be aware of when implementing a wireless network indoors.

Table 7.5 Wireless Obstacles Found Indoors

Obstruction	Obstacle Severity	Example Use
Wood/wood paneling	Low	Inside wall or hollow doors
Drywall	Low	Inside walls
Furniture	Low	Couches or office partitions
Clear glass	Low	Windows
Tinted glass	Medium	Windows
People	Medium	High volume traffic areas where there is considerable pedestrian traffic
Ceramic Tile	Medium	Walls
Concrete blocks	Medium/high	Outer wall construction
Mirrors	High	Mirror or reflective glass
Metals	High	Metal office partitions, doors, metal-based office furniture
Water	High	Aquariums, rain, fountains

NOTE: Wireless and Water   Water is a major interference factor for 2.4GHz wireless networks because water molecules resonate at the frequency in the 2.4GHz band. Interestingly, microwaves cause water molecules to resonate during cooking, which interferes with 2.4GHz RF.

Site Surveys

When placing a wireless access point when troubleshooting wireless signals, a wireless site survey is recommended. The wireless site survey is an important first step in the deployment of a wireless network; it enables the administrator to identify the wireless signal coverage area, potential interference area, and channel overlap and helps determine the best place to put an access point. Without the wireless site survey, it is blind placement.

A site survey will often include two key elements: a visual inspection and an RF inspection. A visual inspection of an area helps the administrator identify elements that might limit the propagation of wireless signals. This can include mirrors, concrete walls, metal racks, and more. The visual survey helps isolate the potential location of the AP.

In addition to the visual survey, testing software on laptops and handheld wireless survey devices can be used to test the signal integrity. These devices test for coverage voids, map any signal leakage from your building, discover the existence and location of rogue access points, channel overlaps, determine effects of neighboring access points, and more. Without using such a device, it would be impossible to detect unforeseen wireless deployment problem areas. For this reason, site surveys are one of the first steps in the deployment of any wireless networks.

Troubleshooting AP Coverage

Like any other network media, APs have a limited transmission distance. This limitation is an important consideration when deciding where an AP should be placed on the network. When troubleshooting a wireless network, pay close attention to the distance client systems are from the AP.

When faced with a problem in which client systems cannot consistently access the AP, you could try moving the AP to better cover the area, but then you might disrupt access for users in other areas. So what can be done to troubleshoot AP coverage?

Depending on the network environment, the quick solution might be to throw money at the problem and purchase another AP, cabling, and other hardware to expand the transmission area. However, you can try a few options before installing another wireless AP. The following list starts with the least expensive solution and progresses to the most expensive:

- **Increase transmission power**—Some APs have a setting to adjust the transmission power output. By default, most of these settings will be set to the maximum output; however, it is worth verifying just in case. As a side note, the transmission power can be decreased if you try to reduce the dispersion of radio waves beyond the immediate network. Increasing the power provides clients stronger data signals and greater transmission distances.

- **Relocate the AP**—When wireless client systems suffer from connectivity problems, the solution can be as simple as relocating the AP to another location. It might be that it is relocated across the room, a few feet away, or across the hall. Finding the right location will likely take a little trial and error.

- **Adjust or replace antennas**—If the AP distance is not sufficient for some network clients, it might be necessary to replace the default antenna used with both the AP and the client with higher-end antennas. Upgrading an antenna can make a big difference in terms of transmission range. Unfortunately, not all APs have replaceable antennas.

- **Signal amplification**—RF amplifiers add significant distance to wireless signals. An RF amplifier increases the strength and readability of the data transmission. The amplifier provides improvement of both the received and transmitted signals, resulting in an increase in wireless network performance.

- **Use a repeater**—Before installing a new AP, you might first want to think about a wireless repeater. When set to the same channel as the AP, the repeater takes the transmission and repeats it. So, the AP transmission gets to the repeater and then the repeater duplicates the signal and passes it forward. It is an effective strategy to increase wireless transmission distances.

> **NOTE: Signal Strength**   Wireless signals degrade depending on the construction material used. Signals passing through concrete and steel are particularly weak-

Wireless Troubleshooting Checklist

Poor communication between wireless devices has many potential causes. The following is a review checklist of wireless troubleshooting presented in this chapter:

- **Auto transfer rate**—By default, wireless devices are configured to use the strongest, fastest signal. If you're experiencing connectivity problems between wireless devices, try using the lower transfer rate in a fixed mode to achieve a more stable connection. For example, you can manually choose the wireless transfer rate and instead of using 11Mbps, the highest rate for 802.11b, try 5.5Mbps, 2Mbps, or 1Mbps. The higher the transfer rate, the shorter the connection distance.

- **AP placement**—If signal strength is low, try moving the AP to a new location. Moving it just a few feet can make the difference.

- **Antenna**—The default antenna shipped with wireless devices might not be powerful enough for a particular client system. Better quality antennas can be purchased for some APs, which can boost the distance the signal can go.

- **Building obstructions**—Wireless RF communications are weakened if they have to travel through obstructions such as metal and concrete.

- **Conflicting devices**—Any device that uses the same frequency range as the wireless device can cause interference. For example, 2.4GHz phones can cause interference with devices using the 802.11g/n standard.

- **Wireless channels**—If connections are inconsistent, try changing the channel to another nonoverlapping channel.

- **Protocol issues**—If an IP address is not assigned to the wireless client, an incorrect SSID or incorrect WEP settings can prevent a system from obtaining IP information.

- **SSID**—The SSID number used on the client system must match the one used on the AP. Typically, the default SSID assigned is sufficient but might need to be changed if switching a laptop between different WLANs.

■   **Encryption**—If encryption is enabled, the encryption type on the client must match what is set up in the AP.

TIP: Troubleshooting   The Network+ exam will likely test knowledge on basic wireless troubleshooting. Be sure to review this section before taking the Network+ exam.

Securing Wireless Networks

Many strategies and protocols are used to secure LAN and WAN transmissions. What about those network transmissions that travel over the airwaves? In the past few years wireless networking has changed the look of modern networks, bringing with it an unparalleled level of mobility and a host of new security concerns.

Wireless LANs (WLANs) require new protocols and standards to handle security for radio communications. As it stands today, wireless communications represent a significant security concern. When working with wireless, you need to be aware of a few wireless security standards, including Wired Equivalent Privacy (WEP), Wi-Fi Protected Access (WPA), WPA-2, and 802.1X. Before we get to describing each, let's define a few terms.

Defining Access Control, Authentication, Authorization, and Encryption

Wireless security, like all computer security, is about controlling access to data and resources. It is important to understand the difference between authentication, authorization, and access control. Though these terms are sometimes used interchangeably, they refer to distinct steps that must be negotiated successfully to determine whether a particular request for a resource will result in that resource actually being returned. This is true for both a wired and wireless network.

Access control refers to any mechanism, software or hardware, used to restrict availability to network resources. To secure a network, it is necessary to determine which users will be granted access to various resources. Access control provides the design strategies necessary to ensure that only permitted users have access to such resources. It is a fundamental concept and forms the basis of a strong and secure network environment.

Although the concept of access control is easily understood, implementing it can be complex. Access to every network resource, including files, folders, hard disks, and Internet access, must be controlled. This is a difficult task in large network environments.

TIP: Access Control   The primary objective of access control is to preserve and protect the confidentiality, integrity, and availability of information, systems, and resources.

Authentication verifies the identity of the computer or user attempting to access a particular resource. Authentication is most commonly done with the presentation of credentials such as a username and a password. More sophisticated identification methods can include the use of the following:

- Smart cards

- Biometrics

- Voice recognition

- Fingerprints

Authorization determines whether the person, previously identified and authenticated, is enabled to access to a particular resource. This is commonly determined through group association; that is, a particular group might have a specific level of security clearance. For instance, a group security policy might enable the school secretaries access to some data while locking students out.

Encryption is the process of encoding the data sent over remote connections, and it involves scrambling the usernames and passwords used to gain access to the remote network. Encryption is the process of encoding data using a mathematical algorithm that makes it difficult for unauthorized users to read the data if they can intercept it. The algorithm is actually a mathematical value known as a *key*. The key is required to read the encrypted data. Encryption techniques use public and private keys; public keys can be shared, and private keys cannot.

A *key* is a binary number that has a large number of bits. As you might imagine, the bigger the number or key, the more difficult it is to guess. Today, simple encryption strategies use 40 to 56 bits. On a 40-bit encryption, there are 2^{40} possible keys; 56-bit encryption has 2^{56} possible keys. That's a lot of keys. Remember that without the correct key, the data cannot be accessed. Although the number of keys associated with lower-grade encryption might seem amazing, they have been cracked by some high-end, specialized systems. That makes necessary higher-grade encryption: Many online transactions require 128-bit encryption, and other applications support encryption as high as 1,024 bits. (If you have time, try to calculate the key combinations for these higher-grade encryption strategies.)

Wireless Authentication and Encryption Methods

Now that we have a better idea of what authorization, authentication, and encryption are, we can look at the protocols and methods used to achieve wireless security. As an administrator for a wireless network, you will certainly be using these security features, and you will certainly be asked questions about them on the Network+ exam.

> **TIP: Wireless Security**   The Network+ exam will have questions about wireless security, including WEP and WPA. Be sure you can identify wireless security protocols before taking the exam.

Wired Equivalent Privacy (WEP)

Wired Equivalent Privacy (WEP) was the first attempt to keep wireless networks safe. WEP was designed to be easy to configure and implement, and originally it was hoped that WEP would provide the same level of security to wireless networks as was available to wired networks. For a time it was the best and only option for securing wireless networks.

WEP is an IEEE standard introduced in 1997 designed for securing 802.11 networks. With WEP enabled, each data packet transmitted over the wireless connection would be encrypted. Originally, the data packet was combined with a secret 40-bit number key as it passed through an encryption algorithm known as RC4. The packet was scrambled and sent across the airwaves. On the receiving end, the data packet passed through the RC4 backward, and the host received the data as it was intended. WEP originally used a 40-bit number key, but later specified 128-bit encryption, making WEP that much more robust.

WEP was designed to provide security by encrypting data from the sending and receiving devices. In a short period of time, however, it was discovered that WEP encryption was not nearly as secure as hoped. Part of the problem was that when the 802.11 standards were written, security was not the major concern it is today. As a result, WEP security was easy to crack with freely available hacking tools. From this point, wireless communication was regarded as a potentially insecure transmission media.

There are two types of WEP security: static and dynamic WEP. Dynamic and static WEP differ in that dynamic WEP changes security keys periodically, or dynamically, making it more secure. Static WEP uses the same security key ongoing. The primary security risks are associated with static WEP, which uses a shared password to protect communications. Security weaknesses discovered in static WEP means that WLANs protected by it are vulnerable to several types of threats. Freely available hacking tools make breaking into static WEP-protected wireless networks a trivial task. Unsecured WLANs are obviously exposed to these same threats as well; the difference being that less expertise, time, and resources are required to carry out the attacks.

Wi-Fi Protected Access (WPA)

Security weaknesses associated with WEP provided administrators with a valid reason to be concerned with wireless security. The need for increased wireless security was important for wireless networking to reach its potential and to bring a sense of confidence for those with sensitive data to use wireless communications. In response, the Wi-Fi Protected Access (WPA) was created. WPA was designed to improve the security weaknesses of WEP and to be backward compatible with older devices using the WEP standard. WPA addressed two main security concerns:

- **Enhanced data encryption**—WPA uses a *temporal key integrity protocol (TKIP)*, which scrambles encryption keys using a hashing algorithm. Then the keys are issued an integrity check to verify that they have not been modified or tampered with during transit.

- **Authentication**—Using the Extensible Authentication Protocol (EAP), WEP regulates access to a wireless network based on a computer's hardware-specific MAC address, which is relatively simple to be sniffed out and stolen. EAP is built on a more secure public-key encryption system to ensure that only authorized network users can access the network.

WPA was designed to address the security shortcomings of WEP by introducing support for mutual authentication and using the Temporal Key Integrity Protocol (TKIP) for data encryption. TKIP is discussed in the next section. The security features of WPA have been improved upon with WPA2. WPA2 enhances security by using Advanced Encryption Standard (AES) instead of TKIP to secure network traffic making it more secure. AES, also known as Rijndael, is a block cipher encryption standard. AES can create secure keys from 128 bit to 256 bit in length.

NOTE: WPA and WPA2   WPA uses TKIP to secure wireless network traffic whereas WPA2 uses the more secure AES encryption method.

Both WPA and WPA2 are vastly more secure than WEP and, when properly secured, there are no currently known security flaws for either protocol. However, due to the AES protocol, wherever possible it is recommend to use WPA2.

Temporal Key Integrity Protocol (TKIP)

As mentioned previously, WEP lacked security. The Temporal Key Integrity Protocol (TKIP) was designed to address the shortcomings of the WEP security protocol. TKIP is an encryption protocol defined in IEEE 802.11i. TKIP was not only designed to increase security but also to use existing hardware, making it easy to upgrade to TKIP encryption.

TKIP is built on the original WEP security standard but enhances it by "wrapping" additional code both at the end and the beginning of the data packet. This additional code modifies the original code for additional security. Because TKIP is based on WEP, it too uses the RC4 stream encryption method, but unlike WEP, TKIP encrypts each data packet with a stronger encryption key than available with regular WEP.

TKIP provides increased security for data communications, but it is far from the final solution. TKIP provides strong encryption for home user and nonsensitive data, but it might not provide a level of security necessary to protect corporate or more sensitive data while in transmission.

802.1X

802.1X is an IEEE standard specifying port-based network access control. 802.1X was not specifically designed for wireless networks; rather, it provides authenticated access for both wired and wireless networks. Port-based network access control uses the physical characteristics of a switched local area network (LAN) infrastructure to authenticate devices attached to a LAN port and to prevent access to that port in cases where the authentication process fails. There are three main components to the 802.1X framework:

■ **Supplicant**—The system or node requesting access and authentication to a network resource.

■ **Authenticator**—A control mechanism that enables or denies traffic to pass though a port.

■ **Authentication server**—The authentication server validates the credentials of the supplicant trying to access the network or resource.

During a port-based network access control interaction, a LAN port adopts one of two roles: authenticator or supplicant. In the role of *authenticator*, a LAN port enforces authentication before it enables user access to the services that can be accessed through that port. In the role of *supplicant*, a LAN port requests access to the services that can be accessed through the authenticator's port. An authentication server, which can be either a separate entity or colocated with the authenticator, checks the supplicant's credentials on behalf of the authenticator. The authentication server then responds to the authenticator, indicating whether the supplicant is authorized to access the authenticator's services.

The authenticator's port-based network access control defines two logical APs to the LAN through one physical LAN port. The first logical AP, the *uncontrolled port*, enables data exchange between the authenticator and other computers on the LAN, regardless of the computer's authorization state. The second logical AP is between an authenticated LAN user and the authenticator.

In a wireless network environment, the supplicant would typically be a network host, the authenticator could be the wireless network switch or AP, and the role of authentication server would be played by a Remote Authentication Dial-In User Service (RADIUS).

RADIUS is a protocol that enables a single server to become responsible for all remote access authentication, authorization, and auditing (or accounting) services. RADIUS functions as a client/server system. The remote user dials in to the remote access server, which acts as a RADIUS client, or network access server

(NAS), and connects to a RADIUS server. The RADIUS server performs authentication, authorization, and auditing (or accounting) functions and returns the information to the RADIUS client (which is a remote-access server running RADIUS client software); the connection is either established or rejected based on the information received.

Securing the Access Point

Any wireless access point ships with a default configuration that is not secure. Before deploying a wireless network it is important to configure the AP not only with encryption but also to secure other settings to prevent attack. The following checklist identifies some of the settings that can be secured.

- **Changing default AP password**—The wireless AP ships with a generic password. One of the first steps is to change this public password to prevent unauthorized access to the AP.

- **SSID broadcast**—The wireless router is configured to broadcast the SSID to make it easy to find for wireless clients. It is possible to choose not to broadcast the SSID making the network invisible to detection.

- **Disabling DHCP on AP and using Static IP**—Many wireless APs distribute IP information automatically using the DHCP protocol. If someone was trying to access the AP and was successful, DHCP makes it easy for them to get a valid IP address. To help secure the AP, it is possible to disable DHCP and create static IP addresses for each legitimate device connected to it. The static IP would need to be configured on the client workstation.

- **MAC filtering**—Most APs enable for MAC filtering, which is enabling only specified MAC addresses to be authenticated to the AP. There are ways to get around MAC filtering, but the average user would not make the effort to find out how. Each client system connecting to the access point would need to have its MAC address listed in the MAC filter.

Summary

Several wireless standards fall under the 802.11 banner, including 802.11a, 802.11b, 802.11g, and 802.11n. Each of these standards has different characteristics, including speed, range, and RF used. Wireless networks are typically implemented using ad-hoc or infrastructure network design. Many types of interference can weaken the wireless signals, including weather, obstructions such as trees or walls, and RF interference.

Three types of spread spectrum technologies are reviewed in this chapter: frequency hopping, direct sequence, and Orthogonal Frequency Division Multiplexing. Each is associated with a particular wireless networking standard.

Many strategies and protocols secure wireless transmissions, including Wired Equivalent Privacy (WEP), Wi-Fi Protected Access (WPA), WPA, AES, and 802.1X. WEP was proven to be insecure but is still widely used. AP uses TKIP to encrypt potentially sensitive data. RADIUS also increases security and acts as an authentication server.

When configuring a wireless network, the client and the AP must be configured with the same characteristics. If the AP uses 802.11a, so must the client. The same holds true for the SSID and the security settings.

Exam Preparation Tasks

 ## Review All the Key Topics

Review the most important topics in the chapter, noted with the key topics icon in the outer margin of the page. Table 7.6 lists a reference of these key topics and the page numbers on which each is found.

Table 7.6 Key Topics for Chapter 7

Key Topic Element	Description	Page Number
Figure 7.1	APs connect WLANs and a wired Ethernet LAN	247
Figure 7.2	Directional antenna signal	250
List	802.11 standards	252
Table 7.1	802.11 wireless standards	253
Table 7.2	RF Channels for 802.11b/g	256
Table 7.3	RF Channels for 802.11a	256
Table 7.4	Comparison of IEEE 802.11 standards	259
Figure 7.3	Wireless configuration information.	260
Table 7.5	Wireless obstacles found indoors	265
List	Troubleshooting access points	266
List	Wireless troubleshooting checklist	267

Complete the Tables and Lists from Memory

Print a copy of Appendix B, "Memory Tables," (found on the CD), or at least the section for this chapter, and complete the tables and lists from memory. Appendix C, "Memory Tables Answer Key," also on the CD, includes completed tables and lists to check your work.

Define Key Terms

Define the following key terms from this chapter, and check your answers in the Glossary.

- 802.11 a/b/g/n
- AES
- AP
- Channels
- Frequency
- Authentication
- Encryption
- Authorization
- WPA
- WPA2
- WEP
- RADIUS
- TKIP
- Omnidirectional antenna
- Directional antenna
- Beaconing
- SSID
- BSS
- ESSID

Apply Your Knowledge

Exercise 7.1 Managing Wireless Security Settings in Windows Vista

You are the network administrator for a large network that has just installed several APs. The APs are configured to use WPA2, but the client stations are not.

In this exercise, you verify the encryption method used for your wireless connection. To complete this exercise, you need a functioning wireless connection.

Estimated time: 5 minutes

Complete the following steps:

1. Right-click the icon for the current wireless network connection, and click Properties.

2. When selected, the Wireless Network Properties window opens. Select the Security tab.

3. From the Security tab, use the drop-down menu to select WPA2.

4. Select OK and the client is configured to use the wireless connection and configured with the WPA2 protocol.

Exercise 7.2 Configuring a Windows XP System to Exclusively Use a Wireless Infrastructure Connection

Configuring and managing wireless connections is an increasing part of the network administrator's role. Windows XP has built-in wizards and features to make working with wireless as easy as possible. In this exercise, we identify the setting used to determine whether a wireless connection is to be configured as an ad-hoc connection or an infrastructure connection.

This exercise assumes that the system has a wireless adapter installed.

Estimated time: 5 minutes

Complete the following steps:

1. In Windows XP, choose Start, Control Panel. (Use the Control Panel in Classic View for this exercise.)

2. From within the Control Panel, double-click the Network Connections Applet to open the Network Connections dialog box.

3. Right-click the wireless connection, and select Properties from the menu screen. This Wireless Network Connection Properties dialog box opens.

4. Select the Wireless Networks tab, and then click the Advanced button on the lower-right side of the dialog box.

5. This displays a small dialog box with three options:
   - Any Available Network (Access Point Preferred)
   - Access Point (Infrastructure) Networks Only
   - Computer-to-Computer (Ad Hoc) Networks Only

6. To configure the XP system to use only an infrastructure wireless connection, select the option button next to the Access Point (Infrastructure) Networks Only option. You need to click Close for the window and click OK for the Wireless Network Connection Properties window. If you click Close and then Cancel, the changes will be dropped.

Review Questions

You can find the answers to these questions in Appendix A.

1. Which of the following wireless protocols operates at 2.4GHz? (Select two.)
   a. 802.11a
   b. 802.11b
   c. 802.11g
   d. 802.11t

2. Under which of the following circumstances would you change the default channel on an access point?
   a. When there is a channel overlap between access points
   b. To release and renew the SSID
   c. To increase the WEP security settings
   d. To decrease WEP security settings

3. A client on your network has had no problem accessing the wireless network, but recently the client moved to a new office. Since the move she cannot access the network. Which of the following is most likely the cause of the problem?
   a. The SSID on the client and the AP are different.
   b. The SSID has been erased.
   c. The client has incorrect WEP settings.
   d. The client system has moved too far away from the access point.

4. Which of the following best describes the function of beacons?
   a. Beacons monitor for wireless security issues.
   b. Beacons advertise the presence of an access point.
   c. Beacons prevent unauthorized access into an AP.
   d. Beacons prevent unauthenticated access into an AP.

5. You have just purchased a new wireless access point that uses no WEP security by default. You change the security settings to use 128-bit encryption. How must the client systems be configured?
   a. All client systems must be set to 128-bit encryption.
   b. The client system will inherit security settings from the AP.
   c. WEP does not support 128-bit encryption.
   d. The client WEP settings have to be set to autodetect.

6. You have just been asked to configure the security settings for a new wireless network. You want the setting that offers the greatest level of security. Which of the following would you choose?
   a. WEP-open
   b. WEP-closed
   c. WEP-shared
   d. WEP-unshared

7. Which of the following best describes 802.1X?
   a. Port-based access control
   b. Wireless standard specifying 11Mbps data transfer
   c. Wireless standard specifying 54Mbps data transfer
   d. Integrity-based access control

8. You are installing a wireless network solution and require a standard that can operate using either 2.4GHz or 5GHz frequencies. Which of the following standards would you choose?
   a. 802.11a
   b. 802.11b
   c. 802.11g
   d. 802.11n

9. You are installing a wireless network solution that uses a feature known as MIMO. Which wireless networking standard are you using?
   a. 802.11a
   b. 802.11b
   c. 802.11g
   d. 802.11n

10. In the 802.1X security framework, which of the following best describes the role of supplicant?
    a. To authenticate usernames and passwords
    b. To encrypt usernames and passwords
    c. The system or node requesting access and authentication to a network resource
    d. A control mechanism that enables or denies traffic to pass through a port

11. Which of the following 802.11 standards can use the nonoverlapping channels of 1, 6, or 11? (Select two.)
    a. 802.11a
    b. 802.11b
    c. 802.11g
    d. 802.11h

12. Which of the following wireless security protocols uses TKIP?
    a. WEP-open
    b. WEP-shared
    c. WPA
    d. WPA-shared

13. Which of the following best describes the role of RADIUS?
    a. RADIUS enables a single IP address to become responsible for all remote access authentication.
    b. RADIUS enables a single server to become responsible for all remote access authentication.
    c. RADIUS encrypts all data leaving the AP.
    d. RADIUS encrypts all data leaving the remote system.

14. Which of the following is associated with OFDM?
    a. 802.11n
    b. WEP
    c. WPA
    d. 802.11b

15. A user calls to inform you that she cannot print. Upon questioning her, you determine that the she has just been moved from the second floor to the third floor. She connects to the printer via a wireless router on the first floor. You need to allow the user to print but do not want to purchase another AP or disrupt other wireless users. Which of the following might you do?
    a. Move the AP to allow the client system to access the network and therefore the printer.
    b. Search for RF interference on the 2.4GHz range.
    c. Change the channel.
    d. Configure an RF repeater to forward the wireless communications.

16. You are deploying a wireless network and decide you need an antenna that provides a 360-degree dispersed wave pattern. Which of the following antennas would you select?
    a. Multipoint
    b. Unidirectional
    c. Omnidirectional
    d. Dispersal

17. You are working with a wireless network that uses channel 1 (2412MHz). What RF range would be used if you switched to channel 3?
    a. 2417
    b. 2422
    c. 2427
    d. 2408

18. You are the network administrator for a small company. Recently you added two remote clients who access the network through an AP. To increase security you decide you need to keep the network name hidden. Which of the following could you do?

   a. Enable WEP broadcast

   b. Disable WEP broadcast

   c. Enable secure SSID broadcast

   d. Disable SSID broadcast

19. Which of the following wireless standards specifies an RF of 5GHz?

   a. 802.11a

   b. 802.11b

   c. 802.11g

   d. 802.11g

20. What is the maximum network speed defined by the 802.11b standard?

   a. 100Mbps

   b. 5.5Mbps

   c. 11Mbps

   d. 10Mbps

This chapter covers CompTIA Network+ objective 2.5. Upon completion of this chapter, you will be able to answer the following questions:

■ What are public and private networks?

■ What are the common switching methods?

■ How are WAN technologies used today?

■ What are the common Internet technologies used today?

■ What are the common wireless wide area networking technologies?

CHAPTER 8

Wide Area Networking

In the beginning, there was a single computer. Soon it connected to other computers and became a local area network (LAN). LANs enabled files, printers, and applications to be shared freely and securely throughout an organization. For a short time, a LAN was sufficient in many organizations, but the need arose to interconnect LANs to provide enterprisewide data availability.

As you might imagine, connecting LANs provided a challenge primarily because of the distances separating them. Some were across town, and some were thousands of miles apart—a long way to run a segment of coaxial cable. Technologies such as X.25 were introduced that could span these distances, and the wide area network (WAN) was born. Some technologies used by WANs are different from those used by LANs; essentially, WANs use different wires and different protocols. In addition, WANs can be far more complex to implement. As far as functionality is concerned, a WAN does exactly what a LAN does: It provides connectivity between computers.

Foundation Topics

Public and Private Networks

To implement a WAN, you need a way to connect two geographically separated networks. Depending on the financial resources of an organization, a WAN can use a dedicated link between networks to establish communication. Or the WAN can be created using a larger public network such as the Internet. Before looking at the various WAN technologies available, we start our examination of WANs by looking at perhaps the most significant consideration facing anyone who is implementing a WAN: whether to use a public or a private network as a means of connectivity. The private and public WAN network services each have their advantages and disadvantages, and knowing the difference between them is a good place to start.

Public Networks

The bottom line for many decisions made in networking is money. This is often true when choosing a WAN networking method. To save money and a certain amount of administrative effort, you can choose to set up a WAN using an existing transmission infrastructure. Two key public networks can establish a WAN: the public switched telephone network (PSTN) and the Internet. The following section discusses each of these.

Public Switched Telephone Network (PSTN)

The Public Switched Telephone Network (PSTN), often called *plain old telephone system (POTS)*, is the entire collection of interconnected telephone wires throughout the world. Elements of the PSTN include all the equipment that goes into connecting two points, such as the cable, the networking equipment, and the telephone exchanges. A detailed discussion of POTS is included later in this chapter in the section "POTS Internet Access."

> **TIP: Use PSTN to Save Money**   If financial cost is a major concern, PSTN is the method of choice for creating a WAN.

The modern PSTN is largely digital, with analog connections existing primarily between homes and the local phone exchanges. Modems convert the computer system's digital signals to analog so that they can be sent out over the analog connection.

Using the PSTN to establish WAN connections has been a popular choice, although the significant drawback is the limited transfer speeds. Transfer on the PSTN is limited to 56Kbps with a regular modem. Today's high-speed networks using videoconferencing, VoIP, large data transfers, and more cannot manage with these limited speeds. Newer WAN technologies have pushed PSTN into the background; however, PSTN is still used by companies that need to send only small amounts of data remotely or have a limited budget. PSTN remains an inexpensive alternative for remote access.

The Internet

The Internet is a popular method for establishing WAN connections. Using the Internet to provide remote access creates a cost-effective and reliable solution for interconnecting LANs. One of the most common methods of using the Internet for connecting LANs is through the use of *virtual private networks (VPN)*. Essentially, a VPN uses a public network, such as the Internet, to create a communication tunnel between two end points. Unlike private networks, VPNs can be used on an as-needed basis. A connection can be established to a remote location and then dropped when no transmissions are required. Many organizations use VPNs as dedicated links that permanently connect private LANs. The security available for VPNs further makes them an attractive option. Figure 8.1 shows a VPN connection over a public network.

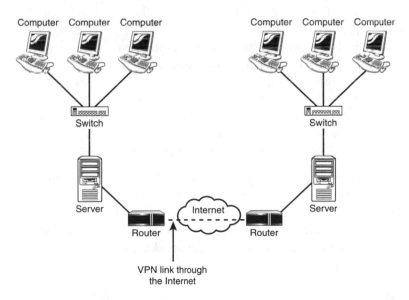

Figure 8.1 A VPN connecting two private LANs.

TIP: Cable and DSL   The availability of cable Internet access and Digital Subscriber Line (DSL) services means that companies can use these technologies as a means to establish VPN connections. Cable and DSL are particularly well suited for such a purpose because they offer high speeds at a low cost. They are also available 24/7 for an inclusive cost, which is a bonus over other methods such as ISDN, which might be billed on a usage basis. Cable and DSL, in concert with VPNs, make it possible for companies to establish low-cost, secure WAN links. Previously, many companies could not have afforded a solution that offers this kind of speed, availability, and security.

Advantages and Disadvantages of Public Networks

The biggest advantages of a public network, such as the PSTN and the Internet, are accessibility and availability. Public network access is almost everywhere, and perhaps more important, it is inexpensive. In addition, the technologies required to use public networks, such as VPNs, are typically easy to configure and can be implemented in a short amount of time. All major client operating systems ship with the software necessary to create a VPN.

You are most likely to see public networks utilized by small organizations, where the money for a private network is simply not available or needed. For many small organizations, the capabilities that the Internet provides are sufficient.

As you might have already surmised, some drawbacks exist in using a public network to interconnect LANs. First and foremost is security. When you establish a link over a public network, there is a risk that another user on that network might compromise your data. Technologies such as VPNs put a lot of emphasis on security measures such as encryption and authentication aimed at reducing the security risk. Commonly a security protocol called IPsec is used on the connection to ensure that data sent over the link is encrypted and that strict authentication requirements are met. However, if you send sensitive data over a public network, there is always a risk. Discussions about the degree of risk are best left to hackers, crackers, and security experts, and that debate is sure to go on for a long time.

In addition to the security risks, numerous other considerations exist concerning public lines, such as disconnections, logon troubles for modems, Internet failures, and a host of other likely and unlikely circumstances. Keep in mind that with a public network you get something for nothing—or at least for very little—and you have to make concessions. If you can't live with the drawbacks, you can always switch to a private network.

Private Networks

If we all had unlimited IT budgets, most of us would use private networking to connect LANs. Private networks provide a solid way to maintain connectivity between LANs, at least for those who can afford them.

A private network does not suffer from the same considerations of a public network. Many technologies create private networks and vary in cost and implementation difficulty. This chapter discusses in detail the specific technologies used to create WANs over private networks in the "WAN Technologies" section.

A private network can be designed and implemented from scratch based on an organization's specific needs. The network can be as complex or simple, expensive or inexpensive, or secure or insecure as enabled by the budget, location, utilization, and data usage demands. The network can also be designed around the security needs of the data carried over the network. For instance, fiber-based networks are more secure and more expensive than copper-based networks or wireless networks. A private network can employ various protocols based on security or performance needs. Basically, a private network gives the designer an opportunity to correct most of the problems and drawbacks associated with public networks.

Probably the biggest disadvantage of a private network is the cost. Whereas the PSTN is yours for the asking at a nominal monthly fee, a private network requires that you purchase or lease every piece of cable, all the network cards, hubs, routers, switches, and so on, until you have enough equipment to go live.

Because of the required networking equipment, private networks often require more administrative effort than public networks, where the networking infrastructure is maintained by outside administrators. Often, a hidden cost associated with private networks is the need for qualified people to manage and maintain them. As the network grows—and it will—it becomes increasingly complex and requires more attention. Good administration is a must; otherwise, inefficiencies and lack of dependability can quickly consume the value of the private network. A company needs to carefully weigh administrative issues before getting into private networking.

Using a private WAN need not be a total do-it-yourself approach; most telephone companies provide managed WAN services, which include all the equipment you need to create a WAN. They also monitor and manage the connection for you, making sure that everything operates as it is supposed to. There is, of course, a price attached to such a service, but for many companies, a managed solution is money well spent.

Switching Methods

Before we discuss the specific WAN technologies, we must first look at the switching methods. For systems to communicate on a network, there must be a communication path between them on which the data can travel. To communicate with another entity, you need to establish a path that can move the information from one location to another and back. This is the function of *switching*: It provides a path between two communication end points and routes the data to make sure that it follows the correct path. Three types of switching are used most often in networks today:

- Packet switching

- Circuit switching

- Message switching

> **TIP: Know the Differences**   For the Network+ exam, you will be expected to identify the differences between the various switching methods.

Packet Switching

In packet switching, messages are broken into smaller pieces called *packets*. Each packet is assigned source, destination, and intermediate node addresses. Packets are required to have this information because they do not always use the same path or route to get to their intended destination. Referred to as *independent routing*, this is one of the advantages of packet switching. Independent routing enables for a better use of available bandwidth by letting packets travel different routes to avoid high-traffic areas. Independent routing also enables packets to take an alternative route if a particular route is unavailable for some reason. Figure 8.2 shows how packets can travel in a packet-switching environment.

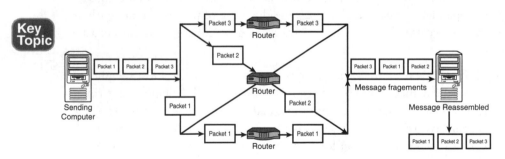

Figure 8.2   An example of packet switching.

> **TIP: Packet Switching**   Packet switching is the most popular switching method for networks and is used on most LANs.

In a packet-switching system, when packets are sent onto the network, the sending device is responsible for choosing the best path for the packet. This path might change in transit, and it is possible for the receiving device to receive the packets in a random or nonsequential order. When this happens, the receiving device waits until all the data packets are received and then reconstructs them according to their built-in sequence numbers.

> **NOTE: Packet Size Restrictions**   The packet size is restricted in a packet-switching network to ensure that the packets can be stored in RAM instead of on a hard disk. The benefit of this size restriction is faster access because retrieving data from RAM is faster than retrieving data from a hard disk.

Two types of packet-switching methods are used on networks: *virtual-circuit packet switching* and *datagram packet switching*. Each of these methods is described in the following sections.

Virtual-Circuit Packet Switching

When virtual-circuit switching is used, a logical connection is established between the source and the destination device. This logical connection is established when the sending device initiates a conversation with the receiving device. The logical communication path between the two devices can remain active for as long as the two devices are available or can be used to send packets once. After the sending process has completed, the line can be closed. There are two types of virtual circuit switching methods, permanent virtual circuits (PVC) and switched virtual circuits (SVC).

- **Permanent Virtual Circuit (PVC)**—A PVC is a permanent dedicated virtual link between the sending and receiving device. The PVC can replace a hardwired dedicated end-to-end line.

- **Switched Virtual Circuit (SVC)**—An SVC represents a temporary virtual circuit established and maintained only for the duration of a data transfer session. The virtual circuit is cleared after the data transfer is completed.

Datagram Packet Switching

Unlike virtual-circuit packet switching, datagram packet switching does not establish a logical connection between the sending and transmitting devices. The packets in datagram packet switching are independently sent, meaning that they can take different paths through the network to reach their intended destination. To do this, each packet must be individually addressed to determine where its source and destination are. This method ensures that packets take the easiest possible routes to their destination and avoid high-traffic areas.

Because in datagram packet switching the packets can take multiple paths to reach their destination, they can be received in a nonsequential order. The information contained within each packet header reconstructs all the packets and ensures that the original message is received in total.

Datagram packet switching technologies are fault-tolerant. As mentioned previously, on a packet switched network, a large message is broken into smaller packets that travel through various paths to reassemble at the destination. These packets travel independently of each other and can take different routes to get to the destination. These multiple routes for packets to travel create fault tolerance, if one path becomes unavailable; there is another way for the packets to travel.

Datagram packet switching networks are connectionless, meaning that they do not require a dedicated active connection for the packets to reach their destination. In a connectionless method, the communications link isn't established between sender and recipient before packets can be transmitted. Connectionless switching use various routes and enable multiple network users to use the circuits simultaneously.

This is in contrast to virtual packet switching, a connection-oriented method in which the communications link is made before any packets transmit. Because the link is established before transmission begins, the packets that constitute a message all follow the same route to their destination.

> **NOTE: Datagram Packet Sizes**   The data packet size used with datagram packet switching is kept small in case of error, which would cause the packets to be re-

Circuit Switching

In contrast to the packet-switching method, *circuit switching* requires a dedicated physical connection between the sending and receiving devices. The most commonly used analogy to represent circuit switching is a telephone conversation, in which the parties involved have a dedicated link between them for the duration of the conversation. When either party disconnects, the circuit is broken, and the data path is lost. This is an accurate representation of how circuit switching works with network and data transmissions. The sending system establishes a physical connection; the data is transmitted between the two; and when the transmission is complete, the channel is closed.

Some clear advantages to the circuit-switching technology make it well suited for certain applications. The primary advantage is that after a connection is established, a consistent and reliable connection exists between the sending and receiving device. This enables for transmissions at a guaranteed rate of transfer.

Like all technologies, circuit switching has downsides. As you might imagine, a dedicated communication line can be inefficient. After the physical connection is established, it is unavailable to any other sessions until the transmission is complete. Again using the phone call analogy, this would be like a caller trying to reach another caller and getting a busy signal. Circuit switching can therefore be fraught with long connection delays. Figure 8.3 shows an example of circuit switching.

Message Switching

In some respects, *message switching* is similar to packet switching, but instead of using and sending packets, message switching divides data transmissions into

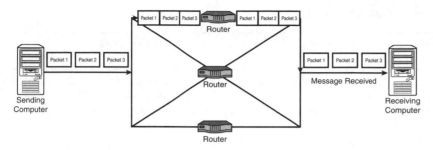

Figure 8.3   An example of circuit switching.

messages. Like packets, each of these messages contains the destination address. Devices on the network that forward the message use this destination address. Each intermediate device in the message's path stores the message momentarily and then forwards it to the next device in the network, until it finally reaches its destination. Message switching is therefore often referred to as the *store-and-forward* method.

NOTE: Email and the Store-and-Forward Method   The store-and-forward method used by message switching makes it well suited for certain applications, including email.

Message switching offers many advantages over circuit switching. Because message switching doesn't require a dedicated connection as does circuit switching, a larger number of devices can share the bandwidth of the network. A message-switching system also has the capability of storing messages, which enables the traffic on the network to clear. This strategy can significantly reduce the traffic congestion on the network.

The main drawbacks are that the store-and-forward method makes it a poor choice for real-time applications, such as videoconferencing, in which the temporary storing of data would be disruptive to the message. A second drawback is that the intermediate devices, often PC systems, must temporarily store messages by using their hard disk space.

Comparing Switching Methods

Table 8.1 summarizes the characteristics of the various switching methods.

Table 8.1   Comparison of Switching Methods

Switching Method	Pros	Cons	Key Features
Packet switching	Packets can be routed around network congestion. Packet switching makes efficient use of network bandwidth.	Packets can become lost while taking alternative routes to the destination. Messages are divided into packets that contain source and destination information.	Packets can travel the network independently, looking for the best route to the destination system. The two types of packet switching are datagram and virtual-circuit packet switching.
Circuit switching	Offers a dedicated transmission channel reserved until disconnected.	Dedicated channels can cause delays because a channel is unavailable until one side disconnects. Uses a dedicated physical link between the sending and receiving devices.	Offers the capability of storing messages temporarily to reduce network congestion.
Message switching	Multiple devices have the capability to share bandwidth.	The store-and-forward system makes message switching impractical for many real-time applications. Intermediate devices temporarily store and then forward messages.	Entire messages are sent during transmissions.

WAN Technologies

Having looked at the differences between the various switching methods, we can now take a better look at the technologies used to create WANs. Several technologies can create a WAN—each varies on speed, cost, and implementation difficulty. In this section we explore the various types of WAN technologies and where they are used in today's networks.

> **TIP: Multiprotocol Label Switching (MPLS)**   MPLS is a technology designed to speed up network traffic flow by moving away from the use of traditional routing tables. The WAN technologies discussed in this section can use MPLS, but because it is associated with network routing, it was included in Chapter 5, "TCP/IP Addressing and Routing."

X.25

X.25 was one of the original packet-switching technologies, but today it has been replaced in many applications by Frame Relay, which you learn about in the next section. Various telephone companies, along with network providers, developed X.25 in the mid-1970s to transmit digital data over analog signals on copper lines. Because so many entities had their hands in the development and implementation of X.25, it works well on many kinds of networks with different types of traffic. X.25 is one of the oldest standards, and therein lies both its greatest advantage and its greatest disadvantage. On the upside, X.25 is a global standard. On the downside, its original maximum transfer speed is 56Kbps, which is reasonable when compared to other technologies in the mid-1970s but slow and cumbersome today. However, in the 1980s a digital version of X.25 was released, increasing throughput to a maximum of 64Kbps. This, too, is slow by today's standards.

Because X.25 is a packet-switching technology, it uses different routes to get the best possible connection between the sending and receiving device at a given time. As conditions on the network change, such as increased network traffic, so do the routes that the packets take. Consequently, each packet is likely to take a different route to reach its destination during a single communication session. The devices that make it possible to use X.25 service are called *packet assemblers/disassemblers (PAD)*. A PAD is required at each end of the X.25 connection.

Frame Relay

Frame Relay was a step up from X.25 and provided a faster form of packet switching networking than X.25. Frame Relay is a wide area networking protocol that operates at the data link layers of the OSI model. Chapter 9, "OSI Model," discusses the OSI model in detail. Frame Relay enables data transmission for intermittent traffic between LANs and between end points in a WAN.

Frame Relay was designed to provide standards for transmitting data packets in high-speed bursts over digital networks, using a public data network service. Frame Relay is a packet-switching technology that uses variable-length packets. Essentially, Frame Relay is a streamlined version of X.25. It uses smaller packet sizes and fewer error-checking mechanisms than X.25 and has less overhead than X.25.

Frame Relay typically operates over permanent virtual circuits (PVC), meaning that data transmissions follow a known route, and no need exists for the transmitting devices to figure out which route is best to use at a destination. Like X.25, Frame Relay uses addressing information in each frame header to determine where packets should go. Frame Relay can be implemented on several WAN technologies, including 56Kbps, T1, T3, and ISDN lines.

TIP: **Packet Switching**   Remember for the Network+ exam that Frame Relay is a packet-switching technology that uses PVCs.

To better understand how Frame Relay works, we look at some of the components of the technology. The following list outlines some of these components and their function:

■ **Frame Relay Access Device or Frame Relay Assembler/Disassembler (FRAD)**—A device located on the local area network designed to modify data packets by placing header and trailer information on outgoing packets to enable them to travel on the Frame Relay network. The addition of information to the data packets is known as encapsulation. On the receiving end, the header and trailer information is stripped from the data packets (decapsulation). The FRAD can be a dedicated hardware device or part of the function of a specialized router.

■ **Frame Relay link**—Refers to the media that connects the local network to the Frame Relay switch. This link can be a T1/T3 link, ISDN, or fiber.

■ **Frame Relay switch**—Responsible for routing the frames after they enter the Frame Relay network. A frame might pass through several Frame Relay switches before reaching its destination. A Frame Relay switch can be part of a private network and owned by a particular company, and often the Frame Relay switch is part of a public network that can be leased.

■ **Backbone media**—Responsible for connecting the Frame Relay switches. This backbone link is often fiber or T1/T3 links. The wiring of the backbone is typically a mesh topology enabling for redundant links interconnecting the Frame Relay switches.

■ **Virtual circuit**—Starts from the local network and the FRAD and connects to the FRAD on the receiving end. The virtual link is often a PVC.

Figure 8.4 shows the components of a Frame Relay network.

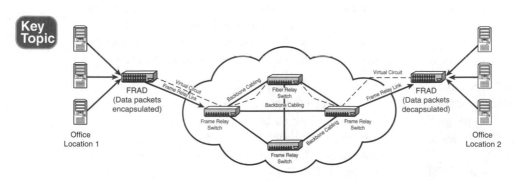

Figure 8.4 Components of a Frame Relay network.

Additional terms you will encounter when reading about Frame Relay networks include data terminal equipment (DTE), data circuit terminating equipment (DCE), and data link connection identifier (DLCI).

- **Data terminal equipment (DTE)**—In the Frame Relay world, the term DTE refers to terminating equipment located with a company's network. Termination equipment includes such hardware as end-user systems, servers, routers, bridges, and switches.

- **Data circuit-terminating equipment (DCE)**—Refers to the equipment owned by the carrier. This equipment provides the switching services for the network and therefore is responsible for actually transmitting the data through the WAN.

- **Data link connectionidentifier (DLCI)**—A number that identifies the logical circuit between the router and the Frame Relay switch.

As previously mentioned, Frame Relay uses virtual circuits to create a communication channel. These virtual circuits establish a bidirectional communication link from DTE devices

T-Carrier Lines

T-carrier lines are high-speed lines that can be leased from telephone companies. T-carrier lines can support both voice and data transmissions and are often used to create point-to-point private networks. Four types of T-carrier lines are available:

- **T1**—Offers transmission speeds of 1.544Mbps and can create point-to-point dedicated digital communication paths. T1 lines have commonly been used for connecting LANs.

- **T2**—Offers transmission speeds of 6.312Mbps. T2 lines accomplish this by using 96 64Kbps B channels.

- **T3**—Offers transmission speeds of up to 44.736Mbps by using 672 64Kbps B channels.

- **T4**—Offers impressive transmission speeds of up to 274.176Mbps by using 4,032 64Kbps B channels.

Of these T-carrier lines, the ones commonly associated with networks are T-1 and T-3 lines, which the following sections discuss.

T1/E1/J1 Lines

T1 (also known as a *leased line*) is a dedicated digital circuit leased from the telephone company. This creates an always-open, always-available line between you and whomever you choose to connect to when you establish the service. T1 lines also eliminate the one-call-per wire limitation by using a method called *multiplexing*, or *muxing*. Using a device called a *multiplexer*, the signal is broken into smaller pieces and assigned identifiers. Multiple transmissions are divided by the multiplexer and transmitted across the wire simultaneously. When the signals reach their destination, they are put back in the proper order and converted back into the proper form.

Having T1 service used to be the way to show someone you were serious about your particular communication needs. T1 lines were expensive; however, their prices have fallen in the past few years, as other technologies have begun to rival their transmission rates. T1 offers data rates up to 1.544Mbps. The obvious advantages of a T1 line are its constant connection—no dial-up or other connection is required because it is always on—and it can be reliably budgeted because it has a fixed monthly cost. In addition, the transfer rate is guaranteed because it, like a telephone call, is a private circuit. Many companies use T1 lines as their pipelines to the Internet.

It is important to point out that T-carrier is the designation to the technology used in the United States and Canada. In Europe, they are referred to as E-carriers and in Japan, J-carriers. Table 8.2 shows the T/E/J carriers.

Table 8.2 Comparing T/E/J Carriers

Name	Transmission Speed	Voice Channels
T1	1.544Mbps	24
T1C	3.152Mbps	48
T2	6.312Mbps	96
T3	44.736Mbps	672
T4	274.176Mbps	4032
J0	64Kbps	1
J1	1.544Mbps	24
J1C	3.152Mbps	48
J2	6.312Mbps	96
J3	32.064Mbps	480
J3C	97.728Mbps	1440
J4	397.200Mbps	5760
E0	64Kbps	1
E1	2.048Mbps	30
E2	8.448Mbps	120
E3	34.368Mbps	480

Table 8.2   Comparing T/E/J Carriers

Name	Transmission Speed	Voice Channels
E4	139.264Mbps	1920
E5	565.148Mbps	7680

T3 Lines

For a time, the speeds offered by T1 lines were sufficient for all but a few organizations. As networks and the data they support expanded, T1 lines did not provide enough speed for many organizations. T3 service answered the call by providing transmission speeds of 44.736Mbps.

T3 lines are dedicated circuits that provide high capacity and are generally used by large companies, ISPs, or long-distance companies. T3 service offers all the strengths of a T1 service (just a whole lot more), but the costs associated with T3 limits its use to the few organizations that have the money to pay for it.

NOTE: Fractional T   Because of the cost of a T-carrier solution, it is possible to lease portions of a T-carrier service. Known as *fractional T*, you can subscribe and pay for service based on 64Kbps channels.

SONET/OCx Levels

In 1984 the U.S. Department of Justice and AT&T reached an agreement stating that AT&T was a monopoly that needed to be divided into smaller, directly competitive companies. This created a challenge for local telephone companies, which were then faced with the task of connecting to an ever-growing number of independent long-distance carriers, each of which had a different interfacing mechanism. Bell Communications Research answered the challenge by developing SONET, a fiber-optic WAN technology that delivers voice, data, and video at speeds starting at 51.84Mbps. Bell's main goals in creating SONET were to create a standardized access method for all carriers within the newly competitive U.S. market and to unify different standards around the world. SONET can transmission speeds between 51.84Mbps to 40Gbps and beyond.

TIP: SONET   For the Network+ exam, remember that SONET is an optical interface standard that enables transmission equipment from multiple vendors to talk together over fiber-optic lines.

One of Bell's biggest accomplishments with SONET was that it created a new system that defined data rates in terms of Optical Carrier (OCx) levels. Table 8.3 contains the OCx levels you should be familiar with.

Table 8.3   OCx Levels and Transmission Rates

OC Level	Transmission Rate
OC-1	51.84Mbps
OC-3	155.52Mbps
OC-12	622.08Mbps
OC-24	1.244Gbps
OC-48	2.488Gbps
OC-96	4.976Gbps
OC-192	9.953Gbps
OC-768	39.813Gbps

NOTE: SDH   Synchronous Digital Hierarchy (SDH) is the European counterpart to SONET.

NOTE: OCx Levels   OC, or optical carrier levels, represent the range of digital signals that can be carried on the SONET fiber-optic network. Each OC level defines the speed at which it operates.

Asynchronous Transfer Mode (ATM)

When it was introduced in the early 1990s, ATM was heralded as a breakthrough technology for networking because it was an end-to-end solution, ranging in use from a desktop to a remote system. Though promoted as both a LAN and WAN solution, ATM did not live up to its hype because of associated implementation costs and a lack of standards. The introduction of Gigabit Ethernet, which offered great transmissions speeds and compatibility with existing network infrastructure, further dampened the momentum of the ATM bandwagon.

ATM is a packet-switching technology that provides transfer speeds commonly ranging from 1.544Mbps to 622Mbps. It is well suited for a variety of data types, such as voice, data, and video. Using fixed-length packets, or cells, that are 53 bytes long, ATM can operate much more efficiently than variable-length-packet packet-switching technologies such as Frame Relay. Having a fixed-length packet enables ATM to be concerned only with the header information of each packet. It does not need to read every bit of a packet to determine the beginning and end of the packet. ATM's fixed cell length also makes it easily adaptable to other technologies as they develop. Each cell has 48 bytes available for data, with 5 bytes reserved for the ATM header.

ATM uses virtual connections to connect end points in an ATM network. The ATM network can use PVCs or SVCs. PVC and SVC were discussed earlier in this chapter. ATM networks using PVCs have the following characteristics:

- PVC is permanent.

- PVC cells cannot take alternative routes to an end point in the event of circuit failure.

- Even when not in use, bandwidth is still reserved for the PVC.

ATM using SVC has the following characteristics:

- SVCs are dynamically connected on an as-needed basis.

- After an SVC connection is released, resources are available for other applications.

- ATM cells can take an alternative route to an end point in the event of failure.

ATM is compatible with the most widely used and implemented networking media types available today, including single-mode and multimode fiber, coaxial cable, unshielded twisted pair, and shielded twisted pair. Although it can be used over various media, the limitations of some of the media types make them impractical choices. ATM can also operate over other media, including FDDI, T-1, T-3, SONET, OC-3, and Fiber Channel.

Integrated Services Digital Network (ISDN)

ISDN is a dial-up technology capable of transmitting voice and data simultaneously over the same physical connection. Using ISDN, users can access digital communication channels via both packet- and circuit-switching connections. ISDN is much faster than a dial-up modem connection. To access ISDN, a dedicated phone line is required, and this line is usually paid for through a monthly subscription. You can expect these monthly costs to be significantly higher than those for a dial-up modem account.

NOTE: ISDN Switching   ISDN is a circuit-switched telephone network system designed to enable digital transmission of voice and data over ordinary telephone copper wires.

To establish an ISDN connection, you dial the number for the end of the connection, much as you would with a conventional phone call or modem dial-up connection. A conversation between the sending and receiving devices is then established. The connection is dropped when one end disconnects or hangs up. The line pickup of ISDN is fast, enabling a connection to be established, or brought up, quickly—much more quickly than a conventional phone line.

Although ISDN uses the same media as PSTN or regular phone wires, it does so in a much different manner. PSTN was not originally designed for data transfer, so a dial-up modem converts PSTN analog signals to digital signals that carry data and network traffic. One of the problems with this has been that not all the communication is digital. The telephone exchange to the modem is an analog signal, and from the modem to the computer is a digital signal.

ISDN, however, uses digital communication right from the ISDN exchange to the network end point. Because the entire communication path is digital, data transfer is faster, and the analog to digital conversion is not necessary. Figure 8.5 shows a simple comparison between PSTN links and ISDN links.

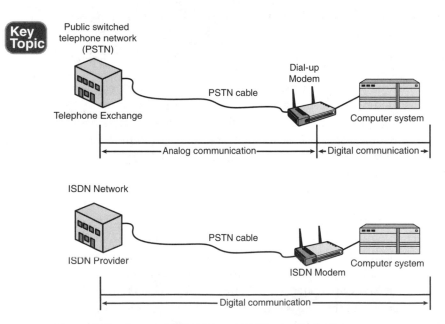

Figure 8.5   Comparing PSTN and ISDN communication.

ISDN has two defined interface standards—Basic Rate Interface (BRI) and Primary Rate Interface (PRI)—which the following sections discuss.

Basic Rate Interface (BRI)

BRI defines a communication line that utilizes three separate channels. There are two B (that is, bearer) channels of 64Kbps each and one D (that is, delta) channel of 16Kbps. The two B channels carry digital information, which can be either voice or data. The B channels can independently provide 64Kbps access or combine to utilize the entire 128Kbps. The D channel is for out-of-band signaling.

NOTE: 2B+D BRI ISDN is sometimes referred to as 2B+D. This abbreviation simply refers to the available channels.

To use BRI ISDN, the connection point must be within 5,486 meters (18,000 feet) of the ISDN provider's BRI service center. In addition, to use BRI ISDN, special equipment is needed, such as ISDN routers and ISDN terminal adapters.

Primary Rate Interface (PRI)

PRI is a form of ISDN generally carried over a T1 line and can handle transmission rates of up to 1.536Mbps. PRI is composed of 23 B channels (30 in Europe), each providing 64Kbps for data/voice and one 64Kbps D channel.

NOTE: Leased Lines ISDN is considered a leased line because access to ISDN is leased from a service provider.

Comparing BRI and PRI ISDN

Table 8.4 compares BRI and PRI ISDN.

Table 8.4 BRI and PRI ISDN Comparison

Characteristic	BRI	PRI
Speed	128Kbps	1.536M
Channels	2B+D	23B+D
Transmission carrier	PSTN	T1

TIP: PRI+BRI For the Network+ exam, be sure you can identify the characteristics of ISDN, including the speeds of BRI and PRI.

WAN Technology Summary

Table 8.5 summarizes the main characteristics of some of the various WAN technologies discussed in this chapter. You can use this table as an aid in reviewing before you take the Network+ exam.

Table 8.5 WAN Technology Overview

WAN Technology	Supported Speed	Switching Characteristic	Key Media	Method Used
ISDN	BRI: 64Kbps to128Kbps PRI: 64Kbps to 1.5Mbps	Copper	Can be used for circuit-switching or packet-switching connections. BRI uses 2B+D channels; PRI uses 23B+D channels. B channels are 64Kbps. ISDN uses the public network and requires dial-in access.	ISDN can transmit all types of traffic, including voice, video, and data.
T-carrier (T1, T3)	T1: 1.544Mbps; T3: 44.736Mbps	Copper/fiber-optic	Circuit switching	T-carrier creates point-to-point network connections for private networks.
ATM	1.544Mbps to 622Mbps	Copper/fiber-optic	Cell switching	ATM uses fixed cells 53 bytes long.
X.25	56Kbps/64Kbps	Copper/fiber-optic	Packet switching	X.25 provides a packet-switching network over standard phone lines.
Frame Relay	56Kbps to 1.544Mbps	Copper/fiber-optic	PVCs and SVCs	Frame Relay is a packet-oriented protocol and uses variable-length packets.
SONET/OCx	51.8Mbps	Fiber optic	N/A	SONET defines synchronous to 40Gbps+ data transfer over optical cable.

Internet Access Technologies

For most organizations, the Internet is an essential component of their business. Many of the business applications such as email, videoconferencing, and VPN connections cannot operate without the Internet. For businesses, the debate is not whether to have an Internet connection but choosing the type of Internet connection that best suits an organization's needs.

In this section we compare the various Internet access technologies. The one chosen by an organization depends on many factors, including transfer speeds, availability, and cost. We start by looking at the oldest and slowest method of Internet access, the plain old telephone system (POTS).

POTS Internet Access

Though slow by today's standards, many people still connect to the Internet using a telephone line and modem. Mainly, POTS Internet access is used in rural areas where higher speed Internet access technologies are not available. Businesses and individuals located in remote areas might have no choice but to use POTS. Others might use POTS if their Internet usage is low and used only for such applications as email.

Internet access through a phone system requires two things: a modem and a dial-up access account through an ISP. As you might recall from Chapter 3, "Networking Components and Devices," modems are devices that convert the digital signals generated by a computer system into analog signals that can travel across a phone line. A computer can have either an internal or external modem. External modems tend to be less problematic to install and troubleshoot because they don't require reconfiguration of the host system. Internal modems use one of the serial port assignments (that is, a COM port) and must therefore be configured not to conflict with other devices.

The second piece of the puzzle, the dial-up ISP account, can easily be obtained by contacting one of the many local, regional, or national ISPs. Most ISPs offer a range of plans normally priced based on the amount of time the user is allowed to spend online. Almost without exception, ISPs offer 56Kbps access, the maximum possible under current standards. Most ISPs also provide email accounts, access to newsgroup servers, and often small amounts of web space.

It is a good idea to research an ISP choice carefully. Free services exist but generally restrict users to a certain number of online hours per month or use extensive banner advertising to pay for the services. Normally, you pay a monthly service fee for an ISP; doing so provides a degree of reassurance because the ISP can be held accountable. Paid-for service also tends to provide a higher level of support.

Another big consideration for dial-up Internet access is how many lines the ISP has. ISPs never have the same number of lines as subscribers; instead, they work on a first-come, first-served basis for dial-up clients. This means that on occasion, users get busy signals when they try to connect. Before signing up for a dial-up Internet access account, ask the company what its ratio of lines to subscribers is, and use that figure as part of your comparison criteria.

With a modem and an ISP account, you are ready to connect. But what happens if things do not run as planned? Welcome to the interesting and sometimes challenging world of troubleshooting dial-up connections.

POTS Troubleshooting Procedures

Troubleshooting a dial-up connection problem can be tricky and time-consuming because you must consider many variables. Of the remote connectivity mechanisms discussed in this chapter, you are far more likely to have problems with a POTS connection than any of the others. The following are some places to start your troubleshooting under various conditions.

NOTE: Technical Support   In some cases, users might not use an ISP and instead dial another system on the corporate network directly. In that case, all the troubleshooting steps in this section apply, except that you have to rely on the technical support capabilities of the person responsible for the remote system rather than the ISP if you have a problem.

If the user cannot dial out, try the following:

■ **Check physical connections**—The most common problem with modem connections is that something has become unplugged; modems rarely fail after they initially work. For an external modem, you also need to verify that the modem has power.

■ **Check for a dial tone on analog lines**—You can do this by plugging a normal phone into the socket and seeing whether you can dial out. Also, a modem generally has a speaker, and you can set up the modem to use the speaker so that you can hear what is going on.

If the user can dial out but cannot connect to the network, try the following:

■ **Make sure that the user is dialing the correct number**—This suggestion sounds obvious, but sometimes numbers change or are entered incorrectly.

■ **Call the ISP**—You can call the ISP to determine whether it is having problems.

■ **Check the modem speaker**—Find out whether you are getting busy signals from the ISP by turning on the modem speaker.

If the user can dial out and can get a connection but is then disconnected, try the following:

■ **Make sure that the modem connection is configured correctly**—The most common modem configuration is 8 data bits, 1 stop bit, and no parity (commonly referred to as *eight-one-none*).

■ **Check the username and password**—Make sure that the correct username and password combination is configured for the dial-up connection.

■ **Verify that the connection settings are correct**—Pay particular attention to things such as the IP address. Nearly all ISPs assign IP addresses through DHCP, and trying to connect with a statically configured IP address is not permitted.

- **Make sure that the user has not exceeded a preset connection time limit—**
  Some ISPs restrict the number of monthly access hours. If the user has such a
  plan, check to make sure that some time credit is left.

- **Try specifying a lower speed for the connection—**Modems are designed to
  negotiate a connection speed with which both devices are comfortable. Sometimes, during the negotiation process, the line can be dropped. Initially setting
  a lower speed might get a connection. You can then increase the modem speed
  to accommodate a better connection.

Call Waiting

If you troubleshoot a dial-up connection that randomly slows down or disconnects
completely, check to see whether the line has a call-waiting function on it. As you
probably know, when call waiting is used, a tone informs you during the call that someone is trying to get through. This tone interferes with the modem connection and can
cause it to either slow down for a period of time or drop the connection altogether.

Call-waiting problems are difficult to troubleshoot because they occur only when a
call is coming in and when you are on that line. Moving the system to another line
might make the connection work properly and leave all concerned scratching their
heads. The good news is that the solution to the call-waiting problem is simple. The
telephone company can give you a code to add to the beginning of the modem dial
string to temporarily disable call waiting for the duration of the call. In most cases,
the telephone company or ISP can help you configure the disabling of call waiting
if you need such help.

Troubleshooting Poor Connection Speeds

Even if you are not having a problem connecting, you might find that the speed of
modem connections is problematic. Such problems are not uncommon. The modem might say it can handle a certain speed, and the ISP might advertise the same,
but often you simply cannot get the maximum supported speed on a dial-up connection. There are many possible reasons; some of them you can do something
about, and some of them you can't. Here are some of the reasons speeds might not
be as fast as expected:

- **Poor line quality—**In some areas, the quality of the telephone lines and exchange equipment can reduce the maximum possible connection speed.

- **Incorrectly configured modem—**The modem configuration is important in
  ensuring the highest possible connection speed. In particular, for external
  modems, you should check the configuration of the serial port the modem
  connects to. Defaults sometimes restrict the speed of the port. Generally,
  though, an incorrectly configured modem or serial port will prevent the modem from making a connection at all, not just impact the speed.

- **Poor-quality modems**—Perhaps less of an issue now than in the past, poor-quality modems can contribute to poor connection speeds and connectivity problems. Paying the extra money for a good-quality modem is worth the savings in frustration alone.

After all this, it is worth mentioning that after you establish a connection, whatever the speed, you are still at the mercy of the ISP. Even a 56Kbps link might be too slow if the ISP's networking equipment or Internet connection can't keep up with demand. Unfortunately, there is no way to know whether the bottleneck is with the ISP or the modem.

Modem-Specific Troubleshooting

Typically, modems are reliable devices. They have no moving parts, and chances are that after you have installed, configured, and tested a modem, you won't have to play around with it again. However, exceptions can occur, and you should be aware of the following modem-specific troubleshooting measures:

- **Make sure that you have the latest drivers**—For any type of modem, make sure that the latest drivers are installed. The drivers supplied with modems typically are not up-to-date, and a visit to the modem manufacturer's website (from another computer) might yield more up-to-date drivers. Try to avoid using generic drivers or those provided with operating systems where possible. Even if they work, which they often don't, they probably won't offer all the features of the proper drivers.

- **Check for resource conflicts**—On older PCs, make sure that no conflicts exist between internal modems and other system resources. For external devices, make sure that serial ports are enabled and configured correctly.

- **Check for firmware updates**—Both internal and external modems have updatable firmware chips. Check the modem manufacturer's website to ensure that you have the latest version of the firmware. (Note that firmware updates should be completed only if they fix a specific problem you are having.)

If you are confident that a modem is installed and configured correctly, but it's still not working properly, you can test and configure it by using special commands called the *AT command set*. These commands are mentioned briefly in Chapter 3 but are worthy of a more detailed discussion here; they are often useful for troubleshooting modems and related connectivity problems.

You can use AT commands through a communications application to talk directly to the modem. On Windows platforms, you can use the Telnet utility. On most common Linux distributions, you can use the `minicom` utility. After you establish a session with the modem, you can issue AT commands directly to the modem, which will respond in different ways, depending on the command. Table 8.6 lists some of the most commonly used AT commands.

Table 8.6 Commonly Used AT Commands

AT Command	Result
ATA	Sets the modem to autoanswer
ATH	Hangs up an active connection
ATD	Dials a number
ATZ	Resets the modem.
ATI3	Displays the name and model of the modem

In general, getting the modem to respond to an ATZ command is a good enough indicator that the modem is functioning.

> **TIP: AT Commands**   Be prepared to identify the function of basic AT commands for the Network+ exam.

xDSL

DSL is an Internet access method that uses a standard phone line to provide high-speed Internet access. DSL is available only in certain areas, although as the telephone companies try to cash in on the broadband Internet access market, the areas of coverage are likely to increase.

DSL offers phone and data transmissions over a standard phone connection. DSL is most commonly associated with high-speed Internet access; because it is less expensive than technologies such as ISDN, it is often used in homes and small businesses. With DSL, a different frequency can be used for digital and analog signals, which means that you can talk to a friend on the phone while you're uploading data.

DSL arrived on the scene in the late 1990s and brought with it a staggering number of flavors. Together, all these variations are known as xDSL:

- **Asymmetric DSL (ADSL)**—Probably the most common of the DSL varieties is ADSL. The word *asymmetric* describes different bands on the line: One band is used for POTS and is responsible for analog traffic, the second band is used to provide upload access, and the third band is used for downloads. With ADSL, downloads are faster than uploads.

- **Symmetric DSL (SDSL)**—Offers the same speeds for uploads and for downloads, making it most suitable for business applications such as web hosting, intranets, and ecommerce. It is not widely implemented in the home/small business environment and cannot share a phone line.

- **ISDN DSL (IDSL)**—A symmetric type of DSL commonly used in environments where SDSL and ADSL are unavailable. IDSL does not support analog phones.

- **Rate Adaptive DSL (RADSL)**—A variation on ADSL that can modify its transmission speeds based on the signal quality. RADSL supports line sharing. RADSL is an asymmetric form of DSL.

- **Very High Bit Rate DSL (VHDSL)**—An asymmetric version of DSL and, as such, can share a telephone line. VHDSL supports high bandwidth applications such as VoIP and HDTV. VHDSL can achieve data rates up to 10Mbps and up, making it the fastest available form of DSL.

- **High Bit Rate DSL (HDSL)**—A symmetric technology withidentical transmission rates in both directions. HDSL does not enable line sharing with analog phones.

Why are there are so many DSL variations? The answer is that each flavor of DSL is aimed at a different user, business, or application. Businesses with high bandwidth needs are more likely to choose a symmetric form of DSL, whereas budget-conscious environments such as home offices are likely to choose an option that enables phone line sharing at the expense of bandwidth. When you work in a home/small office environment, you should expect to work with an ADSL system.

> **TIP: Symmetric or Asymmetric**   For the Network+ exam you should know which DSL options are asymmetric DSL (ADSL) or symmetric (SDSL, HDSL). ADSL is used for Internet access, where fast downstream is required, but slow upstream is not a problem. Symmetric offers high-speed transfers in both directions.

DSL options can be either a shared or a dedicated link. ADSL, for instance, is a shared DSL connection. The shared connection means that a single telephone line can support both voice and Internet service. This is possible because a telephone cable uses two frequencies: high and low. The low frequency is used for DSL Internet, whereas the high frequency is used for voice.

If you see the term *rate adaptive* used with a DSL technology, it means that the speed of the connection fluctuates. This fluctuation is caused by several factors, including the distance between the DSL provider and the Internet system, the condition of the physical line used by the DSL connection, or the interference on the line. This makes technologies such as ADSL inconsistent in terms of speed, but for most day-to-day applications, these speed fluctuations will go largely unnoticed.

If there are shared DSL links, there must be dedicated DSL links. A dedicated DSL link is a more costly Internet solution but provides some clear advantages. Business DSL solutions such as SDSL provide a dedicated DSL link over copper from the service provider to the Internet system. A dedicated DSL line is not used for regular voice transmissions.

Table 8.7 summarizes the expected speeds of the various DSL options.

Table 8.7 Expected DSL Speeds

DSL Variation	Upload Speed	Download Speed	Type
ADSL	1Mbps	8Mbps	Asymmetric
SDSL	1.5Mbps	1.5Mbps	Symmetric
IDSL	144Kbps	144Kbps	Symmetric
RADSL	1Mbps	7Mbps	Asymmetric
VHDSL	1.6Mbps	10Mbps+	Asymmetric
HDSL	768Kbps	768Kbps	Symmetric

Speeds may vary greatly depending on technologies used and quality of connection.

> **NOTE: Broadband**   The term *broadband* refers to high-speed Internet access. Both DSL and cable modem are common broadband Internet technologies. Broadband routers and broadband modems are network devices that support both DSL and cable.

Troubleshooting DSL is similar to troubleshooting any other Internet connection. The following are a few things to check when users are experiencing problems with a DSL connection:

- **Physical connections**—The first place to look when troubleshooting a DSL problem is the network cable connections. From time to time, these cables can come loose or inadvertently be detached and are often overlooked as the cause of a problem. DSL modems typically have a minimum of three connections: one for the DSL line, one for the local network, and one for the power. Make sure that they are all plugged in appropriately.

- **NIC**—While you're checking the cable at the back of the system, take a quick look to see whether the network card LED is lit. If it is not, something could be wrong with the card. It might be necessary to swap out the network card and replace it with one that is known to be working.

- **Drivers**—Confirm that the network card is installed and has the correct drivers. Many times, simply using the most up-to-date driver can resolve connectivity issues.

- **Protocol configuration**—The device you troubleshoot might not have a valid IP address. Confirm the IP address by using the appropriate tool for the operating system being used—for example, `ipconfig` (Windows), or `ifconfig` (UNIX). If the system requires the automatic assignment of an IP address, confirm that the system is set to obtain an IP address automatically. It might be necessary to use the `ipconfig /release` and `ipconfig /renew` commands to get a new IP address.

■ **DSL LEDs**—Each DSL box has an LED on it. The light sequences are often used to identify connectivity problems or problems with the box. Refer to the manufacturer's website for specific information about error codes and LEDs, but remember the basics: A link light should be on to indicate that the physical connection is complete, and a flashing LED indicates activity on the connection.

TIP: Remember the Visual Indicators   When troubleshooting remote connectivity on a cable or DSL modem, use the LEDs that are always present on these devices to aid in your troubleshooting process.

Ultimately, if none of these steps cure or indicate the cause of the problem, you might have to call the DSL provider for assistance.

Cable Internet Access

Cable Internet access isan always-on Internet access method available in areas that have digital cable television. Not all cable TV providers offer Internet access, but an increasing number are taking advantage of the relatively simple jump from being cable providers to being ISPs.

Cable Internet access is attractive to many small businesses and home office users because it is both inexpensive and reliable. In the past, most cable providers did not restrict how much use is made of the access. However, with large data transfers associated with today's Internet usage, many companies are now restricting the amount of upstream or downstream traffic. Additional bandwidth can often be purchased if necessary.

With cable Internet, connectivity is achieved by using a device called a *cable modem*; it has a coaxial connection for connecting to the provider's outlet and an unshielded twisted-pair (UTP) connection for attaching directly to a system, hub, or switch.

Cable providers often supply a cable modem for a monthly fee, or it is possible to buy one from the cable company to avoid the monthly charge. Many cable providers offer free or low-cost installation of cable Internet service, which includes installing a network card in a PC. Some providers do not charge for the network card. Cable Internet costs are comparable to a DSL subscription at about $30 to $50 a month. Business-use cable packages offering many additional features, and increased bandwidth are also available.

Most cable modems supply a 10/100/1000Mbps Ethernet connection for the home LAN, although you wouldn't expect the actual Internet connection to reach these speeds. Business often require more speed and features than a regular home user or small office does. Most cable companies offer different packages to accommodate the various Internet needs. To give you a better idea of the options available, Table 8.8 shows the options available from one cable company.

Table 8.8   Cable Internet Sample Packages

Characteristic	Home Use	Small Business	Medium Business	Large Business
Download speed	5Mbps	5Mbps	10Mbps	25Mbps
Upload speed	512Kbps	512Kbps	1Mbps	2Mbps
Monthly transfer limit	70Gbps	100Gbps	120Gbps	200Gbps
IP addresses	2 dynamic addresses	5 dynamic addresses	2 static and 10 dynamic	5 static and 20 dynamic
Email Accounts	10	10	20	30+

Keep in mind that the information provided in Table 8.8 is an example from a single cable company. Others may offer different packages with various speeds and other features.

> **NOTE: MDI-X ports**   A cable modem is generally equipped with a medium-dependent interface crossed (MDI-X) port, so a straight-through UTP cable can be used to connect the modem to a system.

One disadvantage of cable access is that you share the available bandwidth with everyone else in your cable area. As a result, during peak times, performance of a cable link might be poorer than in low-use periods. In residential areas, busy times are evenings and weekends, and particularly right after school. In general, though, performance with cable systems is good, and in low-usage periods it can be fast.

In general, cable Internet access is a low-maintenance system with few problems. When problems do occur, you can try various troubleshooting measures:

■ **Check the user's end**—Before looking at the cable modem, make sure that the system is configured correctly and that all cables are plugged in. If a hub or switch is used to share the cable Internet access among a group of computers, make sure that the hub or switch is on and functioning correctly.

■ **Check the physical connections**—Like DSL modems, cable modems have three connections: one for the cable signal, one for the local network, and one for the power. Make sure that they are all plugged in appropriately.

- **Ensure that the protocol configuration on the system is valid**—If an IP address is assigned via DHCP, the absence of an address is a sure indicator that connectivity is at fault. Try obtaining a new IP address by using the appropriate command for the operating system platform you use. If the IP addresses are statically configured, make sure that they are set correctly. Trying to use any address other than that specified by the ISP might prevent a user from connecting to the network.

- **Check the indicator lights on the modem**—Most cable modems have indicator lights that show the status of the modem. Under normal conditions, a single light labeled Ready or Online should be lit. Most cable providers provide a manual with the modem that details the functions of the lights and what they indicate in certain states. Generally, any red light is bad. Flashing LEDs normally indicate traffic on the connection.

- **Power down the modem**—Cycling the power on the modem is a sure-fire way of resetting it. However, it has to be done in a particular order. For instance, turn off the computer and then the cable modem; then unplug all devices. Plug devices in after a few seconds; power on the cable modem first and then the computer. Refer to the manufacturer for the recommended reboot and power-down process.

- **Call the technical support line**—If you are sure that the connectors are all in place and the configuration of the system is correct, the next step is to call the technical support line of the cable provider. If the provider is experiencing problems that affect many users, you might get a message while you're on hold, informing you of the fact. If not, you will eventually get to speak to someone who can help you troubleshoot the problem. One of the good things about cable access is that the cable company can remotely monitor and reset the modem. It should tell you whether the modem is functioning correctly.

Unless the modem is faulty, which is not that common, by this point the user should be back on the Internet—or at least you should fully understand why the user cannot connect. If the problem is with the cable provider's networking equipment, you and the user simply have to wait for the system to come back on.

NOTE: The Choice Is Yours   Although the debate about cable versus DSL goes on, it really won't make that much difference which one you choose. Although cable modem technology delivers *shared bandwidth* within the local neighborhood, its speeds are marginally higher but influenced by this shared bandwidth. DSL delivers *dedicated local bandwidth* but is sensitive to distance, which impacts overall performance. With the monthly costs about the same, it really is too close to call.

Broadband Security Considerations

Whether you use DSL or cable Internet access, keep security in mind. Each of these technologies offers always-on service. This means that even when you are away from your computer, it is still on the Internet. As you can imagine, this creates a security risk. The longer you are online, the more chance someone has of remotely accessing your system.

All operating systems in use today have security holes that some people are waiting to exploit. These attacks often focus on technologies such as email or open TCP/UDP ports. Combining OS security holes with an always-on Internet technology is certainly a dangerous mix.

Today, DSL and cable Internet connections have to use mechanisms such as firewalls to protect the system. The firewall system offers features such as packet filtering and network address translation (NAT). The firewall can be a third-party software application installed on the system, or it can be a hardware device.

In addition to a firewall, it is equally important to ensure that the operating system you use is completely up-to-date in terms of service packs and security updates. Today's client systems typically offer automatic update features that alert you when a new security update is available.

If you follow these safety rules, both DSL and cable Internet can provide safe Internet access. You just have to be security diligent.

Satellite Internet Access

Many of us take DSL and cable Internet access for granted, but these technologies are not offered everywhere. For areas where cheaper broadband options are not available, a limited number of Internet options exist. One of the primary ones is Internet via satellite.

Satellite access provides a viable Internet access solution for those who cannot get other methods of broadband. Satellite Internet offers an always-on connection with theoretical speeds advertised anywhere from 512Kbps upload speeds to 2048Kbps download speeds, considerably faster than a 56K dial-up connection. One primary drawback to satellite Internet is the cost, and even with the high price tag, it is not as fast as DSL or cable modem.

Although satellite Internet is slower and more costly than DSL or cable, it offers some attractive features, first of which has to be its portability. Quite literally, wherever you go, you have Internet access with no phone lines or other cables. For businesses with remote users and clients, the benefit to this is clear. But the technology has a far-reaching impact; it is not uncommon to see RVs with a satellite dish on the roof. They have 24/7 unlimited access to the Internet as they travel.

Many companies offer satellite Internet services, as a quick Internet search reveals. These Internet providers offer different Internet packages that vary greatly in terms of price, access speeds, and service. Some target businesses, whereas others aim for the private market.

Two types of broadband Internet satellite services are deployed: one-way and two-way systems. A *one-way satellite system* requires a satellite card and a satellite dish installed at the end user's site; this system works by sending outgoing requests on one link using a phone line, with inbound traffic returning on the satellite link. A *two-way satellite system*, on the other hand, provides data paths for both upstream and downstream data. Like a one-way system, a two-way system also uses a satellite card and a satellite dish installed at the end user's site; bidirectional communication occurs directly between the end user's node and the satellite.

Home satellite systems are asymmetric; that is, download speeds are faster than upload speeds. A home satellite system is likely to use a modem for the uplink traffic, with downloads coming over the satellite link. The exact speeds you can expect with satellite Internet depend on many factors. As with other wireless technologies, atmospheric conditions can significantly affect the performance of satellite Internet access. One additional consideration for satellite Internet is increased *latency*, which is the time it takes for the signal to travel back and forth from the satellite. In networking terms, this time is high and an important consideration for business applications.

Your ability to troubleshoot satellite Internet connections might be limited. Home satellite Internet is a line-of-sight wireless technology, and the installation configuration must be precise. Because of this requirement, many satellite companies insist that the satellite be set up and configured by trained staff members. If you install a satellite system in a way that does not accord with the manufacturer's recommendations, you might void any warranties.

Given this limitation, troubleshooting satellite connections often requires you to concentrate less on connectivity issues and more on physical troubleshooting techniques. Perhaps more than for any other Internet technology, calls to technical support occur early in the troubleshooting process. Be aware of the following issues that are a part of satellite Internet:

- **Rain fade**—Refers to signal loss due to moisture interference. The general rule is that the smaller the dish, the more susceptible it is to rain fade. Home and small businesses use small dishes.

- **Latency**—Refers to the time lapse between sending or requesting information and the time it actually takes to return. As you might expect, satellite communication experiences high latency because of the distance it has to travel.

- **Line of sight**—Despite the distance, satellite is basically a line of sight technology. This means that the path between the satellite dish and the satellite needs to be as unobstructed as possible.

Wireless Wide Area Networking

As discussed in Chapter 7, "Wireless Networking," a wireless LAN (WLAN) enables network users to connect to the local network and move around that network without wires. WLANs are typically restricted to a single location. To use the Internet and remotely access local area networks away from the LAN, wireless wide area networking is used.

A wireless wide area network (WWAN), covers a much larger area than WLANs do. Wireless coverage is generally offered on a city and even nationwide level, with wireless network infrastructure provided by a wireless service carrier. WWANs enable remote access to the Internet, email, and resources of a LAN. Wireless WANs use cellular networks for data transmission, a WAN modem connects to a base station on the wireless networks via radio waves. The radio tower then carries the signal to a mobile switching center, where the data is passed on to the appropriate network.

A few years ago, it would have been inconceivable to walk into your local coffee shop with your laptop under your arm and surf the web while drinking a latte. But today, it is common to see people surfing the web in many public places. This is made possible by subscribing to a wireless Internet service provider (WISP) or connecting to a company's local wireless router.

A WISP provides public wireless Internet access known as *hotspots*. Hotspots provide Internet access for mobile network devices such as laptops, handheld computers, and cell phones in airports, coffee shops, conference rooms, and so on. A hotspot is created using one or many wireless access points near the hotspot location.

Client systems might need to install special application software for billing and security purposes; others require no configuration other than obtaining the network name (SSID). Hotspots are not always a pay-for service because companies use them as a marketing tool to lure Internet users to their businesses.

As of today, hotspots are not everywhere, but finding them is not difficult. Typically, airports, hotels, and coffee shops advertise that they offer Internet access for customers or clients. In addition, WISP providers list their hotspot sites online so that they are easily found.

Establishing a connection to a wireless hotspot is a straightforward process. If not equipped with built-in wireless capability, laptops require an external wireless adapter card. With the physical requirements of the wireless card taken care of, the steps to connect are as follows:

1. When you arrive at the hotspot site, power up your laptop. In some instances, you might need to reboot your system if it were on standby to clear out old configuration settings.

2. The card might detect the network automatically. If this is the case, configuration settings, such as the SSID, will be automatically detected, and the wireless Internet will be available. If Internet access is free, there is little else to do; if it is a paid-for service, you need to enter a method of payment. One thing to remember is to verify that you are using encryption for secure data transfer.

3. If for some reason the wireless settings are not automatically detected, you need to open up your wireless NIC's configuration utility and manually set the configurations. These settings can include setting the mode to infrastructure, inputting the correct SSID, and setting the level of encryption used.

In addition to using a WISP, some companies such as hotels, cafes, and so on provide wireless Internet access by connecting a wireless router to a DSL or cable Internet connection. The router becomes the wireless access point to which the users connect and enables clients to connect to the Internet through the broadband connection. The technology is based on the 802.11 standards, typically 802.11b/g/n, and client systems require only an internal or external wireless adapter.

> **NOTE: Troubleshooting Wireless Connectivity**   There will be times when the Internet connection fails to work. Troubleshooting a wireless connectivity issue is covered in Chapter 11, "Troubleshooting Procedures and Best Practices."

Summary

This chapter outlines the technologies used to create WANs and various Internet access technologies. Each WAN technology has advantages and disadvantages, making some of them well suited for certain environments and completely impractical in others. Each of the technologies varies in terms of media, speed, availability, and cost.

Public networks such as the PSTN and the Internet are the most widely used methods of establishing WANs, due in part to their availability, accessibility, and perhaps most important, their cost. The downsides of using these networks are security and speed issues.

Private networks enable secure communications between devices; however, the costs of dedicated private networks make them unattainable for many small companies. In addition, the implementation and management of private networks can often be more complex than that of public networks.

Several switching methods can establish communication between devices. With packet switching, messages are broken into smaller pieces, with each packet assigned source, destination, and intermediate node addresses. These packets are independently routed toward the destination address. Circuit switching, on the other hand, requires a dedicated physical connection between the sending and receiving devices. Data transmissions follow the dedicated path to the receiving device. Message switching sends the entire message via intermediate devices, such as computers, temporarily storing and then forwarding the messages.

ATM and SONET are examples of packet-switching networks that use virtual circuits, either PVC or SVC, to make a connection between the sender and receiver. ISDN uses the PSTN wires and is most often associated with circuit switching. ISDN provides point-to-point digital communication and requires an ISDN modem on each end of the communication link.

There are several methods of accessing the Internet all varying in terms of speeds, range, cost, and complexity. Cable and DSL Internet are popular Internet access solutions for home users and small business. Many types of DSL versions exist, including VHDLS used for high-speed data transfers. The DSL versions are either symmetric, in which both uploads and downloads are the same speed, or asymmetric, in which uploads are slower than downloads.

Both cable and DSL are a cost-effective solution offering broadband speeds and always-on service. Satellite and wireless Internet access take availability outside the home to practically anywhere. Dial-up Internet access, although slow, remains readily available and a viable solution for many situations.

Exam Preparation Tasks

Review all the Key Topics

Review the most important topics in the chapter, noted with the key topics icon in the outer margin of the page. Table 8.9 lists a reference of these key topics and the page numbers on which each is found.

Table 8.9   Key Topics for Chapter 8

Key Topic Element	Description	Page Number
Figure 8.1	A VPN connecting two private LANs	285
Figure 8.2	An example of packet switching	288
Figure 8.3	An example of circuit switching	291
Table 8.1	Comparison of switching method	292
Figure 8.4	Components of a Frame Relay network	294
Table 8.2	Comparing T/E/J carriers	296
Table 8.3	OCx levels and transmission rates	298
Figure 8.5	Comparing PSTN and ISDN communication.	300
Table 8.4	BRI and PRI ISDN comparison	301

Complete the Tables and Lists from Memory

Print a copy of Appendix B, "Memory Tables," (found on the CD), or at least the section for this chapter, and complete the tables and lists from memory. Appendix C, "Memory Tables Answer Key," also on the CD, includes completed tables and lists to check your work.

Definitions of Key Terms

Define the following key terms from this chapter, and check your answers in the Glossary.

- ATM
- Packet switching
- Circuit switching
- Message switching
- PSTN
- PVC
- SVC
- Modem
- ISDN
- BRI
- PRI
- T-carrier
- T1/E1
- T3/E3
- DSL
- POTS
- Cable Internet
- WWAN

- WISP
- X.25
- SONET/OC-*x*

Apply Your Knowledge

Exercise 8.1 Investigating WAN Options

Estimated time: 30 minutes

Because you are unlikely to have the equipment or facilities to create your own WAN, this exercise requires that you investigate the WAN options that would be available to you if you were to create a WAN from your location to another.

Your research should include visiting the website of a local telecommunications provider and ascertaining the options open to you. Given that financial considerations are generally a major factor in a decision such as this, you should look at the lower-cost options such as cable, DSL, or ISDN in preference to leased-line circuits, such as T1 lines. From your research you should be able to answer the following questions:

- Which services are available in your location?

- Which services offer the best value for the money, based on available bandwidth, cost of installation, ongoing costs (line/equipment rental), maintenance, and call charges if applicable?

- Which of the available services would you choose, and what would the estimated annual cost be for that service?

Although you should not sign up for any of the services during the course of this exercise, through this exercise you can gain valuable information because this is exactly the kind of project you are likely to be assigned when working in a real-world situation as an administrator. Evaluation and recommendation of products is an important element of a network administrator's role.

Review Questions

You can find answers to the review questions in Appendix A, "Answers to Review Questions."

1. Your company currently uses a standard PSTN communication link to transfer files between LANs. Until now, the transfer speeds have been sufficient for the amount of data that needs to be transferred. Recently, a new application was purchased that requires a minimum transmission speed of 1.5Mbps. You have

been given the task of finding the most cost-effective solution to accommodate the new application. Which of the following technologies would you use?

   a. T3
   b. X.25
   c. T1
   d. BRI ISDN

2. You are troubleshooting an ATM network that uses PVC connections. Which of the following is not a characteristic of a PVC?

   a. PVC is permanent.
   b. PVC cells cannot take alternative routes to an end point in the event of circuit failure.
   c. Even when not in use, bandwidth is still reserved for the PVC.
   d. PVCs are dynamically connected on an as-needed basis.

3. Which of the following statements are true of ISDN? (Choose the two best answers.)

   a. BRI ISDN uses 2B+1D channels.
   b. BRI ISDN uses 23B+1D channels.
   c. PRI ISDN uses 2B+1D channels.
   d. PRI ISDN uses 23B+1D channels.

4. You have been hired to establish a WAN connection between two offices—one in Vancouver and one in Seattle. The transmission speed can be no less than 2Mbps. Which of the following technologies could you choose?

   a. T1
   b. PSTN
   c. T3
   d. ISDN

5. You have been asked to recommend a DSL Internet solution for a large company. The company is not concerned about download speeds but wants a fast version of DSL for videoconferencing. Which of the following DSL options would you choose?

   a. VHDSL
   b. SDSL
   c. IDSL
   d. HDSL

6. You are designing a Frame Relay network. Which of the following components are associated with Frame Relay networks? (Choose all that apply.)

   a. FRAD
   b. Frame Relay switch
   c. Frame Relay bridge
   d. Virtual circuit
   e. Rate adaptive switch

7. You are interested in connecting two remote offices over a public network. Which of the following is considered a public network?

  a. ISDN

  b. FDDI

  c. Internet

  d. X.25

8. Which of the following technologies requires a logical connection between the sending and receiving devices?

  a. Circuit switching

  b. Virtual-circuit packet switching

  c. Message switching

  d. High-density circuit switching

9. Which of the following statements is true of satellite Internet access?

  a. Satellite Internet access is available only in urban areas.

  b. Satellite Internet communication is symmetric.

  c. Satellite Internet access is typically faster than DSL.

  d. Satellite Internet access is asymmetric.

10. Which of the following is an advantage of ISDN over the PSTN?

  a. ISDN is more reliable.

  b. ISDN is cheaper.

  c. ISDN is faster.

  d. ISDN uses 53Kbps fixed-length packets.

11. Which of the following best describes the process of creating a dedicated circuit between two communication end points and directing traffic between those two points?

  a. Multiplexing

  b. Directional addressing

  c. Addressing

  d. Circuit switching

12. Which of the following technologies uses fixed-length packets, or cells, that are 53 bytes in length?

  a. ATM

  b. ISDN

  c. VPN

  d. FDDI

13. You need to implement a low-cost WAN implementation. Which of the following are considered public networks? (Choose the two best answers.)

  a. ATM

  b. The Internet

  c. FDDI

  d. The PSTN

14. Which of the following switching methods is associated with the store-and-forward technique?

   a. Packet switching

   b. Message switching

   c. Circuit switching

   d. Virtual-circuit packet switching

15. Which of the following are packet-switching technologies? (Choose the two best answers.)

   a. ATM

   b. X.25

   c. FDDI

   d. Frame Relay

16. Which of the following are disadvantages of a public network?

   a. Lack of security

   b. Lack of accessibility

   c. Lack of availability

   d. Increased cost

17. Which of the following circuit-switching strategies are used by ATM? (Choose the two best answers.)

   a. SVC

   b. VCD

   c. PVC

   d. PCV

18. On an ISDN connection, what is the purpose of the D channel?

   a. It carries the data signals.

   b. It carries signaling information.

   c. It enables multiple channels to be combined to provide greater band width.

   d. It provides a temporary overflow capacity for the other channels.

19. You are creating a frame relay network. Which of the following technologies are associated with frame relay networks?

   a. DTE

   b. DCE

   c. X.25

   d. PAD

20. Which of the following technologies uses independent routing?

   a. Circuit switching

   b. Packet switching

   c. ISDN

   d. PSTN

This chapter covers CompTIA Network+ objective 4.1. Upon completion of this chapter, you will be able to answer the following questions:

- What is the function of the OSI 7 layer model?
- At which level of the OSI model does common network hardware operate?
- At which level of the OSI model do TCP/IP protocols operate?

CHAPTER 9

OSI Model

One of the most important networking concepts to understand is the Open Systems Interconnection (OSI) reference model. This conceptual model, created by the International Organization for Standardization (ISO) in 1978 and revised in 1984, describes a network architecture that enables data to be passed between computer systems. Even though the OSI model is conceptual, an appreciation of its purpose and function can help you better understand how protocol suites and network architectures work in practical applications.

This chapter takes a detailed look at the OSI model and describes how it relates to real-world networking. It also examines how common network devices relate to the OSI model.

Foundation Topics

OSI Reference Model 101

Because we are about to spend some of your valuable time discussing a theoretical model, it is only reasonable that we first discuss why we have such a model and how it can help us.

In simple terms, the OSI model provides a structure that helps us work with networks. By relating services and devices to a certain layer of the model, you can get a better idea of their function and purpose. For example, switches use the Media Access Control (MAC) address of the attached devices to make forwarding decisions. In the OSI model, MAC addresses are defined in the MAC sublayer of the data link layer (Layer 2). If you knew that a bridge was also a data link layer device, you could reasonably draw the conclusion that it, too, works with MAC addresses—and you would be right. This example is perhaps one of the simplest that we can use, but it serves the purpose well: It shows how the theoretical model can be translated into actual scenarios.

The OSI model consists of seven layers, which is why it is sometimes called the OSI seven-layer model. In diagram form, as shown in Figure 9.1, the model is drawn from bottom to top in the following order: physical, data link, network, transport, session, presentation, and application layers. The physical layer is classified as Layer 1, and the application layer is classified as Layer 7. In many cases, devices are referred to in relationship to the numbered layers at which they operate. For example, a router is said to be a Layer 3 (network layer) device.

| 7 - Application |
| 6 - Presentation |
| 5 - Session |
| 4 - Transport |
| 3 - Network |
| 2 - Data link |
| 1 - Physical |

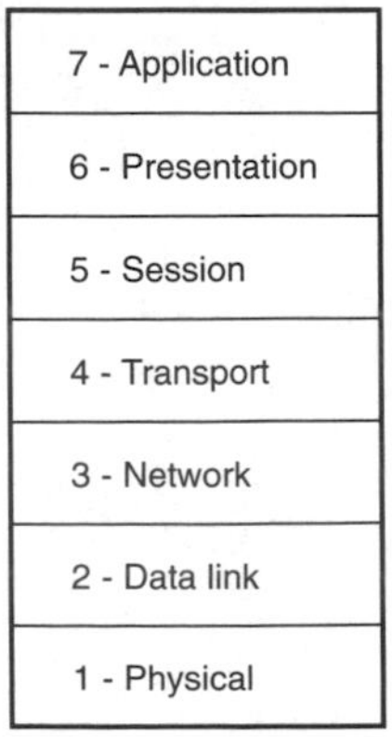

Figure 9.1   The OSI reference model.

TIP: OSI Mnemonics   Many people find it helps to use a mnemonic device to remember the order of the OSI model. Mnemonics are a memory aids and plenty are available, ranging from the surreal to the obscene. One that we particularly like is All People Seem To Need Data Processing. In this example, the first letter in each word matches the first letter of each OSI layer starting with the application layer. If you prefer, you can make up your own or even search the Internet to find some of the alternatives. If a mnemonic device helps you remember the model and the appropriate functions at each layer, it is worth using.

The model is used to relate the transport of data from one host to another. If the data were being sent from an application, such as a web browser, to a web server, it would travel down through all the layers on the sending device, across the network media, and up through all the layers on the receiving device. Figure 9.2 shows a representation of how this works.

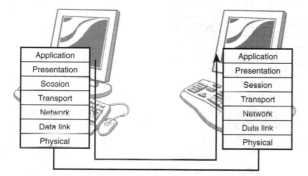

Figure 9.2   How data travels between two devices.

As data is passed up or down through the OSI model structure, headers are added (going down) or removed (going up) at each layer—a process called *encapsulation* (addition) or *decapsulation* (removal). Figure 9.3 shows how this works.

The corresponding layer at the receiving end removes the information added by each device at the sending end. Each layer defines a certain aspect of the communication process, and as data travels up and down the model, the information is sorted into logical groups of bits. The exact term used to refer to the logical group of bits depends on the layer. Table 9.1 contains the terminology used at each layer of the OSI model.

Table 9.1   Terminology Used for Logical Groups of Bits at the Layers of the OSI Model

Layer	Terms Used
Application	Packets and messages

Presentation	Packets
Session	Packets
Transport	Packets, segments, and datagrams
Network	Packets and datagrams
Data link	Packets and frames
Physical	Bits

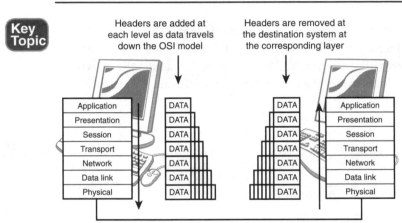

Figure 9.3   Encapsulation and decapsulation.

As you can see, at most layers the term *packet* is used, and in some cases, other terms are used as well. Each layer of the OSI model defines specific functionality. The following sections look at each of the layers separately and discuss the function of each.

Layer 1: The Physical Layer

The physical layer (sometimes referred to incorrectly as the hardware layer) is the layer of the OSI model that defines the physical characteristics of the network. The physical characteristics can include the cable and connector type, the format for pinouts for cables, and so on. It also defines how the data actually travels across the network.

The physical layer also defines the voltage used on the cable and the frequency at which the signals that carry the data are transitioned from one state to another. Such characteristics directly affect the speed of a given media and the maximum distance over which a certain media type can be used.

Because the physical layer defines the physical connection to the network, it also defines the physical topology of the network. Recall that there are a number of common physical topologies, including star, ring, bus, mesh, and hybrid, with star being the most common.

> **NOTE: OSI Numbering**   Some discussions of the OSI model examine it from top to bottom, and others examine it in reverse. Both methods are valid, but remember that the numbering starts from the bottom and works up. Therefore, it seems most logical to us to explain the model starting at Layer 1 and working up.

Various standards can be partially defined at the physical layer—for example, the Institute of Electrical and Electronics Engineers (IEEE) 802.3 Ethernet standard and the 802.5 token ring standard. If you think about it, this is reasonable: An Ethernet network card has different physical characteristics than a token ring network card; however, you should know that some of these standards overlap more than one layer of the OSI model. For example, the Ethernet standard also defines the media access method, which is a function of the data link layer.

Layer 2: The Data Link Layer

The data link layer is responsible for sending data to the physical layer so that it can be transmitted across the network. The data link layer can perform *checksums* and *error detection* on the data to make sure that the data sent is the same as the data received.

The data link layer is different from the other layers of the OSI model because it has two distinct sublayers: the Logical Link Control (LLC) sublayer and the Media Access Control (MAC) sublayer. Each has a specific role:

- **LLC**—The LLC sublayer, which is defined by the IEEE 802.2 standard, controls the access of the media, enabling multiple high-level protocols to use a single network link.

- **MAC**—The MAC sublayer manages and controls access to the network media for the protocols trying to use it. The MAC address is defined at this sublayer.

As discussed in Chapter 1, "Introduction to Computer Networking," a difference exists between the physical topology (how a network looks) and the logical topology (how the network works). Whereas the physical layer sees it from a physical topology perspective, the data-link layer sees the network from a logical topology perspective.

Layer 3: The Network Layer

The network layer of the OSI model is primarily concerned with providing a mechanism by which data can be moved between two networks or systems. The network layer does not define how the data is moved; rather, it is concerned with providing the mechanism that can be used for that purpose. The mechanisms that can be used include defining network addressing and conducting route discovery and maintenance. Common network layer protocols include the following:

- **IP**—IP performs much the same function as IPX, but IP is part of TCP/IP protocol suite.

- **IPX**—Part of Novell's IPX/SPX protocol suite, IPX provides a connectionless transport mechanism.

TIP: Connectionless Transport   Remember, IP is a connectionless transport mechanism that operates at the network layer of the OSI model.

When a system attempts to communicate with another device on the network, network layer protocols attempt to identify that device on the network. When the target system has been identified, it is then necessary to identify the service to be accessed. This is achieved by using a *service identifier*. On Transmission Control Protocol/Internet Protocol (TCP/IP) networks, service identifiers are commonly referred to as *ports*, and on Internetwork Packet Exchange/Sequenced Packet Exchange (IPX/SPX) networks, they are called *sockets*, although technically the terms can be used interchangeably.

Switching Methods

An important concept related to the network layer is switching methods. The switching method describes how the data sent from one node reaches another. Three types of switching are used on networks:

- **Circuit switching**—The best example of circuit switching is a telephone call. The link between caller and receiver is created, after which there is a dedicated communications link between the two points (hence the term *circuit*). The circuit cannot be broken, which is good because it means that no one else can use the line. In a data communications environment, however, this is a disadvantage because the data often **originates from various sources**.

- **Message switching**—In a message-switching environment, transmissions are broken down into messages that can traverse the network by the fastest means available. It might be that all messages travel over the same path, or it might be that messages travel on different paths. At each point in the journey, a node stores the message before it is forwarded to the next hop on the journey. Such a mechanism gives rise to the phrase *store and forward*. The message-switching system works well in environments in which the amount of data being moved around varies at different times, but it also causes problems such as where to store the data before it is forwarded.

- **Packet switching**—Although both circuit switching and message switching can get the job done, both have some serious drawbacks that make them unsuitable for use in a modern network environment. Today, most networks use packet switching, which includes the good points of both circuit and message switching and does not include the bad points. In a packet-switched network, data is broken down into packets that can then be transported around the network. Most modern networks use packet switching as the switching method.

> **TIP:** **Know the Switching Methods** Be prepared to identify switching methods for the Network+ exam.

A more comprehensive discussion of switching methods, in particular how they relate to wide area networks, is included in Chapter 8, "Wide Area Networking."

Network Layer Addressing

From a network administrator's perspective, one of the most important aspects of the network layer is addressing. Network addresses enable a system to be identified on the network by a *logically assigned address*. This is in contrast to the physically assigned MAC addresses used on the data link layer. The logical assignment of addresses means that schemes can be created that enable a more hierarchical approach to addressing than MAC addresses provide. By using a hierarchy, it is possible to assign a certain address to logical groups of systems and to the systems themselves. The result is that network addressing can be used to create portions of the network called *subnets*.

Hierarchical addressing systems are possible only with *routable* network protocols. The most common routable protocol in use today is TCP/IP. Of course, you don't have to use a routable protocol. Other nonroutable protocols, such as the rarely seen protocol NetBEUI, can be used, although they are of limited use in today's modern networking environments, where routable protocols are the order of the day. A more detailed discussion of networking protocols is included in Chapter 4, "Understanding the TCP/IP Protocol Suite."

Another function of the network layer is *route selection*, which refers to determining the best path for the data to take throughout the network. Routes can be configured in two ways: *statically* and *dynamically*. In a static routing environment, the network administrator must manually add routes to the routing tables. In a dynamic routing environment, routing protocols such as Routing Information Protocol (RIP) and Open Shortest Path First (OSPF) are used. These protocols work by automatically communicating routing information between devices on the network.

Layer 4: The Transport Layer

The basic function of the transport layer is, as its name suggests, to transport data from one host to another. The transport layer handles the actual processing of data between devices. This includes functions such as segmenting data so that it can be sent over the network and then reassembling the segmented data on the receiving end. The transport layer also deals with some of the errors that can occur in a stream of data, such as dropped and duplicated packets. In addition, the transport layer deals with some of the problems that can be produced by the fragmentation and reassembly process performed by the network layer.

The protocols that operate at the transport layer are those directly concerned with the transporting of data across the network. The following are some of the most commonly used transport-layer protocols:

- **TCP**—Part of the TCP/IP protocol suite, TCP provides a connection-oriented transport mechanism.

- **User Datagram Protocol (UDP)**—Part of the TCP/IP protocol suite, UDP provides a connectionless transport mechanism.

- **SPX**—Part of connection-oriented transport mechanism.

Connection-Oriented Protocols

As you can see from the descriptions of the protocols in the preceding section, some are connection-oriented and others are connectionless. In a connection-oriented session, the communication dialog between two systems is established, maintained, and then broken when the communication is complete. In technical jargon, this is often referred to as the *setting up* and *tearing down* of a session. While we are on the subject of sessions, we should make something clear: The session layer is also responsible for setting up, maintaining, and closing sessions with other hosts, but it does so at the application level rather than the network level. TCP and other transport-layer protocols maintain the sessions at the network level.

TIP: Connection-Oriented Protocols   Connection-oriented protocols can accommodate lost or dropped packets by asking the sending device to retransmit. You should note this for the exam.

Connection-oriented protocols, such as TCP, enable the delivery of data to be guaranteed because the receipt of each packet sent must be acknowledged by the receiving system. Any packet not received is re-sent. This makes for a reliable communication system, although the additional steps necessary to guarantee delivery mean that connection-oriented protocols have higher overhead than do connectionless protocols.

Connectionless Protocols

In contrast to connection-oriented communication, connectionless protocols offer only a *best-effort* delivery mechanism. A connectionless communication is a "fire and forget" mechanism in which data is sent, but no acknowledgments of receipt are sent. This mechanism has a far lower overhead than the connection-oriented method, and it places the onus of ensuring complete delivery on a higher layer, such as the session layer.

TIP: Know the Protocols   Be prepared to identify both connection-oriented and connectionless protocols on the Network+ exam.

Flow Control

Flow control also occurs at the transport layer. As the name suggests, flow control deals with the acceptance of data. It controls the data flow in such a way that the receiving system can accept the data at an adequate rate. Two methods of flow control are commonly used:

- **Buffering**—Data is stored in a holding area and waits for the destination device to become available. A system that uses this strategy encounters problems if the sending device can send data much faster than the receiving device can accept it.

- **Windowing**—A more sophisticated approach to flow control than buffering. In a windowing environment, data is sent in groups of segments that require only one acknowledgment. The size of the window (that is, how many segments can be sent for one acknowledgment) is defined at the time the session between the two devices is established. As you can imagine, the need to have only one acknowledgment for every, say, five segments can greatly reduce overhead.

Layer 5: The Session Layer

The session layer is responsible for managing and controlling the synchronization of data between applications on two devices. It does this by establishing, maintaining, and breaking sessions. Whereas the transport layer is responsible for setting up and maintaining the connection between the two devices, the session layer performs much the same function on behalf of the application.

NOTE: About the OSI Layers   The Network+ exam touches lightly on the upper layers of the OSI model; therefore, only a basic explanation of them is provided here.

Layer 6: The Presentation Layer

The presentation layer's basic function is to convert the data intended for or received from the application layer into another format. Such conversion is necessary because the way in which data is formatted so that it can be transported across the network is not necessarily readable by applications. Some common data formats handled by the presentation layer include the following:

- **Graphics files**—JPEG, TIFF, GIF, and so on are graphics file formats that require the data be formatted in a certain way.

- **Text and data**—The presentation layer can translate data into different formats such as American Standard Code for Information Interchange (ASCII) and Extended Binary Coded Decimal Interchange Code (EBCDIC).

- **Sound/video**—MPEGs, MP3, QuickTime video, and MIDI files all have their own data formats to and from which data must be converted.

Another important function of the presentation layer is Encryption, which is the scrambling of data so that it cannot be read by anything or anyone other than the intended destination. Data encryption is performed at the sending system, and *decryption* (that is, the unscrambling of data at the receiving end) is performed at the destination. Given the basic role of the presentation layer—that of data format translator—it is the obvious place for encryption and decryption to take place.

Layer 7: The Application Layer

The most common misconception about the application layer, the topmost layer of the OSI model, is that it represents applications used on a system, such as a word processor or a spreadsheet. This is not correct. Instead, the application layer defines the processes that enable applications to use network services. For example, if an application needs to open a file from a network drive, the functionality is provided by components that reside at the application layer.

In simple terms, the function of the application layer is to take requests and data from the user and pass them to the lower layers of the OSI model. Incoming information is passed to the application layer, which then displays the information to the user. Some of the most basic application layer services include file and print capabilities.

OSI Model Summary

Now that we have discussed the functions of each layer of the OSI model, it's time for a quick review. Table 9.2 lists the seven layers of the OSI model and describes some of the most significant points of each layer.

Table 9.2   OSI Model Summary

OSI Layer	Major Functions
Application	Provides access to the network for applications and certain end-user functions
	Displays incoming information and prepares outgoing information for network access

Table 9.2 OSI Model Summary

OSI Layer	Major Functions
Presentation	Converts data from the application layer into a format that can be sent over the network
	Converts data from the session layer into a format that can be understood by the application layer
	Handles encryption and decryption of data; provides compression and decompression functionality
Session	Synchronizes on separate devices
	Handles error detection and notification to the peer layer on the other device
Transport	Establishes, maintains, and breaks connections between two devices
	Determines the ordering and priorities of data
	Performs error checking and verification and handles retransmissions if necessary
Network	Provides mechanisms for the routing of data between devices across single or multiple network segments
	Handles the discovery of destination systems and addressing
Data link	Has two distinct sublayers: LLC and MAC
	Performs error detection and handling for the transmitted signals
	Defines the method by which the media is accessed
	Defines hardware addressing through the MAC sublayer
Physical	Defines the physical structure of the network
	Defines voltage/signal rates and the physical connection methods
	Defines the physical topology

The Layers at Which Devices Operate

Now that we have examined the OSI network layer in some detail, we can look at how it relates to the network connectivity devices discussed in Chapter 3, "Networking Components and Devices": hubs, switches, bridges, routers, and network interface cards (NICs). These devices are said to operate at certain layers of the OSI model based on their functions and roles in the network. Because these devices are covered in Chapter 3, this chapter does not describe them in detail. Instead, this chapter contains a brief description of each device to jog your memory.

Hubs

Hubs act as the connectivity points of the network on systems that use twisted-pair cabling. There are two types of hubs: active and passive. Each performs the same basic function; they both provide a pathway along which the electrical signals that carry the data can travel. The difference between the two types of hubs is that an active hub has power, and a passive hub does not. Even an active hub does nothing with a signal except regenerate it. Therefore, it is said to be a physical-layer device. Recall that the physical layer deals with placing signals on the media.

Switches

In Chapter 3 you learned that, like hubs, switches act as the connectivity points of the network on systems that use twisted-pair cable. You also learned that a switch offers performance benefits over a hub because it forwards data only to the port on which the destination device is connected. This has the benefit of reducing network traffic because data isn't forwarded to all the ports on a switch. The switch does this by examining the MAC address of the devices connected to it. The use of the MAC address as an identifier places the switch at Layer 2 of the OSI model. Therefore, it is a data link layer device. However, modern switches can make routing decisions making them also a Layer 3 or network layer device.

NOTE: Layer 3 Switches and Layer 4 Switches   For the Network+ exam, consider switches as Layers 2 and 3 devices. Switches can be a Layer 3 device because they can route data between devices across single or multiple network segments.

Bridges

Bridges divide a network into smaller areas through a process known as *segmentation*. Then, by learning which devices are located on which interface, a bridge can block or forward traffic between the interfaces. It does this by using the MAC address of the attached devices. The use of the MAC address makes a bridge a Layer 2 (that is, data link layer) device.

Routers

Routers are more complex and more functional than either bridges or switches because they connect networks and then manage the flow of data between the networks. Unlike switches and bridges, routers use software-configured logical network addresses. Because the routing function is implemented at the network layer of the OSI model, routers are referred to as Layer 3 devices.

NICs

A NIC provides the connectivity point to the network for a computer system. Although NICs are physical components, they are defined as data link layer devices because they are used in physical media access (which is handled at the MAC sublayer) and the logical access of the network media (which is handled at the LLC sublayer).

> **NOTE: Debating NIC**   There is some debate as to whether a NIC is just a Layer 2 device, or whether it is both a Layer 1 and Layer 2 device. This debate occurs because although it provides addressing and media access functions (Layer 2 roles), it is also responsible for placing the signal on the network media, which is a Layer 1 task. For the purposes of the Network+ exam, CompTIA considers the NIC to be just a Layer 2 device, which is why we have classified it as such here.

Wireless Access Points (APs)

Wireless access points (APs) are devices that provide connectivity between wireless portions of a network and wired portions of a network. APs are considered data-link layer devices because their primary function is to provide connectivity to the network. This connectivity is independent of the network communications protocol. Like a NIC, APs are involved in both the physical access of the network (which is handled at the MAC sublayer) and the logical access of the network (which is handled at the LLC sublayer).

Summary of the Layers at Which Devices Operate

Table 9.3 summarizes the devices discussed in the previous sections and the corresponding layers at which they operate.

Table 9.3   The OSI Model Layers at Which Various Devices Operate

Device	OSI Layer at Which the Device Operates
Hub	Physical (Layer 1)
Switch	Data link (Layer 2)
Bridge	Data link (Layer 2)
Router	Network (Layer 3)
NIC	Data link (Layer 2)
AP	Data link (Layer 2)

TCP/IP Protocol Suite Summary

Chapter 4 reviewed the various protocols found within the TCP/IP protocol suite. Each of these protocols maps to the OSI model. Knowing what the protocol does helps to identify where it fits within the OSI model. Table 9.4 summarizes the details of each of the various TCP/IP protocols and where they fit into the OSI model. You can use this table for review before you take the Network+ exam.

Table 9.4   TCP/IP Protocol Suite Summary

Protocol	Full Name	Description	OSI Layer
IP	Internet Protocol	Connectionless protocol used for moving data around a network.	Network Layer (3)
TCP	Transmission Control Protocol	Connection-oriented protocol that offers flow control, sequencing, and retransmission of dropped packets.	Transport Layer (4)
UDP	User Datagram Protocol	Connectionless alternative to TCP used for applications that do not require the functions offered by TCP.	Transport Layer (4)
FTP	File Transfer Protocol	Protocol for uploading and downloading files to and from a remote host; also accommodates basic file management tasks.	Application Layer (7)
SFTP	Secure File Transfer Protocol	Protocol for securely uploading and down loading files to and from a remote host. Based on SSH security.	Application Layer (7)
TFTP	Trivial File Transfer Protocol	File transfer protocol that does not have the security or error checking of FTP. TFTP uses UDP as a transport protocol and is therefore connectionless.	Application Layer (7)
SMTP	Simple Mail Transfer Protocol	Mechanism for transporting email across networks.	Application Layer (7)
HTTP	Hypertext Transfer Protocol	Protocol for retrieving files from a web server.	Application Layer (7)
HTTPS	Hypertext Transfer Protocol Secure	Secure protocol for retrieving files from a web server.	Application Layer (7)
POPv3/ IMAPv4	Post Office Protocol version 3/ Internet Message Access Protocol version 4	Used for retrieving email from a server on which the email is stored. Can be used only to retrieve mail. IMAP and POP cannot be used to send mail.	Application Layer (7)

Table 9.4 TCP/IP Protocol Suite Summary

Protocol	Full Name	Description	OSI Layer
Telnet	Telnet	Enables sessions to be opened on a remote host.	Application Layer (7)
SSH	Secure Shell	Enables secure sessions to be opened on a remote host.	Application Layer (7)
ICMP	Internet Control Message Protocol	Used on IP-based networks for error reporting, flow control, and route testing.	Network Layer (3)
ARP	Address Resolution Protocol	Resolves IP addresses to MAC addresses to enable communication between devices.	Data Link Layer (2)
RARP	Reverse Address Resolution Protocol	Resolves MAC addresses to IP addresses.	Data Link Layer (2)
NTP	Network Time Protocol	Used to communicate time synchronization information between devices.	Application Layer (7)
NNTP	Network News Transport Protocol	Facilitates the access and downloading of messages from newsgroup servers.	Application Layer (7)
SCP	Secure Copy Protocol	Enables files to be copied securely between two systems. Uses Secure Shell (SSH) technology to provide encryption services.	Application Layer (7)
LDAP	Lightweight Directory Access Protocol	Protocol used to access and query directory services systems, such as Novell Directory Services and Microsoft Active Directory.	Application Layer (7)
IGMP	Internet Group Management Protocol	Provides a mechanism for systems within the same multicast group to register and communicate with each other.	Network Layer (3)
DNS	Domain Name System	Resolves hostnames to IP addresses.	Application Layer (7)
DHCP	Dynamic Host Configuration Protocol	Automatically assigns TCP/IP information.	Application Layer (7)

Table 9.4   TCP/IP Protocol Suite Summary

Protocol	Full Name	Description	OSI Layer
SNMP	Simple Network Management Protocol	Enables network devices to communicate information about their state to a central system. It also enables the central system to pass configuration parameters to the devices.	Application Layer (7)
TLS	Transport Layer Security	A security protocol designed to ensure privacy between communicating client/server applications.	Application Layer (7)
SIP	Session Initiation Protocol	An application-layer protocol designed to establish and maintain multimedia sessions such as Internet telephony calls.	Application Layer (7)
RTP	Real-time Transport Protocol	The Internet-standard protocol for the transport of real-time data.	Application Layer (7)

Summary

The OSI model is a conceptual model that defines seven layers. Each of these layers performs a specific function that plays an important part in the end-to-end communication between two devices. The model enables us to relate the function of a certain protocol or service to a specific function of the model. For example, IP is responsible for the discovery and establishment of routes through the network. Therefore, it is reasonable to assume that IP is a network-layer protocol because such functions are performed at the network layer. The ability to draw parallels like this can be a useful aid to understanding networking from both conceptual and practical levels.

Because the OSI model defines the functions performed at various layers, it can be said that network devices operate at certain layers of the OSI model. The layer at which a device operates is defined by the function of the device and the information the device uses to complete its task. Of the commonly used network devices, hubs operate at the physical layer; network cards, bridges, and switches operate at the data link layer; and routers operate at the network layer.

Understanding the OSI model is important for networking. Even though it can sometimes be difficult to see how the OSI model is relevant in day-to-day tasks, it helps to reinforce networking theory and provides a framework in which to work.

Exam Preparation Tasks

Review All the Key Topics

Review the most important topics in the chapter, noted with the key topics icon in the outer margin of the page. Table 9.5 lists a reference of these key topics and the page numbers on which each is found.

Table 9.5   Key Topics for Chapter 9

Key Topic Element	Description	Page Number
Figure 9.1	The OSI reference model	326
Figure 9.2	How data travels between two devices	327
Figure 9.3	Encapsulation and decapsulation	328
Table 9.1	Terminology used for logical groups of bits at the layers of the OSI model	327
Table 9.2	OSI model summary	334
Table 9.3	The OSI model layers at which various devices operate	337
Table 9.4	TCP/IP Protocol Suite summary	338

Complete the Tables and Lists from Memory

Print a copy of Appendix B, "Memory Tables" (found on the CD), or at least the section for this chapter, and complete the tables and lists from memory. Appendix C, "Memory Tables Answer Key," also on the CD, includes completed tables and lists to check your work.

Define Key Terms

Define the following key terms from this chapter, and check your answers in the Glossary.

- Application layer
- Buffering
- Circuit switching
- Connectionless protocols

- Connection-oriented protocols
- Data link layer
- Dynamic routing
- Encapsulation
- LLC
- MAC
- Message switching
- Network layer
- OSI
- Packet switching
- Physical layer
- Presentation layer
- Segmentation
- Session layer
- SPX
- Static routing
- TCP
- Transport layer
- UDP
- Windowing

Apply Your Knowledge

Exercise 9.1 Identifying OSI layers

For the Network+ exam, you need to identify the various layers of the OSI model and the network devices that correspond to each level. With that in mind, in lieu of a hands-on project, this chapter provides a practical exercise to reinforce the concepts discussed in this chapter. Your ability to correctly complete this exercise will show sufficient knowledge of the OSI model.

Estimated time: 10 minutes

1. Refer to the worksheet in Figure 9.4 and identify two functions for each layer of the OSI model.

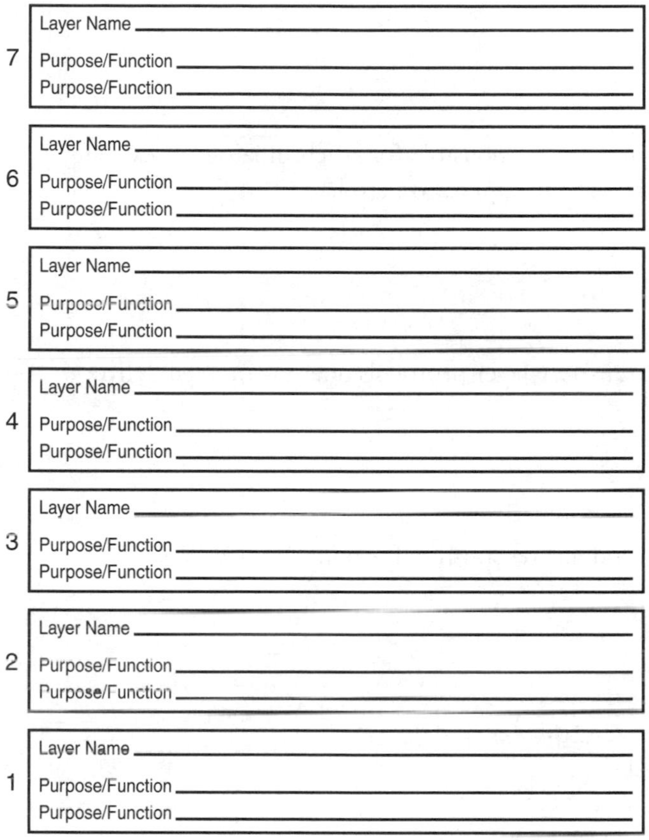

Figure 9.4   A hands-on OSI model project.

2. Check your responses against the information in Table 9.2.

Review Questions

You can find answers to the review questions in Appendix A, "Answers to Review Questions."

1. At which layer of the OSI model does a switch operate?
   a.   Physical
   b.   Data link
   c.   Network
   d.   Session

2. Which of the following devices operate at Layer 2 of the OSI model? (Choose all that apply.)

  a. Switch

  b. Network card

  c. Hub

  d. Bridge

3. Which layer of the OSI model is responsible for synchronizing the exchange of data between two devices at the application level?

  a. Transport

  b. Session

  c. Presentation

  d. Data link

4. Which of the following transport-layer protocols offer guaranteed delivery?

  a. FTP

  b. UDP

  c. HTTP

  d. TCP

5. Which layer of the OSI model is responsible for route discovery?

  a. Session

  b. Data link

  c. Network

  d. Transport

6. What are the two sublayers of the data link layer?

  a. Logical link control

  b. Logical loop control

  c. Media access control

  d. Multiple access control

7. Which of the following are responsibilities of the transport layer? (Choose the two best answers.)

  a. Performs error detection and handling for the transmitted signals

  b. Synchronizes data exchange between two applications

  c. Performs error checking and verification

  d. Establishes, maintains, and breaks connections between devices

8. Which layer of the OSI model defines the method by which the network media are accessed on a logical level?

  a. Data link

  b. Physical

  c. Session

  d. Presentation

9. At which layer of the OSI model does a hub operate?
   a. Application
   b. Network
   c. Physical
   d. Data link

10. Which of the following terms is not used to describe a logical grouping of bits?
    a. Datagram
    b. Segment
    c. Package
    d. Packet

11. Which layer of the OSI model defines the signal rates and voltages that are used?
    a. Data link
    b. Physical
    c. Session
    d. Presentation

12. At which layer of the OSI model does an AP operate?
    a. Physical
    b. Data link
    c. Network
    d. Transport

13. At which layer of the OSI model does a NIC operate?
    a. Physical
    b. Data link
    c. Network
    d. Transport

14. At which layer of the OSI model do encryption and decryption take place?
    a. Physical
    b. Session
    c. Application
    d. Presentation

15. Which of the following are commonly used flow control strategies? (Choose the two best answers.)
    a. Buffering
    b. Segmentation
    c. Windowing
    d. Direct flow management

16. The IP protocol is a connectionless protocol used for moving data around a network. Because it moves data, what layer of the OSI model does IP operate?
    a. Physical
    b. Data link
    c. Network
    d. Session

17. Which of the following OSI layers is responsible for establishing connections between two devices?
    a. Session
    b. Network
    c. Transport
    d. Application

18. At which layer do the protocols that handle route discovery reside?
    a. Transport
    b. Network
    c. Session
    d. Application

19. At the transport layer, two types of protocols are used for sending data to a remote system. What terms are used to describe these protocols? (Choose the two best answers.)
    a. Connection-oriented
    b. Connection-reliant
    c. Connection-dependent
    d. Connectionless

20. At which layer of the OSI model does a router operate?
    a. Application
    b. Session
    c. Network
    d. Transport

This chapter covers CompTIA Network+ objective 4.5. Upon completion of this chapter, you will be able to answer the following questions:

- What is uptime?

- How do you prevent data loss and downtime?

- What are the basics of disaster recovery?

- What are hot and cold spares?

- How are network optimization strategies used?

- What is RAID?

- How are fault tolerant measures used?

CHAPTER 10

Network Performance and Optimization

When you come right down to it, the most important responsibility of network administrators is to ensure data availability. When users, customers, or clients need access to network data, it should be ready to go. Many organizations depend on data availability; without it, they could not function.

Two key strategies help ensure data availability: fault tolerance and disaster recovery. To fulfill the role of network administrator, it is essential that you have a clear understanding of how to use these strategies. These strategies and others have a single goal in mind: uptime.

Foundation Topics

Understanding Uptime

All devices on the network, including routers, cabling, and especially servers, must have one prime underlying trait: availability. Networks play such a vital role in the operation of businesses that their availability must be measured in dollars. The failure of a single desktop PC affects the productivity of a single user. The failure of an entire network affects the productivity of the entire company and potentially of the company's clients as well. A network failure can have an even larger impact than that as new e-commerce customers who look somewhere else for products, and existing customers start to wonder about the reliability of the site.

Every minute that a network is not running can potentially cost an organization money. The exact amount depends on the role that the server performs and the length of time that it is unavailable. For example, if a small departmental server supporting 10 people goes down for 10 minutes, this might not be a big deal. But if the server that runs the company's e-commerce website goes down for an hour, this can cost hundreds of thousands of dollars' worth of lost orders.

The importance of data availability varies between networks but dictates to what extent a server/network implements fault tolerance measures. The projected capability for a network or network component to weather failure is defined as a number or a percentage. The fact that no solution is labeled as providing 100 percent availability indicates that no matter how well we protect our networks, some aspect of the configuration will still, sooner or later, fail.

Assuming we know we can never actually obtain 100 percent uptime, what should we aim for? Consider this—if you were responsible for a server system that was available for 99.5 percent of the time, you might be happy. But if you realized that you would also have 43.8 hours of downtime each year—that's one full work week and a little overtime—you might not be so smug. Table 10.1 compares levels of availability and the resulting potential downtime.

Table 10.1 Levels of Availability and Related Downtime

Level of Availability	Availability %	Downtime per Year
Commercial availability	99.5%	43.8 hours
High availability	99.9%	8.8 hours
Fault-resilient clusters	99.99%	53 minutes
Fault-tolerant	99.999%	5 minutes
Continuous	100%	0

These downtime numbers make it simple to justify spending money on implementing fault-tolerance measures, but remember that to reach the definition of commercial availability, you need to have a range of measures in place. After the commercial availability level, the strategies that take you to each subsequent level are likely to be increasingly expensive, even though they might be easy to justify.

For example, if you estimate that each hour of server downtime can cost the company $1,000, the reduction of 35 hours of downtime—from 43.8 hours for commercial availability to 8.8 hours for high availability—justifies some serious expenditure on technology. Although this first jump is an easily justifiable one, subsequent levels might not be so easy to sell. Working on the same basis, moving from high availability to fault-resilient clusters equates to less than $10,000, but the equipment, software, and skills required to move to the next level can far exceed this figure. In other words, increasing fault tolerance can represent diminishing returns. As your need to reduce the possibility of downtime increases, so does the investment required to achieve this goal.

The role played by the network administrator in all of this can be somewhat challenging. In some respects, you must function as if you are selling insurance. Informing management of the risks and potential outcomes of downtime can seem a little sensational, but the reality is that the information must be provided if you are to avoid post-event questions about why management was not made aware of the risks. At the same time, a realistic evaluation of exactly the risks presented is needed along with a realistic evaluation of the amount of downtime each failure might bring.

In networking, *fault tolerance* refers to the capability for a device or system to continue operating if a failure occurs. Fault-tolerant measures are those used to help ensure uptime. Fault tolerance should not be confused with disaster recovery, which is the capability to respond to and recover from catastrophic events with no loss of data and no loss of data availability.

In practical terms, fault tolerance involves ensuring that when network hardware or software fails, users on the network can still access the data and continue working with little or no disruption of service. Developing a strong fault-tolerant system that ensures continual access to data is not easy and involves attention to many details.

Today's business world relies heavily on networks and network servers. If these networks and servers were to fail, many businesses would be unable to function. Thus, every minute a network is not available costs money. The exact amount of money depends on the size of the organization and can range from a mild economic inconvenience to a crippling financial blow. The potential impact of a network failure often dictates the fault tolerance measures an organization implements.

Unfortunately, no fault-tolerance measures can guarantee 100% availability or up-time to network data or services, and fault-tolerance solutions that strive to meet this goal can be expensive. But the costs associated with any fault-tolerance solution must be compared to the costs of losing access to network services and the reconstruction of network data.

Understanding the Risks

Having established that we need to guard against equipment failure, we can now look at which pieces of equipment are more likely to fail than others. Predicting component failure is not an exact science; different companies have different estimates. Combining the estimates around the Internet, Figure 10.1 shows an approximation of what to expect in terms of hardware failure.

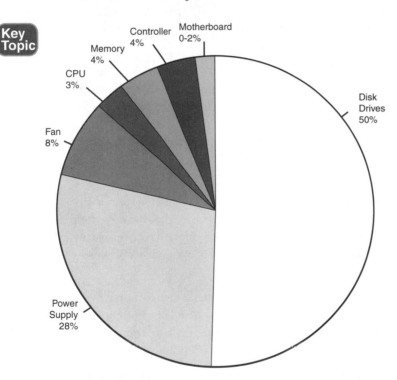

Figure 10.1 Server component failures.

As you can see from the graph, 50 percent of all system downtime can be attributed to hard disk failure. That means that, for instance, a hard disk is more than 12 times more likely to fail than memory is and 50 times more likely to fail than a motherboard is. With this in mind, it should come as no surprise that hard disks have garnered the most attention when it comes to fault tolerance. Redundant array of inexpensive disks (RAID), which is discussed in detail in this section, is a set of standards that enables servers to cope with the failure of one or more hard disks.

NOTE: **Moving Parts**   All system components can fail, but those with moving parts, such as the power supply fan, CPU fans, and hard disk, have a greater chance of failure.

NOTE: **Backup**   Although this chapter discusses various methods of fault tolerance designed to reduce the susceptibility to server failure and downtime, none of these methods is a substitute for a complete and robust backup strategy. No matter how many of these measures are in place, backing up data to an external medium is still an essential consideration.

In fault tolerance, RAID is only half the story. Each of the other components in the chart can also fail, and to varying degrees, there are measures in place to cope with failures of these components as well. In some cases, the fault tolerance is an elegant solution, and in others, it is a simple case of duplication. This might be having duplicate network cards installed in a system so that one takes over if the other fails. We start our discussion by looking at fault tolerance and RAID before moving on to other fault-tolerance measures.

RAID

RAID is a strategy for implementing fault tolerance, performance, and reliability solutions that prevent data disruption because of hard disk failure or enhance performance over capabilities over a single hard disk. RAID combines multiple hard disks in such a way that more than one disk is responsible for holding data. Instead of using a single large disk, information is written to several smaller disks.

Such a design offers two key advantages. First, the failure of one disk does not, in fault-tolerant RAID configurations, compromise the availability of data. Second, reading (and sometimes writing) to multiple smaller disks is often faster with multiple hard disks than when using one large disk, thus offering a performance boost.

The goals of a RAID solution are clear: Decrease the costs associated with downtime, secure network data, minimize network disruption, and (selfishly) reduce the stress on the network administrator(s). Because a well-designed RAID system can accomplish all these goals, RAID is widely implemented and found in organizations of all sizes.

Several RAID strategies are available, and each has advantages and disadvantages. It is important to know what you are protecting and why before you implement any RAID solution; the particular RAID strategy used depends on many factors, including associated costs, the server's role, and the level of fault tolerance required. The following sections discuss the characteristics of the various RAID strategies.

RAID 0

Although it is classified as a RAID level, RAID 0 is not fault-tolerant. As such, RAID 0 is not recommended for servers that maintain mission-critical data. RAID 0 works by writing to multiple hard drives simultaneously, enabling for faster data throughput. RAID 0 offers a significant performance increase over a single disk, but as with a single disk, all data is lost if any disk in the RAID set fails. With RAID 0 you actually increase your chances of losing data compared to using a single disk because RAID 0 uses multiple hard disks, creating multiple failure points. Essentially, the more disks you use in the RAID 0 array, the more at risk the data is. A minimum of two disks is required to implement a RAID 0 solution.

TIP: RAID 0   For the exam, remember that although RAID 0 is known as a RAID solution, it is not fault-tolerant. RAID 0 is used to increase performance by striping data between multiple disks.

RAID 0 writes data to the disks in the array by using a system called *striping*, which works by dividing the hard disks into stripes and writing the data across the stripes, as shown in Figure 10.2. The striping strategy is also used by RAID 2, RAID 3, RAID 4, and RAID 5.

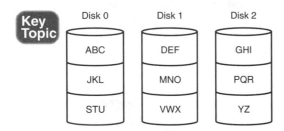

Figure 10.2 RAID 0 with disk striping.

Advantages of RAID 0

Despite that it is not fault-tolerant, RAID 0 is well suited for some environments. The following are some of the advantages of RAID 0:

- **Ease of implementation**—Offers easy setup and configuration
- **Good input/output (I/O) performance**—Offers a significant increase in performance over a single disk and other RAID solutions by spreading data across multiple disks

- **Minimal hardware requirements**—Can be implemented with as few as two hard drives, making it a cost solution for some network environments

Disadvantages of RAID 0

You cannot have the good without the bad. For a number of reasons, a RAID 0 solution might not be appropriate:

- **No fault tolerance**—Employing a RAID solution that does not offer data protection is a major drawback. This factor alone limits a RAID 0 solution to only a few network environments.

- **Increased failure points**—A RAID 0 solution has as many failure points as hard drives. For instance, if your RAID 0 configuration has five disks and any one of those drives fails, the data on all drives will be lost.

- **Limited application**—Because of the lack of fault tolerance, a RAID 0 solution is practical for few applications. Quite simply, it's limited to environments where the performance of I/O outweighs the importance of data availability.

Despite its drawbacks, you might encounter RAID 0.

> **TIP: Data Loss**   Remember for the Network+ exam, if one disk should fail when using RAID 0, all data will be lost. The more disks added to the RAID 0 array, the greater the chance a disk will fail. The more hard disks added, the more failure points there are.

Recovering from a Failed RAID 0 Array

Anyone relying on a RAID 0 configuration to hold sensitive data is bold. The bottom line is, there is no way to recover from a failed RAID 0 array, short of restoring the data from backups. Both the server and the services it provides to the network are unavailable while you rebuild the drives and the data.

RAID 1

RAID 1 is a fault-tolerant configuration known as *disk mirroring*. A RAID 1 solution uses two physical disk drives. Whenever a file is saved to the hard disk, a copy of the file is automatically written to the second disk. The second disk is always an exact mirrored copy of the first one. Figure 10.3 illustrates a RAID 1 array.

RAID 1 writes the same data to the hard drives simultaneously. The benefits of having a duplicate copy of all saved data are clear, and on the surface, RAID 1 might seem like a fault-tolerant solution. However, it has a couple drawbacks. First, RAID 1 has high overhead because an entire disk must be used to provide the mirrored copy. Second, a RAID 1 solution is limited to two hard drives, which limits the available storage capacity.

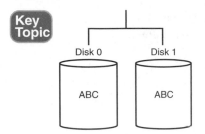

Figure 10.3   A RAID 1 array.

Another RAID strategy that falls under the category of RAID 1 is *disk duplexing*, which is a mirrored solution that incorporates a second level of fault tolerance by using a separate hard disk controller for each hard drive. Putting the hard disks on separate controllers eliminates the controller as a single point of failure. The likelihood of a failed disk controller is not nearly as high as the likelihood of a failed hard disk, but the more failure points covered, the better. Figure 10.4 shows a disk duplexing configuration.

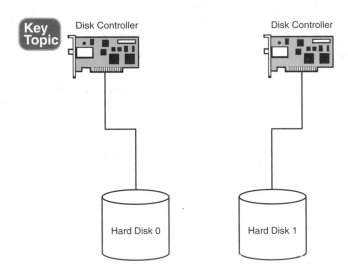

Figure 10.4   A disk duplexing configuration.

NOTE: Sizing the Mirror   Because mirroring involves making a duplicate copy of the data, the volumes used on each disk are the same size. If you set up the mirrored environment with a 500GB volume and a 700GB volume, the result will be only a 500GB volume. The system uses the lowest common amount of free space to construct the mirrored volume.

Advantages of RAID 1

Although it is far from perfect, RAID 1 is widely implemented in many different network environments. The following are a few of the advantages of RAID 1:

- **Fault tolerance**—A fault-tolerance solution that maintains a mirrored image of data on a second hard drive in case of failure. Disk duplexing adds extra fault tolerance by using dual hard drive controllers.

- **Reduced cost**—Provides fault tolerance by using only two hard disks, thereby providing a cost-effective method of implementing a fault-tolerance solution.

- **Ease of implementation**—Is not difficult to implement; it can be set up easily. The procedures and methods for implementing the hardware and software are well documented.

NOTE: Data Loss   RAID 1 uses an exact copy of the data, meaning that if one disk should fail, no data loss occurs when it comes to data transfer rates. RAID 5, however, can lose data when data is written to multiple disks simultaneously.

Disadvantages of RAID 1

Several factors exclude RAID 1 from being used in many network environments. The following are some of the disadvantages associated with RAID 1:

- **Limited disk capacity**—Because RAID 1 uses only two hard disks, limited disk space is available for use. With today's large hard disk capacity, it might not be a problem for most environments.

- **High disk space overhead**—RAID 1 has 50% overhead; that is, half the hard disk space needs to be used for RAID. So for every megabyte used for other purposes, another is needed for RAID. Even if you purchased two 80GB drives, your network would have only 80GB of storage space. The applications and data storage needs of many of today's businesses would exceed this limitation quickly.

- **Hot-swap support**—Some RAID 1 implementations don't support the capability to hot swap drives, meaning that you might have to shut down the server to replace a damaged hard disk. Many hardware RAID solutions do support hot-swap configurations and are the preferred method.

NOTE: Single Failure   Although disk mirroring is a reliable fault-tolerance method, it provides for only a single disk failure.

Recovering from a Failed RAID 1 Array

RAID 1 can handle the failure of a single drive; if one fails, a complete copy of the data exists on an alternative hard drive. Recovering from a failed RAID 1 array typically involves breaking the mirror set, replacing the failed drive with a working one, and reestablishing the mirror. The data will be automatically rebuilt on the new drive.

The recovery process might cause network disruption while a new hard drive is installed. The server can continue to function with a single drive, but no fault tolerance exists until the RAID 1 array is rebuilt. It is possible—however unlikely—for multiple drives to fail, and RAID 1 cannot handle such a situation.

RAID 5

RAID 5 is the preferred hard disk fault-tolerance strategy for most environments; it is trusted to protect the most sensitive data. RAID 5 stripes the data across all the hard drives in the array.

RAID 5 spreads parity information across all the disks in the array. Known as *distributed parity*, this approach enables the server to continue to function if disk failure occurs. The system can calculate the information missing from the failed drive by using the parity information on the disks. A minimum of three hard drives is required to implement RAID 5, but more drives are recommended, up to 32. When calculating how many drives you will be using in a RAID 5 array, remember that the parity distributed across the drives is equivalent to one disk. Thus, if you have four 10GB hard disks, you will have 30GB of storage space.

You can expect to work with and maintain a RAID 5 array in your network travels. Figure 10.5 shows a RAID 5 array.

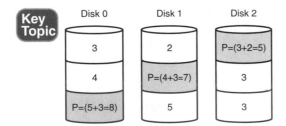

Figure 10.5 A RAID 5 array.

Advantages of RAID 5

RAID 5 has become a widely implemented fault-tolerance strategy for several reasons. The following are some of the key advantages of RAID 5:

- **Minimal network disruption**—When a hard disk crashes in a RAID 5 array, the rest of the drives continue to function with no disruption in data availability.

Network users can keep working, and costs associated with network downtime are minimized. Although there is no disruption to data access, the performance of the system decreases until the drive has been replaced.

- **Performance**—Because RAID 5 can access several drives simultaneously, the read performance over that of a single disk is greatly improved. Increased performance is not necessarily a reason to use a fault-tolerant solution but is an added bonus.

- **Distributed parity**—By writing parity over several disks, RAID 5 avoids the bottleneck of writing parity to a single disk, which occurs with RAID 3 and 4.

Disadvantages of RAID 5

The disadvantages of RAID 5 are few, and the benefits certainly outweigh the costs. The following are the disadvantages of RAID 5:

- **Poor write performance**—Because parity is distributed across several disks, multiple writes must be performed for every write operation. The severity of this performance lag depends on the application used, but its impact is minimal enough to make it a factor in only a few environments. Furthermore, the more drives added to the array, the more it can negatively impact write performance.

- **Regeneration time**—When a hard disk is replaced in a RAID 5 array, the data must be regenerated on it. This process is typically performed automatically and demands extensive system resources.

- **Data limitations**—RAID 5 that is implemented using software might not include the system or boot partitions in the stripe set, so you must use an alternative method to secure the system and boot partitions. For example, some organizations use RAID 5 for data and a mirrored set to provide fault tolerance for the system and boot partitions. This limitation does not include hardware RAID 5 solutions, which can stripe the system and boot partitions.

> **TIP: RAID 5**   RAID 5 is a common fault-tolerant strategy. Ensure you can identify both the pros and cons of RAID 5 for the Network+ exam.

Recovering from a RAID 5 Array Failure

RAID 5 ensures data availability even if hard disks fail. A RAID 5 system can still service requests from clients if a failure occurs, by using the parity information from the other disks to identify the data now missing because it was on the failed drive.

At some point, you must replace the failed hard disks to rebuild the array. Some systems let you remove the failed hard drive (that is, they are hot swappable) and insert the new one without powering down the server. The new hard disk is configured automatically as part of the existing RAID 5 array, and the rebuilding of data on the new drive occurs automatically. Other systems might require you to power down the server to replace the drive. You must then manually perform the rebuild. Because RAID 5 continues to run after a disk failure, you can schedule a time to replace the damaged drive and minimize the impact on network users.

NOTE: RAID 6   Like RAID 5, RAID 6 enables fault tolerance by spreading data across multiple disk drives. Building on RAID 5, RAID 6 adds an extra layer of parity increasing data protection and enabling the restoration of data from an array with up to two failed drives.

Hot Swap Versus Hot Spare

Two strategies are commonly associated with minimizing data disruption with RAID: *hot swappable drives* and *hot spare drives*. A hot spare drive sits unused in a RAID array, waiting to be called into action. For instance, if a hard disk fails in a RAID 5 array, the hot spare is already installed and ready to take over.

Hot swapping, on the other hand, refers to the ability to replace a device such as a hard disk without having to power down the system. Hot swapping is not reserved for hard disks; many other types of server and workstation hardware support hot swapping. You learn more about this topic in the section "Hot Spare and Hot Swapping" later in this chapter.

RAID 10

In some server environments, it makes sense to combine RAID levels. One such strategy is RAID 10, which combines RAID 1 and RAID 0. RAID 10 requires four hard disks: two for the data striping and two to provide a mirrored copy of the striped pair.

NOTE: Implementing RAID 10   There are various ways of implementing RAID 10, depending on how many drives you have available and what the system configuration is.

RAID 10 combines the performance benefits of RAID 0 with the fault-tolerant capability of RAID 1, without requiring the parity calculations. However, RAID 10 also combines the limitations of RAID 0 and RAID 1. Mirroring the drives somewhat reduces the performance capabilities of RAID 0, and the 50% overhead of a RAID 1 solution is still in effect. Even with these limitations, RAID 10 is well suited for many environments, and you might find yourself working with or implementing such a solution. Figure 10.6 shows a possible configuration for a RAID 10 solution.

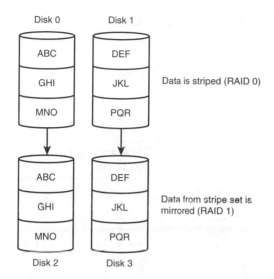

Figure 10.6 A RAID 10 solution.

NOTE: What's in a Name? RAID 10 has many names. It's sometimes referred to as RAID 1/0, RAID 0/1, or RAID 1+0.

Choosing a RAID Level

Deciding whether to use a fault-tolerant solution on a network is the first and most obvious step for you to take when you design a network. The next, less simple, decision is which RAID level to implement. Your first inclination might be to choose the best possible RAID solution, but your budget might dictate otherwise. Consider the following when choosing a specific RAID level:

- **Data protection and availability**—First and foremost, consider the effect of downtime on the organization. If minutes will cost the organization millions, you need a strong fault-tolerant solution. On the other hand, if you can go offline for an hour or more and suffer nothing more than an inconvenience, a costly RAID solution might be overkill. Before choosing a RAID solution, be sure what impact data unavailability will have on you and your network.

- **Cost**—High-end RAID solutions are out of the price range of many organizations. You are left to choose the best solution for the price.

- **Capacity**—Some organizations' data needs are measured in megabytes, and other organizations' needs are measured in gigabytes. Before choosing a RAID solution, you need to know the volume of data. RAID 1, for instance, provides far less space than RAID 5.

- **Performance**—Speed is an important consideration. With some RAID solutions the network suffers a performance hit, whereas with others performance can be increased over the performance using a single disk. Choosing the correct RAID solution might involve understanding the performance capabilities of each of the different RAID levels.

Table 10.2 summarizes the main characteristics of the various RAID levels.

Table 10.2   RAID Characteristics

RAID Level	Description	Key Features	Minimum Disks Required
RAID 0	Disk striping	No fault tolerance; improved I/O performance	2
RAID 1	Disk mirroring	Provides fault tolerance but at 50% overhead; can also be used with separate disk controllers, a strategy known as disk duplexing	2 (2 is also the maximum number of disks used for RAID 1.)
RAID 5	Disk striping with distributed parity	Widely used RAID solution; uses distributed parity	3
RAID 10	Striping with mirrored volumes	Increased performance with striping and offers mirrored fault tolerance	4

Hardware and Software RAID

After you decided to implement a RAID solution, you must also decide whether to use a software or hardware RAID solution. The decision is not easy, and your budget might again be the deciding factor.

Software RAID is managed by the network operating system or third-party software and as such requires server resources to operate. As a result, the overhead associated with software RAID can affect the performance of the server by taking resource time away from other applications. Some variations of RAID require more from the server than others; for example, RAID 1 is commonly implemented using software RAID because it requires less overhead than RAID 5.

Software RAID has one definite advantage: It's inexpensive. For example, Linux, Windows server operating systems and clients, and Mac OS X servers have RAID capability built in, enabling RAID to be implemented at no extra cost, apart from the costs associated with buying multiple disks. These operating systems typically offer support for RAID levels 0, 1, and 5.

Hardware RAID is the way to go if your budget allows. Hardware RAID uses its own specialized controller, which takes the RAID processing requirements away from the server. The server's resources can thus focus on other applications. Hardware RAID also provides the capability to use cache memory on the RAID controller, further adding to its performance capabilities over software RAID.

> **NOTE: Arrays and Volumes**   When discussing RAID, you often encounter the terms *array* and *volume*. An array is a group of disks that are part of a single RAID configuration. For example, you would say, "There are two disks in a RAID 1 array." A volume is a logical disk space within an array. Typically, a volume refers only to data storage and capacity.

Other Fault-Tolerance Measures

Although hard drives represent the single largest failure point in a network, they are not the only failure points. Even the most costly RAID solution cannot save you from a faulty power supply or memory module. To fully address data availability, you must consider all hardware. This section provides a brief overview of some of the other common fault-tolerance measures you can take to further ensure data availability:

- Link redundancy
- Using uninterruptible power supplies (UPSs)
- Using redundant power supplies
- Setting up standby servers and server clusters
- Memory
- Managing processor failures

Link Redundancy

A faulty NIC can disable access to data quickly because a failed NIC effectively isolates a system. Several strategies provide fault tolerance for NICs. Many systems employ a hot spare in the system that can be put to work as soon as the primary NIC fails.

Though a failed network card cannot actually stop a system, it might as well. A network system that cannot access the network isn't much good. Though the chances of a failed network card are relatively low, our attempts to reduce the occurrence of downtime have led to the development of a strategy that provides fault tolerance for network connections.

Through a process called *adapter teaming*, groups of network cards are configured to act as a single unit. The teaming capability is achieved through software, either as a function of the network card driver or through specific application software. Adapter teaming is not widely implemented in smaller organizations; however, the benefits it offers makes it an important consideration. The result of adapter teaming is increased bandwidth, fault tolerance, and the capability to manage network traffic more effectively. These features are organized into three sections:

- **Adapter fault tolerance**—The basic configuration enables one network card to be configured as the primary device and others as secondary. If the primary adapter fails, one of the other cards can take its place without the need for intervention. When the original card is replaced, it resumes the role of primary controller.

- **Adapter load balancing**—Because software controls the network adapters, workloads can be distributed evenly among the cards so that each link is used to a similar degree. This distribution enables for a more responsive server because one card is not overworked while another is underworked.

- **Link aggregation**—This provides vastly improved performance by enabling more than one network card's transfer rate to be combined into a single connection. For example, through link aggregation, four 100Mbps network cards can provide a total of 400Mbps transfer rate. Link aggregation requires that both the network adapters and the switch used support it. In 1999, the IEEE ratified the 802.3ad standard for link aggregation, enabling compatible products to be produced.

NOTE: Warm Swaps   Some systems support warm swaps. Warm swapping involves powering down an individual bus slot to change a NIC. Doing so prevents you from having to power down the entire system to replace a NIC.

Using Uninterruptible Power Supplies

No discussion of fault tolerance can be complete without a look at power-related issues and the mechanisms used to combat them. When sign a fault-tolerant system, your planning should definitely include uninterruptible power supplies (UPSs). A UPS serves many functions and is a major part of server consideration and implementation.

On a basic level, a UPS is a box that holds a battery and a built-in charging circuit. During times of good power, the battery is recharged; when the UPS is needed, it's ready to provide power to the server. Most often, the UPS is required to provide enough power to give the administrator time to shut down the server in an orderly fashion, preventing any potential data loss from a dirty shutdown.

NOTE: Overloading UPSs   One mistake often made by administrators is the overloading of UPSs. This means to attach many devices to a single UPS. The more devices attached, the shorter the battery life. UPSs are designed for server systems, and connecting monitors, printers, or other peripheral devices to them reduces their effectiveness.

A UPS is an essential component for continuation of service and to prevent possible data loss. Home users and network alike can both take advantage of the benefits of using a UPS especially when they clearly understand why a UPS system is used.

Why Use a UPS?

Organizations of all shapes and sizes need UPSs as part of their fault-tolerance strategies. A UPS is as important as any other fault-tolerance measure. Three key reasons make a UPS necessary:

- **Data availability**—The goal of any fault-tolerance measure is data availability. A UPS ensures access to the server if a power failure occurs, or at least as long as it takes to save your file.

- **Data loss**—Fluctuations in power or a sudden power down can damage the data on the server system. In addition, many servers take full advantage of caching, and a sudden loss of power could cause the loss of all information held in cache.

- **Hardware damage**—Constant power fluctuations or sudden power downs can damage hardware components within a computer. Damaged hardware can lead to reduced data availability while the hardware is repaired.

Power Threats

In addition to keeping a server functioning long enough to safely shut it down, a UPS also safeguards a server from inconsistent power. This inconsistent power can take many forms. A UPS protects a system from the following power-related threats:

- **Blackout**—A total failure of the power supplied to the server.

- **Spike**—A short (usually less than a second) but intense increase in voltage. Spikes can do irreparable damage to any kind of equipment, especially computers.

- **Surge**—Compared to a spike, a surge is a considerably longer (sometimes many seconds) but usually less intense increase in power. Surges can also damage your computer equipment.

- **Sag**—A sag is a short-term voltage drop (the opposite of a spike). This type of voltage drop can cause a server to reboot.

- **Brownout**—A brownout is a drop in voltage supply that usually lasts more than a few minutes.

Many of these power-related threats can occur without your knowledge; if you don't have a UPS, you cannot prepare for them. For the investment, it is worth buying a UPS, if for no other reason than to sleep better at night.

> **TIP: Power Threats**   Be sure you can differentiate between the various power threats before taking the Network+ exam.

Using Redundant Power Supplies

If you work with servers or workstations, you know that from time to time a power supply will fail. When it fails in a workstation, you simply power down the system and replace the power supply. On a server, where downtime is often measured in dollars and cents, powering down to replace a faulty power supply can be a major issue.

You can prepare for a faulty power supply by using redundant, hot-swappable power supplies. As you might expect, such a strategy has associated costs that must be weighed against the importance of continual access to data.

Server and Services Fault Tolerance

In addition to providing fault tolerance for individual hardware components, some organizations go the extra mile to include entire servers in the fault-tolerant design. Such a design keeps servers and the services they provide up and running.

When it comes to server fault tolerance, two key strategies are used: *standby servers* and *server clustering*.

Using Standby Servers

In addition to instituting fault-tolerance measures for individual components, many larger organizations use server fault-tolerance measures. In this scenario, if one server fails, a second is fully configured and waiting to take over. Using this configuration, if a server fails, the network services it provided to the network will become available in a short amount of time using the redundant server. The second server is sometimes located in a separate building, in case of fire or flood damage to the location where the first server is kept.

Another strategy used for complete server and network service fault tolerance is *server failover*. A server failover configuration has two servers wired together, with one acting as the primary server and the other acting as the secondary server. The systems synchronize data between them, ensuring that they are always current with each other. If the secondary server detects that the primary is offline, it switches to failover mode and becomes the primary server for the network. It then is responsible for providing any missing network services. The whole procedure is transparent to the network user, and little downtime, if any, is experienced.

As you might imagine, the costs associated with having a redundant server are high. For this reason, few organizations use the failover and standby server measures.

Server Clustering

Continuing our journey into incredibly expensive fault-tolerance strategies, we come to server clustering. For companies that cannot afford even a second of downtime, the costs of server clustering are easily justified.

Server clustering involves grouping several computers into one logical unit. This strategy can, depending on the configuration, provide fault tolerance and increased performance and load balancing. Because the servers within the cluster are in constant contact with each other, they can detect and compensate for a failing server system. A well-configured server cluster provides failover without any disruption to network users.

The advantages of clustering are obvious. Clustering affords the highest possible availability of data and network services. Clusters are the foundational configuration for the "five nines" level of service—that's 99.999% uptime, which translates to less than 10 minutes of downtime in a year.

The fundamental downside to server clustering is its cost. Clustering requires a separate network to be constructed between the servers, installation and configuration of additional software, additional hardware, and additional administrative support.

Specifically, server clustering offers the following advantages:

- **Increased performance**—More servers equals more processing power. The servers in a cluster can provide levels of performance beyond the scope of a single system by combining resources and processing power.

- **Load balancing**—Rather than having individual servers perform specific roles, a cluster can perform a number of roles, assigning the appropriate resources in the best places. This approach maximizes the power of the systems by allocating tasks based on which server in the cluster can best service the request.

- **Failover**—Because the servers in the cluster are in constant contact with each other, they can detect and cope with the failure of an individual system. How transparent the failover is to users depends on the clustering software, the type of failure, and the capability of the application software used to cope with the failure.

- **Scalability**—The capability to add servers to the cluster offers a degree of scalability simply not possible in a single-server scenario. It is worth mentioning, though, that clustering on PC platforms is still in its relative infancy, and the number of machines that can be included in a cluster is still limited.

To make server clustering happen, you need certain ingredients: servers, storage devices, network links, and software that makes the cluster work. Various strategies are available.

Preparing for Memory Failures

After memory is installed and confirmed to be working, it generally works error-free. Sometimes, however, memory is at the root of system problems. Unfortunately, fault-tolerance strategies for memory are limited. Memory doesn't support hot swapping, so you have to power down the server during memory replacement. The best you can do is minimize the impact of the failure.

Some environments have spare memory available at all times in case of failure. When memory does fail, a spare is ready to go. Such planning requires considerable forethought, but when you need such a solution, the preparation pays off.

Managing Processor Failures

Processors are hardy, and processor failure is extremely uncommon. Processor failure is so unusual that few organizations include processors in their fault-tolerance designs. Environments that consider processors might have a spare or, more likely, a standby server (discussed previously in this chapter).

Some multiprocessor machines have a built-in safeguard against a single processor failure. In such a machine, the working processor maintains the server while a replacement for the nonfunctioning processor is found.

Disaster Recovery

Besides implementing fault-tolerance measures in a network, you need to consider disaster recovery—the things to do when your carefully implemented fault-tolerance measures fail. Disaster recovery and fault tolerance are two separate entities, and both are equally important. *Disaster recovery* is defined as measures that allow a network to return to a working state.

Backups and backup strategies are key components of disaster recovery and help ensure the availability of data. The following sections identify the various backup strategies commonly used and why these strategies are such an important part of a network administrator's role.

Backup Methods

You can choose from several backup methods. Don't select one at random; choose carefully, to match the needs of your organization.

TIP: Tape Cleaning   Many backup strategies use tapes as the backup media of choice. When backing up to tape, you must periodically clean the tape drive with a cleaning cartridge. If your system cannot access a tape, you should first try another tape. If that doesn't work, use a cleaning tape. Remember these tips for the exam.

The backup method you choose will most likely be affected by the amount of time you have available. Many organizations have a time window in which backup procedures must be conducted. Outside that window, the backup procedure can impede the functioning of the network by slowing down the server and the network. Organizations with large amounts of data require more time for a backup than those with small amounts of data. Although both small and large organizations require full backups, the strategy each uses will be different. With that in mind, let's look at the various backup methods, which include full backups, incremental backups, and differential backups.

Full Backups

If you have time, a full backup is usually the best type of backup. A full backup, also referred to as a normal backup, copies all the files on the hard disk. In case of disaster, the files from a single backup set can be used to restore the entire system.

Despite the advantages of full backups, they are not always a practical solution. Depending on the amount of data that needs to be backed up, the procedure can take a long time. Many administrators try to run full backups in the off hours to reduce the impact on the network. Today, many networks do not have off hours, making it difficult to find time to squeeze in full backups.

Full backups are often used as the sole backup method in smaller organizations that have only a few gigabytes of data. Larger organizations that utilize hundreds of gigabytes of data storage are unlikely to rely on full backups as their sole backup strategy.

The backup software determines what data has changed since the last full backup, by checking a setting known as the *archive bit*. When a file is created, moved, or changed, the archive bit is set to indicate that the changed file must be backed up.

Backups and Security

Having your entire hard drive stored on a single location, such as a tape or removable hard disk, has obvious advantages but also some not-so-obvious disadvantages, including security concerns. A single device holding all your sensitive data can be restored by you or by anyone who has access to the device. There are well-documented cases of stolen tapes and the resulting stolen data. When you make any backups, you're responsible for storing the backup devices in a secure location.

Incremental Backups

An *incremental backup* is much faster than a full backup because only the files that have changed since the last full or incremental backup are included in it. For example, if you do a full backup on Tuesday and an incremental on Thursday, only the files that have changed since Tuesday will be backed up. Because an incremental backup copies less data than a full backup, backup times are significantly reduced.

On the other hand, incremental backups take longer to restore than full backups. When you restore from an incremental backup, you need the last full backup tape and each incremental tape done since the last full backup. In addition, these tapes must be restored in order. Suppose that you do a full backup on Friday and incremental backups on Monday, Tuesday, and Wednesday. If the server fails on Thursday, you need four tapes: Friday's full backup and the three incremental backups.

NOTE: Incremental   Incremental backups only back up files that have changed since the last full or incremental backup.

Differential Backups

Many people confuse differential backups and incremental backups, but they are different from one another. Whereas an incremental backup backs up everything from the last full or incremental backup, a *differential backup* backs up only the files that have been created or changed since the last full backup.

When restoring from a differential backup, you need only two tapes: the latest full backup and the latest differential. Depending on how dynamic the data is, the differential backup could still take some time. Essentially, differential backups provide the middle ground between incremental and full backups.

NOTE: Differential   Differential backups back up only files that have been changed or modified since the last full backup.

NOTE: What to Use in a Backup Cycle   In a backup cycle, incremental backups and a differential backup must be combined with a full backup to get a complete copy of the data on a drive.

TIP: Understand the Backup Types   For the Network+ exam, make sure that you understand what is involved in backing up and restoring data for all the backup types (for example, how many tapes are used and in what order they must be restored).

A Comparison of Backup Methods

Full backups do not concern themselves with the archive bit because all data is backed up. However, a full backup resets the archive bit after the files have been copied to the tape. Differential backups use the archive bit but do not clear it because the information is needed for the next differential backup. Incremental backups clear the archive bit so that unnecessary files aren't backed up. Table 10.3 summarizes the characteristics of the different backup methods.

Table 10.3 Comparison of Backup Methods

Method	What Is Backed Up	Restore Procedure	Archive Bit
Full	All data.	All data is restored from a single tape.	Does not use the archive bit but clears it after files have been copied to tape
Incremental	All data changed since the last full or incremental backup.	The restore procedure requires several tapes: the latest full backup and all incremental tapes since the last full backup.	Uses the archive bit and clears it after a file is saved to disk
Differential	All data changed since the last full backup.	The restore procedure requires the latest full backup tape and the latest differential backup tape.	Uses the archive bit but does not clear it

> **TIP: Clearing the Archive Bit** On the Network+ exam it is likely that you will be asked to identify what backup methods clear the archive bit from a changed or created file. Remember, to determine whether a file has changed since the last full backup, the backup software checks the *archive bit*. When a file is changed in any way or copied from one area of the disk to another, the archive bit is set to indicate that, at the next time of backup, the file needs to be copied or archived.

Backup Rotation Schedules

You can use a backup rotation schedule with a backup method. Organizations use many different rotations, but most are variations on a single popular rotation strategy: the Grandfather-Father-Son (GFS) rotation.

GFS is the most widely used rotation method. It uses separate tapes for monthly, weekly, and daily backups. A common GFS strategy requires 12 tapes. Four tapes are used for daily backups, Monday through Thursday; these are the son tapes. Five tapes are used for weekly backups, perhaps each Friday; these are the father tapes. Finally, 3 tapes are used for a monthly rotation; these are the grandfather tapes.

Using the GFS rotation, you can retrieve lost information from the previous day, previous week, and several previous months. Adding tapes to the monthly rotation lets you go back even further to retrieve data. Of course, the further back you go, the less current (and perhaps less usable) the information is. More tapes also make the rotation more complex.

Many organizations don't follow the GFS strategy by the book; instead, they create their own backup regimes. Regardless of the backup strategy used, a well-designed backup rotation is an integral part of system administration and should follow guidelines that enable for several retrieval points.

Offsite Storage

The type of backup to use and the frequency of these backups are critical considerations for any organization. Another backup decision that must be made is how and where backups are to be stored. It is easy to perform a backup and store the tapes onsite, perhaps in a locked room, but backup tape rotation schedules should include a consideration for offsite backup.

Offsite data storage is an important element because it enables backups to be accessed if the original location becomes unavailable. Even though the key feature of backups is its role in guaranteeing the availability of data, it is not without its risks.

For many organizations, backups are often the weak link in the security chain because the item of most value to an organization, and to a criminal, is normally the data. Many security measures can protect data while it is inside a controlled environment. But what happens when it is taken outside that environment?

When a data backup leaves your server environment, the degree of control over that tape and the data on it is diminished. An organization can spend millions of dollars building a state-of-the-art server environment, but if the security of data backups is not fully considered, it is a false sense of security. Here are some precautions that you can take to protect your valuable data when it leaves the server environment:

- **Password protection**—Tape backup software commonly has a password feature that enables each tape to be password protected. The password must be entered before the tape is restored or viewed.

- **Physical locks**—Use physically lockable tape cases for transporting the tapes. In addition to providing protection against data theft, tape cases also provide a degree of protection against accidental damage.

- **Registered couriers**—When transferring tapes between sites, use a trusted company employee or a registered secure courier service.

- **Secure storage**—Ensure that the location at which the tapes are stored is sufficiently secure.

- **Verification of data integrity**—If possible, when backup tapes reach their destination, they should be checked to ensure that they are the correct tapes and that they contain the correct data.

- **Encryption**—If facilities exist and the data is deemed sufficiently vital, the use of a data encryption system should be considered.

- **Knowledge restriction**—Confine knowledge of the backup and storage procedures to only those individuals who need the information.

The safety of backed-up data should be given at least the same considerations as the safety of data held inside your environment. When data leaves your site, it is exposed to a wide range of threats. Securing data when it leaves the site is a major security task for any organization.

TIP: Offsite Data   To be effective, the data stored offsite must be kept up-to-date. This means that the offsite data should be included in a backup rotation strategy.

Backup Best Practices

When you design a backup strategy, consider some general best practices. These best practices ensure that when you need it, the backup you depend on is available:

- **Test your backups**—After a backup is completed, you have no idea whether the backup was successful and whether you can retrieve needed data from it. Learning this information after your system has crashed is too late. To make sure that the backups work, it is important to periodically restore them.

- **Confirm the backup logs**—Most backup software generates log files after a backup procedure. After a backup is completed, read the backup logs to look for any documented errors that might have occurred during the backup procedure. Keep in mind that reading the backup-generated logs is no substitute for occasionally testing a restore. A completely unsuccessful backup might generate no documented errors.

- **Label the backup cartridges**—When you use many tapes in a rotation, label the cartridges to prevent reusing a tape and recording over something you need. The label should include the date of the backup and whether it was a full, incremental, or differential backup.

- **Rotate backups offsite**—Keeping all the tape backups in the same location as the server can be a problem. If the server location is damaged (by fire or flood, for example), you could lose all the data on the server and all your backups. Use an offsite tape rotation scheme to store current copies of backups in a secure offsite location.

- **Use new tapes**—Over time, tape cartridges can wear out and become unreliable. To combat this problem, periodically introduce new tapes into the tape rotation and destroy the old tapes.

- **Password protect the backups**—As an added measure of security, it is a good idea to password protect your backups. That way, if they fall into the wrong hands, they are protected by a password.

> **TIP: Write Protection**   Tape cartridges often use a write-protection tab similar to the ones found on 3.5-inch floppy disks. It is a good idea to write protect a tape cartridge after a backup so that it will not be overwritten accidentally.

Designing an effective backup strategy is one of the most important considerations for a network administrator, and therefore, it is an important topic area for the Network+ exam. Remember that the preservation of data is a foremost consideration when approaching network management.

Hot and Cold Spares

The impact that a failed component has on a system or network depends largely on predisaster preparation and on the recovery strategies used. Hot and cold spares represent a strategy for recovering from failed components.

Hot Spare and Hot Swapping

Hot spares give system administrators the capability to quickly recover from component failure. A hot spare, for example, is widely used by the RAID system to automatically failover to a spare hard drive should one of the other drives in the RAID array fail. A hot spare does not require any manual intervention, rather a redundant drive resides in the system at all times, just waiting to take over if another drive fails. With the RAID array continuing to function, the failed drive can be removed at a later time. Even though hot-spare technology adds an extra level of protection to your system, after a drive has failed and the hot spare has been used, the situation should be remedied as soon as possible.

Hot swapping is the capability to replace a failed component while the system is running. Perhaps the most commonly identified hot-swap component is the hard drive. In certain RAID configurations, when a hard drive crashes, hot swapping enables you to take the failed drive out of the server and install a new one.

The benefits of hot swapping are clear in that it enables a failed component to be recognized and replaced without compromising system availability. Depending on the system's configuration, the new hardware will normally be recognized automatically by both the current hardware and the operating system. Today, most internal and external RAID subsystems support the hot swapping feature. Some other hot swappable components include power supplies and hard disks.

Cold Spare and Cold Swapping

The term *cold spare* refers to a component such as a hard disk that resides within a computer system but requires manual intervention in case of component failure. A hot spare engages automatically, but a cold spare might require configuration settings or some other action to engage it. A cold spare configuration typically requires a reboot of the system.

The term cold spare has also been used to refer to a redundant component stored outside the actual system but kept in case of component failure. To replace the failed component with a cold spare, the system would need to be powered down.

Cold swapping refers to replacing components only after the system is completely powered off. This strategy is by far the least attractive for servers because the services provided by the server will be unavailable for the duration of the cold swap procedure. Modern systems have come a long way to ensure that cold swapping is a rare occurrence. For some situations and for some components, however, cold swapping is the only method to replace a failed component.

> **NOTE: Warm Swapping** The term *warm swap* is sometimes applied to a device that can be replaced while the system is still running but that requires some kind of manual intervention to disable the device before it can be removed. Using a PCIe hot plug is technically a warm swap strategy because it requires that the individual PCIe slot be powered down before the PCIe card is replaced. Of course, a warm swap is not as efficient as a hot swap, but it is much better than a cold swap.

Recovery Sites

A disaster recovery plan might include the provision for a recovery site that can be brought quickly into play. These sites fall into three categories: hot, warm, and cold. The need for each of these types of site depends largely on the business you are in and the funds available. Disaster recovery sites represent the ultimate in precautions for organizations that really need it. As a result, they aren't cheap.

The basic concept of a disaster recovery site is that it can provide a base from which the company can be operated during a disaster. The disaster recovery site is not normally intended to provide a desk for every employee but is intended more as a means to enable key personnel to continue the core business function.

Cold Site

In general, a *cold recovery site* is a site that can be up and operational in a relatively short time span, such as a day or two. Provision of services, such as telephone lines and power, is taken care of, and the basic office furniture might be in place, but there is unlikely to be any computer equipment, even though the building might have a network infrastructure and a room ready to act as a server room. In most cases, cold sites provide the physical location and basic services.

Cold sites are useful if there is some forewarning of a potential problem. Generally, cold sites are used by organizations that can weather the storm for a day or two before they get back up and running. If you are the regional office of a major company, it might be possible to have one of the other divisions take care of business until you are ready to go, but if you are the only office in the company, you might need something a little hotter.

Hot Site

For organizations with the dollars and the desire, *hot recovery sites* represent the ultimate in fault-tolerance strategies. Like cold recovery sites, hot sites are designed to provide only enough facilities to continue the core business function, but hot recovery sites are set up to be ready to go at a moment's notice.

A hot recovery site includes phone systems with the phone lines already connected. Data networks are also in place, with any necessary routers and switches plugged in and ready to go. Hot sites might have desktop PCs installed and waiting, and server areas replete with the necessary hardware to support business-critical functions. In other words, within moments, the hot site can become a fully functioning element of an organization. Key to this is having network data available and current.

The issue that confronts potential hot recovery site users is simply that of cost. Office space is expensive at the best of times, but having space sitting idle 99.9 percent of the time can seem like a tremendously poor use of money. A popular strategy to get around this problem is to use space provided in a disaster recovery facility, which is basically a building, maintained by a third-party company, in which various businesses rent space. Space is apportioned, usually, on how much each company pays.

Warm Site

Sitting in between the hot and cold recovery sites is the *warm site*. A warm site typically has computers, but they are not configured and ready. This means that data might need to be upgraded or other manual interventions performed before the network is again operational. The time it takes to get a warm site operational lands right in the middle of the other two options, as does the cost.

> **TIP: Hot, Warm, and Cold**   A hot site mirrors the organization's production network and can assume network operations at a moment's notice. Warm sites have the equipment needed to bring the network to an operational state but require configuration and potential database updates. Warm sites have network data but might not be completely up-to-date. A cold site has the space available with basic service but typically requires equipment and maybe data delivery. Be sure that you can differentiate the three types of recovery sites for the exam.

Network Optimization Strategies

Today's networks are all about speed. Network users expect data and application delivery quickly; consider how impatient many of us get waiting for web pages to load. Networks, however, are saturated and congested with traffic, making it necessary to have strategies to ensure that we use bandwidth in the best possible way. These strategies are collectively referred to as quality of service (QoS). QoS strategies include many areas, such as traffic shaping, load balancing, and caching engines. Each of these are discussed in this section.

QoS

Quality of service (QoS) describes the strategies used to manage and increase the flow of network traffic. QoS features enable administrators to predict bandwidth use, monitor that use, and control it to ensure that bandwidth is available to the applications that need it. These applications can generally be broken down into two categories:

- **Latency sensitive**—These applications need bandwidth for quick delivery where network lag time impacts their effectiveness. This includes voice and video transfer. For example, VoIP would be difficult to use if there were a significant lag time in the conversation.

- **Latency insensitive**—Controlling bandwidth also involves managing latency insensitive applications. This includes bulk data transfers such as huge backup procedures and FTP transfers.

With bandwidth limited and networks becoming increasingly congested, it becomes more difficult to deliver latency-sensitive traffic. If network traffic continues to increase and we can't always increase bandwidth, the choice is to prioritize traffic to ensure timely delivery. This is where QoS comes into play. QoS ensures the delivery of applications, such as video conferencing and VoIP telephony, without adversely affecting network throughput. QoS achieves more efficient use of network resources by differentiating between latency-insensitive traffic such as fax data and latency-sensitive streaming media.

One important strategy for QoS is priority queuing. Essentially what happens is that traffic is placed in an order based on its importance on delivery time. All data is given access, but the more important and latency sensitive data is given a higher priority.

> **TIP: Priority Queuing**   Priority queuing is an important concept of QoS. Be sure you understand the function of priority queuing for the Network+ exam.

Latency-Sensitive High-Bandwidth Applications

Many of the applications used on today's networks require a lot of bandwidth. The past few years have seen considerable growth of two high-bandwidth applications, VoIP and online or networked video applications. Both of these applications, while gaining in popularity, demand resources and can push network resources to their limit.

> **NOTE: High Bandwidth**   CompTIA lists VoIP and video applications as high-bandwidth applications, but there are others. Any application that requires data streaming and is latency-sensitive is likely a high-bandwidth application.

Voice over Internet Protocol (VoIP)

VoIP is designed to transfer human voice over the Internet using IP data packets. In operation, VoIP technology digitizes and encapsulates voice in data packets and then converts them back into voice at the destination.

The ability to "chat" over the Internet has been available for a number of years. Users have been using the Internet to communicate among themselves for some time. However, it has only been in the past few years that network bandwidth, protocols, and customer equipment have advanced far enough to become a viable alternative to a public switched telephone network (PSTN). In addition to voice transfer, communicating over the Internet allows users to exchange data with people you are talking with, sending images, graphs, and videos. That is simply not possible with PSTN conversations.

VoIP communication uses a standard called Real-Time Protocol (RTP) for transmitting audio and video packets between systems. RTP packets are typically used inside UDP-IP packets. Recall from Chapter 4, "Understanding the TCP/IP Protocol Suite," that UDP is a connectionless protocol, whereas TCP is a connection-oriented protocol. UDP does not have the overhead of TCP and therefore can get VoIP data to its destination faster. UDP does not specify an order that packets must arrive at the destination or how long it should take to get there. UDP is a fire-and-forget protocol. This works well because it gets packets to the destination faster and RTP puts the packets in order at the receiving end. UDP ensures a fast continuous flow of data and does not concern itself with guaranteeing the delivery of data packets. Refer to Chapter 4 for more information about RTP and other protocols used for real-time communication.

> **NOTE: UDP and RTP**   VoIP uses both RTP and UDP for maintaining the connection. UDP is preferred over TCP because it does not have error-checking mechanisms and does not guarantee delivery like TCP does.

In addition to latency, another concern with VoIP has been security. Some communications conducted over the Internet can be intercepted, and VoIP is no different. To address these security concerns, RTP was improved upon with the release of Secure RTP (SRTP), which provides for encryption, authentication, and integrity of the audio and video packets transmitted between communicating devices.

Video Applications

The popularity of streaming video applications has increased significantly over the past few years. Many users log on to the Internet to watch streaming video, such as missed TV shows, news broadcasts, entertainment videos found on YouTube, and the like. The capability to click a link and in seconds see content streaming from a remote location is quite amazing. There is much that needs to be in place for this content to display in a speedy fashion.

Like VoIP, streaming videos are typically latency-sensitive and require protocols built for speed. Streaming video can be sent over UDP or TCP data packets. UDP is faster because TCP has a higher overhead and guarantees data delivery using mechanisms such as timeouts and retries.

Working with transport protocols such as TCP and UDP are underlying real-time protocols. Three protocols associated with real-time streaming video applications are RTP, Real-time Streaming Protocol (RTSP), and the Real-time Transport Control Protocol (RTCP); they were specifically designed to stream media over networks.

Traffic Shaping

Traffic shaping is a QoS strategy designed to enforce prioritization policies on the transmission throughout the network. It is intended to reduce latency by controlling the amount of data that flows into and out of the network. Traffic is categorized, queued, and directed according to network policies.

We can shape and limit network traffic using several strategies. The one chosen depends on the needs of the network and the amount of network traffic. Some common traffic shaping methods include the following:

- **Shaping by application**—Administrators can configure a traffic shaper by categorizing specific types of network traffic and assigning that category a bandwidth limit. For example, traffic can be categorized using FTP. The rule can specify that no more than 4Mbps be dedicated for FTP traffic. This same principal can apply to Telnet sessions, streaming audio, or any other application coming through the network.

- **Shaping network traffic per user**—In any network, there are users who use more bandwidth than others. Some of this can be work-related, but more often than not, it is personal use. In such a case, it might be necessary to establish traffic shaping on a per-user basis. Traffic shapers enable administrators to delegate a certain bandwidth to a user; for instance, Bob from accounting is allowed no more than 256Kbps. This doesn't limit what the user can access, just the speed at which that content can be accessed.

- **Priority queuing**—One important consideration when looking at traffic shaping is determining which traffic is mission critical and which is less so. In addition to setting hard or burstable traffic limits on a per-application or per-user basis, traffic shaping devices can also be used to define the relative importance, or priority, of different types of traffic. For example, in an academic network where teaching and research are most important, recreational uses of the network (such as network games or peer-to-peer file-sharing application traffic) can be allowed bandwidth only when higher priority applications don't need it.

Some traffic shaping tasks can be done directly on a regular Cisco or Juniper router, just as a router can also be used to do some firewall-like packet filtering tasks. However, specialized traffic shapers, like any specialized devices, can be optimized to specifically and efficiently handle their unique responsibilities. Specialized devices also typically have a "bigger bag of tricks" to draw from when dealing with problems in their special area of expertise. Doing traffic shaping on a dedicated traffic shaping box also avoids loading up routers with other tasks, leaving the router free to focus on doing its job of routing packets as fast as it can. Figure 10.7 shows an example of traffic priority queuing.

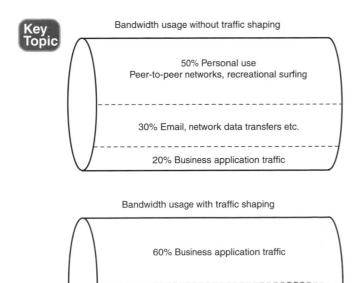

Figure 10.7 Traffic shaping.

TIP: Traffic Shaping   For the Network+ exam, be sure you can identify the function of traffic shaping.

Load Balancing

As the demands placed on an organization's servers and key systems increases, they need to handle the load. One of the strategies used to help facilitate this is load balancing. In networking terms, load balancing refers to distributing the load between different networked systems. In this way, the demand is shared between multiple CPUs, network links, and hard disks. This configuration increases response time, distributes processing, and ensures optimal resource utilization.

Distributing the load between multiple servers is called a server farm. Server farms are often used to ensure the delivery of Internet services. High-performance websites rely on web server farms, which are essentially a few or even hundreds of computers serving the same content for scalability, reliability, and low-latency access to Internet content. Web server farms are used to reliably deliver a range of Internet services, such as Internet Relay Chat networks, FTP servers, DHCP servers, NNTP servers, and DNS servers.

NOTE: Load Balancing   Load balancing distributes the load between multiple systems helping to ensure reliable delivery of data and Internet services.

Caching Engines

Caching is an important consideration when optimizing network traffic. For example, as we discussed in Chapter 3, "Networking Components and Devices," proxy servers use caching to limit the number of client requests that go to the Internet; instead, the requests are filled from the proxy servers cache. Recall from Chapter 3 that, when a caching proxy server has answered a request for a web page, the server makes a copy of all or part of that page in its cache. Then, when the page is requested again, the proxy server answers the request from the cache rather than going back out to the Internet. For example, if a client on a network requests the web page www.comptia.org, the proxy server can cache the contents of that web page. When a second client computer on the network attempts to access the same site, that client can grab it from the proxy server cache, and accessing the Internet is not necessary. This greatly reduces the network traffic that has to be filtered to the Internet, a significant gain in terms of network optimization.

When it comes to determining what to cache, an administrator can establish many rules, including the following:

- What websites to cache
- How long the information is cached

- When cached information is updated

- The size of cached information

- What type of content is cached

- Who can access the cache

The rules established for caching vary from network to network depending on the needs of that network. In networks where a large number of people are accessing similar websites, caching can greatly increase network performance. The advantages to properly configured caching are clear: reduced bandwidth and latency and increased throughput. One possible disadvantage of caching is receiving out-of-date files because you are obtaining content from the caching engine and not the website.

Following are two of the several advantages of using caching strategies:

- **Increasing performance**—Caching can store application data close to the user. That is, cached data is stored on local systems rather than a remote web server for example. This enables for faster retrieval of data and less need for repetitive processing and data transportation to a remote server.

TIP: Cached Data   Caching improves performance because by accessing a cache, servers and systems do not need to re-create and find the same data for multiple user requests. Caching content locally also limits surges in traffic.

- **Data availability**—There may be times when the data or application we are trying to access is unavailable because of failure. For example, a regularly accessed remote website might be down. By having data stored in a cache, it is possible to get that data from the cache. The cache can issue requests from the cache until the failed or unavailable server or database comes back online.

NOTE: Expiring Cache   The information stored in a cache must be kept as fresh and current as possible. To do this, some dynamic content must be updated in the cache regularly. Other content that changes more infrequently can be updated less frequently. Cached content updating is managed using expiration policies. The expiration policy determines how long the content in a cache is kept.

Summary

This chapter explored two important networking concepts: fault tolerance and disaster recovery. Although many people think fault tolerance and disaster recovery are the same, they are different, but equally important, concepts.

Fault tolerance usually refers to the measures network administrators use to ensure that data and network services are always available to network users. A strong fault-tolerance strategy does not happen by accident; rather, you must consider many factors when choosing the best fault-tolerance strategies for a specific organization.

Because availability is such a huge issue and server downtime is so costly, most hardware components within a server need to be considered part of a fault-tolerance solution. Hard drives typically receive the most attention because they're 50% more likely to fail than any other component. The mechanism used to protect against such failures is RAID.

Several RAID levels are available today. The most common are RAID levels 0, 1, and 5. Although RAID 0 is a RAID level, it does not offer any fault tolerance, but it does offer performance improvements over using a single disk. RAID 1 uses disk mirroring to establish fault tolerance but suffers from 50% overhead and limited storage capacity. The RAID level of choice for organizations that can afford it is RAID 5, which stripes data and parity information over several disks. The parity information can be used to re-create data if a hard drive in the array fails.

Other fault-tolerance measures include using UPSs, redundant components, and sometimes redundant servers.

Disaster recovery involves having in place measures that can be used when the system goes down. To protect data from disaster, you need backups. Three key types of backups are available: full, incremental, and differential. A full backup makes a copy of all data, an incremental backup makes a copy of the data that has changed since the last full backup or the latest incremental backup, and a differential backup saves everything that has changed since the last full backup.

In addition to backup methods, a backup rotation strategy ensures that data is sufficiently recoverable. The most common backup rotation strategy is the GFS rotation. This type of rotation requires numerous tapes for daily, weekly, and monthly backups.

Real-time applications such as online video and VoIP are gaining in popularity as the protocols and bandwidth needed to support these applications mature. Video and VoIP applications relay on transport protocols, typically UDP, and real-time protocols such as RTP.

The chapter ended by looking at some of the strategies used to optimize the flow of network traffic. This includes QoS, traffic shaping, caching, and load balancing. One form of load balancing is server farms. Server farms distribute the processing and resource load between multiple systems and help ensure the delivery of Internet services.

Exam Preparation Tasks

Review All the Key Topics

Review the most important topics in the chapter, noted with the Key Topics icon in the outer margin of the page. Table 10.4 lists a reference of these key topics and the page numbers on which each is found.

Table 10.4   Key Topics for Chapter 10

Key Topic Element	Description	Page Number
Table 10.1	Levels of availability and related downtime	350
Figure 10.1	Server component failures	352
Figure 10.2	RAID 0 with disk striping.	354
Figure 10.3	A RAID 1 array	356
Figure 10.4	A disk duplexing configuration.	356
Figure 10.5	A RAID 5 array	358
Figure 10.6	A RAID 10 solution	361
Table 10.2	RAID characteristics	362
Table 10.3	Comparison of Backup methods	371
Figure 10.7	Traffic shaping	380

Define Key Terms

Define the following key terms from this chapter, and check your answers in the Glossary.

- QoS
- Traffic shaping
- Load balancing
- High availability
- Caching engines
- Fault tolerance
- Latency sensitivity

- VoIP

- Video applications

- RTP

- UDP

- TCP

- Archive bit

- Full backup

- Incremental backup

- Differential backup

- Uptime

- Hot swap

- Warm swap

- RAID

- Disaster recovery

- Fault tolerance

Apply Your Knowledge

Exercise 10.1 Performing a Full Backup

You have recently been employed as the network administrator for a large pharmaceutical company. On your first day of work, you notice that no backup has been performed for more than 6 months. You immediately decide to perform a full backup and schedule backups to occur at regular intervals.

You use Windows 2003 Server's Backup Wizard utility to back up a few data files and automate the process to reoccur automatically based on a schedule you construct.

Estimated time: 20 minutes

1. Select Start, All Programs, Accessories, System Tools, Backup. The Backup [Untitled] screen appears.

2. Select the Schedule Jobs tab and click the Add Job button. The Backup Wizard screen appears.

3. Click Next on the Backup Wizard screen.

4. Choose Back Up Selected Files, Drives, or Network Data and click Next.

5. Select the data you want to back up. The window contains a directory of files similar to Windows Explorer, with one added twist: A check box appears next to each directory item. Click the box to select an item to be backed up. Note that if you click a folder, you will back up everything from that point in the directory down.

6. Choose one or two folders that contain a few files. Click Next.

7. Choose the media type to which you want to save your data. In this project, you'll save your backup to disk, so choose the File in the Backup Media Type drop-down box.

8. If the directory you want to use doesn't exist, you can create it by clicking the Browse button and navigating to where you want to put the backup file you are about to create. (Click the New Folder icon in the browse window.)

9. Specify the type of backup you want to perform. Choose Normal and click Next.

10. Select Verify Data After Backup if you want the operating system to check to make sure that the backup has been made. Click Next.

11. Choose whether you want to add this backup to the end of any previous backups or whether you want to replace an old backup with this new one. For this project, choose Replace the Data on the Media with This Backup. Click Next.

12. The next window lets you assign Backup Label and Media Label names. Leave the defaults in place and click Next. A Set Account Information dialog box might appear. Windows 2003 enables you to run the job under another account name/password if you want. If you get this choice, enter your administrator account username and password. (The password will be whatever you established when you installed Windows 2000 Server or whatever you changed it to.)

13. The When to Backup screen appears; give the backup job you are creating the name BackupTest and click Set Schedule.

14. The Schedule Job screen appears, and you can schedule when you want the backup job to occur. Set whatever schedule you want and click OK. You return to the When to Backup Screen; click Next.

15. On the Completing the Backup Wizard screen, click Finish to create the job. The backup utility creates the job, and the folders/files you selected will be backed up according to the schedule you selected.

16. You can view the status of the backup job or make changes to it by using the Task Scheduler. To use the Task Scheduler, choose Start, Settings, Control Panel. When the Control Panel opens, double-click the Scheduled Tasks icon. You should see the backup job you just created. You can double-click it to edit the job.

Review Questions

You can find answers to the review questions in Appendix A, "Answers to Review Questions."

1. What is the minimum number of disks required for a RAID 5 array?
   a. 2
   b. 5
   c. 1 physical and 1 logical
   d. 3

2. What RAID level uses disk mirroring to provide fault tolerance?
   a. RAID 1
   b. RAID 0
   c. RAID 5
   d. RAID 2

3. Which of the following backup methods require the archive bit to be cleared? (Choose the two best answers.)
   a. Full
   b. Incremental
   c. Differential
   d. Mirror image

4. As network administrator, you have been asked to implement a backup and re-store method that requires only a total of two tape sets. Which of the following backup pairs would you use?
   a. Full, incremental, and differential.
   b. Differential, incremental.
   c. Full, differential.
   d. This cannot be done.

5. You are configuring VoIP for a large organization. As part of the process you need to determine the protocols used with VoIP. Which of the following protocols are you likely to use with VoIP? (Choose the two best answers.)
   a. TCP
   b. UDP
   c. RTP
   d. RPT

6. How many hard disks are required to establish a RAID 1 solution?
   a. 8
   b. 4
   c. 6
   d. 2

7. You are the network administrator for a company that operates from 7 a.m. to 9 p.m. Monday through Friday. Your boss requires that a backup be performed nightly but does not want the backup to interfere with network operations. Full backups have been started at 9:30 p.m. and have taken until 8 a.m. to complete. What strategy would you suggest to correct the backup issue?

   a. Weekly full backups, incremental backups on Mondays, and differential backups every other weekday

   b. Full backup performed on the weekend and incremental backups performed on weekdays

   c. Differential backups performed on weekends and a full backup every other weekday evening

   d. Weekly full backups combined with weekend differential backups

8. Which of the following power-related problems is associated with a short-term voltage drop?

   a. Surge

   b. Brownout

   c. Sag

   d. Spike

9. Which of the following fault-tolerant RAID levels offers the best read-and-write performance?

   a. RAID 0

   b. RAID 1

   c. RAID 5

   d. RAID 10

10. Which of the following are fault-tolerance measures associated with network adapters? (Choose the two best answers.)

   a. Warm swapping

   b. Adapter teaming

   c. Packet fragment recovery

   d. Secondary I/O recovery

11. Which of the following devices cannot be implemented in a fault-tolerant configuration?

   a. Power supply

   b. Processor

   c. NIC

   d. Memory

12. What is the storage capacity of a RAID 1 array that uses two 40GB hard disks?

   a. 80GB

   b. 40GB minus the parity calculation

   c. 40GB

   d. 80GB minus the parity calculation

13. Which of the following are valid reasons to use a UPS? (Choose the three best answers.)

   a. Data availability

   b. To prevent damage to hardware

   c. Increased network speeds

   d. To prevent damage to data

14. You have recently helped create an entire duplicate network complete with servers, client systems, and network hardware. It has been created to quickly continue operations if a catastrophic failure occurs. Which of the following terms describe this configuration?

   a. Hot site

   b. Warm site

   c. Hot spares

   d. Cold site

15. As a network administrator, you have been asked to implement a RAID solution that offers high performance. Fault tolerance is not a concern. Which RAID level are you likely to use?

   a. RAID 0

   b. RAID 1

   c. RAID 2

   d. RAID 5

   e. RAID 10

16. Which of the following statements are true of VoIP? (Choose the two best answers.)

   a. VoIP is latency-sensitive.

   b. VoIP is latency-insensitive.

   c. VoIP typically uses TCP as a transport protocol.

   d. SRTP can be used to help secure VoIP communications.

17. Which of the following recovery sites requires the delivery of computer equipment and an update of all network data?

   a. Cold site

   b. Warm site

   c. Hot site

   d. None of the above

18. Which of the following uses redundant hard disk controllers?

   a. Disk duplexing

   b. RAID 0

   c. Disk duplication

   d. RAID 5

19. You have installed five 15GB hard disks into your server in a RAID 5 array. How much storage space will be available for data?

   a. 75GB

   b. 60GB

   c. 30GB

   d. 45GB

20. While digging through an old storage closet, you find two 10GB hard disks. What RAID levels could you implement with them? (Choose the two best answers.)

   a. RAID 5

   b. RAID 0

   c. RAID 10

   d. RAID 1

This chapter covers CompTIA Network+ objectives 4.6 and 4.7. Upon completion of this chapter, you will be able to answer the following questions:

- What are the steps in the troubleshooting process?

- How do you troubleshoot network hardware?

- What issues require escalation?

- What are the procedures when troubleshooting wireless connections?

CHAPTER 11

Troubleshooting Procedures and Best Practices

Even the most well-designed and maintained networks will fail at some point. Such a failure might be as dramatic as a failed server taking down the entire network or as routine as a single computer system being unable to print. Regardless of the problem you face, as a network administrator, you will spend a sizable portion of your time troubleshooting problems with the network, the devices connected to it, and the people who use it. In each case, the approach to the problem is as important as the troubleshooting process. Although some steps are common to the troubleshooting process, few problems you face will be alike because so many variables are involved.

As you see in this chapter, troubleshooting is about more than just fixing a problem; It includes isolating the problem and taking the appropriate actions to prevent it from happening again. The ability to effectively troubleshoot network-related problems goes beyond technical knowledge and includes the ability to think creatively to get to the root of a problem. In addition, strong communication skills can turn a difficult and seemingly impossible troubleshooting task into an easy one. Although the role of the network administrator can be a cellular one, you will be surprised at just how much interaction you'll have with users and how important this element of your role will be.

This chapter provides a comprehensive look into the many facets that make up an effective troubleshooting strategy. In addition, it examines specific skills and techniques you can use to quickly isolate a network-related problem. It also examines scenarios in which these troubleshooting skills come into play.

NOTE: Who Says? Ask 10 network administrators about troubleshooting best practices, and you will no doubt get 15 different answers. There is no universally accepted definition or procedural acceptance of troubleshooting best practices. With this in mind, the information provided in this chapter specifies troubleshooting best practices identified by CompTIA. Whether these are the best practices in real-world application is a matter of debate. However, there is no debate that these are the best practices that will be on the exam.

Foundation Topics

The Art of Troubleshooting

There is no magic or innate ability that makes a good network troubleshooter. You will hear tales of people who have a gift for troubleshooting, but those who can troubleshoot well aren't necessarily gifted. Instead, good troubleshooters have a special combination of skills. The ability to competently and confidently troubleshoot networks comes from experience, a defined methodology, and sometimes just plain luck.

One of the factors that makes troubleshooting such a difficult task is the large number of variables that can come into play. Although it is difficult to preemptively list all the factors you have to consider while troubleshooting networks, this chapter lists a few to help you start thinking in the right direction. When you are troubleshooting, thinking in the right direction is half the battle. Considering that most network administrators spend the majority of their troubleshooting time working on the devices connected to the network rather than on the network infrastructure, it is worth looking at some of the factors that can affect troubleshooting of devices connected to the network. First, let's look at the difference between troubleshooting a server and troubleshooting a workstation system.

Troubleshooting Servers and Workstations

One often overlooked but important distinction in troubleshooting networks is the difference between troubleshooting a server computer and troubleshooting a workstation system. Although the fundamental troubleshooting principles of isolation and problem determination are often the same in different networks, the steps taken for problem resolution are often different from one network to another. Make no mistake: When you troubleshoot a server system, the stakes are much higher than with workstation troubleshooting, and therefore it's considerably more stressful. Let's take a look at a few of the most important distinctions between workstation and server troubleshooting:

- **Pressure**—It is difficult to capture in words the pressure you feel when troubleshooting a downed server. Troubleshooting a single workstation with one anxious user is stressful enough, and when tens, hundreds, or even thousands of users are waiting for you to solve the problem, the pressure can be enough to unhinge even the most seasoned administrator.

- **Planning**—Troubleshooting a single workstation often requires little planning. If work needs to be done on a workstation, it can often be done during a lunch break, after work, or even during the day. If work needs to be done on a server, particularly one that is heavily accessed, you might need to wait days, weeks, or even months before you have a good time to take down the server so that you can work on it and fix the problem.

- **Time**—For many organizations, every minute a server is unavailable is measured as much in dollars as it is in time. Servers are often relied on to provide 24-hour network service, and anything less is often considered unacceptable. Although it might be necessary to take a server down at some point for troubleshooting, you will be expected to account for every minute that it is down.

- **Problem determination**—Many people who have had to troubleshoot workstation systems know that finding the problem often involves a little trial and error. (Swap out the RAM; if that doesn't work, replace the power supply, and so on.) Effective server troubleshooting involves little trial and error—if any at all. Before the server is powered down, the administrator is expected to have a good idea of the problem.

- **Expertise**—Today, many people feel comfortable taking the case off their personal computers to add memory, replace a fan, or just have a quick peek. Although it is based on the same technologies as PC hardware, server hardware is more complex, and those who manage and maintain servers are expected to have an advanced level of hardware and software knowledge, often reinforced by training and certifications.

These are just a few of the differences in the troubleshooting practices and considerations between servers and workstations. As this chapter discusses troubleshooting, the focus is mainly on the server side of troubleshooting. This helps explain why some of the troubleshooting procedures might seem rigid and unnecessary on a workstation level.

> **TIP: Workstations and Servers**   The Network+ exam does not require you to identify any specific differences between workstation and server troubleshooting, but it does require background knowledge of general troubleshooting procedures and the factors that influence how to approach a network problem.

General Troubleshooting Considerations

Knowing the differences between procedures and approaches for troubleshooting servers and for troubleshooting workstations is valuable, but a seemingly endless number of other considerations exist. Each of these other factors can significantly affect the way you approach a problem on the network. The following list contains some of the obvious and perhaps not so obvious factors that come into play when troubleshooting a network:

- **Time**—The time of day can play a huge role in the troubleshooting process. For instance, you are likely to respond differently to a network problem at 10 a.m., during high network use, than at 8 p.m., when the network is not being utilized as much. The response to network troubleshooting during high-use periods is often geared toward a Band-Aid solution, just getting things up and running as soon as possible. Finding the exact cause of the problem and developing a permanent fix generally occurs when there is more time.

- **Network size**—The strategies and processes used to troubleshoot small networks of 10 to 100 computer systems can be different from those used to troubleshoot networks consisting of thousands of computers.

- **Support**—Some network administrators find themselves working alone, as a single IT professional working for a company. In such cases, the only available sources might include telephone, Internet, or manufacturer support. Other network administrators are part of a large IT department. In that type of environment, the troubleshooting process generally includes a hierarchical consultation process.

- **Knowledge of the network**—It would be advantageous if uniformity existed in the installation of all networks, but that isn't the case. You could be working on a network with ring or star topology. Before you start troubleshooting a network, you need to become familiarize with its layout and design. The troubleshooting strategies you employ will be affected by your knowledge of the network.

- **Technologies used**—Imagine being called in to troubleshoot a wide area network (WAN) that includes multiple Linux servers, a handful of NetWare servers, an old Windows NT 4.0 server, and multiple Macintosh workstations. Your knowledge of these technologies will dictate how, if at all, you are going to troubleshoot the network. There is no shame in walking away from a problem you are unfamiliar with. Good network administrators always recognize their knowledge boundaries.

These are just a few of the factors that will affect your ability to troubleshoot a network. There are countless others.

Troubleshooting Methods and Procedures

At some point in your networking career, you will be called on to troubleshoot network-related problems. Correctly and swiftly identifying these problems is not done by accident; rather, effective troubleshooting requires attention to some specific steps and procedures. Although some organizations have documented troubleshooting procedures for their IT staff members, many do not. Whether you use these exact steps in your job is debatable, but the general principles remain the same. The CompTIA Network+ exam objectives list the troubleshooting steps as follows:

Step 1.   Information gathering—identify symptoms and problems.

Step 2.   Identify the affected areas of the network.

Step 3.   Determine if anything has changed.

Step 4.   Establish the most probable cause.

Step 5.   Determine if escalation is necessary.

Step 6.   Create an action plan and solution identifying potential effects.

Step 7.   Implement and test the solution.

Step 8.   Identify the results and effects of the solution.

Step 9.   Document the solution and the entire process.

The following sections examine each area of the troubleshooting process.

Step 1: Information Gathering—Identify Symptoms and Problems

Troubleshooting a network can be difficult at the best of times, but trying to do it with limited information makes it that much harder. Trying to troubleshoot a network without all the information can, and often will, cause you to troubleshoot the wrong problem. Without the correct information, you could literally replace a toner cartridge when someone just used the wrong password.

With this in mind, the first step in the troubleshooting process is to establish exactly what the symptoms of the problem are. This stage of the troubleshooting process is all about information gathering. To get this information, you need knowledge of the operating system used, good communication skills, and a little patience. It is important to get as much information as possible about the problem before you charge out the door with that toner cartridge under your arm. You can glean information from three key sources: the computer (in the form of logs and error messages), the computer user experiencing the problem, and your own observation. These sources are examined in the following sections.

Information from the Computer

If you know where to look and what to look for, a computer can help reveal where a problem lies. Many operating systems provide error messages when a problem is encountered. A Linux system, for example, might present a Segmentation Fault error message, which often indicates a memory-related error. Windows, on the other hand, might display an Illegal Operation error message to indicate a possible memory or application failure. Both of these system error messages can be cross-referenced with the operating system's website information to identify the root of the problem. The information provided in these error messages can at times be cryptic, so finding the solution might be tricky.

In addition to the system-generated error messages, network operating can be configured to generate log files after a hardware or software failure. An administrator can then view these log files to see when the failure occurred and what was being done when the crash occurred. Windows 2000/2003/2008/XP/Vista displays error messages in the Event Viewer; Linux stores many of its system log files in the /var/log directory; and NetWare creates a file called `abend.log`, which contains detailed information about the state of the system at the time of the crash. When you start the troubleshooting process, make sure that you are familiar enough with the operating system used to determine whether it is trying to give you a message.

> **TIP: Error Message Storage**   For the Network+ exam, you might need to know that the troubleshooting process requires you to read system-generated log errors.

Information from the User

Your communication skills will be most needed when you gather information from end users. Getting accurate information from a computer user or anyone with limited technical knowledge can be difficult. Having a limited understanding of computers and technical terminology can make it difficult for a nontechnical person to relay the true symptoms of a problem. However, users can convey what they are trying to do and what is not working. When you interview an end user, you will likely want the following information:

- **Error frequency**—If it is a repeating problem, ask for the frequency of the problem. Does the problem occur at regular intervals or sporadically? Does it happen daily, weekly, or monthly?

- **Applications in use**—You will definitely want to know what applications were in use at the time of the failure. Only the end user will know this information.

- **Past problems**—Ask whether this error has been a problem in the past. If it has and it was addressed, you might already have your fix.

- **User modifications**—A new screensaver, game, or other such programs have ways of ending up on users' systems. Although many of these applications can be installed successfully, sometimes they create problems. When you try to isolate the problem, ask the user whether any new software additions have been made to the system.

- **Error messages**—Network administrators cannot be at all the computers on a network all the time. Therefore, they are likely to miss an error message when it is displayed onscreen. The end user might tell you what error message appeared.

> **NOTE: Installation Policies**   Many organizations have strict policies about what can and cannot be installed on computer systems. These policies are not in place to exercise the administrator's control but rather to prevent as many crashes and failures as possible. Today many harmless-looking freeware and trial programs have Trojan horse or spyware attached. When executed they can cause considerable problems on a system.

Observation Techniques

Finding a problem often involves nothing more than using your eyes, ears, and nose to locate the problem. For instance, if you troubleshoot a workstation system and you see a smoke cloud wafting from the back of the system, looking for error messages might not be necessary. If you walk into a server room and hear the CPU fan grinding, you are unlikely to need to review the server logs to find the problem.

Observation techniques often come into play when you troubleshoot connectivity errors. For instance, looking for an unplugged cable and confirming that the light-emitting diode (LED) on the network interface card (NIC) is lit requires observation on your part. Keeping an eye as well as a nose out for potential problems is part of the network administrator's role and can help in identifying a situation before it becomes a problem.

TIP: Observation Techniques   For the Network+ exam, remember that observation techniques play a large role in the preemptive troubleshooting process, which can result in finding a small problem before it becomes a large one.

Effective Questioning Techniques

Regardless of the method you use to gather information about a problem, you need answers to some important questions. When approaching a problem, consider the following questions:

- Is only one computer affected, or has the entire network gone down?

- Is the problem happening all the time, or is it intermittent?

- Does the problem happen during specific times, or does it happen all the time?

- Has this problem occurred in the past?

- Has any network equipment been moved recently?

- Have any new applications been installed on the network?

- Has anyone else tried to correct the problem; if so, what has that person tried?

- Is there any documentation that relates to the problem or to the applications or devices associated with the problem?

By answering these questions, as well as others, you can gain a better idea of exactly what the problem is.

Step 2: Identify the Affected Areas of the Network

Some computer problems are isolated to a single user in a single location; others affect several thousand users spanning multiple locations. Establishing the affected area is an important part of the troubleshooting process, and it often dictates the strategies you use in resolving the problem.

TIP: Be Thorough   On the Network+ exam, you might be provided with either a description of a scenario or a description augmented by a network diagram. In either case, you should read the description of the problem carefully, step by step. In most cases, the correct answer is fairly logical, and the wrong answers can be identified easily.

Problems that affect many users are often connectivity issues that disable access for many users. Such problems can often be isolated to wiring closets, network devices, and server rooms. The troubleshooting process for problems isolated to a single user often begins and ends at that user's workstation. The trail might indeed lead you to the wiring closet or server, but it is not likely that the troubleshooting process would begin there. Understanding who is affected by a problem can provide the first clues about where the problem exists.

As a practical example, assume that you are troubleshooting a client connectivity problem whereby a Windows client is unable to access the network. You can try to ping the server from that system, and, if it fails, ping the same server from one or two more client systems. If all tested client systems cannot ping the server, the troubleshooting procedure will not focus on the clients but more toward something common to all three, such as the DHCP server or network switch.

Step 3: Determine if Anything Has Changed

Whether a problem exists with a workstation's access to a database or an entire network, keep in mind that they were working at some point. Although many claim that the "computer just stopped working," it is unlikely. Far more likely is that changes to the system or the network caused the problem. As much as users try to convince you that computers do otherwise, computer systems do not reconfigure themselves. Therefore, establishing what was done to a system can lead you in the right direction to isolate and troubleshoot a problem.

Changes can occur on the network, server, or workstation. Each of these is discussed in the following sections.

TIP: Obvious Solutions   In the Network+ exam, avoid discounting a possible answer because it seems too easy. Many of the troubleshooting questions are based on possible real-world scenarios, many of which do have easy or obvious solutions.

Changes to the Network

Most of today's networks are dynamic and continually growing to accommodate new users and new applications. Unfortunately, these network changes, although intended to increase network functionality, may inadvertently cause additional problems. For instance, a new computer system added to a network might be installed with a duplicate computer name or IP address, which would prevent another computer that has the same name or address from accessing the network. Other changes that can create problems on the network include adding or removing a hub or switch, changing the network's routing information, or adding or removing a server. Almost every change that the network administrator makes to the network can potentially have an undesirable impact elsewhere on the network. For this reason, all changes made to the network should be fully documented and fully thought out.

> **NOTE: Faulty Hardware**   Although recent changes to systems or networks account for many network problems, some problems do happen out of the blue. Faulty hardware is a good example.

Changes to the Server

Part of a network administrator's job involves some tinkering with the server. Although this might be unavoidable, it can sometimes lead to several unintentional problems. Even the most mundane of all server tasks can have a negative impact on the network. The following are some common server-related tasks that can cause problems:

- **Changes to user accounts**—For the most part, changes to accounts do not cause any problems, but sometimes they do. If after making changes to user accounts, a user or several users cannot log on to the network or access a database, the problem is likely related to the changes made to the accounts.

- **Changes to permissions**—Data is protected by permissions that dictate who can and cannot access the data on the drives. Permissions are an important part of system security, but changes to permissions can inadvertently prevent users from accessing specific files.

- **Patches and updates**—Part of the work involved in administering networks is to monitor new patches and updates for the network operating system and install them as needed. It is not uncommon for an upgrade or a fix to an operating system to cause problems on the network.

- **New applications**—From time to time, new applications and programs—such as productivity software, firewall software, or even virus software—have to be installed on the server. When any kind of new software is added to the server, it might cause problems on the network. Knowing what has recently been installed can help you isolate a problem.

- **Hardware changes**—Either because of failure or expansion, hardware on the server might have to be changed. Changes to the hardware configuration on the server can cause connectivity problems.

Changes to the Workstation

The changes made to the systems on the network are not always under the control of the network administrator. Often, the end user performs configuration changes and some software installations. Such changes can be particularly frustrating to troubleshoot, and many users are unaware that the changes they make can cause problems. When looking for changes to a workstation system, consider the following:

- **Network settings**—One of the configuration hotspots for workstation computer systems are the network settings. If a workstation cannot access the network, it is a good idea to confirm that the network settings have not been changed.

- **Printer settings**—Many printing problems can be isolated to changes in the printer configuration. Some client systems, such as Linux, are more adept at controlling administrative configuration screens than others; for example, Windows leaves such screens open to anyone who wants to change the configuration. When printing problems are isolated to a single system, changes in the configuration could be the cause.

- **New software**—Many users love to download and install nifty screensavers or perhaps the latest 3D adventure games on their work computers. The addition of extra software can cause the system to fail. Confirm with the end user that new software has not been added to the system recently.

NOTE: Duplicate IP Addresses   Consider a system that could previously log on to the network but now receives an error message, stating that it cannot log on because of a duplicate IP address. A duplicate IP address means that two systems on the network are attempting to connect to the network using the same IP address. As you know, there can be only one. This often happens when a new system has been added to a network where Dynamic Host Configuration Protocol (DHCP) is not used.

Step 4: Establish the Most Probable Cause

There can be many different causes for a single problem on a network, but with appropriate information gathering, it is possible to eliminate many of them. When looking for a probable cause, it is often best to look at the easiest solution first and then work from there. Even in the most complex of network designs, the easiest solution is often the right one. For example, if a single user cannot log on to a network, it is best to confirm network settings before replacing the NIC. Remember, though, that at this point you are trying to determine only the most probable cause, and your first guess might be incorrect. It might take a few tries to determine the correct cause of the problem.

Step 5: Determine if Escalation Is Necessary

Sometimes the problems we encounter fall outside the scope of our knowledge. Few organizations expect their administrators to know everything, but organizations do expect administrators to fix any problem, and to do this, additional help is often needed.

NOTE: Finding Solutions   System administration is often as much about knowing whom and what to refer to in order to get information about a problem as it is about actually fixing the problem.

Technical escalation procedures do not follow a specific set of rules; rather, the procedures to follow vary from organization to organization and situation to situation. Your organization might have an informal arrangement or a formal one requiring documented steps and procedures to be carried out. Whatever the approach, there are general practices that you should follow for appropriate escalation.

Unless otherwise specified by the organization, the general rule is to start with the closest help first and work out from there. If you work in an organization that has an IT team, talk with others in your team; every IT professional has had different experiences, and someone else might know the issue at hand. If you are still struggling with the problem, it is common practice to notify a supervisor or head administrator, especially if the problem is a threat to the server's data or can bring down the server.

Suppose that you are the server administrator who notices a problem with a hard disk in a RAID 1 array on a Linux server. You know how to replace drives in a failed RAID 1 configuration, but you have no experience working with software RAID on a Linux server. This situation would most certainly require an escalation of the problem. The job of server administrator in this situation is to notice the failed RAID 1 drive and to recruit the appropriate help to repair the RAID failure within Linux.

NOTE: Passing the Buck   When you're confronted with a problem, it is yours until it has been solved or until it has been passed to someone else. Of course, the passing on of an issue requires that both parties be aware that it has been passed on.

Step 6: Create an Action Plan and Solution Identifying Potential Effects

After identifying a cause, but before implementing a solution, develop a plan for the solution. This is particularly a concern for server systems in which taking the server offline is a difficult and undesirable prospect. After identifying the cause of a problem on the server, it is absolutely necessary to plan for the solution. The plan must include details around when the server or network should be taken offline and for how long, what support services are in place, and who will be involved in correcting the problem.

Planning is an important part of the whole troubleshooting process and can involve formal or informal written procedures. Those who do not have experience troubleshooting servers might be wondering about all the formality, but this attention to detail ensures the least amount of network or server downtime and the maximum data availability.

As far as workstation troubleshooting is concerned, rarely is a formal planning procedure required, and this makes the process easier. Planning for workstation troubleshooting typically involves arranging a convenient time with end users to implement a solution.

Step 7: Implement and Test the Solution

With the plan in place, you should be ready to implement a solution—that is, apply the patch, replace the hardware, plug in a cable, or implement some other solution. Ideally, your first solution would fix the problem, although unfortunately this is not always the case. If your first solution does not fix the problem, you need to retrace your steps and start again.

It is important that you attempt only one solution at a time. Trying several solutions at once can make it unclear which one actually corrected the problem.

TIP: Rollback Plans   A common and mandatory step that you must take when working on servers and some mission-critical workstations is to develop a rollback plan. The purpose of a rollback plan is to provide a method to get back to where you were before attempting the fix. Troubleshooting should not make the problem worse. Have an escape plan!

After the corrective change has been made to the server, network, or workstation, it is necessary to test the results. Never assume. This is where you find out whether you were right and the remedy you applied actually worked. Don't forget that first impressions can be deceiving, and a fix that seems to work on first inspection might not have corrected the problem.

The testing process is not always as easy as it sounds. If you test a connectivity problem, it is not difficult to ascertain whether your solution was successful. However, changes made to an application or to databases are typically much more difficult to test. It might be necessary to have people who are familiar with the database or application run the tests with you in attendance. For example, suppose that you troubleshoot an accounting program installed in a client/server configuration. Network clients access the accounting program and the associated data from the server. Recently, all network accountants receive only outdated data when using the application. You, being a network administrator and not an accountant, may have never used the program and therefore cannot determine the outdated data from current data. Perhaps you don't even know how to load the data in the application. How can you possibly determine whether you have corrected the problem? Even from this simple example, we can see that the process of testing results may require the involvement of others, including end users, managers, other members of the IT team, support professionals associated with third-party applications, and so on.

NOTE: Avoiding False Starts   When you complete a fix, test it as thoroughly as you can before informing users of the fix. Users would generally rather wait for a real fix than have two or three false starts.

In an ideal world, you want to fully test a solution to see whether it indeed corrects the problem. However, you might not know whether you were successful until all users have logged back on, the application has been used, or the database has been queried. As a network administrator, you will be expected to take the testing process as far as you realistically can, even though you might not simulate certain system conditions or loads. The true test is in a real-world application.

TIP: Virus Activity   Keep in mind when troubleshooting a network or systems on a network that the problem might be virus-related. Viruses can cause a variety of problems that often disguise themselves as other problems. Part of your troubleshooting toolkit should include a virus repair disk with the latest virus definitions. Indicators that you might have a virus include increased error messages and missing and corrupt files.

Step 8: Identify the Results and Effects of the Solution

Sometimes, you apply a fix that corrects one problem but creates another. Many such circumstances are difficult to predict, but not always. For example, you might add a new network application, but the application requires more bandwidth than your current network infrastructure can support. The result would be that overall network performance is compromised.

Everything done to one part of the network can negatively affect another area of the network. Actions such as adding clients, replacing hubs or switches, and adding applications can all have unforeseen results. It is difficult to always know how the changes you make to a network are going to affect the network's functioning. The safest thing to do is assume that the changes you make are going to affect the network in some way and realize that you just have to figure out how. This is where you might need to think outside the box and try to predict possible outcomes.

> **Understanding Potential Impacts of Solutions You Choose**
>
> Remember that the effects of a potential solution can be far reaching. For example, a few years ago, a mid-sized network hired an IT consultant to address a problem of lost data stored on local client hard disks. His solution was to install a new client/server application that would store data and graphics on a centralized file server. With all data stored centrally, data, including backups, could be easily managed and controlled. The solution was implemented and tested on some client systems, and the application worked.
>
> At first only a few users used the application, but within months most users were transferring large files back and forth from the file server. Network monitoring tools revealed that the network could not handle the load of the new application, and network performance was far below an acceptable level, leaving network users frustrated with wait times.
>
> It turned out that the IT consultant failed to identify an infrastructure problem. Although the network used switches and 10/100Mbps NICs, Cat3 cable was used throughout most of the network. Cat3 UTP cable provides 10Mbps network speeds, not enough bandwidth for the number of users accessing the application. This situation provides an example of how the troubleshooting process can easily go wrong. The first problem may have been addressed—decentralized storage on client systems—but the effects of that solution created a much bigger problem. Using a clear troubleshooting process, the troubleshooting procedure is systematic and takes into account the current error and does not stop until all considerations are met.

Step 9: Document the Solution and the Entire Process

Although it is often neglected in the troubleshooting process, documentation is as important as any of the other troubleshooting procedures. Documenting a solution involves keeping a record of all the steps taken during the fix—not necessarily just the solution.

For the documentation to be of use to other network administrators in the future, it must include several key pieces of information. When documenting a procedure, include the following information:

- **Date**—When was the solution implemented? It is important to know the date because if problems occur after your changes, knowing the date of your fix makes it easier to determine whether your changes caused the problems.

- **Why**—Although it is obvious when a problem is fixed while it is done, a few weeks later, it might become less clear why that solution was needed. Documenting why the fix was made is important because if the same problem appears on another system, you can use this information to reduce time finding the solution.

- **What**—The successful fix should be detailed, along with information about any changes to the configuration of the system or network that were made to achieve the fix. Additional information should include version numbers for software patches or firmware, as appropriate.

- **Results**—Many administrators choose to include information on both successes and failures. The documentation of failures can prevent you from going down the same road twice, and the documentation of successful solutions can reduce the time it takes to get a system or network up and running.

- **Who**—It might be that information is left out of the documentation, or someone simply wants to ask a few questions about a solution. In both cases, if the name of the person who made a fix is in the documentation, the person can easily be tracked down. This is more of a concern in environments in which there are a number of IT staff, or if system repairs are performed by contractors instead of company employees.

> **TIP: Log Books**   Many organizations require that a log book be kept in the server room. This log book should maintain a record of everything that has been done on the network. In addition, many organizations require that administrators keep a log book of all repairs and upgrades made to networks and workstations.

Troubleshooting the Network

You will no doubt troubleshoot wiring and infrastructure problems less frequently than you troubleshoot client connectivity problems—and thankfully so. Wiring- and infrastructure-related problems can be difficult to trace, and sometimes a costly solution is needed to remedy the situation. When troubleshooting these problems, a methodical approach is likely to pay off.

Wiring problems are related to the cable used in a network. For the purposes of the Network+ exam, infrastructure problems are classified as those related to network devices such as hubs, switches, and routers.

Troubleshooting Wiring

Troubleshooting wiring involves knowing what wiring your network uses and where it is used. As mentioned in Chapter 2, "Media and Connectors," the cable used has certain limitations in terms of both speed and distance. It might be that the network problems are the result of trying to use a cable in an environment or a way for which it was not designed. For example, you might find that a network connects two workstations 130 meters apart with Category 5 UTP cabling, which is specified for distances up to 100 meters, so exceeding the maximum cable length could be a potential cause of the problem.

TIP: Cable Distances   Look at cable distances carefully. When you run cables along walls, across ceilings, and along baseboards, the distances can add up quickly. For this reason, carefully consider the placement of the wiring closet and ensure that you can reach all extents of your network while staying within the specified maximum cable distances.

Determining the type of cable used by a network is often as easy as reading the cable. The cable should be stamped with its type—whether it is, for example, UTP Category 5, RG-58, or something else. As you work with the various cable types used to create networks, you get to the point where you can easily identify them. However, be careful when identifying cable types because some cable types are almost indistinguishable. After you determine the cable used, you can compare the characteristics and limitations of that cable against how it is used on the network.

TIP: Cable Types   The type of cable used in a network is important and should be included in the network documentation.

Where the Cable Is Used

Imagine that you have been called in to track down a problem with a network. After some time, you discover that clients connect to the network via standard UTP cable run down an elevator shaft. Recall from Chapter 2 that UTP has poor resistance to electromagnetic interference (EMI), and therefore UTP and the electrical equipment associated with elevators react to each other like oil and water. The same can be said of cables that run close to fluorescent light fittings. Such problems might seem far-fetched, but you would be surprised at how many environments you will work in that have random or erratic problems that users have lived with for a long time and nothing has been done.

NOTE: Risers   In many buildings, risers are used for running cables between floors. A riser is a column that runs from the bottom of the building to the top. Risers are used for running all kinds of cables, including electrical and network cables.

Part of troubleshooting wiring problems is to identify where the cable is run to isolate whether the problem is a result of crosstalk or EMI. Be aware of problems associated with interference and the distance limitations of the cable used.

TIP: Test Cable   Never assume that the cable you use is good until you test it and confirm that it is good. Sometimes cables break, and bad media can cause network problems.

If you find a problem with a network's cable, you can do various things to correct it. For cables that exceed the maximum distance, you can use a repeater to regenerate the signal, try to reroute the cable over a more economical route, or even replace the type of cable with one that has greater resistance to attenuation. The method you choose often depends on the network's design and your budget.

For cable affected by EMI or other interference, consider replacing the cable with one that is more resistant to such interference or rerouting the cable away from the source of the interference. If you do reroute cable, pay attention to the maximum distance, and make sure that as you cure one problem you don't create another.

Wiring Issues

Depending on where the cable is used and the type of cable, you might encounter some specific cable-related problems. This section describes some problems you might encounter and their solutions.

Crosstalk

Whether its coaxial cable, or UTP, copper-based cabling is susceptible to crosstalk. Crosstalk happens when the signal from one cable gets mixed up with the signal in another cable. This can happen when cables run too closely together. Some cables use shielding to help reduce the impact of crosstalk. If shielded cable is not used, cables should not be run directly near each other.

Near-End Crosstalk (NEXT)

NEXT refers to interference between adjacent wire pairs within the twisted-pair cable at the near-end of the link (the end closest to the origin of the data signal). NEXT occurs when an outgoing data transmission leaks over to an incoming transmission. In effect, the incoming transmission overhears the signal sent by a transmitting station at the near end of the link. The result is that a portion of the outgoing signal is coupled back into the received signal.

Far-End Crosstalk (FEXT)

FEXT occurs when a receiving station overhears a data signal sent by a transmitting station at the other end of a transmission line. FEXT identifies the interference of a signal through a wire pair to an adjacent pair at the farthest end from the interfering source (the end where the signal is received).

Electromagnetic interference (EMI)

Electromagnetic interference (EMI) can reduce signal strength or corrupt it altogether. EMI occurs when cables are run too close to everyday office fixtures such as computer CRT monitors, fluorescent lighting fixtures, elevators, microwaves, and anything else that creates an electromagnetic field. Again, the solution is to carefully run cables away from such devices. If they have to be run through EMI areas, shielded cabling or fiber cabling needs to be used.

Attenuation

All media has recommended lengths that the cable can be run. This is because data signals weaken as they travel farther from the point of origin. If the signal travels far enough, it can weaken so much that it becomes unusable. The weakening of data signals as they traverse the media is referred to as attenuation. All copper-based cable is particularity susceptible to attenuation. When cable lengths have to be run farther than the recommended lengths, signal regenerators can boost the signal as it travels. If you work on a network with intermittent problems and notice that cable lengths run too far, attenuation can be the problem. To see cable lengths, refer to Chapter 6, "Ethernet Networking Standards."

Open Impedance Mismatch (Echo)

Any network segment can consist of a single continuous section of cable or be constructed from multiple cable sections attached through switches and other hardware. If multiple cable sections are used, it can result in impedance mismatches caused by slight differences in the impedance of each cable section. Impedance refers to the total opposition a circuit or device offers to the flow of a signal, measured in ohms. All media, such as twisted-pair cable, has characteristic impedance. Impedance characteristics for twisted-pair cable include 100, 120, and 150 ohms. UTP typically has an impedance of 100 ohms, and STP has an impedance of 150 ohms. Mixing these two wires in the same cable link can result in an impedance mismatch, which can cause the link to fail. To help prevent impedance mismatch, use cable rated with the same impedance rating.

Shorts

Electrical shorts can occur in any type of cable that has electrical current flowing through it. Shorts occur when the electrical current travels along a different path than what is intended. This can often happen if a network cable is not made correctly and wires are touching each other, improperly grounded, or touching metal. This is another reason to be careful when attaching your own RJ-45 connectors to twisted-pair cable. Sometimes, network cables can become damaged, bent, or mishandled, and shorts can occur. Several networking tools test for shorts, as discussed in Chapter 13, "Network Management Tools and Documentation Procedures." Copper-based media that carries electrical current is susceptible to shorts; wireless and fiber optic cable are not.

Managing Collisions

Collisions occur on a network when two or more networked devices transmit data at the same time. The result is that the data collides, becomes corrupted, and needs to be re-sent. If these collisions keep occurring, the network slows down and can eventually impact network users. Media Access Control (MAC) techniques can help prevent collisions from occurring. Two commonly used MAC methods include Collision Sense Multiple Access/Collision Detection, or CSMA/CD, used with wired Ethernet networks and Collision Sense Multiple Access/Collision Avoidance, or CSMA/CA, used with 802.11 wireless networks.

The more devices that connect to an Ethernet network, the more likely it is that collisions will occur on the network. In other words, the more devices you add to an Ethernet network, the slower, exponentially, the network will become. This decreasing of performance has driven improvements in the structure of how Ethernet networks. Improvements include the substitution of older hubs with new, high-performance Ethernet switches and the reduction of broadcast-intensive applications.

Collisions can mostly be avoided by using switches instead of hubs. Switches enable for the segmentation of Ethernet networks into smaller collision domain. Whereas the use of a hub creates a large single collision domain, each port on a switch represents a separate collision domain. The switch can provide full-duplex communication to the node/nodes connected to that port. In a switched network, systems do not need to use collision detection and can just transmit without hesitation. How a switch functions is covered in Chapter 3, "Networking Components and Devices."

TIP: Switched Network   For the Network+ exam, remember that a switch reduces the need for a contention-based network environment because the switch ports break down the network into smaller collision domains. The smaller the collision domain, the fewer collisions that occur.

Troubleshooting Infrastructure Hardware

If you are looking for a challenge, troubleshooting hardware infrastructure problems is for you. It is often not an easy task and usually involves many processes, including baselining and performance monitoring. Both baselines and monitoring are covered in detail in Chapter 13. One of the keys to identifying the failure of a hardware network device is to know what devices are used on a particular network and what each device is designed to do. Some of the common hardware components used in a network infrastructure are shown in Table 11.1.

Table 11.1 Common Network Hardware Components, Their Function and Troubleshooting Strategies

Networking Device	Function	Troubleshooting and Failure Signs
Hubs	Hubs are used with a star network topology and use twisted-pair cable to connect multiple systems to a centralized physical device.	Because hubs connect multiple network devices, if many devices cannot access the network, the hub might have failed. When a hub fails, all devices connected to it will be unavailable to access the network. Additionally, hubs use broadcasts and forward data to all the connected ports increasing network traffic. When network traffic is high and the network operating slowly, it might be necessary to replace slow hubs.
Switches	Like hubs, switches are used with a star topology as a central point of connection.	The inability of several network devices to access the network can indicate a failed switch. If the switch fails, all devices connected to the switch cannot access the network. Switches forward data only to the intended recipient enabling them to better manage network traffic that hubs.
Routers	Routers separate broadcast domains and connect different networks.	If a router fails, network clients cannot access remote networks connected by the router. For example, if clients access a remote office through a network router and the router fails, the remote office would be unavailable. Testing router connectivity can be done using utilities such as `ping` and `tracert`.
Bridges	Bridges are commonly used to connect network segments within the same network. Bridges manage the flow of traffic between these network segments.	A failed bridge would prevent the flow of traffic between network segments. If communication between network segments has failed, it can be due to a failed bridge.
Wireless Access Points	Wireless access points provide the bridge between the wired and wireless network.	If wireless clients cannot access the wired network, the AP might have failed. However, there are many configuration settings to verify first.

For more information on network hardware devices and their function, refer to Chapter 3.

Configuring and Troubleshooting Client Connectivity

Connecting clients to an existing network is a common task for network administrators. Connecting a client system requires establishing the physical connection,
defining network protocols, assigning permissions, and accessing server services
and resources. This section explores the requirements to connect a client PC to a
network.

Verifying Client TCP/IP Configurations

Configuring a client for TCP/IP can be relatively complex, or it can be simple.
Any complexity involved is related to the possible need to configure TCP/IP manually. The simplicity is related to the fact that TCP/IP configuration can occur automatically via DHCP or through APIPA. This section looks at some of the basic
information required to make a system function on a network, using TCP/IP. At
the least, a system needs an IP address and a subnet mask. The default gateway,
DNS server, and WINS server are all optional, but network functionality is limited
without them. The following list briefly explains the IP-related settings used to
connect to a TCP/IP network:

- **IP address**—Each system must be assigned a unique IP address so that it can
  communicate on the network. Clients on a LAN will have a private IP address
  and matching subnet mask. Table 11.2 shows the private IP ranges. If a system
  has the wrong IP or subnet mask, that client system cannot communicate on
  the network. If the client system has an IP address in the 169.254.0.0 range,
  the system is not connected to a DHCP server and not getting on the network. Refer to Chapter 5, "TCP/IP Addressing and Routing," for information
  on APIPA and automatic IPv4 assignments.

Table 11.2   Private Address Ranges

Class	Address Range	Default Subnet Mask
A	10.0.0.0–10.255.255.255	255.0.0.0
B	172.16.0.0–172.31.255.255	255.255.0.0
C	192.168.0.0–192.168.255.255	255.255.255.0

- **Subnet mask**—Enables the system to determine what portion of the IP address represents the network address and what portion represents the node address. Refer to Table 11.2 to see the right subnet mask associated with each
  private IP range. To be part of the network, each client system needs to have
  the correct subnet mask, and the subnet mask must use the matching one used
  with the rest of the network. Figure 11.1 shows a correct IP configuration and
  an incorrect IP configuration on a Windows Vista system.

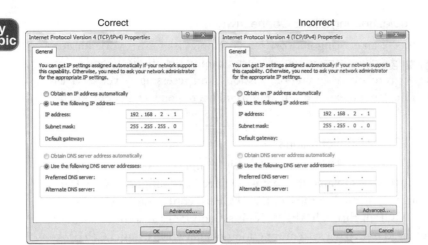

Figure 11.1 A correct and an incorrect IP client configuration.

- **Default gateway**—Enables internal systems to communicate with systems on a remote network. In home use, the gateway would likely be the DSL or cable modem that acts as a router. In a business environment the gateway is the device that routes traffic from the workstation to the outside network. This network device will have an IP address assigned to it, and the client configuration must use this address as the default gateway. If not, the system cannot be routed outside the local network.

- **DNS server addresses**—Enable dynamic hostname resolution to be performed. It is common practice to have two DNS server addresses defined so that if one server becomes unavailable, the other can be used. The client system must be configured with the IP address of the local DNS server. If a client system has the wrong DNS address listed, hostname resolution will not be possible. Figure 11.2 shows the IP configuration for connection to a private network.

NOTE: TCP/IP Connection Requirements   At a minimum, an IP address and a subnet mask are required to connect to a TCP/IP network. With just this minimum configuration, connectivity is limited to the local segment, and DNS resolution is not possible.

When manually configuring a system to use TCP/IP, all information needs to be entered into the respective dialog boxes carefully. Entering a duplicate IP address might prevent the client system from logging on to the network; the wrong gateway will prevent the system from accessing remote networks, and so on. To view the IP settings of a client system, many utilities are used, including the `ipconfig` command for Windows systems and the `ifconfig` for Linux and UNIX systems.

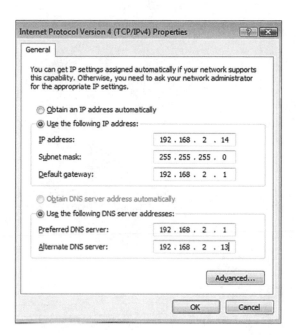

Figure 11.2   The Internet Protocol (TCP/IPv4) Properties dialog box on a Windows Vista system.

When troubleshooting a system, ensure that the IP address, default gateway, subnet mask, and DNS are correctly set. This information can be assigned using DHCP and should not have any errors; however, in networks where DHCP is not used and settings are inputted manually, these settings must be verified.

Setting Port Speeds and Duplex

When configuring a client for the network, you need to be aware of two more settings: port speeds and duplex settings. Adjust these two settings in Windows in the Network Properties area of the Windows operating system. Figure 11.3 shows the port speed and duplex settings of a Windows Vista system.

Figure 11.3 shows several settings for port speed and duplex setting. These settings can be set to autoconfiguration to detect the setting used by the network. It can also be set to one of the other settings to match the network configuration—for example, 100Mbps and half duplex. If you work with a client system that cannot log on to a network, it might be necessary to ensure that the duplex setting and port speeds are correctly set for the network. You can find more information on duplex settings in Chapter 2.

Figure 11.3   The Advanced tab on the properties of a NIC found in Windows Device Manager.

Troubleshooting Incorrect VLANs

As mentioned in Chapter 1, "Introduction to Computer Networking," VLANs provide a method of segmenting and organizing the network. Computer systems can be located anywhere on the network but communicate as if they are on the same segment. For example, VLANs can be segmented according to an organization's departments, such as sales, finance, and secretaries. It can be segmented according to usage, security permissions, and more.

The ability to segment the network provides clear advantages, such as increased security because devices can communicate only with other systems in the VLAN. Users can see only the systems in their VLAN segment. It can help control broadcast traffic and makes moving end systems around the network easier.

Problems can arise when users are moved or otherwise connected to the wrong VLAN. Administrators need to ensure that the user system is plugged into the correct VLAN port. For example, suppose a network uses port-based VLANs, assigning ports 1 through 8 to marketing, ports 9 through 18 to sales, and so on. Plugging a sales client into port 6 would make that sales client part of the marketing network. It sounds simple, but if documentation is not up to date and you walk into a new network, this can be tricky to identify.

One of the keys to preventing VLAN assignment errors is to clearly document the VLAN arrangement. Should systems be moved, it is important to know how to reconnect them and forward them to the correct VLAN port.

Another consideration to keep in mind is that membership to a VLAN can be assigned both statically and dynamically. In static VLAN assignment, the switch ports are assigned to a specific VLAN, and new systems added will be assigned to the VLAN associated with that particular port. For example, plug a new system into port 8 and the user becomes part of the administrator's network. Make sure you have the right port assigned to users.

Dynamic VLAN assignment requires specific software to control VLAN distribution. Using a VLAN server, administrators can dynamically assign VLAN membership based on such criteria as MAC address or a username password combination. As a system tries to access the network, it queries the VLAN server database to ask for VLAN membership information. The server responds and logs the system onto the appropriate VLAN network. When configured correctly, dynamic assignment reduces human error associated with static VLAN assignment.

Identifying Issues That Might Need Escalation

Earlier in this chapter we discussed the procedures that must be followed when issue escalation is required. Although any number of issues might need escalation, the CompTIA Network+ objectives list specific scenarios in which escalation might be necessary. Each of these issues will not always require escalation; an administrator with an Internet connection and a little determination can track these down. Nevertheless, we quickly identify each of the issues listed in the CompTIA objectives:

- **Switching loop**—On an Ethernet network, only a single active path can exist between devices on a network. When multiple active paths are available, switching loops can occur. Switching loops are simply the result of having more than one path between two switches in a network. The Spanning Tree Protocol (STP) is designed to prevent these loops from occurring. If the packet in the loop is a broadcast message, the loop can create a full broadcast storm. Broadcast storms are discussed in this section. Switching loops occur at the data link (Layer 2) of the OSI model.

- **Routing loop**—As the name suggests, a routing loop occurs when data packets continue to be routed in an endless circle. In a proper operation, a router forwards packets according to the information presented in the routing table. If the routing table is correct, the packet takes the optimal path from the source to the destination. It is not common, but if the information in the routing table is incorrect through a manual misconfiguration or a faulty router route detection, routing loops can form. A routing loop is a path through the internetwork for a network ID that loops back onto itself. Routing loops are detectable because they can quickly bog down a network, and some packets are not received by the destination system.

- **Route problems**—Route problems typically occur when routing tables contain information that does not reflect the correct topology of the internetwork. Out-of-date or incorrect routing tables mean that packets cannot be correctly routed through the network, and route problems occur. Verify the routing table to ensure that it is correct. Sometimes static routes are entered and cause problems when the network topology is changed.

■ **Proxy ARP**—The ARP protocol is used to resolve IP addresses to MAC addresses. This is important because on a network, devices find each other using the IP address, but communication between devices requires the MAC address. In a proxy ARP configuration, one system or network device answers ARP requests for another system. It is a proxy ARP because one network system is proxying for another's ARP communications.

■ **Broadcast storms**—A broadcast address is an IP address that you can use to target all systems on a subnet or network instead of single hosts. In other words, a broadcast message goes to everyone on the network. A broadcast storm occurs when a network is overwhelmed with constant broadcast or multicast traffic. Broadcast storms can eventually lead to a complete loss of network connectivity because the network is bogged down with the broadcast storm. As with other network problems, you might suspect a broadcast storm when network response times are poor and people complain of a slow network. These broadcast storms can be caused by faulty hardware, such as a NIC that continually sends out data, switching loops, or even faulty applications running on the network. Baselines work well for identifying broadcast storms.

Troubleshooting Wireless Issues

Because wireless signals travel through the atmosphere, they are subjected to all sorts of elements that can block wireless signals. This includes storms, the number of walls between the sending and receiving devices, ceilings, mirrors, and so on. Just how weakened the signal becomes depends on the building material used, RF interference, the power of the wireless signal, and how far the signal must travel. Every element that a wireless signal must pass through or around weakens the signal, reducing the distance it can travel.

Environmental factors are not the only things to consider when working with wireless networks. This section reviews two key areas to focus on when troubleshooting wireless networks: wireless signals and wireless configurations.

NOTE: Signal Strength   Wireless signals degrade depending on the construction material used. Signals passing through concrete and steel are particularly weakened.

Troubleshooting Wireless Signals

If you troubleshoot a wireless connection that has a particularly weak signal and one that won't reach its destination, you can troubleshoot a signal by checking the following:

- **Antenna type**—As mentioned in Chapter 7, "Wireless Networking," a wireless antenna can be either omnidirectional or directional. Omnidirectional antennas are great in an environment in which there is a clear line of path between the senders and receivers. With omnidirectional antennas, the wireless signal disperses in a 360-degree pattern to all points.

  If environmental obstacles exist, a directional wireless antenna might be a better choice. The directional antenna concentrates the signal power in a specific direction and enables you to use less power for a greater distance than an omnidirectional antenna. Omnidirectional antennas are well suited inside office buildings to accommodate numerous users.

- **Antenna placement**—Many home-use APs have a built-in antenna that is adequate to reach all areas of a home. Network APs can use an external wireless antenna, and placing it correctly is an important consideration. In general, the AP and the antenna should be located as near to each other as possible. The farther the signal has to travel over cabling from the antenna to the AP, the more signal degradation (RF attenuation) there is. Directional antennas connecting locations in a point-to-point configuration should be placed in a clear line of site between each other. Often the outdoor antennas are placed high to prevent the signal being blocked by physical objects. Indoor antennas should be kept away from large metal objects such as filing cabinets and devices that can cause RF interference.

- **Boost signal**—If all else fails, it is possible to purchase devices, such as wireless repeaters, that can amplify the wireless signal. The device takes the signal and amplifies it so that it has greater strength and can travel farther distances. Amplifiers increase the range that the client system can be placed from the AP.

- **Bleed**—Because wireless signals travel through the atmosphere, they are not bound by the same physical limitations of wired media. The dispersed nature of wireless communication can lead to problems. For example, although everyone in an office might be within range of a wireless signal, the signal is not restricted to that office, and someone outside might also use the signal. Wireless signals that travel where administrators might not want is known as bleed. Some APs and antennas enable administrators to restrict the range a wireless signal transmits by reducing the strength of the wireless signal output. Bleed makes wireless security measures essential. To prevent people from using a signal, encryption and other methods are used. So, a user might see the wireless signal but not use the wireless network without the proper security clearance.

- **Distance**—Wireless signals degrade as they travel from their point of origin. While troubleshooting wireless signals, you might need to relocate the AP closer to client systems or add wireless routers to increase the wireless transmission range. Administrators often use wireless signal testers to ensure transmission ranges are adequate before implementing the wireless network.

> **TIP: Relocation**   When troubleshooting wireless signals, it is often necessary to relocate the AP to a more favorable location. This is important to know both for the Network+ exam and for real-world application.

To successfully manage the wireless signals, you need to know the wireless standard that you are using. The standards used today specify range distances, RF ranges, and speeds. It might be that the wireless standard cannot do what you need. More information on all wireless standards is in Chapter 7.

Troubleshooting Wireless Configurations

You can use a number of settings and configurations when working with wireless clients and APs. Some of the more common areas to check when troubleshooting wireless configurations include the following:

- **Incorrect encryption**—The wireless network security features are set on the wireless router or AP. This includes the wireless encryption methods that will be used—for instance, WEP or WPA. When encryption is enabled on the AP, the client must be configured to use the encryption and know the encryption key to be authenticated to the AP. When troubleshooting a connectivity problem between an AP and a wireless client, a common problem is that the encryption security settings do not match.

- **SSID/ESSID mismatch**—Whether your wireless network uses infrastructure mode or ad-hoc mode, an SSID/ESSID is required. The SSID/ESSID is a configurable client identification that enables clients to communicate to a particular base station. Only client systems configured with the same SSID as the AP can communicate with it. SSIDs provide a simple password arrangement between base stations and clients. The ESSID/SSID might be broadcast from the AP and visible to all receiving devices in the area, or it might be configured not to broadcast. Not broadcasting the SSID name adds another level of security because people cannot see the SSID name when browsing for wireless networks in the area. The ESSID/SSID would need to be obtained from the network administrator.

- **Overlapping channels**—When troubleshooting a wireless network, be aware that overlapping channels can disrupt the wireless communications. For example, in many environments, APs are inadvertently placed close together—perhaps two access points in separate offices located next door to each other or between floors. Signal disruption will result if a channel overlap occurs between the access points. You would typically change the channel of a wireless device only if there is a channel overlap with another device. If a channel must be changed, it must be changed to another nonoverlapping channel.

■ **Standard mismatch**—The 802.11 standards commonly used today include 802.11a/b and g, with n as the new standard. When configuring client systems, be sure they are configured to use the same or compatible wireless standard; 802.11a is not compatible with b, g, or n, but b and g are compatible.

NOTE: More Wireless Troubleshooting   When preparing for the Network+ exam, be sure to cross-reference the wireless information in this chapter with Chapter 7.

Summary

Troubleshooting networks is an activity with which network administrators become very familiar. Successful troubleshooting does not happen by accident; rather, the troubleshooting process follows some defined procedures. These procedures include the following:

Step 1.   Information gathering—identify symptoms and problems.

Step 2.   Identify the affected areas of the network.

Step 3.   Determine if anything has changed.

Step 4.   Establish the most probable cause.

Step 5.   Determine if escalation is necessary.

Step 6.   Create an action plan and solution identifying potential effects.

Step 7.   Implement and test the solution.

Step 8.   Identify the results and effects of the solution.

Step 9.   Document the solution and the entire process.

At times, you might troubleshoot wiring and infrastructure problems. Although they are less common than other troubleshooting areas, wiring and network devices should be considered a possible causes of a problem. Tracking down infrastructure problems often requires using documentation and network maps or taking baselines to compare network performance.

Consider several areas when troubleshooting a wireless network. Many problems are related to poor signal strength, low transmission rates, and limited distances. When troubleshooting wireless connectivity, it is important to verify both the signal strength and the AP and wireless client configuration.

Exam Preparation Tasks

Review All the Key Topics

Review the most important topics in the chapter, noted with the Key Topics icon in the outer margin of the page. Table 11.3 lists a reference of these key topics and the page numbers on which each is found.

Table 11.3   Key Topics for Chapter 11

Key Topic Element	Description	Page Number
List	The troubleshooting steps	396
Table 11.1	Common network hardware components, their function and troubleshooting strategies	412
Table 11.2	Private address ranges	413
Figure 11.1	A correct and an incorrect IP client configuration	414
Figure 11.2	The Internet Protocol (TCP/IPv4) Properties dialog box on a Windows Vista system	415
Figure 11.3	The Advanced tab on the properties of a NIC found in Windows Device Manager	416

Define Key Terms

Define the following key terms from this chapter, and check your answers in the Glossary.

- Crosstalk
- Attenuation
- Collisions
- Open impedance mismatch
- Interference
- Port speed
- Port duplex mismatch
- VLAN

- Gateway

- DNS

- Subnet mask

- Switching loop

- Routing loop

- Route problems

- Proxy ARP

- Broadcast storms

- Encryption

- Wireless channel

- SSID

- ESSID mismatch

- 802.11 a/b/g/n

Apply Your Knowledge

Exercise 11.1 Using the Microsoft Support Website to Track Error Codes

As a network administrator, you have the task of installing and configuring a new Windows Vista computer system. However, each time you try to install the new operating system, the process is halted with the following error message:

Stop: 0x000000A5 To install the Windows Vista system, you need to find the solution to the problem.

Estimated time: 10 minutes

1. Go to http://support.microsoft.com.
2. Type Stop: 0x000000A5 in the bing search bar.
3. Select the bing button to continue.
4. One result will be displayed; scroll through the document links.
5. Scroll down the page until you see Stop: 0x000000A5. In this case, you notice that the reason the installation failed is that the computer BIOS is incompatible with the Advanced Configuration and Power Interface (ACPI) standard supported in Windows Vista.

Review Questions

You can find answers to the review questions in Appendix A, "Answers to Review Questions."

1. Considering the following figure, which of the following statements is true?

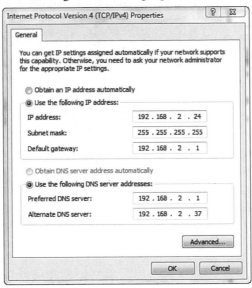

   a. The system cannot access the local network.
   b. The system cannot access remote networks.
   c. The system cannot have hostname resolution.
   d. The system has the wrong subnet mask.

2. Using the following configuration screen, which of the following is true?

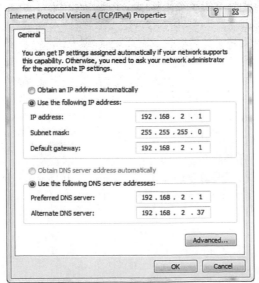

    a. The system cannot access the local network.

    b. The system cannot access remote networks.

    c. The system cannot have hostname resolution.

    d. The system has the wrong subnet mask.

3. Which of the following best describes the function of the default gateway?

    a. Converts hostnames to IP address

    b. Converts IP addresses to hostnames

    c. Enables systems to communicate with systems on a remote network

    d. Enables systems to communicate with routers

4. Which of the following bits of IP information are mandatory to join the network? (Select two answers.)

    a. Subnet mask

    b. IP address

    c. DNS address

    d. Default gateway

5. You are wiring a new network. Because of space limitations, you need to run several cables close to each other. After the setup you find that the signals from each cable are overlapping. Which of the following terms describe what is happening?

    a. Attenuation

    b. Cross talk

    c. Near crosstalk

    d. EMI

6. Which of the following should you consider when troubleshooting wiring problems? (Choose all best answers.)

    a. The distance between devices

    b. Interference

    c. Atmospheric conditions

    d. Connectors

7. You get numerous calls from users who cannot access an application. Upon investigation, you find that the application has crashed. You restart the application, and it appears to run okay. What is the next step in the troubleshooting process?

    a. Email the users and let them know that they can use the application again.

    b. Test the application to ensure that it operates correctly.

    c. Document the problem and the solution.

    d. Reload the application executables from the CD and restart it.

8. A user calls to inform you that she is having a problem accessing her email. What is the next step in the troubleshooting process?

   a. Document the problem.

   b. Make sure that the user's email address is valid.

   c. Discuss the problem with the user.

   d. Visit the user's desk to reload the email client software.

9. You successfully fix a problem with a server, test the application, and let the users back on the system. What is the next step in the troubleshooting process?

   a. Document the problem.

   b. Restart the server.

   c. Document the problem and the solution.

   d. Clear the error logs of any reference to the problem.

10. You are called in to troubleshoot a problem with the NIC on a server that has been running well for some time. The server reports a resource conflict. What would be the next step in the troubleshooting process?

   a. Change the NIC.

   b. Consult the documentation to determine whether there have been any changes to the server configuration.

   c. Download and install the latest drivers for the NIC.

   d. Reload the protocol drivers for the NIC and set them to use a different set of resources.

11. Which of the following can cause switching loops?

   a. Sporadic sending of broadcast messages

   b. Continual sending of broadcast messages

   c. An Ethernet network in which multiple active paths are available for data to travel.

   d. An Ethernet network in which only a single active path is available for data to travel.

12. You are troubleshooting an infrastructure problem and suspect the problem might be the network media. Which of the following must be considered when troubleshooting network media? (Choose two answers.)

   a. Where the media is used

   b. Media frequency output/input ratio

   c. Media type

   d. Media voltage

13. You have been called into a network to troubleshoot a cabling error. You have traced the problem to lengths of cable that have been run too far. Which of the following describes the weakening of data signals as they travel down a given media?

    a. Near crosstalk

    b. EMI

    c. Attenuation

    d. Crosstalk

14. You troubleshoot an intermittent connectivity issue. You suspect the problem might be a form of crosstalk known as NEXT. Which of the following is a symptom of NEXT?

    a. Packets cannot be decrypted.

    b. Packets cannot be encrypted.

    c. Interference exists between wire pairs at the near end of the link.

    d. Interference exists between wire pairs at the far end of the link.

15. You work with several homemade network cables. Which of the following is caused by poorly made cables?

    a. Near End crosstalk

    b. Signal degradation

    c. EMI

    d. Attenuation

16. A client on your network has had no problem accessing the wireless network, but recently the client moved to a new office in the same building. Since the move, she has been experiencing intermittent connectivity problems. Which of the following is most likely the cause of the problem? (Select the two best answers.)

    a. The SSID on the client and the AP are different.

    b. The client WEP settings need to be set to auto detect.

    c. The signal is partially blocked by physical objects.

    d. The client system has moved too far away from the access point.

17. You have been called in to troubleshoot a problem with a specific application on a server system. The client cannot provide any information about the problem except that the application is not accessible. Which of the following troubleshooting steps should you perform first?

    a. Consult the documentation for the server.

    b. Consult the application error log on the server.

    c. Reboot the server.

    d. Reload the application from the original CD.

18. Which of the following is not a concern when troubleshooting connectivity between an AP and a wireless client?

   a. Ensuring both use the same encryption

   b. Ensuring the AP and client are configured not to combine 802.11b/g and n

   c. Ensuring that the same SSID is used

   d. Ensuring that the client system is within range of the AP

19. You have been called in to troubleshoot an intermittent network problem. You suspect that cabling is a problem. You review the documentation and find out that a segment of Category 5e cable runs through the ceiling. Which of the following would you guess would be the problem?

   a. Crosstalk

   b. Near crosstalk

   c. Attenuation

   d. EMI

20. A user is having problems logging on to the server. Each time she tries, she receives a Server Not Found message. After asking a few questions, you deduce that the problem is isolated to this single system. Which of the following are possible explanations to the problem? (Choose the two best answers.)

   a. The protocol configuration on the workstation is incorrect.

   b. A hub might have failed.

   c. The cable has become disconnected from the user's workstation.

   d. The server is down.

This chapter covers CompTIA Network+ objectives 5.1. Upon completion of this chapter, you will be able to answer the following questions:

- How is the `traceroute` command used?

- What are the `ping` and `ipconfig` commands used for?

- What is the function of the `nbtstat` and `netstat` commands?

- What is the function of `arp` and `arp ping`?

- How is the route command used?

CHAPTER 12

Command-Line Networking Tools

There are two certainties in the networking world. The first is that you will work on networks that use Transmission Control Protocol/Internet Protocol (TCP/IP). The second is that at some point, you will troubleshoot those networks. This chapter focuses on identifying the TCP/IP utilities commonly used when working with TCP/IP networks and explains how to use those utilities in the troubleshooting process.

Foundation Topics

Common Networking Utilities

The best way to work through this chapter is to try each of the utilities as they are discussed. This can give you a better idea of how to use the tools and what they are designed to do. These tools are the core utilities used in the troubleshooting of TCP/IP networks and are used extensively in real-world environments. The following sections describe these utilities:

- ping

- traceroute (also called tracert)

- mtr

- arp ping

- netstat

- nbtstat

- ipconfig

- ifconfig

- winipcfg

- nslookup

- dig

- host

- route

Note that not all the tools discussed here are available on every operating system. However, the discussion begins by looking at one that is not only available on all platforms but also is arguably the most used—and most useful—of all troubleshooting utilities: ping.

NOTE: **Help Facility**   Many of the utilities discussed in this chapter have a help facility that you can access by typing the command followed by /? or a -?. On a Windows system, for example, you can get help on the netstat utility by typing the command netstat /? Sometimes, using a utility with an invalid switch will also bring up the help screen.

The **ping** Utility

ping is a command-line utility designed to test connectivity between systems on a TCP/IP-based network. Its basic function is to answer one simple question: "Can I connect to another host?" ping can be a network administrator's right hand; most

TCP/IP troubleshooting procedures begin with the ping utility and, if necessary, work from there. We say "if necessary" because the information provided by the ping command can often isolate the cause of a problem so well that further action from the command line is not needed.

ping works by using Internet Control Message Protocol (ICMP) packets to ascertain whether another system is connected to the network and can respond. A successful ping request requires that a packet, called an *ICMP echo request*, be sent to a remote host. If the remote host receives the packet, it sends an *ICMP echo reply* in return, and the ping is a success. Figure 12.1 shows the output from a successful ping request on a Windows Server system.

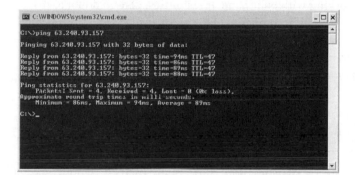

Figure 12.1   A successful **ping** request.

Notice in Figure 12.1 that four packets are sent to the remote host. These packets are 32 bytes in size and took 94ms, 86ms, 89ms, and 88ms to reach their destination. The timo- section of the ping command output is often important because a high number could indicate congestion on the network or a routing problem. The version of the ping utility shown in Figure 12.1 is from a Windows Server system. Other versions of Windows or other operating systems might send more packets or larger packets.

TIP: Command Output   For each of the commands discussed in this chapter, make sure that you can identify the output. On the Network+ exam, you will likely be asked to identify the output from these commands. This aspect of each tool's use is covered in more detail later in this chapter.

NOTE: Sometimes ping requests fail. When a ping fails, you know that you cannot connect to a remote host. Figure 12.2 shows the output from a failed ping command.

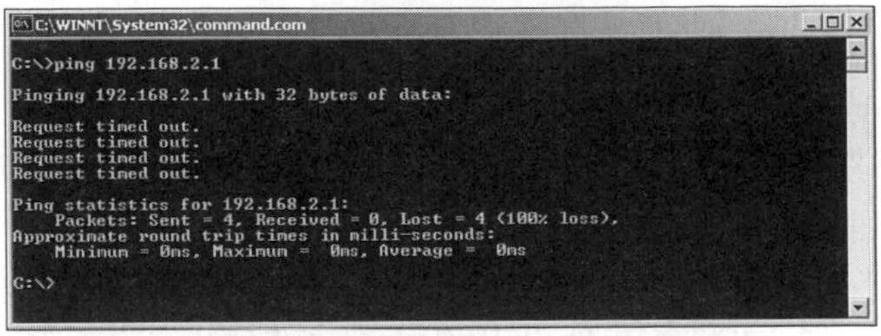

Figure 12.2   A failed **ping** request.

Switches for **ping**

If you've spent any time working with command-line utilities, you no doubt already know that every command is accompanied by a number of *switches*, or options. The switches let you customize the behavior of the command. Although some switches (we'll call them that from now on) are rarely used, others come in handy under a number of circumstances.

> **TIP: Switches**   Even the most obscure switches for the commands discussed in this chapter might appear on the Network+ exam.

The ping command offers several switches. The most widely used, -t, sends continuous packets rather than just a few. This switch sets the ping command to continue to ping the remote host until it is stopped by keyboard input. This switch is particularly helpful when you troubleshoot connectivity issues such as a suspect cable. Table 12.1 shows some of the more useful switches available for the ping command on a Windows Vista system. Some options can vary depending on the Windows version used. Notice the ping switches used for IPv6.

Table 12.1   ping Switches on a Windows Vista System

Switch	Description
-t	ping a network until stopped. To stop it, press Ctrl+C.
-a	Tells the ping utility to resolve the IP address to a hostname as well as perform the ping.
-n count	Specifies the number of ping requests to send to the remote host. Example: ping -n 15 <IP address>.
-l size	Specifies the buffer size of the ping request to send.
-f	Specifies that the Don't Fragment flag is set in the packet.
-i TTL	Specifies the Time-To-Live for the packet.

-v TOS	Specifies the type of service for the packet to be sent.
-r count	Records the route hops that the packet takes on its journey.
-w timeout	Specifies the timeout, in milliseconds, during which the ping utility should wait for each reply.
-R	Use routing header to test reverse route also (IPv6-only).
-S srcaddr	Source address to use (IPv6-only).
-4	Force using IPv4.
-6	Force using IPv6.

One of the main reasons administrators rely on the ping utility is its capability to provide quick information that can be used for troubleshooting. Troubleshooting with ping is something all administrators will do at some point.

Troubleshooting Steps with **ping**

Although ping does not completely isolate problems, you can use it to help identify where a problem lies. When troubleshooting with ping, take the following steps:

1. ping the IP address of your local loopback, using the command ping 127.0.0.1. If this command is successful, you know that the TCP/IP protocol suite is installed correctly on your system and functioning. If you cannot ping the local loopback, TCP/IP might need to be reloaded or reconfigured on the machine you use.

2. ping the IP address assigned to your local network interface card (NIC). If the ping is successful, you know that your interface is functioning on the network and has TCP/IP correctly installed. If you cannot ping the local interface, TCP/IP might not be bound correctly to the card; the network card drivers might be improperly installed; or the computer might not be cabled to the network.

> **NOTE: Loopback Address**   The loopback is a special function within the TCP/IP protocol stack provided for troubleshooting purposes. The Class A IP address 127.X.X.X is reserved for the loopback; although convention dictates that you use 127.0.0.1, you can use any address in the 127.X.X.X range, except for the network number itself (127.0.0.0) and the broadcast address (127.255.255.255). You can also ping by using the default hostname for the local system, which is called localhost (for example, ping_localhost).

3. ping the IP address of another known working node on your local network. By doing so you can determine whether the computer you use can see other com-

puters on the network. If you can ping other devices on your local network, you have network connectivity.

If you cannot ping other devices on your local network you might not be connected to the network correctly, or there might be a cable problem on the computer.

4. After you confirm that you have network connectivity for the local network, you can help verify connectivity to a remote network by sending a ping to the IP address of the default gateway.

5. If you can ping the default gateway, you can verify remote connectivity by sending a ping to the IP address of a system on a remote network. However, this doesn't always work because some routers and firewalls are configured to prevent ICMP echoes (pings). This is done to prevent certain types of malicious attacks that use ICMP.

NOTE: Connectivity Problems   On the Network+ exam, you might be asked to relate the correct procedure for using ping for a connectivity problem.

If you are an optimistic person, you can perform step 5 first. If that works, all the other steps will also work, saving you the need to test them. If your step 5 trial fails, you can go back to step 1 and start the troubleshooting process from the beginning.

TIP: Testing TCP/IP Installations   To test a system to see whether TCP/IP is installed, working, and configured correctly, you can ping the loopback address and then ping the IP address of the local system.

By using just the ping command in the manner described, you can confirm network connectivity to not only the local network but also to a remote network. The whole process requires as much time as it takes to type in the command—and you can do it all from a single location.

NOTE: ping Using DNS   The ping examples used in this section show the ping command using the IP address of the remote host. It is also possible to ping the Domain Name System (DNS) name of the remote host (for example, ping www. comptia.org, ping server1.network.com); this can be done only if your network uses a DNS server. On a Windows-based network, you can also ping by using the Network Basic Input/Output System (NetBIOS) computer name.

Ping Error Messages

When you're troubleshooting with the ping command, four key error messages can be returned: Destination Host Unreachable, Request Timed Out, Unknown

Host, Expired Time-To-Live (TTL). The following sections describe these results of a ping command.

The Destination Host Unreachable Message

The Destination Host Unreachable error message means that a route to the destination computer system cannot be found. To remedy this problem, you might need to examine the TCP/IP configuration or routing information on the local host to confirm that the configuration is correct or, if static routes are used, verify that the local routing table is configured correctly. Listing 12.1 shows an example of a ping failure that gives the Destination Host Unreachable message.

Listing 12.1   A **ping** Failure with the Destination Host Unreachable

```
Pinging 24.67.54.233 with 32 bytes of data:
Destination host unreachable.
Destination host unreachable.
Destination host unreachable.
Destination host unreachable.
Ping statistics for 24.67.54.233:
    Packets: Sent = 4, Received = 0, Lost = 4 (100% loss),
    Minimum = 0ms, Maximum =  0ms, Average =  0ms
```

The Request Timed Out Message

The Request Timed Out error message is common when you use the ping command. Essentially, this error message indicates that your host did not receive the ping message back from the other host within the designated time period. This is typically an indicator that the destination device is not connected to the network, is powered off, or is not configured correctly; however it could also mean that some intermediate device is not operating correctly. In some rare cases, it can also indicate that there is so much congestion on the network that timely delivery of the ping message could not be completed. It might also mean that the ping is sent to an invalid IP address or that the system is not on the same network as the remote host, and an intermediary device is not configured correctly. In any of these cases, the failed ping should initiate a troubleshooting process that might involve other tools, manual inspection, and possibly reconfiguration. Listing 12.2 shows the output from a ping to an invalid IP address.

Listing 12.2   Output for a **ping** to an Invalid IP Address

```
C:\>ping 169.76.54.3
Pinging 169.76.54.3 with 32 bytes of data:
Request timed out.
Request timed out.
Request timed out.
```

```
Request timed out.
Ping statistics for 169.76.54.3:
    Packets: Sent = 4, Received = 0, Lost = 4 (100%
Approximate round trip times in milliseconds:
    Minimum = 0ms, Maximum =  0ms, Average =  0ms
```

When running ping, you might receive some successful replies from the remote host intermixed with Request Timed Out errors. This is often a result of a congested network. An example follows; notice that the example in Listing 12.3, which was run on a Windows Server system, uses the -t switch to generate continuous pings.

Listing 12.3   The **-t** Switch Generating Continuous **ping** Messages

```
C:\>ping -t 24.67.184.65
Pinging 24.67.184.65 with 32 bytes of data:
Reply from 24.67.184.65: bytes=32 time=55ms TTL=127
Reply from 24.67.184.65: bytes=32 time=54ms TTL=127
Reply from 24.67.184.65: bytes=32 time=27ms TTL=127
Request timed out.
Request timed out.
Request timed out.
Reply from 24.67.184.65: bytes=32 time=69ms TTL=127
Reply from 24.67.184.65: bytes=32 time=28ms TTL=127
Reply from 24.67.184.65: bytes=32 time=28ms TTL=127
Reply from 24.67.184.65: bytes=32 time=68ms TTL=127
Reply from 24.67.184.65: bytes=32 time=41ms TTL=127
Ping statistics for 24.67.184.65:
    Packets: Sent = 11, Received = 8, Lost = 3 (27% loss),
Approximate round trip times in milliseconds:
    Minimum = 27ms, Maximum =  69ms, Average =  33ms
```

In this example, three packets were lost. If you experienced this type of error frequently, you would need to determine what was causing packets to be dropped from the network.

The Unknown Host Message

The Unknown Host error message is generated when the hostname of the destination computer cannot be resolved. This error usually occurs when you ping an incorrect hostname, as shown in the following example, or when trying to use ping with a hostname when hostname resolution (via DNS or a HOSTS text file) is not configured:

```
C:\>ping www.comptia.ca
Unknown host www.comptia.ca
```

If the **ping** fails, you need to verify that the **ping** is sent to the correct remote host. If it is, and if name resolution is configured, you have to dig a little more to find the problem. This error might indicate a problem with the name resolution process, and you might need to verify that the DNS or WINS server is available. Other commands, such as nslookup, can help in this process.

> **NOTE: Security Settings and Connection Errors**   A remote host connection error can sometimes be caused by your server's security settings. For example, the IPsec policies might restrict access to certain hosts. You might need to disable security measures temporarily when you troubleshoot errors.

The Expired TTL Message

The Time-To-Live (TTL) is an important consideration in understanding the ping command. The function of the TTL is to prevent circular routing, which occurs when a ping request keeps looping through a series of hosts. The TTL counts each hop along the way toward its destination device. Each time it counts one hop, the hop is subtracted from the TTL. If the TTL reaches 0, the TTL has expired, and you get a message like the following:

```
Reply from 24.67.180.1: TTL expired in transit
```

If the TTL is exceeded with ping, you might have a routing problem on the network. You can modify the TTL for ping on a Windows system by using the ping -i command.

> **NOTE: More on** ping As you can see from each of the ping examples, a common set of information is provided each time you run ping. This summary can be useful for getting an overall picture of the ping information.

The **traceroute** Utility

As great as ping is, sometimes it just isn't enough. In such cases, you need to reach for something a little stronger. traceroute (also called tracert) is a TCP/IP utility used to track the path a packet takes to reach a remote host. Each of the network operating systems used on today's networks provide a route tracing type of utility, but the name of the command and the output vary slightly in each. Table 12.2 shows the tracert command syntax used in various operating systems.

Table 12.2   traceroute Utility Commands

Operating System	traceroute Command Syntax
Windows	tracert <IP address>
Linux/Unix	traceroute <IP address>

What exactly does a traceroute command trace? The simple answer is routes. Local area networks (LANs) and wide area networks (WANs) can have several routes that packets can follow to reach their destinations. These routes are kept in routing tables. Systems use the information from these routing tables to tell the packets how they will travel through the network. The tracert utility lets you track the path a packet takes through the network. Figure 12.3 shows the results of a successful tracert command in a Windows system.

Key Topic

```
Select C:\WINNT\System32\command.com

C:\>tracert comptia.org

Tracing route to comptia.org [216.119.103.72]
over a maximum of 30 hops:

  1    60 ms    20 ms    20 ms  24.67.184.1
  2    50 ms    30 ms    20 ms  rd1ht-ge3-0.ok.shawcable.net [24.67.224.7]
  3    40 ms    30 ms    30 ms  rc1wh-atm0-3-2.vc.shawcable.net [204.209.214.193]
  4    30 ms    30 ms    30 ms  if-8-0.core1.Burnaby.Teleglobe.net [207.45.196.17]
  5    30 ms    40 ms    30 ms  if-7-3.core1.Seattle.Teleglobe.net [64.86.80.210]
  6    60 ms    60 ms    60 ms  if-13-0.core2.Sacramento.Teleglobe.net [64.86.83.193]
  7    50 ms    60 ms    60 ms  if-1-0.core1.LosAngeles.Teleglobe.net [64.86.83.169]
  8    60 ms    81 ms    60 ms  teleglobe-gw.la2ca.ip.att.net [192.205.32.221]
  9    60 ms    60 ms    60 ms  gbr4-p50.la2ca.ip.att.net [12.123.28.134]
 10    90 ms    60 ms    70 ms  gbr2-p30.sd2ca.ip.att.net [12.122.2.121]
 11    90 ms    71 ms    60 ms  gbr1-p60.sd2ca.ip.att.net [12.122.1.109]
 12   100 ms    80 ms    90 ms  gbr1-p30.phmaz.ip.att.net [12.122.2.142]
 13   110 ms    90 ms    90 ms  gar1-p360.phmaz.ip.att.net [12.123.142.21]
 14    91 ms    90 ms    90 ms  12.127.141.26
 15    90 ms    90 ms    90 ms  216.119.107.2
 16   120 ms    90 ms    90 ms  216.119.103.72

Trace complete.

C:\>
```

Figure 12.3 A successful **traceroute** command in a Windows system.

Not all route tracing commands are as successful as the one in Figure 12.3. A tracert command that has an asterisk (*) in the entries shows that the particular hop was timed out. Several consecutive asterisks indicate a problem with the routing information or congestion on the network. Figure 12.4 shows an example of a failed traceroute command.

Key Topic

```
Select C:\WINNT\System32\command.com

C:\>tracert 169.24.35.64

Tracing route to 169.24.35.64 over a maximum of 30 hops

  1    51 ms    20 ms    30 ms  24.67.184.1
  2    40 ms    30 ms    20 ms  rd1ht-ge3-0.ok.shawcable.net [24.67.224.7]
  3     *        *        *     Request timed out.
  4     *        *        *     Request timed out.
  5     *        *        *     Request timed out.
  6    ^C
C:\>
```

Figure 12.4 A failed **traceroute** command from a Windows system.

NOTE: Isolating bottlenecks   Because traceroute reports the amount of time it takes to reach each host in the path, it is a useful tool for isolating bottlenecks in a network. You need to know this for the exam.

In the example shown in Figure 12.4, the route is traced over a number of hops before it times out on the next hop of the route. In this example, pressing Ctrl+C terminates the trace; but if the tracert command were left to its own devices, it could run to 30 hops to complete the trace.

In a network troubleshooting situation, traceroute is often used in concert with ping. First, you use traceroute to determine where on a route the connectivity problem lies. Then, from the point of the problem, you can determine the possible cause of the problem by using ping.

Depending on the version of Windows you use and the type of operating system, switches are available for trace route commands. Table 12.3 identifies some of the switches available for the tracert command on a Windows Vista system.

Table 12.3 Switches for **tracert**

Switch	Description
-h	The –h switch specifies the maximum number of hops to search for target.
-d	Do not resolve addresses to hostnames.
-w	Specifies the wait time in milliseconds for each reply.
-R	Used with IPv6 only, it traces the round-trip path.
-4	Force using IPv4.
-6	Force using IPv6.

Reviewing **tracert** Command Printouts

The tracert command provides a lot of useful information, including the IP address of every router connection it passes through, and in many cases the name of the router. (Although, this depends on the router's configuration.) tracert also reports the length, in milliseconds, of the round-trip the packet made from the source location to the router and back. This information can tell you a lot about where network bottlenecks or breakdowns may be. Listing 12.4 shows an example of a successful tracert command on a Windows Server system.

Listing 12.4 A **tracert** Command

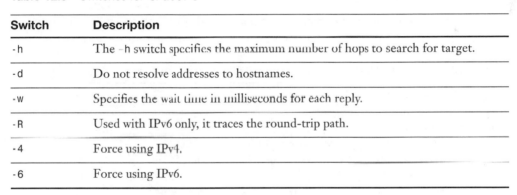

```
C:\>tracert 24.7.70.37
Tracing route to c1-p4.sttlwa1.home.net [24.7.70.37]
over a maximum of 30 hops:
  1    30 ms    20 ms    20 ms   24.67.184.1
  2    20 ms    20 ms    30 ms   rd1ht-ge3-0.ok.shawcable.net
     ➥[24.67.224.7]
```

```
  3     50 ms    30 ms    30 ms   rc1wh-atm0-2-1.vc.shawcable.net
       ➥[204.209.214.193]
  4     50 ms    30 ms    30 ms   rc2wh-pos15-0.vc.shawcable.net
       ➥[204.209.214.90]
  5     30 ms    40 ms    30 ms   rc2wt-pos2-0.wa.shawcable.net
       ➥[66.163.76.37]
  6     30 ms    40 ms    30 ms   c1-pos6-3.sttlwa1.home.net [24.7.70.37]
Trace complete.
```

The tracert display on a Windows-based system includes several columns of information. The first column represents the hop number. The next three columns indicate the round-trip time, in milliseconds, that a packet takes in its attempts to reach the destination. The last column is the hostname and the IP address of the responding device.

Of course, not all tracert commands are successful. Listing 12.5 shows the output from a tracert command that doesn't manage to get to the remote host.

Listing 12.5   A **tracert** Command That Doesn't Get to the Remote Host

```
C:\>tracert comptia.org
Tracing route to comptia.org [216.119.103.72]
over a maximum of 30 hops:
  1     27 ms    28 ms    14 ms   24.67.179.1
  2     55 ms    13 ms    14 ms   rd1ht-ge3-0.ok.shawcable.net
       ➥[24.67.224.7]
  3     27 ms    27 ms    28 ms   rc1wh-atm0-2-1.shawcable.net
       ➥[204.209.214.19]
  4     28 ms    41 ms    27 ms   rc1wt-pos2-0.wa.shawcable.net
       ➥[66.163.76.65]
  5     28 ms    41 ms    27 ms   rc2wt-pos1-0.wa.shawcable.net
       ➥[66.163.68.2]
  6     41 ms    55 ms    41 ms   c1-pos6-3.sttlwa1.home.net
       ➥[24.7.70.37]
  7     54 ms    42 ms    27 ms   home-gw.st6wa.ip.att.net
       ➥[192.205.32.249]
  8      *        *        *       Request timed out.
  9      *        *        *       Request timed out.
 10      *        *        *       Request timed out.
 11      *        *        *       Request timed out.
 12      *        *        *       Request timed out.
 13      *        *        *       Request timed out.
 14      *        *        *       Request timed out.
 15      *        *        *       Request timed out.
```

In this example, the tracert gets only to the seventh hop, at which point it fails; this failure indicates that the problem lies on the far side of the device in step 7 or on the near side of the device in step 8. In other words, the device at step 7 is functioning but might not make the next hop. The cause of the problem could be a range of issues, such as an error in the routing table or a faulty connection. Alternatively, the seventh device might be operating 100%, but device 8 might not be functioning at all. In any case, you can isolate the problem to just one or two devices.

The tracert command can also help you isolate a heavily congested network. In the following example, the trace route packets fail in the midst of the tracert but subsequently can continue. This behavior can be an indicator of network congestion, as shown in Listing 12.6. To test this assumption, you can run the tracert command at different times of the day. If the tracert is successful during low network usage times, such as at night, it could be daytime congestion.

Listing 12.6   A Trace Route Packet Failure During the **tracert**

```
C:\>tracert comptia.org
Tracing route to comptia.org [216.119.103.72]over a maximum of 30 hops:
  1     96 ms      96 ms      55 ms   24.67.179.1
  2     14 ms      13 ms      28 ms   rd1ht-ge3-0.ok.shawcable.net [24.67.224.7]
  3     28 ms      27 ms      41 ms   rc1wh-atm0-2-1.shawcable.net [204.209.214.19]
  4     28 ms      41 ms      27 ms   rc1wt-pos2-0.wa.shawcable.net
        ➦[66.163.76.65]
  5     41 ms      27 ms      27 ms   rc2wt-pos1-0.wa.shawcable.net
        ➦[66.163.68.2]
  6     55 ms      41 ms      27 ms   c1-pos6-3.sttlwa1.home.net [24.7.70.37]
  7     54 ms      42 ms      27 ms   home-gw.st6wa.ip.att.net [192.205.32.249]
  8     55 ms      41 ms      28 ms   gbr3-p40.st6wa.ip.att.not [12.120.44.100]
  9      *          *          *      Request timed out.
 10      *          *          *      Request timed out.
 11      *          *          *      Request timed out.
 12      *          *          *      Request timed out.
 13     69 ms      68 ms      69 ms   gbr2-p20.sd2ca.ip.att.net [12.122.11.254]
 14     55 ms      68 ms      69 ms   gbr1-p60.sd2ca.ip.att.net [12.122.1.109]
 15     82 ms      69 ms      82 ms   gbr1-p30.phmaz.ip.att.net [12.122.2.142]
 16     68 ms      69 ms      82 ms   gar2-p360.phmaz.ip.att.net [12.123.142.45]
 17    110 ms      96 ms      96 ms   12.125.99.70
 18    124 ms      96 ms      96 ms   light.crystaltech.com [216.119.107.1]
 19     82 ms      96 ms      96 ms   216.119.103.72
Trace complete.
```

> **NOTE:** route **Interpretation**   This section explores the results from the Windows tracert command, but the information provided is equally relevant to interpreting traceroute command results from UNIX, Linux, or Macintosh sys-

Generally, tracert enables you to identify the location of a problem in the connectivity between two devices. After you determine this location, you might need to use a utility such as ping to continue troubleshooting. In many cases, as in the examples provided in this chapter, the routers might be on a network such as the Internet and so not be within your control. In that case, there is little you can do except inform your ISP of the problem.

The **traceroute** Command

As discussed previously, the traceroute command performs the same function as tracert but can be used on UNIX, Linux, and Macintosh systems. Output from the traceroute command is almost identical to that produced by tracert on a Windows system, but for the purpose of comparison, you can see an example of the output from a traceroute command run on a Linux system in Listing 12.7.

Listing 12.7   Output from a **traceroute** Command on a Linux System

```
[root@localhost /root]#traceroute 22tecmet44.com
1   d207-81-224-254.bchsia.telus.net (207.81.224.254)   10.304 ms
        ➥10.224 ms   10.565 ms
2   208.181.240.22 (208.181.240.22)   9.764 ms   9.784 ms   9.427 ms
3   vancbc01br01.bb.telus.com (154.11.10.58)   16.771 ms   17.664 ms
        ➥17.456 ms
4   nwmrbc01gr01.bb.telus.com (154.11.10.54)   15.407 ms   14.622 ms
        ➥14.249 ms
5   if-6-0.core1.VBY-Burnaby.Teleglobe.net (207.45.196.17)   14.966 ms
        ➥13.942ms   14.992 ms
6   ix-4-0.core1.VBY-Burnaby.Teleglobe.net (207.45.196.14) 17.653 ms
        ➥17.666 ms   18.356 ms
7   GE3-0.WANA-PACNW.IP.GROUPTELECOM.NET (66.59.190.5)   18.426 ms
        ➥17.626 ms 18.395 ms
8   216.18.31.161 (216.18.31.161)   18.454 ms   17.610 ms   17.467 ms
9   h209-139-197-237.gtst.groulecom.net (209.139.197.237)   19.412 ms
        ➥19.326ms   18.434 ms
10  host-65-61-192-186.inptnet.com (65.61.192.186)   74.120 ms 20.041 ms
        ➥21.091 ms
11  dhweb11.d66534host.com (65.61.222.201)   19.188 ms 20.083 ms
        ➥19.658 ms
```

As mentioned earlier, from a troubleshooting perspective, the information provided by traceroute can be interpreted in the same way as with tracert.

The mtr Utility

The my traceroute (mtr) commandis used on Linux/UNIX systems and essentially combines the functionality of ping with that of traceroute. After it is issued, the command provides details of the path between two hosts (similar to the traceroute command) and additional statistics for each node in the path based on samples taken over a time period (similar to the ping command).

In a Windows environment, a similar command is the pathping command. pathping has been available since Windows NT and is used with modern Windows versions including Windows 2003, Windows 2008, Windows XP, and Windows Vista.

> **TIP:** mtr   Be prepared for the Network+ exam to identify the function of the mtr command. It has features of both the ping and traceroute commands.

The arp Utility

The Address Resolution Protocol (ARP) is the part of the TCP/IP suite and is responsible for resolving IP addresses to Media Access Control (MAC) addresses. Such a translation is necessary because even though systems use IP addresses to find each other, the low-level communication between devices occurs using the MAC address.

When two systems on an IP network want to communicate, they first establish each other's location by using the IP address. Then, ARP requests are sent to ascertain the MAC address of the devices so that they can communicate with each other. In a sense, the IP address can be thought of as the name by which a system can be found in a phone book. The MAC address is the actual phone number used to establish communication.

The arp utility is used to review and modify a host's ARP cache table, which contains mappings between TCP/IP hostnames and IP addresses. The ARP cache is discussed next.

The ARP Cache

ARP translations are typically stored locally on systems in the ARP cache. But how does the MAC address from another computer system end up in your system's ARP cache? Each time you access another host, your system broadcasts to the ARP component of every host on the network. Because the IP address is embedded in the request, all systems other than the chosen one ignore the request, but the target system receives the request and replies accordingly. At this point both hosts record each other's MAC address in their local ARP cache, and these entries remain in the cache until they are timed out, which depends on how often they are accessed. If the ARP entry is reused, the time period is extended further.

The ARP table can hold two types of entries: static and dynamic. Static entries do not expire and can be added to the ARP cache manually via the -s switch. Dynamic entries are added as the system accesses other hosts on the network.

NOTE: ARP and OSI ARP operates at the network layer of the Open Systems Interconnect (OSI) model.

To view the ARP cache on a Windows computer, you use the arp -a command. Figure 12.5 shows an example of an ARP cache, the result of using arp -a.

```
C:\WINNT\System32\command.com                                          _ □ ×

C:\>arp -a

Interface: 24.67.185.183 on Interface 0x1000003
  Internet Address      Physical Address      Type
  24.67.184.1           00-00-77-93-d8-3d     dynamic
  24.67.184.65          00-80-c8-e3-4c-bd     dynamic
  24.67.185.1           00-00-77-93-d8-3d     dynamic

C:\>
```

Figure 12.5 An ARP cache.

Switches for **arp**

As with the other command-line utilities discussed in this chapter, arp has a few associated switches. Table 12.4 lists some of the switches commonly used with the arp command.

Table 12.4 Commonly Used **arp** Command Switches

Channel	Frequency Band
-a (-g)	Both the –a and –g switches display the current ARP entries. If more than one interface exists, ARP resolution for each interface displays.
inet_addr	Resolves the MAC address of a remote system identified in the inet_addr field.
-N if_addr	Displays the ARP entries for a specific network interface.
-d inet_addr	Deletes the entry for the specified host.
-s inet_addr eth_addr	Enables you to add a static entry to the ARP cache. Must be used with both the IP address (inet_addr) and the MAC address (eth_addr).

The **arp** Command Printout

In practical terms, the information provided by the arp utility is of little use beyond the role of identifying the origin of a duplicate IP address. Even so, you still need to identify and interpret the output from an arp command for both the Network+ exam and the real world. With that in mind, Listing 12.8 shows the output from the arp -a command.

Listing 12.8 Output from an **arp -a** Command on a Windows XP Professional System

```
C:\>arp -a
Interface: 192.168.1.100 --- 0x2
  Internet Address      Physical Address     Type
  192.168.1.1           00-0c-41-a8-5a-ee    dynamic
  192.168.1.101         00-60-08-17-63-a0    dynamic
  209.22.34.63          00-fd-43-23-f4-e4    static
```

As you can see, there are three entries in the arp table of this system. For each entry, the IP address and the resolved hardware (MAC) address that corresponds to that address is shown. Two of the entries are dynamic, whereas the other is static. Generally, dynamic entries give you few problems because the automatic resolution process is almost always successful. Static entries, in other words those that have been entered manually, are another matter. If for some reason you decide to add static entries to the arp table, and you then subsequently have problems accessing that host, check the information for the arp entry to ensure that it is correct. Although the arp command will not enable you to add a static entry to the arp table that does not conform to the syntax for either the IP address or the MAC address, it doesn't stop from you entering the *wrong* information for either of these fields.

The **arp ping** Utility

Earlier in this chapter we talked about the ping command and how it is used to test connectivity between devices on a network. Using the ping command is often an administrator's first step to test connectivity between network devices. If the ping fails, it is assumed that the device you are pinging is offline, but this might not always be the case.

Most companies now use firewalls or other security measures that may block Internet Control Message Protocol (ICMP) requests. This means that a ping request will not work. Blocking ICMP is a security measure designed to prevent ICMP-type attacks. These attacks are outlined in Chapter 15, "Security Technologies and Malicious Software."

If ICMP is blocked, there is still another option to test connectivity with a device on the network: the arp ping utility. As mentioned, the arp utility is used to resolve IP addresses to MAC addresses. The arp ping utility uses ARP rather than

ICMP to test connectivity. However, the ARP protocol is not routable and the arp ping cannot be routed to work over separate networks. The arp ping works only on the local subnet.

> **NOTE: Why Block ICMP?**   One type of attack is called an ICMP flood attack (also known as a ping flood). The attacker sends continuous ping packets to a server or network system, eventually tying up that system's resources, making it unable to respond to requests from other systems.

Like a regular ping, an arp ping specifies an IP address; however, instead of returning regular ping results, the **arp ping** responds with the MAC address and name of the computer system. So, when a regular ping using ICMP fails to locate a system, the arp ping uses a different method to find the system. With arp ping, it is possible to ping a MAC address directly. From this, it is possible to determine if duplicate IP addresses are used and, as mentioned, determine if a system is responding.

arp ping is not built into Windows, but you can download a number of programs that enable you to ping using ARP. Linux, on the other hand, has an arp ping utility ready to use. Figure 12.6 shows the results of an **arp ping** from a shareware Windows utility.

IP Address	Mac Address	Computer Name
192.168.001.065	[00:1e:4c:43:fa:55]	mike-PC.domain.invalid
192.168.001.064	[00:1a:a0:12:93:33]	LINDA-PC
192.168.001.254	[00:18:d1:95:f6:02]	
192.168.001.255	[00:1e:4c:43:fa:55]	
192.168.001.065	[00:1e:4c:43:fa:55]	mike-PC.domain.invalid
192.168.001.065	[00:1e:4c:43:fa:55]	mike-PC.domain.invalid
192.168.001.064	[00:1a:a0:12:93:33]	LINDA-PC
192.168.001.060	Timed Out	
192.168.001.061	Timed Out	
192.168.001.062	Timed Out	
192.168.001.063	Timed Out	

Figure 12.6   A third-party **arp ping** utility.

The **netstat** Utility

The netstat utility displays packet statistics such as how many packets have been sent and received from and to the system and other related protocol information. It is also used to view both inbound and outbound TCP/IP network connections. This utility is popular with seasoned network administrators who need more information than what utilities such as ping can provide.

As with the other command-line utilities, you can use a number of available switches with the netstat command. Without using any of these switches, the output from a `netstat` command would resemble the output shown in Figure 12.7. Note that in its default usage, the `netstat` command shows outbound connections that have been established by TCP.

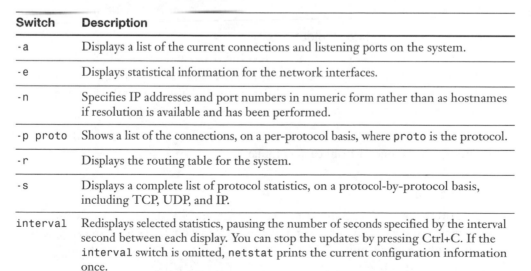

Figure 12.7   Output from a **netstat** command.

A handful of switches are used with the `netstat` command. Table 12.5 shows some of the key netstat switches used from a Windows system.

Table 12.5   netstat Switches on Windows

Switch	Description
-a	Displays a list of the current connections and listening ports on the system.
-e	Displays statistical information for the network interfaces.
-n	Specifies IP addresses and port numbers in numeric form rather than as hostnames if resolution is available and has been performed.
-p proto	Shows a list of the connections, on a per-protocol basis, where proto is the protocol.
-r	Displays the routing table for the system.
-s	Displays a complete list of protocol statistics, on a protocol-by-protocol basis, including TCP, UDP, and IP.
interval	Redisplays selected statistics, pausing the number of seconds specified by the interval second between each display. You can stop the updates by pressing Ctrl+C. If the interval switch is omitted, netstat prints the current configuration information once.

Of these switches, you're likely to use one far more than any other: -r. The netstat -r command provides an easy way to see the routes configured on the system.

In time, you will be able to read a routing table and determine whether a routing problem exists on the network. Figure 12.8 shows the output from the netstat -r command.

```
C:\WINNT\System32\command.com                                    _□×

C:\>netstat -r

Route Table

Interface List
0x1 ....................... MS TCP Loopback interface
0x1000003 ...00 d0 59 09 07 51 ...... Intel 8255x-based Integrated Fast Ethernet

Active Routes:
Network Destination        Netmask          Gateway       Interface  Metric
          0.0.0.0          0.0.0.0      24.67.184.1   24.67.185.183      1
      24.67.184.0    255.255.254.0   24.67.185.183   24.67.185.183      1
    24.67.185.183  255.255.255.255       127.0.0.1       127.0.0.1      1
   24.255.255.255  255.255.255.255   24.67.185.183   24.67.185.183      1
        127.0.0.0        255.0.0.0       127.0.0.1       127.0.0.1      1
        224.0.0.0        224.0.0.0   24.67.185.183   24.67.185.183      1
  255.255.255.255  255.255.255.255   24.67.185.183   24.67.185.183      1
Default Gateway:       24.67.184.1

Persistent Routes:
  None

C:\>
```

Figure 12.8   Output from the **netstat -r** command.

> **TIP: Viewing Routing Information**   In addition to using netstat -r to view routing information, you can use the route print command.

> **TIP:**   netstat -r **Command**   The netstat -r command is commonly used to view routing information. You are likely to be asked about it on the Network+

The **netstat** Command Printouts

The netstat command displays the protocol statistics and current TCP/IP connections. Used without any switches, the netstat command shows the active connections for all outbound TCP/IP connections. In addition, several switches are available that change the type of information displayed by netstat.

The following sections show the output from several netstat switches and identify and interpret the output from each command.

netstat -e

The netstat -e command shows the activity for the NIC and displays the number of packets that have been both sent and received. Listing 12.9 shows an example of the netstat -e command.

Listing 12.9   Example of the **netstat -e** Command

```
C:\WINDOWS\Desktop>netstat -e
Interface Statistics

                         Received              Sent

Bytes                    17412385          40237510
Unicast packets             79129             85055
Non-unicast packets           693               254
Discards                        0                 0
Errors                          0                 0
Unknown protocols             306
```

As you can see, the netstat -e command shows more than just the packets that have been sent and received. The following list briefly explains the information provided in the netstat -e command:

- **Bytes**—The number of bytes that have been sent or received by the NIC since the computer was turned on.

- **Unicast packets**—Packets sent and received directly to this interface.

- **Nonunicast packets**—Broadcast or multicast packets picked up by the NIC.

- **Discards**—The number of packets rejected by the NIC, perhaps because they were damaged.

- **Errors**—The errors that occurred during either the sending or receiving process. As you would expect, this column should be a low number. If it is not, it could indicate a problem with the NIC.

- **Unknown protocols**—The number of packets that were not recognizable by the system.

netstat -a

The netstat -a command displays statistics for both the TCP and User Datagram Protocol (UDP). Listing 12.10 shows an example of the netstat -a command.

Listing 12.10   Example of the **netstat -a** Command

```
C:\WINDOWS\Desktop>netstat -a
Active Connections

  Proto Local Address         Foreign Address        State
```

```
TCP      laptop:1027           LAPTOP:0                      LISTENING
TCP      laptop:1030           LAPTOP:0                      LISTENING
TCP      laptop:1035           LAPTOP:0                      LISTENING
TCP      laptop:50000          LAPTOP:0                      LISTENING
TCP      laptop:5000           LAPTOP:0                      LISTENING
TCP      laptop:1035           msgr-ns41.msgr.hotmail.com:1863
ESTABLISHED
TCP      laptop:nbsession      LAPTOP:0                      LISTENING
TCP      laptop:1027           localhost:50000               ESTABLISHED
TCP      laptop:50000          localhost:1027                ESTABLISHED
UDP      laptop:1900           *:*
UDP      laptop:nbname         *:*
UDP      laptop:nbdatagram     *:*
UDP      laptop:1547           *:*
UDP      laptop:1038           *:*
UDP      laptop:1828           *:*
UDP      laptop:3366           *:*
```

As you can see, the output includes four columns, which show the protocol, local address, foreign address, and state of the port. The TCP connections show the local and foreign destination address and the current state of the connection. UDP, however, is a little different; it does not list a state status because, as mentioned throughout this book, UDP is a connectionless protocol and does not establish connections. The following list briefly explains the information provided by the netstat -a command:

- **Proto**—The protocol used by the connection.

- **Local address**—The IP address of the local computer system and the port number it uses. If the entry in the local address field is an asterisk (*), it indicates that the port has not yet been established.

- **Foreign address**—The IP address of a remote computer system and the associated port. When a port has not been established, as with the UDP connections, *:* appears in the column.

- **State**—The current state of the TCP connection. Possible states include established, listening, closed, and waiting.

netstat -r

The netstat -r command is often used to view the routing table for a system. A system uses a routing table to determine routing information for TCP/IP traffic. Listing 12.11 shows an example of the netstat -r command from a Windows XP system.

Listing 12.11   Example of the **netstat -r** Command

```
C:\WINDOWS\Desktop>netstat -r
Route table


=========================================================================
=========================================================================
Active Routes:
Network Destination        Netmask          Gateway      Interface   Metric
          0.0.0.0          0.0.0.0      24.67.179.1    24.67.179.22     1
       24.67.179.0    255.255.255.0    24.67.179.22    24.67.179.22     1
      24.67.179.22  255.255.255.255       127.0.0.1       127.0.0.1     1
    24.255.255.255  255.255.255.255    24.67.179.22    24.67.179.22     1
         127.0.0.0        255.0.0.0       127.0.0.1       127.0.0.1     1
         224.0.0.0        224.0.0.0    24.67.179.22    24.67.179.22     1
   255.255.255.255  255.255.255.255    24.67.179.22               2     1
Default Gateway:        24.67.179.1
=========================================================================
Persistent   Routes:
  None
```

netstat -s

The netstat -s command displays a number of statistics related to the TCP/IP
protocol suite. Understanding the purpose of every field in the output is beyond
the scope of the Network+ exam, but for your reference, Listing 12.12 shows sample output from the netstat -s command.

Listing 12.12   Example of the **netstat -s** Command

```
C:\>netstat -s


IP Statistics

  Packets Received              = 389938
  Received Header Errors        = 0
  Received Address Errors       = 1876
  Datagrams Forwarded           = 498
  Unknown Protocols Received    = 0
  Received Packets Discarded    = 0
  Received Packets Delivered    = 387566
  Output Requests               = 397334
  Routing Discards              = 0
  Discarded Output Packets      = 0
  Output Packet No Route        = 916
```

```
Reassembly Required               = 0
Reassembly Successful             = 0
Reassembly Failures               = 0
Datagrams Successfully Fragmented = 0
Datagrams Failing Fragmentation   = 0
Fragments Created                 = 0


ICMP Statistics

                                Received      Sent
    Messages                      40641       41111
    Errors                        0           0
    Destination Unreachable       223         680
    Time Exceeded                 24          0
    Parameter Problems            0           0
    Source Quenches               0           0
    Redirects                     0           38
    Echos                         20245       20148
    Echo Replies                  20149       20245
    Timestamps                    0           0
    Timestamp Replies             0           0
    Address Masks                 0           0
    Address Mask Replies          0           0
TCP Statistics

    Active Opens                  = 13538
    Passive Opens                 = 23132
    Failed Connection Attempts    = 9259
    Reset Connections             = 254
    Current Connections           = 15
    Segments Received             = 330242
    Segments Sent                 = 326935
    Segments Retransmitted        = 18851


UDP Statistics
    Datagrams Received    = 20402
    No Ports              = 20594
    Receive Errors        = 0
    Datagrams Sent        = 10217
```

The **nbtstat** Utility

The NetBIOS statistic utility, nbtstat, can display protocol and statistical information for NetBIOS over TCP/IP (sometimes called NetBT) connections. Among other things, the nbtstat utility displays the NetBIOS names of systems that have been resolved.

Because nbtstat is used for the resolution of NetBIOS names, it's available only on Windows systems. Neither NetWare nor Linux supports NetBIOS, or subsequently nbstat.

Table 12.6 shows some of the most frequently used switches for nbtstat.

Table 12.6 nbtstat Switches

Switch	Description
-a	(Adapter status) Lists the NetBIOS resolution table of a remote system identified by its hostname.
-A	(Adapter status) Lists the NetBIOS resolution table for a remote system identified by its IP address.
-c	(Cache) Lists the NetBIOS name cache along with the IP address of each name in the cache.
-n	(Names) Displays the NetBIOS local name table.
-r	(Resolved) Provides statistical information about resolutions.
-R	(Reload) Purges and reloads the NetBIOS names from the LMHOSTS file.
-S	(Sessions) Shows the NetBIOS sessions table, with the state of connection on a hostname basis.

When you look at the output from certain nbtstat commands, you might see reference to a scope ID. Do not confuse this with Dynamic Host Configuration Protocol (DHCP) scopes. In NetBIOS, you can create scopes to logically group systems together. It is this grouping that the scope ID information refers to.

Figure 12.9 shows the output from using nbtstat -r in Windows.

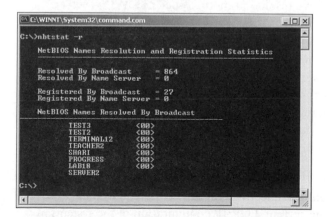

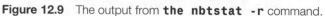

Figure 12.9 The output from **the nbtstat -r** command.

The nbtstat command is used on Windows platforms to show protocol and statistic information for NetBIOS over TCP/IP (NetBT) traffic. Because Microsoft now prefers the Domain Name System (DNS) over the Windows Internet Name Service (WINS) for name resolutions, the need to use nbtstat in troubleshooting scenarios is somewhat reduced. However, you should still be aware of the information that nbtstat provides. Listing 12.13 shows the result of one of the most common uses for nbtstat -r.

Listing 12.13   Output from the **nbtstat -r** Command

```
C:\>nbtstat -r
    NetBIOS Names Resolution and Registration Statistics
    ------------------------------------------------
    Resolved By Broadcast     = 722
    Resolved By Name Server   = 29

    Registered By Broadcast   = 7
    Registered By Name Server = 0

    NetBIOS Names Resolved By Broadcast
    ------------------------------------------------
        SALES               <00>
        ADMIN               <00>
        ROUTER1             <00>
        FWALL-1             <00>
        MAILSERV            <00>
        WORKSTATION2        <00>
        WORKSTATION3        <00>
```

NOTE: Don't Confuse Your Rs   Don't get confused between nbtstat -r and netstat -r. nbtstat -r shows a list of the NetBIOS names that have been resolved via broadcasts or by some other name resolution method such as a WINS server. netstat -r displays the routing table for the system.

As you can see, the information provided by the nbtstat -r command is straightforward. The first part of the listing defines the number of resolutions that have been achieved via broadcast or through a name server. It also shows the number of times that this system has been registered via a broadcast or by a name server. Below that are listed the NetBIOS names of other computers that have been resolved by this system.

The **ipconfig** and **ifconfig** Utilities

When it comes to troubleshooting connectivity on a network, you won't get too far without first determining the current TCP/IP configuration of the systems in question. Two utilities, ipconfig and ifconfig, can provide much of the information you require. The `ipconfig` utility shows the TCP/IP configuration of Windows systems, whereas `ifconfig` is used on Linux, UNIX, and Macintosh systems. In both cases, the same utility that you can use to obtain configuration information can also be used to perform certain configuration tasks. We look at the two utilities separately, beginning with `ipconfig`.

The **ipconfig** Utility

The `ipconfig` utility shows the TCP/IP configuration information for all network cards installed in a Windows system. Information provided includes the IP address, the subnet mask, and the current default gateway. To find additional information, the `ipconfig` command is often used with the `/all` switch, which then yields additional information on Windows Internet Name Service (WINS) servers, DNS configuration, the MAC address of the interface, and whether DHCP is enabled. If DHCP is enabled, information about the DHCP address lease is provided, including how much time is left on the lease.

Because it provides such a wealth of information, `ipconfig` is the utility of choice for network administrators looking for configuration information; therefore, you can expect it to be on the Network+ exam. Figure 12.10 shows the output from the `ipconfig /all` command.

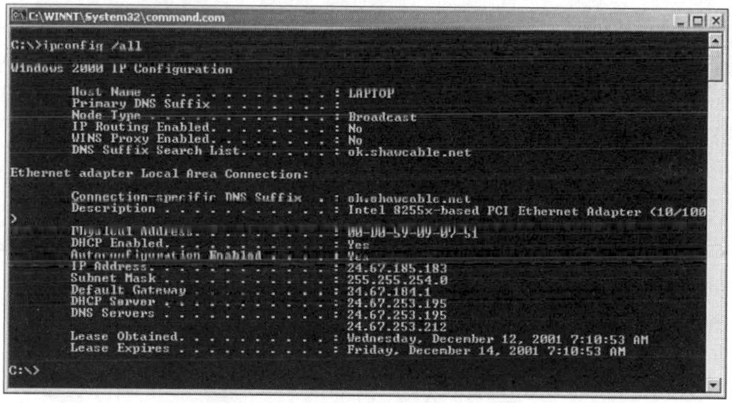

Figure 12.10   Output from the **ipconfig /all** command.

Only a limited number of switches are available for the `ipconfig` command, but they are important. Table 12.7 lists some of the commonly used switches and what they do.

Table 12.7 Commonly Used **ipconfig** Switches

Switch	Description
/?	Provides a list of the switches available for the ipconfig command. Exact switches vary between Windows platforms.
/all	Displays all TCP/IP configuration information.
/renew	Releases all TCP/IP information and then queries a DHCP server for new information. After the command is issued, you can use ipconfig /all to confirm that the ipconfig /renew command was successful.
/renew6	Releases IPv6 TCP/IP information and renews the address from the DHCP server.
/release	Releases the DHCP lease. The result is that the system will not have any IP configuration information until renewed.
/release6	Releases the DHCP lease for IPv6 addresses.
/flushdns	Purges the DNS cache.
/registerdns	Reregisters the system's name with DNS servers and also refreshes the DHCP lease. This command is particularly useful in environments such as Windows server enviroments that use Dynamic DNS (DDNS).

> **NOTE: Multiple NICs** Using the ipconfig command with the switches listed in Table 12.8 can affect all the interfaces on the system. This is fine if you have only one network interface, but on systems with more than one network interface, it's possible to specify the interface rather than have the command applied to all interfaces.

The **ipconfig** Command Printouts

The ipconfig command is a technician's best friend when it comes to viewing the TCP/IP configuration of a Windows system—at least most Windows-based systems. Used on its own, the ipconfig command shows basic information, such as the name of the network interface, the IP address, the subnet mask, and the default gateway. Combined with the /all switch, it shows a detailed set of information, as you see in Listing 12.14.

Listing 12.14 Example of the **ipconfig /all** Command

```
C:\>ipconfig /all
Windows 2000 IP Configuration
    Host Name . . . . . . . . . . . . : server
    Primary DNS Suffix  . . . . . . . : write
    Node Type . . . . . . . . . . . . : Broadcast
    IP Routing Enabled. . . . . . . . : Yes
```

```
    WINS Proxy Enabled. . . . . . . . : No
    DNS Suffix Search List. . . . . . : write
                                        ok.anyotherhost.net
Ethernet adapter Local Area Connection:

Connection-specific DNS Suffix  .  : ok.anyotherhost.net
Description . . . . . . . . . . . : D-Link DFE-530TX PCI Fast Ethernet
Physical Address. . . . . . . . . : 00-80-C8-E3-4C-BD
DHCP Enabled. . . . . . . . . . . : Yes
Autoconfiguration Enabled . . . . : Yes
IP Address. . . . . . . . . . . . : 24.67.184.65
Subnet Mask . . . . . . . . . . . : 255.255.254.0
Default Gateway . . . . . . . . . : 24.67.184.1
DHCP Server . . . . . . . . . . . : 24.67.253.195
DNS Servers . . . . . . . . . . . : 24.67.253.195
                                     24.67.253.212
Lease Obtained.. . . . . : Thursday, February 07, 2002 3:42:00 AM
Lease Expires .. . . . . : Saturday, February 09, 2002 3:42:00 AM
```

TIP: **Check the** `ipconfig` **Information**   When looking at `ipconfig` information, make sure that all information is present and correct. For example, a missing or incorrect default gateway parameter would limit communication to the local segment. Be sure to know this for the exam.

As you can imagine, you can use the output from an `ipconfig /all` command in a massive range of troubleshooting scenarios. Table 12.8 lists some of the most common troubleshooting symptoms, along with where to look for clues about solving them in the `ipconfig /all` output.

Table 12.8   Common Troubleshooting Symptoms That **ipconfig** Can Help Solve

Symptom	Field to Check in ipconfig **Output**
User cannot connect to any other system.	Make sure the TCP/IP address and subnet mask are correct. If the network uses DHCP, make sure DHCP is enabled.
User can connect to another system on the same subnet but cannot connect to a remote system.	Make sure the default gateway is correctly configured.
User cannot browse the Internet.	Make sure the DNS server parameters are configured correctly.
User can browse subnets.	Make sure the DNS server parameters are configured correctly, if applicable.

> **TIP: Identify the `ipconfig` Output**   Be prepared to identify the output from an `ipconfig` command in relationship to a troubleshooting scenario for the Network+ exam.

As mentioned previously, `ipconfig` is a Windows-based utility. The equivalent on a Linux, UNIX, or Macintosh system is `ifconfig`. Because Linux relies more heavily on command-line utilities than Windows does, the Linux and UNIX version of `ifconfig` provides much more functionality than `ipconfig`. On a Linux or UNIX system you can get information about the usage of the `ifconfig` command by using `ifconfig —help`. Figure 12.11 shows the output from the basic `ifconfig` command run on a Linux system.

```
root@localhost.localdomain: /root
File  Sessions  Options  Help
[root@localhost /root]# ifconfig
eth0      Link encap:Ethernet   HWaddr 00:60:08:17:63:A0
          inet addr:192.168.1.101  Bcast:192.168.1.255  Mask:255.255.255.0
          UP BROADCAST RUNNING  MTU:1500  Metric:1
          RX packets:415 errors:0 dropped:0 overruns:0 frame:0
          TX packets:387 errors:0 dropped:0 overruns:0 carrier:0
          collisions:0 txqueuelen:100
          Interrupt:5 Base address:0xe400

lo        Link encap:Local Loopback
          inet addr:127.0.0.1  Mask:255.0.0.0
          UP LOOPBACK RUNNING  MTU:3924  Metric:1
          RX packets:18 errors:0 dropped:0 overruns:0 frame:0
          TX packets:18 errors:0 dropped:0 overruns:0 carrier:0
          collisions:0 txqueuelen:0

[root@localhost /root]#
```

Figure 12.11   Output from an **ifconfig** command on a Linux system.

The **ifconfig** Command Printout

The basic information provided by `ifconfig` includes the hardware (MAC) address of the installed network adapters, and the IP address, subnet mask, and default gateway parameters. It also provides information on the number of packets sent and received by the interface. A high number in any of the error categories might indicate a problem with the network adapter. A high number of collisions might indicate a problem with the network itself. Listing 12.15 shows sample output from the `ifconfig` command.

Listing 12.15   Sample Output from an **ifconfig** Command

```
eth0      Link encap:Ethernet   HWaddr 00:60:08:17:63:A0
          inet addr:192.168.1.101  Bcast:192.168.1.255  Mask:255.255.255.0
          UP BROADCAST RUNNING  MTU:1500  Metric:1
          RX packets:911 errors:0 dropped:0 overruns:0 frame:0
          TX packets:804 errors:0 dropped:0 overruns:0 carrier:0
          collisions:0 txqueuelen:100
          Interrupt:5 Base address:0xe400
```

```
lo          Link encap:Local Loopback
            inet addr:127.0.0.1  Mask:255.0.0.0
            UP LOOPBACK RUNNING  MTU:3924  Metric:1
            RX packets:18 errors:0 dropped:0 overruns:0 frame:0
            TX packets:18 errors:0 dropped:0 overruns:0 carrier:0
            collisions:0 txqueuelen:0
```

Although the `ifconfig` command displays the IP address, subnet mask, and default gateway information for both the installed network adapter and the local loopback adapter, it does not report DCHP lease information. Instead, you can use the `pump -s` command to view detailed information on the DHCP lease, including the assigned IP address, the address of the DHCP server, and the time remaining on the lease. The `pump` command can also be used to release and renew IP addresses assigned via DHCP and to view DNS server information.

The issues and suggested solutions described earlier in Table 12.8 for using `ipconfig` on Windows systems are equally applicable to basic troubleshooting with `ifconfig` on a Linux, UNIX, or Macintosh system. The only thing to remember is that you might need to run both `ifconfig` and `pump -s` to gain all the information required. Also, you might find that the additional statistical information provided by the `ifconfig` command points toward other sources of a problem, such as a faulty network adapter, or a high level of traffic on the network.

The **nslookup** and **dig** Utilities

The `nslookup` and `dig` utilities are TCP/IP diagnostic tools that can be used to troubleshoot DNS problems. They let you interact with a DNS server and locate records by performing manual DNS lookups. `nslookup` is used on Windows systems, whereas Linux, UNIX, and Macintosh systems support both `dig` and `nslookup`.

We can start by reviewing the `nslookup` utility.

The **nslookup** Utility

Using `nslookup`, you can run manual name resolution queries against DNS servers, get information about the DNS configuration of your system, or specify what kind of DNS record should be resolved.

If you provide a server name with `nslookup`, the command performs a DNS lookup and returns the IP address for the server name you entered. If you provide an IP address with `nslookup`, the command performs a reverse DNS lookup and provides you with the server name.

Figure 12.12 shows an example of `nslookup` usage and its output.

Figure 12.12   Output from the **nslookup** command.

Entering nslookup by itself at the command prompt and pressing Enter starts the nslookup utility in interactive mode. Instead of being returned to the command prompt, you stay in the utility and receive a > prompt. At the > prompt, you can issue more commands or switches. A list of some of the nslookup switches is provided in Table 12.9. You can get a full list of the switches by typing ? at the > command prompt.

Table 12.9   nslookup Switches in Interactive Mode

Switch	Description
option	Sets a switch
all	Displays a list of the currently set switches, including the current server and domain
[no]debug	Turns display of debug information print on/off
[no]d2	Turns display of exhaustive debugging information on/off
[no]defname	Causes the domain specified in **defname** to be appended to each query
[no]recurse	Specifies that the query should be recursive
[no]search	Specifies that nslookup should use the domain search list
[no]vc	Specifies that nslookup should use a virtual circuit
domain=NAME	Sets the default domain name to the name specified in NAME
srchlist=N1[/N2/.../N6]	Sets the domain to N1 and the search order to the values specified inside [ ]
root=NAME	Sets the root server to the root server specified in NAME
retry=X	Specifies the number of retries, where X is the number
timeout=X	Sets the timeout value, in seconds, to the value specified in X
type=X	Specifies the type of query that nslookup should perform, such as A, ANY, CNAME, MX, NS, PTR, SOA, or SRV
querytype=X	The same switches as for type

Table 12.9 nslookup Switches in Interactive Mode

Switch	Description
class=X	Specifies the query class
[no]msxfr	Tells nslookup to use the Microsoft fast zone transfer system
server NAME	Sets the default server to the value specified in NAME
exit	Exits the nslookup program and returns you to the command prompt

---

Understanding DNS Records

When reviewing the DNS information retrieved using nslookup, you notice some cryptic acronyms. Each DNS name server maintains information about its zone, or domain, in a series of records, known as DNS resource records. There are several DNS resource records; each contains information about the DNS domain and the systems within it. These records are text entries stored on the DNS server. Some of the DNS resource records include the following:

- Start of Authority (SOA)—A record of information containing data on DNS zones and other DNS records. A DNS zone is the part of a domain for which an individual DNS server is responsible. Each zone contains a single SOA record.

- Name Server (NS)—Stores information that identifies the name servers in the domain that stores information for that domain.

- Canonical Name (CNAME)—Stores additional host names, or aliases, for hosts in the domain. A CNAME specifies an alias or nickname for a canonical hostname record in a domain name system (DNS) database. CNAME records give a single computer multiple names (aliases).

- Mail Exchange (MX)—Stores information about where mail for the domain should be delivered.

- The Service Locator (SRV)—Identifies computers that host specific services. SRV resource records locate domain controllers for the Active Directory.

Now that you know what these acronyms stand for, you have a better idea of how to use and understand the nslookup switches.

The **nslookup** Command Printout

The most common use of nslookup is to perform a simple manual name resolution request against a DNS server. Listing 12.16 shows the output from this process on a Windows XP Vista system.

Listing 12.16 Output from a Manual Name Resolution Using **Nslookup**

```
C:/>nslookup informit.com
Server:   nen.bx.ttfc.net
Address:  209.55.4.155


Name:     informit.com
Address:  63.240.93.157
```

There are two sections to the information provided by nslookup. The first part provides the hostname and IP address of the DNS server that performed the resolution. The second part is the domain name that was resolved along with its corresponding IP address. From a troubleshooting perspective, you can use this information if you suspect that a record held on a DNS server is incorrect.

You can also verify that the DNS server is operating correctly by specifying the DNS server against which the resolution should be performed. For example, consider Listing 12.17, which shows a failed resolution run against a specified DNS server.

Listing 12.17 Sample Output from an **nslookup** Command

```
C:/>nslookup informit.com
Server:   heittm.bx.ttc.net
Address:  209.56.43.130

DNS request timed out.
    timeout was 2 seconds.
```

By adding the IP address of the DNS server to the nslookup command syntax, the resolution request is directed at that server. As you can see, the request timed out, which could indicate that the DNS server is down or inaccessible. The problem also might be with your ISP provider, router, or firewall configurations.

The **dig** Utility

As mentioned previously, on a Linux, UNIX, or Macintosh system, you can also use the dig command to perform manual DNS lookups. dig performs the same basic task as nslookup but with one major distinction—the dig command does not have an interactive mode and instead uses only command-line switches to customize results. Figure 12.13 shows an example of the output from a manual name resolution request with the dig command.

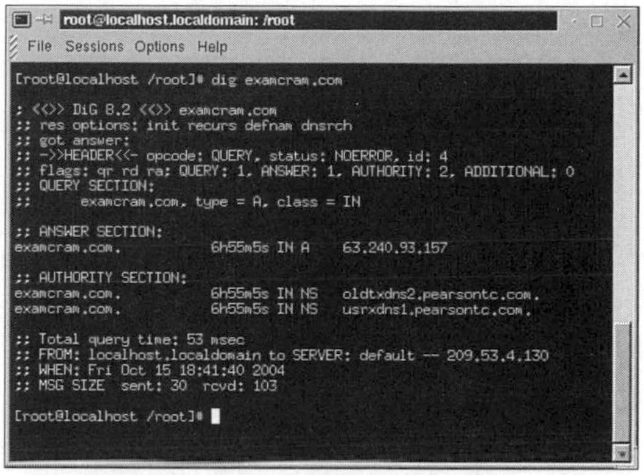

Figure 12.13 Output from **dig** command on a Linux system.

The **dig** Command Printout

The **dig** tool is generally considered a more powerful tool than **nslookup**, but in the course of a typical network administrator's day, the minor limitations of **nslookup** are unlikely to be too much of a factor. Instead, **dig** is often simply the tool of choice for DNS information and troubleshooting on UNIX, Linux, or Macintosh systems. Like **nslookup**, **dig** can be used to perform simple name-resolution requests. Listing 12.18 shows the output from this process.

Listing 12.18 Output from a Name Resolution Request on the Domain examcram.com Performed with **dig**

```
; <<>> DiG 8.2 <<>> examcram.com
;; res options: init recurs defnam dnsrch
;; got answer:
;; ->>HEADER<<- opcode: QUERY, status: NOERROR, id: 4
;; flags: qr rd ra; QUERY: 1, ANSWER: 1, AUTHORITY: 2, ADDITIONAL: 0
;; QUERY SECTION:
;;      examcram.com, type = A, class = IN

;; ANSWER SECTION:
examcram.com.          7h33m IN A     63.240.93.157

;; AUTHORITY SECTION:
examcram.com.          7h33m IN NS     usrxdns1.pearsontc.com.
examcram.com.          7h33m IN NS     oldtxdns2.pearsontc.com.

;; Total query time: 78 msec
;; FROM: localhost.localdomain to SERVER: default — 209.53.4.130
;; WHEN: Sat Oct 16 20:21:24 2004
;; MSG SIZE  sent: 30  rcvd: 103
```

As you can see, dig provides a variety of information in the basic output, more so than nslookup. Administrators can gain information from three key areas of the output: the Answer Section, the Authority Section, and the last four lines of the output.

The Answer Section of the output provides the name of the domain or host being resolved, along with its IP address. The "A" in the results line indicates the record type being resolved. In this case it is an Alias record, the standard type of DNS record used to define IP address to hostname resolutions.

The Authority Section provides information on the authoritative DNS servers for the domain against which the resolution request was performed. This information can be useful in determining whether the correct DNS servers are considered authoritative for a domain.

The last four lines of the output, which don't have a section name, show how long the name resolution request took to process, in this case 78 milliseconds, and the IP address of the DNS server that performed the resolution. It also shows the date and time of the request and the size of the packets sent and received.

The **host** Command

The host command is used on Linux/UNIX systems to perform a reverse or a forward lookup on an IP address. A reverse lookup involves looking up an IP address and resolving the hostname from that. Users running Microsoft Windows operating systems could use the nslookup command to perform a reverse lookup on an IP address, and Linux users can use the host command or nslookup.

Following is an example of the host command:

```
host 24.67.108.119
```

The command would return the hostname associated with the IP address 24.67.108.119. For example, the host command would return www.justmakeiteasy.com if that hostname were associated with 24.67.108.119.

The **route** Utility

The route utility is an often-used and handy tool. Using the route command, you can display and modify the routing table on your Windows or Linux systems. Figure 12.14 shows the output from a route print command on a Windows system.

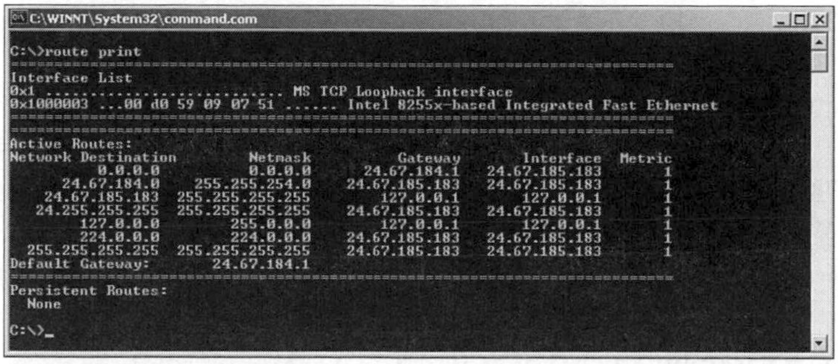

Figure 12.14   The output from a **route print** command on a Windows system.

> **NOTE: Linux and the** route **Command**   The discussion here focuses on the
> Windows route command, but other operating systems have equivalent commands.
> On a Linux system, for example, the command is also route, but the usage and
> switches are different.

In addition to displaying the routing table, the Windows version of the route command has a number of other switches, detailed in Table 12.10. For complete information about all the switches available with the route command in Windows
systems, use the command route at the command line. To see a list of the route
command switches on a Linux system, use the command route --help.

Table 12.10   Switches for the **route** Command in Windows

Switch	Description
add	Enables you to add a route to the routing table.
delete	Enables you to remove a route from the routing table.
change	Enables you to modify an existing route.
-p	When used with the add command, -p makes the route persistent. If the -p switch is not used when a route is added, the route is lost upon reboot.
print	Enables you to view the routing table of the system.
-f	Removes all gateway entries from the routing table.

> **TIP: Know the Command Output**   On the Network+ exam, you will be asked
> to identify the output from a given command. It is also highly likely that you will
> be asked to interpret the information provided by a command.

Summary

Knowing how to troubleshoot network connectivity is an important part of a network administrator's role. Fortunately, many utilities are designed to make the process of determining and correcting connectivity issues easier. The most common utilities for this type of troubleshooting include `ping`, `ipconfig`, `ifconfig`, `tracert`, `traceroute`, `nbtstat`, `mtr Arp`, `arp ping`, `route`, `nslookup`, `host`, and `netstat`.

In addition to knowing what utility to use and where, you need to interpret the output from those commands. This ability allows you to identify configuration problems with a system, the network to which it is attached, and even remote hosts on other networks.

The tools discussed in this chapter represent an important part of any network administrator's toolbox. You will find that your knowledge of these utilities will prove to be useful for much more than just passing the CompTIA Network+ exam.

Exam Preparation Tasks

Review All the Key Topics

Review the most important topics in the chapter, noted with the Key Topics icon in the outer margin of the page. Table 12.11 lists a reference of these key topics and the page numbers on which each is found.

Table 12.11   Key Topics for Chapter 12

Key Topic Element	Description	Page Number
Figure 12.1	A successful `ping` request	433
Figure 12.2	A failed `ping` request	434
Table 12.1	`ping` switches on a Windows Vista system	434
Table 12.2	`traceroute` utility commands	439
Figure 12.3	A successful `traceroute` command in a Windows system	440
Figure 12.4	A failed `traceroute` command from a Windows system	440
Table 12.3	Switches for `tracert`	441
Figure 12.5	An ARP cache	446
Table 12.4	Commonly used `arp` command switches	446

Table 12.11   Key Topics for Chapter 12

Key Topic Element	Description	Page Number
Figure 12.6	A third-party `arp ping` utility	448
Figure 12.7	Output from a `netstat` command	449
Table 12.5	`netstat` switches on Windows	449
Figure 12.8	Output from the `netstat -r` command	450
Table 12.6	`nbtstat` switches	455
Figure 12.9	The output from the `nbtstat -r` command	455
Figure 12.10	Output from the `ipconfig /all` command	457
Table 12.7	Commonly Used `ipconfig` Switches	458
Table 12.8	Common troubleshooting symptoms that `ipconfig` can help solve	459
Figure 12.11	Output from an `ifconfig` command on a Linux system	460
Figure 12.12	Output from the `nslookup` command	462
Table 12.9	`nslookup` switches in Interactive Mode	462
Figure 12.13	Output from `dig` command on a Linux system	465
Figure 12.14	Output from a `route print` command on a Windows system	467
Table 12.10	Switches for the `route` Command in Windows	467

Define Key Terms

Define the following key terms from this chapter, and check your answers in the Glossary.

- traceroute
- ipconfig
- ifconfig
- ping
- arp ping
- arp

- `nslookup`

- `host`

- `dig`

- `mtr`

- `route`

- `nbtstat`

- `netstat`

Apply Your Knowledge

Exercise 12.1 Using the `ipconfig` command

By using the troubleshooting commands, you can reinforce the knowledge you need for the Network+ exam. In this exercise you use a Windows Server 2003 system to view the information provided by the `ipconfig` command. The exercise also works on other versions of Windows, including Windows 2000, Windows XP, and Windows Vista.

Estimated time: 10 minutes

1. Open a command prompt by selecting Start, Run and then typing **cmd** in the Run dialog box. Click OK, and a command prompt dialog box opens.

2. At the command prompt, type ipconfig. Note what information is displayed.

3. At the command prompt, type ipconfig /all. Note what additional information is displayed.

4. Determine whether you use DHCP by looking for the entry for the DHCP server. If you use DHCP, when was your address assigned? How much time is left on the lease?

5. If you use DHCP, attempt to renew the address lease by using the command `ipconfig /renew`. Note whether you can renew the lease.

6. To see the updated lease information, type ipconfig /all. The date and time for the DHCP lease information should now be updated. Leave the command prompt dialog open. You can use it in the next exercise.

Exercise 12.2 Using the `ping` utility

In this exercise, you follow the `ping` troubleshooting sequence. How far you go depends on your network connectivity. If you can connect to the Internet, you should complete all the steps in this exercise.

Estimated time: 10 minutes

1. In the command prompt dialog, `ping` the local loopback of your system by using the command `ping 127.0.0.1`.

2. Determine your IP address by using the `ipconfig` command.

3. `ping` the IP address of your system by using the `ping <IP ADDRESS>` command.

4. Use the `ipconfig` command to determine the address of your default gateway and then `ping` it.

5. `ping` a remote host by IP address. Use the `ipconfig /all` to discover the IP address of your DNS server. If you can determine (from the address) that your DNS server is on a remote network, `ping` that.

6. If you have DNS capability (which is likely, if you connect to the Internet), you can also try to `ping` a remote host by its hostname (for example, `ping comptia.org`). Leave the command prompt dialog open. You can use it in the next exercise.

Exercise 12.3 Using the **arp** Command

In this exercise, you use the `arp` command to look at the local ARP cache and observe the process of the ARP cache being updated. As in the previous exercise, being connected to a network makes a big difference in the amount and variety of information displayed in this exercise.

Estimated time: 10 minutes

1. In the command prompt dialog, view the ARP cache on your local system by using the `arp -a` command. Note how many devices are listed in the ARP cache.

2. Determine the IP address of your default gateway by using the `ipconfig` command. Ping the IP address of your default gateway system. Does the first ping take longer than the subsequent pings? If so, why do you think it does? Immediately run the `ping` utility again. Is the first **ping** quicker than the first **ping** of the first attempt?

3. Using the `arp -a` command again, view the ARP cache. Note whether any entries have been added. Write down the IP address and MAC address of the default gateway; you'll use them later in the exercise.

4. By using the `ipconfig` command, determine the IP address of your default gateway and then **ping** the address.

5. Immediately view the ARP cache again. Note whether any new entries have been added.

6. Wait about 3 minutes and then view the ARP cache again. Is the entry for the default gateway still there?

7. Using the information you wrote down in step 3, add a static entry for your default gateway by using the following command:

```
arp -s <IP ADDRESS OF DEFAULT GATEWAY>
  MAC ADDRESS OF DEFAULT GATEWAY
```

For help with the syntax, type arp at the command line to display the help screen.

8. After you have successfully added the new entry, view the ARP cache. The static entry should now be listed.

9. Delete the static entry you just created by using the following command:

```
arp -d <IP ADDRESS OF DEFAULT GATEWAY>
```

10. View the ARP cache one last time to ensure that the static entry has been removed. Leave the command prompt dialog open. You can use it in the next exercise.

Exercise 12.4 Using the **tracert** utility

In this exercise, you use the tracert command to look at how a trace route works.

Estimated time: 10 minutes

1. In the command prompt dialog, ascertain the IP address of your DNS server by using the ipconfig /all command.

2. Trace the route to your DNS server by using the command tracert <ADDRESS OF DNS SERVER>. Note how many hops you are from your DNS server and how long the trip took.

3. Trace the route to the CompTIA web server by using the command tracert **www.comptia.org**. Note how many hops you are away from the web server and how long the trip took.

4. Use the same command as in step 3, but add the -d switch to the command line, as follows: tracert **www.comptia.org.com** -d. Note what changes in the output from the command.

Review Questions

You can find answers to the review questions in Appendix A, "Answers to Review Questions."

1. Which of the following TCP/IP utilities can be used to view routing tables on a Windows system? (Choose the two best answers.)
   a. netstat
   b. nbtstat
   c. route

   d. `ping`

   e. `tracert`

2. Which of the following commands can be used to purge and reload the remote cache name table?

   a. `nbtstat -R`

   b. `nbtstat -n`

   c. `nbtstat -r`

   d. `nbtstat -S`

3. You are trying to use the `tracert` command to determine the route a packet takes. You receive five successful hops, followed by several asterisks (*). What is the likely cause of the problem?

   a. The destination host is not online.

   b. The router at steps 4 or 5 has a problem.

   c. The router at steps 5 or 6 has a problem.

   d. The router at step 5 is not powered on.

4. Which of the following commands can be used to display the protocol statistics on a per-protocol basis?

   a. `netstat -S`

   b. `netstat -r`

   c. `netstat -R`

   d. `netstat -s`

   e. `netstat -a`

5. The following is output from which of the following commands?

```
Active Connections

Proto Local Address Foreign Address State
TCP     laptop:1026    127.0.0.1:50000 ESTABLISHED
TCP     laptop:50000   127.0.0.1:1026  ESTABLISHED
```

   a. `nbtstat`

   b. `netstat`

   c. `arp`

   d. `ipconfig`

6. You are trying to ping a remote host with the command `ping desertforme.co.uk`. The ping returns an Unknown Host error message. What is the cause of the problem?

   a. The remote host is not responding.

   b. The name of the destination computer cannot be resolved.

   c. The route to the destination computer is incorrect.

   d. WINS is not configured.

7. From your Linux system, you try unsuccessfully to ping a remote host on another network. What utility might you use to determine where the packet was dropped?

   a. `arp`

   b. `tracert`

    c. `traceroute`

    d. `nbtstat`

8. You troubleshoot a client connectivity problem in which a system cannot log on to the network. The client system uses the Linux operating system. Which of the following commands would you use to view the current TCP/IP configuration?

    a. `ipconfig`

    b. `ipconfig /all`

    c. `ifconfig`

    d. `config`

9. Which of the following switches is used on a Windows Server system to perform a continuous ping?

    a. `-c`

    b. `-d`

    c. `-t`

    d. `-ct`

10. Which of the following represents a reason to use `arp ping` over `ping`?

    a. Firewalls or other security measures may block Internet Control Message Protocol (ICMP) requests.

    b. `ping` cannot travel as far.

    c. `arp ping` enables for per protocol statistics.

    d. `ping` rejects CNAME references.

11. You troubleshoot a connectivity problem in which the user cannot connect to any systems on remote networks. Connectivity to systems on the local network appears to work correctly. Based on the following output from an `ipconfig /all` command, what is the most likely cause of the problem?

```
C:\>ipconfig /all
Windows 2000 IP Configuration
    Host Name . . . . . . . . . . . . : server
    Primary DNS Suffix  . . . . . . . : write
    Node Type . . . . . . . . . . . . : Broadcast
    IP Routing Enabled. . . . . . . . : Yes
    WINS Proxy Enabled. . . . . . . . : No
    DNS Suffix Search List. . . . . . : write
                                        ok.anyotherhost.net
Ethernet adapter Local Area Connection:

    Connection-specific DNS Suffix  . : ok.anyotherhost.net
    Description . . . . . . . . . . . : D-Link DFE-530TX PCI Fast Ethernet
    Physical Address. . . . . . . . . : 00-80-C8-E3-4C-BD
    DHCP Enabled. . . . . . . . . . . : Yes
    Autoconfiguration Enabled . . . . : Yes
    IP Address. . . . . . . . . . . . : 24.67.184.65
```

```
Subnet Mask . . . . . . . . . . . : 255.255.254.0
Default Gateway . . . . . . . . . :
DHCP Server . . . . . . . . . . . : 24.67.253.195
DNS Servers . . . . . . . . . . . : 24.67.253.195
                                    24.67.253.212
Lease Obtained.. . . . . : Thursday, February 07, 2002 3:42:00 AM
Lease Expires .. . . . . : Saturday, February 09, 2002 3:42:00 AM
```

    a. The DNS server information is missing.

    b. The node type is set to broadcast.

    c. The default gateway parameter is missing.

    d. DHCP is enabled.

12. Which utility is used to view NetBIOS over TCP/IP statistics?

    a. `ping -t`

    b. `netstat`

    c. `nbtstat`

    d. `arp`

    e. `tracert`

13. Consider the following output from the `netstat -e` command. What might you determine from this information?

```
                       Received           Sent
Bytes                  17412385        40237510
Unicast packets           79129           85055
Non-unicast packets         693             254
Discards                      0               0
Errors                  2233654               0
Unknown protocols           306
```

    a. The NIC in this system is faulty.

    b. This is normal.

    c. Errors are generated on the network but not by this system.

    d. This system is generating errors.

14. Which utility would produce the following output?

```
6 55 ms 27 ms 42 ms so-1-0-0.XL1.VAN1.NET [152.63.137.130]
7 55 ms 41 ms 28 ms 0.so-7-0-0.TL1.VAN1.NET [152.63.138.74]
8 55 ms 55 ms 55 ms 0.so-2-0-0.TL1.SAC1.NET [152.63.8.1]
9 83 ms 55 ms 55 ms 0.so-7-0-0.XL1.SAC1.NET [152.63.53.249]
10 82 ms 41 ms 55 ms POS6-0.BR5.SAC1.NET [152.63.52.225]
11 55 ms 68 ms 55 ms uu-gw.ip.att.net [192.205.32.125]
12 55 ms 68 ms 69 ms tbr2-p013802.ip.att.net [12.122.11.229]
13 96 ms 69 ms 82 ms tbr1-p012801.ip.att.net [12.122.11.225]
14 82 ms 82 ms 69 ms tbr2-p012402.ip.att.net [12.122.11.221]
15 82 ms 83 ms 68 ms gbr2-p20.ip.att.net [12.122.11.254]
16 55 ms 69 ms 69 ms gbr1-p60.ip.att.net [12.122.1.109]
```

```
17 123 ms  96 ms  96 ms  gbr1-p30.ip.att.net [12.122.2.142]
18 83 ms  96 ms  97 ms  gar1-p360.ip.att.net [12.123.142.21]
19 96 ms  82 ms  96 ms  12.127.141.26
20 124 ms  96 ms  96 ms  216.119.107.2
21 124 ms  82 ms  110 ms  216.119.103.72
```

   a. nbtstat -R

   b. netstat -R

   c. arp -s

   d. tracert

15. Examine the following output from the tracert command. What, if anything, is wrong with this trace route?

```
C:\>tracert 24.7.70.37
Tracing route to c1-pos6-3.sttlwa1.home.net [24.7.70.37] over a maximum of
30 hops:
   1    30 ms   20 ms    20 ms   24.67.184.1
   2    20 ms   20 ms    30 ms   rd1ht-ge3-0.ok.shawcable.net [24.67.224.7]
   3    50 ms   30 ms    30 ms   rc1wh-atm0-2-1.vc.shawcable.net
[204.209.214.193]
   4    50 ms   30 ms    30 ms   rc2wh-pos15-0.vc.shawcable.net
[204.209.214.90]
   5    30 ms   40 ms    30 ms   rc2wt-pos2-0.wa.shawcable.net [66.163.76.37]
   6    30 ms   40 ms    30 ms   c1-pos6-3.sttlwa1.home.net [24.7.70.37]
Trace complete.
```

   a. The IP address is invalid.

   b. There is nothing wrong with this output.

   c. The trace was not completed.

   d. The maximum hop count has restricted the number of hops reported.

16. Examine the following output from the ping command. Based on this information, what are you likely to check first in your troubleshooting process? (Choose the two best answers.)

```
Pinging 24.67.54.233 with 32 bytes of data:
Destination host unreachable.
Destination host unreachable.
Destination host unreachable.
Destination host unreachable.
Ping statistics for 24.67.54.233:
    Packets: Sent = 4, Received = 0, Lost = 4 (100% loss),
Approximate round trip times in milliseconds:
    Minimum = 0ms, Maximum =  0ms, Average =  0ms
```

   a. That the remote host is online

   b. The default gateway setting of the system

   c. The routing table on the system

   d. The patch cable for the system

17. Which of the following tools can you use to perform manual DNS lookups on a Linux system? (Choose two.)

- **a.** `dig`
- **b.** `nslookup`
- **c.** `tracert`
- **d.** `dnslookup`

18. Which of the following commands would generate a Request Timed Out error message?

- **a.** `ping`
- **b.** `netstat`
- **c.** `ipconfig`
- **d.** `nbtstat`

19. Which of the following commands would you use to add a static entry to the ARP table of a Windows system?

- **a.** `arp -a IP ADDRESS> <MAC ADDRESS`
- **b.** `arp -s MAC ADDRESS> <IP ADDRESS`
- **c.** `arp -s IP ADDRESS> <MAC ADDRESS`
- **d.** `arp -i IP ADDRESS> <MAC ADDRESS`

20. Which command created the following output?

```
Server:  nen.bx.ttfc.net
Address:  209.55.4.155

Name:    examcram.com
Address:  63.240.93.157
```

- **a.** `nbtstat`
- **b.** `ipconfig`
- **c.** `tracert`
- **d.** `nslookup`

This chapter covers CompTIA Network+ objectives 4.2, 4.3, 4.4, 5.2, and 5.3. Upon completion of this chapter, you will be able to answer the following questions:

- What are the types of management documentation?

- What are the features of wiring schematics?

- How are the network monitoring utilities used?

- What is the function of network scanners?

- What is the difference between IDS and IPS systems?

CHAPTER 13

Network Management Tools and Documentation Procedures

Quality computer wiring is essential to a reliable computer network system. If your network wiring is not installed correctly or in a haphazard manner, chances are good that the network is not getting an appropriate level of performance and reliability. Although the physical placement of cabling is important, equally important is documenting that cabling.

Administrators have several daily tasks, and new ones crop up all the time. In this environment, tasks such as documentation sometimes fall to the background. This is when it is important to understand why administrators need to spend their valuable time sitting down writing and reviewing documentation. A number of advantages exist to having a well-documented network, including the following:

- **Troubleshooting**—When something goes wrong on the network, including the wiring, up-to-date documentation serves as an importance reference to guide the troubleshooting effort. The documentation can save time isolating potential locations of an issue and thereby save money.

- **Training new administrators**—In many networks, new administrators are hired and old ones leave. In this scenario, documentation is critical. New administrators do not have the time to try to figure out where cabling is run, what cabling is used, potential trouble spots, and so forth. By having up-to-date information, new administrators can quickly see the layout of the network.

- **Contractors and consultants**—From time to time, consultants and contractors might need to visit the network. This can be done to make future network recommendations for the network or to add wiring or other components. In such cases, up-to-date documentation is required. If it is not there, it is much more difficult for these people to do their jobs and would likely take more time and, therefore, more money.

Recognizing the importance of documentation is one thing, knowing what to document and when to document is another. In this chapter we look at types of management documentation and how network administrators use them.

Documentation Management

Good quality network documentation does not happen by accident; rather, it requires some careful planning. When creating network documentation, it is necessary to keep in mind who you are creating the documentation for and that it is a communication tool. It is used to take technical information and present it in a manner that can be understood by someone new to the network. When planning network documentation, it is important to decide on what you need to document.

> **NOTE: Write It Down**   Imagine you have just taken over a network as administrator. What information would you like to see? This is often a clear gauge of what to include your network documentation.

All networks are different and so, too, will be the documentation required for each network. However, some elements will always be included in quality documentation:

- **Wiring layout**—Network wiring can be confusing. Much of the network wiring is hidden behind walls and ceilings, making it hard to know where wiring is and what wiring is used on the network. This makes it critical to have up-to-date network wiring documentation.

- **Network topology**—Networks can be complicated, and if someone new looks over the network, it is important to document the entire topology. This includes both the wired and wireless topologies. The network topology documentation typically consists of a diagram or diagrams labeling all critical components used to create the network. These diagrams include such components as routers, switches, hubs, gateways, and firewalls.

- **Server configuration**—A single network typically uses multiple servers spread over a large geographical area. Documentation must include schematic drawings of where servers are located on the network and the services each provides. This would also include server function, server FQDN, server IP address, OS and software information, and the like. This is all the information on servers that you need to manage or administer them.

- **Key applications**—Documentation also needs to include all key applications used on the network. This will includes up–to-date information on their updates, vendors, installation dates, and so on.

- **Network services**—Network services are a key ingredient for all networks. A detailed account of services such as such as DNS, DHCP, and RAS is an important part of documentation. Documentation should include a reference of which server maintains which network service. You should describe in detail how each server is configured and structured.

■ **Network procedures**—Documentation should include information on network policy and procedures. This includes many elements ranging from who can and cannot access the server room, to network firewalls, protocols, passwords, physical security, and so on.

■ **Baselines**—Network documentation can also include the results of baseline testing. For example, after a performance baseline is completed, the results can be documented and stored for later comparison.

Wiring Schematics

Network wiring schematics are an important part of network documentation particularly for midsize to large networks where the cabling is complex. For such networks it becomes increasingly difficult to visualize network cabling and even harder to explain it to someone else. A number of software tools can help document network wiring, but they all enable administrators to clearly detail network wiring. Some examples of this software include Microsoft Visio, SmartDraw, and SolarWinds LAN surveyor. Many of these applications have trial versions that you can download.

Several types of wiring schematics exist. They can be general, as shown in Figure 13.1, or they can include a detailed schematic reference, as shown in Figure 13.2 and Table 13.1.

Table 13.1 Wiring Schematic Reference Sample

Cable	Description	Vendor	Installation Notes
1	Cat5E 350MHz plenum rated cable	King Wiring 350-777-5656 Purchased January 2009.	Cable runs 50ft from the MDF to IDF. Cable placed through ceiling and through a mechanical room. Cable was installed 01/15/2009 upgrading a nonplenum Cat5 cable.
2	Cat5E 350MHz STP cable	King Wiring 350-777-5656 Purchased February 2008.	Horizontal cable runs 45ft to 55ft from IDF to wall jack. Cat5E replaced Cat5 cable February 2008. Section of cable runs through ceiling and above fluorescent lights.

Table 13.1   Wiring Schematic Reference Sample

Cable	Description	Vendor	Installation Notes
3	Cat 5E 350MHz UTP cable	King Wiring 350-777-5656 Purchased June 2007.	All patch cable RJ-45 connectors were attached in-house. Patch cable connecting printer runs 5ft from wall jack to printer.
4	8.3 micron core/125 micron cladding single mode fiber cable	King Wiring 350-777-5656 Purchased June 2007.	Connecting fiber cable runs 2 kilometers between the primary and secondary buildings.

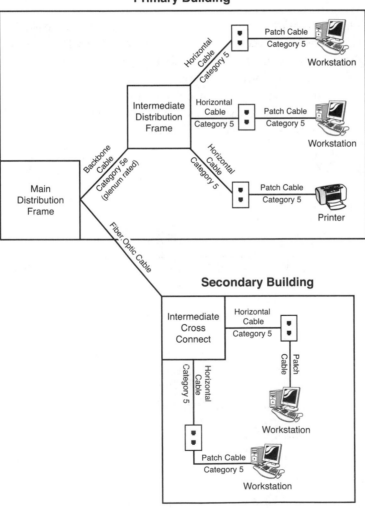

Figure 13.1   General wiring schematic.

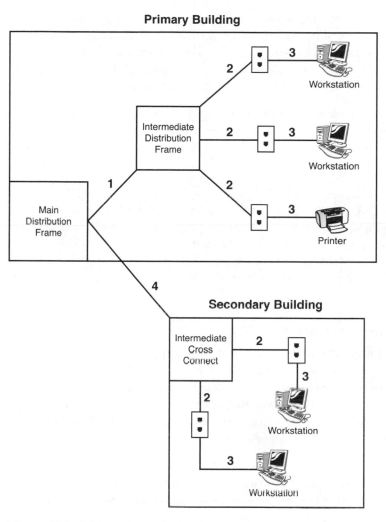

Figure 13.2   Wiring schematic that corresponds to Table 13.1.

Figure 13.1 and Figure 13.2 provide a simplified look at network wiring schematics. Imagine how complicated these diagrams would look on a network with 1, 2, or even 6,000 computers. Quality network documentation software makes this easier, but still the task of network wiring can be a large one for administrators. When documenting wiring, administrators need to ensure that someone could pick up the diagrams and have a good idea of the network wiring.

You might consider documenting network wiring to be a waste of your time. You might, that is, until you need to troubleshoot some random network problems. Without any network wiring schematics, the task will be frustrating and time consuming. Even with simplified information provided in Figure 13.2 and Table 13.1, it is possible to evaluate the network wiring and make recommendations.

In the hypothetical information provided in Figure 13.2 and Table 13.1, several potential problems exist with the network wiring. Any administrator could walk in and review the network documentation and isolate the potential problems. Now it's your turn.

NOTE: Time to Update   Network wiring schematics are a work in progress. Although changes to wiring do not happen daily, they do occur when the network expands or old cabling is replaced. It is important to remember that when changes occur to the network, the schematics have to be updated to reflect the changes. Out-of-date schematics can be frustrating to work with.

Physical and Logical Network Diagrams

In addition to the wiring schematics, documentation should also include diagrams of the physical and logical network design. Recall from Chapter 1, "Introduction to Networking," network topologies can be defined on a physical level or a logical level. The *physical topology* refers to how a network is physically constructed—that is, how it looks. The *logical topology* refers to how a network looks to the devices that use it—in other words, how it functions.

Network infrastructure documentation won't be reviewed daily; however, this documentation is essential for someone unfamiliar with the network to manage or troubleshoot the network. When it comes to documenting the network, you need to document all aspects of the infrastructure. This includes the physical hardware, physical structure, protocols, and software used.

Physical Network Documentation

The physical documentation of the network would include such elements as

- **Cabling information**—A visual description of all the physical communication links, including all cabling, cable grades, cable lengths, WAN cabling, and so on.

- **Servers**—The physical network diagram would include the server names and IP addresses, types of servers, and domain membership.

- **Network devices**—The physical diagram must include the location of the devices on the network. This would include the printers, hubs, switches, routers, gateways, and so on.

- **Wide area network**—The physical network also includes the location and devices of the WAN network and components.

- **User information**—The diagram can include some user information, such as the number of local and remote users.

Figure 13.3 shows a diagram of a physical segment of a network.

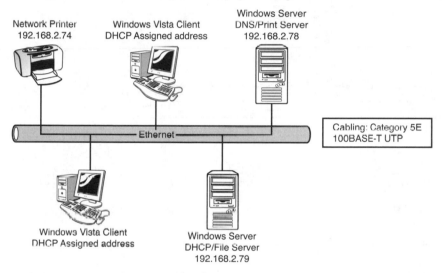

Figure 13.3   Physical network.

Networks are dynamic and changes can happen regularly. The physical network diagrams have to be updated as well. Organizations have different policies and procedures on how often updates should occur. A general rule is that the diagram should be updated whenever significant changes are made to the network, such as the addition of a bridge, change in protocols, or the addition of a new server. These changes impact how the network operates, and the documentation should reflect the changes.

NOTE: Document Change   Documentation should be updated periodically and each time a major change is made to the network. This includes the addition of hardware or setting changes.

Logical Network Documentation

The logical network refers to the direction that data actually flows on the network within the physical topology. The logical diagram is not intended to focus on the hardware of the network but rather how data flows through that hardware. In practice, the physical and logical topologies can be the same. In the case of the bus physical topology, data travels along the length of the cable from one computer to the next. So, the diagram for the physical and logical bus would be the same. Figure 13.4 shows the physical and logical bus.

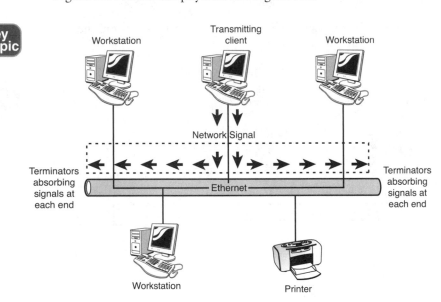

Figure 13.4   Physical and logical bus topology.

This is not always the case. For example, a topology can be in the physical shape of a star, but data is passed in a logical ring. The function of data travel is performed inside a switch in a ring formation. So the physical diagram would appear to be a star, but the logical diagram shows data flowing in a ring formation from one computer to the next. Simply put, looking at a physical diagram it is difficult to tell the way in which data is flowing on the network.

In today's network environments, the star topology is a common network implementation. Ethernet uses a physical star topology but a logical bus topology. In the center of the physical Ethernet star topology is a hub or switch. What happens inside this switch defines the logical bus topology. The switch passes data between ports as if they were on an Ethernet bus segment.

In addition to data flow, logical diagrams can include additional elements, such as the network domain architecture, server roles, protocols used, and so on. Figure 13.5 shows how a logical topology can look in the network documentation.

TIP: Logical Topology   The logical topology of a network identifies the logical paths that data signals travel over the network. Remember this for the Network+ exam.

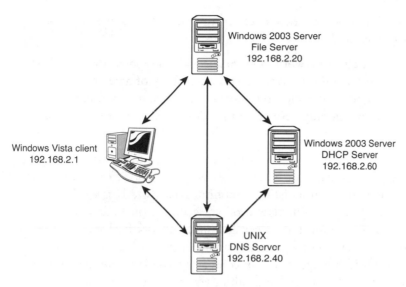

Figure 13.5   Logical topology diagram.

Baselines

Baselines play an integral part in network documentation because they provide the capability to monitor the overall performance of the entire network. In simple terms, a *baseline* is a measure of performance that indicates how hard the network is working and where network resources are spent. The purpose of a baseline is to provide a basis for comparison. For example, you can compare the performance results of the network taken in March to one taken in June, or from one year to the next. More commonly, you would compare the baseline information at a time when the network is having a problem to information recorded when the network was operating with greater efficiency. Such comparisons help you determine if there has been a problem with the system, such as degrading performance, and how significant that problem is and how it impacts users.

To be of any use, baselining is not a one-time task; rather, baselines should be taken periodically to provide an accurate comparison. You should take an initial baseline after the network is set up and operational and then again when major changes are made to the network. Even if no changes are made to the network, periodic baselining can prove useful as a means to determine whether the network is still operating correctly.

All network operating systems (NOS), including Windows, MAC OS, UNIX, and Linux have built-in support for network monitoring. In addition many third-party software packages are available for detailed network monitoring. The system-monitoring tools provided in a NOS give you the means to take performance baselines for either the entire network or an individual segment within the network. Because of the different functions of these two baselines, they are referred to as a *system baseline* and a *component baseline*.

To create a network baseline, network monitors provide a graphical display of network statistics. Network administrators can choose a variety of network measurements to track and use these statistics to perform routine troubleshooting tasks, such as locating a malfunctioning network card, a downed server, or a denial of service (DoS) attack.

Collecting network statistic information is a process referred to as *capturing*. Administrators can capture statistics on all elements of the network. For baseline purposes, one of the most common statistics to monitor is bandwidth usage. By reviewing bandwidth statistics, administrators can see where the bulk of network bandwidth is used. Then administrators can adapt the network for bandwidth use. If too much bandwidth is used by a particular application, administrators can actively control its bandwidth usage. Without comparing baselines, however, it is difficult to see what is normal network bandwidth usage and unusual network bandwidth use.

TIP: Baselines   Remember for the Network+ exam that to provide an effective comparison, baselines need to be performed under the same conditions. If not, the results are not trustworthy.

Policies, Procedures, Configurations, and Regulations

Well-functioning networks are characterized by policies, procedures, and documented configurations. Policies, procedures, and configurations are unique to every network, so every organization should have clear documentation for their network.

Policy Documentation

By definition, policies refer to an organization's documented rules regarding what is to be done, or not done, and why. Policies dictate who can and cannot access particular network resources, server rooms, backup tapes, and so on.

Although networks might have different policies, depending on their needs, some common policies include the following:

- **Network Usage Policy**—Specifies who can use network resources such as PCs, printers, scanners, and remote connections. In addition to stating who can use these resources, the usage policy dictates what can be done with these resources after they are accessed. For example, the policy might state that no outside systems will be networked without permission from the network administrator.

- **Internet Usage Policy**—Specifies the rules for Internet use on the job. Typically, usage should be primarily focused on business-related tasks. The policy might state that incidental personal use is allowed during specified times.

- **Email Usage Policy**—Emphasizes that email must follow the same code of conduct as expected in any other form of written or face-to-face communication. All emails are property of the company and can be accessed by the company. Personal emails should be erased right away.

- **Personal Software Policy**—Outlines what software, if any, users can load onto the network or personal computer. These policies typically dictate that no outside software should be installed on network computer systems. All software installations must be approved by the network administrator.

- **User Account Policy**—Typically states that users are responsible for keeping their password and account information secret. All staff are required to log off their systems when they finish using them. Attempting to log on to the network with another user account is considered a serious violation.

- **Ownership Policy**—Typically states that the company owns all data, including email, voicemail, and Internet usage logs, of users and reserves the right to inspect these at any time.

This list is just a snapshot of the policies that guide the behavior for administrators and network users. Network policies should be clearly documented and available to network users. Often, these policies are reviewed with new staff members or new administrators. Policies are reviewed and updated regularly. As they are updated, they are rereleased to network users.

TIP: Policy Making   For the Network+ exam, remember that network policies dictate network rules and provide the guidelines for network conduct.

Network Procedure Documentation

Network procedures differ from policies in that they identify the way in which tasks are to be performed. For example, each network administrator has backup procedures identifying the time of day backups are done, how often they are done, and where they are stored. A number of procedures apply to networks for practical reasons but perhaps more important for security reasons.

Administrators have to be aware of several procedures when on the job. The number and exact type of procedure depends on the network, the organization, or even the network administrator. The overall goal of the network is to ensure uniformity and ensure that network tasks follow a framework. Without this procedural framework, different administrators might approach tasks differently and cause confusion on the network.

Network procedures can include the following:

- **Backup procedures**—These procedures identify how all backups are to be performed, who can perform them, and who can use them for recovery purposes. They might also include the types of backup such as full, incremental, or differential, and at what frequency these backup types are done. So the backup policy can dictate that a full backup is to be done Monday evenings with incremental backups done Wednesdays, Thursdays, and Fridays.

- **Procedures for adding new users**—When new users are added to a network, administrators typically have to follow certain guidelines to ensure that users have access to what they need but no more. One such procedure might include the principle of lease privilege. This states that users are assigned the minimum privileges to do their jobs—nothing more, nothing less.

- **Security procedures**—Some of the more critical procedures involve security. These procedures identify security monitoring, security researching, and applying security updates, and what the administrator must do if security breaches occur.

- **Network monitoring procedures**—The network needs to be constantly monitored. This includes reviewing such things as bandwidth, application errors, network operating system updates, and the like.

- **Software procedures**—All software needs to be monitored and updated periodically. Documented procedures dictate when, how often, by whom, and why these updates are done.

- **Procedures for reporting violations**—From time to time, users do not follow outlined network policies. This is why documented procedures should exist to handle the violations properly. These policies can include a first verbal warning followed by written reports and account lockouts.

- **Remote access procedures**—Many workers access the network remotely. This remote access is granted and maintained using a series of defined procedures. These can dictate the time remote users can access the network, how long they can access, and what they can access.

These represent just a few of the policies administrators must follow on the job. It is important that all these procedures are documented well and are accessible. To be effective, all network procedures must be reviewed and updated as needed.

Configuration Documentation

Another critical form of documentation is configuration documentation. Many administrators think they could never forget the configuration of a router, server, or switch, but it happens more often than not. Although it's often a thankless, time-consuming task, documenting the network hardware and software configurations is critical for continued network functionality.

Two primary types of network configuration documentation are required: software documentation and hardware documentation. Both types of documentation include all configuration information so that should a computer or other hardware fail, both the hardware and software can be replaced and reconfigured. The documentation is important because often the administrator who configured the software or hardware is not available, and someone else has to re-create the configuration using nothing but the documentation. To be effective in this case, the documentation must be as current as possible. Older configuration information might not help.

Regulations

The terms *regulation* and *policy* are often used interchangeably; however, there is a difference. As previously mentioned, policies are written by an organization for its employees. Regulations are actual legal restrictions with legal consequences. These regulations are not set by the organizations but by applicable laws in the area. The following is an example of network regulations:

> Transmission, distribution, uploading, posting, or storage of any material in violation of any applicable law or regulation is prohibited. This includes, without limitation, material protected by copyright, trademark, trade secret, or other intellectual property right used without proper authorization; material kept in violation of state laws or industry regulations such as Social Security numbers or credit card numbers, and material that is obscene, defamatory, libelous, unlawful, harassing, abusive, threatening, harmful, vulgar constitutes an illegal threat, violates export control laws, hate propaganda, fraudulent material or fraudulent activity, invasive of privacy or publicity rights, profane, indecent or otherwise objectionable material of any kind or nature. You may not transmit, distribute, or store material that contains a virus, "Trojan Horse," adware or spyware, corrupted data, or any software or information to promote or utilize software or any of Network Solutions services to deliver unsolicited email. You further agree not to transmit any material that encourages conduct that could constitute a criminal offense, gives rise to civil liability or otherwise violates any applicable local, state, national, or international law or regulation.

TIP: Regulations Are the Law   For this exam and in real-life networking, remember that regulations are often enforceable by law.

Monitoring the Network to Identify Performance

When networks were smaller, and few stretched beyond the confines of a single location, network management was a simple task. In today's complex, multisite, hybrid networks, however, the task of maintaining and monitoring network devices and servers has become a complicated but essential part of the network administrator's role. Nowadays, the role of network administrator often stretches beyond the physical boundary of the server room and reaches every node and component on the network. Whether an organization has 10 computers on a single segment or a multisite network with several thousand devices attached, the server administrator must monitor all network devices, protocols, and usage—preferably from a central location.

Given the sheer number and diversity of devices, software, and systems on any network, it is clear why network management is such an important consideration. Even though a robust network management strategy can improve administrator productivity and reduce downtime, many companies choose to neglect network management because of the time involved in setting up the system or because of the associated costs. If these companies understood the potential savings, they would realize that neglecting network management could lead to a huge monetary loss.

Network management and network monitoring are essentially methods to control, configure, and monitor devices on a network. Imagine a scenario in which you are a network administrator working out of your main office in Spokane, WA, and you have satellite offices in New York, Dallas, Vancouver, and London. Network management enables you to access systems in the remote locations or have the systems notify you when something goes awry. In essence, network management is about seeing beyond your current boundary and acting on what you see.

Network management is not one thing. Rather, it's a collection of tools, systems, and protocols that, when used together, provide the ability to perform tasks such as reconfiguring a network card in the next room or installing an application in the next state.

NOTE: IDS and IPS   The objectives included in this chapter identified IPS and IDS. However, these topics are included in Chapter 14, "Network Access Security," with a discussion of firewalls.

The capabilities demanded from network management vary somewhat among organizations, but essentially, several key types of information and functionality are required, such as fault detection and performance monitoring. Here are some of the types of information and functions that network management tools can provide:

- **Fault detection**—One of the most important aspects of network management is knowing if anything is not working or is not working correctly. Network management tools can detect and report on a variety of faults on the network. Given the number of devices that constitute a typical network, determining faults without these tools could be an impossible task. Additionally, network management tools can have the capability to not only detect the faulty device but also shut it down. This means that if a network card is malfunctioning, you can disable it remotely. When a network spans a large area, fault detection becomes even more invaluable because it enables you to be alerted to network faults and to manage them, thereby reducing downtime.

- **Performance monitoring**—Another feature of network management is the ability to monitor the performance of the network. Performance monitoring is an essential consideration that provides you with some crucial information. Specifically, performance monitoring can provide network usage statistics and user usage trends. This type of information is essential when you plan network capacity and growth. Monitoring performance also helps you to determine if any performance-related concerns exist, such as whether the network can adequately support the current user base.

NOTE: Performance Monitoring   Performance monitoring can be included with baselines. For more information on this, see the preceding baseline section.

- **Security monitoring**—Any good server administrator has a touch of paranoia built into his or her personality. A network management system provides the capability to monitor who is on the network, what they are doing on the network, and how long they have been doing it. More important, in an environment in which corporate networks are increasingly exposed to outside sources, the ability to identify and react to potential security threats is a priority. Reading log files to learn of an attack is a poor second to knowing that an attack is currently in progress and reacting accordingly.

- **Remote management and configuration**—Want to reconfigure or shut down the server located in Australia? Remote management and configuration are key parts of the network management strategy, enabling you to manage huge multisite locations centrally.

Many tools are available to help monitor the network and ensure that the entire network is functioning properly. Some tools, like the packet sniffer, can monitor traffic for administrators and those wanting to obtain data that doesn't belong to them. In this section we look at several monitoring tools.

Throughput Testing

In the networking world, *throughput* refers to the rate of data delivery over a communication channel. In this case, throughput testers test the rate of data delivery over a network. Throughput is measured in bits per second (bps), for example,

100Mbps. Administrators need to be aware of exactly what the network is doing, so testing throughput is important. It might be that a high-speed network is not functioning with the expected level of throughput, and bottlenecks occur. Testing throughput is done periodically or after any large changes to the network, such as the installation of a new networkwide application or new server.

Any throughput tester is designed to quickly gather information about the network's functionality, and specifically, the average overall network throughput. Many software-based throughput testers are available online, both for free and for a fee. Figure 13.6 shows a software-based throughput tester.

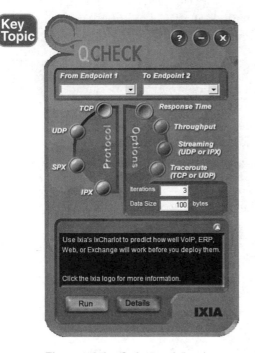

Figure 13.6 Software throughput tester.

As shown in Figure 13.6, throughput testers do not have to be complicated to be effective. To use it, enter the beginning point and then the destination point. The tester sends a predetermined number of data packets to the destination and reports on the throughput level. A throughput tester identifies how long it takes to send the data to the destination point and receive acknowledgment that the data was received. The results display in Kbps or Mbps. Table 13.2 shows the various data rate units.

Table 13.2 Data Rate Units

Data Transfer	Abbreviation	Rate
Kilobits per second	Kbps or Kbit/s	1000 bits per second
Megabit per second	Mbps or Mbit/s	1,000,000 bits per second
Gigabits per second	Gbps or Gbit/s	1,000,000,000 bits per second
Kilobytes per second	KBps	1000 bytes per second or 8 kilobits per second
Megabyte per second	MBps	1,000,000 bytes per second or 8 megabits per second
Gigabyte	GBps	1,000,000,000 bytes per second or 8 gigabits per second

Administrators can periodically conduct throughput tests and keep them on file to create a picture of network performance. If it is suspected that a problem exists with the network functionality, the administrator can compare a test with past performance to see exactly what is happening.

The terms *throughput* and *bandwidth* are often used interchangeably, but there is a difference. When we talk about measuring throughput, we measure the amount of data flow under real-world conditions. That is, measuring with possible EMI influences, heavy traffic loads, improper wiring, and even network collisions. Take all this into account, take a measurement, and you have the network throughput. Maximum bandwidth, on the other hand, refers to the amount of information that can be sent through a particular media under ideal conditions.

TIP: Know the Difference   For the Network+ exam, be sure you know the difference between throughput and bandwidth.

Port Scanners

A port scanner is a software-based security tool designed to search a network host for open ports on a TCP/IP based network. As a refresher, in a TCP/IP based network, a system can be accessed through one of 65536 available port numbers. Each network service is associated with a particular port. Table 13.3 shows some common protocols and associated ports.

Table 13.3 Some of the Most Common TCP/IP Suite Protocols and Their Port Assignments

Protocol	Port Assignment	TCP/UDP Service
FTP	20	TCP
FTP	21	TCP
SSH	22	TCP
Telnet	23	TCP

Table 13.3   Some of the Most Common TCP/IP Suite Protocols and Their Port Assignments

Protocol	Port Assignment	TCP/UDP Service
SMTP	25	TCP
DNS	53	UDP
TFTP	69	UDP
HTTP	80	TCP/UDP
POP3	110	TCP
NNTP	119	TCP
NTP	123	TCP
IMAP4	143	TCP
SNMP	161	UDP
HTTPS	443	TCP
DHCP	67	UDP
DHCP	68	UDP

NOTE: Ports   For the Network+ exam, be sure you can identify the ports used by the more common TCP/IP protocols.

These are just a few of the available ports, and the ports we would expect to be open and available. Many of the thousands of other ports are closed by default; however, many others, depending on the OS, are open by default. These are the ports that can cause us trouble. Like packet sniffers, port scanners can be used both by administrators and by hackers. Hackers use port scanners to try to find an open port that they can use to access a system. Port scanners are easily obtained on the Internet either for free or for a modest cost. After they are installed, the scanner probes a computer system running TCP/IP looking for a UDP or TCP that is open and listening.

When a port scanner is used, several port states might be reported:

- **Open/Listening**—The host sent a reply indicating that a service is listening on the port. There was a response from the port.

- **Closed or Denied or Not Listening**—No process is listening on that port. Access to this port will likely be denied.

- **Filtered or Blocked**—There was no reply from the host, meaning that the port is not listening or the port is secured and filtered.

- **Stealth**—In stealth mode ports are effectively invisible to port scanners.

NOTE: **For Your Protection**   Sometimes an ISP takes the initiative, often blocking specific traffic entering its network before it reaches its customers, or after leaving its customers before it exits its network. This is done to protect customers from well-known attacks.

Because hackers can potentially review the status of our ports, it is important that administrators are aware which ports are open and potentially vulnerable. As previously mentioned, many tools and utilities are available for this. The quickest way to get an overview of the ports used by the system and their status is to use the issue the `netstat -a` command from the command line. A sample of the printout from the `netstat -a` command and active connections for a computer system is shown in Listing 13.1. The output from a Windows XP system might look a little different, but the information would be the same.

Listing 13.1   Output from a **`netstat -a`** Command from a Windows Vista System

```
Proto   Local Address            Foreign Address         State
  TCP    0.0.0.0:135              mike-PC:0               LISTENING
  TCP    0.0.0.0:10114            mike-PC:0               LISTENING
  TCP    0.0.0.0:10115            mike-PC:0               LISTENING
  TCP    0.0.0.0:20523            mike-PC:0               LISTENING
  TCP    0.0.0.0:20943            mike-PC:0               LISTENING
  TCP    0.0.0.0:49152            mike-PC:0               LISTENING
  TCP    0.0.0.0:49153            mike-PC:0               LISTENING
  TCP    0.0.0.0:49154            mike-PC:0               LISTENING
  TCP    0.0.0.0:49155            mike-PC:0               LISTENING
  TCP    0.0.0.0:49156            mike-PC:0               LISTENING
  TCP    0.0.0.0:49157            mike-PC:0               LISTENING
  TCP    127.0.0.1:5354           mike-PC:0               LISTENING
  TCP    127.0.0.1:27015          mike-PC:0               LISTENING
  TCP    127.0.0.1:27015          mike-PC:49187           ESTABLISHED
  TCP    127.0.0.1:49187          mike-PC:27015           ESTABLISHED
  TCP    192.168.0.100:49190      206.18.166.15:http      CLOSED
  TCP    192.168.1.66:139         mike-PC:0               LISTENING
  TCP    [::]:135                 mike-PC:0               LISTENING
  TCP    [::]:445                 mike-PC:0               LISTENING
  TCP    [::]:2869                mike-PC:0               LISTENING
  TCP    [::]:5357                mike-PC:0               LISTENING
  TCP    [::]:10115               mike-PC:0               LISTENING
  TCP    [::]:20523               mike-PC:0               LISTENING
  TCP    [::]:49152               mike-PC:0               LISTENING
  TCP    [::]:49153               mike-PC:0               LISTENING
  TCP    [::]:49154               mike-PC:0               LISTENING
  TCP    [::]:49155               mike-PC:0               LISTENING
  TCP    [::]:49156               mike-PC:0               LISTENING
```

```
TCP     [::]:49157              mike-PC:0               LISTENING
UDP     0.0.0.0:123             *:*
UDP     0.0.0.0:500             *:*
UDP     0.0.0.0:3702            *:*
UDP     0.0.0.0:3702            *:*
```

As you can see from Listing 13.1, the system has many listening ports. Not all these suggest that a risk exists, but it does let us know that they might be vulnerable. To test for actual vulnerability, we use a port scanner. As an example, we can use a free online scanner to probe the system. Many free online scanning services are available. Although a network administrator might use these free online tools for curiosity, for real security testing, a quality scanner should be used.

NOTE: Scan Your System   To find out more about pot scanners and to conduct an online scan of your computer system, go to grc.com and use their ShieldsUP! utility.

TIP: Port Scanning   For the Network+ exam, remember that port scans identify closed, open, and listening ports and can be used by those intending on compromising security by finding open and unguarded ports.

Network Testing

When testing the network, administrators often perform three distinct types of tests: performance, load, and stress. These test names are sometimes used interchangeably, but although some overlap exists, they are different types of network tests, each with different outcome goals in mind.

Performance Testing

A performance test is, as the name suggests, all about measuring the current performance level of the network. The goal is to take ongoing performance tests and evaluate and compare them, looking for potential bottlenecks. For performance tests to be effective, they need to be taken under the same type of network load each time, or the comparison is not valid. That is, a performance test taken at 3:00 a.m. is going to be different from one taken at 3:00 p.m.

TIP: Performance Testing   On the Network+ exam, be prepared to identify the goal of performance testing, which is to establish baselines for the comparison of network functioning.

Load Testing

Load testing has some overlap with performance testing. Sometimes called volume or endurance testing, load tests involve artificially placing the network under a larger workload. For example, the network traffic can be increased throughout the entire network. After this is done, performance tests can be done on the network with the increased load. Load testing is sometimes done to see if there are bugs in the network that are not currently visible but that could become a problem as the network grows. For example, a company's mail server might work fine with the current network load, but if the network grew by 10%, the increased load could overwhelm the server. Load tests are all about finding a potential problem before it happens.

Performance tests and load tests are quite similar; however, the information outcomes are different. Performance tests identify the current level of network functioning for measurement and benchmarking purposes. Load tests are designed to give administrators a look into the future to determine if the current network infrastructure can handle the load.

> **TIP: Load or Performance**   For the Network+ exam, be prepared to identify the difference between performance and load tests. Specifically, performance tests are about the network functioning today, whereas load tests look forward to see if performance might be hindered in the future by growth or other changes to the network.

Stress Testing

Finally, we have stress testing. Whereas load tests do not try to break the system under intense pressure, stress tests sometimes do. They are used to push resources to the limit. Although these tests are not done often, they are necessary and, for administrators at least, entertaining. There are two clear goals of stress testing: the first is to see exactly what the network can handle. That is, where is its breaking point, which is useful to know in terms of network expansion. Second, stress testing enables administrators to test their backup and recovery procedures. If a test knocks network resources out, administrators can verify that their recovery procedures work, and the test enables them to observe network hardware failure. Stress tests assume that someday something will go wrong, and administrators will know exactly what to do when it happens.

Logging

In a network environment, all NOSs and most firewalls, proxy servers, and other network components have logging features. These logging features are essential for network administrators to review and monitor. Many types of logs can be used. In this section we review four of the most common: system, security, history, and events.

On a Windows server system, as with the other operating systems, events and occurrences are logged to files for later review. Windows server and desktop systems such as Vista/XP and 2000 use the Event Viewer to view many of the key log files. The logs in Event Viewer can find information on, for example, an error on the system or a security incident. Information is recorded into key log files, although you also see additional log files under certain conditions, such as if the system is a domain controller or is running a DHCP server application.

Security Logs

A system security log contains events related to security incidents, such as successful and unsuccessful logon attempts and failed resource access. Security logs are customizable, meaning that administrators can fine-tune exactly what they want to monitor. Some administrators choose to track nearly every security event on the system. Although this might be prudent, it often can cause huge log files that are too large and take up too much space. Figure 13.7 shows a Security log from a Windows system.

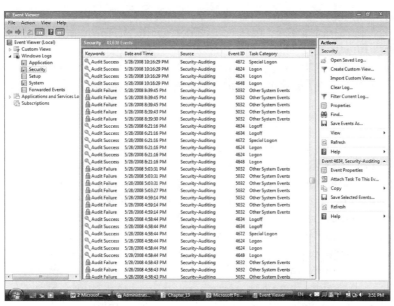

Figure 13.7   Windows Security log.

Notice in Figure 13.7 that there were some successful logons and logoffs. In a potential security breach, there would be some audit failures for logon or logoff attempts. To save space and prevent the log files from growing too big, administrators may choose to audit failed logon attempts, not successful ones.

Each event in a security log contains additional information to make it easy to get the details on the event. To do this, double-click any events listed in the security log. Additional information includes the following:

■ **Date**—The exact date the security event occurred.

- **Time**—The time the event occurred.

- **User**—The name of the user account that was tracked during the event.

- **Computer**—The name of the computer used when the event occurred.

- **Event ID**—The type of event that has occurred. This ID can get additional information about the particular event. Events can be anything from a logon on to logoff to a tracked OS crash.

To be effective, security logs should be reviewed regularly.

Application Logs

Application logs contain information logged by applications that run on a particular system and not just the operating system itself. Vendors of third-party applications can use the application log as a destination for error messages generated by their applications.

The application log works in much the same way as the security log. It tracks events within applications—both successful events and failed events. Figure 13.8 shows the details provided from an applications log in a Windows system.

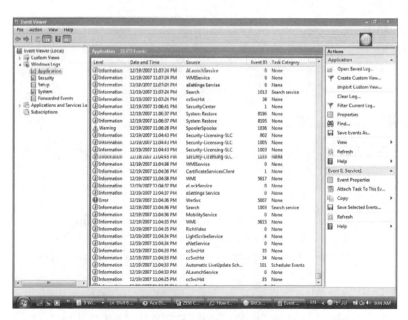

Figure 13.8   Application log.

Notice in Figure 13.8 that three types of events occurred: general application information events, a warning event, and an error event. Vigilant administrators would likely want to check the event ID of both the event and warning failures to isolate the cause.

System Logs

System logs record information about components or drivers in the system. This is the place to look when you troubleshoot a problem with a hardware device on your system or a problem with network connectivity. For example, messages related to the client element of DHCP appear in this log. The System log is also the place to look for hardware device errors, time synchronization issues, or service startup problems. Figure 13.9 shows an example of a System log.

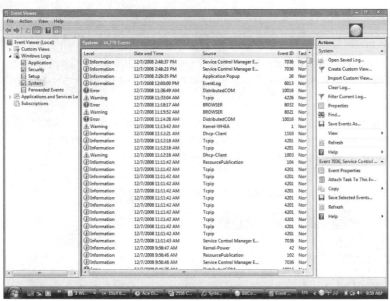

Figure 13.9 System log.

History Logs

History logs are most often associated with the tracking of Internet surfing habits—that is, log files that maintain a record of all sites that a user visits. Network administrators can review these for potential security or policy breaches, but generally these are not commonly reviewed.

Another form of history logs are a compilation of events from other log files. For instance, one history log might contain all significant events over the past year from the security log on a server. History logs are critical because they provide a detailed account of alarm events that can track trends and locate problem areas in the network. This information can help you revise maintenance schedules, determine equipment replacement plans, and anticipate and prevent future problems.

> **NOTE: Log Files**   Application logs, history logs, and system logs can often be viewed by any user. Security logs can be viewed only by users who are use accounts with administrative privileges.

Log Management

Monitoring logs can require significant time and effort. That is where Log Management (LM) strategies come into play. LM describes the process of managing large volumes of system-generated computer log files. LM includes the collection, retention, and disposal of all system logs. LM can be completely designed in-house or you can use many third-party LM applications designed to make the whole process easier. Whichever way you go, LM can be a huge task. It is essential to ensure the proper functioning of the network and applications and keep an eye on network and system security.

Configuring our systems to log all sorts of events is the easy part; trying to find the time to review the logs is an entirely different matter. To help with this process, third-party software packages are available to help with the organization and reviewing of log files.

Networking Tools

A large part of network administration involves having the right tools for the job and knowing when and how to use them. Selecting the correct tool for a networking job sounds like an easy task, but network administrators can choose from a mind-boggling number of tools and utilities.

Given the diverse range of tools and utilities available, it is unlikely that you will encounter all the ones available or even all those discussed in this chapter. For the Network+ exam, however, you are required to have a general knowledge of the tools and what they are designed to do.

Until networks become 100% wireless, network administrators can expect to spend some of their time using a variety of media-related troubleshooting and installation tools. Some of these tools, such as the tone generator and locator, can troubleshoot media connections, and others, such as wire crimpers and punchdown tools, can create network cables and connections.

> **NOTE: Carry a Screwdriver**   Although many costly, specialized networking tools and devices are available to network administrators, the most widely used tool—the standard screwdriver—costs only a few dollars. As a network administrator, you can expect to take the case off a system with amazing regularity—to replace a network interface card (NIC) or perhaps remove the cover from a hub or switch to replace a fan. Advanced cable testers and specialized tools will not help you when you need a screwdriver.

Wire Crimpers

Wire crimpers are tools you might use regularly. Like many things, making your own cables can be fun at first, but the novelty soon wears thin. Basically, a wire crimper is a tool that you use to attach media connectors to the ends of cables. For instance, you use one type of wire crimper to attach RJ-45 connectors on un-shielded twisted-pair (UTP) cable, and you use a different type of wire crimper to attach Bayonet Neill Concelman (BNCs) to coaxial cabling. Figure 13.10 shows an example of a wire crimper for crimping both RJ-11 and RJ-45 connectors.

Figure 13.10   A wire crimper for RJ-45 and RJ-11 cables. (Photo courtesy of TRENDnet, www.trendnet.com.)

NOTE: Cable Caveat   When making cables, always order more connectors than you need; there will probably be a few mishaps along the way.

In a sense, you can think of a wire crimper as a pair of special pliers. You insert the cable and connector separately into the crimper, making sure that the wires in the cable align with the appropriate connectors. Then, by squeezing the crimper's handles, you force metal connectors through the wires of the cable, making the connection between the wire and the connector.

When you crimp your own cables, you need to be sure to test them before putting them on the network. It only takes a momentary lapse to make a mistake when creating a cable, and you can waste time later trying to isolate a problem in a faulty cable.

Strippers and Snips

Two other commonly used wiring tools are strippers and snips. Wire strippers come in a variety of shapes and sizes. Some are specifically designed to strip the outer sheathing from coaxial cable, and others are designed to work best with UTP cable. Any type of strippers is designed to cleanly remove the sheathing from wire to make sure a clean contact can be made.

Many administrators will not have specialized wire strippers unless they do a lot of work with copper-based wiring. However, standard wire strippers are good to have on hand.

Wire snips are tools designed to cleanly cut the cable. Sometimes network administrators will buy cable in bulk and use wire snips to cut the cable in desired lengths. The wire strippers then prepare the cable for the attachment of the connectors.

Punchdown Tools

Within network wiring closets are rows of distribution blocks, or patch panels. A *patch panel* is a freestanding or wall-mounted unit with a number of RJ-45 connections on the front. The patch panel provides a connection point between network equipment such as hubs and switches and the ports to which PCs are connected, which are normally distributed throughout a building.

The individual wires within a twisted pair cable need to be attached to the back of the patch panel for each RJ-45 connector slot. This is where a punchdown tool is used. The punchdown tool presses each of the individual wires within the twisted-pair cable into the connectors at the back of the patch panel. The metal connectors in which the wires are pressed are known as *insulation displacement connectors (IDCs)*. See Figure 13.11.

Figure 13.11   A punchdown tool. (Photo courtesy of TRENDnet, www.trendnet.com.)

A discussion of punchdown tools and how they are used is provided in Chapter 2, "Media and Connectors."

Cable Certifiers

Today's networks are all about speed and for good reason. Whereas the original networks shared simple files and resources such as printers, today's networks see the convergence of voice, data, and video applications on a single network. To accommodate these applications, higher-performance cabling solutions are required to maintain the high demands placed on them. Many existing networks are retrofitted to meet the demands of high-bandwidth applications.

The question for network administrators is, can the existing wiring infrastructure meet the current and future demands of network users? This is where cable certifiers come into the picture. Cable certifiers can determine cable fault locations, cable length issues, cable noise problems, and qualify cables for applications such as VoIP. These handheld devices create a full summary of the cable test results, enabling administrators to see exactly if the current cabling can meet the demands of network users.

Some of the common features of cable certifiers include the following:

- Test telephone and coax cables for continuity and proper termination.

- Determine cable length and distances.

- Verify twisted-pair integrity including opens, shorts, miswires, split pairs, and so on.

- Identify individual cable runs to locate and identify routes

- Obtain accurate reflection of cables' ability by measuring NEXT, FEXT, attenuation, and return loss and bit error rates to determine cable carrying capability.

TIP: **Certifiers** For the Network+ exam, remember that certifiers test the speed of cables, ensuring they can meet the demands of network applications.

Voltage Event Recorders

Voltage event recorders monitor the quality of power used on the network or by network hardware. Voltage event recorders identify potential power-related concerns such as power sags, spikes, surges, or other power variations. Such power irregularities can cause problems for hardware and, in the case of serious spikes, can destroy hardware. Voltage event recorders are attached directly to a wall socket to monitor power. They record their findings, which are reviewed by the administrator.

Temperature Monitors

When we talk about temperature monitoring, we are often referring to the temperature of our server and network equipment rooms. In general, the heat tolerance range for computer equipment is surprisingly wide. Take, for example, a typical server system, which can happily operate in a range between 50°F and 93°F. That is a spread of 43°, which is plenty of room in a normal heated environment. The problem is that if you maintain a computer room at either the upper or lower end of these levels, the equipment will run, but for how long, no one knows.

Although no specific figures exist relating to the recommended temperature of server rooms, the accepted optimum is around 55 to 65°F. At this temperature, the equipment in the room should operate, and those working in the room should not get too cold. Human beings generally require a higher temperature than computer equipment does, which is why placing servers in an office space with staff is not ideal.

Many people assume that the biggest problem with servers and network equipment is that of overheating. To some extent, this is true; servers in particular do generate a great deal of heat and so can overheat to the point where components fail. But this is only one of the heat-related issues. A more significant, and more gradual, problem is that of temperature consistency.

Heat causes components to expand, and cooling causes them to contract. This is known as thermal expansion and contraction. Even the slightest temperature shifts cause the printed circuit boards and chips to shift around, and if they shift too much or too often, the chance of them becoming separated from their connections is greatly increased. Keeping the heat at a moderate and constant level reduces the expansion and contraction of the boards and increases the reliability of the components.

NOTE: Close Doors   Never wedge open a door to an environmentally controlled room, no matter how cold you get. Not only does having an open door defeat the purpose of the controlled environment, but it can also damage air conditioning units.

One way administrators keep their equipment rooms at the right temperature is using temperature monitors. In the equipment room, temperature monitors constantly document changes in room temperature. If the monitor detects radical changes in temperature, it sends an alert to the administrator. This can sometimes occur if someone leaves a door open to the server room, if the air conditioning breaks, or if some piece of network hardware produces a lot of heat. Although network temperature monitors might not often be needed, having them installed adds great peace of mind for administrators.

Keeping It Cool

Fortunately, the solution to the heat problem is relatively simple. You use an air conditioning unit. The problem is, you can't use just any A/C unit. Having a late 1960s window-ledge unit with a pipe hanging out the window might be better than nothing, but we need serious high-quality protection.

High-quality air conditioning systems fall under the domain of industrial heating, ventilation, and air-conditioning (HVAC) equipment. Server-environment-specific air condition units are designed to maintain a constant temperature. High-quality units guarantee an accuracy of plus or minus 1°F. Most units have an audible alarm, but some also have the capability to communicate with management systems so that server-room temperature can be monitored remotely. Although the icy blast of a server-room air conditioning system might not be welcomed by those who have to work in it for an extended period of time, the discomfort is far outweighed by the benefit to server equipment.

Calculating the correct size and type of air conditioning unit can be a tricky proposition. Air conditioning systems are rated on the number of cubic feet that they can safely condition. Using this figure, and estimating the increase in temperature caused by the hardware in the room, gives you the basic information you need to choose an A/C unit. Of course, the calculation should take into account potential future growth. In some cases, a standby A/C unit is also installed. Whether such a system is required depends on how much fault tolerance you need and are willing to pay for.

Toner Probes

A *toner probe*, also called toner and probe, is two devices that can save a network installer many hours of frustration. There are two components to this tool: the tone generator and the tone locator. In the field, you might hear the tone generator and the tone locator referred to as the *fox and hound*.

The purpose of the toner and probe is to generate a signal transmitted on the cable you attempt to locate. At one end, you press the tone locator against individual wires; at the other, the tone generator sends a signal down a specific cable. When the tone locator makes contact with the wire that has the tone generators signal on it, the locator emits an audible signal or tone.

The toner and probe is a useful device, but it does have some drawbacks. First, it often takes two people to operate—one at each end of the cable. Of course, one person could just keep running back and forth; but if the cable is run over great distances, this can be a problem. Second, using the tone generator is time consuming because it must be attached to each cable independently.

NOTE: Labeling Cables   Many problems that can be discovered with a tone generator are easy to prevent by taking the time to properly label cables. If the cables are labeled at both ends, you do not need to use such a tool to locate them.

TIP: Toners   For the Network+ exam, remember that the toner and probe are specifically used for locating the ends of cables hidden in floors, ceilings, or walls, and tracking cables from the patch panel to their destination.

Protocol Analyzer

Protocol analyzers, also known as packet sniffers, can be hardware- or software-based; their primary function is to analyze network protocols such as TCP, UPD, HTTP, FTP, and so on. In use, protocol analyzers help diagnose computer networking problems, alert you of unused protocols, identify unwanted or malicious network traffic, and help isolate network traffic-related problems.

Protocol analyzers capture the communication stream between systems. But unlike the sniffer, the protocol analyzer also reads and decodes the traffic. Decoding enables the administrator to view the network communication in English. From this, administrators can get a better idea of the traffic flowing on the network. When unwanted or damaged traffic is spotted, analyzers make it easy to isolate and repair. For example, if a problem occurs with specific TCP/IP communication, such as a broadcast storm, the analyzer can identify the source of the TCP/IP problem and isolate the system causing the storm. Protocol analyzers also provide many statistical and real-time trend statistics that help for management justification of new hardware.

Protocol analyzers can be used for two key reasons:

- **Identify protocol patterns**—By creating a historical baseline of its analysis, administrators can spot trends for protocol errors. That way, when a protocol error occurs, it can be researched to see if that error has occurred before and what was done to fix it.

- **Decode information**—Capturing and decoding network traffic allows administrators to see what exactly is going on with the network on a protocol level. This helps identify protocol errors and potential intruders.

> **TIP: Statistics**   For the Network+ exam, remember that protocol analyzers enable administrators to examine the bandwidth that a particular protocol is using.

Media/Cable Testers

A *media tester*, also called a *cable tester or continuity tester*, defines a range of tools designed to test whether a cable works properly. Any tool that facilitates the testing of a cable can be deemed a cable tester. However, there are specific tools called media testers and continuity testers. These media testers enable administrators to test a segment of cable, looking for shorts, improperly attached connectors, or other cable faults. All media testers inform you whether the cable works correctly and where the problem in the cable might be. Continuity testers are designed to verify that an electrical path exists between two end points. In the network, this means continuity between your cable jack and termination point. Continuity testers can locate shorts or other wiring problems in a section of network cabling.

Figure 13.12 shows an example of a media tester. Note that there are two parts to the media tester: one for each end of the cable.

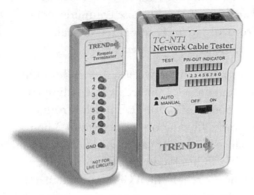

Figure 13.12   An example of a media tester. (Photo courtesy of TRENDnet, www.trendnet.com.)

Media Testers

Although network administrators do not need to use a cable tester every day, it could significantly help in the troubleshooting process. This section describes time domain reflectometers (TDR), which are used on copper cables, and optical time domain reflectometers (OTDR), which are used on optical cables. You also learn about multimeters.

TDR

A time domain reflectometer (TDR) is a device used to send a signal through a particular media to check the continuity of the cable. Good quality TDRs have the capability to locate many types of cabling faults, such as a severed sheath, damaged conductors, faulty crimps, shorts, loose connectors, and the like. TDRs help ensure that data sent across the network is not interrupted by poor cabling that can cause faults in data delivery.

> **TIP: TDR**   For the Network+ exam, you should know that TDRs work on the physical layer of the OSI model, sending a signal through a length of cable looking for cable faults.

OTDR

Because the majority of network cabling is copper-based, most tools designed to test cabling are designed for copper-based cabling. However, when you test fiber-optic cable, you need an optical tester.

An optical cable tester performs the same basic function as a wire media tester, but on optical media. The most common problem with an optical cable is a break in the cable that prevents the signal from reaching the other end. Because of the extended distances fiber-optic cables can cover, degradation is rarely an issue in a fiber-optic LAN environment.

Ascertaining whether a signal reaches the other end of a fiber-optic cable is relatively easy, but when you determine that a break exists, the problem becomes locating the break. That's when you need a tool called an *optical time-domain reflectometer (OTDR)*. By using an OTDR, you can locate how far along in the cable the break occurs. The connection on the other end of the cable might be the source of the problem, or perhaps there is a break halfway along the cable. Either way, an OTDR can pinpoint the problem.

Unless you work extensively with fiber-optic cable, you're unlikely to have an OTDR or even a fiber-optic cable tester in your toolbox. Specialized cabling contractors will have them, though, so knowing they exist is important.

Multimeter

One of the simplest cable-testing devices is a *multimeter*. By using the continuity setting, you can test for shorts in a length of coaxial cable; or, if you know the correct cable pinouts and have needlepoint probes, you can test twisted-pair cable.

A basic multimeter combines several electrical meters into a single unit offering the capability to measure voltage, current, and resistance. Advanced models can also measure temperature. A multimeter has a display, terminals, probes, and a dial to select various measurement ranges. A digital multimeter has a numeric digital display, whereas an analog one has a dial display. Inside a multimeter, the terminals connect to different resistors depending on the range selected.

Network multimeters can do much more than test electrical current. Look for multimeters to do the following:

- **Ping specific network devices**—A multimeter can ping and test response times of key networking equipment such as routers, DNS servers, DHCP servers, and so on.

- **Verify network cabling**—It is possible to use a network multimeter to isolate cable shorts, split pairs, or other faults.

- **Locate and ID cable**—Quality network multimeters enable administrators to locate cables at patch panels and wall jacks using digital tones.

- **Document findings**—Multimeter results can be downloaded to a PC for inspection. Most network multimeters provide a means to link to a PC, such as USB ports.

Network Qualification Tester

The network qualification tester gives administrators a quick glance at the network's bandwidth and whether in its current configuration it can grow to support VoIP or Gigabit Ethernet.

If a network is running slow, the network qualification tester can identify why the network is struggling. For example, it can identify cross talk within a cable and how it impacts the network performance. Most quality network qualification testers can test twisted-pair and coaxial cable, and other models test for fiber-optic cable.

> **TIP: Qualification Testing**   Remember for the Network+ exam, network qualification testers enable administrators to identify the current speeds the network cabling can support and isolate cabling from network problems.

Butt Set

A *butt set* is most often associated with telephony, but it can be used on some data networks as well. A butt set enables the administrator or technician to *butt* or tap into a communication line and use it. In the case of a phone line, a technician can use the line normally—that is, make a call, answer a call, or listen into a call.

The butt set looks somewhat like a regular phone handset with wires attached. The wires from the handset connect to the phone wire and that's it. The technician can test and access the phone line. This device can test network telephony but has limited use on network cable. Some network butt sets enable the access of data on the cable, but many other tools can do the same thing with better results.

Wireless Detector

Wireless media requires its own types of tools. One such tool is a Wi-Fi detector. The intent of such a device is to reveal Wi-Fi hot spots and detect wireless network access with LED visual feedback. Such devices can be configured to scan specific frequencies. When working with 802.11b/g/n networks, you will most certainly require scanning for 2.4GHz RF signals.

Such devices can be used in the troubleshooting process to identify where and how powerful RF signals are. Given the increase in wireless technologies, RF detectors are sure to increase in popularity. Figure 13.13 shows a Wi-Fi detector.

Figure 13.13 Wireless RF detector.

Summary

This chapter focuses on the cable management and documentation. Documentation is an important part of the administrator's role. It involves having documentation of network layout, both physical and logical, and documented network procedures, policies, configurations, and regulations.

Documentation is not a one-time process; keeping up-to-date documentation is necessary to ensure network functionality. In addition to documenting, administrators must review documentation and log files to ensure that they are aware of any security breaches or other issues on the network.

You can use many software- and hardware-based tools to test the network and help in documentation of the network. These tools include packet sniffers, protocol analyzers, load testers, and throughput testers.

Administrators can use many tools to help maintain and troubleshoot network media. These tools include a TDR, OTDR, wireless detector, cable tester, mulitmeter, toner probe, and butt set. In addition, there are tools you can use to work with media, including snips, strippers, and punchdown tools.

Exam Preparation Tasks

Review All the Key Topics

Review the most important topics in the chapter, noted with the Key Topics icon in the outer margin of the page. Table 13.4 lists a reference of these key topics and the page numbers on which each is found.

Table 13.4   Key Topics for Chapter 13

Key Topic Element	Description	Page Number
Figure 13.1	General wiring schematic	482
Figure 13.2	Wiring schematic that corresponds to Table 13.1	483
Table 13.1	Wiring schematic reference sample	481
Figure 13.3	Physical network	485
Figure 13.4	Physical and logical bus topology	486
Figure 13.5	Logical topology diagram	487
Figure 13.6	Software throughput tester	494
Table 13.2	Data rate units	495
Table 13.3	Some of the most common TCP/IP Suite Protocols and their port assignments	495
List 13.1	Output from a `netstat -a`	497
Figure 13.7	Windows security log	500
Figure 13.8	Application log	501
Figure 13.9	System log	502
Figure 13.10	A wire crimper for RJ-45 and RJ-11 cables	504
Figure 13.11	A punchdown tool	505
Figure 13.12	An example of a media tester	510
Figure 13.13	Wireless RF detector	513

Complete the Tables and Lists from Memory

Print a copy of Appendix B, "Memory Tables" (found on the CD), or at least the section for this chapter, and complete the tables and lists from memory. Appendix C, "Memory Tables Answer Key," also on the CD, includes completed tables and lists to check your work.

Define Key Terms

Define the following key terms from this chapter, and check your answers in the Glossary.

- Baselines
- Butt set
- Cable stripper
- Event logs
- History logs
- IP address
- Load testing
- Media testers
- Multimeter
- OTDR
- Packet sniffers
- Physical and logical network diagrams
- Policies and procedures
- Port scanners
- Punchdown tool
- Protocol analyzer
- Regulations
- System logs
- TDR
- Temperature monitor
- Toner probe
- Throughput testers
- Twisted-pair
- Voltage event recorder
- Wire crimpers
- Wiring schematics
- Wireless

Apply Your Knowledge

Exercise 13.1 Testing Network Throughput

In this exercise, you walk through the steps to test the throughput between two points on a network. You download a trial version of a software-based throughput tester and use it to test the connection.

Estimated time: 10 minutes

1. Open your Internet browser and go to the QCheck page on the IxChariot website: www.ixiacom.com/products/display?skey=qcheck.

2. From this screen, click the link that reads Install QCheck.

3. You will be asked to fill out your name and address on a form web page. Then verification will be sent to your email. Click the link in your email to begin the download of the QCheck tester.

4. The installed QCheck throughput tester resembles Figure 13.14.

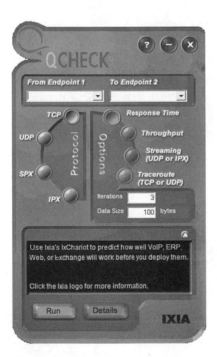

Figure 13.14   QCheck throughput tester.

5. With the throughput tester open, select the protocol you want to test, either UDP or TCP. Select the beginning location and end point IP addresses.

6. Finally, select the brown Throughput button, and click the Run button to test the throughput between the two points you selected.

7. To test the difference in performance, try testing the throughput at different times of day. The throughput readouts should vary according to traffic load.

Exercise 13.2 Diagram Your Network

This exercise assumes you have a home network established or have knowledge of a network design. In this exercise, you document a physical network design.

Estimated time: 10 minutes

1. Open your browser and navigate to the WERESC website at http://www.weresc.com/network.php.

2. Select the Download link. This installs free network diagram software to your computer, as shown in Figure 13.15.

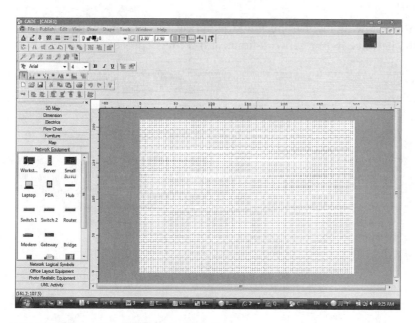

Figure 13.15   Network diagram software.

3. Using the predrawn elements on the left side of the screen, draw the physical layout of your network.

Review Questions

You can find answers to the review questions in Appendix A, "Answers to Review Questions."

1. You have recently installed a new server in a wiring closet. The server shuts down periodically, and you suspect there might be power-related problems. Which of the following tools might you use to isolate a power problem?
   a. Voltage multimeter
   b. Voltage regulator
   c. Voltage monitor
   d. Voltage event recorder

2. While you were away, an air conditioning unit malfunctioned in a server room, and the room and some equipment overheated. Which of the following would have alerted you to the problem?
   a. Multimeter
   b. Temperature monitor
   c. TDR
   d. OTDR

3. Which of the following involves pushing the network beyond its limits, often downing the network to test network limits and recovery procedures?
   a. Crash and burn
   b. Stress test
   c. Recovery test
   d. Load test

4. You have been given a physical wiring schematic. The schematic shows the following:

Description	Installation Notes
Cat5E 350MHz plenum rated CMP cable	Cable runs 50ft from the MDF to IDF.
	Cable placed through ceiling and through a mechanical room.
	Cable was installed 01/15/2009 upgrading a nonplenum Cat5 cable.
Cat5E 350MHz non-plenum cable	Horizontal cable runs 45ft to 55ft from IDF to wall jack.
	Cable 5E replaced Cat5 cable February 2008.

	Section of cable run through ceiling and over fluorescent lights.
Category 5E UTP cable	Patch cables connecting printer runs 15ft because of printer placement.
	8.3 micron core/125 micron cladding single mode Connecting fiber cable runs 2 kilometers between the primary and secondary buildings.

Given this information, what cable recommendation might you make if any?
    a. Nonplenum cable should be used between the IDF and MDF.
    b. Horizontal cable run should use plenum cable.
    c. Patch cable connecting printer should be shorter.
    d. Leave network cabling as is.

5. What tool would you use when working with an IDC?
    a. Wire crimper
    b. Media tester
    c. OTDR
    d. Punchdown tool

6. As a network administrator, you work in a wiring closet where none of the cables have been labeled. Which of the following tools are you most likely to use to locate the physical ends of the cable?
    a. Toner probe
    b. Wire crimper
    c. Punchdown tool
    d. `ping`

7. Which of the following commands can be issued from the command line to view the status of the systems ports?
    a. `netstat -p`
    b. `netstat -o`
    c. `netstat -a`
    d. `netstat -y`

8. You suspect that an intruder has gained access to your network. You want to see how many failed logon attempts there were in one day to help determine how they got in. Which of the following might you do?
    a. Review the history logs.
    b. Review the security logs.
    c. Review the logon logs.
    d. Review the performance logs.

9. You have been called into to inspect a network configuration. All your customer has for reference is a single network diagram. Considering the diagram,
which of the following statements are true?

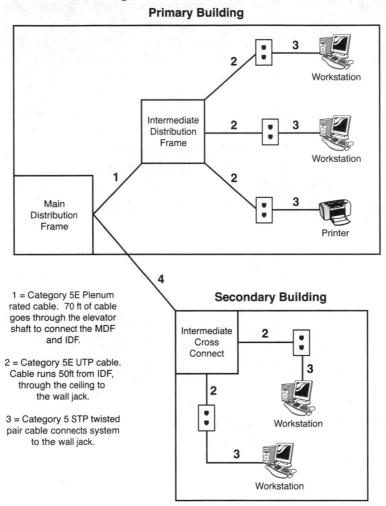

Primary Building

1 = Category 5E Plenum
rated cable. 70 ft of cable
goes through the elevator
shaft to connect the MDF
and IDF.

2 = Category 5E UTP cable.
Cable runs 50ft from IDF,
through the ceiling to
the wall jack.

3 = Category 5 STP twisted
pair cable connects system
to the wall jack.

Secondary Building

a. Cable 1 does not need to be plenum rated.
b. Cable 2 should be STP cable.
c. Cable 3 is incorrect, STP cannot be connected directly to a wall jack.
d. Cable 2 goes beyond recommended length.
e. The network looks good from this diagram.

10. You install a new system into an existing star network and need a cable that is 45 feet long. Your local vendor does not stock cables of this length, so you are forced to make your own. Which of the following tools will you need to complete the task?

   a. Optical tester

   b. Punchdown tool

   c. Crimper

   d. UTP splicer

11. Which of the following network utilities are used by both hackers and administrators to eavesdrop on network transmissions?

   a. Port filters

   b. Packet filters

   c. Data watchers

   d. Packet sniffers

12. You are troubleshooting a problem with a workstation and have managed to narrow it down to a single patch cable. What tool might you use to troubleshoot the problem further?

   a. Tone generator/locator

   b. OTDR

   c. ping

   d. Media tester

13. You have recently been informed that 75 new users will be added to the network over the next 2 months. You are concerned about the impact on overall network functionality. Which of the following could you do to verify that the network can handle the load?

   a. Stress test

   b. Performance test

   c. Load test

   d. Traffic test

14. What tool can find a break in a length of fiber-optic cable?

   a. Tone generator

   b. TDR

   c. OTDR

   d. Fox and hare

15. You have been called in to troubleshoot a network experiencing intermittent connectivity problems. Which of the following documentation might you request to see first?

   a.   Security logs

   b.   History logs

   c.   Physical network diagram

   d.   Logical network diagram

16. Which of the following utilities can measure voltage, current, and resistance?

   a.   Multimeter

   b.   TDR

   c.   OTDR

   d.   Toner probe

17. A toner probe is sometimes referred to as what?

   a.   Fox and rabbit

   b.   Fox and hare

   c.   Fox and hound

   d.   Fox and dog

18. Which of the following describes network procedures?

   a.   Legally enforceable rules.

   b.   Series of rules established by an organization.

   c.   They identify the way in which network tasks are to be performed.

   d.   They identify the way in which policies are to be followed.

19. Your network server maintains several key applications shared to all systems on the network. Recently users have been complaining that the application runs slowly and sometimes they can't access it at all. Which of the following might you do first?

   a.   Move the server closer to the client stations.

   b.   Review the physical network diagram.

   c.   Review the logical logs.

   d.   Review the application logs.

20. On several occasions, your network server has been compromised and a Trojan horse installed remotely. You suspect someone is gaining access to your system. Which of the following might you do? (Choose two.)

   a.   Review the history logs.

   b.   Use a port scanner.

   c.   Use a packet sniffer.

   d.   Use the `netstat -a` command.

This chapter covers CompTIA Network+ objectives 6.1, 6.2, and 6.3. Upon completion of this chapter, you will be able to answer the following questions:

- What are the functions of hardware security devices?

- How are software security devices used?

- What are the common features of firewall systems?

- When are network access security features deployed?

- How are VPN tunnels secured?

- What are remote access security protocols?

CHAPTER 14

Network Access Security

Today, more than ever, the security of networks is a major consideration for network administrators. Security risks come from seemingly everywhere, both from outside of the network from remote attackers and from malicious users from inside the network. Administrators have several tools to help mitigate the risks from attackers. This includes everything from protocols to firewalls.

To fully understand the security risks associated with the network, a network administrator must take a holistic view and consider every aspect, threat, and possible weakness. The network administrator must assume that someone will attempt to gain unauthorized access to the network or the systems attached to it at some point. This might sound a little dramatic, but plenty of network administrators can attest that it is a reality.

There are, of course, certain environments in which security is more of a concern than in others. If you work for, say, a bank or a branch of the government, security is likely to be a high priority and allocate significant resources to security. For a chain of florists in Fresno, network security is likely to be less of an issue due to the nature of the network data, but overall security is still a consideration.

Security today is not just about stopping corporate espionage or preventing theft of equipment. It's about protecting the physical assets and, perhaps more important, the data of the organization. The cracker coming in through your firewall and entering 50 bogus orders for gift hampers might think it's funny. Your boss is likely to find it less amusing.

> **NOTE: Hacker or Cracker?**   The terms *hacker* and *cracker* are tossed about freely when it comes to network security, but the two terms describe different individuals. A *hacker* is someone who attempts to disassemble or delve into a computer program with the intention of understanding how it works, normally to make it better. A *cracker*, on the other hand, is someone who attempts to gain access to a computer system or application without authorization, with the intention of using the application illegally or viewing the data. Crackers, not hackers, are the people network administrators need to be concerned with. However, over time, the term *hacker* has become synonymous with people who attempt to gain access to systems without permission, and the term *cracker* has fallen out of use.

In essence, security is about ensuring the privacy, integrity, and quality of a network's data and the systems that hold it, with the purpose of ensuring business continuity. Determining what measures are required to ensure this security is the concern of the network administrator.

Foundation Topics

Understanding Network Security Threats

Before we look at the measures you can take to secure your network, let's first look at what you need to protect against. The following are some possible threats to a network's security:

- **Internal threats**—It is sad that the most common source of security problems in an organization is from the employees of that organization. For example, a user might decide to "borrow" the apparently unused hub or switch from the equipment cupboard on the third floor, or he might want to know just how much money the president of the company earns. In more extreme cases, a user might attempt to pass valuable corporate information to an outside party. Sound far fetched? It's not; it happens every day.

- **Deliberate data damage**—To most people, the idea of deliberately damaging someone else's property is, to say the least, distasteful. Unfortunately, not everyone operates with the same values. Whether "just for fun" or with more shady intent, some people might delight in corrupting data or deleting it completely. Either way, business continuity will almost certainly be affected.

- **Industrial espionage**—This dramatic sounding security threat involves the process of a person retrieving data from a server for a purpose. The intruder might want to get her hands on the latest blueprints of your new widget, or she might want financial information for a buyout bid. Either way, the integrity (and in some cases, the future viability) of the business can be affected by such events.

- **Physical equipment theft**—Although it is normally less of an issue than theft of data, theft of physical equipment can still affect business continuity. If an important piece of equipment is stolen (for example, the server or a backup tape), the intruder will have access to your data. Insurance normally takes care of replacing the actual equipment, but data is generally not insured, unless specified, so the cost of restructuring the data is not provided for.

You might be fortunate enough not to suffer from any of these threats. Certainly, in a small organization that performs a seemingly uninteresting (to outsiders) business, there might not be any occurrences of security threats. But as an organization grows, so too do the amount of information, the number of methods that can be used to access it, and the number of people interested in finding out about the business. Also, as the number of employees grows, the chance that a "bad apple" will find its way into the cart increases as well.

Security Responsibilities of a Network Administrator

To combat possible security threats, what is expected of you, as a network administrator? The exact network security responsibilities you have depend on the kind of environment in which you work. In large companies, an individual or a group might be responsible specifically for security issues. You might be part of that group or be under its direction. In small companies, the entire onus of network security might be placed on your—the network administrator's—shoulders. This chapter assumes that as a network administrator you are primarily responsible for network security. Assume that you need to do the following to ensure network security in your organization:

- **Ensure that a security policy is in place**—A security policy defines the security measures, how they function, what is involved in their operation, and how problems are dealt with. The security policy should be created with the support of management.

- **Ensure that the security policy is enforced**—There is no point in having a policy if it is not enforced. As the network administrator, you need to make sure that the security policy works and is implemented as described.

- **Ensure that any infractions of the security policy are dealt with**—Perhaps the most undesirable part of a network administrator's security responsibilities involves dealing with infractions of the security policy. Because the majority of security-related incidents occur with people inside the company, this can often be an unpleasant task.

- **Ensure that the security situation is continually evaluated, revised, and updated**—Networks change, as does the company structure. The security needs of an organization should be evaluated constantly. Any changes deemed necessary should be incorporated into the security policy, again with the cooperation of management.

This is a brief look at the responsibilities a network administrator has in implementing security on a network. Depending on the environment you work in, you might need to consider more or fewer security-related responsibilities. Now that you have an idea of some of the basic security responsibilities, let's look at the two types of network security: physical and logical.

Physical and Logical Security

Security can be broken into two distinct areas: physical security and logical security. *Physical security* refers to the issues related to the physical security of the equipment that composes or is connected to the network. Physical security measures include controlling access to equipment, supervising visitors, controlling physical access to areas that contain networking equipment, and ensuring that removable media such as backup tapes are transported and stored securely.

Logical security is concerned with security of data held on devices connected to the network. Logical security involves controlling passwords and password policies, controlling access to data on servers through file system security, controlling access to backup tapes, and perhaps most important, preventing sources outside the network from gaining access to the network through a connection from another network, such as the Internet. Because logical security is a large and complex topic, this chapter covers only topics related to the Network+ exam and some supporting information.

Physical Security

Physical security is concerned with the prevention of unauthorized access to the physical equipment that makes up the network or the systems attached to it.

Perhaps the biggest consideration related to physical security is restricting access to networking equipment and servers. Most commonly, the people you try to protect against in this respect are the employees of the company rather than malicious outsiders. That said, there is always the chance that a miscreant might decide that it is easier to break in to your premises and steal a server rather than access data through a firewall.

Specific physical security considerations include the following:

- **Controlling access to equipment**—Networking equipment should be kept in a secure location. For example, you might have a dedicated, environmentally controlled room in which all the network servers and networking equipment are kept. Alternatively, as in many small organizations, networking equipment might be stored in a cupboard or even a rack. Wherever your equipment is located, access control systems (including locks and keys) should be in place to prevent unauthorized access.

- **Creating and enforcing visitor policies**—Even if you have a dedicated server room, it's highly likely that other equipment will be in the room, such as telephone systems, air-conditioning units, and fire-protection systems. Each of these systems will have a scheduled maintenance program, which will periodically require visitors to be in the server room. Procedures should be in place so that the identities of visitors are verified, and that they are supervised when in the equipment room.

- **Securing the area**—The physical security of the network environment should be examined from a big-picture perspective. If a dedicated room is used for the server, determine the security of the room. Are there windows in the room that might represent a security risk? Are there windows that could facilitate someone outside the building seeing in? All these aspects and more must be factored in when considering physical security.

TIP: Physical Security   The Network+ exam focuses much more on logical security than on physical security. For this reason, the discussion of physical security is confined to just the basics.

Network Hardware and Server Room Access

Access to the server room should be tightly controlled, and all access doors must be secured by some method, whether it is a lock and key or a retinal scanning system. Each method of server-room access control has certain characteristics. Whatever the method of server-room access, it should follow one common principle: control. Some access control methods provide more control than others.

Lock and Key

If access is controlled by lock and key, the number of people with a key should be restricted to only those people who need access. Spare keys should be stored in a safe location, and access to spare keys should be controlled.

Here are some of the characteristics of lock and key security:

- **Inexpensive**—Even a good lock system will cost only a few hundred dollars.

- **Easy to maintain**—With no back-end systems and no configuration, using a lock and key is the easiest access control method.

- **Less control than other methods**—Keys can be lost, copied, and loaned to other people. There is no record of access to the server room and no way of proving that the key holder is entitled to enter.

TIP: Do Not Copy   If you use a lock and key for security, make sure that all copies of the original key are stamped DO NOT COPY. That way, it is more difficult for someone to get a copy because reputable key cutters will not make copies of such keys.

Swipe Card and PIN Access

If budgets and policies permit, swipe card and personal identification number (PIN) entry systems are good choices for managing physical access to a server room. Swipe card systems use a credit-card-sized plastic card that is read by a reader on the outside of the door. To enter the server room, you must swipe the card (run it through the reader), at which point it is read by the reader, which validates it. Usually, the swipe card's use to enter the room is logged by the card system, making it possible for the logs to be checked. In higher-security installations, it is common to have a swipe card reader on the inside of the room as well so that a person's exit can be recorded.

Although relatively few disadvantages exist to swipe card systems, they do need specialized equipment so that the cards can be coded with users' information. They also have the same drawbacks as keys in that they can be lost or loaned to other people. Of course, the advantage that swipe cards have over key systems is that swipe cards are hard to copy.

PIN pads can be used alone or with a swipe card system. PIN pads have the advantage of not needing any kind of card or key that can be lost. For the budget conscious, PIN pad systems that do not have any logging or monitoring capability can be purchased for a reasonable price. Here are some of the characteristics of swipe card and PIN pad systems:

- **Moderately expensive**—Some systems, particularly those with management capabilities, are quite expensive.

- **Enhanced controls and logging**—Each time a person enters the server room, he or she must key in a number or use a swipe card. This process enables systems to log who enters and when.

- **Some additional knowledge required**—Swipe card systems need special software and hardware that can configure the cards. Someone has to learn how to do this.

Biometrics

Although they may still seem like the realms of James Bond, biometric security systems are becoming far more common. Biometric systems work by utilizing some unique characteristic of a person's identity—such as a fingerprint, a palm print, or even a retina scan—to validate that person's identity.

Although the price of biometric systems has been falling over recent years, they are not widely deployed in small to mid-sized networks. Not only are the systems themselves expensive, but the installation, configuration, and maintenance of the systems must be considered. However, biometric solutions are becoming more common; for example, newer laptops can be bought with finger scanners built in. Following are some of the characteristics of biometric access control systems:

- **Very effective**—With biometrics, each person entering the server room must supply proof-of-person evidence. This can be harder to fake than getting a swipe card or stealing a password. Combing these methods can make it even harder to gain unauthorized access.

- **Nothing to lose**—Because there are no cards or keys, there is nothing that can be lost.

- **Expensive**—Biometric security systems and their attendant scanners and software are still relatively expensive and are affordable only by organizations with a larger budget, although prices are sure to drop as more people turn to this method of access control.

Hardware Room Best Practices

Apart from the physical and environmental considerations, server rooms or other areas containing equipment must be managed on a policy and procedural level. In view of this, it is important that procedures, a monitoring schedule, and server-room documentation be in place.

> **TIP: No-Snack Zone**   It may sound obvious, but server rooms should be no-food-or-drink zones. To go to some of the lengths described here and then fall prey to a can of Cherry Coke or to nacho crumbs would be a little ironic. So, the rule is no food, no drinks, no exceptions. Post signs to remind server-room users of this rule. If you want to be creative, you can add a shelf outside the server room so that those entering the server room can save their coffee or snack for later.

As with anything else relating to servers, the server environment should be well documented, and detailed procedures should be in place to cover all possible situations. Anyone working near the server should be made aware of the server environment procedures, and development and enforcement of the procedures should have the backing of management.

Server-room procedures should define the following:

- **Visitor policies**—As discussed earlier, the server environment might not be used exclusively for server hardware, and people other than server administrators might need access to the area. In addition, outside contractors might need to access the server environment. Procedures should state such things as whether outside contractors must be escorted at all times and what identification should be verified before outsiders are granted access to the server area. You would not let engineers from the local utility company come into your home without identification, so why would you let them into your server room without seeing ID?

- **Fire-drill procedures**—Procedures should include guidelines for handling inert gas systems. Different procedures might be needed for a test drill. Procedures should also detail at what intervals fire detection systems are tested and at what intervals they are serviced. Although the companies that service such systems are normally good at reminding you when the system is due for service, it should be noted who is responsible for checking this fact.

- **Flood actions**—As with fire, the procedures should provide information on what actions to take in case of flood detection. If appropriate, the procedures should include the location of valves that can be turned off to limit the flooding and details of whom should be contacted if flooding occurs. Procedures should also define at what point equipment should be removed from the affected area.

- **Staff turnover**—Providing access control mechanisms means that procedures must be in place to cope with employees leaving the organization. The related procedures should define what steps should be taken. These steps can include the changing of network passwords, removal of user IDs, and, in exceptional cases, the changing of door locks.

- **Detailed contact charts**—The procedures should also include information on any internal and external contacts who need to be notified in case of an incident.

Logical Security

Logical security is a much more involved subject than physical security. Not only are there more ways in which data can be threatened logically than physically, but the measures available to secure data are equally diverse. Logical security focuses on the security protocols and procedures to protect data from both internal and remote network users. Logical security measures include authentication (such as username/password), determining access rights (authorization), tracking security logs (accountability). Logical security measures such as authentication, authorization and accountability are discussed in Chapter 15, "Security Technologies and Malicious Software."

Firewalls

A firewall is considered a logical security measure and one of the cornerstone concepts for network security.

A firewall is a either a hardware device or a software application that sits at the edge of the network controlling the flow of traffic between two or more networks. Through configured settings, the firewall controls the type of traffic allowed to flow between networks. The most common use of a firewall is to protect a private network from a public network such as the Internet. However, firewalls are also used as a means to separate a sensitive area of a private network from other, less-sensitive, areas of the private network.

At its most basic, a firewall is a device (it could be a computer system or a dedicated hardware device) that has more than one network interface and manages the flow of network traffic between those interfaces. How it manages the flow and what it does with certain types of traffic depend on its configuration. Figure 14.1 shows the most basic firewall configuration.

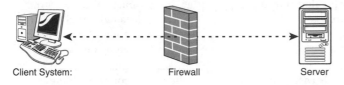

Client System: Firewall   Server

Figure 14.1   A basic firewall implementation.

Strictly speaking, a firewall performs no action on the packets it receives besides the basic functions just described. However, in a real-world implementation, a firewall is likely to offer other functionality, such as Network Address Translation (NAT) and proxy server services. The additional features used with firewalls are discussed in the following section.

When working with firewalls, you might hear the terms host-based and network-based firewalls. Network-based firewall systems are those that monitor traffic on the entire network segment. Typically, a firewall server monitors and controls traffic to the entire network. An administrator monitors and controls the firewall services from a central location. A host-based firewall is installed on an individual system and monitors and controls inbound and outbound traffic for just that system. In general terms, this is how they operate, but which is better? It all depends; they each have their pros and cons. Table 14.1 compares the characteristics of a host-based and network-based firewall system.

Table 14.1   Comparing Host-Based and Network-Based Firewalls

Firewall Characteristic	Host-Based	Network-Based
Network bandwidth usage	Does not use bandwidth.	Uses LAN bandwidth to monitor and update client systems.
Centralized management	No centralized management, each system is managed independently.	Administrators can manage all firewall activities from a centralized location.
Cost	Small for a few systems. Host-based firewall is included with Windows desktop operating systems such as Vista.	Typically a license is required for each client station to be monitored. Depending on the number of client systems on the network, the cost can be high.

Table 14.1   Comparing Host-Based and Network-Based Firewalls

Firewall Characteristic	Host-Based	Network-Based
Logging and auditing	Most host-based firewalls offer logging and auditing features.	Offer a wide range of logging and auditing features. From a central location, the administrator can review logs or auditing to see exactly what is happening on the network.
Specialized knowledge	Typically easy to install and configure. Those shipped with Vista, for example, are preconfigured and can be modified if necessary.	Often more complex and offer more features that must be configured.
Protection when not connected to the network	Monitor traffic on or off the LAN.	Many of the network-based firewalls are dependant on a connection to the firewall server. If it is disconnected, the protection ends. This is a problem in network environments with numerous laptop users.

So which do you choose? It might boil down to whether you are an administrator or network user. In a LAN or WAN, you are likely to see network-based firewall systems. Network-based firewalls are centralized, making it possible for the administrator to update, manage, and monitor the firewall from a single location. All this would be virtually invisible to the end user. Many network administrators opt for the control and ease that a network-based solution holds.

Remote users, with laptops that leave the LAN or WAN, might want a host-based firewall solution that stays active whether they connect to the LAN. Host-based firewalls are versatile for movement and ensure that the system stays protected. However, it is much more difficult for administrators to track and review log files and updates on systems on a one-to-one basis.

The Purpose and Function of a Firewall

Although the fundamental purpose of a firewall is to protect one network from another, you need to configure the firewall to allow some traffic through. If you don't need to allow traffic to pass through a firewall, you can dispense with it entirely and completely separate your network from other networks.

A firewall can employ a variety of methods to ensure security. In addition to the role just described, modern firewall applications can perform a range of other functions, often through the addition of add-on modules. These functions can include the following:

- **Content filtering**—Most firewalls can be configured to provide some level of content filtering. This can be done for both inbound and outbound content. For instance, the firewall can be configured to monitor inbound content restricting certain locations or particular websites. Firewalls can also limit outbound traffic by prohibiting access to certain websites by maintaining a list of URLs and IP addresses. This is often done when organizations want to control employees' access to Internet sites.

- **Signature identification**—A *signature* refers to a unique identifier for a particular application. In the antivirus world, a signature is an algorithm that uniquely identifies a specific virus. Firewalls can be configured to detect certain signatures associated with malware or other undesirable applications and block them before they enter the network.

- **Virus scanning services**—As web pages are downloaded, firewalls can check content within the pages for viruses. This feature is becoming increasingly attractive to companies concerned about the potential threats from Internet-based sources.

- **Network address translation (NAT)**—To protect the identity of machines on the internal network, and to enable more flexibility in internal TCP/IP addressing structures, many firewalls (and proxy servers—see the next section) translate the originating address of data into a different address, which is then used on the Internet. Network address translation is a popular function because it works around the limited availability of TCP/IP addresses.

- **URL filtering**—By using a variety of methods, the firewall can choose to block certain websites from being accessed by clients within the organization. This blocking enables companies to control what pages can be viewed and by whom.

- **Bandwidth management**—Although required only in certain situations, bandwidth management can prevent a certain user or system from hogging the network connection. The most common approach to bandwidth management is to divide the available bandwidth into sections and then make just a certain section available to a user or system.

These functions are not strictly firewalling activities. However, the flexibility offered by a firewall, coupled with its placement at the edge of a network, make a firewall the ideal base for controlling access to external resources.

The following sections describe stateful and stateless firewalls, firewall methods, and the purpose and configuration of a demilitarized zone.

Stateful and Stateless Firewalls

When talking about firewalls, two terms will often come up: stateful and stateless firewalls. These two terms differentiate how firewalls operate. A stateless firewall, sometimes called a packet-filtering firewall, monitors specific data packets and restricts or enables access to the network based on certain criteria. Stateless firewalls look at each data packet in isolation and as such are not aware whether that particular data packet is part of a larger data stream. Essentially, stateless firewalls do not see the big picture or "state" of data flow, only at the individual packets.

Today, we are more likely to use stateful firewalls. Stateful firewalls monitor data traffic streams from one end to the other. A stateful firewall refuses unsolicited incoming traffic that does not comply with dynamic or preconfigured firewall exception rules. A stateful firewall tracks the state of network connections watching data traffic, including monitoring source and destination addresses and TCP and UDP port numbers.

TIP: Stateless Firewall   For the Network+ exam, remember that a stateless firewall examines the information within a data packet and rejects or accepts the packet based on the source or destination address or port number listed within the packet header.

Firewall Methods

This section discusses the various firewall methods commonly used: packet-filtering firewalls, circuit-level firewalls, and application-layer firewalls.

TIP: Three Firewall Methods   The three firewall methods described in this chapter are often combined into a single firewall application. Packet filtering is the basic firewall function. Circuit-level functionality provides NAT, and an application gateway firewall provides proxy functionality.

Network Layer Firewalls

A network layer (also known as a packet-filtering firewall) firewall examines each packet that passes through it and determines what to do with it, based on the configuration. A network layer firewall deals with packets at the network layer of the Open Systems Interconnect (OSI) model. The following are some of the criteria by which packet filtering can be implemented:

- **IP address**—By using the IP address as a parameter, the firewall can enable or deny traffic, based on the source or destination IP address. For example, you can configure the firewall so that only certain hosts on the internal network can access hosts on the Internet. Alternatively, you can configure it so that only certain hosts on the Internet can gain access to a system on the internal network.

- **Port number**—TCP/IP suite uses port numbers to identify which service a certain packet is destined for. By configuring the firewall to enable certain types of traffic, you can control the flow. You might, for example, open port 80 on the firewall to allow Hypertext Transfer Protocol (HTTP) requests from users on the Internet to reach the corporate web server. You might also, depending on the application, open the HTTP Secure (HTTPS) port, port 443, to enable access to a secure web server application.

- **Protocol ID**—Because each packet transmitted with IP has a protocol identifier in it, a firewall can read this value and then determine what kind of packet it is. If you filter based on protocol ID, you specify which protocols you will allow to pass through the firewall.

- **MAC address**—This is perhaps the least used of the packet-filtering methods discussed, but it is possible to configure a firewall to use the hardware-configured MAC address as the determining factor in whether access to the network is granted. This is not a particularly flexible method, and it is therefore suitable only in environments in which you can closely control who uses which MAC address. The Internet is not such an environment.

Circuit-Level Firewalls

Circuit-level firewalls, also called session-layer firewalls, are similar in operation to packet-filtering firewalls, but they operate at the transport and session layers of the OSI model. The biggest difference between a packet-filtering firewall and a circuit-level firewall is that a circuit-level firewall validates TCP and UDP sessions before opening a connection, or circuit, through the firewall. When the session is established, the firewall maintains a table of valid connections and lets data pass through when session information matches an entry in the table. The table entry is removed, and the circuit is closed when the session is terminated. Circuit level firewalls that operate at the session layer, or Layer 5 of the OSI model, provided enough protection in terms of firewalls in their day. As attacks become more sophisticated and included application-layer attacks, they no longer provided sufficient protection.

Application-Layer Firewalls

As the name suggests, application-layer firewalls operate at the application layer of the OSI model. In operation, application-layer firewalls can inspect data packets traveling to or from an application. This enables the firewall to inspect, modify, block, and even redirect data traffic as it sees fit. Application layer firewalls are sometimes referred to as a proxy firewall because they have the capability to proxy in each direction. This means that the source and destination systems do not come in direct contact with each other; rather, the firewall proxy serves as a middle point.

> **TIP: Proxy Service**   For the Network+ exam, remember that application layer firewalls offer a proxy service between the sending and receiving devices. Using proxy services, the firewall can filter the content to and from the object or subject.

Demilitarized Zones

An important firewall-related concept is *demilitarized zones (DMZs)*. A DMZ is part of a network on which you place servers that must be accessible by sources both outside and inside your network. However, the DMZ is not connected directly to either network, and it must always be accessed through the firewall. The military term DMZ is used because it describes an area in which there is little or no enforcement or policing.

Using DMZs provides an extra level of flexibility, protection, and complexity to your firewall configuration. Figure 14.2 shows an example of a DMZ configuration.

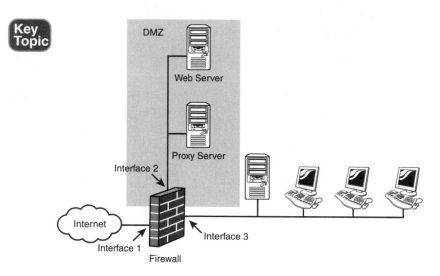

Figure 14.2   A DMZ configuration.

By using a DMZ, you can create an additional step that makes it more difficult for an intruder to gain access to the internal network. In Figure 14.2, for example, an intruder who tried to come in through interface 1 would have to spoof a request from either the web server or proxy server into interface 2 before it could be forwarded to the internal network. Although it is not impossible for an intruder to gain access to the internal network through a DMZ, it is difficult.

Firewalls have become a necessity for organizations of all sizes. As the Internet becomes an ever more hostile place, firewalls and the individuals who understand them are likely to become an essential part of the IT landscape.

Intrusion Detection and Intrusion Prevention Systems

Two other strategies we use to help secure the network are intrusion detection systems (IDS) and intrusion prevention systems (IPS). The IDS device is passive; it monitors the network, watching packets of data travel the network. The IDS compares the traffic it monitors to predefined parameters and rules. Traffic in violation of these rules is flagged as potentially dangerous. The IDSs can detect malware or other dangerous traffic that might pass undetected by the firewall. Most IDSs can detect potentially dangerous content by its signature.

A typical IDS logs incidents and stores these in a database for review. The IDS can be configured to generate alerts sent to the system administrator. The administrator can then take the appropriate action to secure the holes in the network. For those wanting a secure network, IDS and their discovery of potential threats can be an important part. If there is a downside of an IDS, it might be that they can generate false threat reports. The IDS can sometimes erroneously detect and flag harmless traffic. This can be reduced if the administrators carefully configure the IDS rules. As with anything else technology-related, IDSs have progressed, and the false detection errors will and have decreased.

The IPS has all the features of the IDS but also has the capability to prevent dangerous traffic from getting to the network. The IPS is not a passive system; rather, it actively monitors the network traffic and might attempt to block potentially harmful traffic rather than just flag it. The IPS can prevent attacks in a variety of ways; it can block access from a particular user account, IP address, port, or even a specific application.

An IPS is a network device that continually scans the network looking for inappropriate activity and shuts down any potential threats. The IPS scans look for any known signatures of common attacks and automatically tries to prevent those attacks. An IPS is considered a reactive security measure because it actively monitors and can take steps to correct a potential security threat.

Network Access Security

Network access security includes the mechanisms used to filter network traffic to determine who is and who is not allowed to access the network and network resources. Firewalls, proxy servers, routers, and individual computers all have the capability to maintain access control to some degree. By limiting who can and cannot access the network and its resources, it is easy to understand why access control plays an important role in security strategy. This section reviews some network access security concepts, including access control lists and port blocking.

Access Control Lists

As far as security is concerned, an access control list (ACL) typically refers to specific access permissions assigned to an object or device on the network. For example, wireless routers can be configured to restrict who can and who cannot access the router based on MAC address. Another form of access control can be the permissions set on a network printer. The permissions can enable printer access only to a certain network group, whereas another can't access the printer. TCP/IP can also be used as a filtering strategy. TCP/IP filtering involves restricting network traffic based on its IP address.

Access Control and MAC Filtering

Filtering network traffic using the MAC address of a system is typically done using an ACL. The ACL keeps track of all MAC addresses and is configured to enable or deny access to certain systems based on the list. As an example, let's look at the MAC ACL from a router. Figure 14.3 shows the MAC ACL screen.

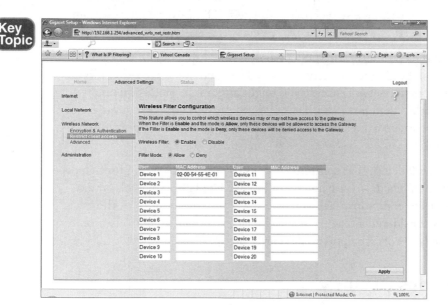

Figure 14.3 Wireless MAC ACL.

Notice from Figure 14.3 that specific wireless MAC addresses can either be denied or enabled depending on the configuration. In this example, only the system with the MAC address of 02-00-54-55-4E-01 can authenticate to this router.

TCP/IP Filtering

TCP/IP filtering also can use an ACL. The ACL determines what types of IP traffic will be let through the router. The IP traffic not permitted according to the

ACL will be blocked. Depending on the type of IP filtering used, the ACL can be configured to enable or deny several types of IP traffic, including the following:

- Protocol type: TCP, UDP, ICMP, SNMP, IP, and so on

- Port number used by protocols (for TCP/UPD)

- Message source address

- Message destination address

Port Blocking/Filtering

Port blocking or filtering is one of the most widely used security methods on networks. Port blocking is associated with firewalls and proxy servers; although, it can be implemented on any system that provides a means to manage network data flow, according to data type.

Essentially, when you block a port, you disable the capability for traffic to pass through that port, thereby filtering that traffic. Port blocking is typically implemented to prevent users on a public network from accessing systems on a private network, although it is equally possible to block internal users from external services, and internal users from other internal users, by using the same procedure.

Depending on the type of firewall system in use on a network, you might find that all the ports are disabled (blocked) and that the ones you need traffic to flow through must be opened. The benefit of this strategy is that it forces the administrator to choose the ports that should be unblocked rather than specify those that need to be blocked. This ensures that you allow only those services absolutely necessary into the network.

What ports remain open largely depends on the needs of the organization. For example, the ports associated with the services listed in Table 14.2 are commonly left open.

Table 14.2 Commonly Opened Port Numbers and Their Associated Uses

Port Number	Protocol	Purpose
80	HTTP	Web browsing
443	HTTPS	Secure web transactions
21	FTP	File transfers
25	SMTP	Email sending
110	POP3	Email retrieval
53	DNS	Hostname resolution

These are, of course, only a few of the services you might need on a network, and allowing traffic from other services to traverse a firewall is as easy as opening the port. Keep in mind, though, that the more ports that are open, the more vulnerable you become to outside attacks. Never open a port on a firewall unless you are absolutely sure that you need to.

> **NOTE: A Complete List of Ports**   You can obtain a complete list of port numbers and their associated protocols from the Internet Assigned Numbers Authority (IANA), at www.iana.org/assignments/port-numbers.

Before you implement port blocking, you should have a good idea of what the port is used for. Although it is true that blocking unused ports does not have any impact on internal network users, if the wrong port is blocked, you can create connectivity issues for users on the network.

For instance, a network administrator was given the task of reducing the amount of spam emails received by his company. He decided to block port 25, the port used by the Simple Mail Transfer Protocol (SMTP). He succeeded in blocking the spam email, but in the process, he also prevented users from sending email.

Remote Access Protocols and Services

Today, there are many ways to establish remote access into networks, including virtual private networks (VPNs) or plain old modem dial-up access. Regardless of the technique used for remote access or the speed at which access is achieved, certain technologies need to be in place for the magic to happen. These technologies include the protocols to enable the access to the server and to secure the data transfer after the connection is established. Also necessary are methods of access control that make sure only authorized users use the remote access features.

All the major operating systems include built-in support for remote access. They provide both the access methods and security protocols necessary to secure the connection and data transfers.

Routing and Remote Access Service (RRAS)

RRAS is a remote access solution included with Windows Server products. RRAS is a feature-rich, easy-to-configure, and easy-to-use method of configuring remote access.

Any system that supports the appropriate dial-in protocols, such as PPP, can connect to an RRAS server. Most commonly, the clients are Windows systems that use the dial-up networking feature; but any operating system that supports dial-up client software will work. Connection to a RRAS server can be made over a standard phone line, using a modem, over a network, or via an ISDN connection.

RRAS supports remote connectivity from all the major client operating systems available today, including all newer Windows OSs:

- Windows Server products

- Windows XP/Vista Home-based clients

- Windows XP/Vista Professional-based clients

- UNIX-based/Linux clients

- Macintosh-based clients

Although the system is called RRAS, the underlying technologies that enable the RRAS process are dial-up protocols such as Serial Line Internet Protocol (SLIP) and Point-to-Point Protocol (PPP).

SLIP

SLIP was designed to enable data to be transmitted via Transmission Control Protocol/Internet Protocol (TCP/IP) over serial connections in a UNIX environment. SLIP did an excellent job, but time proved to be its enemy. SLIP was developed in an atmosphere in which security was not an overriding concern, consequently, SLIP does not support encryption or authentication. It transmits all the data used to establish a connection (username and password) in clear text, which is, of course, dangerous in today's insecure world.

NOTE: Clear Text   *Clear text* simply means that the information is sent unencrypted, and anyone can intercept with a packet capture program and read the data with his or her favorite word processor.

In addition to its inadequate security, SLIP also does not provide error checking or packet addressing, so it can be used only in serial communications. It supports only TCP/IP, and log in is accomplished through a terminal window.

Many operating systems still provide at least minimal SLIP support for backward capability to older environments, but SLIP has been replaced by a newer and more secure alternative: PPP. SLIP is still used by some government agencies and large corporations in UNIX remote access applications, so you might come across it from time to time.

PPP

PPP is the standard remote access protocol in use today. PPP is actually a family of protocols that work together to provide connection services.

Because PPP is an industry standard, it offers interoperability between different software vendors in various remote access implementations. PPP provides a number of security enhancements compared to regular SLIP—the most important being the encryption of usernames and passwords during the authentication process. PPP enables remote clients and servers to negotiate data encryption methods, authentication methods, and support new technologies. PPP even gives administrators the ability to choose which particular local area network (LAN) protocol to use over a remote link; although, today TCP/IP is used almost exclusively.

During the establishment of a PPP connection between the remote system and the server, the remote server needs to authenticate the remote user and does so by using the PPP authentication protocols. PPP accommodates a number of authentication protocols, and it's possible on many systems to configure more than one authentication protocol. The protocol used in the authentication process depends on the security configurations established between the remote user and the server. PPP authentication protocols include CHAP, MS-CHAP v22, EAP, SPAP, and PAP. These authentication protocols are reviewed in Chapter 15.

TIP: Upgrading to PPP   If you work on a network that uses SLIP and you run into connectivity problems, try upgrading to PPP because it is more flexible and secure.

PPPoE

PPPoE (Point-to-Point Protocol over Ethernet) is a protocol used for connecting multiple network users on an Ethernet LAN to a remote site through a common device. For example, using PPPoE it is possible to have all users on a network share the same link such as a DSL, cable modem, or wireless connection to the Internet. PPPoE is a combination of PPP and the Ethernet protocol, which supports multiple users in a LAN. Hence the name. The PPP protocol information is encapsulated within an Ethernet frame.

With PPPoE, a number of different users can share the same physical connection to the Internet, and in the process, PPPoE provides a way to keep track of individual user Internet access times. Because PPPoE enables for individual authenticated access to high-speed data networks, it is an efficient way to create a separate connection to a remote server for each user. This strategy enables Internet access and billing on a per-user basis rather than a per-site basis.

Users accessing PPPoE connections require the same information as required with standard dial-up phone accounts, including a username and password combination. As with a dial-up PPP service, an Internet service provider (ISP) will most likely automatically assign configuration information such as the IP address, subnet mask, default gateway, and DNS server.

There are two distinct stages in the PPPoE communication process: the discover stage and the PPP session stage. The discovery stage has five steps to complete to establish the PPPoE connection: initiation, offer, request, session confirmation, and termination. These steps represent back and forth communication between the client and the PPPoE server. After these steps have been negotiated, the PPP session can be established using familiar PPP authentication protocols.

Tunneling and Encryption

In the mid-1990s, Microsoft, IBM, and Cisco began working on a technology called *tunneling*. By 1996, more companies had become interested and involved in the work, and the project soon produced two new virtual private networking solutions: Point to Point Tunneling Protocol (PPTP) and the Layer 2 Tunneling Protocol (L2TP).

From these developments, virtual private networks (VPNs) became one of the most popular methods of remote access. Essentially, a VPN extends a LAN by establishing a remote connection, a connection tunnel, using a public network such as the Internet. A VPN provides a point-to-point dedicated link between two points over a public IP network.

VPN encapsulates encrypted data inside another datagram that contains routing information. The connection between two computers establishes a switched connection dedicated to the two computers. The encrypted data is encapsulated inside PPP, and that connection is used to deliver the data.

A VPN enables anyone with an Internet connection to use the infrastructure of the public network to dial in to the main network and access resources as if the user were logged on to the network locally. It also enables two networks to connect to each other securely.

Many elements are involved in establishing a VPN connection, including the following:

- **A VPN client**—The computer that initiates the connection to the VPN server.

- **A VPN server**—Authenticates connections from VPN clients.

- **An access method**—As mentioned, a VPN is most often established over a public network such as the Internet; however, some VPN implementations use a private intranet. The network used must be IP-based.

- **VPN protocols**—Required to establish, manage, and secure the data over the VPN connection. PPTP and L2TP are commonly associated with VPN connections.

VPNs have become popular because they enable the public Internet to be safely utilized as a wide area network (WAN) connectivity solution. (A complete discussion of VPNs would easily fill another book and goes beyond the scope of the Network+ objectives.)

> **NOTE: VPN Connections**   VPNs support analog modems, ISDN, and dedicated broadband connections such as cable and DSL. You should remember this for the exam.

SSL VPNs

A VPN creates a virtual link between two end points over the Internet. Because a VPN uses the Internet, security can be a concern. To help alleviate the security issues, VPN transmissions can be secured with the SSL protocol. The SSL VPN functions much the same as a regular VPN but adds the encryption element. An SSL VPN enables encrypted data to travel through the VPN tunnel, making secure communications for such organizations as e-commerce sites, banks, or organizations with sensitive data.

> **NOTE: SSL with HTTP**   Remember that SSL is also used with the HTTP protocol to make it secure for online transactions. HTTPS (HTTP SSL) is used for such transactions as e-commerce and online banking.

SSL VPN does not require any additional software to be installed on the client system, enabling the SSL VPN to be accessed from any computer that has a web browser that supports SSL. The SSL VPN uses the browser as the interface and not other software.

SSL VPN uses something called symmetric encryption. This means that both sides of the communication channel have cryptography keys used to encrypt and decrypt the traffic. Symmetric encryption and cryptography keys are covered in Chapter 15. The purpose of the SSL encryption is to help ensure that you are talking to whom you think you are talking.

> **TIP: SSL Port**   Remember for the Network+ exam that SSL uses TCP port 443, which is normally opened by default on system firewalls. This means that SSL should work through firewalls without any special configuration.

VPN Concentrators

A long time ago, users used to travel to work, sit at their desktop systems, and work. Now, remote users and telecommuting is part of regular business. VPNs make telecommuting possible, and part of this solution is the VPN concentrator.

The VPN concentrator is a device that creates and encrypts a tunnel between the remote user and the network. Traffic is encrypted from the remote user to the VPN concentrator. Figure 14.4 shows a VPN concentrator and encryption range.

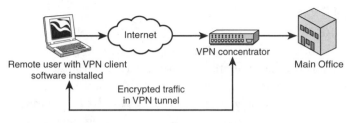

Figure 14.4   VPN concentrator.

Remote access VPN concentrators typically support IPsec or SSL for the VPN. User authentication can be via Remote Authentication Dial In User Service (RADIUS) or Kerberos. Authentication strategies including both RADIUS and Kerberos are discussed in Chapter 15. VPN concentrators also help secure the VPN link by using access lists for remote user sessions.

TIP: SSL or IPsec   Remember for the Network+ exam that a VPN concentrator can use either IPsec or SSL to encrypt the communication between the remote user and the VPN concentrator.

Point-to-Point Tunneling Protocol (PPTP)

PPTP, which is documented in RFC 2637, is often mentioned with PPP. Although it's used in dial-up connections as PPP is, PPTP provides different functionality: It creates a secure *tunnel* between two points on a network, over which other connectivity protocols, such as PPP, can be used. This tunneling functionality is the basis for VPNs.

VPNs are created and managed by using the PPTP protocol, which builds on the functionality of PPP, making it possible to create dedicated point-to-point tunnels through a public network such as the Internet.

To establish a PPTP session between a client and server, a TCP connection known as a *PPTP control connection* is required to create and maintain the communication tunnel. The PPTP control connection exists between the IP address of the PPTP client and the IP address of the PPTP server, using TCP port 1723 on the server and a dynamic port on the client. It is the function of the PPTP control connection to pass the PPTP control and management messages used to maintain the PPTP communication tunnel between the remote system and the server. PPTP provides authenticated and encrypted communications between two end points, such as a client and a server. PPTP does not use a public key infrastructure but does use a user ID and password.

PPTP uses the same authentication methods as PPP, including MS-CHAP, CHAP, PAP, and EAP, which are discussed in Chapter 15.

Layer Two Tunneling Protocol (L2TP)

L2TP is a combination of PPTP and Cisco L2F technology. L2TP, as the name suggests, utilizes tunneling to deliver data. It authenticates the client in a two-phase process: It first authenticates the computer and then the user. By authenticating the computer, it prevents the data from being intercepted, changed, and returned to the user in what is known as a *man-in-the-middle attack*. L2TP assures both parties that the data they receive is exactly the data sent by the originator.

> **NOTE: L2TP Tunneling Without Encryption** It is possible to create an L2TP tunnel without using encryption, but this is not a true VPN and, obviously, lacks a certain amount of security.

> **TIP: L2TP and the Data Link Layer** Unlike IPsec, which operates at the network layer of the OSI model, L2TP operates at the data link layer, making it protocol-independent. This means that an L2TP connection can support protocols such as IPX and AppleTalk.

Advantages of L2TP and PPTP

L2TP and PPTP are both tunneling protocols, so you might be wondering which you should use. Here is a quick list of some of the advantages of each, starting with PPTP:

- Has been around the longest; it offers more interoperability than L2TP.

- Is an industry standard.

- Is easier to configure than L2TP because L2TP uses digital certificates.

- Has less overhead than L2TP.

The following are some of the advantages of L2TP:

- Offers greater security than PPTP.

- Supports common public key infrastructure technology.

- Provides support for header compression.

Inside IPsec

IPsec is an IP-layer security protocol designed to provide security against internal and external attacks. This consideration is important because the reasons and methods for securing against attacks from outside the network are well documented. IPsec provides a way to protect sensitive data as it travels within the LAN. As we know, firewalls do not provide such security for internal networks, so a complete security solution requires both a firewall solution and internal protection provided by such security mechanisms as IPsec.

To create secure data transmissions, IPsec uses two separate protocols: Authentication Headers (AH) and Encapsulating Security Payloads (ESP). Briefly, AH is primarily responsible for the authentication and integrity verification of packets, whereas ESP provides encryption services. Because they are independent protocols, when implementing an IPsec policy, they can be used together or individually. Whether one or both are used depends on the security needs of the network. This section describes AH, ESP, and IPsec transmission modes.

Authentication Headers

Before using AH, it is important to understand what its function is and what it can do. AH provides source authentication and integrity for data communication but does not provide any form of encryption. AH is capable of ensuring that network communications cannot be modified during transmission; however, AH cannot protect transmitted data from being read.

AH is often implemented when network communications are restricted to certain computers. In such an instance, AH ensures that mutual authentication must take place between participating computers, which, in turn, prohibits network communications to occur between nonauthenticated computers.

Encapsulating Security Payloads

Encapsulating Security Payloads (ESP) is used to provide encryption services to network data; however, it can also be used for authentication and integrity services. The difference between AH authentication and ESP authentication is that ESP includes only the ESP header, trailer, and payload portions of a data packet. The IP header is not protected as with AH, which protects the entire data packet. Relative to encryption services, ESP provides encryption with the DES or 3DES encryption algorithms.

In IPsec encryption, you encounter two security protocols: the Data Encryption Standard (DES) and the Triple DES (3DES). The DES encryption method uses a 56-bit encryption key. DES keys are continually regenerated during the communication. This ensures that if one key is compromised, the whole message is not compromised. Unfortunately, DES is not considered secure because 56-bit keys can be cracked with specialized equipment.

Like DES, 3DES used a 56-bit rotating key encryption method; however, as the name suggests, it uses three of them. In total, 3DES is considered a 168-bit encryption method. 3DES is used for environments when communication security is crucial.

IPsec Transmission Modes

IPsec can operate in one of two separate modes: transport mode and tunnel mode. These modes refer to how data is sent throughout the network.

In transport mode, IPsec protection is provided all the way from the issuing client to the destination server. In this way, transport mode is said to provide end-to-end transmission security.

Tunnel mode secures data only between tunnel points or gateways. In this way, tunnel mode provides gateway-to-gateway transmission security. When data is in transmission between the client and the server, it remains unprotected until it reaches the gateway. At the gateway, it is secured with IPsec until it reaches the destination gateway. At this point, data packets are decrypted and verified. The data is then sent to the receiving host unprotected. Tunnel mode is often employed when data must leave the secure confines of a local LAN or WAN and travel between hosts over a public network such as the Internet.

Remote Control Protocols

CompTIA lists three protocols associated with remote control access. The first, the remote desktop protocol (RDP) is used in a Windows environment. Terminal Services provides a way for a client system to connect to a server, such as Windows Server 2000/2003/2008, and by using the Remote Desktop Protocol operating on the server as if they were local client applications. Such a configuration is known as *thin client computing*, whereby client systems use the resources of the server instead of their local processing power.

Windows Server products and XP and Vista have built-in support for Remote Desktop Connections. The underlying protocol used to manage the connection is RDP. RDP is a low-bandwidth protocol used to send mouse movements, keystrokes, and bitmap images of the screen on the server to the client computer. RDP does not actually send data over the connection—only screenshots and client keystrokes. RDP clients are available for multiple platforms including Mac OS X and Linux.

Virtual network computing (VNC) consists of a client, a server, and a communication protocol. It is another system whereby a remote user can access the screen of another computer system. As with the other systems mentioned here, VNC enables remote log-in, where clients can access their own desktop while being physically away from their computer. VNC uses a protocol known as the remote frame buffer (RFB) protocol. RFB is the backbone enabling remote access to another systems graphical interface.

Finally, the Citrix Independent Computing Architecture (ICA) enables clients to access and run applications on a server, using the resources of the server with only the user interface, keystrokes, and mouse movements transferred between the client system and the server. In effect, even though you work at the remote computer, the system functions as if you were actually sitting at the computer. Like with Terminal Services and RDP, ICA is an example of thin client computing.

Summary

Network security is a complex subject, encompassing many elements and factors. Effectively securing a network involves understanding the risks that can be a threat to the network and what the result of a breach in security might entail.

A firewall system provides protection to the network by controlling the traffic that passes between internal and external networks or between two internal networks. Two other forms of network security devices include an IDS and IPS.

Understanding how implementing security features such as port blocking and encryption affect the network and the users on it is another important aspect of network security.

In addition to implementing measures that serve to protect the network, you must also detect intrusions to the network and provide procedures that define what steps should be taken when a breach does occur. All these elements must be combined to have an effective network security policy.

A VPN extends a LAN by establishing a remote connection, a connection tunnel, using a public network such as the Internet. A VPN provides a point-to-point dedicated link between two points over a public IP network. VPN can be established using the PPTP or L2TP tunneling protocols.

Exam Preparation Tasks

Review All the Key Topics

Review the most important topics in the chapter, noted with the Key Topics icon in the outer margin of the page. Table 14.3 lists a reference of these key topics and the page numbers on which each is found.

Table 14.3   Key Topics for Chapter 14

Key Topic Element	Description	Page Number
Figure 14.1	A basic firewall implementation	533
Table 14.1	Comparing host-based and network-based firewalls	533
Figure 14.2	A DMZ configuration	538
Figure 14.3	A wireless MAC ACL	540
Table 14.2	Commonly opened port numbers and their associated uses	541
Figure 14.4	A VPN concentrator	547

Define Key Terms

Define the following key terms from this chapter, and check your answers in the Glossary.

- Application gateway firewall
- Network-based firewall
- Host-based firewall
- IDS
- IPS
- ACL
- DES
- 3DES
- Content filtering
- MAC filtering
- IP filtering

- PPP
- SSL VPN
- VPN
- L2TP
- PPTP
- IPsec
- RRAS
- RDP
- PPPoE
- PPP
- VNC
- ICA

Apply Your Knowledge

Exercise 14.1 Configuring Windows Firewall

Whether you are a network administrator working with a network-based firewall or a home user working with a host-based system, configuring your firewall is an important consideration. In this exercise we filter traffic using the Windows Firewall.

Estimated time: 15 minutes

1. Select Start, Control Panel to open the Windows Vista Control Panel. With the Control Panel open, select the Windows Firewall screen. Figure 14.5 shows the Windows Vista dialog screen.

2. On the left side of the dialog box, click the Allow a Program Through Windows Firewall option. This opens the Windows Firewall Settings dialog box, shown in Figure 14.6.

3. Select the Exceptions tab, as shown in Figure 14.7. The Exceptions tab enables you to configure which programs can and cannot pass through the firewall. Additionally you can open certain ports for communications.

Remember, creating an exception for an application or a port opens an access point into and out of your computer. Each time you do this, the computer becomes a little less secure. The more exceptions or open ports your firewall has, the more your systems can be accessed by malicious users trying to access files or use the exception to spread malicious software.

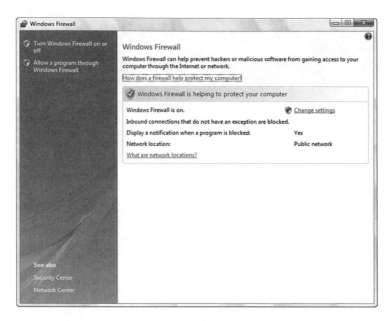

Figure 14.5   Windows Vista Firewall.

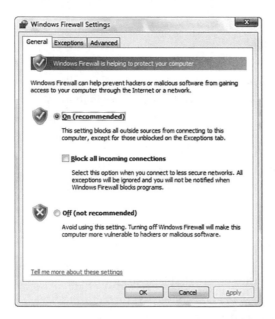

Figure 14.6   Windows Firewall Settings dialog screen.

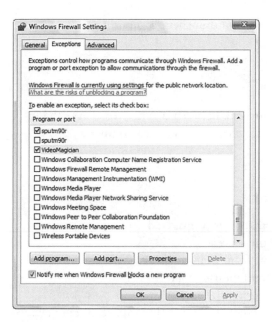

Figure 14.7 Windows Firewall Exceptions tab.

Review Questions

You can find answers to the review questions in Appendix A, "Answers to Review Questions."

1. Which of the following is considered a physical security measure?
   a. Password policy
   b. Locks on equipment cabinets
   c. Auditing policy
   d. Firewall

2. On a packet-filtering firewall, which of the following is *not* used as a criterion for making forwarding decisions?
   a. IP address
   b. MAC address
   c. TCP/IP port
   d. NetBIOS service name

3. What is the basic reason for implementing a firewall?
   a. It reduces the costs associated with Internet access.
   b. It provides NAT functionality.
   c. It provides a mechanism to protect one network from another.
   d. It enables Internet access to be centralized.

4. Which of the following protocols is used in thin client computing?

   a. RDP

   b. PPP

   c. PPTP

   d. RAS

5. Your company wants to create a secure link between two networks over the Internet. Which of the following protocols would you use to do this?

   a. PPP

   b. VPN

   c. PPTP

   d. SLIP

6. In a thin-client scenario, what information is propagated across the communications link between the client and the server?

   a. Any data retrieved by the client from websites

   b. Screen updates and keyboard and mouse input

   c. Any file opened by the client during the session

   d. Only the graphics files used to create the user's desktop, screen updates, and keyboard and mouse input

7. What is the name for an area that is connected to a firewall but is neither in the private network area nor the public network area?

   a. Area of no return

   b. Demilitarized zone

   c. No man's land

   d. Forbidden zone

8. At which two layers of the OSI model does a packet-filtering firewall operate? (Choose the two best answers.)

   a. Network

   b. Data link

   c. Transport

   d. Application

9. Which of the following protocols does PPTP use to establish connections?

   a. DHCP

   b. FTP

   c. SSL

   d. TCP

10. Which of the following protocols provides authentication and integrity verification for the IPsec protocol?

   a. ESP

   b. AH

   c. Kerberos

   d. MD5

11. After noticing that there have been several attempts to access your network from the Internet, you decide to block port 53. Which of the following services is associated with port 53?

   a. NTP

   b. DNS

   c. SMTP

   d. POP3

12. At which level of the OSI model does a circuit-level firewall operate?

   a. Transport

   b. Data link

   c. Network

   d. Physical

13. You need to secure your network using IPsec and you want point-to-point security. Which IPsec transmission mode provides this?

   a. Transport mode

   b. Tunnel mode

   c. Secure mode

   d. Point to point mode

14. Which of the following is considered a passive security measure?

   a. IPS

   b. IDS

   c. AH

   d. ESP

15. To increase security, you decide to block several ports. Afterward, several users complain they cannot access online banking sites. Which of the following ports needs to be reopened to enable users to access secure sites?

   a. 443

   b. 53

   c. 80

   d. 21

16. You are sending sensitive data over the network and want a method of encrypting the data. Which of the following would accomplish this?

   a. ESP used with IPsec

   b. AH used with IPsec

   c. PPP used with IPsec

   d. Kerberos

17. Your company is moving from a client-based email system to a web-based solution. After all the users have been successfully moved to the new system, what are you likely to do on the corporate firewall? (Choose the two best answers.)

   a. Block port 53

   b. Block port 110

   c. Block port 80

   d. Block port 25

18. To increase network security, you have decided that only the company managers need access to a database server. All manager computers range from IP address 192.168.2.15 to 192.168.2.34. Which of the following security measures are you employing? (Select two.)

   a. Create an ACL that enables only the managers' MAC addresses.

   b. Create a TCP/IP exemptions list in the firewall.

   c. TCP/IP port blocking.

   d. TCP/IP filtering.

19. You have been told to use the PPPoE protocol for establishing connections. Which of the following best describes the function of PPPoE? (Select two.)

   a. Multiple users can share a connection to the Internet.

   b. Secures network wide communications.

   c. Provides a way to keep track of individual users.

   d. Provides point to point secure connections.

20. You have configured your wireless router to allow only certain clients according to the MAC address. This is an example of which of the following?

   a. IDS

   b. IPS

   c. ACL

   d. CRT

This chapter covers CompTIA Network+ objectives 6.4, 6.5, and 6.6. Upon completion of this chapter, you will be able to answer the following questions:

- What are the main types of user authentication?

- What issues threaten the security of network devices?

- What are secure network protocols?

- What are common network security threats?

- How are common security threats minimized?

CHAPTER 15

Security Technologies and Malicious Software

Keeping a network secure is not always an easy task for administrators. When securing a network, administrators must considered certain areas. Chapter 14, "Network Access Security," reviewed network security concepts such as access control lists, firewalls, and security protocols. This chapter continues the discussion of network security, focusing on security elements such as authentication methods and protocols, physical and logical security, secure protocols, and one security concept that is always a threat, malware.

We start this chapter with a review of the relationship between three security concepts: authentication, authorization, and accounting.

Foundation Topics

Authentication, Authorization, and Accounting (AAA)

Before it is possible to establish strong network security, it is essential to understand some of the key security concepts. This includes authentication, authorization, and accountability (AAA). AAA defines a spectrum of security measures, policies, and procedures combined to create a secure network.

Authentication

Authentication refers to the mechanisms used to verify the identity of the computer or user attempting to access a particular resource. Several forms of authentication are used on today's networks. A username and password combination is typically the most common form of authentication. Other types of authentication include

- Smart cards

- Biometrics (fingerprints, retina scan)

- Voice recognition

Authentication is a significant consideration for network and system security, and maintaining strong authentication is a primary concern for network administrators.

Although biometrics and smartcards are becoming more common, they still have a long way to go before they attain the level of popularity that username and password combinations enjoy. Apart from the fact that usernames and passwords do not require any additional equipment, which practically every other method of authentication does, the username and password process is familiar to users, easy to implement, and relatively secure. For that reason, they are worthy of more detailed coverage than the other authentication systems previously listed.

> **TIP: Accessing the Network**   For the Network+ exam, remember that in a Windows environment, two pieces of information are required to access the network: a valid username and a valid password. Both are required to gain access.

Password Policies

Passwords are a relatively simple form of authentication in that only a string of characters can be used to authenticate the user. However, how the string of characters is used and which policies you can put in place to govern them make usernames and passwords an excellent form of authentication.

All popular network operating systems include password policy systems that enable the network administrator to control how passwords are used on the system. The exact capabilities vary between network operating systems. However, generally they enable the following:

- **Minimum length of password**—Shorter passwords are easier to guess than longer ones. Setting a minimum password length does not prevent a user from creating a longer password than the minimum, although each network operating system has a limit on how long a password can be.

- **Password expiration**—Also known as the *maximum password age*, password expiration defines how long the user can use the same password before having to change it. A general practice is that a password is changed every month or every 30 days. In high-security environments, you might want to make this value shorter, but you should generally not make it any longer. Having passwords expire periodically is an important feature because it means that if a password is compromised, the unauthorized user will not have access indefinitely.

- **Prevention of password reuse**—Although a system might cause a password to expire and prompt the user to change it, many users are tempted to simply use the same password again. A process by which the system remembers the last 10 passwords, for instance, is most secure because it forces the user to create completely new passwords. This feature is sometimes called *enforcing password history*.

- **Password complexity**—Some systems have the capability to evaluate the password provided by a user to determine whether it meets a required level of complexity. This prevents users from having passwords such as *password* or *12345678*.

> **TIP: Password Policy**   On the Network+ exam, you might need to identify an effective password policy. For example, a robust password policy would include forcing users to change their passwords on a regular basis.

Password Strength

No matter how good a company's password policy, it is only as effective as the passwords created within it. A password that is hard to guess, or *strong*, is more likely to protect the data on a system than one that is easy to guess, or *weak*.

To understand the difference between a strong password and a weak one, consider this: A password of six characters that uses only numbers and letters and is not case-sensitive has more than 2 billion possible combinations. That might seem like a lot, but to a password-cracking program, it's not much security. A password that uses eight case-sensitive characters, with letters, numbers, and special characters has so many possible combinations that a standard calculator cannot display the actual number.

There has always been debate over how long a password should be. It should be sufficiently long that it is hard to break but sufficiently short that the user can easily remember it (and type it). In a normal working environment, passwords of 8 characters are sufficient. Certainly, they should be no fewer than 6 characters. In environments where security is a concern, passwords should be 12 characters or more.

> **TIP: Password Testing**   Want to see how strong your passwords are? Microsoft has a password checker available at http://www.microsoft.com/protect/yourself/password/checker.mspx.

Users should be encouraged to use a password that is considered strong. A strong password has at least eight characters; has a combination of letters, numbers, and special characters; uses mixed case; and does not form a proper word. Examples might include 3E$cc5T0h and e1oXPn$3r. Such passwords might be secure, but users are likely to have problems remembering them. For that reason, a popular strategy is to use a combination of letters and numbers to form phrases or long words. Examples include d1eTc0La and tAb1eT0p. These passwords might not be quite as secure as the preceding examples, but they are still strong and a whole lot better than the name of the user's household pet.

Mutual Authentication Between Client and Server

When designing a security strategy, all possible scenarios must be considered. In terms of the client/server relationship, how does a client system know it is accessing a legitimate server? Conversely, how does the server know the request is coming from a legitimate client?

It is possible for someone to sit between the client and the server claiming to be the server or a client, but who is trying to obtain sensitive information? This attack method is referred to as the *man-in-the-middle attack*. In this scenario, the attacker sits between the sender and receiver of information and listens to any information sent. Users may be sending unencrypted data, which means the man-in-the-middle can easily obtain any unencrypted information. In other cases an attacker may obtain the information from the attack but have to unencrypt the information before it can be read.

To ensure that the computers at either end of a communication link are actually the intended target and not fake, servers and clients can be required to prove their identities before they exchange information. This procedure, called mutual authentication, requires that both server and client demonstrate knowledge of a "shared secret" (like a password) known only to the two of them. Mutual authentication guarantees that servers provide information only to authorized clients and that clients receive information only from legitimate servers. However, if the two entities cannot mutually authenticate, communication between them will not be allowed.

Mutual authentication is designed to protect against eavesdropping, tampering, and information theft. Communication will not occur until the claimed identity of the other party is verified. In a mutual configuration, systems are essentially assumed to be a fake until proven genuine.

Multifactor Authentication

In many environments a username and password combination is an adequate level of authentication security. However, traditional passwords have well-documented problems. Users forget passwords, choose passwords that are easy to guess, and reuse the same password over and over.

Because of such issues, organizations look at other more convenient and secure forms of authentication. Airports, banks, government agencies, and many high-profile companies spend large amounts of time and resources to create more secure environments. An integral part of this effort is the authentication strategy.

Three strategies that can be used to tighten authentication security are tokens, biometrics, and multifactor authentication schemes.

Authentication Tokens

Authentication tokens typically refer to physical hardware devices carried by users for authentication. For example, workers in airports, hospitals, or other organizations might wear cards on neck chains or on belt loops. These tokens are used to authenticate with a computer terminal.

Such tokens can take the form of smart cards or embedded in a commonly used object such as a USB flash drive. Security tokens provide an extra level of assurance through a method known as *two-factor authentication*: The user has a personal identification number (PIN), which authorizes them as the owner of that particular device; the device then displays a number that uniquely identifies the user to the service, allowing the user to log in.

NOTE: Two-Factor Authentication   Two-factor authentication refers to strategies that combine authentication types. Typically two-factor authentication refers to combining something you know (a password) with something you have (a token).

Biometrics

Biometric systems work by utilizing some unique characteristic of a person's identity—such as a fingerprint, a palm print, voice recognition, or even a retina scan—to validate that person's identity.

> **TIP: Biometrics**   For the Network+ exam, remember that biometric authentica-
> tion has a distinct advantage over swipe card and PIN access. Swipe cards can be
> loaned to people, and PINs can be discovered, but unique physical characteristics
> cannot be duplicated.

The price of biometric systems has been decreasing in recent years and is now in
the budget for most organizations. Because each person attempting to authenticate
must supply proof-of-person evidence, verification of the person is very reliable.
Also, because there are no cards or keys, there is nothing that can be lost.

Multifactor Authentication/Two-Factor Authentication

To authenticate a user, there are three primary categories of authentication:

- Something the user knows (passwords, PIN numbers)

- Something the user has (tokens, smart cards, USB key devices)

- Characteristics of a user (fingerprints, retinal scans, voice recognition)

Each of these approaches provides some level of authentication security. Multifactor authentication involves the combination of two of these authentication categories. This approach can be difficult and costly to implement and is often
restricted to environments that require the highest level of authentication security.

Multifactor authentication is also known as two-factor authentication previously
discussed in the token section. Although multifactor authentication provides an increased level of security, users like the convenience of reusable passwords and do
not like the inconvenience of carrying an object around just to log in to a computer
system. Aside from user resistance, the added expense of cards, tokens, and readers
coupled with the logistics of distribution makes it difficult to justify moving away
from a traditional password-based system. The question is whether and when security is preferable to convenience.

Authorization

Authorization is the method used to determine whether an authenticated user has
access to a particular resource. This is commonly determined through group association; that is, a particular group may have a specific level of security clearance.

Figure 15.1 shows an example of authentication and authorization. Marge is authenticated to the network but is not authorized to use the backup server or the
scanner. She is, however, authorized to use other network resources after she has
been authenticated.

A bank transaction at an ATM is another good example of authentication and authorization. When a bank card is placed in the ATM, the magnetic strip is read,
making it apparent that someone is trying to access a particular account. If the

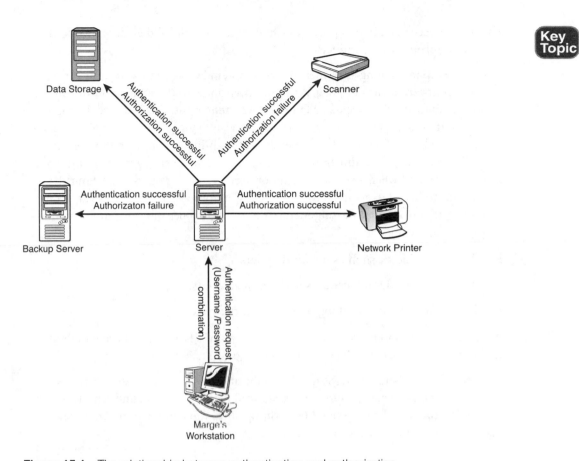

Figure 15.1 The relationship between authentication and authorization.

process ended there and access was granted, it would be a significant security problem because anyone holding the card could gain immediate access. To authenticate the client, after the card is placed in the bank machine, a secret code or PIN is required. This authentication ensures that the PIN number and card match.

With the correct code, the client is verified and authenticated, and access is granted. Authorization addresses the specifics of which accounts or features the user is allowed to access when authenticated, such as a checking or savings account.

Accountability

Accountability refers to the tracking mechanisms used to keep a record of events on a system. One tool often used for this purpose is known as *auditing*. Auditing refers to the process of monitoring events on a system and keeping a log of what has occurred. A system administrator determines the events that should be audited. Tracking events and attempts to access the system helps prevent unauthorized access and provides a record that administrators can analyze to make security changes as necessary. It also provides administrators with solid evidence for looking into improper user conduct.

The first step in auditing is to identify what system events to monitor. After the system events are identified, in a Windows environment, the administrator can choose to monitor the success or failure of a system event. For instance, if "logon" is the event audited, the administrator may choose to log all unsuccessful logon attempts, which may indicate that someone is attempting to gain unauthorized access. Conversely, the administrator can choose to audit all successful attempts to monitor who and when a particular user or user groups log on. Some administrators prefer to log both events. However, overly ambitious audit policies can reduce overall system performance. In general, the common types of events monitored include the following:

- Access to objects, such as files and folders.

- Management of user accounts and group accounts.

- Users logging on to and logging off from the system.

Auditing is an important part of system security and a large part of accountability. It provides a means to track events that occur on a system.

A network administrator might need to audit many events on a system, such as failed/successful logons, printer access, file and directory access, and remote access. Reviewing the log files generated by auditing allows an administrator to better gauge the potential threats to the network.

RADIUS and TACACS+

RADIUS and Terminal Access Controller Access Control System+ (TACACS+) are designed to provide for AAA service. RADIUS and TACACS+ are protocols that enable a single server to become responsible for all remote access authentication, authorization, and auditing (or accounting) services. Although they both provide a function, they do so in a slightly different fashion. This section discusses both protocols and how they are used.

RADIUS

Among the potential issues network administrators face when implementing remote access are utilization and the load on the remote access server. As a network's remote access implementation grows, reliance on a single remote access server might be impossible, and additional servers might be required. RADIUS can help in this scenario.

RADIUS functions as a client/server system. The remote user dials in to the remote access server, which acts as a RADIUS client, or network access server

(NAS), and connects to a RADIUS server. The RADIUS server performs authentication, authorization, and auditing (or accounting) functions and returns the information to the RADIUS client (which is a remote access server running RADIUS client software); the connection is either established or rejected based on the information received.

When RADIUS is used, a client system sends a request to a NAS to gain access to a network or network resource. A NAS can be a wireless access point, VPN server, or even a 802.1x switch. A NAS acts as a gateway between the network and the RAIDUS server. The following outlines the steps in RADIUS authentication:

1. The client system sends its credentials and access request to the NAS system. For instance, attempting to log on to the wireless access point.

2. The NAS forwards this access request message to the RADIUS server. The request message is accompanied with the client credentials (typically username and password combination).

3. The RADIUS server looks over the client request and verifies the credentials using authentication protocols such as PAP, CHAP, and EAP (discussed later in this chapter in the section "Remote Authentication Protocols").

4. Reviewing the user's credentials, RADIUS performs one of the following actions:

   ■ **Deny the request**—If the user's credentials cannot be authorized, the request for access will be denied.

   ■ **Seek more information**—The RADIUS server might request additional information, such as a secondary password or some other means to verify the user's authentication credentials.

   ■ **Accept the client request**—The client system is granted access. The next step is authorization.

Figure 15.2 shows a RADIUS server in action.

With the authentication complete and accepted, the process of authorization and accounting begins. As previously mentioned, authorization refers to the process of granting or denying client access to network resources after authentication. The type and availability of various network resources depends on the user's authorization level.

> **TIP: RADIUS Authorization**   Remember for the Network+ exam that the function of authorization is to establish what a user may do on the network after authentication has been completed.

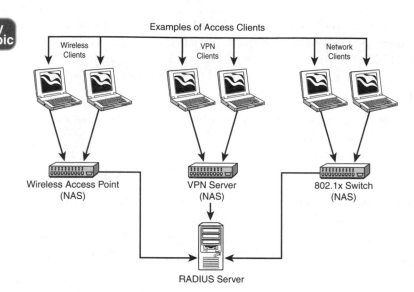

Figure 15.2 RADIUS server.

TACACS+

Terminal Access Controller Access Control System+ (TACACS+) is a security protocol designed to provide centralized validation of users who attempt to gain access to a router or NAS. Like RADIUS, TACACS+ is a set of security protocols designed to provide authentication, authorization, and accounting (AAA) of remote users. TACACS uses TCP port 49 by default.

Although both RADIUS and TACACS+ offer AAA services for remote users, some noticeable differences exist:

- TACACS+ relies on TCP for connection-oriented delivery, whereas RADIUS uses connectionless UDP for data delivery.

- RADIUS combines authentication and authorization, whereas TACACS+ can separate their functions.

> **TIP: RADIUS Versus TACACS+**   For the Network+ exam, remember that TACACS+ relies on the connection-oriented TCP protocol, whereas RADIUS uses the connectionless UDP protocol.

Understanding Cryptography Keys

Before we can continue a discussion of authentication protocols in the following sections, it is important to first understand how cryptography keys work. Cryptography ensures that a client can prove its identity to a server (and vice versa) across an insecure network connection. The term *key* is used for very good reason—public and private keys are used to lock (encrypt) and unlock (decrypt) data. These keys are actually long numbers, making it next to impossible for someone to access a particular key. When keys are used to secure data transmissions, the computer generates two types of keys: a public key and a private key. The distinction between the two follows:

- **Public key**—A nonsecret key that forms half of a cryptographic key pair used with a public key algorithm. The public key is freely given out to all potential receivers.

- **Private key**—The secret half of a cryptographic key pair used with a public key algorithm. The private part of the public key cryptography system is never transmitted over a network.

Keys can be used in two ways to secure data communications: public key encryption (asymmetric) and private (symmetric) key encryption. Private (symmetric) key encryption uses a single key for both encryption and decryption. If a person possesses the key, he or she can both encrypt and decrypt messages. Unlike public keys, this single secret key cannot be shared with anyone except people who should be permitted to decrypt and encrypt messages.

In secret key cryptography, a plain-text message can be converted into ciphertext (encrypted data) and then converted back to plain text using one key. Thus, two devices share a secret key to encrypt and decrypt their communications. Figure 15.3 shows the symmetric key process.

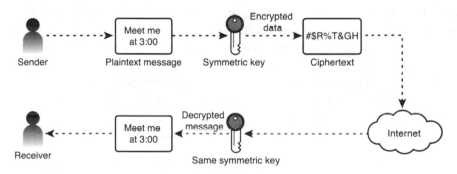

Figure 15.3   Symmetric key process.

Public (asymmetric) key encryption uses both a private and public key to encrypt and decrypt messages. The public key encrypts a message or verifies a signature, and the private key decrypts the message or signs a document. Figure 15.4 shows a public (asymmetric) key encryption.

With an understanding of cryptography keys, we can now look at some of the technologies that use them. First up is the Kerberos protocol.

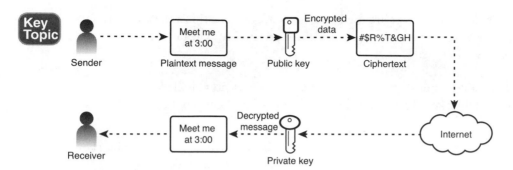

Figure 15.4 Public (asymmetric) key encryption.

Kerberos Authentication

Kerberos is a nonproprietary authentication protocol that provides authentication, which is an integral part of network security. Networks, including the Internet, can connect people from all over the world. When data travels from one point to another across a network, it can be lost, stolen, corrupted, or misused. Much of the data sent over networks is sensitive, whether it is medical data, financial data, or otherwise, and a key consideration for those responsible for the network is maintaining the confidentiality of the data. In the networking world, Kerberos plays a significant role in data confidentiality.

In a traditional authentication strategy, a username and password is used to access network resources. In a secure environment, it may be necessary to provide a username and password combination to access each network service or resource. For example, a user can be prompted to type in her username and password when accessing a database, and again for the printer and again for Internet access. This is a time-consuming process, and it can also present a security risk. Each time the password is typed in, there is a chance it can be seen when typed or, if sent over the network without encryption, it may be viewed by malicious eavesdroppers.

Kerberos was designed to fix such problems by using a method requiring only a single sign-on. This single sign-on enables a user to log in to a system and access multiple systems or resources without the need to reenter the username and password repeatedly. Additionally, Kerberos is designed to have entities authenticate themselves by demonstrating possession of secret information.

Kerberos is one part of a strategic security solution that provides secure authentication services to users, applications, and network devices, by eliminating the insecurities caused by passwords being stored or transmitted across the network. Kerberos is used primarily to eliminate the possibility of a network "eavesdropper" from tapping into data over the network, and particularly usernames and passwords. Kerberos ensures data integrity and blocks tampering on the network. It employs message privacy (encryption) to ensure messages are not visible to eavesdroppers on the network.

For the network user, Kerberos eliminates the need to repeatedly demonstrate possession of private or secret information.

TIP: Kerberos Authentication   For the Network+ exam, remember that Kerberos is a nonproprietary protocol and is used for cross-platform authentica-

Kerberos is designed to provide strong authentication for client/server applications by using secret-key cryptography. After a client and server have used Kerberos to prove their identity, they can also encrypt all their communications to ensure privacy and data integrity.

TIP: Kerberos Security   Remember for the exam, Kerberos enables secure authentication over an insecure network such as the Internet.

The key to understanding Kerberos is to understand the secret key cryptography it uses. Kerberos uses symmetric key cryptography, which was discussed in the previous section. Refer to Figure 15.3 to see how the symmetric key cryptography works.

TIP: Kerberos Keys   For the Network+ exam, remember that Kerberos uses a symmetric key cryptography method.

Kerberos authentication works by assigning a unique key (called a *ticket*), to each client that successfully authenticates to a server. The ticket is encrypted and contains the password of the user, which is used to verify the user's identity when a particular network service is requested. Kerberos works in the same way that you go to a ballgame or a movie. First, you go to a ticket counter, tell the person what game you want to see, and get your ticket. After that, you go to a turnstile and hand the ticket to someone else, and then you're "in." In simplistic terms, that's Kerberos.

TIP: Tickets   For the Network+ exam, you should know that the security tokens used in Kerberos are known as tickets.

Public Key Infrastructure

A public key infrastructure (PKI) is a collection of software, standards, and policies that are combined to enable users from the Internet, or other unsecured public networks, to securely exchange data. PKI is used in a variety of environments and for a range of purposes, including the following:

- **Web security**—As we all know, the Internet is an unsecured network. PKI increases web security by offering server authentication that enables client systems to validate that the server they communicate with is indeed the intended server. Without this information, people can place themselves between the client and the server and intercept client data by pretending to be the server. PKI also offers client authentication, which validates the client's identity.

- **Confidentiality**—PKI provides secure data transmissions using encryption strategies between the client and the server. In application, PKI works with the Secure Sockets Layer (SSL) protocol and the Transport Layer Security (TLS) protocol to provide secure HTTP transfers, referred to as Hypertext Transport Protocol Secure (HTTPS) protocol. To take advantage of the SSL and TLS protocols, both the client system and the server require certificates issued by a mutually trusted certificate authority (CA).

- **Digital signatures**—Digital signatures are the electronic equivalent of a sealed envelope and are intended to ensure that a file has not been altered in transit. Any file with a digital signature verifies not only the publishers of the content or file, but also the content integrity at the time of download. On the network, PKI enables you to issue certificates to internal developers/contractors and enables any employee to verify the origin and integrity of downloaded applications.

- **Secure email**—Today's organizations rely heavily on email to provide external and internal communications. Some of the information sent via email is not sensitive and does not need security, but for those communications that contain sensitive data, a method is needed to secure email content. PKI can be deployed as a method for securing email transactions. In application, a private key can digitally sign outgoing emails, and the sender's certificate is sent with the email so the recipient of the email can verify the sender's signature.

The following sections review the important components of the PKI and how they are combined to provide the services discussed previously.

Components of a PKI

There are services and components working together to develop the PKI. Some of the key components of a PKI include the following:

- **Certificates**—A form of electronic credentials that validates users, computers or devices on the network. A certificate is a digitally signed statement that associates the credentials of a public key to the identity of the person, device, or service that holds the corresponding private key.

- **Certificate authorities (CAs)**—Entities that validate the identity of a network device or user requesting data. CAs issue and manage certificates. CAs can be either independent third parties, known as a *public CA*, or they can be organizations running their own certificate-issuing server software, known as *private CAs*.

- **Certificate templates**—Templates used to customize certificates issued by a certificate server. This customization includes a set of rules and settings created on the CA and used for incoming certificate requests.

- **Certification Revocation List (CRL)**—A list of certificates that have been revoked before they have reached the certificate expiration date. Certificates are often revoked because of security concerns, such as a compromised certificate.

NOTE: PKI keys   PKI uses a public key cryptography method. In public key cryptography, both a private and a public key encrypt and decrypt messages.

Certificates

Certificates are the cornerstones of PKI. A certificate is essentially a form of electronic credentials that validates users, computers, or devices on the network. A certificate is a digitally signed statement that associates the credentials of a public key to the identity of the person, device, or service that holds the corresponding private key. Certificates can provide a number of security services, including the following:

- **Authentication**—An important part of a security strategy. For authentication to happen, users are required to prove their identity to the network device or server to which they try to communicate. Certificates provide the means to ensure that this communication is secure and that the parties involved in the communication are who they say they are.

- **Encryption**—The process of converting something in a plain-text form into an unreadable form. This prevents unwanted eyes from viewing potentially sensitive data. Decryption is the process of taking the unreadable data and converting it to something that can be read. This can be thought of as locking something valuable into a strong box with a key. Using certificates, we have the ability to protect email messages, files on a disk, and files transmitted across the network.

- **Digital signature**—A way to ensure the integrity and origin of data. Integrity involves ensuring that the data received has not been altered since it was signed. Digital signatures also provide a method of verifying the identity of the person or entity who signed the data. This enables the important security features of integrity and nonrepudiation, which are essential for secure electronic commerce transactions.

Discussions of certificates can be quite involved. The following section highlights some of the key concepts surrounding certificates, including certificate stores, trusts, and certificate authorities.

> **TIP: Certificates**   For the Network+ exam remember that a certificate is a form of electronic credentials that validates users, computers, or devices on the network.

Certificate Stores

Certificate stores are essentially a container for certificates and their associated properties. PKI uses five types of certificates stores:

- **Personal**—Stores a user's or a computer's certificates for which the related private key is available.

- **CA stores**—The issuing and intermediate CA certificates to use in the CA hierarchy.

- **Enterprise trust**—Contains certificate trust lists. These are an alternative mechanism that enables an administrator to specify a collection of trusted CAs that must verify to a self-signed CA certificate in the trusted root store.

- **Trusted root**—Contains only self-signed CA certificates that are trust points in the PKI.

- **UserDS**—Stores a logical view of the certificate container located in the Active Directory and simplifies access to certificate stores.

Trusts

The issue of trust is an important consideration when looking at PKI. For instance, in a private key encryption method, the two parties exchanging data trust their shared private key. It is assumed that the private key is stored securely, and therefore, message integrity exists between the sender and receiver. The trust is built on the security of the private key.

A trust built in a public key encryption method is another story altogether. Both parties each secure their own private key, and at the same time, they have to share each other's public key. This means that when we receive a digitally signed message, we need to trust that the digital signature is from whoever claimed to make it. Trusting this public key is a critical consideration for the public key infrastructure to work. The problem is, how can a public key be implicitly trusted?

There are two steps in forming this trust. The first is confirming the validity of the signature using the known public key. Using this key, it is possible to determine the integrity of the signature and ensure that the signature is mathematically valid. The problem is, even if you know the signature is mathematically valid, how do you know you used the right public key? That is, is it the public key from the other end of the communication that made the signature in the first place? It might not be.

To complete the trust in a public key encryption, it is necessary to locate a certificate for the public key that can verify that the key belongs to the right entity. To do this, the certificate must be issued by a CA)that is implicitly trusted by the receiver. If the receiver trusts a particular CA, all certificates issued by that CA are, in turn, trusted.

After a certificate has verified the public key by a trusted CA, the signature is trusted.

Certificate Authorities (CAs)

CAs are entities that validate user identities and that issue and manage certificates. As outlined previously, the CA provides security certificates that ensure that people are who they say they are. CAs can be either independent third parties, known as a public CA, or they can be organizations running their own certificate-issuing server software, known as private CAs.

Public CAs

Public CAs are organizations such as VeriSign or Entrust, which issue publicly accessible certificates. On the Internet, many of the e-commerce sites use these types of third-party CAs for their secured websites. Such a strategy is designed to increase consumer confidence in ensuring that the communication is secure. Public CAs are often used in the following circumstances:

- If you buy or sell products over the Internet, you can use third-party certificates to verify the transaction.

- If the resources or trained personnel are not available to deploy a PKI strategy into an internal network, a public CA can be used.

- If certification use is limited, public CAs have the infrastructure in place to accommodate limited use.

- Third-party CAs can be used for interorganization communication because the certificates are acquired from a common third-party root authority.

Private CAs

Public CAs have found considerable success when conducting transactions over the Internet; however, some organizations choose to create and manage an internal CA. Although it can take more effort to create an internal CA, it also provides an organization with control over all client-issued certificates and as a side benefit, decreases the cost of obtaining certificates from third-party CAs. Private CAs are often deployed under the following conditions:

- An organization requires increased control over client-issued certificates.

- Current infrastructure and expertise are in place to support the PKI.

- An organization wants to reduce the costs associated with obtaining third-party certificates.

Network Access Control

When we talk about network access control, we talk about the mechanisms used to filter network traffic to determine who is and who is not allowed to access the network and network resources. Firewalls, proxy servers, routers, and individual computers all have the capability to maintain access control to some degree. By limiting who can and cannot access the network and its resources, it is easy to understand why access control plays an important role in security strategy. There are a few types of access control:

- Mandatory Access Control (MAC)

- Discretionary Access Control (DAC)

- Rule-Based Access Control (RBAC)

- Role-Based Access Control (RBAC)

The following sections describe each of these access control types.

Mandatory Access Control (MAC)

MAC is the most secure form of access control. In systems configured to use MAC, administrators dictate who can access and modify data, systems, and resources. MAC systems are commonly used in military installations, financial institutions, and because of new privacy laws, medical institutions.

NOTE: MAC x 2 With so many acronyms in the IT world, it makes sense that some of them would overlap. MAC can refer to either the media access control, which is a hexadecimal address that uniquely identifies network cards, and mandatory access control. Both might be referenced on the exam; however, the tests make clear which one is referred to.

MAC secures information and resources by assigning sensitivity labels to objects and users. When a user requests access to an object, his sensitivity level is compared to the objects. A label is a feature applied to files, directories, and other resources in the system. It is similar to a confidentiality stamp. When a label is placed on a file, it describes the level of security for that specific file and permits access only by files, users, programs, and so on with a similar or higher security setting.

Discretionary Access Control (DAC)

Unlike MAC, DAC is not forced from the administrator or the operating system. Instead, access is controlled by an object's owner. For example, if a secretary creates a folder, she decides who will have access to that folder. This access is configured using the permissions dialog box.

DAC uses an ACL to determine access. The ACL is a table that informs the operating system of the rights each user has to a particular system object, such as a file, a directory, or a printer. Each object has a security attribute that identifies its ACL. The list has an entry for each system user with access privileges. The most common privileges include the ability to read a file (or all the files in a directory), to write to the file or files, and to execute the file (if it is an executable file or program).

Microsoft Windows servers/XP/Vista, Linux, UNIX, and MAC OS X are among the operating systems that use ACLs. The list is implemented differently by each operating system.

In Windows server products, an ACL is associated with each system object. Each ACL has one or more access control entries (ACE) consisting of the name of a user or group of users. The user can also be a role name, such as "secretary," or "research." For each of these users, groups, or roles, the access privileges are stated in a string of bits called an *access mask*. Generally, the system administrator or the object owner creates the ACL for an object.

Rule-Based Access Control (RBAC)

RBAC controls access to objects according to established rules. The configuration and security settings established on a router or a firewall are good examples.

When a firewall is configured, rules are set up that control access to the network. Requests are reviewed to see if the requestor meets the criteria to be allowed access through the firewall. For instance, if a firewall is configured to reject all addresses in the 192.168.x.x range of IP addresses, and the requestor's IP is in that range, the request would be denied.

In a practical application, rule-based access control is a variation of MAC. Administrators typically configure the firewall or other device to allow or deny access. The owner or another user does not specify the conditions of acceptance, and safeguards ensure that an average user cannot change settings on the devices.

Role-Based Access Control (RBAC)

In RBAC, access decisions are determined by the roles that individual users have within the organization. Role-based access requires the administrator to have a thorough understanding of how a particular organization operates, the number of users, and each user's exact function in that organization.

Because access rights are grouped by role name, the use of resources is restricted to individuals authorized to assume the associated role. For example, within a school system, the role of teacher can include access to certain data, including test banks, research material, and memos. School administrators might have access to employee records, financial data, planning projects, and more.

The use of roles to control access can be an effective means for developing and enforcing enterprise-specific security policies, and for streamlining the security management process.

Roles should receive just the privilege level necessary to do the job associated with that role. This general security principal is known as the *least privilege* concept. When someone is hired in an organization, the employee's role is clearly defined. A network administrator creates a user account for the new employee and places that user account in a group with those with the same role in the organization.

Least privilege is often too restrictive to be practical in business. For instance, using teachers as an example, some more experienced teachers can have more responsibility than others and require increased access to a particular network object. Customizing access to each individual is a time-consuming process.

NOTE: Where's 802.1x?   802.1x is a standard that specifies port-based network access control. 802.1x is often associated with wireless networks. Information on 802.1x was covered in Chapter 7, "Wireless Networking."

Remote Authentication Protocols

One of the most important decisions an administrator needs to make when designing a remote access strategy is the method by which remote users will be authenticated. Authentication refers to the mechanisms that verify the identity of the computer or user attempting to access a particular resource. The exact protocol used by an organization depends on its security policies. The authentication methods can include the following:

■   **Microsoft Challenge Handshake Protocol (Microsoft-CHAP or MS-CHAP)**—Authenticates remote Windows workstations, providing the functionality to which LAN-based users are accustomed while integrating the hashing algorithms used on Windows networks. MS-CHAP works with PPP, PPTP, and L2TP network connections. MS-CHAP uses a challenge/response mechanism to keep the password from being sent during the authentication process. MS-CHAP uses the Message Digest 5 (MD5) hashing algorithm and the Data Encryption Standard (DES) encryption algorithm to generate the challenge and response and provides mechanisms for reporting connection errors and for changing the user's password.

- **Microsoft Challenge Handshake Authentication Protocol version 2 (MS-CHAP v2)**—The second version of MS-CHAP brings with it enhancements over its predecessor. These enhancements include support for two-way authentication and a few changes in how the cryptographic key is analyzed. As far as authentication methods are concerned, MS-CHAP version 2 is the most secure. MS-CHAP works with PPP, PPTP, and L2TP network connections.

- **Challenge Handshake Authentication Protocol (CHAP)**—CHAP is a widely supported authentication method and works much the same way as MS-CHAP. A key difference between the two is that CHAP supports non-Microsoft remote access clients. CHAP allows for authentication without actually having users send their passwords over the network, and because it's an industry standard, it enables Windows Servers to behave as a remote client to almost any third-party PPP server.

- **Extensible Authentication Protocol (EAP)**—EAP is an extension of PPP that supports authentication methods that go beyond the simple submission of a username and password. EAP was developed in response to an increasing demand for authentication methods that use other types of security devices such as token cards, smart cards, and digital certificates.

- **Password Authentication Protocol (PAP)**—Use PAP only if necessary. PAP is a simple authentication protocol in which the username and password are sent to the remote access server in unencrypted text, making it possible for anyone listening to network traffic to steal both. PAP is typically used only when connecting to older UNIX-based remote access servers that do not support any additional authentication protocols.

- **Unauthenticated Access**—Users are allowed to log on without authentication.

Choosing the correct authentication protocol for remote clients is an important part of designing a secure remote access strategy. After they are authenticated, users have access to the network and servers. It is recommended for administrators to start with the most secure protocol, MS-CHAP v2.

> **TIP: Authentication Protocols**   Before taking the Network+ exam, you should be familiar with the different remote access authentication methods and know where and when they can be used.

Using Secure Protocols

We use many protocols to move information throughout networks. Some of these protocols are secure, whereas others offer little and sometimes no security at all. When administering a network, it is important to choose the right protocol for the job. TCP/IP protocols were discussed in Chapter 4, "Understanding the TCP/IP

Protocol Suite." However, Table 15.1 compares some unsecured protocols with the secure counterpart.

Table 15.1   Comparing Protocols

Protocol	Full Name	Description
FTP	File Transfer Protocol	For uploading and downloading files to and from a remote host; also accommodates basic file-management tasks.
SFTP	Secure File Transfer Protocol	For securely uploading and downloading files to and from a remote host. Based on SSH security.
HTTP	Hypertext Transfer Protocol	For retrieving files from a web server. Data is sent in clear text.
HTTPS	Hypertext Transfer Protocol Secure	Secure protocol for retrieving files from a web server. HTTPS uses SSL for encrypting data between the client and the host.
Telnet	Telnet	Enables sessions to be opened on a remote host.
RSH	UNIX utility used to run a command	Replaced with SSH because RSH sends all on a remote machine data clear text.
SSH	Secure Shell	Secure alternative to Telnet that enables secure sessions to be opened on a remote host.
RCP	Remote Copy Protocol	Copies files between systems but transport is not secured.
SCP	Secure Copy Protocol	Allows files to be copied securely between two systems. Uses Secure Shell (SSH) technology to provide encryption services.
SNMPv1, SNMP v2 and SNMP v3	Simple Network Management Protocol	Network monitoring system used to monitor the network's condition. Both SNMPv1 and 2 are not secured.

Malicious Software

Malicious software, or malware, is a serious problem in today's computing environments. It is often assumed that malware is composed of viruses. Although this is typically true, many other forms of malware exist that by definition are not viruses but are equally undesirable.

The term *malware* is a general term that includes a variety of software threats, including the following:

- **Viruses**—By now, we have all heard of computer viruses. These are the dreaded software programs or code that can unknowingly operate on our computers and cause a range of problems. Often, viruses get blamed for more than they actually do, but as we know, they can cause significant problems.

- **Macro viruses**—One variant of the regular virus is a macro virus. These are the viruses targeted directly at documents. Given that often the data on our systems is the most hard to replace, losing documents or corrupting documents can be a huge loss.

- **Worms**—Worms are programs designed to propagate automatically and silently without modifying software or alerting the user. Inside a system, they can carry out their intended harm, whether it is to damage data or relay sensitive information.

- **Trojan horses**—Trojan horses are particularly tricky and require users to be keenly aware of the programs they install on a computer system. Essentially, Trojan horses appear as helpful or harmless programs but, when installed, carry and deliver a malicious payload. For example, harmless online games might be installed on a system, but they actually might install harmful code at the same time.

- **Spyware**—Spyware covertly gathers system information through users' Internet connection without their knowledge, usually for advertising purposes. Spyware applications are typically bundled as a hidden component of freeware or shareware programs that can be downloaded from the Internet.

Each of these viruses pose a threat to the systems on a network. But how does this malicious software propagate? As a network administrator, you need to be aware of how the various types of malware are distributed.

Malware Distribution

To be effective, malware requires a method to get from one computer to another. Those administering networks or individual systems should know how malware is transported because it helps to determine the strategies used to fight the viruses. Following are some of the common malware delivery types:

- **Removable media**—In the past, floppy disks were the most common mechanism for delivering malware. Today we have many forms of removable media, MP3 players, USB storage devices, and more. All these devices can carry viruses into a network if they go unchecked. Policies, such as checking such devices before using them in a network and restricting access to removable media, are common. USB and FireWire devices can transport both legitimate files and malware because they are commonly used to carry files or applications between computers.

- **Peer-to-peer (P2P) sharing networks**—P2P networks that offer free applications, music, and other software are often ripe with viruses, worms, Trojan horses, and spyware. Many of these malware types can replicate quickly and be tricky to handle. Many network administrators have created policies restricting access to such sites. These policies limit what can be installed on a local computer system.

- **Network shares**—A network share is a file, folder, or resource made available to the network. Malware can use the network shares to propagate itself from system to system over the network. Poorly implemented security on network shares produces an environment where malware can replicate to a large number of computers connected to the network.

- **Email**—Email has traditionally been a hot spot for virus propagation. Many networks have email monitoring software to help determine the presence of viruses in email. Preventing email viruses is important because with the click of a button, malware can be sent to hundreds of thousands of users. Most malware attacks through email require the recipient to activate the attack either by opening an email or downloading something from the email after assuming it is from a trusted source.

These examples show how malware can be transported from system to system. Because the individuals who write and export malware are always designing new programs, they are also continually finding new ways to transport their software. Administrators need to keep abreast of new and existing transport mechanisms.

Malware Payloads

When we talk about a malware payload, we refer to the way in which it impacts the computer system or the description of its intended purpose. To help detect malware, knowing what it is designed to do can help administrators be aware of potential threats. Some of the more common payloads include the following:

- **Attacks on data**—Many of the malicious programs are designed to attack data by corrupting, deleting, or stealing it. These attacks are particularly dangerous because data is the most valuable resource on the network.

- **Backdoor attacks**—If backdoor access to a system is found, an intruder can take complete or partial control over a system. The user might not even know that the takeover is occurring. The intruder can then use that system as a launching point to stage other attacks or steal personal information or data.

- **Overwhelm system resources**—Some malware is specifically designed to overload and ultimately prevent a service form running or to crash the entire system. This is a denial-of-service attack.

- **Applications**—Many malware programs corrupt or take over applications. Applications include everything from the word processor to the firewall software.

More About Viruses

Viruses and their effects are well documented and are feared by users and administrators alike. The damage from viruses varies greatly from disabling an entire network to damaging applications on a single system. Regardless of the impact, viruses can be destructive, causing irreplaceable data loss and consuming hours of productivity.

As mentioned, not all the malware we encounter is by definition a virus. To be considered a virus, the malware must possess the following characteristics:

- It must be able to replicate itself.

- It requires a host program as a carrier.

- It must be activated or executed to run.

TIP: Virus or Not?   For the Network+ exam, remember that a virus must be able to replicate itself.

There are many types of viruses and many terms to describe them, such as the following:

- **Resident virus**—A resident virus installs itself into the operating system and stays there. It typically places itself into memory and from there infects and does damage. The resident virus loads with the operating system on boot.

- **Variant virus**—Like any other applications, from time to time viruses are enhanced to make them harder to detect and modify the damage that they do. Modifications to existing viruses are referred to as variants because they are rereleased versions of known viruses.

- **Polymorphic virus**—One particularly hard to handle type of virus is the polymorphic one. These have the capability to change their characteristics to avoid detection. Polymorphic viruses are some of the most difficult types to detect and remove.

- **Overwriting/nonoverwriting virus**—Viruses can be designed to overwrite files or code and replace them with modified data. In many cases the application can function as normal, so the user will not know the program has been modified. Non-overwriting viruses amend an application by adding files or code.

- **Stealth virus**—A stealth virus is one that hides itself to avoid detection. Such viruses often fool detection programs by appearing as legitimate programs or hiding within legitimate programs.

- **Macro virus**—Macro viruses are specifically designed to infect and corrupt documents. Because documents are commonly shared, these viruses can spread at an alarming rate.

More About Trojan Horses and Worms

Trojan horses, as the name implies, are about hiding. Trojan horses come hidden in other programs. For example, a Trojan horse can be hidden in a shareware game. The game looks harmless but when downloaded and executed, the Trojan operates in the background, corrupting and damaging the system.

Trojan horses are different from viruses because a Trojan horse does not replicate itself and does not require a host program to run. They are commonly found on P2P sharing networks where interesting and helpful looking programs are actually disguised Trojan horses. Trojan horses are also spread when programs are shared using email communications or removable media. In the past, many of the executable jokes sent through email, such as cartoons and amusing games were the front end of a Trojan horse.

Worms are different and have the potential to spread faster than any other form of malware. Worms can be differentiated from viruses. Although they can replicate, they do not require a host and do not require user intervention to propagate. Worms can spread at an alarming rate because they often exploit security holes in applications or operating systems. After a security hole is found, worms automatically begin to replicate, looking for new hosts with the same vulnerability. Worms look for an Internet connection and then use that connection to replicate without any user intervention.

Comparing Malware Types

Table 15.2 identifies the distinctions between worms, Trojan horses, and viruses.

Table 15.2   Comparing Malware Types

Malware Type	Self-Replicates	Requires a Host	Requires User Intervention
Virus	Yes	Yes, requires a host program to propagate.	Sometimes, many viruses require user intervention to be activated. Others can be remotely activated.
Trojan horse	No	No, does not require a host program.	Yes, user must execute a program in which the Trojan horse is hidden.
Worms	Yes, without user intervention	No, self-contained and does not require a host.	No, replicates and activates without requiring user intervention.

Types of Attacks

Life would be easier for network administrators if fewer types of attacks were launched against networks. Unfortunately, numerous attacks exist that administrators must be aware of, with new ones always being discovered. In this section we review some of the more common attacks.

Denial of Service and Distributed Denial of Service Attacks

Denial of service (DoS) attacks are designed to tie up network bandwidth and resources and eventually bring the entire network to a halt. This type of attack is done by flooding a network with more traffic than it can handle. A DoS attack is not designed to steal data but to cripple a network and in doing so may have a significant financial impact on companies.

The effects of DoS attacks include the following:

- Saturating network resources, which then render those services unusable.

- Flooding the network media, preventing communication between computers on the network.

- User downtime because of an inability to access required services.

- Potentially huge financial losses for an organization because of network and service downtime.

Whereas a DoS attack focuses on a single system or a few systems, a distributed denial of service (DDoS) attack takes out entire networks. In a DDoS attack, an influx of traffic halts network functionality. DDoS attacks can also be aimed at specific server types within a network. For example, DDoS attacks can be launched against a network's mail servers, DNS servers, or web servers.

DDoS and Zombies

To target and flood an entire network is no easy task. To aid in this, DDoS attacks often use zombie computer systems. Malware such as a Trojan horse can be used to turn systems into a zombie computer system. A zombie computer system (zombie) is one that has been compromised by a hacker, and the hacker can use that computer for a variety of purposes, such as sending spam, thereby launching DDoS attacks. Users typically have no idea that their system has been compromised because for the users, everything appears to be normal. A collection of these compromised systems is referred to as botnets.

Zombies are often used to launch DDoS attacks. The zombie agent software is surreptitiously installed on a computer system and then sits dormant until activated. This way, it is possible to gather hundreds or thousands of computers to use in an attack. Essentially, attackers can create their own zombie army, a term that refers to the orchestrated flooding of target websites by armies of zombie computers.

Detecting zombie agents installed on a system can be tricky because they often are not detected with outdated antivirus software. Signs that a system might have a zombie agent installed include the following:

- Systems that are constantly accessing the hard disk without user activity

- Slower Internet connection speeds

- Slow boot and shutdown times

- Overall slow system performance

- Unusual occurrences, such as the web browser shutting off unexpectedly or virus checker failures

TIP: DDoS For the Network+ exam, remember that DoS and DDoS attacks are attempts by attackers to prevent use of a system or service from using that service.

There are several types of DoS and DDoS attacks, and each targets a different area. For instance, they can target bandwidth, memory, CPU, and hard drive space. When a server or other system is overrun by malicious requests, one or more of these core resources breaks down, causing the system to crash or stop responding.

- **Fraggle**—In a Fraggle attack, spoofed UDP packets are sent to a network's broadcast address. These packets are directed to specific ports such as port 7 (ICMP) or port 19 (chargen); after they connect, they can flood the system.

- **Smurf**—The Smurf attack is similar to a Fraggle attack, except a ping request is sent to a broadcast network address with the sending address spoofed so that many ping replies come back to the victim and overload the ability of the victim to process the replies.

- **Ping of Death**—With this attack, an oversized ICMP datagram is used to crash IP devices that were manufactured before 1996.

TIP: ICMP Floods For the Network+ exam, remember that attacks that focus on port 7 (ICMP) and use ping are known as ICMP flood attacks. Ping of death, Fraggle, and Smurf are all forms of ICMP flood attacks.

- **SYN flood**—In a typical TCP session, communication between two computers is initially established by a three-way handshake referred to a SYN, SYN/ACK, ACK. At the start of a session, the client sends a SYN message to the server. The server acknowledges the request by sending a SYN/ACK message back to the client. The connection is established when the client responds with an ACK message.

In a SYN attack, the victim is overwhelmed with a flood of SYN packets. Every SYN packet forces the targeted server to produce a SYN-ACK response and then wait for the ACK acknowledgment. However, the attacker won't respond with an ACK or will spoof its destination IP address with a nonexistent address so that there is no ACK response. The result is that the server begins filling up with half-open connections. When all the server's available resources are tied up on half-open connections, it stops acknowledging new incoming SYN requests, including legitimate ones.

Other Common Attacks

Malware and DoS attacks are not the only threats facing network administrators. Other threats include the following:

- **Password attacks**—One of the most common types of attacks. Typically, usernames are easy to obtain, and matching the username with the password allows the intruder to gain system access to the level associated with that particular user. This access is why it is vital to protect administrator passwords. Obtaining a password with administrator privileges provides the intruder with total unrestricted access to the system or network.

- **Social engineering**—A common form of cracking. It can be used both by outsiders and by people within an organization. Social engineering is a hacker term for tricking people into revealing their password or some form of security information. It can include trying to get users to send passwords or other information over email, shoulder surfing, or any other method that tricks users into divulging information. Social engineering is an attack that attempts to take advantage of human behavior.

- **Eavesdropping**—As the name implies, eavesdropping involves an intruder who obtains sensitive information such as passwords, data, and procedures for performing functions by intercepting, listening, and analyzing network communications. An intruder can eavesdrop by wiretapping, using radio, or auxiliary ports on terminals. It is also possible to eavesdrop using software that monitors packets sent over the network. In most cases, it is difficult to detect eavesdropping, making it important to ensure that sensitive data is not sent over the network in clear text.

- **Man-in-the-middle attack**—The intruder places himself between the sending and receiving devices and captures the communication as it passes by. The interception of the data is invisible to those actually sending and receiving the data. The intruder captures the network data and manipulates it, changes it, examines it, and then sends it on. Wireless communications are particularly susceptible to this type of attack. A rogue access point can be an example of a man-in-the-middle attack.

- **Spoofing**—A technique in which the real source of a transmission, file, or email is concealed or replaced with a fake source. This technique enables an attacker, for example, to misrepresent the original source of a file available for download to trick users into accepting a file from an untrusted source, believing it is coming from a trusted source.

- **Rogue access points**—Describes a situation in which a wireless access point has been placed on a network without knowledge of the administrator. The result is that it is possible to remotely access the rogue access point because it likely does not adhere to company security policies. So all security can be compromised by a cheap wireless router placed on the corporate network.

- **Phishing**—Often, users receive a variety of emails offering products, services, information, or opportunities. Unsolicited email of this type is referred to as *phishing* (fishing). The technique involves a bogus offer sent to hundreds of thousands or even millions of email addresses. The strategy plays the odds; for every 1,000 emails sent perhaps 1 person replies. Phishing can be dangerous because users can be tricked into divulging personal information such as credit card numbers or bank account information.

> **TIP: Attack Types**   The Network+ exam is sure to have questions requiring you to identify the types of attacks used. Be sure you can identify the attacks described in the preceding list before taking the exam.

An Ounce of Prevention

The threat from malicious code is a huge concern. We must take the steps to protect our systems, and although we might not eliminate the threat, we can significantly reduce that threat.

One of the primary tools used in the fight against malicious software is *antivirus software*. Antivirus software is available from a number of companies, and each offers similar features and capabilities. The following is a list of the common features and characteristics of antivirus software:

- **Real-time protection**—An installed antivirus program should continuously monitor the system, looking for viruses. If a program is downloaded, an application opened, or a suspicious email received, the real-time virus monitor detects and removes the threat. The virus application sits in the background largely unnoticed to the user.

- **Virus scanning**—An antivirus program must be capable of scanning selected drives and disks either locally or remotely. Scanning can either be run manually or be scheduled to run at a particular time.

- **Scheduling**—It is a best practice to schedule virus scanning to occur automatically at a predetermined time. In a network environment, this would typically occur during off hours when the overhead of the scanning process won't impact users.

- **Automatic updates**—New viruses and malicious software are released with alarming frequency. It is recommended that the antivirus software be configured to receive virus updates regularly.

- **Email vetting**—Emails represent one of the primary sources for virus delivery. It is essential to use antivirus software that provides email scanning for both inbound and outbound email.

- **Centralized management**—In a network environment, it is a good idea to use software that supports managing the antivirus program from the server. Antivirus updates and configurations need to be made only on the server and not on each individual client station.

Managing the threat from viruses is considered a proactive measure, with antivirus software being only part of the solution. A complete virus protection strategy requires many aspects to help limit the risk of viruses, including the following:

- **Develop in-house policies and rules**—In a corporate environment, or even a small office, it is important to establish what information can be placed onto a system. For example, should users download programs from the Internet? Can users bring in their own flash drives or other storage media?

- **Monitoring virus threats**—With new viruses coming out all the time, it is important to check whether new viruses have been released and what they are designed to do.

- **Educate users**—One of the keys to a complete antivirus solution is to train users in virus prevention and recognition techniques. If users know what they are looking for, it can prevent a virus from entering the system or the network. Back up copies of important documents. Be aware that no solution is absolute and care should be taken to ensure the data is backed up. If a malicious attack occurs, redundant information is available in a secure location.

- **Automate virus scanning and updates**—Today's antivirus software can be configured to scan and update itself automatically. Because such tasks can be forgotten and overlooked, it is recommended to have these processes scheduled to run at predetermined times.

- **Patches and updates**—All applications, antivirus programs, and operating systems release patches and updates often; they are designed to address potential security weaknesses. Administrators must keep an eye out for these patches and install them when needed.

The preceding list describes common strategies that can help prevent and manage malware on networks and computer systems. Several strategies are required to mitigate and manage the threats from attacks such as DoS and DDoS, follows:

- Installing an intrusion detection or intrusion prevention system on the network or computer system.

- Use up-to-date antivirus software to help locate possible zombie agents.

- To prevent exploitation of security flaws, ensure your applications and operating systems patches are current.

- Use monitoring software that can identify slow down or unusual behavior on a network or computer system.

- Disable any unused network services.

- Ensure that firewalls are used and properly configured.

Maintaining Operating System Software

One of the key components to keeping systems safe is maintaining the operating system. This includes keeping the network operating software up to date with patches and service that address security issues.

Operating systems are complex systems having to accommodate a dynamic environment while providing services to clients and applications software. This complexity makes it hard to produce products that operate at 100 percent capacity on every level, making it necessary to apply periodic updates to the software. This operation can be one of the more time-consuming and complex server maintenance tasks.

Operating systems are generally updated through the use of patches and service packs. Windows operating systems, for instance, periodically introduce service packs starting with, as most do, service pack 1; they keep producing service packs as issues and security flaws are detected. Each of these service packs provides fixes, updates, and enhanced features for the operating system. However, many servers using Windows do not have the latest service packs installed, leaving them at potential risk of being hacked. To be as secure as possible, you need to know when, why, and how service packs should be used on a server.

> **NOTE: Updating Software**   Service packs are not restricted to operating systems, but can include all application software running on the computer. This abundance of service packs can represent an interesting challenge to server administrators because an update for one product will sometimes necessitate an update for a different product.

Reasons to Use a Service Pack

If you use an operating system out-of-the-box and expect it to provide all the functionality it advertised, you might be out of luck. Before they are released, operating systems are run through a rigorous testing period, including being released in a Beta version to get further testing, with real-world applications, before going live. However, there is no way to cover all real-world applications in a test environment, so when the operating system comes out, its shortcomings are soon discovered. Service packs are released to address problems with the operating system's functionality.

Traditionally, updates to software were distributed individually, with each separate problem necessitating a specific fix. In recent years, the complexity of the software and the need to streamline the application of fixes has led to the use of service packs, which are essentially complete programs designed to easily correct a large number of problems in a single exercise. Even so, software companies still issue specific patches for certain situations.

Although service packs are commonly applied to fix errors or shortcomings of an operating system, some applications will install and run only if the latest service pack is installed. Your server might be functioning well, but when you try to install a new proxy server program, the installation can shut down with a message stating that a newer service pack is required for the installation of the product. These messages are not normally given for the amusement of the software developers; generally, these messages indicate that an unstable situation might arise if the new software is installed on a platform that doesn't have the required service pack installed.

A less-obvious reason for installing services packs is that if you call an operating system manufacturer's technical support line, one of the first questions you will be asked is whether you have the latest service pack installed. The support representative's first recommendation will probably be to upgrade to the latest service pack, and if that doesn't fix the problem, call back. Software manufacturers do not make this stipulation unnecessarily. When someone attempts to troubleshoot a problem, knowing that the underlying operating system is at a given level is an important step in the resolution process.

When to Use a Service Pack

There are some clear guidelines to follow when you consider installing a service pack on a server. Keep in mind that any change to a server—whether it's a software or a hardware change—has the potential for disaster. Therefore, service pack updates are installed only when they're needed to address a known bug with the operating system or when they include a new feature that you need. If you apply a service pack without knowing the reason why, you are guilty of a techno sin—that of blind patching.

Blind patching is the term given to describe the practice of upgrading without knowing the issues you are trying to address. It is a dangerous practice. You must know the specific reasons that a service pack needs to be installed and what it promises to address.

How to Apply a Service Pack

Unfortunately, applying a service pack is not always as easy as simply downloading it and installing it. The installation of service packs is generally well documented by the operating system manufacturer, and the instructions given must be closely followed. The exact instructions for applying service packs can generally be found on the manufacturers' websites (on their support and knowledge base pages).

When you install a service pack, follow these guidelines:

1. **Review the documentation.** Before even downloading the service pack, review the documentation to ensure that there are no last-minute changes and that you are sure that the service pack addresses the problems you have.

2. **Verify free space.** Service packs can be large, so before downloading them, make sure that the server has enough hard disk space for you to apply the patch. If the drive doesn't have the space, you need to free some up.

3. **Test the service pack.** Although it is not always possible, it is recommended that you download and install the service pack on another computer to discover any hidden problems. If you can't do this, check newsgroups for valuable information from other server administrators who have used the service pack. A lot can be gained from the experience of others.

4. **Back up the server.** Make sure that a current backup is done on the system before you apply the service pack. This backup should include the data drives and the main operating system drive. Things can sometimes go wrong, and it's essential to ensure that you can get the server back to the state it was in before you applied the service pack.

5. **Get a baseline.** If the service pack is applied to address a particular problem, it is a good idea to get "before" and "after" pictures. Baselines are often the only means to measure if the service pack has actually addressed the issue it was intended to. If it has, that's good, but if it hasn't, a different fix needs to be applied.

6. **Install the service pack.** As we mentioned, installing a service pack is not always as easy as running an executable file. For instance, is the service pack applied after all the major protocols and services have been installed, or is the service pack applied only after all other server software applications, services, and protocols have been installed and configured? The only way to know how and in what order the service pack is to be installed is to follow the manufacturer's recommendations.

7. **Reinstall and configure as necessary.** Some service packs require some post-installation maintenance and configuration with the operating system. You might need to restart services, reinstall protocols, or update other software.

8. **Test the system.** Before users are allowed back onto the system, it should be thoroughly tested to ensure correct operation. Nothing is likely to annoy users more than being allowed to log back on to the server and then having to log off 5 minutes later because of an unforeseen problem with the service pack.

9. **Perform a comparison baseline.** Whether you expect the update to affect the performance of the server, the baseline must be retaken to ensure that the system has not been detrimentally affected. As we have already discussed, a service pack installation can have far-reaching effects and can, in exceptional cases, affect other system components. A comparison baseline can compare performance before and after the installation of the service pack.

Server Patches

Service packs are released infrequently and are usually used to address numerous issues within an operating system. Patches, on the other hand, provide quick fixes for a program or feature and are more commonplace. Patches are designed to address a specific problem. For instance, you would download a patch to fix a security hole in the operating system when downloading and installing an entire service pack might not be necessary.

NOTE: Hotfix   Patches are sometimes referred to as hotfixes.

The frequency with which patches are released and the relative lack of fanfare that they bring make it difficult to keep ahead of new developments. Maintaining a server involves being aware of the patches that are introduced for both the operating system and other software on the server. Even when the server is running smoothly, hidden problems can exist, such as security holes that patches are designed to fix. Frequently visiting the software manufacturer's website to review the latest patches is not just a good idea, it is an essential part of proactive maintenance.

Another good way of staying up to date with the latest patches and packs is to read related newsgroups and check Internet sites.

Before you even download any patch for the server, first check out the operating system's knowledge base for the specific instructions. Some patches, for instance, work only if applied from within specific directories; some need extra files installed; or some need specific server services shut down. In addition to knowing exactly what the patch is intended to do, you need to know how it must be installed.

Whatever the purpose of the patch, you need to do a full backup because patches invariably change system files. For patches directed toward applications on the server, it can be tempting to skip a backup, but this is not advised. If something goes wrong with the patch, you need to get back to the point you started from before the patch.

> **TIP: Same Rule**   The same rule applies to software patches and service packs: no blind patching is allowed. Know what the patch you are downloading is intended to do, and implement the patch only if it is needed.

Summary

A cornerstone concept of network security is that of authorization, authentication, and accountability (AAA). *Authentication* refers to the mechanisms used to verify the identity of the computer or user attempting to access a particular resource. *Authorization* refers to the ability of the user to access a service or network resource after authentication, and *accountability* is the tracking of users on the network.

Several types of authentication are used on a network, including biometrics and smart cards. The most common is a username and password combination. To be strong, passwords should mix uppercase and lowercase letters with numbers and symbols. In network environments where security is a major concern, passwords should be no shorter than 10 characters.

RADIUS and TACACS+ are designed to provide authentication, authorization, and accountability. RADIUS and TACACS+ are protocols that enable a single server to become responsible for all remote access authentication, authorization, and auditing (or accounting) services. RADIUS uses UDP as a transport protocol whereas TACACS+ uses TCP.

PKI and Kerberos are both used for authentication purposes. Kerberos uses tickets for authentication, whereas PKI uses certificates. PKI uses cryptography keys to secure the communication between the client and the server. Private (symmetric) key encryption uses a single key for both encryption and decryption. PKI uses asymmetric keys that use a public key and a private key for encryption and decryption.

When accessing a network remotely, authentication protocols verify the client. These protocols include CHAP, MS-CHAP, MS-CHAPv2, EAP, and PAP.

Several forms of network access control are used, including mandatory access control, discretionary access control, and rule-based and role-based access control. Mandatory access control is dictated by the network administrator, discretionary is dictated by the owner of an object or resource, role-based is assigned according to the role a user has in a network environment, and rule-based access control is dictated according to settings and policies, such as the settings used to control access in a network router.

Administrators need to be aware of many types of malware. This includes viruses, Trojan horses, and worms. A key part in the strategy for managing malware is to ensure that the firewall is set correctly, that the operating system and other applications are patched, and that the antivirus software is up to date.

Exam Preparation Tasks

Review All the Key Topics

Review the most important topics in the chapter, noted with the Key Topics icon in the outer margin of the page. Table 15.3 lists a reference of these key topics and the page numbers on which each is found.

Table 15.3   Key Topics for Chapter 15

Key Topic Element	Description	Page Number
List	Password policies	563
Figure 15.1	The relationship between authentication and authorization	567
Figure 15.2	RADIUS server	570
Figure 15.3	Symmetric key process	571
Figure 15.4	Public (asymmetric) key encryption	572
Table 15.1	Comparing protocols	582
Table 15.2	Comparing malware types	586

Complete the Tables and Lists from Memory

Print a copy of Appendix B, "Memory Tables" (found on the CD), or at least the section for this chapter, and complete the tables and lists from memory. Appendix C, "Memory Tables Answer Key," also on the CD, includes completed tables and lists to check your work.

Define Key Terms

Define the following key terms from this chapter, and check your answers in the Glossary.

- 802.1x
- Certificate
- CHAP
- DAC
- DoS

- DDoS
- EAP
- Encryption
- Kerberos
- MAC
- MS-CHAP
- PAP
- PKI
- Public key
- Private key
- RADIUS
- RBAC
- Security protocol
- SSL
- TACACS+
- Virus
- Worm

Apply Your Knowledge

Exercise 15.1 Choosing How Windows Applies Updates in Windows Vista

Windows Vista can be configured to automatically or manually download and install updates. In most cases the automatic setting will do for desktop systems such as Vista. But as previously mentioned, the server system will not necessarily want live updates occurring. In this exercise we look at the different update options in Windows Vista, but comparable options can be found in most desktop and server operating systems today.

Estimated time: 15 minutes

1. Select Start, Control Panel, and click the Security link. This opens the Windows Vista Security options dialog screen. This screen is shown in Figure 15.5.

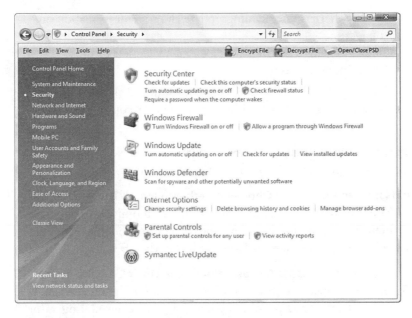

Figure 15.5 Windows Vista Security screen.

2. With the Security window visible, click the Windows Update option. This opens the Windows Update screen as shown in Figure 15.6. The center of the Windows Update screen lists the current status of the system updates. Notice

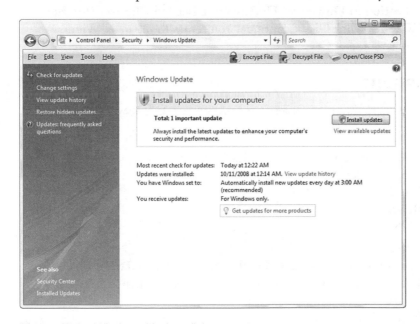

Figure 15.6 Windows Update dialog screen.

from Figure 15.6 that there is one pending update and some information on the most recent updates.

To continue, click the Change Settings link located on the left of the Windows Update Windows screen.

3. In the Change Settings Windows screen, you can configure all the Windows Update features. Windows Vista provides four options for configuring the updates.

- **Install Updates Automatically (Recommended)**—Enables you to set the time of day when you want the automatic updates to occur.

- **Download Updates but Let Me Choose Whether to Install Them**—The updates will be downloaded but not installed until the administrator chooses to install them. This is often done if the update requires too many system resources. The update can then easily be applied in the off hours.

- **Check for Updates but Let Me Choose Whether to Download and Install Them**—Unlike the previous option, in this configuration the update is not downloaded, just flagged as a pending update. This gives the administrator time to review its purpose before deciding to download the update.

- **Never Check for Updates**—This is not the advised option for most configurations. This means that the administrator is responsible to find and download updates if needed.

4. **Select the Option to Download Updates but Let Me Choose Whether to Install Them**—Click OK to continue. You return to the main Windows Update screen.

Review Questions

You can find answers to the review questions in Appendix A, "Answers to Review Questions."

1. Which of the following protocols provides AAA functionality and uses TCP as a transport mechanism?
   a. TACACS+
   b. RADIUS
   c. HTTPS
   d. 802.1x

2. Which of the following terms describes the mechanisms used to verify the identity of the computer or user attempting to access a particular resource?
   a. Authorization
   b. Authentication
   c. Accountability
   d. Accounting

3. Which of the following protocols is used to secure the HTTP protocol?

   a. SSP

   b. PPP

   c. SSL

   d. SFTP

4. What is the function of RADIUS?

   a. RADIUS provides AAA services and uses the UDP protocol.

   b. RADIUS provides AAA services and uses the TCP protocol.

   c. RADIUS provides AAA services and uses the FTP protocol.

   d. RADIUS provides AAA services and uses the HTTP protocol.

5. Which of the following malware types does not replicate itself?

   a. Worm

   b. Trojan horse

   c. Virus

   d. Macro-virus

6. Which of the following is the strongest password?

   a. password

   b. WE300GO

   c. l00#Ka1ivE

   d. lovethemusic

7. Which of the following are PPP authentication methods? (Choose the two best answers.)

   a. SLAP

   b. CHAP

   c. MS-CHAP

   d. POP

8. You are the network administrator for a large network. You have just received an email warning of a potential security flaw in your network operating system. Which of the following should you do first?

   a. Install a service pack to mitigate the threat.

   b. Back up the server and take a baseline.

   c. Review the documentation for the service pack or hotfix.

   d. Back up the server, take a baseline, and apply the fix.

9. SSH is a secure alternative to which of the following?

   a. Telnet

   b. DHCP

   c. PPTP

   d. Kerberos

10. Kerberos is an authentication system that can be used on what operating systems?

   a. Windows 2003/Vista

   b. Linux

   c. Mac OS X

   d. All the options are correct.

11. What is the purpose of auditing?

   a. It allows you to be notified when a security breach is detected.

   b. It allows you to determine whether a security breach has occurred.

   c. It allows you to prevent security breaches.

   d. It allows you to control Internet access from a single point.

12. When defining a password policy for an organization, which of the following would you consider setting? (Choose all the best answers.)

   a. Minimum password length

   b. Password expiration period

   c. Prevention of password reuse

   d. Maximum password length

13. Some of the systems on your network contain sensitive data. Therefore, you have been asked to provide both fingerprint and password authentication. What type of authentication strategy does this represent?

   a. Multilayered authentication

   b. Biometrics

   c. Multifactor authentication

   d. Two-phase authentication

14. Which of the following are not remote access authentication protocols? (Choose all that apply.)

   a. MS-EAP

   b. CHAP

   c. SSL

   d. EAP

15. You suspect that an employee in the company has been logging on to the system from a remote connection and attempting to look through files that he should not have access to. Which mechanism could you use to discover the identity of the person trying to dial in?

   a. Auditing

   b. File permissions

   c. Password policy

   d. Intruder detection

16. Which of the following remote authentication protocols is used with smart card or digital certificates?

   a. Chap

   b. EAP

   c. CHAPv5

   d. PAP

17. You are onsite as a consultant. The client's many remote access users are experiencing connection problems. Basically, when users try to connect, the system cannot service their authentication requests. What kind of server might you recommend to alleviate this problem?

   a. RADIUS server

   b. IPsec server

   c. Proxy server

   d. Kerberos RRAS server

18. You are configuring access control for your network. You decide that you need to implement access control for the network. All access control should be determined by an object's owner. What form of access control does this represent?

   a. DOC

   b. RBAC

   c. MAC

   d. DAC

19. Which of the following best describes an asymmetric key encryption strategy?

   a. Asymmetric key encryption uses both a private and public key to encrypt and decrypt messages.

   b. Asymmetric key encryption uses two private keys to encrypt and decrypt messages.

   c. Asymmetric key encryption uses a single key for both encryption and decryption.

   d. Asymmetric key encryption uses three separate keys for both encryption and decryption.

20. You have been called in to test the security of a network. You notice that a wireless router has been placed on the network without consent and is used by remote users to access the network. Which security risk does this represent?

   a. Rogue protocol use

   b. Malware

   c. Rogue access point

   d. Signal creep

Answers to the Review Questions

Chapter 1

1. **B.** One of the disadvantages of the physical bus topology is that it's prone to cable faults. In addition, a fault on the cable can render the entire network unusable. The advantages of the physical bus topology are that the cabling is simple, and no additional network hardware is required to create the network.

2. **A, B, D.** VLANs can be created by using protocol assignments, by defining the ports on a device as belonging to a VLAN, or by using MAC addresses. VLANs cannot be created by using the NetBIOS computer name.

3. **C.** A VPN provides a secure communication path between devices over a public network such as the Internet. None of the other answers describes a VPN.

4. **A.** In a mesh topology, each device is connected directly to every other device. If there is a break in the connection between two devices, alternative paths between the two systems are available. None of the other topologies provide this level of redundancy.

5. **C.** A VPN extends a local area network by establishing a remote connection using a public network such as the Internet. A VPN provides a point to point dedicated link between two points over a public IP network. The VPN link can be used to connect remote networks via the Internet. A star is a type of topology and does not represent a method of connecting two networks. A VLAN is a virtual LAN and a method of dividing a network for security and performance reasons.

6. **A, B, C.** Many elements are involved in establishing a VPN connection. This includes the VPN client to initiate the session, the VPN server to answer the client requests, and the VPN protocols to secure and establish the connection.

7. **B.** The star-bus topology is a combination of the star topology and the bus topology. The bus topology forms the connection between star networks. The ad hoc topology refers to a wireless network that does not use an access point.

8. **A.** The diagram shows the physical bus topology. None of the other answers are valid.

9. **C.** The infrastructure wireless topology is commonly used to extend a wired LAN to include wireless devices. Wireless devices communicate with the wired LAN through a base station known as an access point or Wireless Access Point. The AP forms a bridge between a wireless and wired LAN, and all transmissions between wireless stations or between a system and a wired network client go through the AP.

10. **C.** A star topology is created when each node on the network is connected to a central device. None of the other answers are valid.

11. **A.** In a point-to-point (PtP) wireless configuration, the communication link travels from one node directly to one other node. Wireless point-to-point systems are often used in wireless backbone systems such as microwave relay communications, or as a replacement for a single wired communication cable. The point-to-point link can be used to connect two locations to share data and resources. A wireless mesh is an interconnection between wireless devices creating a redundant link between all nodes.

12. **D.** The infrastructure wireless topology is commonly used to extend a wired LAN to include wireless devices. Wireless devices communicate with the wired LAN through a base station known as an access point or wireless access point. The AP forms a bridge between a wireless and wired LAN, and all transmissions between wireless stations or between a system and a wired network client go through the AP.

13. **D.** The term WAN (wide area network) describes a network that spans more than one geographic location. A PAN (personal area network) is a small network connecting personal devices such as printers, PDAs and more. A LAN (local area network) is confined to a single geographic location, such as a single building, office, or school. A

14. **D.** The diagram shows a physical ring topology. All the other answers are incorrect.

15. **B.** Physical star networks use centralized devices to connect nodes on the network. Because devices can be plugged and unplugged from these devices without affecting any other systems on the network, star configurations are easy to expand. The disadvantages of a physical star network are that they require more cable than other topologies, require additional networking equipment, and create a single point of failure. For more information, see the section "LAN Topologies" in this chapter.

16. **C.** The IEEE 802.11 standard defines wireless networking architectures.

17. **C.** A mainframe is an example of a centralized computing model. All the other answers are incorrect.

18. **B.** The wired mesh topology requires each computer on the network to be individually connected to every other device. This configuration provides maximum reliability and redundancy for the network. However, it is costly to implement because of the multiple wiring requirements.

19. **A.** A star topology is shown in the diagram. All the other answers are incorrect.

20. **A.** VLANs are used for network segmentation, a strategy that significantly increases the performance capability of the network, removes potential performance bottlenecks, and can even increase network security. For more information, see the section "Virtual Local Area Network (VLAN)" in this chapter.

Chapter 2

1. **A, C.** RS-232 is a TIA/EIA standard for serial transmission between computers and peripheral devices such as modems, mice, and keyboards. RS-232 commonly uses a 25-pin DB-25 connector or a 9-pin DE-9 connector.

2. **C.** The 568A and 568B are telecommunications standards from the Telecommunications Industry Association (TIA) and the Electronics Industry Association (EIA). These 568 standards specify the pin arrangements for the RJ-45 connectors on UTP or STP cables.

3. **C.** F-Type connectors are most commonly associated with the coaxial cable used to connect with cable Internet modems. F-Type connectors are not used on cables with IEEE 1394 or FireWire connectors, nor are they used with STP cabling.

4. **D.** Category 6 high-performance UTP cable is rated and approved for 10GBASE-T networks. Category 6 has a minimum of 250 MHz of bandwidth and specifies cable distances up to 100-meter cable length with 10/100/1000Mbps transfer, along with 10Gbps over shorter distances.

5. **C.** To add a client to an existing network that uses Category 5 UTP, you would work with RJ-45 connectors. SC and ST connectors are used with fiber-optic cable, and RJ-11 is the connector type associated with telephone cable.

6. **B.** Plenum cables are coated with a nonflammable material, often Teflon or Kynar, and do not give off toxic fumes if they catch fire. Plenum-grade cables are typically run in floors and in walls.

7. **C.** RJ-45 connectors are associated with UTP cabling, whereas SC connectors are associated with fiber-optic cabling. Because the network design is high speed (1000Mbps), you would need to use Category 5e cabling or higher. All fiber-optic cable is capable of speeds in excess of 1000Mbps.

8. **B.** The interference created between wires in a cable is called *crosstalk*. *Attenuation* is the term given to the loss of strength in a signal as it travels over the media. Frequency Division Multiplexing (FDM) is a technology that enables more than one signal to be transmitted across a cable at one time. Disruption is not a term used to describe the interference created between wires in a cable.

9. **C.** The rollover cable is a Cisco proprietary cable used to connect a computer system to a router or switch console port. The rollover cable resembles an Ethernet UTP cable; however, it is not possible to use on anything but Cisco equipment. Like UTP cable, the rollover cable has eight wires inside and an RJ-45 connector on each end that connect to the router and the computer port.

10. **B.** The maximum distance for multimode fiber is 412 meters. Single-mode fiber increases the distance to 10,000 meters. Answers C and D are not valid.

11. **A.** A loopback cable is a tool used to test and isolate network problems. The loopback plug redirects outgoing data signals back to the system. The system interprets it as both sending and receiving data, and the corresponding LEDs should light. The loopback cable enables you to connect networking devices directly, without the need for a switch.

12. **C.** Because fiber uses light to transmit data, it is not susceptible to EMI and cross talk. It is the media of choice in high-interference network environments. All the other cable types mentioned are copper-based and are therefore susceptible, to varying degrees, to EMI and cross talk. It is not a type of network media.

13. **A.** Crossover cable are commonly used to interconnect network devices such as routers, switches and hubs. The crossover cable can even be used to directly network two PCs together without using a hub or switch. This is done because the cable performs the function of switching.

14. **C.** There are two main types of punchdown blocks used in industry today, type 66 and type 110. Type 66 is of older design and uses 50 rows of IDC (insulation-displacement connector) contacts to accommodate 25-pair cable. Block 66 was primarily used for voice communication and, although approved for Category 5, might not be suitable due to crosstalk. 110 blocks are used for today's networks and fully support the higher grade twisted-pair cable.

15. **A.** F-Type connectors are used with coaxial cabling. They are not used with fiber-optic cable. SC, ST, and LC connectors are used with fiber-optic cabling.

16. **D.** Attenuation refers to signal degradation as it travels through media. Cross talk is the term used to refer to interference from other cables; EMI is a condition created by electronic or mechanical equipment. Plenum is not a type of interference; it is the term used to classify cables suitable for installation in suspended ceilings and other enclosed areas.

17. **A.** Within the telecommunications room, horizontal cabling connects the telecommunication room to the end user. The horizontal cabling extends from the telecommunications outlet, or network outlet with RJ-45 connectors, at the client end, and includes all cable from that outlet to the telecommunication room. A patch cord finishes the connection between the client system and telecommunication wall jack.

18. **C.** Single-mode fiber enables faster transfer rates than multimode fiber and supports longer data transmissions. SC and ST are types of fiber connectors, not types of cable.

19. **D.** Because of the construction of fiber cable and that it uses light transmission rather than electronic signals, it is resistant to tampering and eavesdropping. All the other cable types listed are copper-based and are therefore less secure than fiber-based media. FTP is a protocol used for transferring files between systems on a network. It is not a type of network media.

20. **D.** The crossover cable can be used to directly network two PCs together without using a hub or switch. This is done because the cable performs the function of the switch. Using a straight-through cable and crossover cable to interconnect hubs and switches is covered in the next chapter.

Chapter 3

1. **D.** The term bandwidth shaping describes the mechanisms used to control bandwidth usage on the network. With this, administrators can control who uses bandwidth, for what, and the time of day bandwidth can be used. Bandwidth shaping establishes priorities to data traveling to and from the Internet and within the network.

2. **A, C.** Multilayer switches are network devices that operate on Layer 2 and Layer 3 of the OSI model. This means that the device can operate both as a switch and as a router.

3. **B.** The function of a DNS server is relatively simple in that it provides name resolution from hostnames to IP addresses.

4. **B.** Bridges make forwarding decisions based on the destination MAC address embedded in each packet. Routers use software addresses, such as IP addresses, to make forwarding decisions. Answers C and D are not valid options.

5. **C.** A switch uses the MAC address of the connected device to determine the port to which data is forwarded. Routers use software addresses, such as IP addresses, to make forwarding decisions. Answer B is not valid. Although there are many addressing schemes used on networks, Ethernet address is not a valid term. Therefore, answer D is incorrect.

6. **A.** A proxy server sits between a client computer and the Internet, looking at the web page requests sent by the client. For example, if a client computer wants to access a web page, the request is sent to the proxy server rather than directly to the Internet. The proxy server first determines whether the request is intended for the Internet or for a web server locally. If the request is intended for the Internet, the proxy server sends the request out as if it had originated the request. Web information can be cached and returned to the client; if no cached information is available, it will go to the Internet to get the information. A DNS server is used for hostname to IP resolution, the DHCP server is used to automatically distribute TCP/IP information and the RAS server is for remote access.

7. **B.** The purpose of Power over Ethernet (PoE) is described in the name. Essentially, PoE is a technology that enables electrical power to be transmitted over twisted-pair Ethernet cable. The power is transferred, along with data, to provide power to remote devices. These devices can include remote switches, wireless access points, Voice over IP (VoIP) equipment, and more.

8. **B, C, D.** The uplink port can connect hubs and switches together, using a standard twisted-pair cable. All the other answers are invalid.

9. **C.** Routers use the software-configured network address to make routing decisions. Bridges use MAC addresses to make decisions. Answer D is not valid. The FCS (that is, frame checksum) field is used for error detection.

10. **D.** Data signals weaken as they travel down a particular media. This is known as attenuation. To increase the distance a signal can travel, we can use repeaters. Repeaters regenerate the data signal as it passes enabling it to travel farther.

11. **A, B.** The Spanning Tree Protocol using the spanning-tree algorithm can place ports in several states. Ordinarily, they are in a forwarding or blocking state, but they can also be in a listening, learning, and disabled state.

12. **D.** An active hub regenerates the data signal before forwarding it to all connected devices. Active hubs come in both managed and unmanaged varieties. Answer B describes the action of a switch. Answer C is invalid.

13. **B.** A firewall is a networking device, either hardware- or software-based, that controls access to your organization's network. This controlled access is designed to protect data and resources from outside threats, such as intruders from a public network.

14. **A.** The purpose of Power over Ethernet (PoE) is to enable electrical power to be transmitted over twisted-pair Ethernet cable. The power is transferred, along with data, to provide power to remote devices. These devices can include remote switches, wireless access points, VoIP equipment, and more.

15. **B.** A 16550 UART chip is capable of speeds up to 115,200bps. None of the other answers represent the speed for the 16550 UART chip.

16. **D.** The bridging method used on Ethernet networks is called transparent because the other network devices are unaware of the existence of the bridge. Source-route bridges are used on Token-Ring networks, invisible is not a type of bridge, and cut-through is a switching method, not a type of bridge.

17. **C.** In computer networking, the term trunking refers to the use of multiple network cables or ports in parallel to increase the link speed beyond the limits of any one single cable or port.

18. **C.** CSUs/DSUs convert the digital signals used on a LAN to the digital signals used on a WAN. The process described in answer A would be performed by a gateway, and the process described in answer B would be performed by a modem. Answer D is not valid because WANs commonly use digital signals.

19. **A.** Routers make routing decisions based on the software-configured network address, which is protocol dependent. ARP is a protocol used to translate IP addresses to MAC addresses. There is no such thing as an ARP address. Answers C and D are invalid.

20. **A, B, C.** You should verify bus compatibility, network compatibility, and hardware compatibility before you buy a new NIC. You do not typically need to concern yourself with cooling requirements of a component.

Chapter 4

1. **A.** Web browsers use HTTP to retrieve text and graphics files from web servers. Answer B describes NTP; answer C describes SSH or Telnet; and answer D describes the function of WINS.

2. **C.** The term lease describes the amount of time a DHCP client is assigned an address. All the other terms are invalid.

3. **A, C.** Both UDP and TCP are transport protocols. IP is a network protocol, and NCP is an application protocol.

4. **C.** The mput command, which is an abbreviation for multiple put, enables more than one file to be uploaded at a time. mget is used to download multiple files in a single command; put is used to upload a single file; and get is used to download a single file.

5. **D.** DNS is a system that resolves hostnames to IP addresses. The term FQDN describes the entire hostname. None of the other services use FQDNs.

6. **C.** ARP resolves IP addresses to MAC addresses. Answer A describes the function of RARP; answer B is incorrect because ARP is not used to secure RARP; and answer D describes the process of DNS resolution.

7. **D.** NTP communicates time synchronization information between systems. NFS is typically associated with accessing shared folders on a Linux system. Utilization information is communicated to a central management system most commonly by using the SNMP protocol.

8. **D.** POP3 uses port 110 for network communication. Port 21 is used for FTP; port 123 is used by NTP; and port 443 is used by HTTPS.

9. **D.** Port 443 is used by HTTPS. Therefore, the application you configure is likely to be a secure website application. A virtual terminal application is most likely to use Telnet on TCP/IP port 23, or SSH on port 22. A web-based email application is most likely to use the HTTP protocol on TCP/IP port 80. An FTP server would need access to the TCP/IP ports for the FTP protocol, which are 20 and 21.

10. **A.** A reverse lookup resolves an IP address to a hostname rather than the hostname-to-IP address resolution normally performed by DNS. Answer B is not valid; answer C describes the process of a standard DNS resolution; and answer D is not a valid answer.

11. **B.** The term that refers to a message sent by an SNMP agent when a condition is met is trap message. None of the other terms describe the message sent by SNMP.

12. **A.** Well-known ports are defined in the range 0 to 1023. Answer B describes the range known as registered ports 1024 to 49151. Answer C describes the dynamic, or private, ports, which range from 49152 to 65535. Answer D is not a valid answer.

13. **D.** FTP is an application protocol. TCP and UDP are transport protocols, and IP is a network protocol.

14. **C.** The Real-time Transport Protocol (RTP) is the Internet-standard protocol for the transport of real-time data, including audio and video. SCP enables files to be copied securely between two systems.

15. **A.** SNMP enables network devices to communicate information about their state to a central system known as a manager. It also enables the central system to pass configuration parameters to the devices. In this way it helps monitor the network.

16. **C.** DNS performs an important function on TCP/IP-based networks. It resolves hostnames, such as www.examcram.com, to IP addresses, such as 209.202.161.67. If DNS is not present or working correctly, it would not be possible for a system to resolve hostnames to IP addresses.

17. **C.** There are several top-level DNS names reserved. These include .com (commercial organizations), .edu (educational organizations/establishments), and .gov (government).

18. **C.** Telnet uses port 23. If an administrator blocked this port, the Telnet service would be unavailable. FTP uses ports 20 and 21, SSH uses port 22, and SMTP uses port 25.

19. **A.** TCP is an example of connection-oriented transport protocol. UDP is an example of a connectionless protocol. Connection-reliant and connection-dependent are not terms commonly associated with protocols.

20. **B, C.** If port 143 were blocked, the IMAP4 protocol would be blocked. IMAP4 is used to retrieve email from a email server. If port 25 were blocked, the SMTP service would be unavailable. SMTP is used to transport email throughout the network. Answer A is incorrect because TFTP uses port 69, and answer D is incorrect because DNS uses port 53.

Chapter 5

1. **C.** OSPF is a link-state routing protocol used on TCP/IP networks. RIP is a distance-vector routing protocol used on both TCP/IP and IPX/SPX networks; ARP is a component of the TCP/IP protocol suite. NLSP is a link-state routing protocol used on IPX/SPX networks.

2. **C.** The term SNAT refers to a configuration whereby a private IP maps address directly to a static unchanging public IP address. Choice B is incorrect because DNAT maps a private IP address to a public IP address using a pool of public IP addresses. The function of NAT is to enable systems to "hide" behind a single IP address. Using NAT means that only one registered IP address is needed on the external interface of the system acting as the gateway between the internal and external networks.

3. **C.** Split horizon is a routing algorithm that dictates that routes are not advertised back on the interface from which they were learned. Choice A describes the operation of the split horizon with poison reverse algorithm. None of the other answers are valid.

4. **C.** In a network that uses distance-vector routing protocols, routers advertise details of the routers they know about. These updates are sent to all the neighbor routers. Answer A describes the actions on a link-state-based network. Answers B and D are invalid.

5. **A.** A count to infinity occurs when two routers provide information on the same destination and so create a routing loop. All the other answers are invalid.

6. **A.** Each step in the path between a router and its destination is called a hop. The other terms are not used in networking.

7. **D.** RIP is a distance-vector routing protocol used on TCP/IP networks. ARP is a component of the TCP/IP protocol suite. NLSP is a link-state routing protocol used on IPX networks, and OSPF is a link-state routing protocol used on TCP/IP networks.

8. **B.** The 131.16 range is from the Class B range and is not one of the recognized private IP address ranges. All the other address ranges are valid private IP address ranges.

9. **A.** Class B addresses fall into the range 128 to 191. Therefore, Answer A is the only one of the addresses listed that falls into that range. Answer B is a Class A address, and Answers C and D are both Class C IP addresses.

10. **B.** The address given is a Class C address; therefore, if you use the default subnet mask, the first three octets represent the network address. None of the other answers are valid.

11. **A.** External Gateway Protocol specifies routing protocols outside the local LAN. In this case the BGP protocol is an EGP protocol. Internal Gateway protocols include RIP and OSPF.

12. **D.** The broadcast address for a network uses the network ID, and all other octets in the address are set to all nodes to indicate that every system should receive the message. Therefore, with a network address of 14, the broadcast address is 14.255.255.255. None of the other answers are valid.

13. **A, C.** The IPv4 address (127.0.0.1) is reserved as the loopback address; IPv6 has the same reservation. IPv6 addresses 0:0:0:0:0:0:0:1 are reserved as the loopback addresses. The address can also be shown using the :: notation with the zeros removed as ::1.

14. **B.** In CIDR terminology, the number of bits to be included in the subnet mask is expressed as a slash value. If the slash value is 24, the first three entire octets form the subnet mask, so the value is 255.255.255.0. None of the other answers are correct.

15. **D.** Using NAT, many computers can "hide" behind a single IP address. The main reason we need to do this is because there aren't enough IPv4 addresses to go around. Using NAT means that only one registered IP address is needed on the external interface of the system acting as the gateway between the internal and external networks.

16. **B, C, D.** A key difference between IPv4 and IPv6 is in the address types. When it comes to IPv6 addresses, there are three main types of addresses: unicast, multicast, and anycast addresses. IPv4 uses broadcast addressing, whereas IPv6 doesn't.

17. **B.** IPv6 addresses are expressed in hexadecimal format and can therefore use only the letters A through F and numbers. They are also expressed in eight parts. None of the other answers fit these criteria.

18. **C.** An IPv4 broadcast address is an IP address that you can use to target all systems on a subnet or network instead of single hosts. In other words, a broadcast message goes to everyone on the network.

19. **B.** In IPv6, unique local addresses are equivalent to the IPv4 private address space (10.0.0.0/8, 172.16.0.0/12, and 192.168.0.0/16). Like IPv4, where private address ranges are used in private networks, IPv6 uses site-local addresses. Site-local addresses are not automatically configured and must be assigned either through stateless or stateful address configuration processes. The prefix used for the site-local address is (FC00::/7).

20. **A.** Link-local addresses are automatically configured on all interfaces. This automatic configuration is equivalent to the 169.254.0.0 automatically assigned IPv4 addressing. The prefix used for a link-local address is fe80::.

21. **D.** The first three bytes (00:D0:59) identify the manufacturer of the card; because only this manufacturer can use this address, the first three bytes are known as the Organizational Unique Identifier (OUI). The last three bytes (09:07:51) are then referred to as the Universal LAN MAC address.

Chapter 6

1. **B.** The 10GBaseER standard specifies a maximum transmission distance of 40,000 meters. The 10GBaseSR standard specifies a maximum transmission distance of 300 meters, whereas 10GBaseLR specifies a maximum transmission distance of 10,000 meters. 10GBaseXR is not a recognized 10 Gigabit Ethernet standard.

2. **A.** Carrier Sense Multiple Access/Collision Detection (CSMA/CD) is defined in the IEEE 802.3 standard. On an Ethernet network using CSMA/CD, when a system wants to send data to another system, it first checks to see whether the network media is free. It must do this because each piece of network media used in a LAN can carry only one signal at a time. If the sending node detects that the media is free, it transmits, and the data is sent to the destination. Collision avoidance is an access method used by 802.11 wireless systems and uses avoidance instead of detection as an access method. Token passing and demand property are access methods rarely used today.

3. **B.** The IEEE 802.3 standard defines the Ethernet networking system, which uses CSMA/CD as its media access method. 802.2 defines specifications for the LLC sublayer of the 802 standard series. 802.4 defines the use of a token-passing system on a linear bus topology. 802.5 defines token ring networking.

4. **D.** 100BaseFX has the potential to transmit distances that exceed 600 meters. However, to reach distances of 600 meters, you need to use single-mode fiber. Of the other standards, 100BaseT can reach only 550 meters when using Category 5e or Category 6 cabling.

5. **C.** The 10GBaseT standard specifies 10-gigabit speeds over twisted-pair cable. It is possible for networks using Category 6 cable to upgrade to these speeds;

however, the transmission range is limited to 55 meters with Category 6 cable. Transmission range is limited to 100 meters with Category 6a cable.

6. **B.** The 10GBaseER standard provides 10GBps transmission speeds over distances up to 10,000 meters. It is a currently ratified IEEE 802.3 standard. 100BaseFX runs at only 100Mbps, which makes it the slowest of the technologies listed in the answer. 10GBaseSR can be used only over distances up to 330 meters. 10GBaseWR is not a recognized 10Gbps standard.

7. **A.** 10GBaseSR/SW is designed for LAN or MAN implementations, with a maximum distance of 300 meters using 50 micron multimode fiber cabling. 10GBaseSR can also be implemented with 62.5 micron multimode fiber cabling but is limited to 33 meters.

8. **D.** Many substandards fall under the 802.3 Ethernet banner. One is the 802.3an standard for 10GBaseT networking. The 10GBaseT standard calls for 10-gigabit networking over Category 6 or 6a twisted-pair cable.

9. **D.** 100BaseT4 is a Fast Ethernet standard that can use existing Category 3 cable and have transmission speeds of up to 100Mbps. 100BaseVG-AnyLAN can also use Category 3 cable, but it uses a demand priority access method. 100BaseTX requires Category 5 cable, and 100BaseFX uses fiber-optic cable.

10. **B, C,** and **D.** Fast Ethernet standards are specified in the IEEE 802.3u standard. Three standards are defined by 802.3u: 100BaseTX, 100BaseT4, and 100BaseFX. Of the three, the FX standard uses fiber-optic cable and. 10GBaseT uses the 802.3an designation.

11. **A, B,** and **D.** Three standards are associated with 802.3z: 1000BaseLX, 1000BaseSX, and 1000BaseCX. 10GBaseSR is a 802.3ae Gigabit Ethernet standard.

12. **D.** The 10GBaseLW standard is designed to be used over long-wavelength single-mode fiber, giving it a potential transmission range of anywhere from 2 meters to 10 kilometers. This transmission range makes the standard available for LAN, MAN, and WAN deployments. 100BaseCX uses STP cable and has a transmission distance of 25 meters, 100BaseT uses UTP/STP cabling category 5 or higher and has a transmission range of 100meters, and 10GBaseT using copper-based media reaches segment distances of up to 100 meters.

13. **B.** The 1000BaseT standard uses UTP/STP cabling category 5 or better and offers a segment maximum of 100 meters.

14. **D.** 100BaseFX is a Fast Ethernet standard implemented on fiber-optic cabling. It is more expensive and more difficult to install than 100BaseTX, which uses twisted-pair cabling. Both standards have a maximum speed of 100Mbps; however, 100BaseFX can be used over greater distance than 100BaseTX.

15. **A** and **C**. Both 1000BaseCX and 10GBaseT high-speed standards specify twisted-pair cable for transfer. The drawback is shorter transmission range. The 1000BaseCX standard calls for STP copper and is limited to 25 meters. The 10GBaseT standard calls for Category 6/6a cable and is limited to 55 and 100 meters, respectively.

16. **A**. The 802.3ab standard specifies Gigabit Ethernet over Category 5 UTP cable. The standard enables for full-duplex transmission using the four pairs of twisted cable. To reach speeds of 1000Mbps over copper, a data transmission speed of 250Mbps is achieved over each pair of twisted-pair cable.

17. **B**. 1000BaseLX can transmit up to 5,000 meters, using single-mode fiber. 1000BaseCX uses copper-based cabling restricted to 25 meters; 1000BaseSX distance ranges from about 275 meters to 316 meters depending on fiber cabling used; and 10GBaseT uses copper-based media with a transmission range per segment of about 100 meters.

18. **C**. Single-mode fiber enables faster transfer rate than multimode fiber and supports longer data transmissions. SC and ST are types of fiber connectors, not types of cable.

19. **C**. The 802.3an standard specifies 10-gigabit transfer speeds over copper cable. 10GBaseT offers these speeds over both Category 6 and 6a cable.

20. **A**. Baseband transmissions use digital signaling. Analog signaling is associated with broadband.

Chapter 7

1. **B** and **C**. Wireless standards specify an radio frequency (RF) range on which communications are sent. The 802.11b and 802.11g standards use the 2.4GHz range. 802.11a is incorrect because it uses the 5GHz range, and 802.11t is not a valid standard.

2. **A**. Ordinarily the default channel used with a wireless device is adequate; however, it might be necessary to change the channel if there is overlap with another nearby access point. The channel should be changed to another nonoverlapping channel. Changing the channel would not impact the WEP security settings.

3. **D**. An AP has a limited distance that it can send data transmissions. When a client system moves out of range, it can't access the AP. Many strategies exist to increase transmission distances, including RF repeaters, amplifiers, and buying more powerful antennas. The problem is not likely related to the SSID or WEP settings because the client had access to the network before and no settings were changed.

4. **B.** Beacons are an important part of the wireless network because they advertise the presence of the access point so systems can locate it. Wireless clients automatically detect the beacons and attempt to establish a wireless connection to the access point. Answers A, C and D are invalid.

5. **A.** On a wireless connection between an access point and the client, each system must be configured to use the same WEP security settings. In this case, they must both be configured to use 128-bit encryption.

6. **C.** Both WEP-open and WEP-shared are forms of wireless security. WEP-open is the simpler of the two authentications methods because it does not perform any type of client verification. It is a weak form of authentication because there is no proof of identity. WEP-shared requires that a WEP key be configured on both the client system and the access point. This makes authentication with WEP-shared mandatory and therefore more secure for wireless transmission.

7. **A.** 802.1X is an IEEE standard specifying port-based network access control. Port-based network access control uses the physical characteristics of a switched local area network (LAN) infrastructure to authenticate devices attached to a LAN port and to prevent access to that port in cases where the authentication process fails.

8. **D.** The IEEE standard 802.11n can use either the 2.4GHz or 5GHz radio frequencies. 802.11a uses 5GHz, 802.11b uses 2.4GHz, as does the 802.11g standard.

9. **D.** Multiple input multiple output (MIMO) is used by the 802.11n standard and takes advantage of multiplexing to increase range and speed of wireless networking. Multiplexing is a technique that combines multiple signals for transmission over a single line or media. MIMO enables the transmission of multiple data streams traveling on different antennas in the same channel at the same time. A receiver reconstructs the stream that has multiple antennas.

10. **C.** There are three main components of the 802.1X security framework. The supplicant is the system or node requesting access and authentication to a network resource. The authenticator usually is a switch or AP that acts as a control mechanism enabling or denying traffic to pass though a port. Finally, the authentication server validates the credentials of the supplicant trying to access the network or resource.

11. **B** and **C.** The 802.11b and 802.11g standards use channels 1–11 in the 2.4GHz frequency range. Of the channels, 1, 6, and 11 are considered nonoverlapping, which means there is less chance for interference.

12. **C.** The WPA wireless security protocol uses TKIP (temporal key integrity protocol), which scrambles encryption keys using a hashing algorithm. Then the

keys are issued an integrity check to verify that they have not been modified or tampered with during transit. TKIP encryption is not used with WEP.

13. **B.** RADIUS is a protocol that enables a single server to become responsible for all remote access authentication, authorization, and auditing (or accounting) services. RADIUS functions as a client/server system.

14. **A.** Orthogonal Frequency Division Multiplexing (OFDM) is a transmission technique that transfers large amounts of data over 52 separate, even-spaced frequencies. OFDM splits the radio signal into these separate frequencies and simultaneously transmits them to the receiver. By splitting the signal and transferring over different frequencies, the amount of cross talk interference is reduced. OFDM is associated with the 802.11n wireless standard.

15. **D.** By the description, it sounds like the client has moved beyond the reach of the AP. To try to accommodate the client, an RF repeater could be used to duplicate and forward the wireless signal. It would not be wise to move the wireless access point because the move might put it out of reach for other network users. Changing the wireless channel would not help but would prevent the user from accessing the AP altogether.

16. **C.** An omnidirectional antenna is designed to provide a 360-degree dispersed wave pattern. This type of antenna is used when coverage in all directions from the antenna is required. Omnidirectional antennas are good to use when a broad-based signal is required. This is in contrast to a directional antenna, which works more for a point-to-point connection.

17. **B.** IEEE 802.11g/b wireless systems communicate with each other using radio frequency signals in the band between 2.4GHz and 2.5GHz. Neighboring channels are 5MHz apart. Therefore, channel 3 would use the 2422 RF (2412+5+5).

18. **D.** Disabling the SSID broadcast would prevent the SSID name from being displayed on wireless systems. In their default configuration, wireless access points typically broadcast the SSID name into the air at regular intervals. This feature of SSID broadcast is intended to enable clients to easily discover the network and roaming between WLANs. The problem with SSID broadcasting is that it makes it a little easier to get around security. SSIDs are not encrypted or protected in any way.

19. **A.** The 802.11a wireless standard uses the 5GHz frequency range. 802.11b/g use the 2.4GHz range.

20. **C.** The IEEE 802.11b standard for wireless networks defines a maximum speed of 11Mbps. With today's wireless networking standards operating significantly faster, 802.11b deployments are increasingly rare.

Chapter 8

1. **C.** A T1 line has a transmission capability of 1.544Mbps and is considerably cheaper than a T3 line. X.25, and BRI ISDN cannot provide the required transmission speed.

2. **D.** A PVC is a permanent virtual circuit between two points, in this case over an ATM network. The PVC can be used to replace a hardwired dedicated end-to-end line. A PVC circuit is permanent. PVC cells cannot take alternative routes to an end point if circuit failure occurs, and even when not in use, bandwidth is still reserved for the PVC. An PVC represents a temporary virtual circuit established and maintained only for the duration of a data transfer session. PVCs are dynamically connected on an as-needed basis.

3. **A** and **D.** BRI ISDN uses 2B+1D channels, which are two 64Kbps data channels, and PRI-ISDN uses 23B+1D channels. The other answers are not valid.

4. **C.** The only technology in this question capable of transfer speeds above 2Mbps is a T3 line. None of the other technologies listed can provide the transmission speed required.

5. **A.** Several versions of digital subscriber line (DSL) exist; each is designed for a different purpose, and each offers different upload and download speeds. DSL can be symmetric, high-speed upload and download speeds, and asymmetric, slower upload speeds. VHDSL is an asymmetric version of DSL and offers speeds of 10Mbps and beyond. Answers B, C, and D are symmetric versions of DSL.

6. **A, B,** and **D.** Many elements are needed to make the connections in a Frame Relay network. This includes a FRAD (Frame Relay Assembler/Disassembler) designed to encapsulate and decapsulate information on packets to make them compatible with Frame Relay. The Frame Relay switch is responsible for routing the frames when they enter the Frame Relay network. The virtual circuit starts from the local network and the FRAD and connects to the FRAD on the receiving end. The virtual link is often a PVC. Answer C is incorrect because Frame Relay bridge is not a valid technology. Answer E, rate adaptive, refers to RADSL that can modify its transmission speeds based on the signal quality.

7. **C.** The Internet is a public network and commonly used to interconnect remote offices. To do this, technologies such as VPN and appropriate security protocols must be used.

8. **C.** When virtual circuit switching is used, a logical connection is established between the source and the destination device. None of the other answers are valid.

9. **D.** Home satellite systems are asymmetric; that is, download speeds are faster than upload speeds. A home satellite system is likely to use a modem for the up-

link traffic, with downloads coming over the satellite link. Symmetric communication involves equivalent upload and download speeds. All other answers are invalid.

10. **C.** One clear advantage that ISDN has over the PSTN is its speed. ISDN can combine 64Kbps channels for faster transmission speeds than the PSTN can provide. ISDN is no more or less reliable than the PSTN. ISDN is more expensive than the PSTN. Answer D describes ATM.

11. **D.** Circuit switching is the process of creating a dedicated circuit between two communication end points and directing traffic between those two points. None of the other answers are valid types of switching.

12. **A.** ATM uses fixed packets, or cells, with lengths of 53 bytes—48 bytes for data information and 5 bytes for the header. None of the other technologies listed use this cell format.

13. **B** and **D.** The Internet and the PSTN are considered public networks and are therefore the most cost-effective data transmission solutions. ATM and FDDI are examples of private networking technologies.

14. **B.** Message switching uses a store-and-forward switching method. This method is impractical for real-time data transmissions but well suited for other applications, such as email. None of the other switching methods are associated with store-and-forward.

15. **B** and **D.** X.25 and Frame Relay are both packet switching technologies. ATM and FDDI are not considered packet-switching technologies.

16. **A.** A public network has many advantages, but security is a concern because data transmissions can be intercepted. All the other answers are advantages of using a public network.

17. **A** and **C.** ATM uses two types of circuit switching: PVC and SVC. VCD and PCV are not the names of switching methods.

18. **B**. The D channel on an ISDN link carries signaling information, whereas the B, or bearer, channels carry the data. The other answers are not valid.

19. **A** and **B.** DTE and DCEs are associated with Frame Relay networks. The term DTE refers to terminating equipment located with a company's network. Termination equipment includes such hardware as end-user systems, servers, routers, bridges, and switches. The DCE is the equipment owned by the carrier. This equipment provides the switching services for the network and therefore is responsible for transmitting the data through the WAN.

20. **B.** In a packet switching network, packets do not always use the same path or route to get to their intended destination. Referred to as independent routing, packet switching enables for a better use of available bandwidth by letting packets travel different routes to avoid high-traffic areas. Answer A is incorrect

because circuit switching does not use independent routing; rather, it established a physical circuit that all packets follow. Answers C and D are incorrect because ISDN and PSTN are examples of circuit switching technologies.

Chapter 9

1. **B.** A switch uses the MAC addresses of connected devices to make forwarding decisions; therefore, it can operate at the data link layer of the OSI model. Additionally, today's switches can operate at Layer 3, network layer because they provide mechanisms for the routing of data between devices across single or multiple network segments. Components at the physical layer define the actual connection to the network. Physical layer components include cabling and connectors. Protocols at the network layer handle addressing and route discovery. Protocols at the session layer deal with establishment and termination between systems or applications on the network. None of the other answers apply.

2. **A, B,** and **D.** Switches, bridges, and NICs operate at the data link layer of the OSI model, which is also known as Layer 2. A hub is defined as a physical layer (that is, Layer 1) device.

3. **B.** The synchronization of data between applications is performed at the session layer of the OSI model. Protocols at the transport layer establish, maintain, and break connections between two devices. Protocols at the presentation layer convert data so that it can be received from or sent to the network. Devices at the data link layer define the media access method and hardware addressing.

4. **D.** TCP is a connection-oriented protocol, which means that it guarantees delivery of data. Other protocols, such as UDP, are known as connectionless protocols because data delivery is not guaranteed. Both have advantages; UDP is faster because error checking mechanisms are not required. If data is not delivered, UDP will just keep sending. TCP uses error checking mechanisms to ensure data has been delivered but has a higher overhead due to this extra step.

5. **C.** Route discovery is performed by protocols that operate at the network layer of the OSI model. Devices at the data link layer define the media access method and hardware addressing. Protocols at the network layer handle addressing and route discovery. Protocols at the transport layer establish, maintain, and break connections between two devices.

6. **A** and **C.** The data link layer of the OSI model is divided into two distinct sublayers: the LLC sublayer and the MAC sublayer. None of the other answers are valid.

7. **C** and **D.** The transport layer is responsible for, among other things, performing error checking and verification, and establishing, maintaining, and breaking connections between devices. Synchronizing data exchange between applica-

tions occurs at the session layer. Error detection and handling for the transmitted signals occur at the data link layer.

8.   **A.** Standards at the data link layer define how the network is accessed on a logical level. Do not confuse the function of the data link layer with that of the physical layer, which performs similar functions but at a physical rather than a logical level. The session layer handles the synchronization of data between applications on networked devices. Protocols at the presentation layer prepare data for transmission on the network or prepare data from the network to be passed to the application layer.

9.   **C.** A hub operates at the physical layer of the OSI model. Components at the application layer are software-based. A router is an example of a network layer device. A switch can operate at level 2 and 3 of the OSI model.

10. **C.** The term package is not valid when referring to a logical grouping of bits. All the other answers are valid terms.

11. **B.** The physical layer of the OSI model defines the physical characteristics of the network, including voltages and signaling rates. The data link layer performs error detection and handling for transmitted signals. It also defines the method by which the media is accessed. The session layer handles the synchronization of data between applications on networked devices. Protocols at the presentation layer prepare data for transmission on the network or prepare data from the network to be passed to the application layer.

12. **B.** APs provide connectivity between wireless and wired portions of a network. They are classified as data link layer devices because they provide logical connectivity but are protocol-independent. Components at the physical layer define the actual connection to the network. Physical layer components include cabling and connectors. A router is an example of a network layer device. Protocols at the transport layer establish, maintain, and break connections between two devices.

13. **B.** NICs operate at the data link layer of the OSI model. Physical layer components include cabling and connectors. A router is an example of a network layer device. Transport layer components are typically software.

14. **D.** Encryption is a function that takes place at the presentation layer of the OSI model. Components at the physical layer define the actual connection to the network. Physical layer components include cabling and connectors. The session layer handles the synchronization of data between applications on networked devices. Protocols at the presentation layer prepare data for transmission on the network or prepare data from the network to be passed to the application layer.

15. **A** and **C.** Windowing and buffering are commonly used flow control strategies. Segmentation is the term used to describe the division of packets to enable them to be transported across the network. Answer d is not valid.

16. **C.** The network layer of the OSI model provides mechanisms for moving data between devices on a network. IP uses this layer to move data. The physical layer defines the physical structure of the network; the data link layer is responsible for getting the data signals onto the media; and the session layer synchronizes the data exchange between applications on separate devices.

17. **C.** The transport layer is responsible for establishing connections between two devices. The session layer handles the synchronization of data between applications on networked devices. Protocols at the network layer handle addressing and route discovery. The application layer provides access to the network for applications and certain end-user functions.

18. **B.** Protocols at the network layer are responsible for route discovery. Protocols at the transport layer establish, maintain, and break connections between two devices. The session layer handles the synchronization of data between applications on networked devices. Protocols at the application layer provide access to network functions.

19. **A** and **D.** The two terms used to describe protocols at the transport layer are connection-oriented and connectionless. The terms in Answers B and C are not used.

20. **C.** A router uses the logical network address to make decisions and is therefore a network layer device. Application, session, and transport level components are software-based.

Chapter 10

1. **D.** At least three hard disks are required in a RAID 5 array. None of the other answers are valid.

2. **A.** Disk mirroring is defined by RAID 1. Raid 0 is disk striping, which offers no fault tolerance. RAID 5 is disk striping with parity. RAID 2 is not a commonly implemented RAID level.

3. **A** and **B.** The archive bit is reset in both a full backup and an incremental backup. Differential backups do not change the status of the archive bit. Mirror image is not an accepted backup type.

4. **C.** A full backup combined with a differential backup requires only two tapes to do a complete restore, assuming that each backup set fits on a single tape. Full and incremental backups might need more than two tapes. Differential and incremental backups must be combined with a full backup to be effective. Answer D is not valid.

5. **B** and **C**. RTP and UDP are both protocols used with VoIP. UDP is the transport protocol used because it has less overhead and error-checking mechanisms than does TCP. TCP guarantees message delivery, which adds an unnecessary element to real-time applications. RTP is used with UDP to complete the video of VoIP data stream. Answer D is not valid.

6. **D**. Two disks are required to create a RAID 1 array. All the other answers are invalid.

7. **B**. By making a full backup on the weekend and incremental backups during the week, you should be able to complete the backups without interfering with the normal working hours of the company. All the other answers are invalid.

8. **C**. A sag is a short-term voltage drop. A brownout is also a voltage drop, but it lasts longer than a sag. A surge is an increase in power that lasts a few seconds. A spike is a power increase that lasts a few milliseconds.

9. **D**. RAID 10 offers the performance advantages of RAID 0 and the fault-tolerance capabilities of RAID 1. RAID 0 is not a fault-tolerant solution. RAID 1 and RAID 5 offer fault tolerance but do not increase performance.

10. **A** and **B**. In server systems, warm swapping enables network adapters to be swapped out without the server being powered off. Adapter teaming enables multiple NICs to be logically grouped together. If one of the NICs fails, the other NICs in the group can continue to provide network connectivity. Adapters in a team can also be grouped together to increase the available bandwidth. Answers C and D are not valid answers.

11. **D**. There is no accepted fault-tolerance strategy for coping with a failed memory module. All the other hardware components listed can be implemented in a fault-tolerant configuration.

12. **C**. A RAID 1 array requires an amount of disk space equivalent to that of the mirrored drive. Therefore, in a RAID 1 array of 80GB, only 40GB will be available for data storage. None of the other answers are valid.

13. **A, B,** and **D**. UPSs can prevent damage to hardware and damage to data caused by fluctuations in the power supply. They can also promote the availability of data by keeping a server running if a power outage occurs. A UPS does not increase the speed of the network.

14. **A**. A hot site is a complete network ready for operation if a catastrophic failure occurs. The hot site will typically include all hardware and data to quickly continue service. Hot sites are not typically deployed due to the costs of the redundant network. However, large financial institutions and government agencies can deploy a hot site. A warm site can refer to an alternative network that is not completely ready for a network switch and might need a few days to get the network operational. A hot spare is a piece of hardware such as a hard disks that

can be replaced without needing to power down a system. A cold site is often just an alternative location from which a network can be created if a failure occurs. Limited hardware and infrastructure is located at a cold site.

15. **A.** RAID 0 offers the highest level of performance but does not offer any fault tolerance. If the performance of RAID 0 is required along with fault tolerance, RAID 10 is a better choice. RAID 1 offers fault tolerance but no increase in performance.

16. **A** and **D.** VoIP is a latency-sensitive application. This means that lags in delivery time negatively impact its capability to function properly. VoIP communications can be secured using the secure real-time transfer protocol (SRTP). Answer C is incorrect because VoIP typically uses UDP as a transport protocol and not TCP.

17. **A.** A cold site provides an alternative location but typically not much more. A cold site often requires the delivery of computer equipment and other services.

18. **A.** Disk duplexing is an implementation of RAID 1 (disk mirroring) that places each of the drives on a separate controller. None of the other answers are valid.

19. **B.** In a RAID 5 configuration, a space equivalent to one whole drive is used for the storage of parity information. In this question, this requirement equates to 15GB. Therefore, in a 75GB RAID 5 array, 60GB is available for data storage. None of the other answers are valid.

20. **B** and **D.** Both RAID 0 and RAID 1 use two disks. The difference between the two implementations is that RAID 1 offers fault tolerance through disk mirroring, whereas RAID 0 stripes the data across the drives but does not offer any fault tolerance. RAID 5 requires at least three disks, and RAID 10 requires at least four disks if the entire hard disk is to be used.

Chapter 11

1. **D.** Internal networks are assigned one of the private address ranges. Each of these ranges have a corresponding subnet mask. In this example, the wrong subnet mask has been entered.

2. **B.** Notice from the dialog screen that the default gateway address is incorrectly entered as the same address as the system's IP address. Because of this, the system could not likely connect to remote networks. The DNS, IP, and subnet mask settings are correct.

3. **C.** The default gateway enables the system to communicate with systems on a remote network without the need for explicit routes to be defined. The default gateway can be assigned automatically using a DHCP server or manually inputted.

4. **A** and **B.** Configuring a client requires at the least the IP address and a subnet mask. The default gateway, DNS server, and WINS server are all optional, but network functionality is limited without them.

5. **B.** Crosstalk can occur when the signal from one cable overlaps with the signal from another. This can sometimes happen when cables are run too close together. The remedy is to run the cables farther apart or use quality shielded cable.

6. **A, B,** and **D.** When you troubleshoot a wiring problem, consider the distance between devices, interference such as crosstalk and EMI, and the connection points. Answer C is not correct because bound media (that is, cables) are not affected by atmospheric conditions.

7. **B.** After you fix a problem, you should test it fully to ensure that the network operates correctly before allowing users to log back on. The steps described in Answers A and C are valid but only after the application has been tested. Answer D is not correct; you would reload the executable only as part of a systematic troubleshooting process, and because the application loads, it is unlikely that the executable has become corrupt.

8. **C.** Not enough information is provided to make an accurate decision about what the problem might be. In this case, the next troubleshooting step would be to talk to the user and gather more information about exactly what the problem might be. All the other answers are valid troubleshooting steps, but only after the information gathering has been completed.

9. **C.** After you fix a problem, test the fix, and let users back on to the system, you should create detailed documentation that describes the problem and the solution. Answer A is incorrect because you must document both the problem and the solution. It is not necessary to restart the server, so Answer B is incorrect, and Answer D would be performed only after the documentation for the system has been created.

10. **B.** In a server that has been operating correctly, a resource conflict could indicate that a device has failed and is causing the conflict. More likely, a change has been made to the server, and that change created a conflict. Although all the other answers represent valid troubleshooting steps, it is most likely that there has been a change to the configuration.

11. **D.** On an Ethernet network, only a single active path can exist between devices on a network. When multiple active paths are available, switching loops can occur. Switching loops are the result of having more than one path between two switches in a network. The spanning-tree protocol is designed to prevent these loops from occurring.

12. **A** and **C.** When troubleshooting media, you need to know the type of media used. This enables you to know the characteristics of the media and if it is used

correctly on the network. You also need to know where the media is used. If it is used in an area that causes interference, another media type or another location might be required.

13. **C.** Data signals weaken as they travel farther from the point of origin. If the signal travels far enough, it can weaken so much that it becomes unusable. The weakening of data signals as they traverse the media is referred to as *attenuation*.

14. **C.** NEXT refers to interference between adjacent wire pairs within the twisted-pair cable at the near end of the link (the end closest to the origin of the data signal). NEXT occurs when an outgoing data transmission leaks over to an incoming transmission. Answer D refers to FEXT, which is interference at the far end of the link. Answers A and B are invalid.

15. **A.** Near End crosstalk, or NEXT, occurs when connectors are not properly attached to UTP cable. Specifically, the crosstalk can occur if the wires pushed into the RJ-45 connector are crossed or crushed. When this occurs, the signal can experience intermittent problems.

16. **C** and **D.** An AP has a limited distance that it can send data transmissions. When a client system moves out of range, it cannot access the AP. Many strategies exist to increase transmission distances, including RF repeaters, amplifiers, and buying more powerful antennas. Also, client systems might be moved, and the signal can be weakened by a physical issue, such as a concrete wall, mirror, or other obstacles. This too can explain intermittent connectivity problems. The problem is not likely related to the SSID or WEP settings because the client had access to the network before and no settings were changed.

17. **A.** When you work on an unfamiliar system, the first step should be to consult the documentation to gain as much information as you can about the server and the applications that run on it. All the other troubleshooting steps are valid, but they would be performed only after the information-gathering process is complete.

18. **B.** Wireless standards 802.11b/g and n are compatible, so either one could be used in a configuration. Encryption, SSID, and distance all have to be verified for a client to authenticate to an AP.

19. **D.** The Category 5e cable run through the ceiling is likely an indication of EMI. Recall from Chapter 2 that UTP has poor resistance to electromagnetic interference (EMI); therefore, UTP and the electrical equipment do not mix. Cables that run close to fluorescent light fittings can cause intermittent problems because of EMI.

20. **A** and **C.** The information provided indicates that this user is the only one experiencing a problem. After determining the scope of the problem, we can assume that the issue must lie with something directly connected with that system. In this case, it is likely that the configuration of the workstation or the physical connectivity is the problem.

Chapter 12

1. **A** and **C.** Both `route` and `netstat` can be used to view the routing table on a Windows system. `nbtstat` is used to view NetBIOS over TCP/IP statistics, and `ping` is used to test connectivity between two devices. `tracert` is used to trace the route between two devices on a network.

2. **A.** The `nbtstat -R` command purges and reloads the remote cache name table. The `-n` switch displays the local name table, `-r` provides resolution information, and `-s` shows the NetBIOS session table.

3. **C.** The router at steps 5 or 6 is the likely source of the problem. Because all steps up to and including step 5 have been successful, the problem lies either on the far side of Router 5 or the near side of the router in step 6. Answer A is incorrect because if the destination host were not online, you would receive no successful replies. Answer B is incorrect because if the router at step 4 were having a problem, you would receive only four successful replies and not five. Answer D is incorrect because if the router were powered off, you would receive no successful replies.

4. **D.** The `netstat -s` command displays statistics on a per-protocol basis. The `-S` and `-R` switches are not valid with `netstat`. Answer B (`-r`) causes `netstat` to display the routing table, and Answer E (`-a`) checks connections.

5. **B.** The output is from a `netstat` command. All the other utilities listed provide different output.

6. **B.** In this case, the problem is caused because the hostname of the destination computer cannot be resolved. In Answer A, the hostname would have to first be resolved before you could draw this conclusion. Answer C is incorrect; if the route to the destination could not be determined, you would receive a Destination Unreachable message. Answer D is incorrect because WINS is not used for name resolution on the Internet.

7. **C.** On a Linux system, the `traceroute` command can be used to track the path a packet takes between hosts on the network. Of the commands listed, only `traceroute` can perform this function on a Linux system. `Tracert` is the equivalent of the `traceroute` command on Windows systems. The `arp` utility is used to view IP address to MAC address resolutions that have been performed by the system. The `nbtstat` utility is used to view NetBIOS over TCP/IP statistics.

8. **C.** The `ifconfig` command displays the configuration of the network interfaces on a Linux system. Answers A and B are Windows-based utilities, and Answer D is a NetWare command.

9. **C.** The `ping -t` command issues a continuous stream of ping requests until it is interrupted. None of the other answers are valid switches for the `ping` command.

10. **A.** Many routers and firewalls are configured to block ICMP echoes, which is used by the `ping` command. ICMP is blocked because it can be used as a method of attack—specifically, denial of service attacks in which ICMP is used to overwhelm a system. With ICMP blocked, `ping` will not work. This is where `arp ping` is the better utility to use.

11. **C.** The default gateway parameter is missing from the TCP/IP configuration.

12. **C.** The `nbtstat` command can be used to view NetBIOS over TCP/IP statistics. The `ping` command is used to test connectivity between devices; `netstat` is used to view TCP/IP protocol statistics; the `arp` command is used to view a list of IP address to MAC address resolutions; and `tracert` is used to track the path between two devices on the network.

13. **C.** A high number of errors in the Received column in the `netstat -e` output indicates that errors are generated on the network. However, the 0 value in the Sent column suggests that this system is not generating the errors. The other answers for this question are not valid.

14. **D.** The output is from the Windows `tracert` command. The `tracert` command is used for troubleshooting to help identify where data packets travel and where they are dropped. All the other utilities listed provide different output.

15. **B.** This is normal output from a `tracert` command.

16. **B** and **C.** A Destination Host Unreachable message in response to a ping suggests either a problem with the default gateway or a possible error in the routing table. Answer A is incorrect; if the remote host were online, the ping should be successful. Answer D would result in a series of Request Timed Out errors.

17. **A** and **B.** Both the `dig` and `nslookup` commands can be used to perform manual DNS lookups on a Linux system. You cannot perform a manual DNS lookup with the `tracert` command. There is no such command as `dnslookup`.

18. **A.** The `ping` command generates a Request Timed Out error when it can receive a reply from the destination system. None of the other commands produce this output.

19. **C.** This command would correctly add a static entry to the ARP table. None of the other answers are valid ARP switches.

20. **D.** The output shown was produced by the `nslookup` command. The other commands listed produce different output.

Chapter 13

1. **D.** Voltage event recorders monitor the quality of power used on the network or by network hardware. Voltage event recorders identify potential power related concerns such as power sags, spikes, surges, or other power variations.

2. **B.** Temperature monitors are used in server and network equipment rooms to ensure that the temperature does not fluctuate greatly. In the case of a failed air conditioner, the administrator would have been alerted of the drastic changes in temperature. Multimeters, and TDRs, work with regular network media. OTDRs are used with optical based media.

3. **B.** Whereas load tests do not try and break the system under intense pressure, stress tests sometimes do. There are two clear goals of stress testing: The first is to see exactly what the network can handle. That is, where is its breaking point, which is useful to know in terms of network expansion. Secondly, stress testing enables administrators to test their backup and recovery procedures.

4. **B.** In this scenario, the section of horizontal cable runs through the ceiling and over fluorescent lights. This cable run might be a problem as such devices can cause EMI. Alternatively to plenum cable used in this scenario, STP might have worked as well.

5. **D.** You use a punchdown tool when working with an IDC. All the other tools are associated with making and troubleshooting cables, but they are not associated with IDCs.

6. **A.** The toner probe tool, along with the tone locator, can be used to trace cables. Crimpers and punchdown tools are not used for locating a cable. The `ping` utility would be of no help in this situation.

7. **C.** Administrators can quickly determine the status of common ports by issuing the `netstat -a` command from the command line. This command output lists the ports used by the system and whether they are open and listening.

8. **B.** The security logs can be configured to show failed or successful logon attempts. In this case, the administrator can review the security logs and failed logon attempts to get the desired information. The failed logs show the date and time when the failed attempts occurred.

9. **B.** In this diagram, Cable 1 is plenum rated and should be fine. Cable 3's are patch cable are do not need to be STP rated. However, STP cables can attach directly to the wall jack. Cable 2 however goes through walls and ceilings; therefore, it would be recommended to have a better grade of cable than regular UTP. STP provides greater resistance to EMI. In ceilings, lights or other devices can cause interference.

10. **C.** When attaching RJ-45 connectors to UTP cables, the wire crimper is the tool you use. When in use, the individual wires from twisted-pair cable is inserted into the RJ-45 connector. When carefully inserted, the RJ-45 connector is placed into the crimpers. The crimpers force a metal connector to pierce the individual wires and the connections is made. None of the other tools are used in the construction of UTP cable.

11. **D.** Packet sniffers are commonly used on networks. They are either a hardware device or software and eavesdrop on network transmissions traveling throughout the network. The packet sniffer quietly captures data and saves to be reviewed at a later time.

12. **D.** If you suspect a problem with a patch cable, you can use a media tester to test it. An OTDR tests optical cables, and so it would not be used on UTP, which is copper-based cable. The other tools discussed in this question would not be used.

13. **C.** A load test enables administrators to put the network and specific network hardware under increased loads to test their functionality. In this case the number of users on the network is due to grow. The administrator can run a load test to see what impact the new users will have on the network. A simulated load test will reveal potential problems before the new user are added.

14. **C.** An OTDR can find a break in a length of fiber-optic cable. The other tools listed cannot be used to troubleshoot a break in a fiber-optic cable.

15. **C.** In this case, there are intermittent transmission problems that might be related to cables being used and cable placement. If you could see a physical network diagram, you might notice that the wrong cable type is used. Reviewing the logical diagram might be done after verifying that the physical one looked okay. It would not necessarily help in this case to review security or history logs.

16. **A.** A basic multimeter combines several electrical meters into a single unit offering the ability to measure voltage, current, and resistance. Advanced models can also measure temperature. A multimeter has a display, terminals, probes, and a dial to select various measurement ranges. A digital multimeter has a numeric digital display, whereas an analog has a dial display. Inside a multimeter, the terminals connect to different resistors depending on the range selected.

17. **C.** A toner probe is sometimes referred to as the fox and hound. None of the other answers are valid. A toner and probe can locate the ends of a cable; the toner probe generates a signal transmitted on the wire you are attempting to locate. At the other end, you press the tone locator against individual wires. When it makes contact with the wire that has the signal on it, the locator emits an audible signal or tone.

18. **C.** Network procedures differ from policies in that they identify the way in which tasks are to be performed. For example, each network administrator has backup procedures identifying the time of day backups and done, how often they are done, and where they are stored. A network is full of a number of procedures both for practical reasons but perhaps more important for security reasons. Policies are established rules from a particular organization.

19. **D.** The application log contains information logged by applications that run on a particular system rather than the operating system. Vendors of third-party ap-

plications can use the application log as a destination for error messages generated by their applications. In this case it would be necessary to review the application logs on the server to determine the problems with the application.

20. **B** and **D**. For security reasons, administrators must know what ports are open and potentially accessible from outside sources. Some ports are left open by default in operating systems making them vulnerable to outside attacks. Port scanners provide a way to check the status of all system ports ensuring that they cannot be compromised. Additionally, the `netstat -a` command can be used on Windows systems to quickly identify the status of the systems ports.

Chapter 14

1. **B.** Locks on a cabinet would be considered a physical security measure. Logical security measures have more to do with securing communications with protocols, using firewalls and such. All the other answers are considered logical security measures.

2. **D.** Firewalls do not make forwarding decisions based on the NetBIOS service name, which is fictitious. All the other answers are valid means by which a firewall can make filtering decisions.

3. **C.** Implementing a firewall enables you to have protection between networks, typically from the Internet to a private network. All the other answers describe functions offered by a proxy server. Note that some firewall systems do offer NAT functionality, but NAT is not a firewall feature; it is an added benefit of these systems.

4. **A.** The RDP protocol is used in thin-client networking, where only screen, keyboard, and mouse inputs are sent across the line. RDP has been used for Windows Terminal Services and now is used with the Remote Desktop feature with Windows XP. PPP is a dial-up protocol used over serial links; PPTP is a technology used in VPNs, and RAS is a remote access service.

5. **C.** To establish the VPN connection between the two networks, use PPTP. PPP is a protocol used on dial-up links. A VPN is a type of network, not a protocol. VPNs create a virtual tunnel between two end points, such as creating a tunnel through the Internet to create a point-to-point connection. SLIP is a nonsecure dial-up protocol remote access protocol.

6. **B.** Only screen, keyboard, and mouse inputs are sent across the communications link in a thin-client scenario. This enables the processing to be handled by the server, and with limited information sent, it reduces the amount of bandwidth required for the remote connection. None of the other answers are valid.

7. **B.** A DMZ is an area of a network where you would place systems that must be accessed by users outside the network.

8. **A** and **B.** Packet-filtering firewalls work at the network and data link layers of the OSI model. They do not operate at the application or transport layers of the OSI model.

9. **D.** PPTP uses TCP to establish a connection. DHCP is used to automatically assign IP information to client systems. FTP is used to transfer files between an FTP server and an FTP client. FTP enables for large file transfers. SSH is a security protocol used to encrypt network communications.

10. **B.** To create secure data transmissions, IPsec uses two separate protocols: Authentication Headers (AH) and Encapsulating Security Payloads (ESP). Briefly, AH is primarily responsible for the authentication and integrity verification of packets, whereas ESP provides encryption services.

11. **B.** DNS uses port 53. NTP uses TCP/IP port 123, SMTP uses port 25, and POP3 uses port 110.

12. **B.** A circuit-level firewall works at the transport layer of the OSI model. The biggest difference between a packet-filtering firewall and a circuit-level firewall is that a circuit-level firewall validates TCP and UDP sessions before opening a connection, or circuit, through the firewall. None of the other answers are valid.

13. **A.** IPsec can operate in one of two separate modes: transport mode and tunnel mode. These modes refer to how data is sent throughout the network. In transport mode, IPsec protection is provided all the way from the issuing client to the destination server. In this way, transport mode is said to provide end-to-end transmission security. Tunnel mode provides gateway to gateway security, leaving some areas unprotected by IPsec.

14. **B.** An IDS is considered a passive security measure because it monitors the network looking for potential threats but does not actively seek to correct the threats. An IPS is considered reactive; it can detect threats and take steps to manage those threats. AH and ESP are security protocols used with IPsec.

15. **A.** Port 443 is used by the HTTPS protocol and is used for secure web transactions. If this port is blocked, users cannot perform secure online transactions. Port 53 is used by DNS, port 80 is used by regular HTTP, and port 21 is used by FTP.

16. **A.** Encapsulating Security Payloads (ESP) is used to provide encryption services for IPsec and secure network traffic. AH is used with IPsec to provide authentication services.

17. **B** and **D.** Because users will access their email via a web browser, the firewall will not need to accommodate POP3 (port 110) and SMTP (port 25). Blocking port 53 would disable DNS lookups, and blocking port 80 would disable web browsing (HTTP).

18. **A** and **D.** Common ACL filters use MAC addresses and TCP/IP addresses. A MAC ACL enables or denies certain MAC addresses to the network or a network resource. Similarly, a TCP/IP ACL enables or denies access based on the system's IP address.

19. **A** and **C.** With PPPoE, a number of users can share the same physical connection to the Internet, and in the process, PPPoE provides a way to keep track of individual user Internet access times.

20. **C.** As far as security is concerned, an ACL typically refers to specific access permissions assigned to an object or device on the network. Restring access to a router by a MAC address is an example of an ACL. Only those MAC addresses listed on the list can authenticate to the router.

Chapter 15

1. **A.** Although both RADIUS and TACACS+ offer AAA services for remote users, some noticeable differences exist. TACACS+ relies on TCP for connection-oriented delivery, whereas RADIUS uses connectionless UDP for data delivery.

2. **B.** Authentication refers to the mechanisms used to verify the identity of the computer or user attempting to access a particular resource. Authorization controls who can and who cannot access a resource after authentication. Accountability and accounting are mechanisms used to track who does what on a system or a network.

3. **C.** SSL provides a mechanism for securing data across a network. When used with the unsecured HTTP protocols, HTTP becomes HTTP secured (HTTPS).

4. **A.** RADIUS is a protocol that enables a single server to become responsible for all remote access authentication, authorization, and auditing (or accounting) services. RADIUS uses the UDP protocol for communication.

5. **B.** A Trojan horse does not replicate itself and does not require a host program to run. This is in contrast to viruses that self-replicate. Worms self-replicate without user intervention.

6. **C.** Strong passwords include a combination of letters and numbers and upper- and lowercase letters. In this question Answer C is by far the strongest password because it has nine characters—a symbol, numbers, and letters. Answer A is not a strong password because it is a standard word, contains no numbers, and is all in lowercase. Answer B mixes letters and numbers, and it is not a recognized word, so it is a strong password, although it is not as strong as Answer C. Answer D is too easy to guess and contains no numbers.

7. **B** and **C.** Both CHAP and MS-CHAP are PPP authentication methods. The other answers are not valid authentication protocols.

8. **C.** Often overlooked is the need to read the documentation for the service pack or hotfix. The documentation tells the administrator what the patch is intended to fix and how it should be applied. After the documentation is read and the administrator is sure of the process to apply the patch, a backup and possibly a baseline should be taken before applying the fix.

9. **A.** Many of the protocols used on today's networks have a secure and a not secure option, meaning that data is sent in clear text. In this instance, SSH is a secure alternative to Telnet. Other examples include HTTPS (HTTP secure) and HTTP. None of the other answers are valid.

10. **D.** Kerberos is available for all the major operating systems.

11. **B.** Auditing is a process of reviewing security logs so that breaches can be detected. Answer A describes the function of alerting. The other answers are not valid.

12. **A, B,** and **C.** When creating a password policy, you should set a minimum password length, parameters limiting reusing the old password, and a password expiration period. You may even want to set a maximum password length, though most operating systems have a built in maximum.

13. **C.** In many network environments, two types of authentication are used to help ensure that only those who should gain network access actually do. Combing authentication methods is known as multifactor authentication. It combines, for instance, a username-password combination with a smart card or finger scan.

14. **A** and **C.** MS-EAP and SSL are not remote access authentication protocols. Remote authentication protocols such as CHAP and PAP are used by RADIUS or other applications to authenticate remote user credentials.

15. **A.** To determine the user ID of a person trying to log on, you would implement auditing. All major operating systems provide auditing services to record events that occur on a system. This includes tracking logons, logoffs, who accesses certain systems resources, and so on. File permissions, password policies, and intruder detection would not help you to do this.

16. **B.** EAP is an extension of PPP that supports authentication methods that go beyond the simple submission of a username and password. EAP was developed in response to an increasing demand for authentication methods that use other types of security devices, such as token cards, smart cards, and digital certificates.

17. **A.** By installing a RADIUS server, it is possible to move the workload associated with authentication to a dedicated server. A proxy server would not improve the dial-up connection's performance. There is no such thing as a Kerberos RRAS server or an IPsec server.

18. D. With discretionary access, control is not forced from the administrator or the operating system. Instead access is controlled by an object's owner. DAC uses an ACL to determine access. The ACL is a table that informs the operating system of the rights each user has to a particular system object, such as a file, directory, or printer.

19. A. Asymmetric key encryption uses both a private and public key to encrypt and decrypt messages. The public key is used to encrypt a message or verify a signature, and the private key is used to decrypt the message or to sign a document. In a symmetric key encryption strategy, a single key is used for both encryption and decryption.

20. C. A rogue access point describes a situation in which a wireless access point has been placed on a network without knowledge of the administrator. The result is that it is possible to remotely access the rogue access point because it likely does not adhere to company security policies.

Index

Numerics

A

C

T

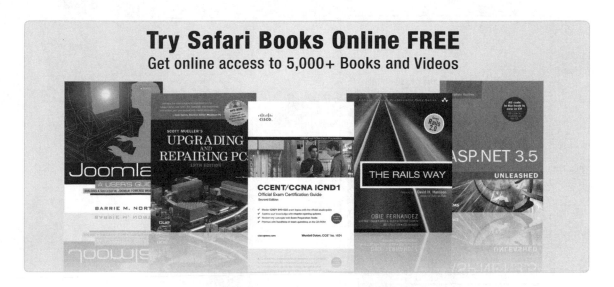

MIKE HARWOOD

Cert Guide
Learn, prepare, and practice for exam success

▶ Master every topic on the newest 2010 Network+ exam.

▶ Assess your knowledge and focus your learning.

▶ Get the practical workplace knowledge you need!

CompTIA
Network+
N10-004

CD FEATURES
1 COMPLETE
SAMPLE EXAM

PEARSON

FREE Online Edition

Your purchase of **CompTIA Network+ (N10-004) Cert Guide** includes access to a free online edition for 45 days through the Safari Books Online subscription service. Nearly every Pearson IT Certification book is available online through Safari Books Online, along with more than 5,000 other technical books and videos from publishers such as Addison-Wesley Professional, Cisco Press, Exam Cram, IBM Press, O'Reilly, Prentice Hall, Que, and Sams.

SAFARI BOOKS ONLINE allows you to search for a specific answer, cut and paste code, download chapters, and stay current with emerging technologies.

Activate your FREE Online Edition at
www.informit.com/safarifree

> **STEP 1:** Enter the coupon code: XFDYAZG.

> **STEP 2:** New Safari users, complete the brief registration form.
> Safari subscribers, just log in.

If you have difficulty registering on Safari or accessing the online edition, please e-mail customer-service@safaribooksonline.com